THE CLASSICS BOOKSHOP
3, TURL STREET, OXFORD, OX1 3DQ.

Telephone / Fax . 01865 726466.

We have the largest secondhand stock of Latin and Greek Classics in the United Kingdom. We always have a wide selection of secondhand and Antiquarian Classics on view in our shop.

The stock includes texts and commentaries, translations, general works, Archaeology, Ancient History, Philosophy and periodicals.

We usually have runs of periodicals available, although these are not kept in the shop.

We issue three catalogues a year, free in the U.K.

WE ARE ALWAYS KEEN TO BUY CLASSICS AND RELATED MATERIAL, FROM SINGLE VOLUMES TO COLLECTIONS IN THE U.K. AND ABROAD.

The Bulletin of British Byzantine Studies

The *Bulletin of British Byzantine Studies* is an essential periodical for all libraries serving Byzantinists or scholars in related fields. The *Bulletin* provides information concerning publications and research being carried out by British and international Byzantine scholars, abstracts of recent theses, announcements of conferences and seminars throughout the world, abstracts of communications delivered to the annual Byzantine Spring Symposia, short reviews and articles on current events and exhibitions, bibliographical listings and many other items. Published annually in March, the *Bulletin* can be mailed anywhere in the world.

Price of subscriptions to institutions: £15 annually in pounds sterling only

Please send cheques or write for more information to Dr M. B. Cunningham, Editor, *BBBS*, 44 Church Street, Littleover, Derby DE23 6GD.
(Email: Mary_B_Cunningham@iconex.mactel.org)

THE JOURNAL OF HELLENIC STUDIES

VOLUME CXVI

1996

PUBLISHED BY THE COUNCIL OF THE SOCIETY
FOR THE PROMOTION OF HELLENIC STUDIES

MDCCCCXCVI

CONTENTS

ARTICLES

NOTES

MUSEUM SUPPLEMENT

Journal of Hellenic Studies cxvi (1996) pp 1-32

HYBRIS, DISHONOUR, AND THINKING BIG

THE focal point of this article is the detailed study of the concept of *hybris* recently published by N.R.E. Fisher,[1] and the differences of interpretation which exist between that study and other recent work on the concept.[2] Though I dispute much of what Fisher has to say about *hybris*, I also defend many of his most important insights, and readily admit that my own task has been made immeasurably lighter by his industry and integrity in the presentation of a wealth of valuable data. That I take issue with his thesis is no token of disesteem, rather a recognition that he has made a strong case for his interpretation and that disagreement with a study as well documented as his must rest on detailed discussion of individual passages.

I

Fisher sees the essence of *hybris* in 'the committing of acts of intentional insult, of acts which deliberately inflict shame and dishonour on others'.[3] MacDowell, on the other hand, argues that *hybris* need not involve a victim, and so need not refer to dishonour; its essence, instead, lies in self-indulgent enjoyment of excess energy. Similarly, Dickie argues that *hybris* is essentially a disposition of over-confidence or presumption, as a result of which one fails to recognize the limitations and precariousness of one's human condition.[4] The dispute between Fisher and his opponents thus centres on the importance or otherwise of the subjective disposition of the *hybristês* in the definition of *hybris*.

The reference to intention in Fisher's definition indicates that he is aware of a certain dispositional aspect, and so his definition is not wholly 'behaviourist'—it does not focus only on external behaviour and its effects on others. He also recognizes that in some cases the dispositional aspect of *hybris* may be to the fore,[5] and that the word *hybris* can be used as a name for the disposition as well as for the act;[6] but he consistently locates the essence of the concept in the commission of concrete acts, and defines the disposition of *hybris* with reference to the commission of such acts, as merely the intention, desire, drive, or tendency to commit hybristic acts.[7] Thus the act of *hybris* is prior to any dispositional aspect, and the intention which is part of the definition is necessarily an intention to perpetrate an act of dishonour on a particular victim.[8] My position is that this view must be modified; for I do not believe that

---

[1] *Hybris: a study in the values of honour and shame in ancient Greece* (Warminster 1992; henceforth 'Fisher'); for remarks preliminary to what follows, see my review in *CR* xliv (1994) 76-9.

[2] Especially D.M. MacDowell, *G&R* xxiii (1976) 14-31, *Demosthenes, Against Meidias (Oration 21)* (Oxford 1990) 18-22; A.N. Michelini, *HSCP* lxxxii (1978) 35-44; M.W. Dickie, in D.E. Gerber (ed.), *Greek poetry and philosophy: studies ... L. Woodbury* (Chico 1984) 83-109. J. T. Hooker (*Arch. f. Begriffsgesch.* xix [1975] 125-37) is misguided in his search for an original, neutral meaning, but he focuses on phenomena which are also important in MacDowell's account. In closest agreement with Fisher is E. Cantarella, in *Symposium 1979: Actes du IVe colloque international de droit grec et hellenistique* (Athens 1981) 85-96 = *Incontri Linguistici* vii (1982) 19-30. See also A.F. Garvie in A. Machin, L. Pernée (eds.), *Sophocle: le texte, les personnages* (Aix-en-Provence 1993) 243.

[3] Fisher 148; *cf.* 1.

[4] This, as Dickie is aware, has much in common with the 'traditional view' in opposition to which Fisher defines his own thesis; see Dickie (n. 2) 101-9, esp. 102; *cf.* Fisher 2-4 and *passim*.

[5] See 130, 133, 148, 173, 402.

[6] See 493; *cf.* 125, 242, 281.

[7] See esp. 1: '*Hybris* ... most often denotes specific acts or general behaviour directed against others, rather than attitudes; it may, though, on occasions ... denote the drive or the desire ... to engage in such behaviour directed against others.' *Cf.* 212-13, 229, 323, 393; also K. Latte, *Kleine Schriften* (Munich 1968) 13.

[8] *Cf.* Fisher in P. Cartledge *et al.* (eds.), *Nomos: essays in Athenian law, politics, and society* (Cambridge 1990) 126 and n. 14.

the act is prior to the disposition in the definition of *hybris*, nor that *hybris* must be defined in terms of an intention to insult a specific victim.

II

Fisher's definition of *hybris* takes its authority from Aristotle's treatment in the *Rhetoric*.[9] It is true that Aristotle does define *hybris* in terms of actions of verbal or physical affront, and that his references to the concept elsewhere in the *Rhetoric* and in other works are consistent with his definition. Nevertheless, it becomes clear from a closer examination of the relevant passages that Aristotle's definition places more emphasis on the dispositional element than Fisher's, and that the latter, despite the meticulousness of his research, has not quite succeeded in identifying the place of *hybris* in Aristotle's ethical theory.

Aristotle's definition of *hybris* in the *Rhetoric* falls within his discussion of the *pathos* of anger, and more specifically of its cause, *oligôria*, of which *hybris* is one of the three kinds (1378b13-15). The statement that *hybris* is a kind of *oligôria* is backed by a definition of the former: 'For *hybris* is doing and saying things[10] at which the victim incurs *aischynê*, not in order that the agent should obtain anything other than the performance of the act,[11] but in order to please himself' (1378b23-5). *Hybris*, we are then told, requires the initiation of harm, and the pleasure of *hybris* lies in the thought of one's own superiority (b25-30). Fisher is thus right to regard Aristotle as supporting him in referring *hybris* to acts (including speech acts), and it is also true that Aristotle lends support to his insistence that *hybris* is fundamentally a matter of causing dishonour (*cf.* 1378b29-30, 'Dishonour is part of *hybris*, for the one who dishonours slights'). Already, however, one can discern certain differences of emphasis; Fisher has said that *hybris* has more to do with specific acts than with attitudes, yet Aristotle begins by classifying *hybris* as a type of attitude (*oligôria*), albeit one which is necessarily manifested in word and deed. Similarly, Fisher has characterized his own approach as placing more emphasis on 'the intention specifically to insult and the effects of dishonour achieved';[12] whereas Aristotle regards the intention which is necessary for *hybris* not primarily as a wish to bring about a certain state of affairs or to affect a patient in a particular way, but as the desire to please oneself by demonstrating one's own superiority. It seems to me that Aristotle gives rather more prominence to the attitude and motivation of the agent than Fisher allows.

Yet Aristotle does define *hybris* in terms of its actualization in word and deed, and Fisher can argue that his own reference to the intentions of the agent covers the subjective aspects to which I have drawn attention. The intention to please oneself and feel superior, after all, is only the obverse of the intention to dishonour another, as Aristotle himself makes clear at 1374b13-15—not every case of striking is a case of *hybris*, but only when one strikes for a reason, such as dishonouring the other person or pleasing oneself. Aristotle clearly regards the intention to dishonour as parallel to the intention to obtain the pleasure of feeling or appearing

---

[9] Fisher 7-11.

[10] Translating τὸ πράττειν καὶ λέγειν (A; Ross, Kassel), rather than τὸ βλάπτειν καὶ λυπεῖν as in some later Mss. (and earlier eds.). MacDowell, *Meidias* (n. 2) 20 argues that this sentence is not an exhaustive definition of *hybris*, on the grounds that ὕβρις, minus the article, must be the complement and τὸ πράττειν κτλ. the subject. But the article is omitted with the subject, ὕβρις, as often with abstract nouns, esp. the names of virtues and vices, while its presence in τὸ πράττειν is explained by the need to mark the infinitive as substantival.

[11] I follow E.M. Cope (*The Rhetoric of Aristotle* ii [Cambridge 1877] 17) and Fisher (8) in the interpretation of the phrase, μὴ ἵνα τι γένηται αὐτῷ ἄλλο, ἢ ὅτι ἐγένετο; the alternative proposed by W.M.A. Grimaldi, *Aristotle: Rhetoric* ii (New York 1988) *ad loc.*, seems to me very unlikely.

[12] (n. 8) 126 n. 14.

superior,[13] and this seems to bring us back to Fisher's definition. In fact, however, close attention to the context of this passage reveals that Aristotle's view of *hybris* and Fisher's are somewhat different and that Fisher has failed to follow up certain leads which show precisely where *hybris* fits in Aristotle's ethical theory.

Aristotle's remarks on *hybris* belong in the context of a discussion of the forensic branch of oratory, which is concerned with acts involving an individual or a community as victim; thus Aristotle discusses the motives, conditions, and circumstances of injustice, and gives a short account of what injustice, the subject-matter of forensic oratory, consists in. Any ascription of injustice to an agent depends on an assessment of his motivation; a bare description of an action, in external terms, is insufficient. Thus some admit that they took but deny that they stole, or admit that they struck but deny that they committed *hybris*, and so on (1373b38-1374a6). These are disputes about what it is to be unjust or wicked and the opposite, and therefore about *prohairesis*, for wickedness and wrongdoing lie in the *prohairesis*, and terms such as *hybris* and *klopê* connote *prohairesis* (1374a6-13).

Fisher translates *prohairesis* here as 'intention',[14] but *prohairesis* is a technical term in Aristotle's ethical writings which signifies much more than intention.[15] It is important in both ethical treatises (and the *Magna Moralia*) in the discussion of the various states of character which are classified as excellences or defects, but is discussed in particular detail in *EN* iii 2-3 (cf. *EE* ii 10-11, *MM* 17-19) and vi 2.[16] From these and other passages we learn that all actions which result from *prohairesis* are voluntary, but not all voluntary actions result from *prohairesis* (thus *prohairesis* is already distinguished from mere intention),[17] and that *prohairesis* follows deliberation *qua* deliberative desire to perform actions which contribute to the ends set by one's rational desire for the good.[18] Thus it requires that concept of the end of one's conduct which is supplied by one's developed and settled state of character (*hexis*), be

---

[13] Fisher (10 n. 17; *cf*. 57 n. 71) is right to claim (against M. Gagarin in G. Bowersock *et al.* [eds.], *Arctouros* [Berlin and New York 1979] 231-2; MacDowell, *Meidias* [n. 2] 20) that the pleasure mentioned here is, as at 1378b26-8, that of demonstrating one's superiority, and so entails asserting one's own claim to honour at others' expense.

[14] Fisher 10.

[15] W.D. Ross, *Aristotle*[5] (London 1949) 200 distinguishes a 'technical sense' of *prohairesis* (relating to means) in *EN* iii 2 and vi 2 from its supposed use elsewhere to mean 'purpose' (relating to ends), but see R. Sorabji in A.O. Rorty (ed.), *Essays on Aristotle's Ethics* (Berkeley and Los Angeles 1980) 202-4.

[16] For recent discussion of *prohairesis*, see esp. A. Kenny, *Aristotle's theory of the will* (London 1979) 69-107; D.S. Hutchinson, *The virtues of Aristotle* (London 1986) 88-107; N. Sherman, *The fabric of character* (Oxford 1989) 79-94, 106-16; *cf*. G E.M. Anscombe in J. Barnes *et al.* (eds.), *Articles on Aristotle* ii (London 1977) 61-6; Sorabji (n. 15) 201-5; D. Wiggins in Rorty (n. 15) 222-7; D. Charles, *Aristotle's philosophy of action* (London 1984) 137-42, 151-5.

[17] *EN* 1112a14-15, 1135b8-11, *EE* 1223b38-1224a7, 1226b34-6; *cf*. Anscombe (n. 16) 61, 66, 69-70; T.H. Irwin in Rorty (n. 15) 127-33, id., *Aristotle's first principles* (Oxford 1988) 340-2; Sherman (n. 16) 67.

[18] Follows deliberation: *EN* 1112a15-1113a14, *EE* 1226a20-b30, 1227a5-18; deliberative desire: *EN* 1113a10-11, 1139a22-b5, *EE* 1226b2-20; chooses τὰ πρὸς τὰ τέλη: *EN* 1112b11-1113a14, 1113b3-4, *EE* 1226a7-13, 1226b9-20, 1227a5-18; *telos* set by *boulêsis*: *EN* 1113a15-b3, *EE* 1226a13-17, *EE* 1227a28-31, 1227b37-1228a2; cf. *EN* 1142b28-33 on *euboulia*. For detailed discussion of *prohairesis*, deliberation, practical wisdom, and their relationship to means and ends, see L.H.G. Greenwood, *Aristotle: Nicomachean Ethics. Book 6* (Cambridge 1909) 46-7; D.J. Allan in Barnes *et al.* (n. 16) 72-8; J.M. Cooper, *Reason and human good in Aristotle* (Cambridge Mass. 1975) ch. 1 *passim*; W.F.R. Hardie, *Aristotle's ethical theory*[2] (Oxford 1980) 160-81, 212-39; Sorabji (n. 15) 201-14; Wiggins (n. 16) 222-7; Sherman (n. 16) 70-1. Despite passages such as *EN* 1111b9-10, 1135b8-11, *EE* 1224a4, not every action that is with *prohairesis* need follow *actual* deliberation: see *EN* 1117a17-22; Cooper 6-10; W.W. Fortenbaugh, *Aristotle on emotion* (London 1975) 70-5; Sorabji (n. 15) 204-5; Charles (n. 16) 187; Irwin, *Principles* (n. 17) 344; Sherman (n. 16) 82.

it virtuous or vicious;[19] in order, therefore, for a *prohairesis* to be good, the agent must possess excellence of character,[20] and, by the same token, excellence of character requires the exercise of *prohairesis* (the choice of the specific moral action for its own sake in the light of one's overall conception of the end).[21] It is in the *prohairesis* that we see virtue or vice, and the praise and blame which presence or absence of virtue rightly attracts respond not to the act but to the *prohairesis*.[22]

Certain aspects of this picture are particularly relevant to the account of *hybris* in *Rhetoric* i 13 and ii 2. First, the *Rhetoric* agrees with the *Ethics* that *prohairesis* is the mark of virtue or vice: 'Wickedness and wrongdoing [μοχθηρία καὶ τὸ ἀδικεῖν] lie in the *prohairesis*, and such terms (e.g. *hybris* and theft) connote the *prohairesis*' (1374a11-13). Secondly, *hybris* was defined as gratuitous insult, motivated by a desire not to achieve any ulterior purpose, but to obtain the intrinsic pleasure of demonstrating one's own superiority through the dishonouring of another (1378b23-8; *cf.* 1374a13-15). *Hybris*, then, is explicitly said to be a kind of action performed for its own sake, one which implies a *prohairesis*, and if the summary indications given in the relevant passages of the *Rhetoric* presuppose the developed framework of the *Ethics*, then the *prohairesis* which *hybris* connotes is much more than an intention.

That the reference to *prohairesis* at *Rhetoric* 1374a11-13 does presuppose the technical sense of that term is apparent from the context in which it occurs, for the entire discussion of *adikia* in i 10-13 is clearly related to that of justice and injustice in *EN* v.[23] Thus τὸ ἀδικεῖν is defined as voluntary injury in contravention of the law (1368b6-7), the criteria of the voluntary are summarily rehearsed (b9-10; *cf. EN* 1135a15-b8), and voluntary action is distinguished from action on *prohairesis* (b10-12; *cf. EN* 1135b8-11), which is a sign of vice. Injustice in the fullest sense exists when the agent acts on *prohairesis*, and this is a sign of the possession of a vicious *hexis* (1374a9-13; *cf.* 1374b13-16); but acts of injustice may also be committed by those who do not possess this *hexis*, for example by those who act in anger (1373b33-8); and acts which harm others may be committed unintentionally, though ignorance of some relevant particular, or by pure accident (1374b4-10).[24] This is clearly a simplified version of *EN* v's distinction between *atychêmata*, *hamartêmata*, *adikêmata*, and 'being an unjust person' (1135a5-1136a5). The important point for our purposes is that it is only in the last case that the

[19] Requires *hexis*: *EN* 1139a33-5; see Cooper (n. 18) 48 n. 59; D.J. Furley in Barnes *et al.* (n. 16) 59; Anscombe (n. 16) 64-6; Kenny (n. 16) 97-9; T. Engberg-Pedersen, *Aristotle's theory of moral insight* (Oxford 1983) 166; N.O. Dahl, *Practical wisdom, Aristotle, and weakness of the will* (Minneapolis 1984) 36; Hutchinson (n. 16) 88-92, 100-7. Charles (n. 16) 151-5 disputes the idea (see Anscombe [n. 16] 64) that every *prohairesis* requires a state of character and a grasp of the end of human action (*cf.* Engberg-Pedersen 21 n. 27); but see Irwin, *Principles* (n. 17) 598 n. 22.

[20] Excellence of character makes the *prohairesis* right: *EN* 1144a20; *cf.* 1145a4-5, *EE* 1227b34-1228a2.

[21] Virtue requires *prohairesis*: *EN* 1106a3-4, 1110b31, 1111b5, 1117a5, 1127b14, 1134a17-23, 1135b25, 1139a22-6, 1144a13-22, 1145a2-6, 1157b30, 1163a22, 1178a34-b1, *EE* 1227b1-5; vice also requires *prohairesis*: *EN* 1110b31, 1135b25, 1146a32, 1146b22-3, 1148a4-17, 1150a19-21, 1150b29-30, 1151a6-7, 1152a4-6. Not only virtue (*EN* 1105a32,1144a13-20), but also vice involves choosing the action for its own sake in the light of one's view of *eudaimonia*. See, e.g., 1127a26-b17 (with Hutchinson [n. 16] 103-4).

[22] *EN* 1111b6, *EE* 1228a2-18.

[23] Cope (*An introduction to Aristotle's Rhetoric* [Cambridge 1867] 176, 182-5, etc.) exaggerates the extent to which use of important concepts of Aristotelian ethics and politics in *Rhet.* is to be distinguished from more technical applications in the *Ethics* and *Pol.*, but even he (188-93, esp. 189 and n. 1) recognizes that *Rhet.* i 10-13 presupposes the account of justice in *EN* v. The *Rhet.* does avoid detailed discussion of problems appropriate to more specialized contexts, but its assumptions in many aspects of politics, ethics, and psychology are those of the treatises devoted to those subjects. See (e.g.) Fortenbaugh (n. 18) 16, *id.* in Barnes *et al.* (eds.), *Articles on Aristotle* iv (London 1979) 133-53 (followed by Fisher 9).

[24] That the treatment of justice and injustice is concluded by a discussion of *epieikeia* (1374a26-b23; *cf. EN* 1137a31-1138a3) is another sign that the framework of the *EN* is being applied.

agent acts with *prohairesis*; this has the consequence that one can actually commit an unjust act, and commit it intentionally, and yet still not be an unjust person—one can steal and yet not be a thief, commit adultery and yet not be an adulterer (1134a17-23);[25] in order to be a thief or an adulterer (etc.) one must possess a settled disposition to choose such vicious acts for their own sake, *qua* acts of injustice.[26] Thus if the act of *hybris* is to connote *prohairesis* it will demand more than an intention to dishonour another, for such an intention is possible even in cases where no *prohairesis* is present.

That Aristotle's first expression of his view of *hybris* occurs in the context of a discussion of justice and injustice already suggests that he sees *hybris* as a form of injustice,[27] and that the *hexis* from which *hybris* springs is that which is identified in *EN* v (1129a31-b10, 1130a14-b18, b30-1132b20, and *passim*) as 'particular injustice' (ἡ ἐν μέρει/κατὰ μέρος ἀδικία). This is confirmed when we see that the characteristics of particular injustice match those of *hybris* very closely. First, particular injustice is concerned with *pleonexia*, with wanting more of some external good (1129a32-b11); this greed, however, is not purely material, as it covers desire not just for money, but also for *timê*, safety, and other things of that type (1130b2-4).[28] This kind of injustice can be manifested in the distribution of goods, but also in the context of 'involuntary transactions' in which an agent creates an unfair inequality between himself and a patient in respect of some good, whether by stealth or by force (*EN* 1131a1-9). Thus particular injustice can be concerned with honour, requires a specific victim, and can be manifested in words or in deeds, by physical assault (*aikeia*, 1131a8) or by verbal insult (*propêlakismos*, 1131a9;[29] with all this, cf. *Rhet.* 1374a13-15, 1378b23-8). Just as the *hybristês* is motivated by desire for a particular kind of pleasure (*Rhet.*, ibid., cf. 1380b4-5, also *EN* 1149b21), so particular injustice seeks the pleasure that comes from the *kerdos* (*EN* 1130b4);[30] particular injustice also requires the initiation of wrongdoing, and is not found in

---

[25] As in *Rhet.* 1373b33-8, the sign of 'doing injustice' as opposed to 'being unjust' is action in the grip of a *pathos*, typically anger; cf. 1135b20-9. (The remarks at 1134a17-23 are clearly out of place; Gauthier-Jolif, *L'Éthique à Nicomacque* ii 1 [Louvain 1959] 385-6, 406, and Irwin, *Aristotle: Nicomachean Ethics* [Indianapolis 1985] 335, would transpose the whole section, 1133b29-1134a23; Irwin's transposition *post* 1135a5 seems better than Gauthier-Jolif's *post* 1136a9.)

[26] For the distinction between 'doing injustice' and 'being unjust', cf. 1134a32-3, 1137a4-9, 17-26. It may seem that this is ignored in the passage of the *Rhet.* under discussion; the point of 1373b38-1374a18, after all, is not that of *EN* 1134a17-23 (the former distinguishes between [e.g.] theft and justifiable removal, the latter between [e.g.] being a thief and committing a theft), and at 1374a11-12 τὸ ἀδικεῖν, in apparent contradiction of the *EN*, is said to lie in *prohairesis*; similarly, 1374b4-10 fails to distinguish between *adikêmata* and 'being unjust', attributing *adikêmata* to *ponêria*. Thus Cope (n. 11) i 257-8 argues that the *EN*'s distinction between 'doing injustice' and 'being unjust' is not operative in the *Rhet.*; but, as Grimaldi observes (*Aristotle: Rhetoric* i [New York 1980] 293-4, 304), precisely that distinction is made at 1373b35-6. There may be no real problem here: perhaps τὸ ἀδικεῖν at 1374a12 and ἀδικήματα at 1374b8-9 are used in a non-technical sense, of the unjust actions of an unjust character, and we might say that the refinement of the schema, introducing non-prohaeretic *adikêmata* as a category distinct from possession of a vicious character, though presupposed, is not explicitly activated; but if instead we prefer to see inconsistency, it will be an inconsistency within the *Rhet.* passage itself, not between *Rhet.* and *EN*.

[27] Cf. the explicit references to *hybris* as a type of unjust act at *Rhet.* 1373a34-5, 1374a11-12, 1389b7-8, 1391a18-19; cf. also [Arist.] *De Virt.* 1251a30-6) and [Pl.] *Def.* 415e12 (Fisher 11).

[28] Aristotle is aware that he is using *pleonexia* in an extended sense (cf. 1132a7-14, b11-18), and so it is no objection to the interpretation of *hybris* as a kind of particular injustice/*pleonexia* that elsewhere *hybris* and *pleonexia* are distinguished (e.g. *Pol.* 1302b5-9; Fisher 22-4).

[29] According to Ammonius (*De Adfin. Vocab. Diff.* 20; cf. Fisher 53 n. 52) *hybreis* are distinguished from *aikeiai* by the fact that *propêlakismos* is necessary for the former; on *propêlakismos* and *hybris*, cf. Fisher 44 n. 31, 48, 93, 107.

[30] *Kerdos* is to be understood here not as gain *per se*, but as that gain at another's expense which is characteristic of particular injustice; the *pleonexia* in which particular injustice consists is essentially comparative; cf. Irwin, *Principles* (n. 17) 426, 429 and 624 nn. 4-6. This notion of comparison is, as we shall see, also fundamental to *hybris*.

retaliation (1138a20-2; *cf.* on *hybris, Rhet.* 1378b23-8 once more, also 1379a30-5, 1402a1-5). Both *hybris* and particular injustice, then, involve taking the initiative in exalting oneself at the expense of others, for no other motive than the pleasure of the offence itself.[31] That the characteristics of *hybris* are those of a form of particular injustice seems to me indisputable.[32]

If *hybris* is a type of conduct which results from the vicious *hexis* of particular injustice, then Fisher has not only failed to identify the place of *hybris* in Aristotle's scheme, he has also underestimated the extent to which Aristotle's remarks on *hybris* form part of a systematic ethical theory, which, while it starts from the opinions of the many (and the wise), not infrequently has to revise the significance of popular terms in order to accommodate them.[33] The main upshot of this is that Fisher places too little emphasis on the dispositional aspect of the concept. Aristotle would probably have allowed that, just as one can commit an unjust act without being an unjust person, so one can commit an act of *hybris* without possessing the *hexis* necessary for action with *prohairesis*; and he is as capable as other authors of using *hybris*-words in 'behaviourist' senses (less with reference to the motivation of the agent than to the objective infliction of dishonour on a patient);[34] but in the paradigm case, in which *hybris* connotes vice and requires *prohairesis*, it requires a specific sort of motivation rooted deeply in a developed and settled state of character, a state of character which, in the sphere of honour, leads one to enjoy unfairly pressing one's own claims in the face of the legitimate claims of others. This, the disposition which is necessary for *hybris*, is something rather more than a simple intention or tendency to act, and thus Aristotle's definition in terms of *prohairesis* differs markedly from Fisher's in terms of intention; at the same time, Fisher's stress on the actual infliction of dishonour and its effects on the patient underestimates Aristotle's emphasis on the agent's attitude to his own honour, which is both apparent in the definition at *Rhet.* 1378b23-8, and necessary if *hybris* is to be a form of injustice, of the *pleonexia* which seeks more for oneself at the expense of others. The comparative nature of the concept of *pleonexia*/particular injustice in *EN* v isolates what I shall argue to be a fundamental feature of *hybris*—that as a way of going wrong about one's own claim to honour it inevitably involves going wrong about the claims to honour of others (and *vice versa*).

True, Aristotle does define *hybris* in terms of acts, but even though *hybris* is, for him, always a particular way of treating another person, it is not the nature of the act or the effect on the

---

[31] *Hybris* thus meets the criteria for vicious action in the fullest sense—it springs from a settled disposition to choose the vicious course for its own sake, in so far as it is pleasant. This also answers to a typical feature of *hybris* in ordinary usage, in which to say that someone acted 'not out of *hybris*, but ... [for some further motive]' is to deny acting 'just for badness', as a demonstration of one's insolent disregard for law or convention; see (e.g.) Lys. vii 13; *cf.* Thuc. iv 95.8, Xen. *Anab.* v 5.16, Dem. xxi 181-2; Fisher 49, 98, 103.

[32] This helps explain why Aristotle imagines that *hybris* must always have a victim—all forms of injustice are necessarily πρὸς ἕτερον (*EN* 1129b25-1130a13; *cf.* 1130b20; 1130b1-5), and, as a form of particular injustice, *hybris* must occur in 'involuntary transactions' involving two parties. Aristotle's discussion of 'involuntary transactions', moreover, focuses on cases where correction will be forthcoming from a judicial source (1130b33-1131a9, 1131b25-1132b20); likewise in the *Rhet.* the reference to *hybris* in i 13 (1373b38-1374a18) is specifically related to the needs of the forensic orator (esp. 1374a7-9). The account of *hybris* in ii 2 (1378b13-34) forms part of a discussion of the *pathê* which frequently goes far beyond these needs, but even there *hybris* is discussed *qua* form of *oligôria* and cause of anger, and so the context demands concentration on affronts involving an agent and a patient; it should thus be no surprise that forms of *hybris* which would be unlikely to form the basis of a court action or at least of a dispute between two parties are not considered in Aristotle's definition. *Cf.* MacDowell (n. 2) *G&R* 28, *Meidias* 20, against Fisher 9. This is not to say that Aristotle is defining a distinct 'legal' sense of *hybris*, merely that apparently victimless cases do not occur to him, given the contexts in which he expresses his views on *hybris*.

[33] See (e.g.) his account of *nemesis, Rhet.* 1386b9-1387b20; *cf.* n. 35 below.

[34] E.g. *hybris* of homosexual practices thought objectively to involve the dishonour of the passive partner, regardless of the motive of the agent or of the partner's consent; *EN* 1129b22, 1148b31, *Rhet.* 1384a18-19. Cf. Fisher 13-14, 109-10; D. Cohen, *Law, violence and community in classical Athens* (Cambridge 1995) 147-51, 155-6.

honour of the patient which makes an act hybristic, but the motive; and that motive is a *prohairesis*, a particular choice of a developed character. Aristotle does not explicitly (unlike other authors)[35] refer to this state of character as *hybris*,[36] but be does have a name for it, since by virtue of the possession of such a state one is called a *hybristês*. Now, the term *hybristês* is derived from *hybris*, and thus the latter is prior in definition to the former; but we can be sure that to be a *hybristês* for Aristotle is not just to be liable to commit hybristic acts; *qua* unjust acts manifesting *prohairesis*, hybristic acts must be defined as those which the possessor of a particular *hexis* would perform. The *hexis* from which *hybris* springs is that of injustice in its narrower sense. That in itself allows us to adumbrate the typical characteristics of the hybristic agent to a certain extent. But other contexts provide further help in narrowing down the precise nature of the disposition to choose from which *hybris* results.

Our best evidence comes in a handful of passages in which Aristotle discusses *hybris* as typical of particular character types. The *Rhetoric*'s discussions of pity and fear, for example, consider not only the dispositions which give rise to these emotions (ὡς διακείμενοι αὐτοὶ φοβοῦνται, 1382b29), but also those which do not. Both pity and fear require the notion of one's own vulnerability to misfortune; by contrast, those who believe that their current good fortune renders them invulnerable to reversal are disposed not to pity or to fear, but, being *hybristai* (1383a2), and 'in a hybristic condition (*diathesis*)' (1385b30-1), to *hybrizein* (1385b21). Even if *hybrizein* here does imply the expression of contempt for the unfortunate in word or deed,[37] Aristotle can refer to a hybristic disposition from which such concrete expressions spring, a disposition which entails a blind over-valuation of oneself caused by the experience or the illusion of excessive prosperity. All the stress in these passages is on the subjective attitude of the *hybristês*;[38] in these accounts of people who are disposed to manifest *hybris* it is the agent's sense of his own superiority that is emphasized, rather than its expression in acts which affect others. Clearly, dishonouring others is the obverse of over-valuing oneself, but these passages provide further evidence that the latter side of the coin figures more prominently in Aristotle's concept of *hybris* than the former, and they should be used to emphasize the element of the sense of one's own superiority in the definitions of *hybris* at the expense of the mere intention to cause a diminution of honour in others.

The sketches of the characteristics of the young, the rich, and the powerful in the *Rhetoric* and *Politics* also consistently attribute the *hybris* of those groups to their failure to form an appropriate conception of their own worth *vis-à-vis* that of others. The characterization of the young at *Rhet.* 1389a2-b12, for example, stresses their naiveté, their inexperience of misfortune, and their acute attachment to *timê*.[39] When *hybris* enters this picture, it is with specific reference to acts of insult or mockery (their acts of injustice tend more towards *hybris* than to petty wrongdoing, and they are witty, since wit is educated *hybris*, b7-12), but these acts spring from a particular type of character, one which lacks the experience which should set limits to one's self-confidence and self-assertion.

Being hybristic and arrogant is likewise one of the 'characters' (*êthê*, 1390b32) which attend wealth, and the acquisition of wealth creates the illusion that one possesses all good things,

---

[35] As Fisher (493) admits. *Cf.* above, n. 6. Aristotle's account of *hybris* thus resembles his discussions of *aidôs* in failing to recognize that *hybris*, like *aidôs*, can be the name of a disposition; see my *Aidôs* (Oxford 1993) 393-431.

[36] The only instance I can find in the Aristotelian corpus of *hybris* used as the name of a character trait is in the spurious *Oec.* (1344a35-b1).

[37] I am not sure that we need follow Fisher (19-20) in thus limiting the reference of the verb; on his treatment of transitive and absolute uses of *hybrizein*, see below, nn. 48, 69.

[38] *Cf.* D. Armstrong and C.W. Peterson, *CQ* xxx (1980) 69; Dickie (n. 2) 97-8, 102.

[39] Several of these points emerge again by contrast in the characterization of the old at 1389b13-1390a28.

which is the basis of the disposition of being *hybristai* and *hyperêphanoi* (1390b34-1391a1). As a result of this error, the rich have a false idea of their own worth and a misplaced confidence in their own good fortune (1391a1-14).[40] The *Politics* also recognizes the tendency of the excessively fortunate to become *hybristai* and commit *hybris* (1295b6-11); again, the specific reference of the noun, *hybris*, is to a type of unjust act (b10-11), but one which springs from a mistaken belief that one's particular good fortune entitles one to a greater share of honour than it should. Similarly, at 1334a25-8 we read that war compels men to be just and to *sôphronein*, whereas enjoyment of good fortune and leisure in time of peace makes them *hybristai*. All the terms here are dispositional; war fosters a disposition of modesty and self-restraint, prosperity and peace one of over-confidence and self-assertion;[41] to be sure, these are dispositions to act, but still this passage resembles the others cited in making it clear that to possess the disposition which is necessary for *hybris* is to have a particular mistaken view of oneself and one's lot in life.

In *Pol.* 1295b8-9 it is the absence of reason which explains the mistaken attitude to good or bad fortune. The same point is made at *EN* 1124a26-b6; the *megalopsychos* has the right attitude to *timê* and the goods for which one receives *timê*; others who enjoy the same external advantages, but lack virtue, are wrong in thinking themselves worthy of great things and should not be called *megalopsychoi*. These people instead become supercilious (*hyperoptai*) and *hybristai*, because without *aretê* it is hard to deal appropriately with good fortune; unable to bear their good fortune and thinking themselves superior they despise others and do whatever they please. In this they resemble the *megalopsychos*, but his contempt for others is rational where theirs is not. It could not be made clearer that one's attitude to oneself and one's own worth is for Aristotle a more important constituent of *hybris* than one's attitude to others; to be a *hybristês* one's contempt for others must be based on a mistaken conception of one's own worth.

It cannot be said that Fisher ignores such passages;[42] but he uses them simply to establish what he sees as the conditions or causes of *hybris*, which properly consists in intentional acts of affront. But Aristotle's definitions of *hybris* presuppose a reference to a source of motivation which provides the crucial criterion for differentiating a hybristic act from an apparently similar non-hybristic act; hence these dispositional factors are not mere concomitants or causes, but characteristics of the *hexis* which is necessary for *hybris*. To be a *hybristês* is not just to possess a drive, tendency, or intention to commit hybristic acts, but to entertain a misguided and inflated conception of oneself and one's place in the world. Aristotle's sketches of hybristic character-types concentrate much more on the subject's excessive concern for his own honour than on his assaults on the honour of others.

III

Aristotle's view of *hybris* thus diverges from Fisher's at precisely the point where Fisher and his modern critics also differ, on the importance of the disposition of the hybristic agent. Yet Aristotle and Fisher remain close in that they both believe that *hybris* is essentially a way of behaving towards other people. Aristotle may place more emphasis on the dispositional aspect,

---

[40] The same misapprehension which makes the rich *hybristai* and *hyperêphanoi* makes the powerful *hyperêphanoteroi* at 1391a33-b1; it is difficult to avoid the conclusion that the adj. *hyperêphanos* reinforces the connotation of *hybristês* at 1390b33. *Cf.* Armstrong and Peterson (n. 38) 69.

[41] The frequent opposition between *hybris* and *sôphrosynê* (see Fisher, Index, s.v.) contrasts two ways of coping with one's self-assertive urges, and reinforces my contention that the element of over-valuation of one's own honour in *hybris* is more important than Fisher allows. Fisher (111) argues that *sôphrosynê* is an antonym of *hybris* only in so far as it restrains that desire to wrong others which *hybris* primarily denotes, but the falsity of this follows from that of the view of *hybris* it employs.

[42] See Fisher 12, 19-25.

but he agrees with Fisher in so far as he gives no explicit indication of believing that the word *hybris* may be used as the name of a disposition which need not issue in acts infringing the *timê* of a particular victim. Our task now is to decide whether this restriction of the reference of *hybris* applies across the board.

First we shall look at some passages in which it seems to me that the dispositional aspect is decisive for the application of the *hybris*-term; these are passages in which either specific acts or victims are not mentioned or else the effects of acts on victims are not constitutive of the *hybris* described. My focus here is partly on the requirement that *hybris* entails a conscious intention to dishonour, partly on Fisher's dictum that 'in almost all cases the victim of *hybris* is patently present in the context; where it can or has been doubted [*sic*] that there is a victim, in all cases it can be plausibly argued that one is supposed by the argument' (148). Both these requirements, it seems to me, need to be relaxed.

Several of the relevant passages come from Fisher's general discussion of the links between luxury (*tryphê*) and *hybris* (113-17). At Demosthenes xxxvi 42 the *hybris* envisaged is that of Apollodorus: if the Athenians turn the disputed sums over to him they will see his opponent, Phormio, in extreme need, while Apollodorus behaves with *hybris* and spends money on the things he usually spends it on. For Fisher (113), the verb *hybrizein* here is not merely a condemnation of Apollodorus' 'extravagant and dissolute behaviour', but signals that such behaviour would constitute an affront against the unjustly defeated Phormio. I agree that the contrast between Apollodorus and Phormio is emphasized in the text, and thus that Apollodorus' reaction to his success at Phormio's expense is an important part of the meaning of *hybrizein* in the passage, but there is little warrant for believing that Apollodorus is to be imagined as *deliberately* spending his ill-gotten gains on luxuries and depravities with the specific intention of further dishonouring his defeated opponent; rather, those who witness his extravagant behaviour are invited to construe it as *hybris* on the grounds that it manifests a shameless self-absorption which others, especially those who have suffered at Apollodorus' hands, will find offensive. The affront to Phormio and others is not Apollodorus' intention in enjoying his luxurious lifestyle in his usual way; rather, his behaviour constitutes an implicit affront to those at whose expense he carouses and those whose claim to honour he ignores. If *hybrizein* may refer to excessive self-assertion which dishonours others simply by failing to take their claims into account, then there is no specific intention to commit a particular act of dishonour, and this case does not fit Fisher's definition of *hybris*.[43]

Two passages in Euripides' *Troades* demonstrate that, while *hybris* (*qua* luxuriating in a misplaced sense of one's own superiority) can be construed as an affront to a particular group of other people (because they have more reason than others to resent the agent's self-assertion), it can also be seen as an attitude which affronts other people in general. At 993-7 there is no hint that the *hybris* of which Hecuba accuses Helen was intended by the latter to dishonour anyone in particular; Fisher's suggestion, that in οὐδ' ἦν ἱκανά σοι τὰ Μενέλεω / μέλαθρα ταῖς σαῖς ἐγκαθυβρίζειν τρυφαῖς (996-7) Hecuba refers to a kind of 'extravagance and dominant "queening it" [which] would be felt to involve an assertiveness against a husband, characteristic of foreign queens',[44] is a rather desperate attempt to maintain his schema—Helen's

---

[43] [D.] xlviii 55 (Fisher 114; *cf.* 440-1) is an even clearer example of the same thing. Here again *hybrizein* is a matter of excessive enjoyment of (illegitimately acquired) prosperity and again there is an element of comparison, between Olympiodorus' *hetaira* and the women of the speaker's own household; there is no implication that the former does or says anything which is specifically designed to bring disgrace on the latter. Rather, they are imagined as 'taking it personally' that she should lay claim to a greater degree of honour than is felt appropriate for a person in her position.

[44] Fisher 114.

hybris does consist in extravagant 'queening it', but there is no reference to a specific victim. Instead, Hecuba represents Helen's behaviour as signifying an excessive claim to honour which entails an implicit lack of regard for the honour of anyone in Helen's group or vicinity.[45]

The occurrence of *hybrizein* in Eumaeus' denunciation of Melanthius at *Od.* xvii 244-6 is comparable:[46] Eumaeus prays that Odysseus will return and put an end to the *aglaiai*, the 'splendour' or 'ostentation', with which the goatherd, behaving with *hybris* (ὑβρίζων), now conducts himself. Fisher sees Melanthius' deliberate insult in his disobedience towards his masters, and possibly also his specific acts of violence and abuse towards his fellow servants and their guests, but the reference of the participle is clearly to the goatherd's ostentatious behaviour and demeanour;[47] this is an insult to anyone who has reason to resent such presumption, but the reference of the *hybris*-word is once again to a misplaced exaltation of the agent's own honour which only implicitly constitutes an attack on the honour of others. Those who may feel themselves dishonoured by the goatherd's conduct do not figure in the thoughts of the agent at all; the dishonour to them consists precisely in his focusing on his own honour to the exclusion of theirs.[48]

In all these passages[49] the relevant *hybris*-word refers to a particular attitude to one's own prosperity or good fortune. The emphasis is on the disposition of the agent, but this is a disposition which inevitably has implications for the relationship between the agent and other people; this seems to me to answer very well to the emphases of the Aristotelian passages considered above, where it was clear that both the disposition of the agent (involving a feeling of superiority and a confidence that one is invulnerable to the misfortunes which plague others) and the effects on the honour of the patient must be given due weight in any discussion of *hybris*. *Hybris* is a concept to which both one's own and others' honour are relevant, and this not merely in the sense that specific acts of insult are typically intended to increase one's own prestige at others' expense.

IV

At this point it may seem that Fisher and I are not terribly far apart; with regard to the passages just discussed, we agree that the behaviour described as *hybris* can be construed as an insult against someone. But whereas Fisher demands a conscious intention deliberately to insult a particular victim, I argue that *hybris* may be a subjective attitude or disposition which can be construed as an implicit affront. My emphasis is on that element of *hybris* which relates to one's

---

[45] Equally, at 1019-22 the *hybris* manifested in Helen's enjoyment of barbarian *proskynêsis* involves no intention to insult anyone in particular, but an excessive conceit of her own worth, implicitly insulting to all those who do not accept that Helen's honour is superior to their own. It is this lack of a proper appreciation of the interplay between her own and others' honour that Hecuba misses in Helen at 1025-8 (Cairns [n. 35] 298).

[46] Fisher 171.

[47] Pompous ostentation (rather than deliberate insult) is the sense of *hybris* at Athen. 522c (a rejected motive for the wearing of Persian dress); cf. *hybrismenos* of clothing at Xen. *Cyr.* ii 4.5 and (negatively) of a shield-device at E. *Pho.* 1111-12; also of excessively expensive and ostentatious hospitality at Ael. *VH* i 31 (on all these, see Fisher 116-17). In the passages which Fisher (*ibid.*) cites from Clearchus (*frr.* 43a, 46, 47, 48 Wehrli), *hybris* is a consequence of luxury, and most of the applications of *hybris*-words refer to concrete acts of dishonour; but in 43a the phrase, καὶ πόρρω προάγοντες ὕβρεως, which links the *tryphê* of the Lydians' gardens and their gross acts of *hybris* against others' womenfolk, must indicate that the former as well as the latter involve *hybris*.

[48] In this passage, as in the others quoted above (this section), Fisher takes an absolute use of the verb *hybrizein* as equivalent to a transitive. But my interpretation suggests that the distinction made by LSJ s.v. between transitive and absolute uses is wholly warranted, even if in some instances it is impossible to be sure whether an unstated object is to be assumed.

[49] *Cf.* Theopompus, *FGrH* 115 F 213 (Fisher 115).

own honour, and I argue that the state of mind which over-values one's own honour is decisive for *hybris*, even though *hybris* regularly involves an assault on the honour of others, and even though over-valuation of one's own honour virtually always constitutes at least a potential affront. This may still not seem like much of a difference, and it may look as though Fisher could accommodate my criticisms without drastically altering his overall thesis; but the real distance between our positions will emerge in this section, when we look at Fisher's arguments for excluding the disposition of 'thinking big', pride, or presumption from his definition. Terms such as *mega phronein* are, I shall argue, ways of referring to the subjective, dispositional aspect of *hybris*, and thus, since *hybris*-words can be used in purely dispositional senses, *hybris* and 'thinking big' can amount to the same thing. Fisher repeatedly denies this;[50] even when the two ideas occur in close proximity with reference to the behaviour of the same agent, they remain (he maintains) conceptually distinct.

Many passages in which the relevant locutions occur are too general to provide much help in settling the matter; whether we distinguish or associate 'thinking big' and *hybris* in these cases will depend on our interpretation of passages which offer more hope of establishing the relationship between the two sets of terms. The most obvious of these is to be found in Sophocles' *Ajax*,[51] at the end of the speech in which Menelaus, justifying his prohibition of burial, attempts to set Ajax's behaviour in the context of the norms of military and civic discipline. He concludes: 'These things go by turns. Previously he was a flagrant *hybristês*, now it is my turn to think big. And I forbid you to bury this corpse, or else you yourself will meet an early grave if you bury him' (1087-90).

According to Fisher, Menelaus' 'assertion that Ajax was a "blazing hybristês", but that he now "thinks big" proclaims that committing *hybris* is the arrogant, violent crime of those who possess, or seek, power, and merely "thinking big" is acceptable and justified self-confidence in one's capacity to exercise power and achieve a satisfactory revenge over one's defeated enemies'. But this falsifies the relationship between the terms; Menelaus' language has become precisely antithetical,[52] and he says explicitly that ἕρπει παραλλὰξ ταῦτα (1087); the things which alternate should be parallel, and that Ajax's *hybris* and Menelaus' 'thinking big' are parallel is indicated by the use of the adverb, αὖ (1088)—it is now Menelaus' turn to play a role similar to that played by Ajax before, when he was a *hybristês*. This must mean that *hybristês*, applied to Ajax, refers not to his commission of specific acts, but to his general demeanour as one who, as Menelaus represents it, found military discipline impossible to bear. It is to this attitude of self-assertion that Menelaus' 'thinking big' now responds, and so 'being a *hybristês*' and 'thinking big' must, at the least, be two ways of describing a disposition of confidence in one's own power.

One must concede, however, that Menelaus is unlikely to be describing his own attitude explicitly as hybristic; thus, while the logic of his remarks demands that 'being a *hybristês*' must involve 'thinking big',[53] it is likely that by terming his own attitude 'thinking big' he means to differentiate it from *hybris*. And Fisher repeatedly points out that the expression 'thinking big' differs from *hybris* in that it may be used of justifiable self-assertion, where *hybris* is

[50] Fisher 125, 148, 224 n. 122, 238, 244, 374.

[51] See Fisher 315-16, Dickie (n. 2) 106.

[52] See 1084-6: ἀλλ' ἑστάτω μοι καὶ δέος τι καίριον
καὶ μὴ δοκῶμεν δρῶντες ἂν ἡδώμεθα
οὐκ ἀντιτείσειν αὖθις ἂν λυπώμεθα.

[53] As Dickie ([n. 2] 106) argues, and Fisher (316) concedes.

generally pejorative.[54] But the very wording of Menelaus' observation suggests that there is a far closer parallel between himself and Ajax than he means to draw, and it is virtually certain that his description of himself as 'thinking big' alerts the audience to the possibility of *hybris* on his own part. Menelaus intends a parallel between unjustified and justified 'thinking big'; but the logic of ἕρπει παραλλὰξ ταῦτα is best preserved if the audience take him at his word, and see both forms of 'thinking big' as illegitimate.

This interpretation is confirmed by the chorus-leader (1091-2): 'Menelaus, do not lay down wise maxims and then yourself become a *hybristês* on the dead.' Fisher maintains that the *hybris* against which Menelaus is now warned is the prohibition of burial and nothing else, and thus (as usual) an action bringing dishonour on a specific victim. There is little warrant for this in the text; but even if the primary reference of the chorus-leader's words is to non-burial, it remains significant that he uses the same word as Menelaus had used of Ajax at 1088, and that he uses the dispositional term, *hybristês*, rather than the verb, *hybrizein*. There is a clear sequence of thought running from the description of Ajax as a *hybristês* at 1088, through Menelaus' avowal of his own *megalophrosynê* in the same line, to the chorus-leader's warning that Menelaus is becoming hybristic at 1092; 'thinking big' is the feature common to both the *hybris* of Ajax, as identified by Menelaus, and the *hybris* of Menelaus, as identified by the chorus-leader. The sequence of thought in this passage is just too neat and precise to admit the *a priori* distinctions that Fisher maintains.

This interpretation of Menelaus' remarks and the Coryphaeus' response to them also sits better with the dialectic of *hybris* in the play as a whole, where *hybris* has been applied to what 'they' do to 'us', rather than to what 'we' do to 'them'.[55] Even if Menelaus does not go so far as sanguinely to proclaim himself a *hybristês*, his remarks none the less encapsulate this process of retaliatory *hybris*.[56] The same pattern is exemplified in the ensuing confrontation between Teucer and Menelaus, in another passage which reveals the connexion between 'thinking big' and *hybris* (1120-5):

Με.   ὁ τοξότης ἔοικεν οὐ σμικρὸν φρονεῖν.

Τευ.   οὐ γὰρ βάναυσον τὴν τέχνην ἐκτησάμην.

Με.   μέγ' ἄν τι κομπάσειας, ἀσπίδ' εἰ λάβοις.

Τευ.   κἂν ψιλὸς ἀρκέσαιμι σοί γ' ὡπλισμένῳ.

Με.   ἡ γλῶσσά σου τὸν θυμὸν ὡς δεινὸν τρέφει.

Τευ.   ξὺν τῷ δικαίῳ γὰρ μέγ' ἔξεστιν φρονεῖν.

References to a person's temper, spirit, or cast of mind can in fact refer to that person's acts or utterances;[57] Menelaus' οὐ σμικρὸν φρονεῖν (1120) is a comment on the insulting language of Teucer's speech; likewise, when he refers to Teucer's δεινὸς θυμός (1124), he is

---

[54] See Fisher 112 n. 193, 316, 323, 374-5 n. 144; for neutral/positive applications of *mega phronein*, etc., cf. Xen. *Ages.* 11.11; S. *Aj.* 1125; Hdt. vii 135-6.

[55] See Cairns (n. 35) 229-30, 234-8.

[56] Thus R.P. Winnington-Ingram (*Sophocles* [Cambridge 1980] 62) may not be absolutely right to say that Menelaus regards *hybris* as a reciprocal process, if Menelaus is not actually confessing to *hybris*; but Menelaus' remarks do reveal the reciprocity of *hybris* once we see through his implication that his own thinking big is justified. He therefore does, as M.W. Blundell points out (*Helping friends and harming enemies* [Cambridge 1989] 91), manifest a form of *hybris* which answers that which he blamed in Ajax.

[57] Fisher 377 recognizes this phenomenon in another connexion, but draws no conclusions for his view of the relation between 'thinking big' and *hybris*.

commenting on a disposition currently being manifested in speech. The same is true of Teucer's defence of his own 'big thoughts' at 1125; Menelaus has identified a formidable spirit of self-confidence behind Teucer's language; Teucer then justifies the spirit *and* the insulting language/behaviour with the claim that such are permissible when right is on one's side. 'Thinking big' in 1125, like *thymos* in 1124 and 'thinking no small thought' at 1120, refers to a demeanour manifested in behaviour, and there is no great difference between saying 'This fellow thinks big' and 'This fellow is insulting me': the reference to the disposition is a comment on the behaviour. This being so, we can understand the logic of Teucer's defence of his own 'thinking big'; Menelaus' references to Teucer's spirit and to his 'thoughts' accuse him of insolence; Teucer realizes that, in effect, he is being accused of *hybris*, and so defends himself. As all the dispositional terms in this short passage are used to refer to actual behaviour, there cannot be as sharp a distinction as Fisher maintains between *hybris*, the act, and 'thinking big', the state of mind. We have seen that a disposition of excessive self-assertion can be construed as an effective insult; now it appears that an actual insult can be described in terms of a disposition of excessive self-assertion. As *hybris* can refer to a disposition which can be described as 'thinking big', so 'thinking big' can refer to behaviour which might otherwise be called *hybris*.

That 'thinking big' and *hybris* can be identical in reference is also demonstrated by three passages of Herodotus vii involving the response of Artabanus to Xerxes' proposed invasion of Greece. Xerxes outlines his intentions and his motives in vii 8, and it is clear that the pursuit of honour is high among his priorities—he does not wish to be left behind in honour *vis-à-vis* his ancestors, and sees the expedition as a means of obtaining *kudos* and winning back *timê* lost as a result of the burning of Sardis and the failure of the previous expedition (vii 8α.2-γ.1); this concern for honour, too, is presented in extravagant terms—Xerxes intends to yoke the Hellespont (β.1), and cherishes an image of the Persian empire, after the conquest of Greece, encompassing all the lands on which the sun shines, equalling 'Zeus' heaven' in extent (γ.1-2). So Xerxes is motivated by honour, believes that he possesses a status sufficient to consider subduing the elements, and dreams of making his dominion co-extensive with the sovereignty of Zeus. Xerxes is also a typical *hybristês* in believing that his good fortune and that of his nation can only continue—god is guiding Persian destiny for the best, and the Persians themselves have merely to follow (α.1).

Artabanus sees the dangers in his nephew's plan; he points out that confidence does not always precede success, as in the case of Darius' expedition against the Scythians (vii 10α), and gives good grounds for caution in undertaking any enterprise against the Greeks, making particular reference to the (apparently pragmatic) dangers of bridging great waterways (α-δ). Having stressed the importance of *euboulia* (10δ), he offers a general, theological warning against over-confidence: 'the god' blasts those creatures which stand out, and does not allow them to 'show off' (*phantazesthai*), but is not irritated by the insignificant; the same applies to houses and trees, for the god is wont to cut back all things that stand out. Thus a great army can be destroyed by a small, because the god allows no one but himself to think big (10ε).[58] This last argument clearly constitutes a response which is very closely focused on Xerxes' proposals, on their dangerous over-confidence which threatens to encroach even upon the *timê* of the gods.

Artabanus' second evaluation of Xerxes' plan comes at vii 16α, after Xerxes has relented from his previous fury at his uncle's opposition, but has been warned by a dream-figure against calling off the expedition. Xerxes now wishes Artabanus to sit on his throne and sleep in his

---

[58] Artabanus' argument shifts from the notion of divine resentment of all forms of prominence to particular resentment of human presumption; the latter is his main point, the former merely an illustration, and the function of the warning as a whole is to provide another perspective on the unexpected failure of great armies when they cross significant natural frontiers to take on apparently inferior opponents.

bed, in order that the same dream may appear to him and he may judge that it is sent by the gods, and although Artabanus is reluctant to accept this invitation, he feels himself under compulsion. He prefaces his acceptance, however, with a rehearsal of his previous opposition to a proposal which 'increased *hybris*' and involved 'always seeking to have something more than what is present'. Even when convinced by the dream-figure that the expedition must go ahead, Artabanus reiterates his earlier position, referring (with examples) to the failure of the strong to overcome the weak, stressing Xerxes' youth, and contrasting the dangers of 'desiring many things' with the virtues of 'keeping quiet' (vii 18.2-3).

This third comment on the merits of the expedition has elements in common with each of the previous; it returns to the central point of the first, that great forces have often been overcome by weaker, and with the second it shares an awareness of the dangers of seeking more. *Hybris* is associated with 'desiring many things' in the second passage, while in the third 'desiring many things' is associated with disastrous attempts by greater forces to subdue weaker; this brings us full circle back to the first passage, where one reason for the failure of such attempts is 'thinking big'. All three passages concern attempts to increase power and prestige beyond a vague limit of what is 'enough'; *hybris* is one way of describing the drive to do this, 'thinking big' is another, and the connexions between the three passages suggest that there is not much to choose between them.[59]

Another reason for assuming that *hybris* and 'thinking big' are virtually interchangeable here is the presumption that Artabanus' characterization of the proposal to invade Greece should refer to identifiable characteristics of Xerxes' original speech. We saw that that speech was strong on self-assertion, manifesting a desire to restore and enhance the monarch's prestige; there were also hints that this concern for individual royal *timê* was somewhat in excess of the norm, envisaging a degree of success which no mortal had hitherto attained. This is readily construed as 'thinking big'; but *qua* extravagant exaltation of one's own claim to honour, stemming from youth, existing good fortune, inexperience of failure, and blind faith in continued success, it also patently deserves the title of *hybris*. In this case it is not merely other mortals who are imagined as affronted, but the gods themselves; Artabanus' statement that 'the god does not allow anyone other than himself to think big' is a recognition that Xerxes' excessive pursuit of honour constitutes an implicit assault on those who possess the most *timê* of all; that the god is the party affected in this case does not alter the fact that we have here what is, on my account, a perfectly standard case of *hybris* involving the pursuit of greater honour for oneself in a way that threatens the honour of others.

Fisher's interpretation,[60] on the other hand, demands that we dissociate Artabanus' first and second evaluations from what Xerxes actually said; on his account, the 'thinking big' of the first speech does not refer to a specific offence on Xerxes' part, but is rather an aspect of Persian

---

[59] See Dickie (n. 2) 104-6. Of particular importance are Artabanus' references to the expeditions against the Massagetae, the Ethiopians, and the Scythians; all three, *qua* attempts to extend power beyond natural limits, have a symbolic function both in themselves and in the presentation of Xerxes' expedition; thus, although Artabanus advances sound pragmatic reasons against the crossing of important natural frontiers and the attempt by greater powers to subdue smaller, his reference to these campaigns is not simply intended to stress the material dangers of expansionism (*pace* Fisher 372), and this constitutes another link between the three passages, esp. between the warning against 'thinking big' and divine *phthonos* in the first and the reference to the three previous campaigns in the third. See J. Gould, *Herodotus* (London 1989) 100-9, and *cf.* F. Hartog, *The mirror of Herodotus* (Berkeley 1988) 331 and (on the Scythian campaign as a prefiguration of Xerxes' invasion) 34-40; on the 'river motif' *cf.* H. R. Immerwahr, *Form and thought in Herodotus* (Cleveland 1966) 75, 84, 91-2, 130, 132, 166, 183 n. 103, 293, 316; Fisher 352-8, 377, 383.

[60] Fisher 367-74, 384.

power which attracts (non-moral) divine jealousy;[61] whereas the *hybris* which Artabanus identifies in his second speech is not Xerxes' own, and has little to do with his acute concern for his own honour, but rather refers to a political characteristic of the Persian nation, its tendency towards imperialist expansionism, bringing 'dishonour' on the autonomous peoples who are its victims. This explanation fails, first because there is no warrant for distinguishing Persian *hybris* as an abstract national characteristic from the *hybris* of those who formulate and carry out Persian policy, and secondly because the relevant passages have much more to say about the dangers of the growth of pride and prosperity in the Persians themselves than about the effects of their actions on others. Fisher treats as discrete and heterogeneous passages which are more plausibly seen as contributing to one consistent presentation of the metaphysical aspect of Xerxes' invasion, in which the elements of human pride, *hybris*, and divine *phthonos* combine. The divine hand is clearly at work in the dreams which appear to both Xerxes and Artabanus (vii 12-19), the attempts of previous potentates to cross natural boundaries provide thematic and symbolic parallels for Xerxes' enterprise (n. 59 above), and an oracle promises divine retribution for the Persians' *hybris* (viii 77);[62] the judgement of Themistocles (viii 109.3) draws all these threads together—the gods and heroes caused Xerxes' defeat at Salamis, because they grudged (ἐφθόνησαν) one man rule over Asia and Europe, impious and *atasthalos* as he was. Thus divine *phthonos* is explicitly associated with the expansionism, sacrilege, and impiety which even Fisher concedes are hybristic, and referred specifically to Xerxes' desire to rule Europe and Asia in vii 8;[63] Themistocles' verdict is the fulfilment of the warning uttered by Artabanus in vii 10ε, which clearly forms part of a presentation of the whole expedition in terms of human *hybris* as infringement of the prerogatives of the gods.[64]

Fisher's treatment of two passages from Euripides' *Hippolytus* indicates the lengths to which he has to go to preserve his absolute distinction between *hybris* and 'thinking big'. At 443-6 the Nurse argues that 'The Cyprian is not a thing to be borne if she flows in full spate; the one who yields she attends with gentleness, but whomever she finds excessive and thinking big, she takes and treats with incredible *hybris*'. 'Thinking big', then, is resisting the power of the goddess, the sort of thing that provokes her to anger to such a degree that she retaliates by subjecting her victim to degrading and dishonouring treatment. Compare 473-6: 'Please, my dear child, give up your perverse thoughts, stop behaving with *hybris*—for this is nothing but *hybris*, wishing to be superior to the gods—and endure in your passion.' Both passages comment on the same sort of conduct; the one sees resistance to the goddess as 'thinking big', the other as *hybris*, and both designations identify that attitude which magnifies the honour of oneself and diminishes that of others. Fisher, however, sees the matter entirely differently; *mega phronein* is a mere condition or concomitant of *hybris*,[65] while the *hybris* which is actually identified

---

[61] The interplay between *hybris*. 'thinking big', and *phthonos* is discussed below. In the present context Fisher (374) may be right to say that the description of the divine reaction as *phthonos* soft-pedals the offensiveness of Xerxes' or the Persians' 'big thoughts' (whereas the description *hybris* calls attention to a moral offence), but it remains clear that 'the god' regards such presumption as an affront. Fisher (*ibid.*) states that the suffering of great armies, which, through divine *phthonos*, fall victim to small, is 'undeserved'; but this is not the implication of ἀναξίως ἑωυτῶν, which contrasts the potential of the greater force for victory with the actual outcome of defeat; defeat was unworthy of them because it was incommensurate with their strength in numbers, abilities (etc.). (See A.W.H. Adkins, *CQ* xvi [1966] 90-4, and M. Heath, *The poetics of Greek tragedy* [London 1987] 82.)

[62] Discussed by Fisher 375-6, and distinguished by him from other evaluations in terms of 'thinking big' and divine *phthonos*. N.b., however, the oracle's conviction that the gods will punish Persian *koros*, a term which emphasizes the extravagant growth of Persian confidence.

[63] Fisher 380 does not make the connexion.

[64] *Cf.* in general H. Lloyd-Jones, *The justice of Zeus*[2] (Berkeley 1983) 60-9.

[65] Fisher 414.

is explained away as 'a cunning sophistry', a 'persuasive definition'. There is no persuasive definition; the gods participate in a hierarchy of honour in which the *timê* they possess is quantitatively but not qualitatively different from that of mortals; to think big to the extent of considering oneself equal or superior to a god is hopelessly to inflate one's own *timê* and provocatively to ignore the *timê* of the god; thus the conditions of *hybris* are satisfied. The sophistry of the Nurse's argument lies not in any redefinition of *hybris*, but in the equation of resistance to (illicit) sexual passion with a challenge to the honour of the goddess of sexual love; this might well be considered an illegitimate dialectical move, but the move from 'challenging the honour of the gods' to *hybris* is perfectly justified in terms of Greek usage; it is consonant even with Fisher's restricted definition of the term. There is a degree of confusion in Fisher's argument here, but behind that lies a desire to create as much distance as possible between *hybris* and 'thinking big'; it will not work.

The same is true of the discussion of *hybris* and *mega phronein* in connexion with Aphrodite's account of her grievance against Hippolytus, rendered in the prologue. Fisher recognizes that Aphrodite complains in general of an insult to her honour, and that she is now set on revenge precisely because she wishes to establish that mortals may not so lightly seek to deny her her due; he also points out that the goddess' complaint against Hippolytus' verbal insults (13) is justified by Hippolytus' attitude towards her in his dialogue with the Servant (102, 106, 113).[66] Yet according to Fisher, the insult constituted by Hippolytus' attitude is a mild one, one at which Aphrodite 'should not' take offence, and which Fisher himself 'would prefer not' to label hybristic. This is not the place for a discussion of the seriousness of Hippolytus' offence; but the point is that he surely does give offence.[67] Whether Fisher would or would not choose to label Hippolytus' behaviour hybristic is neither here nor there, for what we are dealing with is the *goddess*' evaluation of the situation. Of course some people (or gods) are more sensitive to perceived affronts than others; some see an insult where no normal person would; thus what one person considers *hybris* might not be so regarded by another; but if an individual sincerely regards another's behaviour as manifesting unwarranted self-assertion at his/her expense, then that individual is linguistically and culturally justified in describing it as *hybris*. Others may disagree with Aphrodite's perception of *hybris* in Hippolytus, but there can be little doubt that it is *hybris* of which she accuses him. The expression she uses, however, is not *hybris*, but *mega phronein* (6); yet it is clear that Hippolytus' 'large thoughts' have a target—σφάλλω δ' ὅσοι φρονοῦσιν εἰς ἡμᾶς μέγα, says Aphrodite, and she explains her statement with reference to the gods' paramount concern to receive *timê* from mortals (7-8). Not only can 'thinking big' in practice constitute an affront, but the phrase itself can be used actually to refer to the commission of an affront. Thus there is no possibility of a neat separation of 'thinking big' from *hybris*.[68]

---

[66] Fisher 416-17.

[67] Fisher (417) sees the Servant's attempt to avert Aphrodite's anger (114-20) as evidence that Hippolytus' lifestyle, demeanour, and specific remarks do not constitute a major insult; but the Servant only feels driven to make this attempt because of his concern at the danger of what Hippolytus has said, and his wish that Aphrodite show forgiveness is a reminder that gods take such attacks on their honour extremely seriously.

[68] *Cf.* A. *Pers.* 800-31 (Fisher 259-61); *hybris* (808, 820) certainly refers to concrete acts, including failure to recognize the honour of the gods (807-12), but it is also associated with 'godless thoughts' (808), 'thinking excessively for a mortal' (820), 'despising one's present fortune' (825), 'excessively boastful thoughts' (827-8), and 'harming the gods with over-boastful boldness' (831); if the disastrous results of *hybris* (821-2) give a reason for avoiding excessive, unmortal thoughts (820; n.b. γάρ, 821), then 'thinking more than mortal thoughts' must be a form of *hybris*; see Dickie (n. 2) 107. Fisher answers Dickie by making the dangerous concession that 'having excessive thoughts' may be 'an element' in *hybris* here, but maintains that not all such self-assertion is hybristic. The (fallacious) argument that, because *hybris* and 'thinking big' are not identical in definition, they are never identical in reference is also used (308-9) to distinguish *hybrizein* and *hybris* in S. *Ant.* 480 and 482 from *mega phronein* in 479.

The previous paragraphs have discussed those passages which contain references to both *hybris* and 'thinking big' etc. and which offer some hope of establishing the relationship between the two. They have shown that subjective dispositions of self-assertion, describable as 'thinking big', can be considered as genuine cases of *hybris* and that even where *hybris* also encompasses acts which have an impact on the honour of others, *mega phronein* etc. can refer to its dispositional aspect. The overlap of *hybris* and *mega phronein* corroborates what was said above about the importance of the subjective, dispositional side of *hybris*, and it should be obvious that the kind of inflated opinion of one's own worth conveyed by expressions such as *mega phronein* or *phronêma* is a regular feature of *hybris* even where these expressions do not occur. The passages in which *mega phronein* etc. constitute part of *hybris* only make explicit what is latent in the other passages considered above.[69]

V

The question of offences against the gods and their *phthonos* has already been touched upon; we now need to decide to what extent *hybris* may be an offence which arouses the anger of the gods, and whether divine *phthonos* can be a reaction to human *hybris*. Fisher's exhaustive study has performed an enormous service by refuting the misconception that there is something fundamentally 'religious' about the concept of *hybris*, whether that misconception be what he assails as the 'traditional view' (*hybris* as a form of human presumption which meets with divine *nemesis*, especially in tragedy)[70] or the more interesting, but equally unsubstantiated thesis of Gernet (on the essentially religious quality of *timê*).[71] Nevertheless, even under Fisher's conception of *hybris* it is clear that the victim of insulting or dishonouring behaviour can be a god as well as a mortal; and so he discusses a number of passages in which *hybris*-words are used explicitly to denote attacks on divine *timê*.[72] In the previous section, too, we saw that the 'thinking big' which can often be construed as *hybris* could impinge upon divine as well as human honour.[73] A species of 'thinking big' is 'thinking more than mortal thoughts', and we saw in connexion with Darius' speech in *Persae* (n. 68) that such thoughts could be part and parcel of *hybris*. Another example might be the description of Capaneus in the *Septem*; Capaneus' boast οὐ κατ' ἄνθρωπον φρονεῖ (425), and he is openly contemptuous of Zeus and the gods (427-31); Eteocles sees him as a thinker of 'vain thoughts' and comments on his dishonouring of the gods through his boasts (438-43). That this behaviour can be described as *hybris* is clear, and Fisher concedes that, 'When verbal *kompoi* and *mataia phronemata* take these forms and are expressly directed against the honours and powers of the gods, they clearly constitute *hybris*;' but 'that is not to say that all boasting and foolish thoughts can be so

---

[69] *Cf.*, e.g., the Aristotelian passages in sect. II in which *hybris* is associated with wealth, power, and misplaced confidence in continued good fortune; *cf.* E. *Supp.* 463-4, 726-30, 741-4 (Fisher 420-1; the first and third of these passages contain absolute uses of *hybrizein*, and again Fisher's translation, 'commit *hybris*', begs the question by assuming specific acts against particular victims). *Cf* also the *hybris* of Cyrus' sacred white horse (Hdt. i 89; Fisher 353-4; MacDowell, *G&R* [n. 2] 15), which is not disobedience towards its master (Fisher's standard explanation of the *hybris* of domestic animals, 119-20), but the creature's misplaced confidence that it is able to ford a river which in fact is only crossable by ship (νηυσιπέρητον i 89.1).

[70] See Fisher 2-3, 32, 142-8, and *cf.* 484-5, 491-2 on the (untypically) religious aspect of *hybris* in Pl. *Laws*. (But see below, VI.)

[71] Fisher 5, 56, 62.

[72] Fisher 144 (Ar. *Nub.* 1506-9), 146 (Lys. *fr.* 73 Thalheim), 147 (Lys. ii 9), 412-14 (E. *Hipp.* 473-6), 415 (*Or.* 1641-2), 445-6 (*Ba.* 516-17, 553-5, 1297, 1347). *Hybris* may also concern the gods in the sense that they are felt to punish *hybris* among mortals; but here again *hybris* is no more specifically religious in nature than any other form of human injustice; see Fisher, Index, s.v. 'gods, concern at *hybris*/injustice, etc.', and *cf.* MacDowell *G&R* (n. 2) 22.

[73] Most explicitly in the case of E. *Hipp.* 6-8, 13, and Hdt. vii 10ε.

described'.[74] That this is not an admission that 'thinking more than mortal thoughts' is always *hybris* is made clear by his discussion of Clytemnestra's speech at *Ag.* 958-74; 'such over-confident boasting of one's good-fortune [*sic*] and its permanence should ... be classified rather as a strong form of "saying things too great for mortals" (etc.), that, because they can be offensive to other humans and to the gods, may conceivably be considered as (mildly) hybristic'.[75] Fisher's position seems to be that 'thinking (and expressing) more than mortal thoughts' and *hybris* are conceptually distinct, but that a strong form of the former may (as a matter of contingency) constitute a mild form of the latter, even in the absence of the desire deliberately to inflict dishonour on a specific victim. This attempt to have one's cake and eat it will not work;[76] 'thinking more than mortal thoughts' is unlike 'thinking big' in that the latter can, apparently, be justified; the former, however, entails the notion of excess and always involves reprehensible self-assertion in the face of legitimate claims to *timê*; thus it always constitutes a standard case of *hybris* in its unattenuated sense.[77]

There is in many passages a strong connexion between 'thinking more than mortal thoughts' and divine *phthonos*. Fisher accepts the existence of a notion of divine *phthonos* which focuses on recognized moral offences on the part of human beings;[78] he is less willing, however, to accept that such moralized *phthonos* may have human *hybris* as its object. Yet Herodotus' account of Xerxes' invasion of Greece, as we have seen, draws clear links between *hybris*, human presumption, dishonouring the gods, and divine *phthonos*. Themistocles' retrospective explanation of the success of Greek resistance (viii 109.3) contains traces of all these notions. Greek victory, he says, was not achieved by merely mortal means, but the gods and heroes resented (begrudged, were envious—ἐφθόνησαν) that one man, an impious and wanton (*atasthalos*) man, a man who committed gross acts of sacrilege, who actually lashed and bound the sea, should rule Asia and Europe. The *phthonos* identified here focuses not only on the presumption first made apparent in Xerxes' initial proposal to add Europe to his rule (vii 8β-γ), the kind of presumption which Artabanus could describe both as a form of 'thinking big' liable to attract divine *phthonos* (7. 10ε) and as *hybris* (vii 16α.2), but also on the specific acts of impiety and *atasthalia* which even Fisher agrees may be regarded as *hybris*.[79] This *phthonos* clearly bears a considerable moral charge, and responds both to hybristic deeds and to hybristic attitudes. We should expect that wherever divine *phthonos* bears a similar reference to more than mortal thoughts which directly impugn the *timê* of the gods it should also be regarded as responding to *hybris*.[80]

---

[74] Fisher 253.

[75] Fisher 290.

[76] *Cf.* his discussion of S. *Aj.* 756-77 (342-8).

[77] On *hybris* and 'thinking more than mortal thoughts' *cf.* Dickie (n. 2) 85 against Fisher 445. Dickie does, however, import notions of 'mortal limits' or 'the human condition' rather too freely into the discussion.

[78] See Fisher 360, 362, 374.

[79] See Fisher 377-8, on Herodotus' account of the bridging of the Hellespont, where he recognizes that the use of *atasthala* (vii 35.2) identifies conduct which might also be described as *hybris*.

[80] *Cf.* Hdt. i 34.1; Croesus' presumption, Herodotus conjectures, attracted divine *nemesis*. Fisher (357-60, esp. 358 n. 1) is right to argue that the mere occurrence of the term *nemesis* is no proof that Croesus is to be regarded as guilty of *hybris*, for the supposed correlation between human *hybris* and divine *nemesis* which is such a feature of the 'traditional view' is poorly attested. Instead, Fisher agrees with Gould (n. 59) 79 that *nemesis* bears its Homeric sense of 'indignation'; but when he claims that this *nemesis* is merely 'the "indignation" of an "envious" deity' (358) he ignores the fact that Homeric *nemesis* always focuses on some perceived offence (see Cairns [n. 35] 51-4; *cf.* J. M. Redfield, *Nature and culture in the Iliad* [Chicago 1975] 117); if Fisher and Gould are right about the sense of *nemesis* (and I am sure they are), then they must locate the focus of that *nemesis* in a failure to accord honour where honour is due; Croesus' prosperity has led him to place himself on a level higher than other men and to presume to know and control what no mortal can know or control. The signs of *hybris* are all there. N.b., then,

This is clearly the case in the 'carpet-scene' of the *Agamemnon*.[81] *Timê* is central to the scene; Clytemnestra's invitation is an attempt to persuade Agamemnon to lay claim to a greater share of honour than a mortal should possess (922, 925), and her decisive argument, after which Agamemnon ceases to resist, appeals explicitly to his desire to be honoured (939). Agamemnon realizes, too, that Clytemnestra is urging him to exalt his own honour to the extent of dishonouring the gods, and is fully aware of the dangers of *phthonos* as a divine response (921, 946-7); unlike Herodotus' Croesus, he is determined to avoid counting himself happy before he is dead (927-30);[82] and he remains uneasy even as he prepares to tread the crimson path, his *aidôs* in 948-9 a sign that he realizes he is pushing his own claim to *timê* too far and failing to pay honour where honour is due.[83] The *phthonos* of the gods which is so prominent in this context, then, does not focus only on human prosperity or success; rather, Agamemnon is persuaded to act in a way which demonstrates an illegitimate response to success, a response of over-valuation of one's own *timê* clearly classifiable as the *hybris* which proceeds from prosperity. Fisher's insistence that Agamemnon's actions and motives, while representing 'more than mortal thoughts', constitute at most only a 'mild' form of *hybris*,[84] becomes explicable when we realize that for him it is only the gravity of the act itself which really matters. But the importance of the scene lies in what it tells us about Agamemnon's motivation and his sense of his own honour *vis-à-vis* that of others; the *phthonos* envisaged focuses on Agamemnon's excessive self-assertion, and this is hybristic precisely because its 'victims' are those who enjoy the greatest *timê* of all. The scene suggests not only that 'thinking more than mortal thoughts' is necessarily a form of *hybris* but also that *phthonos* and *hybris* can be correlatives.

It remains to be seen, however, whether they are necessary correlatives, or only contingently so, where *phthonos* has become a just response to human offences rather than mere jealousy. We need, therefore, to explore the concept of *phthonos* in greater detail. As a human emotion, *phthonos* bears no essential reference to *hybris*. Human *phthonos* focuses on another's possession of goods which one would like for oneself; it presupposes no moral offence, but is a malicious reaction to others' success or good fortune which is frequently said to demonstrate the viciousness not of its target, but of its patient.[85] Yet this *phthonos* does operate within the same milieu as *hybris*, in that it enjoys a fundamental relationship with the notion of honour. *Phthonos* can be directed at the possession of any good,[86] but in practice the relationship between *phthonos* and competition for honour is intimate, first because it is typical of the *phthoneros* to resent not only the other's success, but also the enhanced reputation and status which success brings; *phthonos*, as a feeling that others' success somehow diminishes one's own standing, thus belongs with the competitive impulse of *philotimia*.[87] Secondly, as a reaction to the possession of some admired good or quality, *phthonos* is the negative obverse of that

---

that the statement at i 34.1 is referred in context to Solon's warning that the divine is φθονερόν and ταραχῶδες (i 32.1). Fisher is right to assimilate *nemesis* and *phthonos* in this case (contrast Gould [n. 59] 80), but wrong to deny their focus on an offence on Croesus' part.

[81] For a recent discussion of the scene, with bibl., see G. Crane, *CP* lxxxviii (1993) 117-36.

[82] See Crane (n. 81) 130-1.

[83] *Cf.* Cairns (n. 35) 194-8, 210-11 n. 129.

[84] Fisher 287-9, with repeated doubts as to whether 'the walking on tapestries should be called hybristic at all' (289).

[85] See (e.g.) Arist. *Rhet.* 1388a35-8; *cf.* Pl. *Laws* 731a-b; Isoc. ix 6, xv 259; Plut. *Quaest. Conv.* 681e; P. Walcot, *Envy and the Greeks* (Warminster 1978) 72-5; *cf.* P. Bulman, *Phthonos in Pindar* (Berkeley 1992) *passim*.

[86] See Arist. *Rhet.* 1386b18-20, 1387b21-1388a28.

[87] See Arist. *Rhet.* 1387b31-1388a23 on *phthonos* and *philotimia*, esp. the remarks on the grounds of *phthonos* (1387b34-1388a5) and on its typical targets (1388a5-23). *Cf.* Walcot (n. 85) 16-20, 34, 62, 97-8; H. Lloyd-Jones, *Greek comedy, Hellenistic literature, Greek religion, and miscellanea* (Oxford 1990) 255-7.

positive acclaim which is conveyed by terms such as *timê*, *kleos*, etc. Hence the commonplace that others' *phthonos*, though possibly harmful and certainly to be deprecated, is at least a sign of one's own achievement, that *phthonos* is better than pity.[88]

There is no question of a total separation of meaning between human and divine *phthonos*, and the conception of divine *phthonos*, I take it, will have grown out of the deeply rooted belief that the gods are givers of both good and evil on an apparently indiscriminate basis, and that they are particularly stinting (*phthoneroi*) in their granting of good fortune or in allowing it to continue.[89] The idea that the gods somehow resent mortals' success has its roots in Homer,[90] but is expressed in terms of *phthonos* (etc.) only in later authors such as Pindar, Aeschylus, and Herodotus. It is generally accepted that in these authors moral factors enter into the notion of divine *phthonos* to a greater or lesser degree, but there is real disagreement as to where the line should be drawn between ('unmoralized') conceptions which focus on success alone and those ('moralized') which focus on human transgression.[91] Fisher is firmly on the side of those who see real persistence of the unmoralized view (especially in Herodotus), and he draws an absolute distinction between the gods' punishment of *hybris* and their non-moral resentment of human prosperity; there may be a degree of overlap between the fields in which *hybris* and *phthonos* are operative (because divine *phthonos* may focus on human offences), but where the 'unmoralized' form of *phthonos* is in play, no overlap can exist; the gods' resentment of human prosperity in itself cannot be regarded as outrage at human *hybris*.[92]

This is debatable, for there are certain differences between human and divine *phthonos* which make it difficult to consider a conception of the latter which totally excludes the possibility of a relationship between divine *phthonos* and human *hybris*. In achieving the kind of success which annoys a god, a human being has transgressed a boundary in a way that the target of human *phthonos* has not; for, though it may be virtually impossible to know for certain where the limit lies, there certainly exists an unbridgeable gap in status between men and gods. Since this is true, and since it is well known that the gods resent all incursions into their sphere, it behoves any prosperous mortal to avoid antagonizing the gods by the appearance of rivalry; accordingly, if such a person's success does antagonize the gods, he has failed to be cautious, to exhibit the proper attitude of mind. Thus in divine resentment of human prosperity there will always be an element which focuses on the attitude of the human victim, either on his failure

---

[88] See Clytemnestra at A. *Ag.* 939; better to be envied than pitied, see Pi. *Pyth.* 1. 85, Hdt. iii 52, Thales 17 DK, Epicharmus 285 Kaibel/B34 DK. The Pindar passage is perversely interpreted by Bulman (n. 85) 5, 21. For the standard interpretation, see A.W.H. Adkins, *Moral values and political behaviour in ancient Greece* (London 1972) 77; see further G.M. Kirkwood in Gerber (n. 2) 169-83.

[89] See W.C. Greene, *Moira* (Cambridge Mass. 1944) 20, 28, 36-7, 39-42, 47-8, etc. The verb *phthonein* does not occur in the context of divine responses to human affairs in Homer, but its sense of 'begrudging', 'refusing to grant' (see Walcot [n. 85] 26; Bulman [n. 85] 15-17) is shared by *agasthai*, which is used of the gods' grudging attitude towards mortal happiness (*Il.* xvii 70-1, *Od.* iv 181-2, v 118-20, viii 565-6, xiii 173-4, xxiii 209-12; *cf.* Greene 19-20; Lloyd-Jones [n. 64] 57; Walcot [n. 85] 26).

[90] See *Il.* v 440-2, vii 446-53, *Od.* iv 78-81, xii 287-9, with Greene (n. 89) 20; Lloyd-Jones (n. 64) 4, 56; Walcot (n. 85) 26.

[91] Broadly, commentators divide into those who find that all or most instances of divine *phthonos* found in Pindar, Aeschylus, and Herodotus are, in some sense, 'moral', and those who believe that even in (one or other, or some passages of) these authors traces of the unmoralized version remain. For the first view see E. Fraenkel, *Aeschylus: Agamemnon* ii (Oxford 1950) 349-50; Lloyd-Jones (n. 64) 56-70, (n. 87) 255-6; Bulman (n. 85) 1, 31-4, 88 n. 66; for the second, see Greene (n. 89) 6-7, 48, 74-5, 84-8, 103, 106, 113 n. 54; Adkins (n. 88) 78-82; Walcot (n. 85) 22-51; R.P. Winnington-Ingram, *Studies in Aeschylus* (Cambridge 1983) 1-13.

[92] See esp. Fisher 363: 'the chorus of the *Agamemnon* (750 ff.) analysed in Chapter Seven [pp. 275-7] is ... strong evidence that explanations in terms of divine jealousy at human prosperity and those in terms of divine anger at human crime are felt to be incompatible contraries'. *Cf.* Garvie (n. 2) 243-4, 249, 252. For Fisher's distinction between 'moralized', 'unmoralized', and 'ambiguous' forms of divine *phthonos*, *cf.* 360, 362.

to manifest the correct attitude (to recognize the gulf between human and divine prosperity, as well as the role of the gods in human achievement), or on his active adoption of the wrong attitude (deliberate rejection of mortal limits, through an inflated conception of himself as master of his destiny and guarantor of his prosperity). The target of human *phthonos*, by contrast, is not necessarily deluded as to his real status and worth. Thus divine *phthonos*, even when focusing on the prosperity of its target, must always be a form of resentment in which the divine agent feels justified, in that the target has failed (by commission or omission) to recognize the boundary which separates his *timê* from that of the gods.[93]

This can be demonstrated by passages in which the concept of divine *phthonos* is felt to be at its most 'unmoralized'. In Aeschylus' *Persae*, the divine *phthonos* which Xerxes, according to the Messenger, did not understand (362) is not explicitly referred either to great prosperity alone or to some more specific offence; it certainly belongs with the Messenger's ascription of the defeat at Salamis to the influence of an *alastôr* or *kakos daimôn* (354), as with similar Persian pronouncements on the unpredictability of (unnamed) *daimones*, but there is also stress in the context on Xerxes' confidence (352, 372-3), which the Queen later explains in terms of the human tendency blindly to believe that present good fortune will continue forever (601-2). The unpredictability of fortune or of the gods who grant and withhold good fortune has been a theme since the beginning of the play (see 93-100, 157-8, 161-4); it was with the help of 'some god' that Darius amassed his great prosperity, and the correct attitude in anyone who would retain such prosperity is caution. The Messenger's reference to *phthonos* belongs with these hints of a mistaken attitude to prosperity and to the decisive role played by the gods in all human affairs which are later broadened into an account of the Persians' deluded pride, impiety, and *hybris* by the authoritative pronouncements of Darius' ghost.[94]

Similarly, in Herodotus' presentation of the warnings delivered by Solon to Croesus and Amasis to Polycrates (i 32.1, iii 40.2)[95] the emphasis is more on the need to manifest the proper attitude in success than on the notion that success in itself provokes the gods to envy; Croesus, Solon implies, should be more circumspect and less confident of his own happiness, given that prosperity is in the lap of the gods, with their tendency to disrupt human affairs. This point is just as clear in the case of Amasis' advice to Polycrates, which urges him, in view of the divine propensity to *phthonos*, to acknowledge the role of the gods in all human prosperity and to manifest a proper sense of perspective with regard to his wealth by jettisoning something he values highly. That the gods are not simply concerned with material wealth emerges in sinister fashion from the fact that even this propitiatory offering proves unsuccessful—the offence cannot be undone by material propitiation (and Polycrates' display of caution and humility comes too late to save him).[96] In all these cases there exists at least a minimal idea of offence, and the conditions for describing the behaviour and motivations of the humans involved as *hybris* are, at least from the divine point of view, satisfied.

Neither in *Persae* nor in Herodotus, moreover, do apparently non-moral conceptions of divine *phthonos* constitute the last word on the subject. In *Persae*, the Persians' complaints

---

[93] *Cf.* (broadly) Lloyd-Jones (n. 64) 4, 56-8, 67-70, (n. 87) 255-6; N. Yamagata, *Homeric morality* (Leiden 1994) 97-8 makes a similar point.

[94] Winnington-Ingram (n. 91) and Fisher 261-2 agree that the interpretation offered by the Ghost is authoritative, but contrast this moral explanation of Persian failure with the supposedly non-moral interpretation of the other characters; M. Gagarin (*Aeschylean drama* [Berkeley 1976] 49-50) denies that the Ghost's interpretation has any special authority. Others (Fraenkel [n. 91] ii 349; Lloyd-Jones [n. 64] 69) regard the Messenger's reference to *phthonos* as itself a moral explanation.

[95] See Fisher 357-60, 362-3 (resp.).

[96] In the case of the *phthonos* against which Artabanus warns Xerxes the element of moral offence is, as we have seen, even clearer (confirmed at viii 109.3).

against the evil deities who have struck them down at the height of their fortunes are partisan,[97] and belong with a perspective which seeks to minimize the notion of Persian offence; the true perspective is offered by the ghost of Darius, but it is one which the Athenian audience will already have formed for themselves as they set the remarks of the Persian characters in the context of all that is said about Persian prosperity and presumption. Likewise in Herodotus, most of the references to divine *phthonos* come in speeches,[98] and in the cases of Solon, Amasis, and Artabanus their purpose is precisely to warn without giving offence; all three try to promote the correct attitude to one's own prosperity and the prerogatives of the gods, and so remind their interlocutors of the dangers of offending jealous and resentful deities, as a way of stressing the dangers without actually accusing them of *hybris*. The suggestion of *hybris*, however, is there; Solon, Amasis, and Artabanus are not denying that divine *phthonos* is a response to a perceived human offence; they are rather suggesting that the gods have a tendency to perceive offence where none is intended. The implication that divine resentment is sometimes excessive and unjustified allows the warning to be conveyed without explicit accusation of *hybris*. But the gods themselves believe their *phthonos* to be justified, and the author or the reader can always endorse this interpretation.[99] Thus Solon, diplomatically, speaks of the instability of good fortune and reminds his host of the grudging meddlesomeness of the divine; but the reader will have noted the dangerous moral blindness involved in Croesus' conviction that his prosperity is paramount and permanent, and the notion that forthcoming *phthonos* would be directed not merely at his great wealth but at his mistaken attitude to that wealth is confirmed by the sequel, where Croesus is declared liable to divine *nemesis* because he thought himself (*not*, as Lloyd-Jones points out,[100] because he was) the most fortunate of men.[101]

An evaluation in terms of *phthonos*, then, can never entirely rule out an interpretation of the same state of affairs in terms of human *hybris*. In all behaviour which attracts divine *phthonos* will be found the same elements of the transgression of limits, of the offender's excessive pursuit of honour and status, and of the corresponding insult to the *timê* of the gods.

VI

The final area in which I wish to test Fisher's view of *hybris* concerns the role of exuberance, energy, and high spirits. This will lead us into an examination of certain instances of *hybris* in Plato which Fisher regards as anomalous, but which I believe can be accommodated in an account which lays proper emphasis on the dispositional aspect. We come now to the central point of disagreement between Fisher and MacDowell. For MacDowell,[102] the notion of excess energy or exuberance stands very close to the heart of the concept, whereas for Fisher

---

[97] See 345-7, 353-4, 472-3, 513-16, 724-5, 909-11, 920-1, 942-3, 1005-7; *cf.* Winnington-Ingram (n. 91) 13-14, Fisher 261.

[98] *Cf.* Immerwahr (n. 59) 313, who argues that the one occurrence of the notion in narrative (iv 205) proves that 'the great advisers do indeed propound a Herodotean idea'. The *phthonos* of iv 205 is moral in scope, and Immerwahr's statement will, I think, be true only if we construe divine *phthonos* in moral terms.

[99] *Cf.* Lloyd-Jones (n. 87) 255-6.

[100] See Lloyd-Jones (n. 64) 63; *cf.* 68.

[101] That divine *phthonos* is by definition justified seems to be the view favoured by Aeschylus in *Pers.* and *Ag.*, and to be implied in Herodotus. Similarly Pindar's references to divine *phthonos* (*Ol.* 13.24-8, *Pyth.* 8.71-2, 10.20-1, *Isth.* 7.39-42) belong with warnings such as 'Seek not to become Zeus' (*Isth.* 5.14, cf. *Ol.* 5.24) and his stress on the objective limits dividing man and god (*Nem.* 6.1-4). See Lloyd-Jones (n. 64) 69; Bulman (n. 85) 31. Kirkwood (n. 88) imagines that the use of divine *phthonos* as a 'rhetorical formula of praise' (174-6) entails the absence of 'the Herodotean religious meaning' (182; *cf.* 176, 179). The two are not incompatible; even if the former is primary, it implies the latter.

[102] And for Hooker (n. 2).

the essence of *hybris*, even when associated with such ideas, is always to be found in a more immediate and specific reference to dishonour. Crucial to MacDowell's case are those passages in which *hybris* is attributed to animals and plants, which he maintains cannot simply be dismissed as metaphorical, but must contribute to an overall definition.[103]

On the basic question of the status of the *hybris* of animals and plants I agree with Fisher that such manifestations must be regarded as metaphorical and therefore as parasitic on standard applications of the term. None the less, there must be a ground for the metaphorical extension, and we are entitled to look for the point of comparison in something that vehicle and tenor may be thought to have in common, the identification of which may prove enormously helpful in establishing the flavour or character of a concept.[104] For Fisher, the point of comparison in the case of domestic animals and plants lies in a sense that they are 'disobedient', dishonouring human beings by 'refusing' to behave as required;[105] in wild animals and natural forces such as the winds and the sea, on the other hand, the point of comparison is the violence and aggression which the elements share with hybristic humans.[106] According to Xenophon, *Cyr.* vii 5.62-3, for example, horses which are *hybristai* cease to bite and to *hybrizein* once castrated; similarly, bulls cease to *mega phronein* and *apeithein*, and dogs to desert their masters. The notion of disobedience, which can certainly be construed as offering dishonour to a superior, is clearly there, and Fisher (119) sees this as the main reference of the *hybris*-words in this passage. Equally, however, both *mega phronein* and *apeithein* may convey some of the force of *hybris* here, and indeed the aspect of arrogant pride and wilfulness will be difficult to separate from that of disobedience, given that, in a domestic animal, the latter can always be construed in terms of the former and the former always furnish the explanation for the latter. This passage is compatible with Fisher's definition, although it also offers scope for an interpretation which lays more stress on the dispositional aspect.

Elsewhere, however, and indeed in general, the metaphor is better explained with reference to dispositional factors. Common to a number of metaphorical applications, for example, is a reference to food.[107] The analogy between the over-feeding which produces *hybris* in animals and plants and the wealth or good fortune which commonly leads to *hybris* in standard, human cases is well explained by Michelini, who also notes how the opposition between the *hybris* of plants and that of humans is mediated by the frequent association of the latter with both *koros*[108] and vegetation imagery.[109] This notion of nurture and growth in itself suggests those ideas of 'being full of oneself, 'becoming too great' which I have argued to be important, and surely implies a process in the hybristic organism itself, a process resulting in a condition of

---

[103] See MacDowell (n. 2) *G&R* 15-16, *Meidias* 21.

[104] *Cf.* R. Osborne in Cartledge *et al.* (n. 8) 85.

[105] See Fisher 19, 119-20.

[106] Fisher 121.

[107] See Arist. *GA* 725b35 (Fisher 19); Ar. *Vesp.* 1306, 1310 (Fisher 120); Theophr. *HP* 2.7.6, *CP* 2.16.8, 3.1.5, 3.6.8, 3.15.4 (Michelini [n. 2] 36-8). Previous pampering rather than excessive nutrition *per se* is what leads to *hybris* in both horses and subjects at Xen. *Hiero* 10.2 (Fisher 119), but the common idea of sufficiency/surfeit still underlies the comparison.

[108] See Michelini (n. 2) 36 on Solon *fr.* 4. 8-10 (West) and Pi. *Ol.* 1. 55-6, where the connexion between *koros* and food is explicit; *cf.* Fisher 70-3, 240-2, on these passages, and 21, 75, 154-5, 212-13, 219, 221-3, 230-2, 233-5, 272-3, 336, 347-8, 375-6 on others. *Cf.* also MacDowell *G&R* (n. 2) 15-16 and n.b. the association between nutrition, youth, and *hybris* at Pl. *Laws* 835e (Fisher 486). For a recent (brisk) survey of *koros* in archaic poetry, see J.J. Helm, *CW* lxxxvii (1993) 5-11.

[109] See Solon *fr.* 4. 34-5 (West) (Michelini [n. 2] 40, Fisher 73), Bacch. 15. 57-63 (Michelini 39, Fisher 227-9); A. *Pers.* 821-2 (Michelini 40, Fisher 258-61), 104-11 (Michelini 39, Fisher 265); S. *OT* 873-9 (Fisher 329-38), *fr.* 786 Radt (Fisher 97); *cf.* the rapprochement between human and animal *hybris* at Pl. *Phd.* 81e (Fisher 456 n. 13) and *Laws* 808d (Fisher 480); also the physical and psychological forms of *hybris* at *Laws* 691c (see below).

satiety in which the potency or energy of the subject exceeds the norm; in a human being this will be the disposition of excessive self-assertion which arises from having had too much of a good thing and entails the feeling that one's own claims are superior to those of others.[110]

This notion of excessive energy or power is present even in the passage from the *Cyropaedia* (above). The point of the reference to the *hybris* of horses (the *megalophrosynê* of bulls, etc.) is that it can be cured by castration (as it can in humans—the ultimate point is an analogy between castrated male animals and eunuch bodyguards). We do not have to look far to discover why it is that castration should be felt to cure *hybris*—there is clearly a link between the powerful forces of masculinity and a headstrong spirit which values self over others and rejects external restraint.[111] Even if the verb *hybrizein* refers to the commission of concrete acts in this passage, the association with an excess of natural energy and power constitutes an important part of the context which helps give *hybris* its meaning.[112] This association is, as MacDowell points out,[113] apparent in the attribution of *hybris* to donkeys: Fisher explains the 'erect *hybris*' of the donkeys about to be sacrificed by the Hyperboreans (P. *Pyth*. 10.34-6) with reference to 'the rampantly ithyphallic prancing that donkeys are often held to display in ritual and folk-tale contexts, and are often shown displaying in Greek art'.[114] But where does this leave his definition of *hybris*? No doubt the donkeys' prancing coincides with their notorious recalcitrance, and no doubt this could be construed as a form of disobedience or dishonour; but there is no mention of such things in the context, and the application of the adjective *orthios* to the creatures' *hybris* locates the latter quite firmly in their phallic display, a self-absorbed and self-indulgent manifestation of their frivolous masculine energy.[115]

In passages like these *hybris* is envisaged as a force which grows and wells up within the organism, a force which has its origins in the energy-giving properties of food or in the inherent fertility or fecundity of the subject itself, and which eventually grows so powerful that it can be contained no longer and 'breaks out'.[116] This idea of *hybris* as a form of unchecked energy is present not only in its associations with plants and animals, not only in the use of plant and food imagery in the context of human *hybris*, but also in many of the standard contexts in which the concept is at home—in the common link between *hybris* and wealth;[117] in those passages in which *hybris* is associated with *tryphê*;[118] in the association of *hybris* with the

---

[110] *Cf.* Michelini (n. 2) 38-9: 'The ὑβρίζων organism—whether human, animal, or vegetable—puts self-aggrandizement before the performance of the social role assigned to it'.

[111] For the *hybris* of the bull, that most masculine of animals, *cf.* E. *Ba*. 743-4; Fisher (121; *cf.* 450) sees the reference of *hybristai* here in 'frightening hostility to men', but I should prefer to see it in the creature's general 'machismo', its brutish demeanour, and its exuberant sexual energy.

[112] This is another passage where Fisher's translation, 'committing *hybris*', assumes no distinction in sense between transitive and absolute uses. See above, nn. 48, 69.

[113] *G&R* (n.2) 15-16.

[114] Fisher 232-3 (quotation, 233). On the opposition between *hybris* and festive *hêsychia* in this and other passages, see Fisher 216-42 *passim* and Dickie (n. 2); *cf.* W.J. Slater, *ICS* vi (1981) 205-14.

[115] For asinine *hybris*, *cf.* Hdt. iv 129 and Ar. *Vesp*. 1306, 1310; I doubt whether the point of comparison in these passages lies in 'acts of disobedience' or 'insolence to one's betters' (Fisher 120) rather than in the general skittish exuberance of a particularly self-willed creature.

[116] Such, I think, is the normal connotation of the compound *exhybrizein*; see below, n. 140. On the imagery of plant-like growth and efflorescence in the content of human psychology, see R. Padel, *In and out of the mind* (Princeton 1992) 134-7.

[117] See Fisher 19-21, 102-4, 113-17, and Index, s.vv. '*olbos*', 'wealth'.

[118] See above Sect. III, Fisher 113-17.

young;[119] and in the connexion between *hybris* and alcohol in sympotic contexts,[120] where the significance of the concept is not exhausted by reference to the concrete acts of dishonour undoubtedly perpetrated by drunken *hybristai*, but also resides at least partly in the fact that alcohol unleashes energies which are normally repressed.[121] The notion of exuberance and excess energy is thus to be linked to the element of self-assertion, over-confidence, and presumption in *hybris*, in both metaphorical and non-metaphorical passages;[122] it gives us a great deal of the flavour of *hybris*—not, indeed, the essence of the concept, but an important aspect of its phenomenology, and, I should say, of its 'meaning'.

If this is correct, there are important consequences for the treatment of *hybris* in Plato. Fisher contends that Plato revalues *hybris*, greatly extends its range, and adapts it to his own, highly individual philosophy. 'Platonic' forms of *hybris* emerge in works of Plato's middle period, especially in the *Phaedrus*, and are atypical in that they represent *hybris* as any form of excessive desire (though the paradigm of such *hybris* is sexual desire) and oppose *hybris* to *sôphrosynê* in what Fisher claims is a much more general sense than is normally the case.[123] While I would not deny that Plato does very occasionally extend the application of *hybris*, I do not agree that he ever redefines the concept, and I believe that, if we give the dispositional aspect of *hybris* and its frequent representation in the language of exuberance and energy their due importance,[124] then we can dispense with the distinction between 'Platonic' and 'traditional' uses.

Fisher's identification of a Platonic revaluation of *hybris* starts from a discussion of the relevant terms in the *Phaedrus*. In the first passage discussed in this connexion (237d-238c), it is indeed clear that some extension of the regular meaning has occurred, for *hybris* is explicitly applied to the rule in the soul of any form of irrational desire, opposed to *sôphrosynê qua* rule of reason over desire, and specifically said to include excessive desires for food, drink, and sex. The surprise in this passage is the extension of *hybris* to cover gluttony and dipsomania; but the surprise is softened, first (as Fisher himself points out, 468) by the regular association of *hybris* with food and drink—food and drink can be seen as leading to *hybris*, and one can eat and drink in a hybristic manner.[125] But this association with food and drink does not normally extend to the identification of the specific desires for such things with *hybris*, and to that extent the use of *hybris* here is anomalous. The anomaly, however, is slight, and it is further reduced by the antithesis with *sôphrosynê* (which is regular and traditional). Furthermore, as Fisher again makes clear (*ibid.*), the personificatory language of (here) bipartition facilitates an understanding of

[119] See esp. Arist., *Rhet.* 1389b8-9, 11-12, to be seen in the context of the spirited impulsiveness of youth (1389a2-b12 *passim*); *cf.* Pl. *Laws* 835e, where the *hybris* of youth is explicitly associated with being well fed; *cf.* n. 108 above, and Fisher 20, 97-9, and Index, s.v. 'youth'.

[120] See Fisher 16-17, 57-8, 98-102, 145, 203-7, 488; also Index, s.vv. '*symposia*', 'drink'.

[121] N.b. esp. Panyassis *fr.* 13 Davies (Fisher 206). The links between drink, the control of passions, and the terminology of honour and shame are explored below *re* Plato's *Laws*.

[122] We should perhaps remember that the notion of 'flourishing' is typically opposed to *hybris* not only in the case of plants but also in connexion with both youth and the symposium (see [e.g.] B. MacLachlan, *The age of grace* [Princeton 1993] 39, 57-64, 91-3).

[123] See Fisher 467-79, 485-92, 499-500. 'Platonic' instances constitute a problem for Fisher's definition in that they often refer to forms of self-assertion in which no other person is harmed (453). Fisher (468-9) recognizes that these uses have developed from standard cases, for *hybris* is associated with the desires for food and drink, and is often found as a description of pederastic sexual activity (n. 34 above); *hybris qua* disobedience is also relevant, in so far as 'Platonic' *hybris* presupposes the tripartite or bipartite soul, in which the lower elements rebel against the higher. Nevertheless, he still sees the Platonic development as 'radical', and 'startling' (492).

[124] Fisher (e.g. 489, 491) recognizes the presence of many of the complex, traditional, and metaphorical associations in Plato's uses of *hybris*, but does not see these as mitigating the novelty of Plato's view of the concept.

[125] See (e.g.) *Od.* i 227 (Fisher 163, MacDowell *G&R* [n. 2] 16).

hybris as the refusal to fulfil one's allotted role, which can readily be construed as the dishonouring of superior by inferior. In so far as *hybris* is attributed to the quasi-personified desiderative part, then, its sense is quite regular and traditional; the departure from tradition comes only when this *hybris* of one part of the soul against another is said to account for *hybris* of the whole person. But this extension, as we have seen, is mitigated; and it is further mitigated by the fact that the main point of the passage is the condemnation of pederastic sexual desire, for in pederastic contexts *hybris* has come to be used as a descriptive term for practices which as a matter of fact involve the dishonour of a submissive by a dominant party.[126] Also relevant, however, is the fact that *hybris* is not just the name for a type of act or intention to act, but can refer more generally to self-indulgent and egotistical self-assertion; such self-assertion, in the Greek context, is always a matter of honour, in that it inevitably involves an image of oneself and one's status which implies as a correlative a certain attitude towards the claims of others. In applying *hybris* to all forms of excessive desire (desires which involve excessive self-assertion both on the part of the whole person and on that of the desiderative part of the soul), Plato is exploiting the most fundamental of all significances of *hybris*, the idea that *hybris* involves a disposition in the agent which overvalues self and undervalues others. The *hybris* identified in this passage, then, is less startling under an interpretation which gives the dispositional aspect of *hybris* its due than it is under one which stresses the actual over the dispositional.

This is as far as Plato goes in extending the sense of *hybris*. The other passages in the *Phaedrus* are fully explicable in traditional terms; at 250e the opposition of psychic parts is not in question, and the *hybris* of the man who, on seeing the earthly manifestation of the Beautiful, conceives the desire to 'go the way of a four-footed animal and sow children' is opposed both to reverence (*sebas*) for the beautiful object and to *aischynê* at pursuing unnatural pleasure; it is thus fully at home in its normal context of honour and shame, of the disgrace of pederastic desires,[127] and of the pursuit of self-assertion in the face of the honour of others. The next relevant passage comes in the description of the horses which draw the chariot of the soul, and so the opposition of psychic parts is relevant, but once again the personification of the parts makes the *hybris* of the bad horse analogous to that of a whole person; the good horse is a 'lover of *timê* with *sôphrosynê* and *aidôs*', the bad 'a companion of *hybris* and *alazoneia*' (253d-e). Both sides of this antithesis deal with attitudes to honour; the good horse values honour, but observes limit in its pursuit, its *aidôs* recognizing the point at which excessive pursuit of *timê* violates the honour of others and so becomes dishonourable for oneself, while the bad exaggerates its own importance (*alazoneia*) and pursues its selfish goals in excessive ways which dishonour others (*hybris*).[128] *Hybris* here, to be sure, is used in the service of a highly individual Platonic doctrine, but its actual significance in the description of the personified psychic force is wholly traditional.

Of course, the implication is there that the *hybris* of the 'bad horse', which represents the purely selfish, irrational, appetitive aspect of the human personality, will, if it prevails, translate into *hybris* of the lover against his *paidika*, and so there is a close link between these passages and the earlier at 237d-238c; but the application of *hybris* to all desires, while perhaps not totally abandoned, is at least not mentioned in these later passages, and so the *hybris* of the individual in whose soul the *hybris* of the appetites prevailed would be readily explicable as the

---

[126] *Cf.* Fisher 109-10 (and above, n. 34).

[127] See G. Vlastos, *Platonic studies* (Princeton 1973) 25 n. 76, and contrast A.W. Price, *Love and friendship in Plato and Aristotle* (Oxford 1989) 228-9 n. 8. K.J. Dover, *Greek homosexuality* (London 1978) 163 n. 15, and Fisher 474 see a reference to both homosexual and heterosexual intercourse.

[128] For the opposition between the two horses in terms of *hybris* against *aidôs*/*aischynê*, cf. 254c, 254e.

standard *hybris* of the pederast, abandoning proper self-control in favour of selfish desires which take no account of the honour of the other party. The real importance of the attribution of *hybris* to the bad horse lies in the recognition that this kind of self-assertion or self-indulgence springs from forces within the personality which subvert the individual's concern for the honourable; the personificatory allegory is Plato's way of locating *hybris* in a defective disposition of character, in which basic human drives have been allowed to run riot.[129] His account thus combines stress on the dispositional aspect of *hybris* with the portrayal of this aspect in traditional terms as the product of the growth of powerful forces within the individual.[130]

The arbitrariness of Fisher's distinction between 'Platonic' and 'traditional' uses of *hybris* is demonstrated by his treatment of the discussion of the proper task of the statesman which concludes the *Politicus* (305e-311e). Fisher (479-80) is happy to classify the two instances of *hybris*-words in this section of the dialogue as 'traditional', denoting 'anti-social and unjust aggression', but this does scant justice to the argument. The discussion of the Statesman's task begins with the opposition of *sôphrosynê* and *andreia* as traits of character; these two are then analysed into simpler terms, as quietness and quickness, which can be either praiseworthy or excessive; excessive quickness is called 'hybristic' and 'manic', excessive slowness or softness cowardly and indolent (307b-c). This temperamental opposition is then traced in the state, where the political consequences of the ascendancy either of the *kosmioi* or of those who tend towards *andreia* are equally disastrous, and so the role of the true Statesman must be to weave these elements into a harmonious whole, both in the individual and in the state; those who are incapable of sharing in a manly and *sôphrôn* character, but instead are driven to atheism, *hybris*, and injustice by their evil nature, he must eliminate (308e-309a).

In both applications of *hybris*-words here we are dealing with states of character in which an excess of vigour, 'quickness', or manliness leads to a breakdown in the personality; this aspect of the context is much more prominent than any implicit reference to aggression against others (though aggression is the consequence of the relevant character defect which makes it so problematic). The references to *hybris* must be understood in terms of the general opposition between self-control and self-assertion as dispositions of character; this is confirmed in the ensuing discussion of the twin methods of interweaving of *andreia* and *sôphrosynê*, through education and eugenics, which emphasizes the importance of avoiding intermarriage within the two character-types—continued intermarriage between brave and brave with no admixture of *sôphrosynê* will issue in madness, while that between souls 'too full of *aidôs* and unmixed with manly daring' will eventually produce complete passivity (310d-e). Two points in this last

---

[129] In manifesting *hybris* and *alazoneia*, the bad horse, which represents the *epithymêtikon*, is being credited with thymoeidic responses; but this phenomenon, in which each 'psychic part' possesses the capacities which typify the others, is a regular feature of Plato's tripartition, not a sign that the categories of the *Rep.* are breaking down. See J. Annas, *An introduction to Plato's Republic* (Oxford 1981) 142-6; G.R.F. Ferrari, *Listening to the cicadas* (Cambridge 1987) 185-203.

[130] Cases of 'Platonic' *hybris* in other works prove equally or more traditional. At *Phd.* 81e-82a (Fisher 476), *hybreis* are associated with vices (love of drinking, gluttony) which involve lack of self-control and contrasted with those (injustice, tyranny, rapacity) which entail action in infringement of others' rights. At *Rep.* 402e-403b (Fisher 477) pederastic sex is said to involve excessive, maddening pleasures which signify *hybris* and *akolasia* and are incompatible with *sôphrosynê*; the view that *sôphrosynê* and excessive pleasure are incompatible because the latter 'makes one go out of one's wits' shows that *sôphrosynê* is being used in its everyday, quasi-intellectual sense. *Hybris* and *akolasia*, regular antonyms of *sôphrosynê*, connote the pursuit of self-assertion beyond the limits which *sôphrosynê* observes; *akolasia* is always liable to be reformulated in terms of *hybris*, because self-indulgence implies a view of one's *timê* which takes little account of the *timê* of others. It is partly this that makes such instances of *hybris* recognizably traditional; but also relevant are the elements of undisciplined, riotous exuberance (expressed several times by Plato in terms of *mania*) and the consequent failure to fulfil one's social role which are constitutive of the *hybris* of plants. For the opposition, *hybris/akolasia/*madness *versus sôphrosynê/*limit, cf. *Phlb.* 26b, 45d-e, *Soph.* 228d-229a (Fisher 478-9).

passage indicate that we are still dealing with matters pertinent to the earlier occurrences of *hybris*: first, madness is the ultimate consequence of an excess of manliness or daring, as at 307b; we note, therefore, that manliness is said eventually to 'burst into bloom' (*exanthein*) with 'madnesses of all sorts'; the botanical metaphor is familiar in the context of *hybris*, and it cannot be that *hybris* is not in Plato's mind here.[131] This suggests that we are to regard *hybris* and *mania* in 307b as close associates; both are, here as elsewhere in Plato (particularly in cases classified by Fisher as 'Platonic'), the result of an excess of vital, masculine energy, analogous to the excess of growth potential which produces *hybris* in plants. The reference to *aidôs* is the second indication that we are still dealing with a form of *hybris* as an unbalanced, undisciplined, diseased state of character, for *aidôs* is, even more clearly than *sôphrosynê*, that recognition of the balance between one's own and others' *timê* which inhibits excessive self-assertion. The discussion in which *hybris*-terms occur thus deals exclusively with the dispositions of self-assertion and self-control, expressed in terms which both invite a construction of these notions in terms of *timê* and locate their origins in innate character-traits which must be regulated, educated, and harmonized. The *Politicus* thus effaces the distinction between 'Platonic' and 'traditional' uses of *hybris*. It is 'Platonic' in seeing *hybris* as a character-trait antithetical to *aidôs* and *sôphrosynê*, but thereby also 'traditional', for *hybris* traditionally has its roots in a disposition of excessive self-assertion.

The *Politicus* in many respects looks forward to the *Laws*, in which Plato's interest in the dispositional basis of *hybris* may also be traced. The roots of *hybris* in unrestrained drives are apparent in the long discussion of the utility of controlled alcohol abuse which dominates the early part of the work; *symposia* as they currently exist encourage pleasure, *hybreis*, and every sort of senselessness (637a-b), but in the controlled *symposion* advocated by the Athenian, through which one repeatedly comes to terms with one's own hybristic and other passions, repeated relaxation of one's *aidôs* can eventually foster an ingrained form of *aidôs* which keeps *hybris* safely under control. *Hybris* occurs only once in the discussion of the reformed *symposion* (649d5),[132] but its one appearance has to be understood in the context of the discussion of *methê* as a whole. Basic to this is the opposition between *sôphrosynê* and *andreia* which was operative in the *Politicus* but goes back ultimately to the *Republic*.[133] In the discussion of alcohol as a drug which removes one's inhibitions and, paradoxically, facilitates the acquisition of an ingrained inhibitory mechanism, we are dealing with the same two educable drives as in the *Politicus*, one of self-assertion, described in terms of *anaischyntia*, *anaideia*, and boldness, and one of self-control, relying on the good *phobos*, *aidôs/aischynê*.[134] It is with these self-assertive, bold, and dangerous drives that *hybris* belongs, as 649c-d makes clear: just as *andreia* has to be developed by confronting circumstances in which we naturally feel fear, so the avoidance of *anaischyntia* and boldness must be practised when we are affected by factors which naturally incline us to be exceedingly confident and bold, to wit *thymos*, *erôs*, *hybris*, *amathia*, and *philokerdeia*,[135] which arise from the conditions of being wealthy, physically attractive, or strong; all these things make us drunk with desire for pleasure and make us mad. It is clear from the list in which *hybris* occurs that the term is being applied in a

---

[131] L. Campbell, *The Sophistes and Politicus of Plato* (Oxford 1867) *ad loc.*, is right to compare A. *Pers.* 821.

[132] See Fisher 488.

[133] See 646e-647a: *andreia* is a matter of dealing with fear of pain and danger in the correct way, and *sôphrosynê* is closely associated with *aidôs/aischynê*, which, *qua* fear of ill-repute, opposes the strongest pleasures.

[134] See 647a-d, 649b (the *anaideia* of the drunk), 649d, 671c-e; for wine as a drug which both relaxes and develops *aidôs*, *cf.* 666a-c and 672b-d, with Cairns (n. 35) 374-5.

[135] Not *deilia*, rightly deleted by Ast (*cf.* E. B. England, *The Laws of Plato* i [Manchester 1921] 270). *Amathia* here is probably the effrontery involved in thinking one knows what one does not.

dispositional sense; the other terms are all dispositions or drives of agents, not forms of behaviour, and the purpose of the list is to name affections which naturally incline us to be confident and bold; it is thus impossible that *hybris* should refer to 'insulting violence and [unfortunate phrase] straight sexual excesses'.[136]

So *hybris* is here a dysfunctional trait of character involving excessive boldness or confidence and a desire for some form of pleasure. The same characteristics recur in a specifically sexual context at 782e-783a.[137] Where in the *Phaedrus* all excessive desires, including *erôs*, were called *hybris*, here excessive desires for food and drink as well as for sex are called *erôs*, and it is the last, the keenest form, which most sets people on fire with *maniai* burning with the greatest *hybris*; all three desires, however, are *nosêmata* and their growth and onrush are to be quenched.[138] The 'growth and onrush' are those of the *nosêmata*, not of *hybris*,[139] but still the fact that the *erôs* which is regarded as a disease can 'burn with *hybris*' and produce madness reveals that we are dealing with that complex of ideas in which the deviant psychological drives which cause disturbances within human beings have much in common with the uncontrolled vital·forces which are described as *hybris* in plants.[140] We thus have the *Phaedrus*' identification of sexual and non-sexual desires as manifestations of one drive with different objects; this assimilation of other desires to the sexual urge combines with the presence of the metaphorical associations of *hybris* with exuberance, fertility, and turmoil in regularizing the application of *hybris* to all forms of desire (for *hybris* is regularly linked with *erôs* in its everyday sense, and if all desires are forms of *erôs*, then *hybris* can be associated with all desires). But this *hybris* is also a matter of excessive self-assertion at others' expense, whether we regard it specifically as the lack of deference of a personified desire towards a superior *logistikon*, or more generally as an experience of the individual in the grip of *erôs*—a desire for self-gratification which takes no account of the honour of the object of desire, or a desire to indulge one's own passion regardless of the role in life laid down for one by *logos*.[141]

That Plato's view of hybristic desires is firmly rooted in the traditional significance of *hybris* is made clear by the discussion of three types of *philia* at 837a-d. The essential distinction is between the love of the body, a form of *philia* which is based on the lover's desire to obtain from the beloved something that he lacks, and a form which exists between equals and is reciprocated, the desire of one soul for another like itself. These forms can, however, be

---

[136] Fisher 488.

[137] Discussed by Fisher 485-6, and classified as 'Platonic'.

[138] England's explanation of the Mss. σβεννύντων as scribal error is persuasive, and it would be better to read σβεννύναι with the Aldine.

[139] *Hybris* does, however, occur as the object of *sbennumi* at 835d-e, where *hybris* is a fire/disease/desire which burns and grows within the (well-fed) individual and leads to self-indulgent sexual behaviour.

[140] The notion of *hybris* as a form of disease or madness which results from too much of a good thing (n.b. *tryphê* at 691a) is active at 691c: giving 'more to the less' and disregarding moderation (e.g. sails to ships, food to bodies, and rule to souls) results sometimes in disease, sometimes in 'the offspring of *hybris*', injustice. The participle ἐξυβρίζοντα applies both to those things which break out into disease and those which produce injustice; we thus have a notion of physical disease as the result of a form of *hybris* in the organism which comes of over-feeding. The verb *exhybrizein* suggests in itself the bursting out of a *hybris* hitherto contained, and this fits very well with the statement that *adikia* is the offspring of *hybris*; *hybris* is thus the disposition, the force which grows out of control within the individual, and injustice is its issue in concrete acts. Fisher (19, 112, 120-1, 129-30, 135, 147, 299, 344, 388, 393-4, 427, 489 [this passage]) typically refers the verb to the commission of acts.

[141] *Cf.* 835d-e (above n. 139) and 83lc-e, where the elements of *erôs*, shamelessness, and selfishness strongly suggest a *hybris* which lies in neglecting one's proper concerns as a human being in favour of a hedonistic conception of advantage.

combined within one individual, which inevitably causes a conflict of desires,[142] between the motivation of one whose passion is a physical craving like hunger and who 'awards no *timê* to the character of the beloved's soul' and that of one 'who considers the desire for the body to be a matter of no importance', and who 'regards the fulfilment of the body with the body as *hybris*, and because he both respects and reveres *sôphrosynê*, bravery, magnificence, and *phronêsis*, would wish to remain pure forever with a pure beloved' (837b-d).

The *hybris* which the pure lover rejects is traditional in two ways; first, it involves that lack of regard for the honour of the beloved that is attributed to the base, physical lover, and concentrates instead on selfish gratification of extravagant desires; and secondly, it constitutes a failure to live up to the standards of behaviour proper for one who aspires to virtue. This last makes contact with *hybris* in its traditional guise because Plato sees good performance of one's allotted role as a human being as a matter of paying honour where honour is most due—to reason, to the soul rather than the body, and ultimately to the gods. Indulgence of one's baser desires is *hybris* because it involves exalting oneself, and the inferior part of oneself, in the face of the much weightier claims to consideration of reason, the good, and the divine. Plato's ideas of what sorts of action or desire qualify as *hybris* may be idiosyncratic and extreme, but his view of what *hybris* is is entirely traditional; *hybris* is still a matter of illegitimately placing oneself, one's desires, and one's own claim to honour before the legitimate claims of others.

One final passage may help to draw these ideas together. At 713c the Athenian begins a myth which is used to illustrate the disasters which ensue when human beings order their lives and their communities without deference to an ultimate, divine authority. Human nature is insufficient to order human affairs without *hybris* and *adikia* (713c), and so Kronos placed human communities under the rule of *daimones*, whose kingship made for peace, *aidôs*, *eunomia*, and an abundance of justice, and made human peoples free from faction and happy (713c-e). Contemporary communities must, as far as possible, recreate this kind of regime, in which the divine rather than the human is the ultimate source of authority, and foster obedience to the divine in us (713e-714a); the alternative, be it rule of one man, few men, or many, is irremediable disaster, caused by the insatiable urge to gratify extreme desires (714a).[143] These remarks are presently followed by an appeal to the colonists of the new city, which extols humility before 'the god' and his attendant, Justice, and warns:

> if anyone, raised up by pride [*megalauchia*], whether exulting in money or honours, or again in bodily beauty along with youth and senselessness, blazes in his soul with *hybris*,[144] as if he needed neither ruler nor any leader at all, but were actually sufficient to lead others, he is left behind deserted by god, and, once left behind, he takes to himself yet others of the same kind and romps [σκιρτᾷ], throwing everything at once into confusion; to a good many people he seems to be someone, but after a short time he pays to justice no negligible penalty, and utterly destroys himself, his household, and his city (715e-716b).

---

[142] This conflict is not presented as one between psychic parts, but as one between the two other types of lover, concrete persons representing abstract types of motivation. Thus we do not quite have the personification of the good and the bad horse of the *Phaedrus* myth, and the *hybris* which is associated with the inferior form of *erôs/philia* is that of a type of individual rather than of one part of the soul against another. *Cf.* England (n. 135) ii 344, on 837a2, and 345 on 837b8.

[143] The paradosis would introduce the metaphor of disease at this point (714a5-6); but England's ([n. 135] i 442) defence of Hermann's seclusion of νοσήματι is persuasive.

[144] It is unclear what text Fisher (489) is translating, but the Mss. ὁ δέ τις ἐξαρθεὶς...φλέγεται ...καταλείπεται, printed by Burnet, will not do. We need either the εἰ δέ τις of some quotations or the ὁ δέ τις explained by England ([n. 135] i 448-9). N.b. that the conditions described in ἢ χρήμασιν...ἀνοίᾳ are those which are typically associated with *hybris*; if, therefore, England is right to take this phrase as subordinate to ἐξαρθεὶς ὑπὸ μεγαλαυχίας, this is a sign of the closeness of *hybris* and *megalauchia* here.

Fisher calls this passage 'a mixture of old and new ideas', but there is no element which is not thoroughly traditional. The *hybris* of the unjust type is, as usual, something which results from too much of a good thing, a powerful force, associated with youth and high spirits, which builds up within the individual until it can be contained no more,[145] and which involves over-valuing one's own qualities to the extent that one under-values the claims of others and neglects one's social role. The novelty of the passage for Fisher seems to lie first in the stress placed on the role of the divine, and secondly in the notion of *hybris* in the soul; but although in both these directions Plato is using *hybris* as an element in a moral theory that is certainly highly individual, his application of the term is in no way revisionary. Fisher is right to link this passage with others on the need to honour the soul, or the immortal in us,[146] but while this does introduce the idea of the divided soul it implies no novel extension of the meaning of *hybris*, for *hybris* in such a context remains the insolent and self-centred failure to pay honour where honour is due.

The exhortations to honour the soul and to refrain from *hybris* belong very closely with similar exhortations to honour the gods; in the immediate sequel to the passage quoted the hybristic way of life is contrasted with following the divine, behaving with *sôphrosynê*, and honouring especially the gods and one's parents (716c-718a); this exhortation is then followed by a coda in which one's obligations to honour other relatives, *philoi,* and guests are also mentioned (718a). The emphasis on the need to honour the gods above all is typical of the *Laws*, but it entails no revaluation of the concept of *hybris* in the direction of a specifically religious offence; rather, since the gods are firmly entrenched at the top of a hierarchy of honour, *hybris* against them is the worst *hybris* of all.[147] Similarly, the *hybris* which involves a failure to honour the best part of oneself is a matter of withholding due deference; in dishonouring what should be an internal source of authority one is also giving in to a powerfully disruptive psychic force and failing to fulfil one's social role;[148] these are traditional elements in the concept, and this way of looking at the matter is not a Platonic revaluation of *hybris*, but rather Plato's way of explaining what *hybris*, in its traditional guise, really is. The extreme over-valuation of the self that is *hybris* is, for Plato, a failure to control disruptive forces within the personality, a refusal to accept one's place within a rational system, and an exaltation of the merely human (or less than human) at the expense of the divine. Plato's recognition of the associations of *hybris* with exuberance, vigour, disease, and madness is, because it forms such an obvious point of contact between his view and some of the earliest poetic applications, valuable evidence of the dispositional basis of *hybris*. Since Plato does give the dispositional aspect its full significance and does connect *hybris* with failure to know one's place in society and in the universe as a whole, he is in some ways less revisionary in his approach to the concept than is Aristotle.

---

[145] Excess energy and high spirits, I think, are the basic connotations of σκιρτᾷ at 716b2; *cf.* Ar. *Vesp.* 1303-6. Fisher (491) would specify 'sexual excitement or over-confident violence'.

[146] *Cf.* 697c-d, 726a-728c (Fisher 490).

[147] *Cf.* the hierarchy of kinds of *hybris* at 884a-885b (Fisher 483-5).

[148] In Cairns (n. 35) 373-8 I underestimate the extent to which Plato's emphasis on 'honouring the soul' implies an internalized form of *aidôs*; but see 378 n. 103 on 837c.

CONCLUSION

We are now in a position to compare Fisher's definition of *hybris* with that of his most persuasive opponent; and it must be said that MacDowell's 'having energy or power and misusing it self-indulgently' can now be seen to have a great deal in its favour.[149] But its great demerit is its failure to recognize that, as social phenomena, the excess energy and self-indulgence of someone who is 'full of himself' must be construed in terms of *timê*. For *timê* is the concept with reference to which are balanced the claims of the individual and the rights of others. Expressing one's excess energy self-indulgently means placing oneself and one's pleasure first, and thus losing sight of one's status as one among others. Self-aggrandisement constitutes an incursion into the sphere of others' honour, because the concept of honour is necessarily comparative.[150] Thus the reason why MacDowell, Dickie, and others ought to recognize that their accounts of *hybris* should be firmly located within the concept of honour is also the reason why Fisher should accept that the essential relationship between *hybris* and dishonour can accommodate purely dispositional, apparently victimless forms of self-assertion. Both sides, in fact, make the same error, in working with a view of dishonour which is too narrowly focused on the perpetration of acts of physical or verbal affront; but both demonstrate valuable insights into the nature of *hybris* which should be incorporated into an account of *hybris* as a way of going wrong about the honour of self and others.[151]

DOUGLAS L. CAIRNS

University of Leeds

---

[149] The element of self-indulgence is central to my view of *hybris* as excessive self-assertion in the face of others' claims; it also emerges in the frequent association of *hybris* with *akolasia* and in the antithesis of *hybris* and *sôphrosynê* or *aidôs*; but it is especially prominent where acting 'just for *hybris*' is contrasted with action for some further motive (see n. 31 above).

[150] This is noticed by Aristotle in so far as he recognizes that *hybris* is a form of particular injustice which seeks to increase one's own honour at the expense of another (*cf*. n. 30 above); the comparative aspect of *timê* also plays a major role in his account of *phthonos* at *Rhet*. 1387b25-30, 1388a12-24 (esp. 18-21). Aristotle's view has much (and mine a little) in common with the modern description of honour in terms of a 'zero-sum game'; but the very existence of the term *hybris*, referring to a way of dishonouring others which brings no honour to the agent, proves that the zero-sum view is an over-simplification. See Cairns (n. 35) 94 n. 141 (*cf*. 56 n. 42) and *PLLS* vii (1993) 162, 166 n. 32; *cf*. (and contrast) now Cohen (n. 34) 63.

[151] This paper was written at the Seminar für klassische Philologie (Göttingen) in the summer of 1993; I am grateful to the Alexander von Humboldt Stiftung (and to Professor Dr C. J. Classen) for making my stay possible. I also wish to thank Dr Roger Brock, Dr Malcolm Heath, Professor Alan Sommerstein, and two anonymous referees for their helpful suggestions. I am especially grateful to Mr A.F. Garvie for stimulating discussion and criticism, and for generous communication of his own work on *hybris*, both published and unpublished.

Journal of Hellenic Studies cxvi (1996) pp 33-46

NOMOS IN ATTIC RHETORIC AND ORATORY

FORENSIC oratory must of necessity deal with the subject of law, and rhetoric which aspires to be of use in the courts must offer the potential litigant or logographer guidance on the way to deal with questions of law. Accordingly, Aristotle devotes some space to this issue in the *Rhetoric*. Although the morality of Aristotle's advice has been debated, little attention has been paid to the more basic question of the soundness of his advice.[1] The aim of this paper is to examine Aristotle's presentation of the rhetoric of law in the *Rhetoric* in comparison with actual practice in surviving forensic speeches. The fourth century *Rhetorica ad Alexandrum*, commonly ascribed to Anaximenes of Lampsakos, also offers advice on the manipulation of argument from law, and the general similarity of that advice to Aristotle's suggests either direct influence or a common source. Anaximenes' discussion of the use of law in forensic oratory is both more brief and less systematic, and will be given more cursory treatment.

I

Aristotle begins his discussion of the law in the *Rhetoric* with what to the modern reader at least is a paradox, a paradox which has profound implications for his treatment of law in oratory. For he lists laws among the *atechnoi pisteis*. Aristotle divides the means of persuasion into two groups, *entechnoi pisteis* or 'artful proofs', those means of persuasion which are the province of rhetoric,[2] and *atechnoi pisteis* or 'artless proofs' which 'have not been provided through us but were already in existence'. He lists as examples witnesses, tortures and contracts. When he returns to the subject of artless proofs in 1375a22 ff. he adds two more items, oaths and laws. For Aristotle therefore law is, at least in forensic contexts, a means of persuasion.[3] Formally, at least, his inclusion of law among the artless means of persuasion reflects current practice. There were no lawbooks, and there was no text of relevant laws available to the jurors. It was up to the individual litigant to provide his own excerpts from the laws in order to prove his case. So laws are introduced in court exactly like other documents pertaining to the case. In the late fifth and early fourth century the formulae for introducing laws differ significantly from those used for introducing witnesses;[4] but this merely reflects the fact that witnesses were required to depose in person at this period, while laws were read out by the clerk of the court. Once the procedure for witness testimony was altered in the 380s, so that witness depositions were read out by the clerk, the formulae tended to coalesce,[5] with the result that there was no perceptible difference in the lawcourts between the law and depositions, contracts, tortures and oaths. The procedures for the citation of laws inevitably mean that the use of laws by litigants

---

[1] See W.K.C. Guthrie, *The sophists* (Cambridge 1971) 125 f., W.M.A. Grimaldi S.J., *Aristotle Rhetoric I, a commentary* (New York 1980) 317 f., for the ethical question. Problems of application are noted in passing by D.C. Mirhady, 'Aristotle on the rhetoric of law', *GRBS* 31 (1990) 397, E.M. Harris 'Law and oratory', in *Persuasion* ed. I. Worthington (London 1994) 130-150, 140.

[2] Arist. *Rhet.* 1355b35 ff.

[3] Although Anaximenes recognizes a similar category of proof (*Rhet. Alex.* 1428a16 ff.), it is interesting to note that his four types of 'supplementary proof' do not include law. D. Mirhady, 'Non-technical *pisteis* in Aristotle and Anaximenes', *AJP* 112 (1991) 5-28, 10 f. suggests that Aristotle's item 'law' corresponds to Anaximenes' item 'opinions of the speaker' and that both reflect an original item *enklema*, 'the statement of accusation' in their shared source. However, since nothing is said by Anaximenes in any of his references to this *pistis* to indicate that it is to be confined to any one or other aspect of the factual or other issues dealt with in oratory, forensic or otherwise, I find it difficult to accept the identification. It is easier to suppose that the two authors have independently expanded a simpler schema which they have inherited.

[4] Witnesses, e.g. Lys. 13.64 καί μοι ἀνάβητε μάρτυρες: laws, e.g. Lys. 14.5 ἀνάγνωθί μοι τὸν νόμον.

[5] See e.g. Isai. 2.16 καί μοι τὰς μαρτυρίας ἀνάγνωθι ταύτας καὶ τὸν νόμον.

approximates them in some respects to the status of depositions etc. For although considerable space is given to laws relating unambiguously to the main issue in order to demonstrate substantive points, that is to prove that the speaker's conduct in the matter under dispute has been, or the opponent's has not been, in accordance with the law, we also find speakers using laws to support tangential issues, for instance to demonstrate allegations of the sort classified by rhetoricians under the heading *diabole* (that is, intended to create hostility toward the opponent) or to overwhelm the jury with a seemingly compelling array of legal support.[6] Laws, like depositions, tortures etc., form part of the speaker's strategy. It is important however to distinguish between the formal presentation of laws and the role of law in the courts. Firstly, laws were protected procedurally in a way which distinguished them from other *atechnoi pisteis*. We are told that the penalty for introducing a non-existent law was death.[7] Procedures were in place to prevent abuse in relation to other *atechnoi pisteis*. For false witness there was the *dike pseudomartyrion*; this action would also prevent abuse in cases of torture, since both the challenge to torture and the torture session itself would be witnessed, and also in cases of contracts for similar reasons. But the penalty in such cases consisted of damages to the prosecutor. Law is privileged in its protection by the death penalty. It is also privileged in the decision-making process, since the jurors swore to vote according to the laws and decrees of the Athenian assembly and Boule.[8] Law is thus treated in an ambiguous way. Formally it is treated as a means of proof; but it is given a status quite distinct from other means of persuasion.

Aristotle subdivides law in the *Rhetoric* into different types, though not with complete consistency. He defines law at *Rhet.* 1368b5 ff. as follows:

ἔστω δὴ τὸ ἀδικεῖν τὸ βλάπτειν ἑκόντα παρὰ τὸν νόμον. νόμος δ' ἐστὶν ὁ μὲν ἴδιος, ὁ δὲ κοινός· λέγω δὲ ἴδιον μὲν καθ' ὃν γεγραμμένον πολιτεύονται, κοινὸν δὲ ὅσα ἄγραφα παρὰ πᾶσιν ὁμολογεῖσθαι δοκεῖ.

Let unjust action be defined as doing harm voluntarily contrary to the law. There are two types of law, individual and common. By individual I mean the written law which forms the basis of the constitution, by common all the unwritten laws which seem to be universally agreed.

At 1374a25 *idios nomos* and *gegrammenos nomos* are again identical. However, at 1373b he says:

λέγω δὲ νόμον τὸν μὲν ἴδιον, τὸν δὲ κοινόν, ἴδιον μὲν τὸν ἑκάστοις ὡρισμένον πρὸς αὑτούς, καὶ τοῦτον τὸν μὲν ἄγραφον, τὸν δὲ γεγραμμένον, κοινὸν δὲ τὸν κατὰ φύσιν.

---

[6] I discuss this issue in 'Artless proofs in Aristotle and the orators', *BICS* xxxix (1994) 95-106.

[7] [Dem.] 26.24 καὶ θάνατον μὲν ὡρικέναι τὴν ζημίαν, ἐάν τις οὐκ ὄντα νόμον παράσχηται, τοὺς δὲ τοὺς ὄντας εἰς τὴν τῶν οὐκ ὄντων νόμων τάξιν ἄγοντας, τούτους ἀτιμωρήτους περιορᾶν. As with so much else in the Athenian system, enforcement (by legal action) was presumably left to the volunteer, either the opponent or *ho boulomenos*.

[8] For this and other clauses in the dikast's oath see A.R.W. Harrison, *The law of Athens* II (Oxford 1971) 48, R.J. Bonner and G. Smith, *The administration of justice from Homer to Aristotle* II (Chicago 1938) 152 ff. S.C. Todd, *The shape of Athenian law* (Oxford 1993) 60 underrates the force of law when he attributes to it only a persuasive power. It is of course true that the litigant in citing a law seeks to persuade the jurors of its applicability to his own or his opponent's conduct, and, where conflicting laws are cited, of the greater applicability in context of one law rather than another. Thus the law forms part of the process of persuasion. But this does not mean that the jurors, once convinced of the relevance of a law to the subject at issue, feel that its authority in court is merely to suggest a response. The juror's oath, and the strenuous efforts of Athenian litigants to prove that the law supports their stance on the subject at issue, indicate that the jurors did feel bound by the law and that for the most part they consciously sought to make their decisions conform to the law. That the jurors might allow other factors to outweigh the law indicates only that its authority was not absolute, not that it did not take priority over other considerations. Here I am in general agreement with Harris (n. 1), though I do not share his belief (p.137) that we can dismiss occasions on which emotional appeal obfuscated legal considerations as rare aberrations.

I term one type of law individual, another common, individual being that which is defined by a group with reference to themselves, consisting of two categories, unwritten and written, common being that which accords with nature.

The definitions at 1368b and 1373b are not entirely compatible as formulated.[9] In the first, unwritten law is identical with common/shared law, as distinct from individual law; in the second, unwritten law is a species of individual law. For our present purposes it is the first formulation which matters, for this is the definition which forms the basis of Aristotle's guidance on appropriate use of the law in oratory. The unwritten local law is of no further significance for the treatise. What Aristotle meant by unwritten or common law is never fully clarified, since the distinction between written and unwritten law does not play a major role in the *Rhetoric*; as with the other *atechnoi pisteis*, once he has dealt with law he abandons it. In 1373b7 ff. and 1375a33 ff. he exemplifies common law with reference to the famous speech of Antigone justifying her decision to bury Polyneikes in contravention of Kreon's decree.[10] This would appear to identify common law with rules of conduct, as does 1374a23 ff.,[11] where he lists gratitude for a good turn, requital of benefactions, helping friends. This agrees with Perikles' famous formulation of unwritten laws in Thucydides as rules whose breach results in informal rather than formal sanctions, and with the (possibly) dependent passage in Lysias 6, which quotes Perikles to the effect that one should obey the unwritten as well as the written laws.[12] But Aristotle also cites Alkidamas' maxim that nature made no man a slave.[13] Evidently therefore he has in mind something broader than non-statutory imperatives.

II

Since Aristotle has characterized law as a species of artless proof, he proceeds to analyse the treatment of law in the context of the lawcourts according to a simple schema for dealing with such proofs. Aristotle is not, of course, particularly interested in the artless proofs themselves, for they are not in his opinion the real business of rhetoric.[14] The orator's role is to use rhetorical proof (specifically argument) to maximize the impact of his own artless proofs and to minimize the impact of his opponent's. This means undermining the general validity of such

---

[9] See in general M. Ostwald, 'Was there a concept of ἄγραφος νόμος in classical Greece' in *Exegesis and argument: studies in Greek philosophy presented to Gregory Vlastos*, ed. E.N. Lee, A.P.D. Mourelatos, R.M. Rorty, 70-104, 71f., Grimaldi (n. 1) 287.

[10] *Rhet.* 1375a34-b2 τὸ μὲν ἐπιεικὲς ἀεὶ μένει καὶ οὐδέποτε μεταβάλλει, οὐδ' ὁ κοινός (κατὰ φύσιν γὰρ ἐστιν), οἱ δὲ γεγραμμένοι πολλάκις, ὅθεν εἴρηται τὰ ἐν τῆι Σοφοκλέους Ἀντιγόνηι· ἀπολογεῖται γὰρ ὅτι ἔθαψε παρὰ τὸν τοῦ Κρέοντος νόμον ἀλλ' οὐ παρὰ τὸν ἄγραφον,

οὐ γάρ τι νῦν γε κἀχθές, ἀλλ' ἀεί ποτε...

[11] *Rhet.* 1374a18 ff. ἐπεὶ δὲ τῶν δικαίων καὶ τῶν ἀδίκων ἦν δύο εἴδη (τὰ μὲν γὰρ γεγραμμένα τὰ δ' ἄγραφα), περὶ ὧν μὲν οἱ νόμοι ἀγορεύουσιν εἴρηται, τῶν δ' ἀγράφων δύο ἐστιν εἴδη· ταῦτα δ' ἐστὶν τὰ μὲν καθ' ὑπερβολὴν ἀρετῆς καὶ κακίας, ἐφ' οἷς ὀνείδη καὶ ἔπαινοι καὶ ἀτιμίαι, καὶ τιμαὶ καὶ δωρεαί (οἷον τὸ χάριν ἔχειν τῷ ποιήσαντι εὖ καὶ ἀντευποιεῖν τὸν εὖ ποιήσαντα καὶ βοηθητικὸν εἶναι τοῖς φίλοις καὶ ὅσα ἄλλα τοιαῦτα), τὰ δὲ τοῦ ἰδίου νόμου καὶ γεγραμμένου ἔλλειμμα.

[12] Thuc. 2.37.3 ἀνεπαχθῶς δὲ τὰ ἴδια προσομιλοῦντες τὰ δημόσια διὰ δέος μάλιστα οὐ παρανομοῦμεν, τῶν τε αἰεὶ ἐν ἀρχῆι ὄντων ἀκροάσει καὶ τῶν νόμων, καὶ μάλιστα αὐτῶν ὅσοι τε ἐπ' ὠφελίᾳ τῶν ἀδικουμένων κεῖνται καὶ ὅσοι ἄγραφοι ὄντες αἰσχύνην ὁμολογουμένην φέρουσιν. Lys. 6.10 καίτοι Περικλέα ποτέ φασι παραινέσαι ὑμῖν περὶ τῶν ἀσεβούντων μὴ μόνον χρῆσθαι τοῖς γεγραμμένοις νόμοις περὶ αὐτῶν ἀλλὰ καὶ τοῖς ἀγράφοις καθ' οὓς Εὐμολπίδαι ἐξηγοῦνται.

[13] *Rhet.* 1373b18 f. καὶ ὡς ἐν τῷ Μεσσηνιακῷ λέγει Ἀλκιδάμας, 'ἐλευθέρους ἀφῆκε πάντας θεός, οὐδένα δοῦλον ἡ φύσις πεποίηκεν'. More precisely, the Mss. have a lacuna after Ἀλκιδάμας; the quotation is supplied by the scholiast.

[14] *Rhet.* 1354a11 ff. In 'Artless proofs in Aristotle and the orators' (n. 6) I argue that Aristotle exaggerates the distinction between artful and artless proofs.

proofs where they favour the opponent and stressing the validity of such proofs where they favour ourselves. The same approach is adopted by Anaximenes; though (as was noted above) he does not explicitly classify laws as proofs, his treatment of laws at 1443a11 ff. (where they figure in his advice on the anticipation of the opponent's case) is very similar to his treatment of depositions, tortures and oaths at 1431b20 ff., 1432a14 ff., 1432a33 ff. At first sight this looks like a promising approach. It reflects a strand in Greek rhetoric which was represented for instance in the teaching of Protagoras, who taught his pupils to argue the same case from diametrically opposing sides, and which in surviving works is represented by the *Dissoi Logoi* and the *Tetralogies* of Antiphon. But in fact the value of what Aristotle and Anaximenes have to say lies, in general, less in the direct applicability of the advice than in the insight it gives into some areas of ambiguity in the Athenian attitude to the law.

In advising on the use to be made of law in oratory, Aristotle begins with arguments to adopt when the law is against us.[15] Presumably he does not here mean 'when we are patently guilty' or 'when the person we are accusing is patently innocent'. Rather, he appears to have in mind a situation in which the law, interpreted strictly, supports our opponent. In such a context, it would appear to be in our interests to subvert the authority of law, and accordingly Aristotle proposes that we should utilize the *koinos nomos* and base our argument on *epieikeia*, equity, and justice.[16] When we attempt to exemplify Aristotle's advice from contemporary oratory, however, we encounter a problem. Inevitably, newly proposed laws are subjected to rigorous criticism through the *graphe nomon me epitedeion theinai*. But we do not find assaults on statute law as a category. Although Aristotle makes much of the distinction between the different types of *nomos*, the word *nomos* itself, applied to written law or customs and values, commanded enormous respect. To judge from surviving oratory, there appears to have been a fundamental inhibition against frontal assaults on the authority of law. Even when speakers misuse the laws, when they cite irrelevant laws or seek to distort their significance, they are still drawing on an enormous reservoir of respect for *nomos*. This attitude is not merely Athenian but more generally Greek. Subservience to impersonal laws, as distinct from the authority of a single figure, is one of the features which distinguish the Hellene from the barbarian. Although few Athenians would go as far as Sokrates in Plato's *Crito* in obedience to the laws,[17] the rhetorical force of the *Crito* as part of Plato's continuing apologia for Sokrates derives in no small part from the ideology of obedience to *nomos*, in any form, to which it appeals.

This is a rhetorical as well as a moral problem. Whatever logic may say, any theoretical gain in force of argument from an outright attack on the laws is immediately counteracted by a disproportionate loss in the area of *ethos*. It is important to remember that the speaker had only a limited amount of time available to present his case, and that he faces an opponent ready to exploit any vulnerable points in his case. In this context the speaker cannot afford to present an *ethos* of which disregard for *nomos* is a salient characteristic. It is standard practice to associate

---

[15] *Rhet.* 1375a27 ff. Grimaldi (n. 1) objects to the translation of ἐὰν μὲν ἐναντίος ᾖ ὁ γεγραμμένος νόμος τῷ πράγματι as 'when the written law is opposed to our case', but offers no argument. His alternative, to take πρᾶγμα as 'that which took place, the actual fact, the specific action at issue' gives an inferior sense. The question is not whether the law is relevant to the *subject under dispute* (for throughout his discussion of *nomos* Aristotle clearly envisages the citation of law by one side or the other) but which side the law favours.

[16] There is a textual problem at 1375a28 f. Mss. and editors are divided between τῷ κοινῷ χρηστέον καὶ τοῖς ἐπιεικεστέροις καὶ δικαιοτέροις and τῷ κοινῷ χρηστέον καὶ τοῖς ἐπιεικέσιν ὡς δικαιοτέροις. I agree with Mirhady (n. 1) 396 in preferring the second of these two readings; the context requires a firm distinction between τὸ ἐπιεικές and written *nomos*, and the positive is therefore to be preferred to the comparative. For my present purposes, however, all that matters is that *epieikeia* is offered as an alternative to *gegrammenos nomos*.

[17] Plat. *Crit.* 50c-53a.

oneself with observance both of moral rules and of statutes and to dissociate the opponent from such observance. As will be shown below, obedience to the statutes is characteristic of the good litigant. In real trials, there was more advantage to be gained from evasion of issues or straight falsification of the facts than in undermining the laws. Accordingly, it is actually difficult to exemplify in oratorical practice the advice which Aristotle gives.

Aristotle's first argument in support of the application of *epieikeia* rather than the written law is that this is what is meant by 'using our best judgement'. The last phrase here refers to the clause in the juror's oath which prescribed that in matters where there were no laws the juror was to use his 'most just opinion'. However, the dikasts' oath does not *oppose* law and justice; nor do real speeches on the rare occasions when this clause of the oath surfaces. At Dem. 39.41 in fact quite the opposite use is made of the oath, *viz.* that law and just judgement coincide.[18]

A second line of argument offered by Aristotle is that written law is subject to change, while common law, being the product of nature (*physis*), is of eternal validity. But although Athenians had personal experience of the legislative process, so that they knew in practice that laws could and did change, the orators do not in the citations of laws or their general references to the laws reflect this awareness. Quite the reverse, in fact, for there is a tendency to associate laws with the name of Solon, irrespective of the date at which the laws referred to were enacted. There is a 'doublethink' at work, which was probably typical of Athenian attitudes in general; the laws are the product of legislation involving ordinary people, but at the same time individual laws are felt to reflect the antiquity of the lawcode as a whole. This of course reflects the more conservative approach to *nomos* prevalent in the fourth century. Moreover, the more ponderous processes for new legislation and revisions to existing legislation in the fourth century made the representation of the law as something impermanent considerably less plausible that it might have been in the fifth century. The effect of all this was to provide the laws with a patina of antiquity, to suggest fixity, not fluidity. The scope for exploiting the antithesis between change and continuity was therefore restricted. If the argument from fixity and fluidity seems unhelpful, the point that the superiority of unwritten law resides in its relation to *physis* is positively dangerous. The antithesis between *nomos* and *physis*, and the preference for *physis*, would probably suggest the sophistic movement to the average Greek, and therefore create an impression of *deinotes*, cleverness. But it is a general rule in the orators, not surprisingly in view of the hostility of Athenian juries to anything resembling professionalism in legal matters, that *deinotes* is a characteristic of the opponent, not the speaker. The persistence of the stereotype of the sophist through the fourth century, and the ease with which hostility to this stereotype could be aroused in court, can be seen from [Dem.] 35.40 f.

Aristotle's third, fourth and fifth *topoi* may be taken together, since all rest on the superiority of unwritten law as being more just. The third argument is that justice is something real and beneficial, not mere semblance; written law is not just and does not perform the function of *nomos*, which is justice. The fourth, closely related, argument is that it is the dikast's task to distinguish between true and specious justice. The fifth is that it is a sign of moral superiority to utilize the unwritten rather than the written laws. None of this is to be found in the orators. Not surprisingly; for to elevate one type of *nomos* over another in this way is in effect to reduce the validity of the non-privileged category. This devaluation of written *nomos* is most explicit in the third line of argument, a bold paradox in which the status of written *nomos* as *nomos* is challenged. The nearest parallel from the orators known to me for Aristotle's downgrading of

---

[18] Dem. 39.41 ὥστε καὶ κατὰ τὴν δικαιοτάτην γνώμην καὶ κατὰ τοὺς νόμους καὶ κατὰ τοὺς ὅρκους καὶ κατὰ τὴν τούτου προσομολογίαν ἐγὼ μὲν μέτρι' ὑμῶν, ὦ ἄνδρες Ἀθηναῖοι, δέομαι ... For the general compatibility of oath and laws see e.g. Aischin. 3.8 τῶν ὅρκων οὓς ὠμόσατε μεμνημένοι καὶ τῶν νόμων ... and Lys. 10.32 (n. 41).

statute law is the occasional suggestion that the jurors are not merely adjudicating on the basis of law but acting as lawmakers in their interpretation of law.[19] But this is still both more subtle and more insidious than Aristotle's prescriptions, since at most it argues for a broad interpretation of the law while still upholding the authority of law; it does not oppose another authority to that of the written law.

Aristotle's sixth line of argument concerns the exploitation of contradiction. His advice has two aspects, the manipulation of disagreement between laws and the exploitation of internal contradiction within a law. The first type of argumentation can be seen, for instance, in Aischines' insistence that the law does not allow proclamations of honours to be made in the theatre (2.44-5) and Demosthenes' citation of a law which allows exceptions (18.120). The Athenians were themselves aware of the existence of contradictory laws,[20] and it was natural that such contradictions should be exploited. However, the scope for exploitation of internal inconsistency within a law, as distinct from disagreements between laws, was considerably limited by the procedural orientation of Greek laws. Although some laws in Athens were substantive (inheritance laws, for instance), there is a marked tendency for Athenian laws to be procedural, to define means of redress rather than offences.[21] Accordingly, although it was certainly possible to question the applicability of a given law in a given situation, in general there was less room for quibbling about the content of a law. There is accordingly far less interest in the precise wording of laws than Aristotle's general discussion might lead one to expect. There are, of course, exceptions. *Paragraphai* by their very nature must appeal to specific clauses in the laws dealing with special pleas. And of course cases of *graphe paranomon* and *graphe nomon me epitedeion theinai* must deal with questions of law in detail. In most surviving forensic speeches however there is not much interest in the precise details of law, beyond the demonstration (certainly important in itself) of basic legal support for a position. Lysias 10 is most unusual in its interest in the details of law, as is Hypereides' speech *Against Athenogenes*. The same objections may also be advanced against Aristotle's seventh line of opposition to the law, the exploitation of ambiguities in the written law.

The eighth and final argument concerns laws which are obsolete. Again, I find no trace of the argument in the orators.

Like Aristotle, Anaximenes advocates a frontal assault on the laws where necessary (1443a20 ff.), though he confines himself to attacks on specific laws, rather than on statute law as a category. His first suggestion has something in common with Aristotle's third line of argument. Where the laws which oppose us are held to be bad (*mochtheros*), we should argue that the law in question is not *nomos*, 'law', but *anomia*, 'lawlessness', 'negation of law', since it is harmful to the state, while the law is meant to confer benefit. In the same vein, Anaximenes suggests (1443a12 ff.) that we should praise the laws which support our case and criticize the laws put forward by our opponents. Not surprisingly, however, the laws are never described by litigants as *mochtheroi*. And not only do we not find litigants objecting to statute law as a type, they also avoid questioning the wisdom of specific established laws. His second proposed argument is that the jurors are not acting illegally in ignoring the law but legislating for the future. Again, we never find litigants explicitly urging the jurors to vote in contravention of the laws; this is hardly surprising, given the dikast's oath. And although we do (as was noted above) find speakers urging the jurors to regard themselves as legislators, this is always in the context of the application of a law rather than the outright subversion of a law. Anaximenes' third point

---

[19] Lyk.1.9 διὸ καὶ μάλιστ', ὦ ἄνδρες, δεῖ ὑμᾶς γενέσθαι μὴ μόνον τοῦ νῦν ἀδικήματος δικαστὰς ἀλλὰ καὶ νομοθέτας. Cf. Lys.14.4, [Dem.] 56.48.

[20] See Dem. 20.91, Aischin.3.38.

[21] See especially S.C. Todd (n. 8) 64 ff.

is that there is no law which prevents a man from helping society, and that annulling bad laws is helping society. Again the orators are silent.

Anaximenes agrees with Aristotle in suggesting that we exploit ambiguities in the law (1443a31 ff.). The limitations of this approach were noted above. He also agrees with Aristotle in advising appeal to *epieikeia* where a defendant cannot take a stand on the legality of his conduct (1444a10 ff.), but since he does not explicitly oppose the authority of the law, his advice does not present the moral and rhetorical problems raised by Aristotle's approach.

Taken as a whole, the advice on means of counteracting appeal to the law by the opponent is difficult to square with what actually happened in the courts. Such a marked deviation from actual practice requires explanation. There are several factors at work. First, the treatment of written law by Aristotle is the direct result of his categorization of law as a species of proof. As was observed above, although Aristotle's taxonomy has a basis in contemporary practice, law occupies an ambiguous position; it cannot be assimilated completely to other documentary means of proof. Accordingly, problems arise when Aristotle imposes on law the schema he applies to artless proof as a category. His purpose in this section of the *Rhetoric* is to exemplify ways in which the presence or absence of support from different types of artless proofs can be exploited by the litigant. For each category of artless proof he offers means of strengthening or weakening the impact of the *pistis* itself by rhetorical means. Within this schema laws, like witnesses, must allow for opposed modes of argumentation. The same is essentially true of Anaximenes, who approaches the law exactly as he approaches depositions, oaths, and evidence from torture, all of which are to be strengthened or undermined by argument according to immediate need. In both cases, the advice is the product of the theoretical structure imposed rather than of observation of actual practice.[22]

A second problem common to Aristotle and Anaximenes is a failure to take due account of the form of Athenian law. In defining law, both concentrate on its normative function. This is implied in Aristotle's definition of wrongdoing (τὸ ἀδικεῖν) at 1368b5 (quoted above) as harm done contrary to the law. This conception of law is explicit in Anaximenes (1422a2 f.; *cf.* 1424a11 f.):

νόμος δ' ἐστὶν ὁμολόγημα πόλεως κοινόν, διὰ γραμμάτων προστάττον πῶς χρὴ ποιεῖν ἕκαστα.

Law is a common agreement of the state prescribing in writing how people should act in various matters.

The emphasis here on the role of the laws in regulating conduct in general and not merely the processes of dispute settlement is perfectly natural as a description of the social function of the laws. It reflects a widespread conception of the role of law, found for instance in Perikles' statement at Thuc. 2.37.3 that the Athenians obey the laws or in the assertion of Euphiletos at Lys. 1.26 that the adulterer Eratosthenes chose to transgress the law. However, both Aristotle and Anaximenes ignore the fact that the laws fulfil their role largely by prescribing procedures for obtaining punishment and reparation. The emphasis on function leads to misunderstanding when applied rhetorically to the manipulation of the form of the laws. Aristotle may also be influenced by his own ideal formulation of the law in 1354a31 ff.; there he tells us that good laws should be as complete as possible, containing few omissions.[23] Very few real Athenian laws would meet Aristotle's ideal.

---

[22] For other examples of the rigidity of rhetorical theory in comparison with actual practice see C. Carey, 'Rhetorical means of persuasion', in *Persuasion* ed. I. Worthington (London 1994) 26-45, esp. 29, 35 f., 39 f., 43f.

[23] 1354a31 ff μάλιστα μὲν οὖν προσήκει τοὺς ὀρθῶς κειμένους νόμους, ὅσα ἐνδέχεται, πάντα διορίζειν αὐτούς, καὶ ὅτι ἐλάχιστα καταλείπειν ἐπὶ τοῖς κρίνουσιν. This suggestion was also made to me independently by Dr. R.G. Osborne.

The third common factor is an overly cerebral approach to the task of persuasion, which leads both authors to pursue lines of argument which, whatever their intellectual appeal, would carry grave risks of alienating the hearer. In Aristotle's case this is typical of his whole overall approach to the art of rhetoric. On pragmatic grounds he accepts the importance of *ethos* and *pathos*, but he regards these as accommodations to the inadequacy of the hearer. The proper business of the art of persuasion is to argue.[24] This intellectual approach is visible in the relative space afforded to the different means of persuasion.

A further factor at work in Aristotle's treatment, which is generally both more sophisticated and more abstract than that of Anaximenes, is the transformation of a distinction into an antithesis. At *Rhet.* 1375a25 ff. Aristotle sees written and unwritten laws not merely as two distinct parts of a comprehensive set of imperatives and prohibitions, but as two alternative and potentially competing sources of authority. This is not in fact a common view. It is familiar to us above all through the famous speech of Antigone which is quoted by Aristotle to exemplify the dichotomy. There Antigone sets Kreon's *psephisma* against the abiding and unwritten *nomima* of the gods. But in general we find that Greek thinkers present these systems as complementary and mutually supportive. Inevitably, the two categories of *nomos* overlap, most obviously in the sphere of religion, where the speaker of Lysias 6 appeals simultaneously both to written and to unwritten *nomos*.[25] But in general the two categories are seen as governing different areas of conduct, with the unwritten laws supplementing written laws and providing additional sanctions to deal with activities not covered by the written statutes. This complementarity is seen for instance in the Thucydidean Perikles,[26] and it is true also of the other classical reference to Perikles on unwritten laws, Lysias 6. Both (with their formulation 'not only but'/'both and') presuppose written and unwritten laws as interlocking parts of a system of constraint which makes civilized society possible. This approach is also exemplified by Aristotle himself in *Rhet.* 1374a, where he associates unwritten justice with non-judiciary penalties and informal reward and with omissions in the written law; a similar definition is offered by Anaximenes at 1421b36 ff.[27] Likewise Aristotle at *E.N.* 1180a sees unwritten and written laws as mutually supportive inducements to proper conduct; so also Dem. 18.275 and Xen. *Mem.* iv.4.19.[28] It is difficult to see how this general consensus on the compatibility and complementarity of written and unwritten *nomoi* could persist if the different types of *nomos* were perceived as opposed.

However, although this aspect of the advice on the forensic use of law offered by fourth century rhetoric is of limited value, the awareness of ambiguity in the Greek attitude to law on which it rests is of use. It would for instance be a mistake to conclude from the inadequacy of Aristotle's opposition between written and unwritten law that the distinction between law and

[24] At 1354a15 ff. Aristotle asserts that logical arguments are the σῶμα τῆς πίστεως, while emotional appeals are ἔξω τοῦ πράγματος and are directed πρὸς τὸν δικαστήν. *Cf.* 1415b5 ff.

[25] See n. 12.

[26] See n. 12.

[27] Anaximenes 1421b36 ff. δίκαιον μὲν οὖν ἐστὶ τὸ τῶν ἁπάντων ἢ τὸ τῶν πλείστων ἔθος ἄγραφον, διορίζον τὰ καλὰ καὶ τὰ αἰσχρά, ταῦτα δ' ἐστὶ τὸ γονέας τιμᾶν καὶ φίλους εὖ ποιεῖν καὶ τοῖς εὐεργέταις χάριν ἀποδιδόναι· ταῦτα γὰρ καὶ τὰ τούτοις ὅμοια οὐκ ἐπιτάττουσι τοῖς ἀνθρώποις οἱ γεγραμμένοι νόμοι ποιεῖν, ἀλλ' ἔθει ἀγράφῳ καὶ κοινῷ νόμῳ νομίζεται. For Aristotle see n. 11.

[28] Arist. *E.N.* 1180a34 ff. αἱ μὲν οὖν κοιναὶ ἐπιμέλειαι δῆλον ὅτι διὰ νόμων γίγνονται, ἐπιεικεῖς δὲ αἱ διὰ τῶν σπουδαίων· γεγραμμένων δ' ἢ ἀγράφων, οὐδὲν ἂν δόξειε διαφέρειν. Dem.18.275 φανήσεται ταῦτα πάνθ' οὕτως οὐ μόνον ἐν τοῖς νόμοις, ἀλλὰ καὶ ἡ φύσις αὐτὴ τοῖς ἀγράφοις νομίμοις καὶ τοῖς ἀνθρωπίνοις ἤθεσιν διώρικεν. Xen. Mem. iv.4.19 ἀγράφους δέ τινας οἶσθα, ἔφη, ὦ Ἱππία, νόμους· τούς γ' ἐν πάσῃ, ἔφη, χώρᾳ κατὰ ταὐτὰ νομιζομένους. ... ἀλλὰ δίκην γε διδόασιν οἱ παραβαίνοντες τοὺς ὑπὸ τῶν θεῶν κειμένους νόμους, ἣν οὐδενὶ τρόπωι δυνατὸν ἀνθρώπῳ διαφυγεῖν, ὥσπερ τοὺς ὑπὸ τῶν ἀνθρώπων κειμένους νόμους ἔνιοι παραβαίνοντες διαφεύγουσι τὸ δίκην διδόναι.

natural justice is without value in the lawcourts. There is a clear awareness on the part of speakers addressing the courts of a potential for abuse of the laws. The efforts of litigants to present themselves as pitchforked into litigation indicates that there is a reluctance to resort to litigation. Individual litigants may of course be misrepresenting themselves; but what matters is the ideology to which they appeal rather than the veracity of individual claims. The laws are seen as a final means of resolving a dispute, not a remedy to be applied casually. There is therefore a degree of discomfort felt by speakers citing the laws in detail, and a consequent tendency to apologize for legal knowledge displayed, as at Hyp. *Athen.* 13,[29] where the speaker prefaces a dazzling display of legal expertise with a complaint that his enemy has forced him to study the law. This attitude underlies the accusation hurled at Dem. 57.5 that the opponent Euboulides possesses excessive knowledge of the laws.[30] Most potent of all as a source of miscarriage of justice is the mixture of legal expertise and rhetorical training. So the laws can be manipulated. In addition, there is a marked tendency for speakers to lay claim to a reluctance to assert their legal rights. We find litigants presenting themselves as fair-minded people who are ready to forego the advantages which they could claim under the law in an effort to be reasonable; so for instance [Dem.] 44.8, where the speaker expresses a readiness to give up the legal advantage afforded him by the law if the case presented by his opponents is reasonable; similar is the speaker of [Dem.] 56.14, who is ready to take less than he might under the letter of the law, so as not to appear *philodikos*.[31] This attitude to law is prevalent in the *paragraphe* cases in the Demosthenic corpus; by definition, the *paragraphe* is based in technical irregularities in the prosecution, and will therefore involve reliance on specific clauses of the relevant law. However, speakers are never satisfied with the demonstration of the legal base for their objection to the prosecution, since there is always the possibility that legal expertise is being used to win an unjust victory. This suspicion of excessive legalism arises naturally from the orientation of the laws toward procedure. Although the laws deter certain types of behaviour of which society disapproves, they do so largely by prescribing remedies rather than by forbidding the acts themselves. Accordingly *nomos* and *dike* (in the sense 'lawsuit') are irrevocably linked. It is important to note, however, that this is not a straight opposition between the laws and justice. The potential for manipulation is not perceived, or at least not presented, by litigants as a flaw in the laws but simply a result of individual unscrupulousness. The laws are themselves fair in intention, but they are open to abuse. Although we find contexts in which the laws and justice are distinguished, it is usually assumed that the laws and justice are on the same side.[32] And in many contexts the laws and justice are treated as identical.[33]

---

[29] Hyp. *Athen.* 13 ἐξ αὐτῶν δέ σοι τῶν νόμων ἐγὼ φανερώτερον ποιήσω. καὶ γὰρ οὕτω με διατέθεικας καὶ περίφοβον πεποίηκας μὴ ἀπόλωμαι ὑπὸ σοῦ καὶ τῆς δεινότητος τῆς σῆς ὥστε τούς τε νόμους ἐξετάζειν καὶ μελετᾶν νύκτα καὶ ἡμέραν, πάρεργα τἄλλα πάντα ποιησάμενον.

[30] Dem. 57.5 οὗτος εἰδὼς τοὺς νόμους καὶ μᾶλλον ἢ προσῆκεν ἀδίκως καὶ πλεονεκτικῶς τὴν κατηγορίαν πεποίηται. *Cf.* Lys. 10.13 πότερον οὕτως σὺ δεινὸς εἶ ὥστε, ὅπως ἂν βούλῃ, οἷός τ' εἶ χρῆσθαι τοῖς νόμοις....

[31] [Dem.] 44.8 καὶ ἐὰν ἐκ μὲν τῶν νόμων μὴ ὑπάρχῃ, δίκαια δὲ καὶ φιλάνθρωπα φαίνωνται λέγοντες, καὶ ὡς συγχωροῦμεν. [Dem.] 56.14 ἡμεῖς μὲν ταῦτα συνεχωροῦμεν, οὐκ ἀγνοοῦντες, ὦ ἄνδρες δικασταί, τὸ ἐκ τῆς συγγραφῆς δίκαιον, ἀλλ' ἡγούμενοι δεῖν ἐλαττοῦσθαί τι καὶ συγχωρεῖν ὥστε μὴ δοκεῖν φιλόδικοι εἶναι. The effect is to present the speaker as an ἐπιεικής, a reasonable/equitable man, whom Aristotle (*E.N.* 1138a1 f.) characterizes as disinclined to insist rigidly on his rights, even when the law is on his side (ὁ μὴ ἀκριβοδίκαιος ἐπὶ τὸ χεῖρον ἀλλ' ἐλαττωτικός, καίπερ ἔχων τὸν νόμον βοηθόν).

[32] *Cf.* Isai. 1.35 πρὸς δὲ τούτοις ἡμεῖς ὑμῖν ἀποφαίνομεν ἐναντίας οὔσας [sc. τὰς διαθήκας] καὶ τῷ νόμῳ καὶ τοῖς δικαίοις . Dem. 19.179 φαίνεται δ' οὗτος πάντα τἀναντία τοῖς νόμοις, τοῖς ψηφίσμασι, τοῖς δικαίοις πεπρεσβευκώς. See also Dem. 35.45, 39.41.

[33] *Cf.* [Dem.] 42.2 ὥσπερ ἐξουσίαν δεδωκότος αὐτῷ τοῦ νόμου ποιεῖν ὅ τι ἂν βούληται καὶ μὴ ὡς δίκαιόν ἐστιν. See also Isai. 4.21, Hyp. *Athen.* 13.

It is from this tacit acceptance that the laws are just that Lys. 1.49 derives its force:

πολὺ γὰρ οὕτω δικαιότερον ἢ ὑπὸ τῶν νόμων τοὺς πολίτας ἐνεδρεύεσθαι, οἳ κελεύουσι μέν, ἐάν τις μοιχὸν λάβῃ, ὅ τι ἂν βούληται χρῆσθαι, οἱ δ' ἀγῶνες δεινότεροι τοῖς ἀδικουμένοις καθεστήκασιν ἢ τοῖς παρὰ τοὺς νόμους τὰς ἀλλοτρίας καταισχύνουσι γυναῖκας.

This [i.e. to annul the laws] is far better than to have the citizens ambushed by the laws, which prescribe that if someone captures a *moichos* he should treat him as he sees fit, while the trials have become far more dangerous for the victims of injustice than for those who bring shame on the wives of others in contravention of the laws.

Here the speaker sees the citizens as being entrapped by the laws. In fact, he does not mean the laws at all, but the application of the laws by those sitting in judgement; but the paradox of laws as ensnarers is a powerful reflection of the prevailing ideology of the laws as fundamentally just.

The notion of *epieikeia*, as a counterweight to the rigid application of the written statutes, shared by Aristotle and Anaximenes also plays a significant role in forensic contexts. At *Rhet.* 1374b1 ff. Aristotle sees the exercise of *epieikeia* as the tempering of the strictness of the law with reference to factors such as the circumstances in which an act is committed, the motive, and the general character of the parties to a suit; both there and at *E.N.* 1143a21 ff., *epieikeia* is closely associated with forgiveness, συγγνώμη.[34] Again, however, rhetorical guidelines prove less subtle than actual practice. The blunt opposition of *epieikeia* and law favoured by rhetoricians is avoided. *Epieikeia* figures in surviving oratory not as text but as sub-text; explicit appeal for *epieikeia* is in fact not found in the orators.[35] Where *epieikeia* is mentioned explicitly, it is as a characteristic of parties to a suit rather than a quality to be displayed by the jurors. It is important to bear in mind however that we lack the brief speeches allowed for the assessment in *agones timetoi*, where explicit appeals for *epieikeia* might naturally figure. The avoidance of pleas for *epieikeia* by defendants in the defence speech proper is readily understood; a plea based on extra-legal considerations will inevitably be taken as an acceptance of the weakness of the defendant's legal position and therefore an admission of guilt. What the speaker can do, however, is excite sympathy for his situation, or for his relatives, or request gratitude for past services. Alternatively, he may present his opponent as a man of low character, an habitual malefactor, a figure worthy only of hostility from the jury. Better still, he may present the opponent as someone who habitually uses the legal system for his own profit and advantage. These all amount to a means of inducing the jurors to hesitate before applying the rigour of the law. Pity for relatives is meant to induce the jurors to reflect on the injustice of punishing the innocent along with the guilty. Mention of past services to the city is meant to give the jurors a countervailing impression of the overall worth of the speaker which will have the effect of reducing the significance of his offence. Character assassination is intended to make the jurors ask whether the opponent deserves a favourable verdict. It is of course an impossible task to distinguish clearly the different effects sought through these devices. Some are obviously intended in part to affect the jurors' view of the veracity of the parties to the

---

[34] *Cf.* also Anaximenes 1444a10 ff. Mirhady (n. 1) 396 n. 7, 399 argues that *epieikeia* in Aristotle is to be distinguished from common law. It is however difficult to disentangle the two concepts completely. Evidently the two are not completely identical, but they are closely associated for Aristotle, who makes no attempt to distinguish them precisely. At *Rhet.* 1374a27 ff., he discusses *epieikeia* in the context of his definition of written and unwritten *dikaia*; he defines it as 'justice contrary to written law', particularly associated with imprecision and omission in the law (cf. *E.N.* 1137b11 ff.), which in context is explicitly one of two aspects of unwritten *dikaia* (for the close relationship between *epieikeia* and *to dikaion* see *E.N.*1137a33 ff.). *Epieikeia* and unwritten *nomos* are associated at 1375a29 ff.

[35] *Cf.* Harris (n. 1) 140.

action and therefore their decision on questions of fact. But all are in part a tacit insurance policy against the possibility that the factual case will go against the litigant. That there was a real, if unquantifiable, possibility that such extra-legal considerations would carry weight with the jurors is clear from the attempts of prosecutors to close the possibilities for leniency and urge harshness.[36] The jurors' readiness to give weight to such considerations is in harmony with the ideology of law implied by the disinclination (affected or real) of litigants to insist on their legal rights, which was discussed above. The application of the laws must be tempered with broader considerations of fairness and with the knowledge that the laws are subject to abuse.

Aristotle's notion of common or universal law is not entirely without value. It is however used in ways not anticipated by Aristotle. Although the laws of Athens carry great authority, it appears that they gain still more authority if they can be shown to be in agreement with laws elsewhere in Greece, and even beyond. This is the case, for instance, with Isaios' discussion of the laws of adoption at 2.24;[37] the same law, allowing a man without children to adopt an heir, is according to Isaios observed not only throughout Greece but also among barbarians; i.e. this is a truly universal law. A similar point is made by Isokrates 19.50. Likewise, when Lysias wishes to stress for the jurors the seriousness of the offence of *moicheia* at 1.2, he insists that all Greek cities regard *moicheia* as the most serious of offences, irrespective of the political system; as a result even oligarchies, which discriminate in favour of the rich and powerful, allow equal rights to all where this offence is concerned. The appeal to laws outside Athens implies an opposition between the law of the individual community (*idios nomos*) and law which is recognized in most or all communities (*koinos nomos*), along the lines of Aristotle's distinction; and this in turn implies the *nomos/physis* antithesis,[38] and the superiority of universal law. But the antithesis is never drawn explicitly, and the tacit notion of universal law is used not to subvert the authority of written law, as Aristotle prescribes, but to enhance that authority.

III

The opposite set of arguments offered by Aristotle, on the treatment of the law when it is in our favour, is less contentious. Aristotle argues that the phrase 'most just opinion' relates to areas where the juror does not know the law. This is closer to the juror's oath than his counter-formulation. He also offers the argument that there is no difference between having no laws and not using the laws. This can be exemplified in surviving oratory.[39] He also offers the argument

---

[36] As Dem. 21.148 μὴ τοίνυν ὑμῖν, πρὸς τῷ μὴ καλόν, μηδὲ θεμιτὸν νομίζετ', ἄνδρες δικασταί, μηδ' ὅσιον εἶναι τοιούτων ἀνδρῶν οὖσιν ἀπογόνοις, πονηρὸν καὶ βίαιον καὶ ὑβριστὴν λαβοῦσιν ἄνθρωπον καὶ μηδένα μηδαμόθεν, συγγνώμης ἢ φιλανθρωπίας ἢ χάριτός τινος ἀξιῶσαι, 225 δεῖ τοίνυν μήτε λητουργίας μήτ' ἔλεον μήτ' ἄνδρα μηδένα μήτε τέχνην μηδεμίαν εὑρῆσθαι, δι' ὅτου παραβάς τις τοὺς νόμους οὐ δώσει δίκην, 24.175 οὔκουν δεῖ δοκεῖν, νῦν μαλακισθέντας, τότε τῶν ὁμωμοσμένων ὅρκων ἀμελήσαντας ὑμῖν αὐτοῖς χαρίσασθαι παρὰ τὸ δίκαιον, ἀλλὰ μισεῖν καὶ μηδ' ἀνέχεσθαι φωνὴν μήτε τούτου μήτ' ἐκείνου, τοιαῦτα πεπολιτευμένων. Cf. 25.81.

[37] Isai. 2.24 καὶ τοῖς μὲν ἄλλοις ἅπασιν ἀνθρώποις καὶ Ἕλλησι καὶ βαρβάροις δοκεῖ καλῶς οὗτος ὁ νόμος κεῖσθαι, ὁ περὶ τῆς ποιήσεως, καὶ διὰ τοῦτο χρῶνται πάντες αὐτῷ. Cf. Isokr. 19.50 ἥκω πρὸς ὑμᾶς ἔχων...νόμον ταύταις [sc. ταῖς διαθήκαις] βοηθοῦντα, ὃς δοκεῖ τοῖς Ἕλλησιν ἅπασι καλῶς κεῖσθαι, Lys. 1.2 περὶ τούτου γὰρ μόνου τοῦ ἀδικήματος καὶ ἐν δημοκρατίᾳ καὶ ὀλιγαρχίᾳ ἡ αὐτὴ τιμωρία τοῖς ἀσθενεστάτοις πρὸς τοὺς τὰ μέγιστα δυναμένους ἀποδέδοται ...

[38] It also implies that this antithesis had permeated from intellectual debate into the collective consciousness.

[39] Cf. Lys. 14.11 εἰ ἐξέσται ὅ τι ἄν τις βούληται ποιεῖν, οὐδὲν ὄφελος νόμους κεῖσθαι, Dem. 21.57 ἀλλὰ μὴν οὐδέν ἐστ' ὄφελος καλῶς καὶ φιλανθρώπως τοὺς νόμους ὑπὲρ τῶν πολλῶν κεῖσθαι, εἰ τοῖς ἀπειθοῦσι καὶ βιαζομένοις αὐτοὺς ἡ παρ' ὑμῶν ὀργὴ τῶν ἀεὶ κυρίων μὴ γενήσεται.

that one should not seek to be more clever than the laws. Though I can find no specific example of such blunt advice to the jury (it is the opponent who tends to be represented as aspiring to be cleverer than the laws), the orators are full of examples of exhortations to the jurors to apply the full rigour of the laws,[40] and reminders of the dikasts' oath to judge according to the laws.[41] In general this clause of the juror's oath is invoked much more frequently than the 'just opinion' clause, precisely because of the explicit restriction in the oath on the exercise of 'just opinion'.

Anaximenes has considerably less to say on this subject, presumably because the rhetorical demands of a situation in which the laws may be cited with confidence are considerably less. The logical counterpart to the advice that the opponent's laws be denigrated (1443a12 ff.) is that we should praise the usefulness of laws which we cite. It is not uncommon for citation of the law to be accompanied by praise of the law.[42] He also suggests that the jurors be reminded of their oath to judge according to the laws and be discouraged from tampering with them; specifically, they are to be told that they are to judge the facts not the laws, and to legislate on other occasions rather than in court. The latter advice can be exemplified in oratory;[43] the frequency of the reminder of the oath to vote according to the laws has already been noted.

However, the real limitation in the treatment of the utilization of the support of the laws by Aristotle and Anaximenes is that it appears to be envisaged solely in terms of the direct support of specific laws cited on substantive issues. As with the inadequacy of the arguments against the authority of statute law, individually and collectively, this limitation arises from excessive schematism, together with an emphasis on the intellectual element in the act of persuasion to the detriment of the affective. The superimposed schema makes the treatment of the topic unduly specific, since it ties the rhetoric of law to citations of specific laws and leads the rhetoricians to ignore the broader uses of law in oratory. Although the citation of laws intended to convince the jury of the legal support for the speaker on the main issue plays a major role in the orators, there is a broader rhetoric of law which is not tied to artless proofs. Essentially, the aim of this rhetoric is to tap the reservoir of respect for *nomos* which the Athenians shared with other Greeks. The effect is partly to assist the speaker in projecting an appealing *ethos*, partly to stimulate the audience to the appropriate emotion, rarely to appeal to reason. In this respect again, actual usage deviates from Aristotle's instructions. Moreover, the rhetoric of law appears to bear no discernible relation to the most important discriminator for Aristotle in terms of usage, that is, whether the law is with us or against us. For Aristotle the law is to be pressed or undermined in court according to its precise support for our case or our opponent's. But the rhetoric of law is martialled irrespective of the precise legal position, in fact in some cases where a precise appeal to the law would probably be damaging to the speaker. Put simply, the law is more often a blunt instrument than the sharp instrument Aristotle envisages. We find the authority of law marshalled not only in the context of a specific appeal to one or more laws but in portions of the speech where *ethos* is the primary effect sought or where emotional appeal is the dominant effect. I offer a few examples of this broader rhetoric.

---

[40] Dem. 21 is particularly rich in examples: *cf.* 21.34. 57, 177, 224.

[41] E.g. Lys. 10.32 ὧν μεμνημένοι καὶ ἐμοὶ καὶ τῶι πατρὶ βοηθήσατε καὶ τοῖς νόμοις τοῖς κειμένοις καὶ τοῖς ὅρκοις οἷς ὀμωμόκατε; Dem. 21. 177 τοῦτο γάρ ἐσθ' ὃ φυλάττειν ὑμᾶς δεῖ, τοὺς νόμους, τὸν ὅρκον, 18.121 ἀλλ' οὐδ' αἰσχύνει ... νόμους μεταποιῶν, τῶν δ' ἀφαιρῶν μέρη, οὓς ὅλους δίκαιον ἦν ἀναγιγνώσκεσθαι τοῖς γ' ὀμωμοκόσιν κατὰ τοὺς νόμους ψηφιεῖσθαι. See in general Harris (n. 1) 149 nn.6-7.

[42] *Cf.* Isai.6.49 ταυτὶ τὰ γράμματα, ὦ ἄνδρες, ὑμεῖς οὕτω σεμνὰ καὶ εὐσεβῆ ἐνομοθετήσατε ..., Dem. 21.48 ἀκούετε, ὦ ἄνδρες Ἀθηναῖοι, τοῦ νόμου τῆς φιλανθρωπίας, ὃς οὐδὲ τοὺς δούλους ὑβρίζεσθαι ἀξιοῖ, 36.26 f.

[43] *Cf.* Lys.15.9 καὶ μὲν δή, ὦ ἄνδρες δικασταί, εἴ τῳ δοκεῖ μεγάλη ἡ ζημία εἶναι καὶ λίαν ἰσχυρὸς ὁ νόμος, μεμνῆσθαι χρὴ ὅτι οὐ νομοθετήσοντες περὶ αὐτῶν ἥκετε, ἀλλὰ κατὰ τοὺς κειμένους νόμους ψηφιούμενοι.

(*i.*) There is a strong tendency for litigants to associate themselves with the laws or to appropriate for themselves the discourse of law. There is no simple correlation here with the amount of legal support for the speaker's case; accordingly this aspect of the rhetoric of law does not fall neatly into the 'law on our side' half of Aristotle's antithesis. The clearest case is in Lys. 1, where the speaker bases his case on his strict adherence to the law, to the extent of asserting at one point that he is merely the physical agent of the law,[44] despite the fact that (as is generally recognized) he is at the very least interpreting the law over-narrowly. But this is merely the most dramatic instance of the invocation of *nomos*. When Antiphon praises the homicide laws, he is in part drawing for his own purposes on the widespread respect for these laws.[45] There is of course an ambiguity here, already noted, for although the speaker aligns himself with the laws he dissociates himself (unless his status makes such dissociation implausible) from knowledge of the laws.

(*ii.*) There is an equally strong tendency to associate the opponent with breach of the laws. The opponent is someone who despises the laws.[46] The opponent can be represented as the enemy of the laws, or otherwise placed into outright opposition to the laws. Thus at Lys. 6.10 the jurors are told that they cannot have both the laws and Andokides; either the laws must be expunged or they must be rid of Andokides.[47] At [Dem.] 59.115 the laws are envisaged as actually presenting the case against Neaira.[48] Even where the opponent is obedient to the letter of the law, he may still be represented as abusing the laws; he may be represented as someone who knows the laws but exploits them for personal advantage. Strict legality is not enough. The rhetoric of law is not just about legality but about justice and reasonableness.

(*iii.*) The future of the laws themselves is in the balance. The jurors must give aid not just to the litigant but also to the laws.[49] The right decision in the present case will confirm the validity of the laws.[50] The wrong decision in the present case will have the effect of invalidating the laws. The jurors thus have the choice of voting for the opponent or siding with the laws. The laws are the basis for ordered society, as we are reminded on occasion.[51] As such they are a source of fear.[52] The deterrent power of the law prevents unscrupulous men

[44] Lys. 1.26 ἐγὼ δ᾽ εἶπον ὅτι 'οὐκ ἐγώ σε ἀποκτενῶ ἀλλ᾽ ὁ τῆς πόλεως νόμος...'.

[45] Ant. 6.2, καὶ τοὺς μὲν νόμους οἳ κεῖνται περὶ τῶν τοιούτων πάντες ἂν ἐπαινέσειαν κάλλιστα νόμων κεῖσθαι καὶ ὁσιώτατα.... The use of the same motif at 5.14, though rather closer to Aristotle's general treatment of law (since it is closely linked to the speaker's objection to the procedure used against him), again seeks to achieve an emotional effect rather than to prove a substantive point.

[46] *Cf.* [Dem.] 42.2 καταφρονήσας ἀμφοτέρων, καὶ ἡμῶν καὶ τοῦ νόμου..., Lys. 14.9 οὕτως ὑμῶν κατεφρόνησε ... καὶ τῶν νόμων οὐκ ἐφρόντισεν.

[47] Lys. 6.8 οὐκ οἷόν τε ὑμῖν ἐστιν ἅμα τοῖς τε νόμοις τοῖς πατρίοις καὶ Ἀνδοκίδῃ χρῆσθαι.

[48] [Dem.] 59.115 ἡγεῖσθε δὲ μήτ᾽ ἐμὲ τὸν λέγοντα εἶναι Ἀπολλόδωρον μήτε τοὺς ἀπολογησομένους καὶ συνεροῦντας πολίτας, ἀλλὰ τοὺς νόμους καὶ Νέαιραν ταυτηνὶ περὶ τῶν πεπραγμένων αὐτῇ πρὸς ἀλλήλους δικάζεσθαι.

[49] [Dem.] 26.27 παρακαλέσαντες οὖν ὑμᾶς αὐτούς, ἄνδρες Ἀθηναῖοι, βοηθήσατε μὲν τοῖς νόμοις.... *Cf.* Lys. 10.32 (n. 41), Dem.21.225 (n. 50).

[50] Lys. 1.34 ἐν ὑμῖν δ᾽ ἐστὶ πότερον χρὴ τούτους ἰσχυροὺς ἢ μηδενὸς ἀξίους εἶναι, Dem. 21.224-5 ἡ δὲ τῶν νόμων ἰσχὺς τίς ἐστιν; ἀρ᾽ ἐάν τις ὑμῶν ἀδικούμενος ἀνακράγῃ, προσδραμοῦνται καὶ παρέσονται βοηθοῦντες; οὔ· γράμματα γὰρ γεγραμμέν᾽ ἐστίν, καὶ οὐχὶ δύναιντ᾽ ἂν τοῦτο ποιῆσαι. τίς οὖν ἡ δύναμις αὐτῶν ἐστιν; ὑμεῖς ἐὰν βεβαιῶτ᾽ αὐτοὺς καὶ παρέχητε κυρίους ἀεὶ τῷ δεομένῳ. οὐκοῦν οἱ νόμοι θ᾽ ὑμῖν εἰσιν ἰσχυροὶ καὶ ὑμεῖς τοῖς νόμοις. δεῖ τοίνυν τούτοις βοηθεῖν....

[51] [Dem.] 58.56, [Dem.] 59.115; *cf.* Dem.21.221 ff.

[52] Lys. 14.15 ἀλλ᾽ ὅμως οὐκ ἐτολμᾶτε ἀπολιπεῖν τὰς τάξεις οὐδὲ τἀρεστὰ ὑμῖν αὐτοῖς αἱρεῖσθαι, ἀλλὰ πολὺ μᾶλλον ἐφοβεῖσθε τοὺς πόλεως νόμους ἢ τὸν πρὸς τοὺς πολεμίους κίνδυνον. *Cf.* [Dem.] 59.86.

from exploiting their advantages over others. Yet the laws themselves are also perceived as weak. The clearest statement (and the nearest Demosthenes comes to a devaluation of written law in line with Aristotle's examples in the *Rhetoric*) is Dem. 21.224.[53] The laws, we are told, have no power in themselves. They are inert. It is through their enforcement by the jurors that the laws become a force for order in society. The same image of the laws lies behind the many other passages in which the jurors are asked to make the laws *kyrios*. There is thus a paradox in the presentation of the laws in oratory.

IV

In conclusion, it seems that, on the issue of the role of law in oratory, the advice of Aristotle and Anaximenes should come with a health warning, that use of the arguments proposed could seriously damage a litigant's chances of success, at least as far as the attempts to undermine the authority of law, general and specific, are concerned. Accordingly we find that speakers who have to face real juries in real trials do not use the arguments favoured by the rhetoricians. Both authors also, in concentrating on the specific question of the extent to which the litigant's factual case finds support in the laws, ignore the broader uses to which law was put in oratory of the period. But although the discussion of *nomos* in surviving fourth century rhetoric is flawed, it offers a useful starting point for an examination of the ambiguities in the Athenian attitude to law, and used with caution it may still provide a useful approach to reading the orators.[54]

C. CAREY

Royal Holloway, University of London

---

[53] See n. 50.

[54] This article is a revised version of a paper presented to research seminars at the Institute of Classical Studies in London and at Oxford University in November 1993. I wish to express my thanks to all who commented on both occasions. I am also grateful to the anonymous referees for a number of helpful suggestions.

Journal of Hellenic Studies cxvi (1996) pp 47-61

HOMER'S SENSE OF TEXT

HOMERIC 'TEXT', CYCLIC 'TEXT'

IN this article[1] I am concerned to form a view of the interaction of Homer's *Iliad* with other texts prior to his. This is an issue whose legitimacy, particularly in English-language scholarship, has been rather obscured by scholarly discourse in terms of oral poetics, an issue I shall discuss presently. Yet, unless they are completely new fictions, the Cyclic epics do show us some of the material with which Homer was bound to be interacting, and it has been the achievement of the Neoanalysts to detail that interaction. In the following I do not claim to add greatly to the repertoire of neoanalytic data, but I do hope to build on it some sense of Homer's achievement in this area and to make clear our entitlement to respond to Homer's intertextuality.

By the word 'text' I refer to a *fixed* poem. There is some telling, e.g. of the *Aithiopis*, which is sufficiently fixed for Homer to allude to it specifically, to inform his work by it, and for his audience to recognise this interaction. A narrative may indeed become such a text thanks to writing, but only because writing *fixes* it, not because there is something special about writing. It is perfectly possible to have a fixed (memorised) text in an oral tradition, and Nagy, noting

[1] The oral tradition of this paper goes back to the Annual General Meeting of the Classical Association in Canterbury in April 1990 ('Homer and the Mythology Game') and to the West Midlands Classical Seminar in February 1994. I am grateful for advice and correction given by participants at both and to Professor C.D.N. Costa for his advice and encouragement. In addition I have benefited to a very considerable extent from the advice of editors and referees and, above all, Ahuvia Kahane. The following items of bibliography are referred to frequently or need to be grouped for clarity:

E. Bethe, 'Homer und die Heldensage: die Sage vom troischen Kriege', *NJ* vii (1901) 657-76.

E. Bethe, *Homer: Dichtung und Sage*, vol. i 'Ilias' (Leipzig-Berlin 1914); vol. ii 'Odyssee, Kyklos, Zeitbestimmung' (1922); vol. iii 'Die Sage vom Troischen Kriege' (1927).

M.E. Clark, 'Neoanalysis: a biblographical review', *CW* lxxix (1986) 379-94.

M. Davies, *The Epic Cycle* (Bristol 1989).

G.F. Else, *Homer and the Homeric problem* [*Lectures in memory of Louise Taft Semple*] (Cincinnati 1965).

H. Erbse, 'Nestor und Antilochos bei Homer und Arktinos', *Hermes* cxxi (1993) 385-403.

J.M. Foley, *Immanent art: from structure to meaning in traditional oral epic* (Bloomington-Indianapolis 1991).

J. Griffin, 'The Epic Cycle and the uniqueness of homer', *JHS* xcvii (1977) 39-53.

J. Griffin, *Homer on life and death* (Oxford 1980).

A. Heubeck, *Die Homerische Frage* [*Erträge der Forschung* xxvii] (Darmstadt 1974).

A. Heubeck, 'Homeric studies today: results and prospects', in Fenik 1978: 1-17.

R. Janko, *The Iliad: a commentary*, vol. iv 'books 13-16' (Cambridge 1992).

M.S. Jensen, *The Homeric Question and the oral-formulaic theory* (Copenhagen 1980).

J.T. Kakridis, *Homeric researches* (Lund 1949).

G.S. Kirk, *The songs of Homer* (Cambridge 1962).

G.S. Kirk, *The Iliad: a commentary*, vol. i 'books 1-4' (Cambridge 1985).

W. Kullmann, *Die Quellen der Ilias (troischer Sagenkreis)* [*Hermes* Einzelschrift xiv] (Wiesbaden 1960).

W. Kullmann, 'Zur Methode der Neoanalyse in der Homerforschung', *WS* xv (1981) 5-42.

A.B. Lord, *The Singer of tales* (Cambridge, Mass. 1960).

A.B. Lord, 'Homer as oral poet', *HSCP* lxxii (1967) 1-46.

A.B. Lord, *Epic singers and oral tradition* (Ithaca 1991) [ch.2, pp. 38-47 reprints 'Homer's originality: oral dictated texts', *TAPA* lxxxiv (1953) 124-33].

R. Merkelbach, 'Die pisistratische Redaktion der homerischen Gedichte', *RhM* xcv (1952) 23-47.

G. Nagy, *Greek mythology and poetics* (Ithaca 1990) 23.

J.A. Notopoulos, 'Studies in early Greek oral poetry', *HSCP* lxviii (1964) 1-77.

H. Pestalozzi, *Die Achilleis als Quelle der Ilias* (Erlenbach 1945).

N.J. Richardson, *The Iliad: a commentary*, vol. vi 'books 21-24' (Cambridge 1993).

W. Schadewaldt, *Von Homers Welt und Werk*[2] (Stuttgart 1951).

R. von Scheliha, *Patroklos: Gedanken über Homers Dichtung und Gestalten* (Basel 1943).

G. Schoeck, *Ilias und Aithiopis: Kyklische Motive in homerische Brechung* (Zürich 1961).

O. Taplin, *Homeric soundings* (Oxford 1992).

D. Young, 'Never blotted a line? formula and premeditation in Homer and Hesiod', *Arion* vi (1967) 279-324.

the archaic accentuation preserved by rhapsodes, has argued that Homer's own text is a case in point, preserved fixed in an oral tradition.[2] Between the two extremes of total fixity and utter fluidity lie various levels of semi-fixity. Amongst these, and sufficient for most of my argument, lies a firm and standard sense of how the story goes (Proklos' summaries of the Cyclic epics may serve as a model for this), which I shall later refer to with Kullmann's term, *Faktenkanon*. But I think it is also worth envisaging a stronger case, where Homer interacts with specific implementations of the standard story (those, indeed, which standardise stories), if only to see that the problem with demonstrating that he referred to specific texts is not that the critical method is illegitimate but that the evidence runs out, i.e. earlier epic and Cyclic epic are not known *verbatim* to us, a few fragments apart.

A fixed text is more visibly owned and authored, and whoever borrows it owes an acknowledgement. Thus, the supposed author, Homer himself, if he is not a projection from the textuality of later ages, testifies to the fixed character of *Iliad* and *Odyssey*. The *Iliad* was a 'text' already for Homer. Construction of an architecturally accomplished poem on that scale (or delivery over a practical minimum of three days) implies some impressive—probably life-long—degree of premeditation and planning, a sense of text, and suggests something which in principle is capable of being repeated. Such a construction does not necessitate the use of writing (Taplin 36), though it is interesting that the age of the first authors is also an age during which writing is coming into more general circulation.[3] The difficulty with Homer's use of writing is more at the practical level: 15,693 lines of *Iliad* and 12,110 lines of *Odyssey*, and who paid for all that parchment or papyrus?[4] A 'Peisistratean recension' might indeed explain the funding, as indeed it would explain much else.[5]

The author of the *Kypria* already regarded the *Iliad* as a text. Any reading of the *Kypria* will show it preparing events in readiness for (specifically) the *Iliad* to refer back to them, for instance the sale of Lykaon to Lemnos and the kitting out of Achilles with Briseis and Agamemnon with Chryseis.[6] The *Kypria* very obviously does refer to the *Iliad* and was designed to lead up to it. It has rightly been described by Davies as 'a hold-all for the complete story of the Trojan War up to the events of the *Iliad*'.[7] Therefore, in the form in which it is reported to us by Proklos, it is later than Homer, in dialogue with Homer, and presupposes Homer as text. To reach this form of Homeric supplement from any earlier form would require more than mere adaptation: it would require severe re-editing and re-composition, by the author of the *Kypria*, let us say Stasinos, himself. The *Kypria* is clearly embedded in textual thinking.

The *Aithiopis*, however, unlike the *Kypria*, can be read as an independent work not necessarily presupposing the *Iliad*,[8] though one was clearly influenced by the other. It cannot

---

[2] Fixed preservation in other traditions, e.g. R. Finnegan, *Literacy and orality: studies in the technology of communication* (Oxford 1988) 95; *ead., Oral poetry: its nature, significance and social context*[2] (Bloomington 1992) 73-8. Nagy 40-3. Yet the assumption that fixity and writing are the same thing remains prevalent, e.g. A. Ford, *Homer: the poetry of the past* (Ithaca 1992) 132.

[3] A. Lesky, 'Homeros', *RE* Suppl. xi (1968) 687-846, at p. 706 views the architecture in particular as ruling out 'oral improvisation'—though 'improvisation' is not quite the right term.

[4] Kirk 1962: 99. Economics, Jensen 94. Other objections to writing: Kirk 1985: 13.

[5] It would have to be invented if it did not exist, *cf.* Merkelbach 40.

[6] Observed by Bethe 1922: 202, who concludes (241) 'Ein selbständiges Werk hatten sie niemals sein sollen.' For the question, 'why was Chryseis at Thebe?', obligingly answered by the *Kypria*, see Taplin 85 & n. 4.

[7] Davies 4. The opening of the poem appears to have been stylistically late—Davies 3, referring to J. Wackernagel, *Sprachliche Untersuchungen zu Homer* (Göttingen 1916) 1-159.

[8] Notopoulos 34 f.; Bethe 1922: 243: 'Die Aithiopis, d.h. Memnons Aristie und Tod, liegt in einheitlicher Überlieferung vor. Sie bildet ein geschlossenen Ring, ein selbständiger Gedicht.' Insufficient allowance for differences between Cyclic epics in Davies 4 f. Dating of the *Aithiopis*: 775 or 760 according to Eusebios *Chron.*

wholly be excluded that Arktinos was an 8th-century poet and antedates Homer, a view which Notopoulos was prepared to entertain. The *Aithiopis* would then be one of those predecessors of Homer in the (by now?) relatively fixed tradition which inspired him and led to his work. Though it is conventional to stress the brevity of the Cyclic Epics, they are only brief in comparison with Homer, who could readily be conceived as carrying forward a tendency to greater length which the newly fixed tradition was now displaying; this would dispose of some of the romantic oddity of the sudden appearance of the 'monumental poet'. Some Cyclic epics remain very long works compared with a standard recitation length, on Notopoulos's reckoning, of around one book (a 'lay'). The *Aithiopis*, though not rising to the eleven books of the (perhaps later) *Kypria*, was of substantial length at five books, suggesting that it was as fixedly designed as Homer's works were. Its plot at least was of elegant and compelling structure, it sought 'une grandeur et une émotion' (Severyns)[9] and, if *Odyssey* 24.48-49 is anything to go by, it must have contained one of the most thrilling moments in Cyclic epic as an uncanny scream rising over the sea heralds the arrival of Thetis and the Muses to lament the body of Achilles.

'Cyclic epic' is a term of convenience: these were works composed by different poets at different times and stand in different relationships to Homer. The *Aithiopis* is at one extreme, the *Telegony* of Eugammon of Kyrene (*fl.* 567 BC according to Eusebios)[10] at the other. Eugammon looks to be the most innovative and the least typical—it does not seem appropriate, on the basis of his *Telegony*, to read Homer's Circe in the light of her son Telegonos and Telemachos' later marriage to her.[11] But most Cyclic epics were as traditional as the *Iliad* and *Odyssey*,[12] indeed probably more so (see below on the 'Uncanonical *Iliad*'), and their access to tradition should not be funnelled exclusively through Homer. Rather, Homer may draw on the material that they are using. If they too were transmitted orally, some of them from early dates, they too must surely have received their definitive written form and definitive statement of their future careers as cyclic supplements to Homer at the 'Peisistratean recension'.

I think it is an attractive conceptual model that Homer was exploiting a tradition which had developed recognised, quite fixed, 'texts' and that his works were not the first 'texts'. Thus however much his manner may be derived from an oral tradition, he is so far towards being a literary text that non-oral literary analytical techniques should not be disqualified. In distinguishing between oral and non-oral criticism, the analysis of Foley provides a useful focus.[13] For him, in the oral-traditional mode of composition the power of the poem depends on its resonance with the established elements and strategies of tradition—the meaning of any part of the poem is 'inherent' in the (typical) scene, motif, or expression. In the 'modern'[14] literary mode of composition, meaning is newly and distinctively 'conferred' on the text. Foley also speaks here of the relative balance between these two extremes in any given work, an important point if one is not to exaggerate the orality of Homer. Clearly, the economy of the

---

(ed. R. Helm *GCS* xlvii, Berlin 1956); born *c*. 744 and a 'pupil of Homer' according to Artemon of Klazomenai (4th century BC?) *FGrH* 443F2.

[9] A. Severyns, *Le Cycle épique dans l'école d'Aristarque* (Liége-Paris 1928) 322.

[10] The date of Eugammon may indeed, as often thought (e.g. Davies 6), simply be based on a decent interval after the foundation of Cyrene (c. 630), but, if so, that is a perfectly reasonable ground for the dating, not a refutation of it. It is fair to assume that Eugammon belongs to the last generation of poets before the Peisistratean recension.

[11] It is, however, somewhat disturbing that a *Telegony* is also ascribed to Kinaithon of Sparta, which would take the story much further back. For supposed influence of the *Telegony* on our *Odyssey*, see Davies 87 f.

[12] See Notopoulos, esp. 18-45.

[13] Foley 8.

[14] One feels the influence of Romanticism in this formulation and it becomes clear that Homer and Vergil are indeed not poles apart. Vergil is rather an oral poet in his closeness to tradition, his focus on recitation, and his tendency to sound patterns.

Homeric formula implies a significant leaning towards the oral-traditionalist pole when discussing, e.g., πόδας ὠκὺς ᾿Αχιλλεύς in 1.58. But my contention in this article is that Homer had a sufficient sense of text to allow us to move towards the literary pole when discussing his use of other 'authors'. Specifically, the following description by Lord of Bosnian performers does not apply to him:[15]

> We have learned that a tradition is made up not of discrete songs but of songs, or preferably, stories about a limited number of heroes, tales that overlap and intertwine, in such a way that in the experience of both the singer and his traditional audience any one traditional song can evoke subconsciously a large group of other songs, or stories, in the tradition.

Homer, we will find, did more than evoke subconsciously, through the tradition, a corpus of stories. He evoked particular stories at particular points for particular effect and could well have had particular tellings, 'texts', in mind.

On this model, then, he emulated, and advanced on, earlier masters—and perhaps advanced on his own work through incremental variation of an original, much shorter, quarrel poem. The expansion involved the composition of new episodes, which were assigned a place in his growing 'supertext', but his implied total text was probably never performed in its entirety (see below).[16] Goold in particular has argued forcefully for Homer's works being formed by continual additions and has made clear that the additions were made to a very fixed text, which Goold interprets as therefore written.[17] Furthermore, Goold has observed that the additions so respect book divisions and the book divisions in any case make such sense that, like Notopoulos, he thinks they must be Homer's own. There would indeed be a certain literate virtuosity, a degree of *epideixis*, in ultimately creating a poem that consists of one recitation for every letter of the alphabet (if, as could be the case, that is the number of letters his alphabet had), though this may be too small a unit of recitation.[18] There is however an alarming corollary if Goold is wrong on one essential point: have we recovered not the 'Nature of Homeric Composition', but the method of the Peisistratean recension as it gathered songs supposedly by 'Homer', conceived of as hitherto 'scattered'? There is no evidence that we have Homer's *Iliad* other than the perceived unity of the poems (is that enough?)—which only Merkelbach (42) has denied, if not with such devastating consequences in mind.

But even if we do not go to that extreme, there remains something strange about Homer's textuality. It is hard to be convinced by any of the suggested occasions for the oral performance of Homer's lengthy works (unless a festival performance is conceived of as a Bayreuth[19] with, unusually for the Greek world, no competitors performing their own monster-epics). Nor,

---

[15] Lord, unpublished, cited by Foley 11.

[16] Similarly, Young 306.

[17] See G.P. Goold, 'The nature of Homeric composition', *ICS* ii (1977) 1-34, esp. pp. 9, 10-12, 26-30 for the points cited here.

[18] I am realigning Notopoulos's argument (11 f.). The consensus is, however, firmly against the book-division being Homer's own, and gently in favour of its being Alexandrian (Taplin 285; Richardson 20 f.). The ultimate reason is less the apparent absence of book divisions from papyri (in fact there are some signs of recognition of book divisions, S. West, *The Ptolemaic Papyri of Homer* [Köln-Opladen 1967] 22 f.) than the absence of any awareness of book divisions in any author before the fourth century BC (West 18). But West is now inclined to push the book division back to the Peisistratean recension; and Jensen (87) is 'inclined to interpret the arrangement of each poem into twenty-four songs as resulting from the process of dictation'—making the scribe responsible for the assignation of one letter of the 'Ionic alphabet' to each book (at the Peisistratean recension, on Jensen's view). Larger units: an anonymous referee of this article comments: 'The *Odyssey* falls so neatly into six nearly equal parts (each of four present-day books, except that the third part ends at 13.92), that I find irresistible the inference that it was composed specifically with a view to performance in six instalments.'

[19] The comparison of an anonymous referee.

evidently, can it have been designed *in toto* for a readership.[20] It is apparently unperformable.[21] Unless we should simply accept the endurance of singer (with assistants?) and of audience on some occasion not yet accurately envisaged (there are, worryingly, no close parallels), there may be a fault in our conception of this problem. I therefore ask a radical question, returning us almost to the views of Bentley:[22] *do we have any reason to suppose the Iliad was ever in fact performed complete before the Peisistratean Panathenaia?* If not, it is up to us to conceive of a way in which an *Iliad* only told in isolated episodes might nonetheless have an identity. The *Iliad* would on this supposition be the environment, the sense of total story, the 'supertext', within which Homer and his successors sang episodes to audiences. Yet this 'supertext' was sufficiently designed, developed and fixed for it to be theoretically possible to put together the episodes and create the monumental whole that no-one in fact had heard before: possibly this was the grandiose scheme of Peisistratos. The 'supertext' itself was a remarkable invention. Just as other poets operated, for instance within an environment of a 'Trojan War' saga, ultimately collected together as what we know as 'the Cyclic epics', so Homer created a tauter environment—of Achilles' withdrawal from, and return to, battle—to which he transferred by allusion much of the Trojan War material. He designed and constructed his rhapsodies within that context, and these rhapsodies were finally collected together as 'the *Iliad*'. He expanded his work, as it were, by oral word-processing, but the hard copy of the whole document was only printed in 6th-century Athens. This is not so very different from the known features of certain oral traditions, where only selected episodes from the 'whole story' are ever performed, where 'Mr Rureke ... repeatedly asserted that never before had he performed the whole story within a continuous span of days'.[23]

FAKTENKANON, INTERTEXT

Homer does not, of course, refer to other historical poets. But he does refer to other poems, or subjects for poems. How defined are these poems? And how defined is his own?

I have argued elsewhere that Greek Mythology is an intertext formed from all tellings of myth that 'readers' (or listeners) have ever encountered.[24] Thus for any particular myth there is a sense of how the story goes, which need not be dependent on a single telling. Any new telling of a myth positions itself in relation to the intertext and gains its sense and ambience from that relationship. This model is applicable equally to oral and literary traditions. Indeed, there is an important intertextual element to heroic-epic tradition, which for instance leads Hatto to speak of its oral and post-oral form as consisting of the 'totality of its texts' or performances.[25] For each myth/subject, regardless of whether there is reference to a specific hypotext

---

[20] Nagy 38.

[21] This is particularly well shown by Kirk 1962: 280 f., who finds himself driven by an entirely reasonable argument to the desperate solution of a genius-Homer defying normal performance conditions. Kirk 1985: 12 talks of its having 'been performed in a special way at which we can only guess', rejecting as unlikely that it 'was never intended to be heard as a whole'. The suggestion of assistants (or sons/apprentices) comes from an anonymous referee and would somewhat recall the recitals of Vergil. Ford (n. 2) 133 also arrives at this position, speaking of 'a still largely illiterate age in which they would have been rarely read and nearly impossible to perform in toto'.

[22] H. Lloyd-Jones, 'Remarks on the Homeric question', in: *Greek epic, lyric and tragedy: the academic papers of Sir Hugh Lloyd-Jones* (Oxford 1990) ch.1 [reprinting H. Lloyd-Jones, V. Pearl, and B. Worden (eds.), *History and imagination: essays in honours of H.R. Trevor-Roper* (London 1981) 15-29], at p. 3.

[23] Foley 12 on the Pabuji epic in Rajasthan and on the Mwindo tradition, citing this particular passage from D. Biebuyck, *The Mwindo epic from the Banyanga* (Berkeley 1969) 14.

[24] K. Dowden, *The uses of Greek mythology* (London 1992) 7-9.

[25] A.T. Hatto, 'Towards an anatomy of heroic/epic poetry', in: J.B. Hainsworth (ed.), *Traditions of heroic and epic poetry*, vol. ii 'Characteristics and techniques' (London 1989) 145-306, at pp. 147 f.

(this or that poet's telling), there is an intertext which, except in some peculiarly disputed or little-known myth, will amount to what Kullmann called a *Faktenkanon*, a standard event-list.[26] On the larger scale, it is obviously unthinkable that Homer's tradition was so fluid that he had no sense at all of how the story of Troy went and what incidents were generally included. Lord too, consistently with his stress in the *Singer of Tales* on 'the stable skeleton of narrative', has stated that there is a 'more or less stable core' in response to Smith's observation, in the case of the performers of the Rajasthani epic of the warrior-prince Pabuji, of 'substantial agreement amongst them as to what kinds of story-element are "necessary".'[27] Without such a sense of how the story goes, it would be impossible for Avdo Medjedović to have claimed a repertoire of 58 (therefore identifiable) epics, or for Lord to envisage that Homer 'sang these two songs often'.[28] Homer's Phemios, after all, knew various songs from which the audience might wish to choose (*cf.* Jensen 116-8). This is an important point to grasp about limitations on fluidity. Jensen (49), for instance, regards Lord's views as confirmed by a West-Central African tradition where 'two performers are never exactly alike, yet the singers are engaged in various definite songs and by no means improvising freely'.

The *Faktenkanon* is the bottom line of Homeric intertextuality. It is because of its existence that Homer is able to allude—in a way, notably, that Bosnian bards do not[29]—to other epic subjects:

- *Iliad:* the two expeditions against Thebes (4.365-410), the hunting of the Kalydonian Boar (9), Herakles (e.g. 14.266 with 15.25, 14.324, 15.640), Perseus (14.320), Semele and Dionysos (14.323-5), Pylian epics (e.g. 11.670-761), and Oedipus (23.679).

- *Odyssey*: *Nostoi* and the vengeance of Athene (as told by Phemios, 1.326-7), the Argonaut myth (12.69-72), Oedipus (11.271), Herakles (8.224, 11.267) and his murder of Iphitos (21.22-30).

There is no way of telling from these references whether Homer refers here to common stories or particular poems. The number of these references, however, does show his concern to place his own work in a context of other epics and to give it a sense of reaching out to the rest of the legendary world. Slatkin rightly speaks of Homer establishing 'bearings for the poem as it unfolds and linking it continually to other traditions and paradigms and to a wide mythological terrain'.[30]

HOMERIC SILENCE

Homer's manipulation of the *Faktenkanon* can also be discerned in negative. As part of his self-definition, he has a policy of exclusion.[31]

Homeric silence about a tradition does not necessarily mean that it was unknown to him.

---

[26] Kullmann 1960: 12 f.

[27] J.D. Smith, 'How to sing a tale: Epic performance in the Pabuji tradition', in: J.B. Hainsworth (ed.), *Traditions of heroic and epic poetry*, vol. 2 'Characteristics and techniques' (London 1989) 29-41, at p. 36; Lord 1987: 67; Lord 1960: 99. *Cf.* Milman Parry, *The making of Homeric verse: the collected papers of Milman Parry*, ed. A. Parry (Oxford 1971) 446 on '*stable* or *essential*' themes.

[28] Finnegan 1992 (n. 2) 174. Lord 1960: 151.

[29] Lord 1960: 159, Young 305.

[30] L.M. Slatkin, *The power of Thetis: allusion and interpretation in the* Iliad (Berkeley 1991) 108.

[31] *Cf.* also Slatkin (n. 30) 15 on the 'exclusion of such traditional mythological material, or its displacement into more or less oblique references'.

One instance is the sacrifice of Iphigeneia.[32] Because it is not overtly referred to in the *Iliad*, the scholiast comments, 'Homer does not know the sacrifice of Iphigeneia'. Yet Agamemnon's words to Calchas, accusing him of a habit of evil prophecy (1.106-8), gain point if they react with a knowledge of that tradition shared by Homer and his audience. Homer also does not know: the education of Achilles by the Centaur Cheiron, and his invulnerability but for his heel; the theft of the Palladion; Kassandra the prophetess; and, but for 24.29 (damned by Aristarchos), the Judgment of Paris. To create his *verismo* he is prepared to blank out parts of traditions. Bellerophon may (in a narration of ancestry) kill the Chimaira, but winged horses are proscribed.[33] Prophets like Calchas and Helenos may exist and may be said to be able to foresee the future; but they must not do any actual foreseeing—that would disrupt the human tone and they must make do with advising.[34] Homer's Kassandra is no prophetess—she is simply the most beautiful of Priam's daughters, ready to be married off at 13.365 (or to be raped by Aias?) and first to perceive the return of Priam with Hektor at 24.699 (almost prophetic?). As Griffin has shown, Homer deliberately cultivates a very special tone that distances him from the more tolerant (or less discriminating) cyclic epics: he is most reluctant to allow elements that are 'fantastic, miraculous, romantic ... sensational, ignoble'.[35] So, absent details are not necessarily post-Homeric inventions—even if, indeed especially if, they display garish taste, because Homer establishes his idiosyncratic good taste precisely by excluding details that fail his test. The sacrifice of Iphigeneia was either too gross or, if we think of the replacement of her by a deer at the moment of sacrifice, too miraculous—hence Homer's 'sedulous silence' (Davies 46).

This is not a quaint characteristic of Homer, but a deliberate choice. If he meant his work to be so perceived, it could only be so perceived in contrast to the prevailing character of a tradition, which therefore included these motifs and *to which, by refusing reference, he made reference*. This is once again indicative of his method, to create the literary effect of his own poem by manipulation of the audience's experience of other poems.

THE UNCANONICAL *ILIAD*

How much of the *Iliad* itself belongs to the *Faktenkanon*? Which canonical or generally recognised events of the Trojan War is it its business to relate?

The *Iliad* has a narrow time span, measured in days, and rather a lack of incident compared with the Cyclic epics (just as Aristotle observed in the cases of epics of Herakles and Theseus). It concerns neither the beginning nor the conclusion of the war. Instead it focusses on a moment in the war when there was a quarrel between Achilles and Agamemnon, Achilles withdrew from the action, and as a result Patroklos and Hektor were slain. Neither Patroklos nor Hektor seem to be figures particularly well embedded in the epic tradition,[36] and however much Homer tries to persuade us that Achilles' death follows upon that of Hektor, it is not strictly true that Hektor's death makes it come any sooner (except that a few hours have been divertingly filled

---

[32] Homeric ignorance: K. Dowden, *Death and the maiden* (London 1989) 11 f.

[33] J.H. Gaisser, 'Adaptation of traditional material in the Glaucus-Diomedes episode', *TAPA* c (1969) 165-76, at p. 170.

[34] No foreseeing: Griffin 1977: 48, Kullmann 1960: 221-4.

[35] Griffin 1977: 40 f. The qualitative distinction is an important point in Schadewaldt's work too, see Heubeck 1974: 43.

[36] Patroklos invented by Homer: Scheliha 236-51, 391; Schadewaldt 178-81; raised from obscurity by Homer: Kullmann 1960: 44 f., 193 f.; Janko 313. Hektor: J.W. Scott, *The Unity of Homer* (Berkeley 1921) ch.vii esp. 226; Scheliha 221 f.; Kullmann 1960: 182-8; Janko 312. According to Bethe 1901: 674, H. Usener tried to reconstruct an *Iliad* with Paris replacing Hektor.

for Achilles). Hektor, as used by Homer, is a figure who inventively encapsulates 'the new realm in which man is son and husband and father and citizen as well as fighter' (Else 39) in contrast to the brutal heroic world that is one aspect of Achilles. In fact the originality of Homer's plot is precisely that it stands aside from the *Faktenkanon*, but continually echoes it whilst evaluating men and war. It depends on the *Faktenkanon* for its context and resonance, but is largely untraditional in its ostensible choice of subject.

This has the most curious corollary for the *Iliad* as battle epic: it is very difficult for anyone to die in the *Iliad* unless they have been specially, non-traditionally, invented for it. This is because, if they have an existence independent of the *Iliad*, then the *Iliad*, as a non-traditional work, does not embrace previously significant moments in their life, such as their loss of it. A striking case is that of Achilles, to whom in a psychological sense everything happens in the *Iliad*, but to whom in cold fact nothing happens—except the loss of an (invented or severely overhauled) friend and the defeat of a (similarly untraditional) enemy. He himself, as we have seen, despite Homer's nudgings is no closer to death than he was earlier. In the case of other heroes, Kullmann showed[37] that so far as one can tell, of the Greek heroes found in the *Catalogue of Ships*,

1. the thirty-six who do not die in the *Iliad* figure somewhere else also in the story of Troy; depending on one's prejudices, it is quite possible to view all of them as belonging to pre-Homeric poetry;

2. this is also true of five of the ten who die (Askalaphos, Schedios, Amphimachos, Elephenor—who all figure in posthomeric events—and Tlepolemos who does not);

3. the other five (Arkesilaos, Prothoenor, Klonios, Diores & Medon) are inventions who exist to be killed.[38]

Obviously Achilles has a story, his personal *Faktenkanon*, including for instance the wounding of Telephos, the slaying of Troilos (whence his epithet, πόδας ὠκύς, 'swift-footed'),[39] and the death by arrow to the heel. Other heroes too will have had their stories, but one reading of these researches of Kullmann is that conceivably as many as thirty-six heroes are preserved from death in the *Iliad* precisely because they are part of, belong to, another story, a story of their own perhaps unknown to us—these are not just miscellaneous heroic names used at will.

Thus when Homer uses a hero, in principle we should be aware of the rest of his text, or some central, perhaps different, way of telling his story. When Telamonian Aias performs so majestically in the great fight for the body of Patroklos (17, e.g. 274-318, 626-55), we should compare his role in recovering the body of Achilles (which leads to the contest over the armour). In his instruction (715-21) to Meriones and Menelaos to remove the body of Patroklos while he and his namesake fight rearguard, we see the displacement of the motif in which he personally removes the body of Achilles as Odysseus fights rearguard. And when he wrestles

---

[37] Kullmann 1960: 122 f. Kullmann challenged, e.g. by Heubeck 1974: 45; for such criticism and its validity, see Clark 382.

[38] On the Trojan side, surely Pandaros is of this type: he is a Paris-avatar, who exists to break the truce and be killed (on Pandaros as Paris, now see Taplin 104 f.); Euphorbos is a similar figure, who in killing Patroklos foreshadows Paris killing Achilles (16.812), *cf.* Janko 410, 414 and Clark 385, referring to H. Mühlestein, 'Euphorbos und der Tod Patroklos', *SMEA* xv (1972) 79-90. For this avatar technique, *cf.* Phoinix who is a Nestor-avatar who can be left at Achilles' tent (Phoinix as Nestor, *cf.* Erbse 387).

[39] Just as πολύτλας points forward to the return of Odysseus from Troy, Nagy 23.

with Odysseus (23.708-37), we should look ahead to that other contest between them.[40] When Aias son of Oileus behaves badly in the games (23.473-98), we should perceive the character failing that will lead him to sacrilege; and the intervention of Athene later in the book and his complaint against her (23.782) look forward to the storm in which she will have him destroyed.[41] This twenty-third book conducts its own, final, review of the Greek heroes and their society, thereby balancing the parades that introduced them in the *Catalogue*, the *Teichoskopia*, and the *Epipolesis*,[42] but also reaching out to other stories in which the heroes figure.

It is less clear to me how other heroes with a pre-existing identity have been incorporated in Homer's narrative. If it is true, as Bethe alleged, that the conflict of Tlepolemos (of Rhodes)—appearing at Troy here only, to be slaughtered—and Sarpedon (of Lykia) looks like a local combat re-set in Troy, then what continuity does it carry with it, in what does 'diese Sage' consist?[43] I think it might, just conceivably, be a celebrated case where the slayer was himself slain: Sarpedon retires very wounded from this combat, πατὴρ δ' ἔτι λοιγὸν ἄμυνεν ('but his father still warded destruction from him', *Iliad* 5.662) so that he might provide the poet with a distinguished victim for his invented, or much revamped, Patroklos and undergo a special (Memnonic) death, as we shall see. The poet certainly, when one examines the dialogue (5.640-54), is labouring overtime to assert the relevance of the contest to its (now?) Trojan setting. Hektor too poses difficulties: if his tomb at Thebes is to be taken seriously, then the firmest supporting argument is his propensity for killing Boiotians and the like in the *Iliad*, as Bethe once observed. Yet I still do not understand the mechanics of this phenomenon in the *Iliad*. Is it traditional for Hektor to kill Teuthras, Orestes, Trechos and Helenos (5.705-10) of Boiotia and not A, B, C of Pylos, without there being any further thematic or textual implications, just a link of name with name? Does it just 'feel right'?

So, the *Iliad*, being less than canonical, cannot legitimately include the direct telling of events from the *Faktenkanon* of the Trojan War and the lives of the Greek heroes. How else, then, can it respond to known events?

ILIAD, MIRROR OF THE WHOLE WAR

The *Iliad* tells within itself and is meant to tell within itself, by allusion, by reflection and by replay, the whole story of the Trojan expedition up to the fall of Troy and beyond.[44] It does not just accidentally and inevitably reflect other events, by virtue of its being situated in that war, or by virtue of Homer's head being full of oral stuff. There is a clear and deliberate intention to reach out, embrace, and mould his poem on, major events in the war and to *evoke* those specific events. I can scarcely imagine any perception more fundamental to the understanding of the *Iliad* than this—and it is one which is shared by scholars of quite different persuasions who have been less concerned with oral issues.[45]

---

[40] Kullmann 1981: 23-5, now accepted by Richardson 202, 246.

[41] Proklos' summary of Hagias of Troizen, *Nostoi*; Eur. *Tro.* 65 ff., 70, 90.

[42] *Cf.* Richardson 78.

[43] *Iliad* 5.627-98: Bethe 1901: 668 f.; C. Robert, *Studien zur Ilias* (Berlin 1901) 402; P. Cauer *Grundfragen der Homerkritik*³ (Leipzig 1923) 242; Bethe 1927: 65. 'Bethe's fundamental elements, the duels, are very meagre and somewhat uninteresting myths', M.P. Nilsson, *Homer and Mycenae* (London 1933) 48.

[44] For a list of possible allusions to *Antihomerica* and *Posthomerica* see Kullmann 1960: 6-11.

[45] E.g. Kullmann 1960: 365 f. ('In der ganzen Ilias kann man die Beobachtung machen, dass dies Epos in seinem Aufbau den ganzen Krieg zu repräsentieren scheint' plus detailed table); Griffin 1980: 1 ('The wrath of Achilles and its consequences are made to represent the whole story').

The *Catalogue of Troops*, with its emphasis on ships and its rather slighter Trojan pendant, evokes the mustering of the Greek fleet at Aulis and is overtly linked to that scene by Odysseus' recall of the prophecy of the sparrows and snake. The *Teichoskopia* belongs with the first sighting of the Greek leaders, perhaps even on the occasion of the Duel between Menelaos and Paris, which must surely be the opening event. The *Epipolesis* presumably follows the failed duel, but in any case has the atmosphere of an initial event. Achilles' withdrawal from the fighting is associated in the first book with Thetis and her fears for him, which caused her elsewhere in the mythology to hide him on Skyros. He had to be retrieved from there by an Embassy, which is replayed in the ninth book and strongly associated there with the inverse movement, namely his prospective return home. The *Doloneia*, an apparently ill-motivated night-expedition against Troy, eliminates Rhesus, who in order to leave room for Hektor has to be scaled down from the man who would have saved Troy, had he tasted its water.[46] But it also surely mirrors the expedition of Odysseus and Diomedes to steal the Palladion. Attention had already been drawn to the Palladion in the sixth book, with particular irony when the Trojan Women call on Athena to demolish Diomedes (6.307), but with a second irony, that she should do so at the Skaian Gate, where of course Achilles will in fact be killed by the Paris to whom Hektor is currently heading. And of course, to linger a little in Book 6, the starting point for the meditation on Astyanax is the fate which the audience knows will befall him on the capture of Troy.

The later part of the book is especially, and more than merely typologically,[47] affected by intertextuality with what we know as the *Aithiopis* of Arktinos, focused in particular on Achilles' defeat of Memnon and his own death (Pestalozzi 7).[48] The observation of this relationship has been the major achievement of the neoanalytic school of criticism, as Janko (312-3) has recently recognised. There can be no doubt that the events of the two poems, the *Aithiopis* and the *Iliad*, mirror each other; the only question is the direction—which in the light of the non-canonical nature of the Homeric plot seems to me to flow from *Aithiopis* to *Iliad*. There is room for difference of view on this issue, but the view I suggest is that, although it can be argued that this similarity or that similarity makes better sense in the context of the *Aithiopis* than in that of the *Iliad*, it is more important to perceive that the aggregation of references forward to the sequence of events leading to Achilles' death gives us a fine, resonant *Iliad* and an allowable and consistent method on Homer's part: his poem looks forward just as it looks backward.

Achilles' death was an event before the *Iliad* and his death was doubtless regularly lamented by Thetis, as depicted in *Odyssey* 24 (from Arktinos?). It is not in itself hard to realise that the death of Patroklos, who had gone into battle masquerading as Achilles, knowingly foreshadows the death of Achilles himself. Other connections include: the role of Apollo in both (*cf.* 22.359); the role of Aias in the fight over the body (a theme which, as Else has observed, is here in Book 17 'fully expanded');[49] the reception of Achilles' mourning as a pointer to his death by the Thetis who must eventually mourn him (18.35), and who accidentally will mourn Patroklos (23.14); the deathlike posture of Achilles, lying μέγας μεγαλωστί ('huge, hugely',

---

[46] B.C. Fenik, *Iliad X and the Rhesus: the myth* [*Collection Latomus* 73] (Bruxelles 1964).

[47] Notopoulos 34 f.

[48] Pestalozzi was in effect the first to adumbrate the full picture of the influence of the *Aithiopis* on the *Iliad*, though the way was pointed by Kakridis 1949: 93-5 (1944 in Greek). This picture has subsequently been developed, notably by Schadewaldt (155-202, 'Einblick in die Erfindung der Ilias: Ilias und Memnonis'), Kullmann 1960 (from his Habilitationsschrift of 1957) and Schoeck. In my opinion, the most thoroughgoing and dependable of these texts is Kullmann's. For a full account of neoanalysm, see Clark.

[49] Else 39.

18.26, on which more below). All this, and maybe the funeral games too, point unmistakeably forward.

A particular part in all this is played by Nestor's son Antilochos. In the *Aithiopis* he is Achilles' closest friend, as (derivatively) at *Odyssey* 24.79—μετὰ Πάτροκλόν γε θανόντα ('after, that is, the death of Patroklos'), is patched in to maintain consistency with the *Iliad*.[50] But he is killed by the new arrival Memnon as he saves his father Nestor, trapped because Paris has shot down one of his horses. This *Nestor in Danger* scene appears in Pindar (*Pythian* 6.28, presumably on the basis of Arktinos) and is anticipated at *Iliad* 8.80-129, where this time Diomedes plays the part of Antilochos, much more than just a typical scene (X rescues Y in a chariot).[51] This time Diomedes rescues Nestor; next time Antilochos will—and it will cost his life. Diomedes and Nestor are very close in *Iliad* 8-9; and Nestor himself says that Diomedes could be his own youngest son (9.57). At the very least, this depiction of Diomedes as Antilochos enhances the warmth with which we, like Nestor, view his character. If we had the full text of the *Aithiopis* perhaps there would be more: is there something lurking behind the either cowardly or deaf figure of Odysseus running away as only Diomedes is left to save Nestor (8.92 ff.)? Does this, as Kullmann suggested, represent (and superimpose) an agonising moment as Antilochos appeals, is ignored and realises he must die for his father?[52]

Memnon is a hero with a divine mother like Achilles (Eos) and armour made by Hephaistos (Vergil, *Aeneid* 8.383-4). The major duel between them perhaps reached its climax through appeals of their respective mothers to Zeus, and Memnon's death was settled through the weighing of the sons' souls, the Ψυχοστασία (the title of Aeschylus' play on the subject)—which Homer presses into service (though he weighs dooms not souls) for rhetorical, amplificatory effect in that other climax, at *Iliad* 22.208-13.[53] Memnon is, however, at his mother's request granted immortality and to judge by art his body is taken off by Sleep and Death (transferred to Sarpedon in Patroklos' mock-Achillean *aristeia*, 16.666-83).[54] Slatkin has observed the relationship of this mother and child story to the Eos and, e.g., Tithonos story and to Sanskrit mythology of the cognate dawn-figure, Uṣás-.[55] If this Indo-Europeanising approach represents the origins of the tradition, then the fact that Dawn is Memnon's mother (and that Thetis is merely, as Slatkin observes, associated with events at dawn) would seem to indicate a direction of flow from the less innovative, Arktinos, to the more innovative, Homer. Achilles' revenge is complete but now he assaults the city of Troy itself, the fatal point at which Paris and Apollo kill him (like Homer's Patroklos, warned by Apollo and killed by a Paris-substitute, Euphorbos, and Apollo).[56]

---

[50] 24.77 and 24.79 look artificial.

[51] Connection of the scenes: Bethe 1914: 109-12, Pestalozzi 10, Schoeck 20-2. Accepted and, revealingly, muddled by Davies 4—it is hard to hold the scenes apart. Typical or meaningfully borrowed?—fair, if cautious, discussion in B.C. Fenik, *Typical battle scenes in the Iliad: studies in the narrative techniques of Homeric battle description*, [*Hermes* Einzelschrift xxi] (Wiesbaden 1968) 231-40. For a different view, that Arktinos is here developing Homer, see Erbse.

[52] Kullmann 1960: 32. The replay in the *Iliad* is taken rather lightly by Kullmann 1981: 25, who sees it as the Aithiopis minus the tragedy. In contrast, Erbse 394-7, though I disagree with his ultimate conclusion, shows that the episode has a proper function in the Homeric text.

[53] Pestalozzi 11 f., Schadewaldt 164, Schoeck 29 f.

[54] Schadewaldt 165 f.; M.E. Clark & W.D.E. Coulson, 'Memnon and Sarpedon', *Museum Helveticum* xxxv (1978) 65-73. There is the problem of why Death should remove someone granted immortality (Davies 57), but perhaps it is no more a problem than why a dead Sarpedon should be anointed with ambrosia, given immortal clothing and transported if permanently, and Homerically, dead (in implicit contrast not only to Memnon, but also to Achilles on Leuke).

[55] Slatkin (n. 30) 28-33. On Uṣás-, see also J. Puhvel, *Comparative Mythology* (Baltimore 1987) 60.

[56] 16.651-5. Clark-Coulson (n. 54) 66 f. Euphorbos as Paris-avatar, above n. 38.

Patroklos' death anticipates the death of Antilochos, as Hektor's triumph and defeat anticipate those of Memnon, already signalled in the death of Sarpedon. The consequence of the Memnon-story is the death of Achilles himself, itself also immanent in the death of Patroklos. The Wagnerian *Leitmotifs* of the story of Achilles' death have become very dense and overshadow this whole area of the text, from 16 to 23—perhaps he is already dead, even Lord of the Dead,[57] in 24, given the *katabasis*-quality of Priam's journey. Memnon, naturally, does not appear in the *Iliad*, but Antilochos does and some of his movements seem to prepare for the *Aithiopis*:[58] he is proposed out of thin air by Aias (wondering, perhaps meaningfully, if he is still alive, 18.653) to carry the news of Patroklos' death to Achilles (Bethe 1914: 100); and both in his protectiveness to Achilles when he makes the report (18.32-4) and in the Funeral Games (23.540 ff., 785 ff.), the growing cordiality between the two is apparent. Even Achilles' final and fatal attack on Troy is prefigured in his passing thought of trying out the Trojans (22.378-84; Schadewaldt 168-9).

The end of Troy, symbolised by the death of Hektor (Schoeck 117), is within sight at the end of the *Iliad*, visible in the pathetic Priam and Hekabe of 22 and 24. Perhaps too it was not Vergil's Priam that was the first to have in mind a contrast between Achilles and Neoptolemos in their treatment of Priam—they do after all talk of fathers and sons and death and it is no casual irony that it is the son of Achilles who will finish Priam, conversely entering *his* home and with converse behaviour. The ransoming of his dead son by Priam also reflects (and may be the model for) the failed attempt by Chryses to ransom his daughter at the outset of the poem—a scene which itself reflects an earlier one.[59] Having rejected the ransom, Agamemnon finds himself in dispute with Achilles over a woman that he has taken with some injustice from him. This could be a typical scene, but here it serves to recall the cause of the Trojan War, the dispute between Paris and Menelaos over Helen, with Agamemnon this time cast as Paris, belonging with other replays in Books 1-4 of the beginning of the war.[60] And moving one step back to Chryseis, it will be seen that Kalchas intervenes decisively to ensure that Agamemnon loses a daughter (not in this case his own) because of the wrath of Apollo (not this time Artemis), an allusion surely underlined by Agamemnon's complaint that Kalchas has never spoken a useful word for him—referring then to the sacrifice of Iphigeneia (see above).

Willcock, who went further than other English scholars in the 1970s to pay attention to this relationship between Homer and the *Aithiopis* material, observed 'interaction between parts of the poet's own repertoire' and 'thematic association, in the way that his "Muse" directed him' and reckoned that these facts 'show us something of the method of the oral poet'.[61] That, I think, was to stay too close to the oral-'inherent' pole. This was Homer's conscious use of other texts (inasmuch as artistic creation is a conscious process), a use which any student of Vergil would recognise, but for misplaced guilt at the illegitimacy of our sense of text.[62]

---

[57] A long shot, this, but see H. Hommel, 'Der Gott Achilleus', *SB Heidelberg* Abh. i (1980).

[58] M.M. Willcock, 'The final scenes of *Iliad* XVII', in: J.M. Bremer, I.J.F. de Jong & J. Kalff, *Homer: beyond oral poetry: recent trends in Homeric interpretation* (Amsterdam 1987) 191 ('as if to prepare for what will happen after the end of the *Iliad*'); Kullmann 316 ('bereiten offenbar bewusst den Aithiopisstoff vor').

[59] D. Lohmann, *Die Kompositio der Reden in der Ilias* (Berlin 1970) 169-73; Richardson 5 f., 17.

[60] Briseis and Helen functionally compared already by Bethe 1901: 667.

[61] M.M. Willcock, *A companion to the Iliad* (Chicago 1976) 287. Even Kullmann, in a concessive mood, allows the concept 'zumindest assoziativ von ihr beeinflusst', 1981: 20.

[62] Thus I think Page's sarcasm recoils on itself, when he derides the neoanalysts for treating Homer's use of his predecessors like Vergil's use of Homer and contrasts them with 'those of us who have long understood the process of growth of the traditional oral epic' (D.L. Page, 'Homer and the Neoanalytiker', *CR* xiii [1963] 21-4).

QUOTATION (OF OTHERS, OF SELF)

The question of fixed texts would be definitively solved if we could identify non-formular verbatim quotations. But even if Homer was able to allude to texts in this way, our loss of all earlier texts would seem to exclude knowledge of his having done so. All the same, there may be two dimly visible instances:

1. As Patroklos is mourned, we read μετὰ δέ σφι Θέτις γόου ἵμερον ὦρσε ('and amidst them Thetis aroused the desire for lament', *Iliad* 23.14), but as Kakridis pointed out, she has not arrived and is not there—these lines have been taken 'bodily from an epic description of Achilles' funeral'. It is hard to justify the lines and they give the impression of a poet on auto-pilot who has let the evoked text take over.

2. At *Iliad* 18.26 we see an Achilles, overcome by grief at the death of Patroklos, ἐν κονίῃσι μέγας μεγαλωστὶ τανυσθείς ('stretched out huge, hugely in the dust'). It takes no great imagination to see this as an iconic anticipation of his own death, but the words μέγας μεγαλωστὶ ('huge hugely') are unusually powerful and in fact recur to describe the fallen Achilles at *Odyssey* 24.39-40: ἐν στροφάλιγγι κονίης | κεῖσο μέγας μεγαλωστὶ λελασμένος ἱπποσυνάων ('in the swirl of dust you lay huge, hugely, forgetful of your horsemanship').[63]

In addition, on the larger scale, the *Catalogue of Ships* and the *Catalogue of Women* in Odyssey 11 point towards pre-existing verbatim texts.[64]

Beyond quotation, there is the question of how far repetitions in the text of the *Iliad* are meant to remind us of their earlier occurrences.[65] A fairly negative answer to this question would be expected from an oralising perspective, but the text does seem to invite a different view, such as that of Heubeck that Homer's formulaic diction has developed (through writing, he thinks) into a poetic vehicle allowing reminiscence and foreshadowing (1974:149). Yet, on any view, oral poetry cannot be completely disposable ('hear it, forget it'). Indeed Taplin has argued that the rapt attention of oral audiences promotes cross-reference and his recent book depends on its validity, whilst retaining a non-written Homer. One example, if perhaps rather a debatable one, is at 5.278: here Pandaros speaks of the πικρὸς ὀϊστός ('bitter arrow') he has fired against Diomedes, reminding us (according to Else 34-5) of the equally 'bitter arrow' which he scandalously fired against Menelaos 700 lines earlier (4.118).[66] A stronger example, however, is the incident where Hektor admits that Troy will perish at 6.447-9, thereby confirming for the audience the judgment of Agamemnon, given earlier in the same three lines

---

[63] *Cf.* Schadewaldt 168; Kullmann 1960: 38 f. There is of course a problem here with whether 'forgetful of your horsemanship' is appropriate, something which it is in the one other use at *Iliad* 16.776 of Kebriones; but equally one may query whether 'huge hugely', a rare 'formula', is justly deployed on such a minor and expendable figure and it is this that is the issue, not the tagging on of the second half-line. On the other hand, Kebriones' death is sited somewhere near the Skaian Gate (16.712) in an area of text where Apollo is very active, and may confront Patroklos-Achilles with a vision of the death and fight for the body (16.765-80) awaiting Achilles in person.

[64] References: Kakridis 84, Gaisser (n. 33) 176. Catalogue of Ships: Kullmann 1960: 157-68, 1981: 23, 38 ('offenbar der Katalog zum grössten Teil wörtlich von anderswoher übernommen wurde').

[65] On verbatim repetitions scarcely attributable to formulaic composition, see Young 311 f.

[66] πικρὸς ὀϊστός, or the accusative, are very Iliadic. The phrase occurs 10 times and the word πικρός occurs only another three times with different substantives. (In the *Odyssey* it occurs only seven times, once of an ὀϊστός; in Apollonius only four times, of which only one occurrence is associated with ὀϊστῶν ; in Quintus only once, of πόλεμον.) The first six references in the *Iliad* are at 4.19, 134, 217, 5.99, 110, 278. The first three references are to the wounding of Menelaos; the second three to the wounding of Diomedes. The two scenes are linked in our minds, but perhaps more by the rarity of arrows than by the word πικρός.

(at 4.163-5), that the fall of Troy will be the reward for Pandaros' Trojan treachery (Else 36).[67] Indeed, Agamemnon's comfort of Menelaos in the sure knowledge of punishment of Trojan treachery mirrors the basis of the whole expedition in the first place. (*cf.* Else 35-6).

CONCLUSION

Throughout this article I have taken the Neoanalytic view that where Homer's material reflects Cyclic material, except in obvious deviant inventions, notably of Eugammon, Homer knows that material and constructs his text with reference to it. But if one were not prepared to accept this direction of flow and were to suppose instead that Cyclic material, such as the story of Antilochos, was based on Homer, it is not clear that the reading of Homer which I propose would necessarily fall. Doubtless if we were in the original audience of Homer, at the longest festival in history, events surrounding Antilochos would have no significance but the obvious. But if we had been in the audience of a post-Homeric Arktinos, or even if in modern times we think about Arktinos' material (perhaps after reading Kullmann), it is inevitable that Homer's Antilochos, for example, has found a place in a larger intertext and gained in depth and resonance thereby. One achievement, then, of the Cyclic poets would be to have created a greater Homer in which the death of Patroklos and the closing development of Antilochos' character is given a larger, doom-laden forward reference. This would be a marvellous and paradoxical result, but it is not the most economical solution. The economical solution remains that Homer is responsible for the greatness of his own work precisely because he had harnessed the power of reference to other texts.

I have raised the question whether oral poetry ever, or Homer's tradition in particular (if he must be treated as an 'oral poet' within some meaning of that term), excludes the evocation of specific scenes in other 'poems'. There is clearly a model which excludes specific evocations—in Foley's terminology in such a case the poem would operate through the 'inherent' meanings of oral-traditional poetry rather than meanings 'conferred' on it by the literary artist.[68] It is, however, questionable whether this extreme oral poetry has actually existed. It would seem psychologically unlikely that *specific* associations can be prevented and that the use of literary techniques can ever be fully excluded, any more than that, on the other hand, life and art can wholly cease to be formulaic. There is no need, then, to adopt the consistent but pernicious view of Jensen (30) that excludes the search for what is new and special in Homer, a view which is, after all, as unacceptable to Lord as to Kakridis' vision of Homer 'who stands alone in his greatness'.[69] But equally this does not have to lead us to the other extreme, where

> "oral" is only an empty label and "traditional" is devoid of sense. Together they form merely a façade behind which scholarship can continue to apply the poetics of written literature.
>
> Lord 1967: 46

It would, however, be less worrying to abandon oral criticism of Homer than to adopt it exclusively. If we did adopt an all-oral Homer, we have too little left of alleged Greek oral poetry to have any feel for the effects which Homer creates and to estimate his merit. The texts would be simply inaccessible, because they depend for their inherent meaning on a tradition

---

[67] A different link between these scenes is found by Taplin 107, unaware, I think, of Else's argument.

[68] Foley 8.

[69] J.T. Kakridis, *Homer revisited* (Lund 1971) 23.

which is lost.[70] The meaning of Homer depends on what we are able to perceive.

So my conclusion is that Homer, his contemporaries and his immediate predecessors—recognised experts in something more than a trade—were knowingly producing fairly fixed products. In the rhapsodies constituting his *Iliad* Homer makes conspicuous use either of Arktinos' *Aithiopis* itself or of a predecessor with practically the same contents. The density of reference to that particular poem's *Faktenkanon* seems to guarantee that the connection is of special importance. So far from this demeaning Homer or rendering him in some way derivative, defective and ill-motivated (one cause of resistance to the neoanalytic method which looked as though it was picking holes in Homer), in fact it shows Homer's understanding of the power of textual interaction; it enriches and deepens the *Iliad*, showing something of what makes it so very special. From the *Iliad*—the framework, if I am right, that encompasses so many of his (episodic) performances—Homer looks out to the world of heroic poetry, and in particular to its sense of tragedy, and somehow calls upon us to evaluate the worth of heroic life and our own. Homer's use of such material and his wonderful control over ambience, evocation and undertone make that coherent sense of this work and of its author which a critical vocabulary reduced to identifying exceptional formulae and deviations from typical scenes never could.

KEN DOWDEN

University of Birmingham

---

[70] Foley 247 addresses this problem by deriving 'extratextual meanings' from the text itself, but it is plain—*cf.* 247 n. 6—that, even if effective, this method can only lead to a poor-quality understanding of the text. The real problem is the legitimation, and disqualification, of critical language: Foley's excellent chapter on *Iliad* 24 acquires legitimacy through conforming to his oral-'inherent' discourse, but it does not say anything which is specially surprising or categorically different, i.e. which reveals an unperceived Homer.

Journal of Hellenic Studies cxvi (1996) pp 62-87

HERODOTOS AND HIS CONTEMPORARIES*

Real data is messy.
Tom Stoppard, *Arcadia* I iv

AMONG early Greek historians, Herodotos and Thukydides, owing to their survival, inevitably dominate our attention. But of course they were not alone. We have some substantial citations and numerous shorter fragments of many contemporaries. Difficulties of interpretation and the authority of their greatest modern interpreter, Felix Jacoby, have for many years prevented a thorough re-evaluation of early historiography and the position of Herodotos within it. The present paper is a contribution to this effort. In the first section, the list of Herodotos' contemporaries is drawn up as a necessary starting-point. We shall find that Jacoby's assessment of the evidence, and in particular his late date for some historians, is to be rejected, and that his conclusions about Herodotos' position in the development of historiography, which still dominate the field, lack at least part of their foundation. In section II an alternative method, in the absence of certain chronology, is developed for identifying the salient characteristics of the individual historian; the method owes something to narratology. It is illustrated from the fragments of the authors listed in section I, together with those of other historians down to the beginning of the fourth century. Section III then focuses on Herodotos; it will emerge that the most distinctive thing about him is his constant talk about sources and how to assess them. Other historians (and, indeed, poets) knew that sources contradict each other, but Herodotos first realised that this situation exists as a theoretical problem requiring the development of new methods. His is a second-order, or meta-cognitive awareness. Section IV goes on to deal, as seems necessary, with Detlev Fehling's theory about Herodotos' sources, since if he is right Herodotos is not really serious about them. An epilogue draws attention to a fifth-century passage in the Theognidean corpus with striking parallels to a passage in Plato's *Protagoras*; the two together throw light on Herodotos' proem, and confirm the picture drawn in this paper of his historical activity.

I. WHO WERE HERODOTOS' CONTEMPORARIES?

Discussion must begin with the well-known passage of Dionysios of Halikarnassos in which he assesses the contributions of Thukydides' predecessors:[1]

Dion. Hal. *Thuc.* 5.1 (i 330.7 Usener-Radermacher, 48.17 Aujac). μέλλων δὲ ἄρχεσθαι τῆς περὶ Θουκυδίδου γραφῆς ὀλίγα βούλομαι περὶ τῶν ἄλλων συγγραφέων εἰπεῖν, τῶν τε πρεσβυτέρων καὶ τῶν κατὰ τοὺς αὐτοὺς ἀκμασάντων ἐκείνῳ χρόνους, ἐξ ὧν ἔσται καταφανὴς ἥ τε προαίρεσις τοῦ ἀνδρός, ᾗ χρησάμενος διήλλαξε τοὺς πρὸ αὐτοῦ, καὶ ἡ δύναμις. (2) ἀρχαῖοι μὲν οὖν συγγραφεῖς πολλοὶ καὶ κατὰ πολλοὺς τόπους ἐγένοντο πρὸ τοῦ Πελοποννησιακοῦ πολέμου (a. 431)· ἐν οἷς ἐστιν Εὐγαίων τε ὁ Σάμιος (*FGrH* 535 Τ 1) καὶ Δηίοχος ὁ Προκοννήσιος (*FGrH* 471 Τ 1) καὶ Εὔδημος ὁ Πάριος (*FGrH* 497 Τ 1) καὶ Δημοκλῆς ὁ Φυγελεὺς (*FHG* ii p. 20) καὶ Ἑκαταῖος ὁ Μιλήσιος (*FGrH* 1 Τ 17a), ὅ τε Ἀργεῖος Ἀκουσίλαος (*FGrH* 2 Τ 2) καὶ ὁ Λαμψακηνὸς Χάρων

* Versions of this paper were delivered at the Oxford Philological Society in February, 1995, and at the University of Rome 'La Sapienza' in May, 1995. I am most grateful to both audiences for lively discussion and suggestions, to Dr. D.C. Innes for advice and information on Demetrios, *De Elocutione* discussed below, and to the journal's referees.

[1] For treatments of the passage see L. Pearson, *Early Ionian historians* (Oxford 1939) 3 f.; W. Kendrick Pritchett, *Dionysius of Halicarnassus: on Thucydides* (University of California Press 1975); T.S. Brown in *AHR* lix (1953-54) 834 ff.; Sandra Gozzoli, 'Una teoria antica sull'origine della storiografia greca', *SCO* xix-xx (1970-71) 158-211; David L. Toye, 'Dionysius of Halicarnassus on the first Greek historians', *AJP* cxvi (1995) 279-302. For details of the textual criticism I may refer to my forthcoming edition of the early mythographers.

(*FGrH* 262 T 3a) καὶ ὁ Χαλκηδόνιος <...> ᾿Αμελησαγόρας (*FGrH* 330 T 1), ὀλίγῳ δὲ πρεσβύτεροι τῶν Πελοποννησιακῶν καὶ μέχρι τῆς Θουκυδίδου παρεκτείναντες ἡλικίας ῾Ελλάνικός τε ὁ Λέσβιος (*FGrH* 4 T 5 = 323a T 2a) καὶ Δαμάστης ὁ Σιγειεὺς (*FGrH* 5 T 2) καὶ Ξενομήδης ὁ Κεῖος (*FGrH* 442 T 1) καὶ Ξάνθος ὁ Λυδὸς (*FGrH* 765 T 4) καὶ ἄλλοι συχνοί. (3) οὗτοι προαιρέσει τε ὁμοίᾳ ἐχρήσαντο περὶ τὴν ἐκλογὴν τῶν ὑποθέσεων καὶ δυνάμεις οὐ πολύ τι διαφερούσας ἔσχον ἀλλήλων, οἳ μὲν τὰς ῾Ελληνικὰς ἀναγράφοντες ἱστορίας, οἳ δὲ τὰς βαρβαρικάς, {καὶ} αὐτάς τε ταύτας οὐ συνάπτοντες ἀλλήλαις, ἀλλὰ κατ᾿ ἔθνη καὶ κατὰ πόλεις διαιροῦντες καὶ χωρὶς ἀλλήλων ἐκφέροντες, ἕνα καὶ τὸν αὐτὸν φυλάττοντες σκοπόν, ὅσαι διεσῴζοντο παρὰ τοῖς ἐπιχωρίοις μνῆμαι {κατὰ ἔθνη τε καὶ κατὰ πόλεις} <ἢ>[2] εἴτ᾿ ἐν ἱεροῖς εἴτ᾿ ἐν βεβήλοις ἀποκείμεναι γραφαί, ταύτας εἰς τὴν κοινὴν ἁπάντων γνῶσιν ἐξενεγκεῖν, οἵας παρέλαβον, μήτε προστιθέντες αὐταῖς τι μήτε ἀφαιροῦντες· ἐν αἷς καὶ μῦθοί τινες ἐνῆσαν ἀπὸ τοῦ πολλοῦ πεπιστευμένοι χρόνου καὶ θεατρικαί τινες περιπέτειαι πολὺ τὸ ἠλίθιον ἔχειν τοῖς νῦν δοκοῦσαι· (4) λέξιν τε ὡς ἐπὶ τὸ πολὺ τὴν αὐτὴν ἅπαντες ἐπετήδευσαν, ὅσοι <γε>[3] τοὺς αὐτοὺς προείλοντο τῶν διαλέκτων χαρακτῆρας, τὴν σαφῆ καὶ κοινὴν καὶ καθαρὰν καὶ σύντομον καὶ τοῖς πράγμασι προσφυῆ καὶ μηδεμίαν σκευωρίαν ἐπιφαίνουσαν τεχνικήν· ἐπιτρέχει μέντοι τις ὥρα τοῖς ἔργοις αὐτῶν καὶ χάρις, τοῖς μὲν πλείων, τοῖς δ᾿ ἐλάττων, δι᾿ ἣν ἔτι μένουσιν αὐτῶν αἱ γραφαί. (5) ὁ δ᾿ ῾Αλικαρνασεὺς ῾Ηρόδοτος, γενόμενος ὀλίγῳ πρότερον τῶν Περσικῶν (480/79), παρεκτείνας δὲ μέχρι τῶν Πελοποννησιακῶν, τήν τε πραγματικὴν προαίρεσιν ἐπὶ τὸ μεῖζον ἐξήνεγκε καὶ λαμπρότερον... καὶ τῇ λέξει προσαπέδωκε τὰς παραλειφθείσας ὑπὸ τῶν πρὸ αὐτοῦ συγγραφέων ἀρετάς.

Before beginning my account of Thukydides I wish to say a few things both about the writers who preceded him and about his contemporaries, so that the plan of his work, in which he surpassed his predecessors, as well as his overall ability will become apparent. The old writers, then, were many and came from many places; among those living before the Peloponnesian War were **Eugaion of Samos, Deiochos of Prokonnesos, Eudemos of Paros, Demokles of Phygela, Hekataios of Miletos, the Argive Akousilaos, the Lampsakene Charon, the Chalkedonian** <...and **the Athenian**> **Amelesagoras**; born a little before the Peloponnesian War and living down to the time of Thukydides were **Hellanikos of Lesbos, Damastes of Sigeion, Xenomedes of Keos, Xanthos the Lydian** and many others. These writers had a similar plan in respect of subject matter, and did not differ greatly from one another in ability. Some wrote about Greece, others about barbarians, not joining their inquiries together into a continuous whole, but separating them by nations and cities and bringing them out individually, with one and the same object in view, that of bringing to the attention of the public traditions preserved among the local people {by nations and by cities} <or> written records preserved in sacred or profane archives, just as they received them, without adding or subtracting anything. Among these sources were to be found occasional myths, believed from time immemorial, and dramatic tales of upset fortunes, which seem quite foolish to people of our day. The style which they all employed was for the most part the same (at any rate among those who used the same dialect): clear, ordinary, unaffected, concise, suited to the subject and displaying none of the apparatus of professional skill; nonetheless a certain grace and charm attends their works, some more than others, and this has ensured their preservation. But **Herodotos of Halikarnassos,** who was born a little before the Persian Wars and lived down to the time of the Peloponnesian War, both raised the choice of subject to a more ambitious and impressive level... and added to his style those virtues which had been omitted by writers before him.

Dionysios divides the early historians into two groups: first those who lived before the Peloponnesian War, then those who lived or flourished from a date not long before the war down to the time of Thukydides. Then there is Herodotos, who Dionysios says was born just before the Persian Wars and lived to see the start of the Peloponnesian War. The lower terminus we know to be correct from Herodotos' own words (ix 73.3), and the higher one is in all likelihood correct as well. Dionysios' list is partly chronological, but also schematic, in that he is attempting to sketch, no doubt after Theophrastos, the history of early prose style. It is possible that the chronological lines have been stretched in some cases in order to accommodate

---

[2] Following Usener's deletion and Aujac's supplement. Dionysios, of course, has no independent knowledge of early archives and pre-literary chronicles; he infers their existence from the text of the historians, especially Herodotos and Thukydides.

[3] For the reading ὅσοι <γε> cf. *Thuc.* 23.4 sqq., where Dionysios carefully reminds us that each dialect has its own character.

an author's perceived place in the history of style. In one instance he has been taken in by a forgery, that of Amelesagoras. His list has some remarkable omissions, but as there seems to be a lacuna in the manuscripts, the fault may not be his.

On the other hand, where we can test his information directly, he scores not badly. We must take his word for the very early date of the first four authors he mentions, Eugaion or Euagon,[4] Deiochos,[5] Eudemos[6] and Demokles,[7] but he is right about the date of Hekataios and Akousilaos.[8] Damastes of Sigeion[9] is said to be a contemporary of Herodotos by the *Suda* (δ 41 = *FGrH* 5 T 1), which, however, also says that he was a student of Hellanikos, and indeed he can occasionally be seen to follow that writer's version of events. Damastes also named as a source for details of Persian geography Diotimos son of Strombichos, who was strategos in 433/32.[10] On the other hand, the testimony that Hellanikos' book *Barbaric Customs* was pillaged from Damastes and Herodotos tends rather to support an earlier date for the Sigeian (or a later date for Hellanikos).[11] For the precise date of Xenomedes of Keos[12] we have really no other indications than those Dionysios gives us. As for Xanthos,[13] his book on Lydian history contained some spectacular information which it is hard to believe Herodotos would have omitted had he known about it, e.g., that King Kambles ate his wife (*FGrH* 765 F 18), or that the magi have sexual relations with all their female relatives (F 31). A stronger indication than this argument from silence is that Xanthos dated an event by its Olympic year (*FGrH* 765 F 30), using a technique we do not expect to find in advance of the publication of Hippias of Elis' list; but for this very reason some scholars reject the fragment as spurious.[14] Ephoros (*FGrH* 70 F 180) explicitly says that Xanthos gave Herodotos his ἀφορμαί, either 'starting-point' or 'source material',[15] and Athenaios, who preserves the fragment, took him to mean (if he did not say so himself) that the Lydian was the earlier of the two. A *terminus a quo* is provided by a reference to Artaxerxes (*FGrH* 765 F 12), who reigned from 465-425. On balance, H. Herter's assessment—'an older contemporary of Herodotos'[16]—is probably right.

---

[4] The truest form of the name (Euagon) is given in *IPriene* 37 = *FGrH* 535 F 3. He wrote local history of Samos (no title transmitted).

[5] Transmitted titles are Περὶ Κυζίκου and Περὶ Σαμοθρᾴκης.

[6] Parian or Naxian; no titles transmitted.

[7] No titles transmitted.

[8] Hekataios wrote Γενεαλογίαι (also cited as Ἱστορίαι and once as Ἡρωολογία, *FGrH* 1 F 8) and the *Periodos*; Akousilaos wrote Γενεαλογίαι.

[9] Transmitted titles are Περὶ τῶν ἐν Ἑλλάδι γενομένων, Περὶ γονέων καὶ προγόνων τῶν εἰς Ἴλιον στρατευσαμένων, Ἐθνῶν κατάλογος καὶ πόλεων, Περὶ ποιητῶν καὶ σοφιστῶν, Περίπλους.

[10] Strabo i.3.1 p. 47 = *FGrH* 5 T 7, F 8.

[11] Porph. *fr.* 409 Smith apud Eus. *Praep. Evang.* x.3.16 p. 466b = *FGrH* 5 T 5 = Hellan. *FGrH* 4 T 17.

[12] Wrote local history (no title transmitted).

[13] Λυδιακά, Μαγικά, Περὶ Ἐμπεδοκλέους.

[14] See Pearson (n. 1) 115. The Olympic date in this fragment, which is preserved by Clement, might be someone else's calculation on the basis of some synchronism in Xanthos; on this assumption the fragment may be accepted as genuine.

[15] See R. Drews, *The Greek accounts of eastern history* (Princeton 1973) 102, who, however, thinks that Ephoros may have drawn an incorrect inference about their chronological relationship from Xanthos' subject matter which for the most part seems to treat an earlier period than Herodotos. Against this see Peter Kingsley, 'Meetings with magi: Iranian themes among the Greeks, from Xanthus of Lydia to Plato's Academy', *JRAS* v (1995) 173-209 at 174 n. 12.

[16] *RE* ix A.2 (1967) 1354.

That leaves Hellanikos[17] and Charon.[18] Jacoby argued repeatedly that Herodotos knew nothing of either writer, even though Charon is placed in Dionysios' first group. At most Jacoby would concede that some of their works, like those of some of the other early historians, might have been published before Herodotos' *logoi*, but *not* before his travels, so that he could play out his part in *Entwicklungsgeschichte* unencumbered by familiarity with anybody but the old ethnographers.[19] Jacoby's view is tied up with his still influential theory of the development of Greek historiography, which held that the ethnography and geography of Hekataios was first succeeded by the panoramic *Hellenika* of Herodotos, who indeed first set out to write ethnography, but changed into an historian as a result of his experience in Athens, and of the Persian Wars.[20] Local history, Jacoby held, originated in the desire of the individual city to 'secure in Greek history a place for herself, which Great Historiography [i.e., Herodotos] did not assign to her... The local chronicles... deliberately place the history of one city in the framework of the general history of the Greek people as designed by "scientific" historiography.'[21] So local history had to wait for Herodotos. But *some* Greek sense of an historical framework had existed for a long time. We must not forget the poets. Mimnermos had written historical verse at the end of the seventh century.[22] Xenophanes wrote the foundation of Kolophon and the colonization of Elea.[23] Herodotos' own uncle (or cousin) told the story in verse of the colonization of Ionia,[24] which is to say the starting-point for many prose histories. Epic poems in which legendary local history played a leading role are the *Korinthiaka*, the *Meropis*, the *Naupaktia*, the *Phoronis*, and the *Phokais*; many lyric poems such as Alkman's or Pindar's, though not historical in purpose, display detailed knowledge of local traditions.[25] A local history in prose before Herodotos would be in no way surprising; the argument from a theory of development is no stronger than that which placed the *Supplices* of Aischylos at the

---

[17] Φορωνίς, Δευκαλιωνεία, Ἀτλαντίς, Ἀσωπίς, Τρωϊκά, Αἰολικά / Λεσβι(α)κά, Ἀργολικά, Περὶ Ἀρκαδίας, Ἀτθίς, Βοιωτιακά, Θεσσαλικά, Αἰγυπτιακά, Εἰς Ἄμμωνος ἀνάβασις, Κυπριακά, Περὶ Λυδίας, Περσικά, Σκυθικά, Κτίσεις ἐθνῶν καὶ πόλεων, Περὶ Χίου κτίσεως, Βαρβαρικὰ νόμιμα, Ἱέρειαι τῆς Ἥρας αἱ ἐν Ἄργει, Καρνεονῖκαι οἱ καταλογάδην, Καρνεονῖκαι οἱ ἔμμετροι. Of course this list and the others I have given are attended by the usual problems, but there is no need here to discuss the various efforts of scholars to combine or otherwise modify the list of Hellanikos' works, which must remain impressive on any reconstruction.

[18] Αἰθιοπικά, Περσικά, Ἑλληνικά, Περὶ Λαμψάκου, Λιβυκά, Ὧροι Λαμψακηνῶν, Πρυτάνεις {ἢ ἄρχοντες} (deleted by editors as a gloss) τῶν Λακεδαιμονίων (but see below, p. 67), Κτίσεις πόλεων, Κρητικά, Περίπλους τῶν ἐκτὸς τῶν Ἡρακλέους στηλῶν.

[19] F. Jacoby, *Atthis* (Oxford 1949) 184; introduction to *FGrH* 323a pp. 8 f.

[20] 'Über die Entwicklung der griechischen Historiographie und den Plan einer neuen Sammlung der griechischen Historikerfragmente', *Klio* ix (1909) 80-123 = *Abhandlungen zur griechischen Geschichtsschreibung* ed. H. Bloch (Leiden 1956) 16-64; *RE* articles on Hekataios (vii.2 [1912] 2666-2769), Hellanikos (viii.1 [1912] 104-53), and Herodotos (suppl. ii [1913] 205-520), all reprinted in *Griechische Historiker* (Stuttgart 1956); *Atthis* ch. III §4 *et passim*; introduction to *FGrH* 323a. Support (with some qualifications) in K. von Fritz, *Die griechische Geschichtsschreibung* (Berlin 1967); more recently in S. Hornblower, *Greek historiography*, ed. S. Hornblower (Oxford 1994) 15 f.; compare his *Thucydides* (London 1987) 19 n. 14.

[21] *Atthis* 201.

[22] Frr. 13-13a West.

[23] *Vorsokr.* 21 A 1.

[24] Panyasis Test. 1 Davies. *Cf.* also Kallinos *fr.* 7 West. On ktisis-poetry see now C. Dougherty, 'Archaic Greek foundation poetry: questions of genre and occasion', *JHS* cxiv (1994) 35-46; to her discussion of the occasion of elegy add R.L. Fowler, *The nature of early Greek lyric* (Toronto 1987) ch. 3. Her general scepticism about the genre's separate existence does not affect the point made here.

[25] The ἀρχαιολογία Σαμίων attributed to Semonides of Amorgos (test. 1 West), though scarcely a title originating with the author, presumably treated the island's foundation. *Cf.* F. Lasserre, 'L'historiographie grecque à l'époque archaïque', *QS* iv (1976) 113-42 at 119 ff.

head of his surviving tragedies.[26]

Jacoby further argued that Herodotos shows no sign of knowing any such local histories or chronicles.[27] If we could be sure of that, it would be a stronger argument. Jacoby's main reason for his diagnosis was that Herodotos uses very few archon-dates or similar devices. But we do not know how frequent these were in the earliest chronicles, in spite of their name,[28] nor what use Herodotos might have chosen to make of them. His aims were quite different. Scholars disagree strongly about how much of Hekataios made its way into his pages, when we do in fact have a respectable number of fragments of that author; how much more hazardous must it be to make any statement about works represented by a mere handful of citations. The gaps in the record are simply too great for dogmatism.

Hellanikos, as we know from his fragments, was still active towards the end of the Peloponnesian War;[29] tradition held that he lived a long life,[30] and indeed he must have lived to mature, if not very ripe years to compose so many works. If his name is really connected with the victory of the Greeks over the Persians,[31] we may reasonably conjecture that his happy parents chose to commemorate a recent event in such a manner; but if his name is to be read Ἑλλάνῖκος, with short iota,[32] one may rather think that the tradition of his longevity is owed to someone who scanned the iota long and drew the appropriate inference. At all events, while Dionysios here places his career as a whole after Herodotos, other testimonies unequivocally place him before;[33] and even Dionysios in another place says that some work(s) of Hellanikos came first.[34] The evidence really presents no serious difficulties: Hellanikos was almost exactly contemporary with Herodotos, lived a long life, and died sometime after 406 BC.

---

[26] Jacoby repeatedly questioned Dionysios' evidence because it was ultimately based only on the style of the authors concerned; consequently he simply ignored him (e.g. 'ganz unbrauchbar' *RE* viii.1 109). But style is no very bad criterion—indeed, it is a better one than Jacoby's, if you have nothing else to go on.

[27] *Atthis* 182; *RE* suppl. ii 404.

[28] Jacoby, 'Über die Entwicklung' (n. 20) 49 ff., insists that anything called Ὧροι must have proceeded κατ' ἔτος. But we do not know if these titles were assigned by their authors (note the variance in the title of Aristophanes' work, below n. 54, and see on Charon, below n. 44), and anything that proceeded in chronological order using expressions such as 'during King X's reign', 'in the time of his son', 'a few years later', 'twenty years after the destruction of Y' (expressions we often see in the fragments of early historiography and in Herodotos) might have earned such a title from a later scholar looking for the right pigeon-hole in which to place the work.

[29] *FGrH* 4 FF 171-172 = 323a FF 25-26 (references to events of 407/6 BC).

[30] [Lucianus] *Macr.* 22 = *FGrH* 4 T 8, 323a T 6 (lived to 85 years of age).

[31] *Vit. Eurip.* (i 2.5 Schwartz) = *FGrH* 4 T 6, 323a T 4 (he and Euripides both born on the day of Salamis). Wilamowitz, *Kleine Schriften* iv 673 n. 1 explains the name on the analogy of Πυθιόνικος and Ὀλυμπιόνικος as 'victor over the Greeks' in athletic contests (he might have cited also Ἀνδρόνικος). *Cf.* L. Pearson, *The local historians of Attica* (Philadelphia 1942) 5 f.

[32] The name is then the ethnic with changed accent. For other occurrences of the name see P.M. Fraser and E. Matthews, *A lexicon of Greek personal names* i (Oxford 1987) s.v. (One example from the 3rd century AD is written -νεικος, for what it is worth; the name of the historian himself may also occur, so spelled, twice in *POxy* liii 3711.)

[33] Aul. Gell. 15.23 = *FGrH* 4 T 3, 323a T 5; *Suda* δ 41 = Damastes *FGrH* 5 T 1, Hellan. 4 T 9 (quoted above p. 64). Aulus' source is Pamphila, *FHG* iii 521 *fr.* 7, who places his birth in 496/5 (reckoning inclusively; she says he was 65 in 432/1); this would place his ἀκμή in 457/6, close to the year of Euripides' first production (456/5), which F. Rühl, *RhM* lxi (1906) 475, argued was the foundation of her (Apollodoros') date; Hellanikos' *Suda* article (= *FGrH* 4 T 1, 323a T 1) synchronises the two writers. See further Alden A. Mosshammer, 'The Apollodoran *Akmai* of Hellanicus and Herodotos', *GRBS* xiv (1973) 5-13. At Eus. (Hieron.) *Chron.* p. 107ᵉ Helm = *FGrH* 4 T 4a, Hellanikos is said to have been '*clarus*' in Ol. 70.1 (a. 500/499; the Armenian version gives Ol. 69.3, the *Chronicon Paschale* Ol. 67.1); on the assumption that this date represents a misreading of γέγονε as a *floruit* rather than a birthdate, we have another testimony to the standard ancient view, which should not be tossed aside without reason: whether born in 495 or 480, he was born early in the century like Herodotos.

[34] *Pomp.* 3.6 = *FGrH* 4 T 12, 323a T 2b, 687a T 1, referring to work(s) which treated the same subject as Herodotos; there are several candidates (Αἰγυπτιακά, Εἰς Ἄμμωνος ἀνάβασις, Περὶ Λυδίας, Περσικά, Σκυθικά, Βαρβαρικὰ νόμιμα). The *Suda* entry synchronises him with Herodotos.

Within that life we know the approximate dates of only a few of his works.

For Charon, the one secure fact is a reference to the beginning of the reign of Artaxerxes: Charon said that Themistokles in exile went not to Xerxes' court but to his son's.[35] Artaxerxes acceded in 465/4 and died in 425/4. This accords well enough with the date given by Dionysios, and with the admittedly confused indications in the *Suda*[36] (none of which, however, point to a later date, rather the opposite). Jacoby's arguments for dating Charon to after the end of the fifth century are weak.[37] The reference to an event near the beginning of Artaxerxes' reign he managed to change into a reference to the end: 'Der Ansatz [by chronographers] im ersten Jahr eines Königs bedeutet oft, dass man den Autor überhaupt nach seiner Regierungszeit bestimmt; und das Jahr 425/4 wäre an sich ein passender Schluss auch für ein Werk über persische Geschichte.'[38] Another argument has little more to recommend it. Thukydides i.97.2 says that apart from Hellanikos no one before him has treated the Pentakontaetia. Therefore Charon had not yet written his *Hellenika*.[39] We do not know, however, what the scope of this book was.[40] Just as importantly, one cannot know what books Thukydides might disdain to mention in so polemical a passage. A final argument is that Charon's book Πρυτάνεις Λακεδαιμονίων, described by the *Suda* as χρονικά, was presumably inspired by Hellanikos' *Priestesses of Hera in Argos* (*FGrH* 4 FF 74-84), which we infer from Thukydides iv 133 was published sometime after 423, or at any rate (since the inference is not quite secure) sometime after 429, on the basis of Thukydides ii 2.1.[41] Furthermore, Jacoby argues, interest in the officials of Sparta is much more likely after 404 with the rise of Sparta to hegemony.[42] This third argument is no stronger than the first two. Sophists were interested in systems of government long before 404; Kritias (*ob.* 404/3) in fact wrote a book entitled Πολιτεία Λακεδαιμονίων, of which several fragments are preserved.[43] Anyhow the title of Charon's book is suspicious. Sparta never had πρυτάνεις. Anton Westermann in 1838 emended to Πρυτάνεις τῶν Λαμψακηνῶν.[44] This still leaves the argument about possible influence from Hellanikos untouched, but even if this book was produced late in Charon's career (late 420s?), there were many others that preceded it. Like Dionysios, both in *Thuc.* and *Pomp.* (3.6, cited above), Plutarch is perfectly clear that Charon was the older writer.[45]

---

[35] Plut. *Them.* 27.1 = *FGrH* 262 F 11.

[36] *Suda* χ 136 = *FGrH* 262 T 1.

[37] F. Jacoby, 'Charon von Lampsakos', *SIFC* xv (1938) 207-42 = *Abhandlungen* (n. 20) 178-206. H.D. Westlake, 'Thucydides on Pausanias and Themistocles—a written source?', *CQ* xxvii (1977) 95-110 at 108 n. 74, finds Jacoby's arguments weak; detailed criticism in Gozzoli (n. 1) 169 n. 33; Drews (n. 15) 24 ff.; Mauro Maggi, 'Autori greci di *Persika*. II: Carone di Lampsaco', *ASNP* vii (1977) 1-26 at 5 n. 17; Silvio Accame, 'La leggenda di Ciro in Erodoto', *MGR* viii (1982) 1-43 at 26 ff.

[38] P. 179.

[39] P. 182.

[40] Drews (n. 15) 25. One might think a discussion of Themistokles' exile points to a treatment of the Pentekontaetia; but he could have looked briefly forward to the admiral's demise after a treatment of Salamis. (Jacoby p. 178 calls this idea 'very improbable'; the reasons given on pp. 202 ff. in support of this judgment are of a very general kind. Obviously, it is perfectly possible.)

[41] See Jacoby, intro to *FGrH* 323a p. 4; Gomme on Thuk. iv 133.2-3.

[42] P. 187. He might have added, given his penchant for arguments from silence, that Thukydides might have been expected to use the data of such a book at least once or twice, just as he used Hellanikos' book of priestesses.

[43] *Vorsokr.* 88 B 32-7.

[44] In his re-edition of Vossius' *De historicis graecis*, p. 21 n. 63. If the emendation is correct (it is certainly plausible, though Jacoby p. 187 thought it 'most improbable'), the further question arises whether this is not simply an alternative title for the Ὧροι Λαμψακηνῶν listed immediately before in the *Suda*. It is possibly relevant that a Spartan king bore the name Prytanis (Hdt. viii 131).

[45] *De Hdt. mal.* 20 p. 859b = *FGrH* 262 F 9. Similarly Tert. *De Anim.* 46 = *FGrH* 262 F 14.

In brief, Herodotos could have known the works of many of the writers mentioned by Dionysios, as well as others not mentioned by him. These include Skylax of Karyanda[46] and the other early periegetes Euthymenes of Massilia and Hanno of Carthage,[47] Dionysios of Miletos,[48] Pherekydes of Athens,[49] Antiochos of Syracuse,[50] Ion of Chios,[51] and Simonides of Keos the Genealogist.[52] These are all authors for whom a sufficiently early date is attested. In addition we must mention the names of others whom various indications assign to a date at least as early as the first half of the fourth century, and who could for all we know be earlier: Aethlios of Samos,[53] Aristophanes of Boiotia,[54] Armenidas,[55] Kreophylos of Ephesos,[56] Menekrates of Xanthos,[57] and Skythinos of Teos.[58]

Jacoby's theory of early Greek historiography, though a work of undeniable genius, thinks too much in terms of development, a self-evident concept to scholars of the day. A theory in which all the characteristics of the first stage of historiography are found in one author, Hekataios, and all the characteristics of the logical second stage in another, Herodotos, all of the logical third stage in another, Hellanikos, and all of the fourth stage, in another, Thukydides, all of whom fit together like ashlar blocks, squeezing out anyone caught between, is inherently unlikely. Jacoby based the arrangement of his edition on his theory; consequently it is very easy to forget just how many historians were active during Herodotos' lifetime, since everybody after volume I (indeed, everybody after number 3 in volume I) is conceptually post-Herodotos in Jacoby's scheme. We have compiled a lengthy list of Herodotos' contemporaries. If a god could restore all the works of these people to us, with dates helpfully attached, we would surely receive many shocks.

Was there then a Herodotos before Herodotos? In theory one must admit the possibility. Practically speaking, one would expect to have *some* inkling of the fact, if (say) Charon's *Hellenika* was a book of similar scope. We can at least say this much, that of all the early titles known to us, Charon's is the *only* one which suggests a work anything like Herodotos'; and that is encouraging.[59] Herodotos, on any reconstruction, is likely to remain the cardinal turning-

---

[46] *FGrH* 709; pseudo-Skylax in *GGM* i 154 ff. Transmitted titles are Περίπλους τῶν ἐκτὸς [ἐντὸς coni. quidam] τῶν Ἡρακλέος στηλῶν, τὰ κατὰ Ἡρακλείδην τὸν Μυλασσῶν βασιλέα, Γῆς περίοδος. Herodotos, of course, names Skylax himself at iv 44.

[47] *FHG* iv 408; *GGM* i 1 ff.

[48] *FGrH* 687. Only transmitted title, Περσικά. Synchronised by the *Suda* s.v. Ἑκαταῖος (= *FGrH* 1 T 1) with Dareios; the same entry says Herodotos borrowed from him.

[49] Wrote genealogical Ἱστορίαι (once cited as Θεογονία, *FGrH* 3 F 54, no doubt by confusion with the Syrian). He is probably to be dated to about 470: see G. Huxley, 'The date of Pherekydes of Athens', *GRBS* xiv (1973) 137-43; R. Thomas, *Oral tradition and written record in classical Athens* (Cambridge 1989) 161 ff.

[50] *FGrH* 555; Περὶ Ἰταλίης, Σικελικά. Died sometime after 424/3 (below, n. 109).

[51] *FGrH* 392, *Vorsokr.* 36, *TrGF* 19, *IEG* ii 79; wrote Χίου κτίσις plus poetic, philosophical, and other works. First tragedy produced Ol. 82 (452/48); dead by 421 (Ar. *Pax* 827 ff.).

[52] *FGrH* 8; son of the poet's daughter κατά τινας. Wrote Γενεαλογία, Εὑρήματα, perhaps also Σύμμικτα.

[53] *FGrH* 536; Ὧροι Σαμίων.

[54] *FGrH* 379; Θηβαῖοι Ὧροι (also cited as Θηραϊκά and Βοιωτικά).

[55] *FGrH* 378; Θηβαϊκά.

[56] *FGrH* 417; Ἐφεσίων Ὧροι.

[57] *FGrH* 769; Λυκιακά.

[58] *FGrH* 13, *IEG* ii 97; Ἱστορίη.

[59] Damastes' Περὶ τῶν ἐν Ἑλλάδι γενομένων (a phrase, as Jacoby ad loc. remarks, presumably taken from the proem) was, it seems, a *Hellenika*, but was probably later than Herodotos. The fragments of Charon contain tantalizing references to Persian affairs; for discussion of possible connections with Herodotos see Accame (n. 37) and L. Piccirilli, 'Carone di Lampsaco e Erodoto', *ASNP* v (1975) 1239-54.

point in the history of historiography. But it has long been recognized that Herodotos drew on various kinds of material for his history, and if (as I think we have now established as a strong possibility) Herodotos knew works of local history and others mentioned here, no one can really know how many of these writers might have shaped his thinking, or schooled him in the technique of *historie*.

Of course Greek historiography developed in some sense, but one must be careful to describe developments in appropriate terms. Rather than thinking of a step-by-step development, we would be wise to think in terms of a long and mutually beneficial exchange of work and ideas between Herodotos and his many contemporaries. Therefore if we wish to prove Herodotos' uniqueness, it is best to do so by demonstrating that those qualities which seem most characteristic of him are intimately bound up with his *own* perception of his task as an historian. If that is the case, it becomes less likely that he was anticipated by a predecessor in any essential point, and would not matter anyway if he was.

II. THE HISTORIAN'S VOICE

Scholars have looked again and again at Herodotos' proem, where indeed insight into his self-perception is most likely to be found. Close examination of Herodotos' proem shall here be postponed to the end. In the meantime it will be useful to look at various aspects of what may be termed the 'historian's voice'. Any historiographical text involves the historian and the object of study. In reading the text, we are frequently aware of the intercession of the investigator between ourselves and the data. Most obviously, this obtrusion may take the form of first-person statements or self-reference of some kind. The proem is a place where such statements are apt to occur. A surprisingly large number (ten) of beginnings of fifth-century prose works by named authors is known.[60] The first-person deictic pronoun (in Hekataios, ὧδε μυθέεται and τάδε γράφω; in Herodotos, ἀπόδεξις ἥδε; in Antiochos, ᾿Αντίοχος... τάδε συνέγραψε, and so on) is a well-known stylistic habit of these passages, as if to say, here I am, this is my work. The pronoun is often accompanied by assertions of the importance of the subject or the accuracy of the information.[61] The historian's voice is strong and egotistical already in the first Greek historian. It need not have been so; but in a time when even the poets had arrogated to themselves the inspiration of the Muses, such pride in individual achievement is perhaps not surprising. Thukydides, as usual, differs from the others in style (no deictic pronoun), though not in the forcefulness with which he announces his subject, nor the implied

[60] The qualification 'by named authors' excludes the works in the Hippocratic corpus. Known beginnings are: Hekataios *FGrH* 1 F 1; Herakleitos *fr.* 1 Marcovich; Ion of Chios Τριαγμός *fr.* 20 von Blumenthal; Antiochos of Syracuse Περὶ ᾿Ιταλίας *FGrH* 555 F 2; Alkmaion of Kroton *Vorsokr.* 24 B 1; Philolaos of Kroton 44 B 1; Diogenes of Apollonia 64 B 1; Kritias Πολιτεία Λακεδαιμονίων 88 B 32; Herodotos and Thukydides. Depending on the reading, Anaxagoras 59 B 1 may be included as an eleventh example: that is, whether '...λέγων ἀπ' ἀρχῆς· "ὁμοῦ πάντα ἦν..."' or '...λέγων· "ἀπ' ἀρχῆς ὁμοῦ πάντα ἦν..."' is correct.

[61] This chest-thumping habit of early writers is commented on by Aristeides (xxviii 68) in a minor testimonium that escaped Jacoby's notice: ἔστι δὲ ταῦτα οὐδὲν ἕτερον ἀλλ᾿ ἢ ἐνδείκνυται τῷ ᾿Ηροδότῳ καὶ τοῖς ᾿Ελλανίκοις καὶ τοῖς ᾿Εκαταίοις καὶ πᾶσι τούτοις ὅτι ἐγὼ ὑμῶν προέχω τῇ κρίσει πρῶτος· τὰ γοῦν κράτιστα ἐξειλεχὼς, ταῦτα καὶ περὶ τούτων γράφω, τὰ δὲ πλείω παιδιά. *Cf.* Joseph. *Ap.* i 16 = Eus. *Praep. Evang.* x 7.12 p. 478c = Akous. *FGrH* 2 T 6, Hell. 4 T 18 on the frequent disagreement between Hellanikos and Akousilaos; Thuk. i 97.2 = *FGrH* 4 T 16, 323a T 16 (the celebrated attack on Hellanikos); Aristophanes *FGrH* 379 F 5 (attacking Herodotos). See also Hippias *FGrH* 6 F 4, a verbatim quotation of a passage that might well be from a proem, in which Hippias brags about his καινὸς καὶ πολυειδὴς λόγος. L. Koenen, 'Der erste Satz bei Heraklit und Herodot', *ZPE* xcvii (1993) 95-6, argues that the deictic pronoun refers to the book itself; ultimately (once the book was deposited somewhere) it must have that effect, but the original reference is to the performance, and thus effectively to the author.

pride in his accomplishment.[62]

First-person statements are only the most obvious form in which the historian's voice might manifest itself. At the other end of the scale are the decisions implied by the basic shape of the narrative, and turns of phrase that direct the reader's attention to different objects as the narrative unfolds itself; some of these devices, as narratologists have demonstrated, can be very inconspicuous indeed. In Greek the tiniest of particles can betray the involvement of the author. Here is a small example from Herodoros of Herakleia (*fl.* ca. 400), which, though slight, is pleasing enough in that it has to be rescued by philology (*FGrH* 31 F 63 *bis*):

δράκοντες δέ που ἦσαν ἐν τῷ Καυκάσῳ <θαυμαστοὶ τὸ> μέγεθος, καὶ μέγεθος καὶ πλῆθος

Demetr. *Eloc.* 66. καὶ ἀναδίπλωσις δ' ἔπους εἰργάσατο μέγεθος ὡς ʽΗρόδωρος (Orth: –δοτος cod.)· ʽδράκοντες δέ που' φησίν ʽἦσαν–πλῆθος'. δὶς ῥηθὲν τὸ μέγεθος ὄγκον τινὰ τῇ ἑρμηνείᾳ παρέσχεν.

1 add. Kroll apud Radermacher

Radermacher and Roberts and no doubt earlier editors gave the little word που to Herodoros, but Orth,[63] who restored the name of Herodoros and identified the Argonautic context of the fragment, strangely gave the particle to Demetrios; he was followed by Jacoby. This creates a very difficult word order, in that a break exists after δέ, so that we have πού φησιν, instead of φησίν που; the enclitic has nothing to lean on. If we give the particle to Herodoros we get an attractive result. που does not here mean 'somewhere', as Orth thought (which then seemed to him difficult with ἐν τῷ Καυκάσῳ), but 'I suppose';[64] I conjecture that Herodoros is rationalizing the story of the serpent which guarded the Golden Fleece. He frequently rationalized in this manner. The tone of 'I suppose there were amazingly big snakes in the Kaukasos' is casual and self-assured, as if such rationalizations were a routine and well accepted technique of scientific study. There is something conspiratorial in the way the reader is assumed to understand the method and invited to share in the writer's sophistication. A century earlier Hekataios had to argue hard for his new method.

Many particles imply judgment, assessment, evaluation of the relative priority of different facts, and many other operations which involve the intercession of the historian. Every γάρ might be thought to imply such intercession. A character's motive for some action is usually only surmised by the historian; this is almost certainly the case when alternative motivations are given, for instance at i 86.2 where Herodotos offers three possible reasons why Kyros put Kroisos on the pyre.

Between the two extremes of explicit and inferred self-assertion there are many other ways in which the historian's voice might be heard. Here is a list of such ways, compiled by reading through Herodotos and looking out as diligently as possible for any sign of the historian at work; no doubt ingenuity might discover many more:

1. Explicit or implicit first-person statements, e.g.:
general statements of purpose (e.g. in proem); discussion of methods; statements about what comes next, went before, or will be omitted in the narrative; value judgments or editorial comments about events, characters, sources' credibility; avowals of ignorance; ridicule of or disagreement with other practitioners; use of particles.

---

[62] For Thukydides' proem see the study of A.M. Bowie, 'The beginnings of Thucydides', in *Tria lustra. Essays and notes presented to John Pinsent* (Liverpool Classical Monthly, Liverpool 1993) 141-7.

[63] *B.phil.Woch.* xlv [1925] 778 ff.

[64] A referee helpfully notes Hdt. i 114.2 and iii 72.3 as parallels for this position and meaning of δέ που (κου); at i 181.4, by contrast, κου is spatial, at iii 120.1, temporal.

2. Using scientific tools, e.g.:
rationalization; chronography; etymology; testing a report or theory by comparing it to similar phenomena or by inquiry with those likely to know; appeal to τὸ εἰκός; providing a σημεῖον, τεκμήριον, or μαρτύρια.

3. Referring to sources:
explicitly named; implied by λέγεται; giving alternative sources and weighing their merits; saying no source is available.

4. Giving unusual information that implies special knowledge or research, e.g.:
oddities of local customs, beliefs, nomenclature, climate, flora, fauna, etc.; catalogues of places, people, objects; genealogies; statistics; dates; former names of places; foreign language equivalents; 'the first / the only / the most X (where 'X' is an adjective) τῶν ἡμεῖς ἴδμεν'; 'ἔτι ἐς ἐμέ'.

These are all, it is hoped, self-explanatory, except perhaps the last two in group 4. The first of these, τῶν ἡμεῖς ἴδμεν, which is always in Herodotos (and Thukydides, for that matter) accompanied by a superlative or an equivalent such as πρῶτος, implies that the historian has eliminated all contenders but one for a title such as 'first to harm the Greeks' or 'most productive land of any known to us'. The second phrase, ἔτι ἐς ἐμέ (or an equivalent), is often used by Herodotos to refer to some monument or practice that still exists in his day; it shows the historian researching and establishing the links that exist between past and present. All the other devices in the list similarly betray the working hand of the researcher.

By carefully describing the frequency and use of these devices in a given historian—or 'markers' of the historian's voice, as I shall call them—one may in theory obtain a kind of voiceprint, which must be unique in every case. Of course the voice of the fragmentary historian can never be clearly heard. Yet some of the main contours can be made out, and with due regard to the gaps in our evidence and the danger of arguments from silence, one can also suggest what is unique about Herodotos, or at any rate highly characteristic. Close study of all these particulars can hardly be attempted here; but an exploratory effort to hear the louder echoes may at least determine the main contours of the graph and suggest possibilities for further work.[65]

Rationalization of legend is one item on the list that figures in every discussion of early historiography. As everyone knows, it is a method especially associated with Hekataios (perhaps his invention); his proem, 'I write these stories, as they seem true to me; for the tales of the Greeks, as they seem to me, are many and ridiculous', is commonly and plausibly taken to refer to the supernatural element of traditional tales which Hekataios proposes to eliminate, or at any rate reduce, by his rationalizations. He made Kerberos into a big snake, and Geryones into an ordinary human king.[66] These innovations, and what part they might have played in the march from μῦθος to λόγος, have long exercised scholars. What I should particularly like to draw attention to here is the quaver in the voice: at the same time as Hekataios seeks to reduce Kerberos to realistic proportions, he is able to accept the story that Orestheus' bitch gave birth to a stump, and much else besides.[67] It is one thing to develop a revolutionary new method;

[65] In looking for interesting examples I have extended the list of authors to include slightly later ones, but no later than the early fourth century: Agias/Derkylos (*FGrH* 305); Anaximander of Miletos the younger (*FGrH* 9); Andron of Halikarnassos (*FGrH* 10); pseudo-Epimenides (*FGrH* 457); pseudo-Eumelos (*FGrH* 451); Herodoros of Herakleia (*FGrH* 31); Metrodoros of Chios (*FGrH* 43); Polos of Akragas (*FGrH* 7); Skamon of Mytilene (son of Hellanikos; *FGrH* 476); Hippias of Elis (*FGrH* 6); Stesimbrotos of Thasos (*FGrH* 107); Kratippos of Athens (*FGrH* 64); Akesandros (*FGrH* 469); Thibron (*FGrH* 581); Kritias (*Vorsokr.* 88 B 32-7). I cast an occasional glance sideways at Thukydides; at Xenophon not at all.

[66] *FGrH* 1 FF 27, 26

[67] *FGrH* 1 F 15.

it is another to realize all its possibilities and to think instinctively of applying it at every opportunity. In a similar way Hellanikos rejects the story of Niobe's petrifaction, saying instead that there is a spring on Mt. Sipylos whose water turns the bellies of those who drink from it to stone—a version only superficially more realistic than the myth and obviously invented.[68] Geoffrey Lloyd has said much about a similar failure to universalize among early scientists, who, indeed, could hardly be expected to discover the truth about, say, epilepsy with the means at their disposal; while espousing admirably rational principles and rejecting the nonsense of their opponents, they often substitute equally arbitrary theories of their own.[69] The point will be relevant later in our discussion of Herodotos' methods. For the moment we may note, in respect of rationalization, that the second book and much of the fourth are wholly imbued with its spirit. An example among many is his argument that the 'speaking dove' of Dodona was really only a foreign woman whose barbaric utterances sounded like the chirping of birds, since birds cannot speak with human tongue.[70] Herodoros presents a peculiar mixture of rationalism, allegory, and fantastic zoology.[71] Among major figures, only Pherekydes affords no example of rationalization; nor is there any other trace in this author of the Greek enlightenment. Akousilaos has perhaps two examples; neither is particularly striking.[72]

Etymology as a scientific method became especially favoured in the late fifth century, but of course popular etymology is as old as Homer.[73] Hekataios thinks that Mykenai got its name from μύκης, the cap of Perseus' scabbard.[74] Pherekydes tells a charming story of how Teos got its name from the conjunction τέως; '*while* you were looking for a spot to build your city,' said Athamas' daughter as she built little castles out of stones, 'I have found one.'[75] Ion and Metrodoros of Chios derived Chios' name from χιών.[76] Herodotos certainly makes play with so-called 'speaking names', for instance Atys and Adrastos in the story of Kroisos, but the only example of the scientific use of etymology seems to be found at ii 52, where he derives θεοί from τίθημι, and (a novelty) a Skythian etymology of 'Arimaspians' at iv 27.[77] If the potential of etymology has not yet been fully realized in these earlier authors, it is again and again the weapon of choice for Hellanikos. He is capable of some astonishing claims in this respect—for

---

[68] *FGrH* 4 F 191; further examples at *frr.* 28, 72, 104b, 148, 168a.

[69] G.E.R. Lloyd, *Magic, reason and experience. Studies in the origin and development of Greek science* (Cambridge 1979); *id., The revolutions of wisdom. Studies in the claims and practice of ancient Greek science* (Berkeley 1987).

[70] On rationalization in Herodotos see A. Lesky, 'Aithiopika', *Hermes* lxxxvii (1959) 27-38 = *Gesammelte Schriften* (Bern/Munich 1966) 410-21; A.B. Lloyd, *Herodotus Book II* (Leiden 1975) i 135 ff., 162 ff.; Virginia Hunter, *Past and process in Herodotus and Thucydides* (Princeton 1982) 107 ff.

[71] *FGrH* 31 FF 4, 13, 14, 19, 21, 22, 28, 30, 57, 58, 63 *bis*. On the other hand Kerberos growls still at *fr.* 31.

[72] *FGrH* 2 F 29: the Cretan bull captured by Herakles was the one that bore Europa—which was not, therefore, Zeus metamorphosed; 2 F 37: the fleece was not golden, but dyed purple from the sea. See also Agias/Derkyllos 305 F 6; Xanthos 765 F 20.

[73] On etymology see E. Risch, 'Namensdeutungen und Worterklärungen bei den ältesten griechischen Dichtern', in *Eumusia, Festschrift Ernst Howald* (Erlenbach/Zurich 1947) 72-91 = *Kleine Schriften* (Berlin/New York 1981) 294-313; M. Salvadore, *Il nome, la persona. Saggio sull' etimologia antica* (Genova 1987); and other references listed by L.E. Woodbury, *Phoenix* xxxiv (1980) 114 n. 12 = *Collected writings* (Atlanta 1991) 341 n. 12.

[74] *FGrH* 1 F 22; further in Hekataios note *fr.* 15 ('Oineus' from οἶναι, what the ancients called ἄμπελοι).

[75] *FGrH* 3 F 102.

[76] *FGrH* 392 F 1; 43 F 3 *bis*.

[77] Something like an etymology at iv 189: the Greeks, it is argued, got their custom of dressing Palladia in αἰγίδες (something like a goatskin) from the Libyans, who use αἰγέαι (real goatskins) for the same purpose. See Henry R. Immerwahr, *Form and thought in Herodotus* (Cleveland 1966) index s.v. 'etymologies'. If pressed to state how 'popular' and 'scientific' etymology are to be distinguished, one might not be successful in stating universally valid criteria, but the latter usually seems more self-conscious and displays a pretence of being based on some theoretical understanding of the phenomenon; in particular, it may be used to construct or confirm an historical hypothesis.

instance, that the Idaian Daktyloi got their name because they touched Rhea's fingers, or that Hermes Philetes was so named because he was conceived in love.[78] These are as arbitrary as any in Plato's *Kratylos*, and should always be presumed to be his own invention unless proof to the contrary can be supplied. Consequently his explanation of the Apatouria—that it was originally named Apatenouria, because it commemorated a 'trick' of Melanthos in his fight with Xanthios—is most unlikely to represent genuine Athenian tradition about the origin and purpose of the festival.[79]

The typical Herodotean locution ἔτι ἐς ἐμέ does not occur in any surviving verbatim quotation of the people on our list, but it is implied in the second fragment of Charon, who, we are told, claimed to have seen, still extant in Sparta, the cup (designated καρχήσιον) that Zeus gave to Alkmene when disguised as Amphitryon. The καρχήσιον was also mentioned by Pherekydes and Herodoros, and under the name σκύπφος by Anaximander.[80] It was plainly a fixture in the myth; the moment when Zeus handed it over was depicted also on the Kypselos chest,[81] and one may suspect that it did in fact exist as a cult object. A kind of equivalent of ἔτι ἐς ἐμέ which is very common is to identify a character in myth as the eponym of an existing city; this occurs dozens of times in Hekataios, who set the pattern for everybody else.[82] Also a writer might identify by-the-bye a still existing landmark near which the story is supposed to have taken place, for instance the Seven Pyres at Thebes in a fragment of Armenidas,[83] the wild olive tree in the marketplace at Herakleia in a fragment of Herodoros,[84] or the Hypelaios fountain, the sacred Harbour, a temple and two sanctuaries at Ephesos in a fragment of Kreophylos.[85] Very frequent too is the habit of identifying former names of cities or countries, with an appended relative clause 'which is now called so-and-so'.[86]

To turn from ἔτι ἐς ἐμέ to τῶν ἡμεῖς ἴδμεν: again, although the phrase does not occur in the verbatim quotations of any of the people on our list, the πρῶτος εὑρετής was a favourite theme, which would easily occasion the use of the phrase πρῶτος τῶν ἡμεῖς ἴδμεν.[87] Hekataios, Dionysios of Miletos, Anaximander, Herodotos, and Andron of Halikarnassos all

---

[78] *FGrH* 4 FF 89, 19b; *cf.* 33 (Maloeis), 38 (Areopagos), 71 (Sinties), 108 (Agammeia), 111 (Italy), 123 (Pelias), 130 (Aphetai), 188 (Helots). Instances in other writers: Andron 10 FF 4 (Selloi), 8 (Parnassos); Aristophanes of Boiotia *apud* Phot. p. 237 Porson = *Suda* λ 867 s.v. λύσιοι τελεταί (Arist. of Byzantium *fr. dub.* 421 Slater; not in *FGrH* 379; the rites were so named διὰ τὸ λυτρώσασθαι Θηβαίους παρὰ Ναξίων ἄμπελον); Charon 262 F 12 (Hamadryads); Herodoros 31 F 45 (Miletos); Hippias 6 F 6 (τύραννος); Menekrates 769 F 2 (Lykia); Stesimbrotos 107 FF 12 (Daktyloi), 13 (Dionysos); Xanthos 765 F 15 (Mysoi); Xenomedes 442 F 4 (Telchines). The concentration of this activity in the later part of the fifth century is obvious.

[79] *FGrH* 4 F 125 = 323a F 23. Unfortunately this assumption is crucial to P. Vidal-Naquet's enormously influential theory of the Black Hunter: 'The black hunter and the origin of Athenian ephebe', *PCPS* xiv (1968) 49-64; reprinted with corrections most recently in *id., The black hunter. Forms of thought and forms of society in the Greek world* (Baltimore 1986) 106-28. See also 'The black hunter revisited', *PCPS* xxxii (1986) 126-44.

[80] *FGrH* 3 F 13; 31 F 16; 9 F 1. The words ἔτι καὶ νῦν in a paraphrased fragment of Xanthos (*FGrH* 765 F 29) may well come from him.

[81] Paus. v 18.3.

[82] The use of eponyms is so common and universal that I have not bothered to illustrate it.

[83] *FGrH* 378 F 6 (a verbatim quotation).

[84] *FGrH* 31 F 51; cf. *fr.* 31.

[85] *FGrH* 417 F 1.

[86] Further instances of the phenomena discussed in this paragraph: Hek. *FGrH* 1 FF 10, 84, 119, 127-9, 234, 239, 275, 308-9, 372; Pher. 3 FF 54, 64a, 79a, 84, 125, 145, 155; Hell. 4 FF 4, 6, 23, 25, 26a, 51, 59-60, 77, 79a, 109, 115, 117, 150, 163, 165, 197 *bis*; Aethlios 536 F 3; Agias/Derkyllos 305 FF 4, 7, 8, 8 *bis*; Andron 10 FF 6, 16a; Antiochos 555 FF 3, 11, 12; Aristophanes 379 FF 2, 4, 9; Armenidas 378 FF 3, 5; Charon 262 FF 7, 8, 12; Deilochos 471 FF 3, 5, 7a, 9; Epimenides 457 F 11; Eumelos 451 F 4; Herodoros 31 FF 34a, 48; Menekrates 769 F 2; Xanthos 765 F 17; Xenomedes 442 F 1.63.

[87] As for instance Hdt. i 94.1: '[The Lydians] are the first people we know of to mint coins of gold and silver.' On the theme generally see A. Kleingünther, Πρῶτος εὑρετής, *Philol.* suppl. xxvi.1 (1933). In addition to the examples listed in the text, note Hellanikos *FGrH* 4 FF 71b, 86, 175, 189; Damastes 5 F 6; Xanthos 765 F 4; Hippias 6 F 8; Andron 10 F 13.

discussed the inventor of the Greek alphabet.[88] Andron discussed the origin of cremation.[89] Hellanikos knew who invented letter-writing, not to mention trousers, eunuchs, and tiaras,[90] and his son Skamon wrote a whole book on inventions, as did Simonides the Genealogist. In a similar vein Charon tells us that Phobos son of Kodros of Phokaia was the first to hurl himself from the White Rocks, and also that white doves first appeared in Greece after Mardonios' disaster at Mount Athos.[91]

We have so far discussed devices that are more or less universally employed by the early historians, with exceptions as noted. The fragmentary nature of our sources means that we cannot always be sure if lack of attestation of this or that device is significant. Thus the word μαρτύριον does not occur in any author but Herodotos and Thukydides; the word τεκμήριον only once outside these authors, in a fragment of Hippias;[92] and σημεῖον only once, in a fragment of Herodoros.[93] Some of our voice-markers (for instance, in group one, discussing how a narrative will be organized) are apt to be found only in lengthy texts; others are apt to be found only in certain kinds of texts: foreign language equivalents are a feature of ethnography, so it is not surprising that they are absent from Akousilaos and Pherekydes.[94] Oddities of local customs, climate, etc., are also at home in ethnography, as are statistics about distances or catalogues of peoples, but similar material can crop up in local histories, and even occasionally in genealogy.[95]

Chronography is a more difficult question.[96] Eduard Meyer, in a famous article,[97] inferred from the way Herodotos uses chronography that it was not original with him; indeed, with marvellous nineteenth-century confidence in the powers of analysis, he inferred that Herodotos' chronography was *two* steps away from its inventor. This must have been Hekataios, to whom a system of 40-year generations was attributed, even though its use is not attested in the

---

[88] Hekataios *FGrH* 1 F 20; Dionysios 687 F 1; Anaximander 9 F 3; Hdt. v 58; Andron 10 F 9.

[89] *FGrH* 10 F 10.

[90] *FGrH* 4 F 178.

[91] *FGrH* 262 FF 7, 3.

[92] Diog. Laert. i 24 = *FGrH* 6 F 5 (τεκμαιρόμενον); but the word may be Diogenes' (and is in fact attributed, via Hippias and Aristotle, to Thales!). However, the word appears also in Pindar and the tragedians, so nothing much should be made of this.

[93] *FGrH* 31 F 22a. This word is not so common in the two surviving historians, either: in Herodotos, only at ix 71 (ἀποσημαίνομαι); in Thukydides, at i 6.2, 10.1, 21.1, ii 42.2.

[94] In Hekataios note *fr.* 21, τῇ Δανᾷ μίσγεται Ζεύς: Herodian, who reports the fragment (Π. μον. λέξ. ii 912.23 Lentz), says that Hekataios himself reports that this is the Phoenician equivalent of Δανάη ('ὡς αὐτός φησι'). Further examples are Hek. *FGrH* 1 FF 322, 370; Charon 262 F 5; Hell. 4 FF 54, 60, 111; Xanthos 765 FF 16, 20d, 23; Menekrates 769 F 1. Similar is Hek. *fr.* 15: Hekataios says that οἴνη is the older word for ἄμπελος, and draws therefrom an historical inference.

[95] Local curiosities etc.: many fragments of Hekataios and Skylax; Aethlios *FGrH* 536 FF 1, 3; Agias/Derkyllos 305 F 7; Antiochos 555 F 1; Armenidas 378 F 4a; Charon 262 FF 1, 5; Damastes 5 F 5 = Hellanikos 4 F 195 (a marvel: some Epeians live 200, even 300 years); Demokles *fr.* 1 Müller; Hell. 4 FF 53, 54, 66, 67, 71a, 137, 174, 184, 190; Herod. 31 F 31; Kritias *Vorsokr.* 88 B 32 sqq.; Metrodoros 43 F 3; Pher. 3 F 47; Xanthos 765 FF 13, 31; Xenomedes 442 F 1. For statistics see Damastes 5 FF 2 (distance between the pillars of Herakles), 10 (size of Kypros); Pher. 3 F 30 (size of Ares' field); Hek. 1 FF 197 (size of the Aegean, though the stade figure is not his), 332 (three days to cross the Ψυλλικὸς κόλπος). Catalogues of Niobids and the like as a feature of mythography need hardly be illustrated. The geographer's list of cities along a coastline makes a telling reappearance in Herodoros 31 F 2 (a verbatim quotation), where the Iberian coast is charted, Hekataios-like, in an account of Herakles' westward progress. It is all part of Herodoros' rationalistic programme.

[96] References to earlier literature may be found in E. Vandiver, *Heroes in Herodotus. The interaction of myth and history* (Frankfurt a.M. 1990) 133 n. 1 and Alden A. Mosshammer, *The chronicle of Eusebius and Greek chronographic tradition* (Lewisburg and London 1979) 105-11; see also the important work of Pietro Vannicelli, *Erodoto e la storia dell'alto e medio arcaismo (Sparta - Tessaglia - Cirene)* (Rome 1993) 9 ff.

[97] E. Meyer, *Forschungen zur alten Geschichte* i (Halle 1892) 153-209.

fragments. The weaknesses in Meyer's argument have long been exposed. Inconsistencies in Herodotos' application of the technique prove nothing. For instance, he has not noticed that the date implied for Herakles (*ca.* 1180) by his three-generations-to-the-century formula (ii 142), when calculated from the twenty-one generations in the Spartan king-lists (vii 204, viii 131), contradicts his date of 900 years before his own time (say, *ca.* 1330) given at ii 145. The Spartan king-lists were, however, a given, and it need not have occurred to Herodotos to apply his new technique in every circumstance.[98] If it could be established that his date for Herakles was derivative, of course that would mean someone else had first invented chronography; but the date could be Herodotos' own calculation, if we assume that the 505 years for the 22 Heraklid kings at i 7 (which notoriously produces a very short generation, and does not look like the result of chronographical calculation) was given to him by some other source; after the Heraklids we have five Mermnads who reigned for 170 years (i 14, 16, 25, 86), which is 167 years on the three-to-a-century rule plus the three extra years accorded Kroisos for his piety (i 91); from Agron, the first Heraklid king (i 7), back to his great-great-grandfather Herakles was five generations = one and one third centuries reckoned inclusively; all these added to the date of Kroisos' downfall (which cannot be exactly determined from Herodotos' indications, but is certainly somewhere in the mid-sixth century) bring us back almost precisely to 1330, a date thus produced by Herodotos on the basis of information available to him and his (own?) formula of three generations to a century.[99] It is quite impossible to judge from Herodotos' tone or the manner with which he introduces his chronological data whether some or all aspects of his method were original with him or someone else.[100] Certainly Meyer's statement[101] that Herodotos wasn't really interested in chronography—he simply took over what was given to him by others, applied the data inconsistently and made mistakes in his calculations, showing that this wasn't his invention at all—is not justified by Herodotos' text; surely he *was* keenly interested in chronography, and conscientiously gives his audience many indications of time passed. Indeed, this looks like a new-found tool whose usefulness for historical inquiry has quite impressed Herodotos.

Of course Hekataios has genealogies, but there is no indication in the fragments that he ever assigned a standard length to the generation or did chronological calculations on such a basis; nor is there any certain instance in Hekataios of synchronistic fiddling—that is, padding a genealogy with invented names in order to make contemporaries in different branches of the tree line up. Nor do Akousilaos or Pherekydes use such a technique; it is, however, typical of Hellanikos, who also produced several works of a purely chronographical nature. Whether he was the first to do so is hardly known (perhaps Charon's *Prytaneis of the (?) Lampsakenes* came first),[102] but chronography was certainly where Hellanikos made his reputation. On general grounds the sort of methodological awareness implied by such devices is not to be

---

[98] See above p. 72 on the failure to universalize.

[99] *Cf.* D.W. Prakken, *Studies in Greek genealogical chronology* (Lancaster, PA 1943) 22 f. If this conjecture is correct, it removes the basis for Meyer's inference of a 40-year generation, which was this figure of 900 divided by the number of Spartan kings. The only real hint of a 40-year generation left in early sources, therefore, is Thuk. i 12.3 (Dorian invasion 80 years after Troy). Multiples of 40 in Herodotos at i 163.2 and iii 23.1 are suggestive, but hardly probative. See now W. Burkert, 'Lydia between East and West, or how to date the Trojan war: a study in Herodotus', in J.B. Carter, S.P. Morris, edd., *The ages of Homer. A tribute to Emily Townsend Vermeule* (University of Texas 1995) 139-48, who argues with much probability that the 505 years are ultimately derived from Assyrian records.

[100] Von Fritz (n. 20) ii 177 n.3 argues that the last sentence of Hdt. ii 146.2 implies that others before him had produced chronological calculations based on genealogies.

[101] P. 169, 184 f. *Cf.* Mosshammer (n. 96) 326 n. 6; Lloyd (n. 70) i 193 concludes after a lengthy discussion: 'That he was interested in chronological questions admits of no doubt.'

[102] See above, p. 66. I do not share Toye's (n. 1) view of the *Priestesses of Argos.*

expected in the naive early days of historiography. Of course, one can never be too careful when treading on general grounds, and Hekataios may indeed be the inventor of a rudimentary system. But on the evidence available it seems more prudent to date the advent of these methods to the lifetime of Herodotos. Perhaps he and Hellanikos had a few discussions.[103]

Rationalization, etymology, study of foreign languages, and other devices thus far mentioned, with the possible exception of chronography, are not first found in Herodotos, and cannot in themselves identify the distinctive elements in his voiceprint. We need now to inquire what those elements might be.

III. THE VOICE OF HERODOTOS

The first candidate is one of those obvious things too easily forgotten. As far as our record goes one of the distinguishing features of Herodotos' work is precisely the frequency with which he makes his voice heard. His is an extraordinarily self-conscious performance. Voice-markers occur so often that in reading through him one begins to notice their *absence* more than their presence. Thukydides, by comparison, has few markers, and thus gives the superficial impression of being the more 'objective' historian. Interestingly the places where Herodotos steps aside and allows the eye of the reader to behold the events directly are those places where his imagination as a story-teller is given the freest rein: in telling anecdotes and in composing speeches. The absence of markers is no guarantee of objectivity; by the same token, a plethora of markers does not imply an historian who is allowing his own personality to get in the way of his job.

After a lengthy stretch of straight narrative the historian's voice may reappear with particularly telling effect. A superb example is the end of the story of Harpagos and his son, i 119. 'Thus answering he gathered up what was left of the flesh and went home, intending, I suppose, to collect it all and bury it.' There has been no marker of any kind for a very long time (since chapter 110), and the quiet intrusion of Herodotos' voice, 'I suppose', breaks the spell. We realize that we have been lost in a gripping narrative; its horror and pathos become even more apparent to us.[104]

There are two noteworthy occasions in Thukydides when markers do become frequent: the *archaiologiai* of Books i and vi.[105] His language and technique in these sections are thoroughly Herodotean, suggesting that his methods were acknowledged as the appropriate way to determine the truth about the remoter past.[106] Since imitation is the sincerest form of

---

[103] For further indications of chronographical activity see Agias/Derkyllos *FGrH* 305 F 2; Andron 10 F 13; Damastes 5 F 7; Hell. 4 FF 74 sqq. (the *Priestesses of Argos*), 85-6 (the *Karneonikai*), 152, 168, 169, 201 *bis*; Herod. 31 F 33; Ion 392 F 1; Xanthos 765 F 32.

[104] τούτοισι δὲ ἀμειψάμενος καὶ ἀναλαβὼν τὰ λοιπὰ τῶν κρεῶν ἦιε ἐς τὰ οἰκία. ἐνθεῦτεν δὲ ἔμελλε, ὡς ἐγὼ δοκέω, ἁλίσας θάψειν τὰ πάντα. *Cf.* J.D. Denniston, *Greek prose style* (Oxford 1952) 6 (reminder from H. Lloyd-Jones).

[105] *Cf.* S. Hornblower, 'Narratology and narrative technique in Thucydides', in S. Hornblower, ed., *Greek historiography* (Oxford 1994) 131-66 at 151; L. Canfora and A. Corcella, 'La letteratura politica e la storiografia', in *Lo spazio letterario della grecia antica* edd. G. Cambiano, L. Canfora, D. Lanza (Rome 1993) i 1.433-71 at 454 ff.; and especially Hunter (n. 70) chs. 1 and 3.

[106] In i 1-21, ii 15-16, and vi 1-5, I count the following markers: τεκμήριον or the like (including δῆλον and congeners, which demonstrably have the same force), 18 examples; use of an expression such as ἔτι καὶ νῦν, or 'which is now called', 26 examples; use of an expression like ὧν ἀκοῇ ἴσμεν, or reference to the first inventor, 10 examples; chronological markers, whether in terms of a span of years to his own day, or more vaguely 'a few years later', 'shortly before the Persian War', 'some generations later' and the like, 28 examples; appeal to εἰκός, 7 examples; references to sources or possibilities of discovery, 8 examples, including two instances of λέγονται, one οὐκ ἔχω εἰπεῖν, and one instance of alternative versions; one foreign language equivalent; and, revealingly, five instances of δοκεῖ μοι or the like: Thukydides cannot here command the truth in his usual sovereign manner. This is an astonishing list and is a very powerful argument against Fehling's thesis (see the last section of the article). *Cf.* also vi 54-9.

flattery, one may wonder whether Thukydides' celebrated gibe at the end of the archaeology in Book i against those more interested in τὸ μυθῶδες than the truth, was really directed at Herodotos, as we are so often told. If we are to think of charlatans, an obvious choice would be a Sophist like Hippias, who in the *Hippias Major* of Plato says that his audiences' favourite subject by far is 'the genealogies of heroes and men, how the cities were founded in ancient days, in a word, the whole of ἀρχαιολογία'.[107] This is not in the least a description of Herodotos' book, and the greater part of Thukydides' archaeology (though admittedly not all) treats subjects lying wholly outside Herodotos' purview.

One of the things Herodotos likes to talk about more than anything else is his sources. He frequently gives alternative versions of events derived from different informants, and sometimes comments on their relative merits. He is careful to tell us what he has seen for himself and what he knows only from hearsay. He sometimes merely says λέγεται, leaving the source unnamed; at other times, he tells us explicitly that a certain piece of information is not reported. He uses an extensive vocabulary to discuss his relationship with his sources: words like ἀκούω, ὄψις, πυνθάνομαι, εὑρίσκω, συμβάλλομαι, ἱστορέω, οἶδα, δοκέω, λογίζομαι, γνώμη, σταθμόομαι, οὐ πιστά, ἀτρεκέως εἰπεῖν, and so on. So far as we can tell this is original with him, and it certainly strikes every reader as a large part of his literary persona. One might expect to find a certain amount of talk about sources in Antiochos of Syracuse, in view of the proem to the Περὶ Ἰταλίης (*FGrH* 555 F 2): Ἀντίοχος Ξενοφάνεος τάδε συνέγραψε περὶ Ἰταλίης ἐκ τῶν ἀρχαίων λόγων τὰ πιστότατα καὶ σαφέστατα. Antiochos' surviving fragments unfortunately do not confirm or belie this expectation; but one may note that in the archaeology of Sicily at the beginning of Book vi, where as we have noted Thukydides suddenly becomes quite Herodotean in his diction, critics are agreed he is following Antiochos.[108] However, most of Antiochos' working career probably came after Herodotos', since the fragments of the Περὶ Σικελίης provide a *terminus post quem* of 424/3;[109] it is most unlikely, then, that he is the innovator.

In writers before Herodotos there is no sign of this talk of alternative sources. Certainly *sources* are occasionally mentioned. For instance, in *fr*. 21 (quoted in n. 94) Hekataios tells us that the Phoenicians do not say Danae but 'Dana'. In *fr*. 79a it appears that Pherekydes reports what the 'locals' called a certain landmark; in other fragments he appears to show knowledge of local cults at Thorikos, Thebes, and Delphi, which bespeaks a certain amount of ἱστορίη, getting out and seeing things for yourself; but he may have obtained his knowledge from literary tradition.[110]

Pherekydes once appears to say that a certain name in a genealogy is *not* reported; if we could be sure of that, it would be important, for you would normally expect an early mythographer, like a poet, to make up the name, whereas declining to do so on the grounds that tradition is silent implies that one is not part of that tradition, and that it might present problems to the researcher—in other words, it implies a different kind of awareness and self-conception altogether from that of the poet. The fragment (Schol. Ap. Rhod. 2.373-76a = Pher. *FGrH* 3 F

---

[107] *Hipp. Maior* 285d = *FGrH* 6 T 3. *Cf.* Toye (n. 1) 289, 297.

[108] After K.J. Dover, 'La colonizzazione della Sicilia in Tucidide', *Maia* vi (1953) 1-20 = 'Die Kolonisierung Siziliens bei Thukydides', in H. Herter, ed., *Thukydides* (Darmstadt 1968) 344-68; see also *HCT* iv 198 ff.

[109] *FGrH* 555 T 3 explicitly gives this as the last year covered by the work.

[110] Thebes: *FGrH* 3 F 84, an aetiological myth concerning Alkmene; Delphi: 3 F 64, an aetiological myth concerning Neoptolemos; Thorikos: 3 F 34, conjectured to be aetiological by R.L. Fowler, 'The myth of Kephalos as an aition of rain magic (Pherekydes *FGrH* 3 F 34)', *ZPE* xcvii (1993) 29-42. For the citation of local sources *cf.* Hell. 4 FF 23, 71a, 137, Herod. 31 F 31, Metrod. 769 F 2 (λέγουσι in a verbatim quotation), and Arist. 379 F 6, who quotes from local archives (ὑπομνήματα).

15b) runs: Δοίας καὶ "Ακμων ἀδελφοί· τίνος δὲ πατρός, οὐ φέρεται, ὥς φησι Φερεκύδης. Unfortunately one can never be sure in these scholiastic paraphrases what the original wording might have been. In scholiasts' Greek the locution 'Pherekydes does not say X but Y', where X is a proposition such as 'the father of Doias and Akmon is so-and-so', does not normally mean that in Pherekydes there was an explicit denial that X was the case; it means that Pherekydes is silent about X, and says rather Y. The expression was noted in many fragments of Pherekydes long ago by Karl Luetke,[111] and much more recently A.B. Bosworth has drawn important inferences about the Peace of Kallias based on the same turn of phrase in Plutarch.[112] It is possible that behind this fragment of Pherekydes lies a misunderstanding of the expression 'Pherekydes does not say that', and that Pherekydes was simply silent on the subject.

Herodotos normally records the absence of information by saying οὐ λέγεται; much more often, he records the existence of tradition by saying λέγεται. This impersonal use of the verb in itself implies a certain distance in one's stance vis-à-vis the tradition, as if it is there to be tested. In the verbatim quotations of Hekataios, Akousilaos and Pherekydes, no example is recorded. There are enough such quotations that the absence seems significant. After Herodotos, λέγεται is routinely employed in historiography and mythography.[113]

In Akousilaos discussion of alternative or non-existent sources can be excluded completely, if the report is true that he composed his book out of ancient tales written on bronze tablets discovered by his father while digging in his house.[114] I suspect that these tablets were in fact mentioned by Akousilaos in his proem, and that he claimed to be merely the promulgator of ancient lore; he would thus be a mythographical counterpart to an oracle-monger like Onomakritos. If this conjecture is correct, it explains the report in the *Suda*[115] that the work was a forgery, and therefore not a candidate for the title of oldest prose work (as some people, therefore, did believe); it also explains how some more gullible authorities placed Akousilaos on the list of the Seven Wise Men.[116] In the light of all this it is not to be expected that Akousilaos adopted the pose of a disinterested inquirer, honestly appraising the merits of different sources.

In Hekataios there is one prominent disagreement with a source, in *fr.* 19 where he says 'Aigyptos himself did not come to Argos, but his sons, who were fifty in number, as Hesiod said, but as I say, no more than twenty'. His grounds are presumably that fifty is an unrealistically high number, so he rationalistically lowers it. But he does not tell us his grounds, unless he went on to do so after the fragment breaks off; but that would be quite out of keeping with everything we know of the style of these early writers. We can often catch them changing the details of a myth to avoid unpleasant implications, and to that extent we can see that they are wrestling with a problem in their sources. We can sometimes infer the reason why they have changed the details—for instance, local patriotism. With such inferences we must be satisfied, for we are seldom told the reason. In this procedure the early mythographers do not differ from

---

[111] Carolus Luetke (a pupil of Wilamowitz), *Pherecydea* (Diss. Göttingen 1893) 26. See Pher. *FGrH* 3 FF 26, 54, 60, 72, 82, 133; Hell. 4 FF 104a, 117; Andron 10 F 13; Deilochos 471 F 5.

[112] A.B. Bosworth, 'Plutarch, Callisthenes, and the peace of Callias', *JHS* cx (1990) 1-13.

[113] *Cf.* H.D. Westlake, 'λέγεται in Thucydides', *Mnem.* xxx (1977) 345-62, who finds interesting similarities to and differences from Herodotos' usage.

[114] *Suda* α 942 = *FGrH* 2 T 1.

[115] ε 360 = *FGrH* 2 T 7 = Hec. *FGrH* 1 T 1a.

[116] Diog. Laert. i 41 = *FGrH* 2 T 11a; Clem. Al. *Strom.* i 59.5 = 2 T 11b.

poets, who after all routinely reject, sometimes explicitly, myths they do not like.[117] But awareness of the disagreement or absence of sources as a general problem requiring theoretical attention and the development of critical tools is not found in either poets or early mythographers. It *is* found in Herodotos.

His thoughts on the reliability of knowledge are expressed frequently and with a subtle and consistent vocabulary. One of the most important passages in this regard comes in the second book (ii 23), in the course of discussing various theories of the flooding of the Nile:

ὁ δὲ περὶ τοῦ Ὠκεανοῦ λέξας ἐς ἀφανὲς τὸν μῦθον ἀνενείκας οὐκ ἔχει ἔλεγχον· οὐ γάρ τινα ἔγωγε οἶδα ποταμὸν Ὠκεανὸν ἐόντα, Ὅμηρον δὲ ἤ τινα τῶν πρότερον γενομένων ποιητέων δοκέω τοὔνομα εὑρόντα ἐς ποίησιν ἐσενείκασθαι.

The man who spoke of Ocean, thus removing his tale into the realm of the invisible, cannot be refuted; for I do not know that any river Ocean exists, but rather think that Homer or one of the earlier poets invented the name and introduced it into his poetry.

Herodotos here has pronounced the important principle of falsifiability: a true proposition must not only be capable of being verified, it must also have the potential of being falsified. A proposition of a kind that offers no handle to anyone who might wish to test it is refused admission to the discussion on principle. Such propositions may have value in the world of imagination or poetry, but they lie outside the realm of positivistic truth or falsehood. Herodotos is not interested in such propositions.

In the world of the city-state, especially in the developed democracies, citizens had long been used to hearing alternative points of view expressed, and to adjudicating between them when they cast their votes in the law-courts and assemblies. In the middle of the fifth century, the science of rhetoric was furnishing a theoretical framework and a practical set of tools for use in such arenas. The orators argued from analogy, from contrast, from probability, from experience—just like Herodotos. Poets had long been instinctive philosophers, just as they had been instinctive rhetoricians, but it was sophists who first realized that knowledge can be expressed in the form of propositions, which can be tested, and whose properties *qua* propositions can be examined.[118] About the time that Herodotos was writing his histories, if we accept the conventional chronology, Sokrates was confronted with a mysterious proposition by the god of Delphi: that he was the wisest of men; he set out to refute this statement, ἐλέγχειν; and, again if we follow the conventional outline of Sokrates' career, it was from this experience that his own distinctive contribution to philosophy developed, the ἔλεγχος.[119] The contribution of autopsy to the acquisition of knowledge relative to other forms of sensory perception and to ratiocination, so familiar from Herodotos, was a commonplace in the philosophy of his youth.[120]

[117] See T.C.W. Stinton, '"Si credere dignum est": some expressions of disbelief in Euripides and others', *PCPS* xxii (1976) 60-89 = *Collected papers on Greek tragedy* (Oxford 1990) 236-64.

[118] On Herodotos and the Sophists, see Albrecht Dihle, 'Herodot und die Sophistik', *Philologus* cvi (1962) 207-20 (p. 218 on arguments from probability); on contemporary methods of reasoning, see G.E.R. Lloyd, *Polarity and analogy* (Cambridge 1966) index s.v. Herodotus; on early rhetoric, see the references given by R.L. Fowler, *HSCP* xciii (1987) 15 n. 24. A.B. Lloyd (n. 70) i 149 f., 156 ff. provides a detailed discussion of the connections between Herodotos and the intellectual climate of his day; *cf.* also Hunter (n. 70) 93 n. 1.

[119] Pl. *Apol.* 21; for the chronology, W.K.C. Guthrie, *History of Greek philosophy* (Cambridge 1969) 405 ff.; for a carefully reasoned explanation of the connection between the oracle and the ἔλεγχος see T.C. Brickhouse and N.D. Smith, *Socrates on trial* (Oxford 1989) 87-100.

[120] E.g. Herakleitos *frr.* 5-6 Marcovich; Xenophanes *Vorsokr.* 21 B 34-6; Alkmaion 24 B 1; Anaxagoras 59 B 21a; see further E. Hussey, 'The beginnings of epistemology: from Homer to Philolaus', in *Epistemology*, ed. S Everson (Cambridge 1990) 11-38. *Cf.* Donald Lateiner, *The historical method of Herodotus* (Toronto 1989) 66; G. Schepens, *L' 'autopsie' dans la méthode des historiens grecs du Ve siècle avant J.-C.* (Brussels 1980).

The language of Herodotos shows him to be a man of his day. He was not a Sophist, but he was a thinker, and he profited from discussions with other thinkers. He brought the old science of ἱστορίη, critical inquiry, up to date by employing new critical tools, and applied ἱστορίη itself to new subjects. The strength and insistence of the historian's voice is perhaps no different from Hekataios; but the combination of this extraordinary self-projection with a sophisticated awareness of the problem of sources—their nature and reliability, and the historian's relation to them: this is the unique voiceprint of Herodotos. The imitation of Thukydides and Antiochos acknowledges that his tools were the appropriate ones for finding out the truth about the past. One first obtains whatever λόγοι are available, and then tests them by various means: by gauging their inherent probability; by detecting their bias, if any;[121] by comparing them to similar stories; by appealing to everyday experience; by comparing the evidence of surviving monuments or practices; by applying elementary logic, for example by finding contradictions. Herodotos occasionally represents characters in his own story engaging in this kind of activity, which is helpful in clarifying for us what he means by ἱστορίη;[122] but even without that, we can judge for ourselves what he is up to. Herodotos' explicit awareness of the problems of sources and his development of methods of dealing with them are his distinctive contribution to historiography.

IV. HERODOTOS' SOURCES AND THE PROEM

Readers familiar with current controversies may be thinking that the picture being drawn of Herodotos will not be so brightly burnished if the sources he so persistently refers to do not really exist. One could try to evade the issue by saying everything so far established as new and different remains new and different in Herodotos' *text*, whatever the relationship of that text to external reality. But that would hardly be satisfactory. If 'inquiry' was not meant by Herodotos as seriously as it was meant by contemporary mathematicians, doctors, astronomers, scientists, philosophers, and others (or, indeed, by characters in Herodotos' own text), then his contribution to 'history' is accidental at best. Therefore it is necessary to confront any theory that would have us believe otherwise.

In a forcefully argued book, Detlev Fehling has shown that many of Herodotos' source citations are questionable.[123] They follow fixed patterns; they are always the most appropriate source possible for whatever fact is being reported or theory propounded, no matter how fantastic or unreal; credibility is carefully preserved—for instance, in the case of information from the edges of the known world, by stressing that it has come through several intermediaries, and implicitly allowing for distortion; bias is always preserved (e.g., so that Egyptians always praise Egyptians); supplementary accounts and confirmations are forthcoming from the most widespread locations, yet always dovetail perfectly with each other, even in support of what is wildly wrong. The list of indictments could be continued. Fehling concludes that almost all of Herodotos' source citations are fictive. To report Fehling fairly, it should be stressed that he is

---

[121] See e.g. i 95 on Kyros: 'In my account I will follow those Persians who do not want to glorify Kyros, but rather to tell the truth—though I know there are several other versions of Kyros' tale.' *Cf.* iii 16.

[122] See i 24.7-8, 117, 122, 209 (a passage which clearly illustrates Herodotos' own awareness of the problem of knowledge), ii 2, 119. *Cf.* W.R. Connor, 'The *histor* in history', in *Nomodeiktes. Greek studies in honor of Martin Ostwald*, edd. Ralph M. Rosen, Joseph Farrell (University of Michigan 1993) 3-15, who stresses the old sense of 'arbitration' in the root (ἵστωρ already in *Il.* xviii 501, xxiii 486). Connor's rather speculative explanation of why the word is less common in the last books seems to overlook one pertinent factor, which is that they treat a period much closer to Herodotos' own time and place, thus needing less ἱστορίη.

[123] Detlev Fehling, *Herodotus and his 'sources'. Citation, invention, and narrative art*, tr. J.G. Howie (Leeds 1989; German original 1971).

not trying to call Herodotos a simple liar or a fraud, even if many of his remarks seem to have no other implication. He thinks Herodotos has invented a new art form, which is not history, but a kind of narrative based loosely on historical facts. The alternative to Herodotos the historian is not Herodotos the fraud, but Herodotos the poet.[124] He takes whatever information he has and spins a tale from it, using his imagination to fill in the gaps.

Numerous objections have been made to these startling ideas.[125] The considerations advanced so far in this paper raise a further difficulty: the only assessment Fehling can make of Herodotos' constant discussion of the basis of his knowledge is to say that he is an exceptionally clever liar.[126] This does not give an adequate account of Herodotos' place in the intellectual milieu of his time and particularly his relationship with other historians. Fehling seems at one point uncomfortable with his position; on p. 121 he allows that Herodotos' use of the devices of 'lying literature' has a 'more serious end in view than the mere enhancement of the credibility of his account... Many of the passages involved must also have been intended as object lessons on the conditions and limitations within which historical knowledge is acquired and on likely sources of error.' This qualification seems to give the game away; it is very hard to see why an expression of scepticism about a source's statement which, on Fehling's view, exists only in Herodotos' mind, should be read as an 'object lesson' on historical method, if the author is not interested himself in doing real history. Why would Herodotos bother? And how could the ancient audience have understood his real meaning from the text? How could they know he was really only 'playing' at research?[127] Fehling does not discuss the passage on the ἔλεγχος; but Thukydides, whom Fehling regards as the one true historian[128] (begging the question, where Thukydides got the inspiration for such a revolutionary new idea),[129] acknowledges the methodological insight of Herodotos in the most famous of his own methodological passages, by rejecting all stories that are ἀνεξέλεγκτα (i 21). Thukydides, as we saw above, knew that Herodotos was serious about doing history; he knew that his were the best available methods of discovering truth about the past. So far from faking his sources,

---

[124] Fehling 154 f.; cf. 11, 214 f.

[125] E. Will, review of Fehling, *Rev. de phil.* xlviii (1974) 119-21; Hartmut Erbse, 'Über Herodots Kroisoslogos', *Ausgewählte Schriften zur klassischen Philologie* (Berlin and New York 1979) 180-202 at 181 f.; *id.*, 'Fiktion und Wahrheit im Werke Herodots', *GGN* 1991, 131-50 (in my judgment the best reply yet); Oswyn Murray, 'Herodotus and Oral History', in H. Sancisi-Weerdenburg and A. Kuhrt, edd., *Achaemenid history II: the Greek sources* (Leiden 1987) 93-115 at 101 n. 12; Simon Hornblower, *Thucydides* (London 1987) 19 ff.; *id.*, introduction to *Greek historiography*, ed. S. Hornblower (Oxford 1994) 18 f. with further references; J.A.S. Evans, review of Fehling in *EMC/CV* xi (1992) 57-60; *id.*, 'The Faiyum and the Lake of Moeris', *AHB* v.3 (1991) 66-74; W. Kendrick Pritchett, *The Liar school of Herodotus* (Amsterdam 1993); Canfora and Corcella (n. 105) 448 ff.; P.J. Rhodes, 'In defence of the Greek historians', *G&R* xli (1994) 156-71 at 160 f. Qualified support and sensible remarks from H.R. Immerwahr in P.E. Easterling, B.M.W. Knox, edd., *The Cambridge history of classical literature* i (Cambridge 1985) 439 f. Evans well notes that Herodotos compares very favourably in point of accuracy with other early travelers, for instance reporting from the Americas (a point made again in his *Herodotus, explorer of the past* [Princeton 1991] 135, 141). I might add that Fehling makes little allowance for the distortions of memory, for instance when he writes (243): 'Could anyone who had ever seen the Pyramids get it all so wrong?' I recently re-visited Kenilworth after seventeen years and was amazed to discover that someone had put up two 400-year-old buildings in my absence.

[126] See 120 ff. on the features Herodotos shares with 'lying literature' (e.g. wealth of detail, occasional expression of scepticism, avowal of inability to discover the truth on some points); *cf.* 8, 33. Fehling grants that some history is found in Herodotos, but only the merest amount (213 f.); although Herodotos worked into his account all the genuine information he had (83), his primary purpose was not the discovery of such information, but the construction of an entertaining narrative.

[127] Fehling 252. On his hypothesis, even if the audience was duped, many other historians who decided to play at the same game were not; did Herodotos then take them into his confidence backstage after the performance?

[128] Fehling 154 f. To put everybody but Thukydides out of the historian's court is absurd. Fehling has not considered the differences that result from Thukydides' decision to concentrate on contemporary history; see below, p. 83.

[129] An objection to Fehling first raised by Dover and reported by S. Hornblower, *Thucydides* (London 1987) 22.

Herodotos found new ways to deal with them.

Yet it cannot be denied that Fehling has put his finger on some real peculiarities in Herodotos' procedures. There does appear to have been considerable manipulation of the facts between their discovery and their presentation. The many responses to Fehling's thesis have so far failed to identify the middle way that must be found between his extreme position and the pleasant but equally indefensible picture of Herodotos as a researcher faithful to the 'facts' as we understand them.

One must consider Herodotos' mentality, the conditions under which he worked, and the prevailing intellectual atmosphere. I referred earlier to Geoffrey Lloyd's admirable work on contemporary scientists; Stephanie West, in her careful study of Herodotos' use of inscriptions, has seen how his findings may be applied to Herodotos.[130] It is to be expected that Herodotos' critical tools will be imperfectly and inconsistently applied. It is to be expected that he will fill in gaps in the record with conjectures that make sense to him; he could hardly proceed in any other way. Given the state of contemporary knowledge, many of his conjectures, which seemed as true to him as any propositions have ever seemed true to anybody, will seem ridiculous to us. Reality is passed through conceptual filters en route to representation. Herodotos' filters required him to think that a true account of any event must have no loose ends. Corroborative accounts must dovetail perfectly. Maps must be symmetrical.[131] History has no irregularities. Instead it has patterns, for instance that nemesis follows hybris. To us, a true historical account acknowledges the endless complexity of the record; indeed, Fehling thinks Herodotos must have known this, and therefore knew that his source-citations were fictive.[132] Herodotos would say that *our* accounts are unhistorical, because they leave all the bumps in; as any number of contemporary philosophers would tell you, τὸ ἐόν—one of Herodotos' words for truth—is not like that.

If he massages his data to produce typical patterns, it is because, to him, that is the structure of truth and reality. Future historians of historiography will identify ways of thinking that have affected our explanations of historical events, and with a similar lack of generosity accuse us of lying, or at any rate, of writing nothing better than historical fiction. We have no way of knowing what these might be, and if they could be pointed out to us, we would in all likelihood simply not understand the force of the objection. Nor would Herodotos understand Fehling.[133] Thus, for instance, it may readily be admitted that Herodotos fills out his account of the Persian forces to include nations from one end of the world to the other, a cosmopolitan muster very reminiscent of the *Iliad*. This is not lying nor even fiction; it is, to Herodotos, reasonable

---

[130] S. West, 'Herodotos' epigraphical interests', *CQ* xxxv (1985) 278-305 at 303: 'The confident assurance of his historical reconstructions is bluff... The inadequacies of his argumentation may well be a matter of period rather than personality. Certainly we find rather similar procedures in the early Hippocratic writings...'; she goes on to cite Lloyd's work, and draws a telling parallel with the 'confident rationalism of a Victorian scientist confuting a literal interpretation of the opening chapters of *Genesis*'.

[131] Even though Herodotos criticises others for imposing symmetry on their maps (iv 36), he notoriously does the same himself (ii 33-4).

[132] Fehling 84, 188. The presence of any literary motif and the imposition of any pattern on the data (Fehling catalogues many of them) must, in his theory, fall under the same verdict; pressed to its logical limits it would probably condemn not only ancient but modern historians, including Gibbon, Mommsen, and maybe Fehling himself. As will become clear, I too find much in common between Herodotos' methods and those of the poet; but I differ *toto caelo* from Fehling in my assessment of Herodotos' intentions.

[133] Contrast Fehling 97: 'A remarkable thing about all these passages is that they reveal that Herodotus' standards of credibility and incredibility are little different from those of the twentieth century.'

conjecture. And there is genuine research behind it, as David Lewis as shown.[134] Modern historians, at bottom, are no different; consider what mental processes are going on every time one of them uses an expression like 'must have' or 'surely'. The difficulty for Herodotos is that the point at which he must resort to surmise comes a great deal sooner than it does for the modern historian, who has far superior tools for research. The same applies to ancient and modern scientists and other researchers. Fehling's assessment of Herodotos could apply equally well to ancients doctors, physicists, etc.; but to speak of pseudo-medicine and pseudo-science is not particularly helpful. Nor is it helpful to speak of pseudo-history.[135]

This weakness in Fehling's assessment of Herodotos' procedures is particularly visible in his treatment of the proem, to which we may now turn. After relating the Persian account of who was responsible for the aggression, which is based on the interpretation of certain legends, Herodotos goes on to say that he will not discuss whether or not the Persian account is true, but will rather say who first *in his knowledge* (τὸν δὲ οἶδα αὐτός) committed acts of injustice against the Greeks. I follow those who say that Herodotos is not here rejecting all legends *qua* legends, since such a proposition is not consistent with his behaviour elsewhere in the book; rather, he is rejecting *these* stories because they cannot be verified or falsified.[136] They have no ἔλεγχος. Just as in the passage on the Nile discussed earlier, Herodotos appeals to reliable knowledge as the basis for further discussion. Similarly at iii 122, Polykrates is the first thalassocrat 'of those we know'; that is (Herodotos adds by way of explanation) the first 'of the so-called human generation'. The two qualifiers are equivalent, and exclude legendary thalassocrats like Minos. If information were forthcoming that would allow the legends to be tested, then Herodotos would admit them to the discussion. Elsewhere he is quite willing to accept legends that seem plausible to him for one reason or another. These reasons might not always seem adequate to us, and might even, on investigation, seem to contradict the principles Herodotos espouses in the proem (another example of the failure to universalize). No matter; this is what he says here, and he means it. He cannot know the truth of these stories; and therefore (to make explicit the implicit logic of the ring-composition, as the λέξις εἰρομένη often requires us to do),[137] they are insufficient to answer the question posed in the opening words, why the Greeks and Persians fought one another. So Herodotos restricts the scope of his inquiry, his ἱστορίη, to a more recent period where results are more likely to be obtained. Unlike Hekataios, whose personal genealogy began sixteen generations ago with a god, and unlike Hellanikos and others, whose local histories began with the foundation by a hero, Herodotos does not pretend that a continuous record from the remotest period of time to the present day is possible.[138] He starts about two centuries before his own day; Thukydides, with

---

[134] D.M. Lewis, 'Persians in Herodotus', in *The Greek historians. Literature and history, Festschrift A.E. Raubitschek* (Saratoga 1985) 101-17. Contrast Fehling 213 ff.: a very small amount of real historical information, he says, would account for Herodotos' narrative; he knew no more about the past than the rhapsodes knew about the Trojan War. At 243 ff. Fehling develops the view that Herodotos may have composed the whole work sitting in Athens, without ever having travelled anywhere.

[135] Fehling 179 ff. For him, it seems, Herodotos must be a perfect positivist historian (a thing that never existed anyway) or no historian at all. Historians are still a cross between scientists and artists. *Cf.* E. Will (n. 125) 121.

[136] See J.A.S. Evans, *Herodotus, explorer of the past* (Princeton 1991) 105 f., who also connects the passage on Ocean with the prologue; Erbse (n. 125) 183; *cf.* Donald Lateiner, *The historical method of Herodotus* (Toronto 1989) 41; K. Nickau, 'Mythos und Logos bei Herodot', in *Memoria rerum veterum, Festschrift C.J. Classen* (Stuttgart 1990) 83-100; Hunter (n. 70) 104 ff.

[137] For a study of the thought-processes of λέξις εἰρομένη see R.L. Fowler, *The nature of early Greek lyric* (Toronto 1987) ch. 2.

[138] Hdt. ii 143.1 = Hekataios *FGrH* 1 T 4.

even severer standards, starts as it were the day before yesterday.[139] There is much in Thukydides that Herodotos never dreamed of; but there is much too that is only Herodotos taken one step further.

This proem makes no sense if it is not taken seriously. Fehling's theory cannot take it seriously. The significant expression τὸν δὲ οἶδα αὐτός, whose strategic position gives it obvious rhetorical force, and which is followed immediately by the first announcement of one of the history's great leitmotifs, that of the mutability of fortune, Fehling is obliged to call a mere transitional formula.[140] He is obliged to condemn the words ἱστορίης ἀπόδεξις as misleading, since this 'inquiry' must be bound up with the source-citations; the words must be interpreted 'from a literary point of view', and are 'of no value as a guide in any investigation of Herodotos' real practice'.[141] We ask again, how on earth was the audience to know this? What reason would they have to think that the proem, unlike the proem of every other work of Greek literature (to speak from a purely literary point of view), was *not* a guide to the author's practice? What clue would they have that the words did not bear their ordinary Greek meaning? They had none; Fehling must therefore say that they were completely taken in, and thought Herodotos was *not* just telling stories, but giving them facts; and since, according to Fehling, every other 'inquirer' from Hekataios on (except Thukydides) was doing the same thing, we must believe that the confusion in Greek minds about reality and the possibility of historical inquiry was of truly stupendous proportions. Again one wonders where Thukydides got his idea from.

Now the proem, as everyone knows, attributes a fairly extensive knowledge of Greek myths to Persians and Phoenicians; more than that, it attributes knowledge of rationalized Greek myths to them. This has always seemed difficult to defenders of Herodotos' integrity, and it seems tailor-made for Fehling's theory. Yet looked at in the right way, this passage teaches us much about Herodotos' procedures. In the first place, there is no difficulty at all in thinking that Persians could honestly be represented as knowing these stories. Whether they really did know them is another question; David Lewis demonstrated that contacts between Greeks and Persians were a great deal more extensive than we might be inclined to believe *a priori*, but let us not pursue that here.[142] More to the point is that Hekataios had already represented Phoenicians as knowing Greek myth, when (in the fragment cited earlier)[143] he tells us the Phoenician form of the name Danae. Again, it does not matter if he made this up, though I doubt he did; it is part of his representation, and was accepted by his audience, if we may judge from the behaviour of subsequent writers. That the ancestor of the Persians was Perses, son of Perseus, is a belief reported by both Herodotos and Hellanikos, probably independently;[144] his father-in-law Kepheus, eponym of the Kephenes, one of the peoples of the Persian empire, also figures prominently in early tradition.[145] This arrogation of Persian genealogy to Greek was routine,

[139] *Cf.* Evans' review of Fehling (n. 125) 60; D. Asheri, *Erodoto: Le storie* i² (Fondazione Lorenzo Valla 1989) xxxviii; and P. Vannicelli's book (n. 96), which develops the thesis that Herodotos' focus throughout his work is on the three generations preceding the Persian Wars.

[140] Fehling 58.

[141] Fehling 247.

[142] See above p. 83; *id.* in A.R. Burn, *Persia and the Greeks*² (London 1984) 597 ff.; *id.*, *Sparta and Persia* (Leiden 1977) 12 ff.; *cf.* J. Diggle, *Euripidea* (Oxford 1994) 447. With respect to Phoenicians, apart from the well known connection at Al Mina, note that Phoenicians and Greeks resided together at Pithekoussai from the mid-eighth century; see D. Ridgway, *The First Western Greeks* (Cambridge 1992) 111-18.

[143] Above, n. 94.

[144] Hdt. vii 61, Hellanikos *FGrH* 4 F 60.

[145] Kepheus father of Andromeda already in Hes. *fr.* 135 Merkelbach-West; Hdt. vii 61, Hellanikos *FGrH* 4 F 59.

and it was natural for Greeks to believe that the Persians accepted it. It is, to be sure, possible that Greeks persisted in this belief in spite of Persian denials. Fortunately we have an important passage of Herodotos to help us. At vii 149 ff., Herodotos is explaining why the Argives remained neutral in the war. He gives first the Argive story, then another, which is 'told up and down Greece', λεγόμενος ἀνὰ τὴν Ἑλλάδα. This story is that Xerxes sent ambassadors to Argos reminding them of their common ancestor Perseus, and urging them for this reason not to fight. Citations attributed to all the Greeks Fehling excludes from his general theory, and regards as reflections of generally accepted lore;[146] thus we may affirm that, in a widely held Greek view, the Persians accepted these stories.[147]

That Herodotos could not have got the information in his prologue from a source as he pretends to do, is disproved by the passage in Book viii and the fragment of Hekataios. That he invented it all thus becomes an unnecessary hypothesis, unless a special reason is forthcoming for thinking so. The rationalized Greek myths he imputes to the Persians may be thought to provide such a reason. But this is not in fact such a serious obstacle; whether the version Herodotos thought the Persians believed was a rationalized version or some other kind matters not, so long as Herodotos thought it was the true version of the myth. We have already posited a real source for these stories; it is natural to suppose that the rationalized version is that source's version. If we remove from the myth as presented by Herodotos those elements that are bound up with his immediate purposes, *viz.* the causes of the war, we are left with straightforwardly comprehensible stories: Io was not really a cow, but an ordinary human princess, who wound up in Egypt because foreign sailors carried her off. Europe was similar. These look like good Hekataian rationalizations. But even if the source here was Greek, like the source of much of the Egyptian *logos*, so long as Herodotos regarded it as a trustworthy guide to Persian belief, he will not say 'X says the Persians say', but simply 'the Persians say'. This is perfectly honest in Herodotos' way of thinking; indeed, such scrupulous care in verifying references is rare to this day. Thus at ii 156, he says Chembis island 'is said by the Egyptians to be floating', although the original is in all probability Hekataios *FGrH* 1 F 305. Again, at ii 73 where the information about the phoenix is reported from an Egyptian source ('the Heliopolitans say'), the source is Hekataios 1 F 324a.[148] A similar situation exists with regard to Aristeas and Herodotos' statements about the Skythians.

That the source of the individual rationalized stories is Greek thus presents no problem. But who first worked them all together into a tally of offences committed by one race against the other, and advanced these events as causes of the great war? The section as it stands is a carefully constructed unity; the old guess that it came from Dionysios of Miletos' *Persika* is not so foolish. But let us suppose that Herodotos is the culprit. Suppose he never actually heard any Persian claim these events were the cause of the war. Can we still save his integrity? Admittedly, it becomes more difficult; but we may do so, if Herodotos sincerely believed that this is what the Persians *would* say and therefore *did* say.[149] The speeches in Thukydides, after all, work that way. Even if Herodotos' account is spun out of a single chance remark from some Persian to the effect that the campaign was undertaken to avenge wrongs committed long ago,

---

[146] Fehling 118 f.

[147] *Cf.* Erbse (n. 125) 187 f. At vii 62 Herodotos says the Medes were named after Medeia—as the Medes themselves say.

[148] *Cf.* Hek. *FGrH* 1 F 322 and Hdt. ii 77.4.

[149] Thus I can agree partly with Fehling 152: Herodotos' work is 'a carefully thought-out picture of what any enquiries would have had to yield', though 'any enquiries' suggests (consistently with Fehling's theory) that the whole process of inquiry is just pretence. But I think he inquired, thought a bit, inquired some more, then thought some more; he did not intend to deceive, and thought he was telling the truth.

with nothing further than that specified, his procedure remains defensible. His account is not 'fictive' in any helpful sense, but an intelligent putting together of all the information available to him. That information would include the prevailing Greek world-view, with its universal tendency to evoke mythological exempla. The Persians therefore do the same. The response of the Phoenicians could also be conjectural; but it is not necessary to think so. Any Phoenician would quite naturally take umbrage at the suggestion of rapine, and reply that Io came of her own accord, naughty girl that she was.[150] However that may be, out of all of this—Greek tradition, conversations with foreigners, Herodotos' own theorizing, and even connections or shadings suggested to him at the last minute by the exigencies of a good performance—out of all this comes an amalgam which Herodotos can present with perfect honesty as the account of the Persian λόγιοι. That account is then dismissed. To think that the whole thing is a straw man of Herodotos' invention, is to mistake entirely his relationship with his sources; to think that the great words τὸν δὲ οἶδα αὐτός are simply a way of leaving behind this pleasant fiction, is to miss utterly his contribution to historiography.[151]

Herodotos' constant discussion of sources is the unique element in his voiceprint, so far as our evidence goes; we see now that it is an integral part of his self-perception as an historian. In accordance with the principle laid down earlier,[152] we may impute these methodological innovations to him with little fear of contradiction. He has applied to historical problems the latest methods of other branches of inquiry, making at the same time his own contribution to their development. He did not invent his sources; he discovered the *problem* of sources.

* * *

To close I should like to suggest that two passages may be relevant to the understanding of the famous expression ἱστορίης ἀπόδεξις, and further confirm the general picture drawn in this paper. The first is from the Theognidean corpus, vv. 769-772:

χρὴ Μουσῶν θεράποντα καὶ ἄγγελον, εἴ τι περισσόν
εἰδείη, σοφίης μὴ φθονερὸν τελέθειν,
ἀλλὰ τὰ μὲν μῶσθαι, τὰ δὲ δεικνύεν, ἄλλα δὲ ποιεῖν·
τί σφιν χρήσηται μοῦνος ἐπιστάμενος;

In the *Collected Writings* of the late Leonard Woodbury, a study of the Theognidean poem has been published.[153] It is the only posthumous piece in the book, and may not be well known. The poem says that the servant and messenger of the Muses ought not to begrudge others his σοφίη, for then it is of no use to anyone; instead, he ought to seek out knowledge, present or perform it, and ποιεῖν, compose the results of his inquiry into a coherent piece of

---

[150] No doubt this reply was improvised on the spot (though Fehling 54 f. finds the idea ridiculous), and strictly speaking it implies nothing about the extent of Phoenician knowledge of Greek myth. On such improvisations cf. J.A.S. Evans in his review of Fehling (n. 125). Fehling is contemptuous of the 'suggestive questioning' theory, but his characterization of a complex process, at all events tendentious, comes close to parody (e.g. at pp. 5, 54). At all stages of an inquiry conducted over a period of decades Herodotos will have laid before his interlocutors knowledge already obtained elsewhere; in the course of conversation he will have obtained new information from them, engendering modifications in the views of both sides. On the complexity of the decades-long process by which the final text was produced see also Canfora and Corcella (n. 105).

[151] Erbse, 'Fiktion und Wahrheit' (n. 125) 137 ff. is particularly cogent on this point, showing that the line reveals genuine historical thought, and is of a piece with many other examples of such thought in Herodotos. He also advances some reasons for thinking that the Persians really pushed this line about vengeance for the Trojan War as a kind of official propaganda.

[152] See above, p. 69.

[153] Leonard E. Woodbury, 'Poetry and publication: Theognis 769-772', *Collected writings,* edd. C.G. Brown, R.L. Fowler, E. Robbins, P. Wallace Matheson (Atlanta 1991) 483-90.

work. Woodbury points out that to us it seems that the three aspects of the operation are presented in the wrong order—it ought to be seek, compose, present—but that this betrays our allegiance to a literate culture; in an oral culture, the act of composition, in whole or part, occurs simultaneously with the act of performance. In a footnote Woodbury also suggested that the poem displays a rationalistic reduction of τέχνη into three parts, and should therefore be suspected of Sophistic influence and a fifth-century date.[154] Had he lived to put the *ultima manus* to this article, he would surely have quoted the parallel that in my view clinches his case; this is the second passage:

ἐγὼ οὖν, ὦ Πρωταγόρα, εἰς ταῦτα ἀποβλέπων οὐχ ἡγοῦμαι διδακτὸν εἶναι ἀρετήν· ἐπειδὴ δέ σου ἀκούω ταῦτα λέγοντος, κάμπτομαι καὶ οἶμαί τί σε λέγειν διὰ τὸ ἡγεῖσθαί σε <u>πολλῶν μὲν ἔμπειρον γεγονέναι, πολλὰ δὲ μεμαθηκέναι, τὰ δὲ αὐτὸν ἐξηυρηκέναι· εἰ οὖν ἔχεις ἐναργέστερον</u> ἡμῖν ἐπιδεῖξαι ὡς διδακτόν ἐστιν ἡ ἀρετή, <u>μὴ φθονήσῃς, ἀλλὰ ἐπίδειξον</u>.

Plato, Prot., 320b.

The context could hardly be more significant. The dialogue is Plato's portrayal of the master Sophist. Protagoras is about to deliver a showcase speech expounding his great theory of cultural development. At this juncture Sokrates says, 'I think you probably have something to say, because I think you have had great experience, have learned much, and have made your own discoveries as well. So if you have a clearer way to demonstrate how virtue may be taught, please do not begrudge it to us, but give us your demonstration.' As will readily be seen, the thought and the words are very close to those of the Theognidean passage. The σοφός has sought information and experience; this is μῶσθαι. On this basis he has made personal discoveries, αὐτὸν ἐξηυρηκέναι. Since ἐξηυρηκέναι is here distinguished from learning and experience, it presumably refers (as often in Herodotos) to drawing inferences on the basis of that learning and experience. That too is μῶσθαι, but it is also ποιεῖν. The σοφός then presents, ἐπιδεῖξαι, the results of his inquiry. Only unnatural anti-social sentiment, φθόνος, would induce a person to withhold beneficial knowledge; if he possesses it (εἴ τι περιοσσόν / εἰδείη ~ εἰ οὖν ἔχεις ἐναργέστερον), it should be shared.

The two passages are clearly related to one another; I suggest they are also pertinent to Herodotos. What is described in both of them is precisely ἱστορίης ἀπόδεξις. Like his opening, they are both proems: the Theognidean piece is self-evidently introductory to something else; in Plato, Sokrates is in a way providing Protagoras' proem for him, and it seems most likely that Plato has borrowed the language here from Protagoras' own works. The connection once again allows us to see Herodotos in the context of his own times. The opening up of vast new areas to human inquiry is one of the great characteristics of the age, in which Herodotos played his full part. He sought knowledge and, good Greek that he was, shared it publicly; we may be grateful that, if Herodotos' gods were φθονεροί, he was not. If his ἱστορίη occasionally involved more ποιεῖν—creation or individual discovery, filling in the gaps, last-minute adjustments in performance—than it did experience or learning, it is not to be wondered. For that matter, what did Protagoras really know about evolution? Not much; but it would be a most superficial use of words to say he made it all up. So too Herodotos. We should not require him to meet the standards of modern historiography. Instead, we should allow him to be what any admiring Greek would have called him: σοφός.

ROBERT L. FOWLER

University of Bristol

---

[154] 488 n. 16.

THE CONSTRUCTION OF XERXES' BRIDGE OVER THE HELLESPONT*

THE bridging of the Hellespont by Xerxes was a unique achievement. How was it done? The Chorus of Elders in Aeschylus' *Persians* expressed their wonder at 'the flax-bound raft', and Herodotus described the construction of the two bridges, each with warships as pontoons, with cables well over a kilometre long, and with a roadway capable of carrying a huge army. Classical scholars have generally found these accounts inadequate and even inexplicable, especially in regard to the relationship between the pontoons and the cables. The Hellespont has strong currents which vary in their direction, turbulent and often stormy waters, and exposure to violent winds, blowing sometimes from the Black Sea and sometimes from the Mediterranean. How were the warships moored in order to face the currents and withstand the gales? Did the warships form a continuous platform, or was each ship free to move in response to weather conditions? What was the function of the enormous cables? How and where were they made? Did they bind the pontoons together? Did they carry the roadway? How were they fixed at the landward ends? This article attempts an answer to these questions through the collaboration of a classical scholar and a mechanical engineer.

In 1988 I expressed my conclusions on this subject in the limited space which was available in *The Cambridge Ancient History* iv 527-32. They were based on the description by Herodotus, which I, unlike Macan, found to be neither 'inadequate' nor 'unintelligible', and on an amateurish knowledge of bridge-structures which I had acquired for purposes of demolition in time of war. A justification of some of those conclusions is attempted here; others are superseded. Moreover, while teaching in the University of Washington in 1993, I had the good fortune to discuss the technical problems with a mature student of history, Lawrence J. Roseman, who had retired as the Program Manager of the AWACS Airplane 'Radome' of the Boeing Company, whose engineering expertise is in stress analysis. As he had further new ideas, we decided to undertake a joint article. I have written 'Testimonia' and 'Commentary', which deal with the ancient evidence, and Mr. Roseman has written the section 'Feasibility of the Reconstruction'. Finally we give a 'Summary of the Main Arguments', to which we both subscribe.

N.G.L. HAMMOND

A. TESTIMONIA IN TRANSLATION

1. Herodotus vii 25.1. For 'the bridges' over Strymon 'Xerxes was preparing also cables of papyrus and white-flax, issuing his orders to Phoenicians and Egyptians.'

2. Herodotus vii 33. 'Between Sestus city and Madytus there is a rugged headland coming down to the sea opposite Abydus' (*cf.* ix 120.4).

---

* The following abbreviations are used:

Burn	A.R. Burn, *Persia and the Greeks* (London 1962)
CAH	*The Cambridge Ancient History* iv (Cambridge 1988) eds. J. Boardman, N.G.L. Hammond, D.M. Lewis and M. Ostwald
Casson	Lionel Casson, *Ships and seamanship in the ancient world* (Princeton 1971)
Chapman	Charles F. Chapman, *Piloting, seamanship and small boat handling* (New York 1958)
H. and W.	W.W. How and J. Wells, *A commentary on Herodotus* i and ii (Oxford 1912)
Kutz	Myer Kutz ed., *Mechanical engineer's handbook* (New York 1986)
LSJ	H.G. Liddell, R. Scott and H.S. Jones, *A Greek-English lexicon* (Oxford 1953)
Macan	R. Macan, *Herodotus vii-ix* (London 1908)
Maurice	F. Maurice, 'The size of the army of Xerxes in the invasion of Greece, 480 BC', *JHS* i (1930) 210-35
Myres	J.L. Myres, *Herodotus: father of history* (Oxford 1953)

3. Herodotus vii 34. 'Starting from Abydus the appointed persons were bridging, Phoenicians the bridge of white-flax and Egyptians that of papyrus. From Abydus to the land opposite is seven stades. But a great storm chopped it all up and broke it apart.'

4. Herodotus vii 36.1. 'They bridged as follows. Placing penteconters and triremes together, 360 under the bridge facing the Black Sea and 314 under the other; and in the Black Sea one (they were) at an angle and in the Hellespont one (they were) according to the current,[1] in order that he might relieve[2] the tension of the cables.'

5. Herodotus vii 36.2. 'After placing them together, they let down very long anchors, those facing the Black Sea in the one (bridge) because of the winds that blow out from within (that sea), and those in the other (bridge) facing the evening and the Aegean because of the west wind and the south wind. And they left a narrow space as a way through the penteconters and (? the triremes at three places)[3], in order that anyone wishing to sail in light craft both to and from the Black Sea could do so.'[4]

6. Herodotus vii 36.3. 'After doing that, they began to extend the cables from the land [cf. Hdt. iv 72.4 χαλινοὺς...κατατείνουσι ἐς τὸ πρόσθε, and see LSJ s.v. κατατείνω i 4 and 6] twisting the cables with wooden donkeys (i.e. capstans), no longer employing the two types separately but for each bridge dividing them so as to be two of white-flax and four of papyrus. Thickness and fine quality were the same, but the flax ones, of which a cubit weighed a talent, were heavier relatively.'

7. Herodotus vii 36.4-5. 'When the strait was bridged, they sawed up tree-trunks, and making them equal to the width of the raft they arranged them in order on top of the taut cables, and after placing them there in order they joined them at the top thereafter. That done, they piled brushwood, and placing the brushwood in order they piled up earth, and beating the earth down firmly they drew a palisade alongside, on this side and on that, to prevent the draught-animals looking over at the sea and being frightened.'

8. Herodotus viii 117. 'They did not find the rafts still tight-stretched but broken apart by a storm.'

Herodotus ix 114. 'They found the bridges broken apart, which they expected to find tight-stretched.'

9. Herodotus ix 115. 'Oeobazus a Persian had brought the cables from the bridges' (to Sestus).

Herodotus ix 121. 'They sailed off to Greece, taking the cables of the bridges . . . to dedicate at the shrines.'

---

[1] The words τοῦ μὲν Πόντου and τοῦ δὲ Ἑλλησπόντου resume τὴν πρὸς τοῦ Εὐξείνου Πόντου and τὴν ἑτέρην. They are not dependent on ἐπικαρσίας and on κατὰ ῥόον, as Grote, Rawlinson and Macan suggested (H. and W. ii 142); for that interpretation would reqire a different order of words and there is no sense in the proposed translation 'at right angles to the Black Sea.' See Myres 222, who translated as I do. D. Hill, *A history of engineering in classical antiquity* (London 1984) 65 followed Rawlinson.

[2] The subject of ἀνακωχεύῃ is uncertain. H. and W. ii 143 supposed it was 'the bridge (i.e. here the moored ships)', but they had just said that 'Herodotus regarded the cables with the roadway as the true bridge.' I suppose that Herodotus had Xerxes' engineer in mind as the personal subject.

[3] See the *apparatus criticus* of the Oxford Classical text for suggested emendations. Since τριηρέωνand τριχοῦ begin with the same three letters, one word could easily be omitted by a scribe. There are no paleographical grounds for emending τριχοῦ to διχοῦ (H. and W. *ad loc.*)

[4] The importance of providing more than one bridge, for instance at the Hellespont, was appreciated by Maurice 224-5. But H. and W. ii 169 wrote of 'the bridge' despite the plural word at vii 25.1 and vii 114-5.

10. Aeschylus, *Persae* 68-73. 'The royal army . . . crossed the strait on a flax-bound raft, casting a much-bolted way as a yoke upon the neck of the sea.' 104 'trusting in light-made ropes and people-carrying devices.' 130-1 'crossing the sea-washed headland which yokes both sides in common of the two continents.' 722 'he yoked the Hellespont with devices.' 736 'he was glad to reach the bridge which yokes two continents.' 745 'he hoped to check the flow of the sacred Hellespont like a slave, with shackles, the Bosporus a god's river, and he devised a new form of crossing, and throwing hammer-wrought fetters around it he created a great pathway for a great army.'

11. Arrian, *Anabasis* v 7.2. 'If the narrows (of the Indus) were bridged with vessels, I cannot decide whether it was the case that, as Herodotus says of the bridging of the Hellespont, the warships being set together with ropes and lying at anchor in a row were sufficient to constitute the bridging.'

B. Commentary on the Testimonia

1. The first mention of cables in bridges was during the preparations for the invasion by Xerxes. For the bridge which was built for Darius over the Bosporus *c.* 513 BC was described as a 'raft' both by its architect, Mandrocles of Samos, and by Herodotus in his text (iv 88.1-2; 97.1; 98.3); and it seems that part of it was removed for the passage of Darius' flagship (iv 85.1). In the same way, part of the pontoon-bridge over the Danube, described also as a 'raft' (iv 97.1 and 98.3 σχεδίη), was removed and later replaced (iv 139.1 and 141). If this had been a cabled bridge, the cables would have been left in position.

Herodotus was interested in the material from which the cables for Xerxes' bridges over the Strymon were made. Papyrus, grown in Egypt, was probably well-known to the Greeks. But 'white-flax' (λευκόλινον), later called λευκέα 'from Spain' (Athenaeus, 206 F) and evidently brought from there by the Phoenicians, was a form of esparto-grass, less well known. At least two bridges were built over the Strymon (not one, as Myres 219 and 228 wrote), in order not to have a bottleneck for Xerxes' huge forces. One was at Nine Ways (vii 114.1). Another was presumably at the mouth of the Strymon, then near Eion, where Xerxes had laid a dump of supplies (vii 25.2 Ἠιόνα τὴν ἐπὶ Στρυμόνι; *cf.* vii 113.1). The terrible winds which blew 'from the Strymon river' were famous (Aesch. *Ag.* 192 and Arist. *Vent.* 973 b 17, cited by H. and W. ii 274).

2. The headland (ἀκτή) was 'rugged' because it was rocky; and it was with reference to this headland that Strabo wrote of Xerxes' landing-place on the European side as the 'Apobathra' at the 'Sestian promontory' (591 and 331 fr. 55 Ἀποβάθρα καθ' ὃν ἐζεύγνυτο ἡ σχεδία). The starting-place for this bridge was not at Abydus city, which lay to the south of the strait, but within its territory.[5] It was undoubtedly somewhere on the low-lying coast east of Nagara Burnu. We are not told where the other bridge started and ended. Myres was probably correct in having it start at Nagara Point and end at the 'firm beach' west of the 'gravelly delta' of the stream on the European side. Stanley Casson[6] provided views of the very low-lying coast at and east of Nagara Burnu in his figs. 78 and 79. He noted from personal observation that 'the one long stretch of route along the European shore fit for lateral traffic and capable of being

---

[5] Maurice, taking Abydus to mean 'Abydus city', carried the bridges from the city over to the coast not of Sestus but of Madytus, reckoned the length of each bridge there as 4,220 yards, and exposed both bridges to changing currents (217). For the site of Abydus city, see J.M. Cook, *The Troad* (Oxford 1973) 56.

[6] *Macedonia, Thrace and Illyria* (Oxford 1926).

made fit for wheeled transport' was 'between Sestus and Gallipoli town' (214; *cf.* x [7]). This, he maintained, was the route used by Xerxes' army.[7]

3. Herodotus here stressed the novel feature of the bridges, namely the cables of white-flax and of papyrus; and it was with reference, it seems, to the cables that he added the distance of seven stades (1,295 m.),[8] as at iv 85.4. They were indeed very long cables. The width of the strait from Sestus to Abydus was given as 'not more than eight stades' (1,480 m.) by Xenophon, who knew the area well (*Hell.* iv 8.5). Strabo (125 and 591) and Pliny (*NH* iv 75) agreed with Herodotus. It seems best to accept Xenophon's figure and round it up to 1,500 m.

The distance today across the strait is some two kilometres. Since this crossing was much used throughout antiquity, and since the measurement was needed in 481 BC for instance, for making the cables, it is sensible to accept the ancient traditions. How and Wells wrote 'the difference may be explained by the washing away of the coasts by the strong currents' (ii 140). This would apply especially to the south coast, which is 'fringed, almost throughout its length, by a shallow bank which extends over half a mile offshore in some places' (*Black Sea Pilot*[10] 83). Another factor is the lower level of the Aegean by some five feet in antiquity.[9] Neither can a change in the level of the land since antiquity be excluded.

The destruction of the two bridges through 'a violent storm', such as is common in these waters (*Black Sea Pilot*[10] 21 and 84), was graphically described: 'a great storm chopped it all up and broke it apart' (χειμὼν μέγας συνέκοψέ τε ἐκεῖνα πάντα καὶ διέλυσε). Wind and wave evidently tore the warships of the pontoons from their moorings and snapped all the cables, of which some parts would be swept away waterlogged. For the emphatic 'all' included both ships and cables.

Herodotus completed his description of the first bridging and its after-effects, ending with the decapitation of the overseers. He begins the new bridging with the appointment of other directors (vii 36.1). There is no indication that any cables from the first bridging were re-used.

4. We may note that in the Persian fleet the triremes were decked (Plut. *Them.* xiv 2), and thus could carry more than thirty marines or other passengers (Hdt. vii 184.2; viii 118.2 *katastroma* in the singular). Since the Persian tactic was to ram and then to board an enemy vessel, the 'Ionian' triremes in the Persian fleet carried numerous marines (Hdt. viii 90.2, Samothracian javelin-men). The same was true of the penteconters; for they carried thirty men in addition to their fifty oarsmen (Hdt. vii 184. 3). The decks on the ships of the bridges made the roadway on them more stable and spread the load on each ship.

Herodotus described the stages of the construction one by one. In the first stage the warships (which were to become the pontoons) were placed in two lines across the channel, the eastern line being longer than the western line. The warships facing the Black Sea were at a right angle to the center line of the bridge. Those facing the Hellespont (τοῦ δὲ Ἑλλησπόντου being contrasted with τοῦ μὲν Πόντου) were 'according to the current', i.e., not at a precise right angle.[10]

The reasons for these different alignments are to be found in the local conditions. The warships of the eastern bridge were at a right angle to the center line of the bridge, because they

---

[7] Maurice, who seems to have been unaware of Stanley Casson's work, proposed an inland route on his map (218). The huge army certainly used more than one route (*pace* Casson and Maurice) in the Chersonese as in Thrace (see *CAH* iv 537-9), and not just the one route even for a 'double column, one of troops and one of transport' (Maurice 224).

[8] Maurice's location for the bridges made the distance to the other coast 4,220 yards, which is vastly more than seven stades (217). In making the stade 185 m. I follow P.A. Brunt, *Anabasis Alexandri* i (Harvard 1976) 488.

[9] For this calculation see Hammond's summary in *Ancient World* xxv (1994) 23-4.

[10] See (n. 1) above.

were facing 'the main current' which 'fills the whole width of the strait between Nagara Burnu and Bigali Kalesi (Fort)' (*Black Sea Pilot*[10] 25). Polybius commented on 'the swiftness and the violence of the current in the strait' (xvi 29.14). On the other hand, 'at a bend' (in the channel) 'the main current sets strongly towards the convex side', and this causes 'an eddy with a counter-current flowing northward along the shore' (*Black Sea Pilot*[10] 22). These antithetical currents could be exploited by merchant ships in making the crossing (Strabo 591).[11] It is evident that the warships of the western bridge were at somewhat different angles in relation to the center line of the bridge in order to face the current bow on, in each case. The purpose of these alignments was to offer the least possible resistance to the flow of water and thus to put the least possible strain on the cables of the anchors (which Herodotus described next). The reference in his word 'cables' (ὅπλα) here is not to the kilometre-and-a-half cables, which were affected only very remotely, but to the anchor-cables.

5. The unusually long anchors were evidently designed to hold fast against both the wind and the current which may reach a speed of three knots in the narrows and, under abnormal conditions, as much as five knots (*Black Sea Pilot*[10] 23). 'The holding ground is good' off the south shore (*ibid*. 83). I take it that the warships, when in position as pontoons, were anchored bow and stern.

'The narrow space' was to be used by 'light craft' (πλοίοισι λεπτοῖσι; *cf.* viii 137.2 τὰ λεπτὰ τῶν προβάτων), presumably low barges either under oar or under tow. The narrow space lay presumably between triremes, in order to give more headroom. The text, reading τριχοῦ or τριχῇ, can best be emended to τριηρέων τριχοῦ which would mean that there were three such spaces at places where the best use could be made of the main current and of the counter-currents.[12]

6. The translation which I have given described the twisting of the strands to make a cable. This was done with capstans, as they proceeded 'from the land' and reached the other coast. For the technique of cable-making see C 1. Capstans or 'donkeys' (as in the modern term 'donkey engine') had long been in use (probably since the seventh century; see J.J. Coulton in *JHS* xciv [1974] 12. n. 69).

The usual translation of this passage is that of G. Rawlinson. 'When all this was done, they made the cables taut from the shore by the help of wooden capstans'. Here he omitted the important word 'twisting' (στρεβλοῦντες, the tense being contemporary with κατέτεινον). Once the cables were made, 'tightening and twisting' them would have damaged them beyond repair. See C 1. How were the ends of the cables secured on land? Herodotus did not say. However, in *CAH* iv 531 I made what was, I think, an original suggestion, that the capstans and the cables were attached to land-piers. 'These piers', I wrote, 'had to take an immense strain. I imagine that narrow shafts (as in ancient mining) were sunk in the rock and that large timbers, reinforced perhaps with metal rods, were placed in the shafts, so that their tops formed the land-anchors of the cables. The cable-ends were set at about the same level as the roadway which they were intended when taut to carry.' The cables were continuous from shore to shore, each being some 1,500 m. long.[13] The slack in a cable was taken up when it was attached to its second land-pier. A method of doing so is suggested in C 5. Thereafter the cable was described as 'taut'.

---

[11] See H. and W. ii 143, whereas Maurice did not consider the currents in his siting of the bridges (216-7 with fig. 1).

[12] Thus corn-barges, running downstream, would have used a central opening in the bridges where the current ran fast, whereas the light craft, going up the Hellespont, would have used openings near the coast and taken advantage of the counter currents.

[13] Burn 320 judged the cables to be continuous and so 'about a mile long', and he reckoned that the heavier kind of cable would have weighed 'close on 100 tons'.

The landward ends of the roadway which was to lie on top of the taut cables were not described by Herodotus. We may suppose that on the south side the roadway was entered from the low-lying ground of Nagara Burnu and of the nearby plain (see B 2 above). On the European side, the northern end of the western bridge would have led onto the firm gravelly beach, and that of the eastern bridge would have reached the foot of the hill where the Apobathra was located. But the level of water was lower in ancient times, as we have noted.

Map: Xerxes bridges at the narrows of the Hellespont, based on British Admiralty Chart No. 1429.

Note:
In the time of Xerxes, the coast at either end of Bridge B was roughly the 20 metres dotted line, and the coast at either end of Bridge A was very roughly on the 30 metres dotted line. In the map, the bridges are shown extending from present shorelines, so that the reader can visualize them more easily.

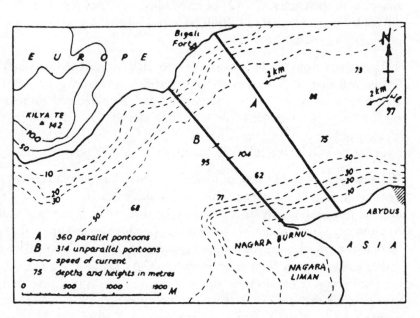

Herodotus was more interested in the materials used for the six cables of each bridge, and in the weight of the flax-cables. Where did he obtain this information? The answer is probably Samos, where he may have lived as a young man some twenty years after the building of the bridges; for Samos was the home of Mandrocles, the architect of Darius' bridges, and perhaps also of Harpalus, one of the architects of Xerxes' bridges (Hdt. iv 87-9 and *Laterculi Alexandrini* 8, ed. Diehls), and it is certain that Samos was one of the subject-states which provided manned warships for the bridges. For that reason the cubit was probably the royal Samian cubit of 527 mms. (H. and W. i 138), and the talent was that of Samos, namely the Euboic talent, which was in Ionia 'the basis of all calculation' (C. Seltman, *Greek Coins* [London 1933] 37). This talent weighed about 25.86 kilogrammes = 57.01 lbs. Herodotus made the point that the cables of flax were heavier than those of papyrus 'relatively' (LSJ s.v. λόγος ii 1), which I take to mean individually and not, as H. and W. ii 144 argued, 'the four byblos (papyrus) cables were absolutely heavier than the two esparto-grass', which would have been a glimpse of the obvious.

7. With the pontoons anchored in place and the cables taut over them 'the strait was bridged'. Next, as I understand the passage, they made planks as wide as the tree-trunks, placed a number of planks together so as to equal the width of the 'raft', i.e. the pontoon whether a trireme or a penteconter, and arranged the groups of planks in order on top of the cables and joined the groups together 'at the top', probably with a loose tie. The aim was to have the planking flexible where it passed from one pontoon to the next pontoon, so that, if one pontoon should rise and its neighbour should fall somewhat, the planked roadway would not be disrupted. The addition of brushwood and then of compacted earth provided the continuous roadway which ran

on over the junction of one pontoon and its neighbour and which rested on the cables. The result was a natural track for cavalry horses and for draught animals yoked to a waggon. The palisades were erected at the edges of the planks.[14]

8. Herodotus used different expressions when he described (1) the destruction of the original bridges of Xerxes and (2) that of the bridges used by the army crossing to Asia. For (1) he used two verbs συνέκοψέ τε...καὶ διέλυσε (vii 34), where I suggested that συνέκοψέ meant the snapping of the cables. For (2) he used only one verb διαλύω. The implication is that in (2) the cables were not snapped. Both pontoons and cables were parts of 'the bridges' which had previously been 'taut' (ix 114).

9. The cables from the bridges (ix 115 τὰ ἐκ τῶν γεφυρέων ὅπλα) were safeguarded first at Cardia and then at Sestus as the best fortified stronghold, in case they were needed for the construction of other bridges. Since they had been secured to land-piers, they had not been carried away by wind and wave during the storms. Thus there were twelve cables, each 1,500 m. long, at Sestus. When the Athenians sailed from Sestus to Athens, they took presumably only a section or two of the cables to be offerings to the gods.

10. Aeschylus probably served in the fleet which laid siege to Sestus in 479/8 BC. He produced his *Persae* in 472 BC, when many of his audience had seen the cables and the sites of the original bridges. Aeschylus referred to the distinctive features of Xerxes' bridges: (1) 'a raft' (σχεδία); (2) 'flax-bound' (λινοδέσμῳ), 'finely-wrought ropes' (λεπτοδόμοις πείσμασι); (3) 'people-carrying devices' (λαοπόροις μαχαναῖς), 'a much-bolted way' (πολύγομφον ὅδισμα), and 'a great pathway for a great army' (πολλὴν κέλευθον πολλῷ στρατῷ). Of these phrases the third group referred to the skilfully devised roadway. In the first and the second we have the two main features of the structure, as in the account by Herodotus. In addition, Aeschylus seems to have referred in an allusive phrase to Xerxes' landing-place, the 'Apobathra', when he wrote that 'the host together with its commander, having passed the sea-washed promontory which yokes both sides in common of either continent, has disappeared' (τὸν ἀμφίζευκτον ἐξαμείψας ἀμφοτέρας ἅλιον | πρῶνα κοινὸν αἴας, vv.131-3); for no news of what had happened in Europe had reached the capital at Susa.

11. Arrian seems to be in error. His phrase 'the warships being set together with ropes' (ξυντεθεῖσαι αἱ νῆες σχοίνοις) implied that the ropes tied the ships one to the other (see C 3 below). That is not what Herodotus wrote; for at vii 36.1-2 there was no mention of cables (see B 4 and 5 above). Arrian was probably misled by his knowledge of the Roman method of bridging wide rivers, according to which one ship was tied to another by planks (*Anab.* v 7.4). Myres made the same mistake: 'the ships (of the eastern bridge) were lashed four-square to the cables' and 'the remedy was to lash each ship first by the bows to the upstream cable ... and to lash it astern to the downstream cable' (222). He thought too that 'each bridge, being to leeward of the other, needed no moorings on its own inward side', as if a northerly wind and a southerly wind were blowing simultaneously and meeting one another at the bridges continuously. Macan, followed by H. and W., thought that each cable consisted of eight or ten separate pieces, and that each piece tied a number of pontoons together, which could be moved about as a unit, a sort of 'mulberry' in the terms of 1944. H. and W. put forward an

---

[14] Herodotus vii 55.1 reported that the armed forces and Xerxes himself crossed on the eastern bridge, while the draught animals and the retainers crossed on the western bridge. If the camels crossed on the latter bridge, the palisade would have been high to prevent them seeing the water. On the other hand they might have been transported by ships, for the fleet was also available.

incongruous argument. 'If Herodotus means that the cables were all in one piece, he is of course wrong as the weight would be too great; doubtless each was made in eight or ten pieces; the length of modern cables is 720 ft.'(ii 144). The weight of a cable was the same whether it was in one piece or in ten pieces, and the length of modern cables is irrelevant.

Additional comment. R. Macan criticised Herodotus for not explaining in his account how the warships were manoeuvred into position alongside one another. What Herodotus did tell us was that 674 penteconters and triremes were provided on Xerxes' orders by some of his subject states (vii 21.2). We can guess that those states included Greek states in the islands and in Asia which were under Persian rule. These ships were of course manned, were brought by their crews to the Hellespont, and were therefore manoeuvred by them into the two lines. No doubt one warship was towed into position by a warship under oar, was anchored, and then set free. Arrian described a similar technique in Roman times (*Anab.* v 7.3). There are of course other points which we should like him to have told us: for instance, how the cables and the capstans were secured on land, whether all the pontoons were anchored bow and stern, whether the very long anchors were additional to these, and so on. But we have to remember that Herodotus was not writing a monograph on the construction of these bridges. Instead he told us what he judged would enable us to understand how the Hellespont was bridged and how Xerxes' army was able to cross from Asia to Europe in seven days and seven nights (vii 56.1). How wide, for instance, was the roadway? The Greek road from the Megarid towards Plataea which was used by waggons in 479 BC was some 9 ft. wide, and a later road near the top of the pass through Mt. Gerania averaged some 12 ft. wide. Because penteconters, even when not at right angles to the line of the bridge, could accommodate a roadway of 12 ft., I suggest that the roadways on Xerxes' two bridges were of that width.[15]

C. FEASIBILITY OF THE RECONSTRUCTION

The bridges described in Herodotus were well within the capacity of the engineers of the day to design and build. Herodotus' description provides the clues to the design but, since he was not an engineer, those clues are ambiguous and have given rise to several varying interpretations of the bridge's construction. Joining basic engineering principles to Herodotus' account allows us to create a credible reconstruction: we argue that Herodotus was describing the construction of a pontoon bridge, the cables for which were made in place. The cables are the key to this argument.[16]

---

[15] This would allow for a column of four armed men abreast and of two cavalrymen abreast. Maurice thought of 'a column of troops in fours' at narrow places on the route, of which the bridge-roadways are examples. It is thus credible that the crossing of the two bridges did take a week, day and night.

[16] Basic articles in the *Encyclopaedia Britannica* 1957 and 1993 describe a process which is entirely compatible with Herodotus' account. Both show that 'capstans' ('donkeys') are used in several phases of the manufacturing process: 'Friction on the revolving capstans draws the yarn through the machine' (1957, xix 546). 'Strands also known as readies are formed by twisting yarns...together' (1993, x 176). Three or more strands are twisted (laid) into a rope (the 1993 edition is more apt to use the word 'flyer' than capstan). 'The three subassemblies of the rope-laying machine arranged in tandem horizontally, are the foreturn flyers (rotating strand bobbins), the capstan flyer (pulling mechanism), and the receiving flyer (rope-twisting and storage bobbin mechanism)' (1993, x 176). Instead of winding the rope 'onto a heavy steel bobbin', the floating 'raft' was used as a 'ropewalk' (before removing any ships to make the gaps described in Herodotus) over which the rope was laid *in situ* and the final capstan was on land. It should be noted that any twisting of a finished cable or rope will either create kinks or unlay (unwind) the strands of the rope. Therefore, the words of Herodotus *cannot* be describing what was done to the finished cables.

1. Feasibility of making cables *in situ*

The elements of a cable are ropes, made in three basic stages. First, raw fibres are spun into yarn by twisting together a continuous series of overlapping fibres so that the force of friction will grip them and provide its strength. Second, a chosen number of yarns are twisted together to form a strand in a manner similar to that of spinning yarn, except that one starts with 20, 30 or more twisted yarns instead of a series of loose fibres. And third, strands are 'laid' or twisted together to form a rope in a process called 'closing the rope'. Most ropes have three strands. The key to cohesion is in the direction of the twist. At each of the three stages the twist is in a different direction: the strands are twisted against the direction of the yarns and the rope against the strands. The result is a balanced energy pattern which stops any tendency for the rope to unwind.

Using those tools, techniques and material handling capacities available at the time, we can reconstruct a process of cable-making for the bridge. It would seem that bales of fibre were brought to the bridges' site in ships. First the bales were opened and sorted into bundles small enough for one man to handle. Then the flax was drawn through a coarse 'heckle' (some call it a hatchel) which is a wooden board with perhaps forty iron pins, each a foot long, arranged in rows—one side inclining from the workmen. The men would grasp a handful of flax and draw it through the heckle pins, dividing the fibres, cleaning and straightening them in preparation for spinning.

Spinning frames would be erected on land (in pits similar to that of FIG. 4 but upright) well back from each bridge-end. We may think of a frame technologically akin to those of the early 1800s, which had eight hooks extending from the rim of a stationary wheel, each hook inserted into a small capstan on the other side of the rim. The capstans were rotated at a very high speed by a pulley rope connected to a large driving wheel turned by hand. Each spinner would wrap a bundle of fibre around him and, taking hold of the middle of the fibres, attach them to the rotary motion of his hook that supplied the twist. As the hooks spun, he would walk backwards away from the frame, keeping the fibres taut. With one hand he would feed new fibres from his bundle into the forming yarn and with his other hand he would keep the newly spun yarn round and smooth. All spinners would walk backwards the full length of the pontoons 'extending the yarns from the land'; a simple yoke with men at either end walking forward and a harness in the center around a spinner would provide stability when moving from one ship to another or when the ships moved up and down. When they reached the opposite spinning frame, the yarns would have been taken off the hooks. So that the yarns would not sag on the ship decks, they were supported (every few yards) by trestles with vertical pegs on them to separate the yarns. The spinners were able to continue making yarn by using the spinning frames positioned on the 'far' shore and working their way back to the 'near' shore. This process continued until all the yarn required was spun; to account for subsequent twisting operations, it would be much longer than the finished cable. The 125 ft. length of each penteconter, tied to adjacent ships, created cross-channel pontoons which could accommodate several spinners working side by side with multiple spinning frames erected at each bridge site to speed the process.

The number of yarns per strand for our cable can be calculated by reference to early modern rope-making; 'To find the number of yarns . . . per . . . strand for any three-strand cable laid: multiply the square of the cable by the size of the yarn, and divide by 36.'[17] For our 27 in. cable (see C 4(2) below) and assumed yarn:

---

[17] Robert Chapman (formerly foreman to Mssrs. Huddart & Co., Limehouse; and Master Ropemaker of H.M. Dockyard, Deptford), *A treatise on ropemaking as practiced in private and public ropeyards, with a description of the manufacture, rules, tables of weights, etc., adapted to the trade, shipping, mining, railways, builders, &c.,* (Philadelphia 1869) 22.

$$\frac{(27)^2}{36} \times 18 \; = \; 364 \;\; yarns \; per \; strand$$

Before recent technological developments, a strand had to be made by 'attaching' the required number of yarns to one hook on a stationary 'donkey' and to another hook on a travelling 'donkey'. The stationary 'donkey', anchored in the ground in a rock lined pit, had the capacity to twist the yarns together by a rotary motion which contracts the forming strand and pulls the travelling 'donkey' towards the stationary 'donkey'. The yarns on the outside of the strand would bear more stress than the others and would break first. The object is to maintain a certain speed in a given time with respect to the travelling 'donkey', in order that the strand will receive a proper degree of twist in a certain length.

The third and final stage is that of 'closing' or laying the rope. At the 'near' shore were the stationary 'donkeys', and at the 'far' shore the travelling 'donkeys' were set up as sledges on smooth surfaces. Each pair was connected by a continuous drive-rope taken round capstans at the 'far' shore end of the rope walk. These capstans were operated by hand winches, with up to 220 men employed to close such large cables. The strands to be made into rope were laid out along the rope walk, supported and kept apart by the trestles, their ends connected to separate hooks on both the stationary and travelling 'donkeys'.

The first phase of this third stage was to 'tension' or 'harden' the strands, done by turning the hooks of both donkeys in a clockwise direction. As the strands were twisted they shortened and became tense. When the ropemaker in charge felt that the strands had received sufficient hardness of twist, the hooks were stopped: at the travelling donkey, the three strands were placed upon one hook; at the stationary 'donkey', the three strands remained on separate hooks. Then a cone of wood—a 'top', with three grooves cut into it to receive the strands—was inserted between the strands a short distance from the travelling 'donkey'. The 'top' acted as a guide which caused the strands to come together evenly. When the 'top' was fitted between uprights of an arch, then mounted on a horse, the hooks at both ends of the ropewalk were rotated. The travelling donkey had its hook put into reverse, so that it turned in an anti-clockwise direction, twisting the strands together into rope as they passed through the top-grooves. This action forced the 'top' (with the horse supporting it) down the ropewalk, and the ropemaker in charge walked alongside the horse, controlling the speed by means of a small piece of rope twisted around the newly formed rope. As the strands combined to form the rope, the distance between the two donkeys shortened, pulling the travelling 'donkey' down the 'far' shore. Weights were placed on the sledge to maintain tension in this phase. During closing, the strands were twisted together in the opposite direction to that of the forming process. To prevent them from unwinding, the hooks of the stationary donkey continued to turn in a clockwise direction. Once the 'top,' mounted on the horse, had travelled the length of the ropewalk, the rope had been made. The ends were tied off to prevent unravelling and then the hooks cut off. Then the 'spliced eyes' were completed at either end of a cable and inserted in the end restraint configuration of C 5.

The above reconstruction has been reviewed by England's last remaining Master Ropemaker, Mr. Fred Cordier who has spent 29 years (since a small boy) working at the Chatham Historic Dockyard, Kent. He has served in all phases of ropemaking, and today heads the ropewalk workforce. Mr. Cordier finds no fault in the concepts proposed here and while not being able to 'approve' some unknown details, he feels men of 480 BC could have made the cables *in situ*.

The cables were crucial to the bridge construction but there were several other, equally essential, elements: penteconters and triremes, anchors, roadway and end-restraints.

2. The Penteconters and Triremes

These represent the pontoons or rafted floats. Most of the ships are likely to have been penteconters because they were lighter and thus would offer less resistance to the currents. According to L. Casson 'a single-banked penteconter would run some 125 ft. in length. The beam would be about 13 ft.'[18] Triremes were probably used only at either side of the gaps, both for additional height (i.e. 8 ft. 6" waterline to deck) and to handle the extra loading.[19] Each trireme would handle one-half of the load over the gap, plus that sustained on its 16 ft. wide deck. The total weight of the bridge was supported by all the penteconters' and triremes' buoyant capacities which are well within any possible loadings. (See maximum loading configuration below).

3. The Anchors (fore and aft) (Fig. 1)

These were no doubt the design with removeable stock: the words 'very long anchors' (A 5 above) refer to the length of stock. As Casson points out (253), 'The essential weight the ancients put into the stock—the reverse of subsequent practice which was to put it principally into the arms and shank.' What he does not say is that they did not use chain in their 'ground tackle' (a general term for anchors, cables, chain, etc., anything used in securing a vessel at anchor) until years later. So the function of keeping the pull on the arms as horizontal as possible was performed by a heavy (removeable) lead stock, allowing the arms to 'stay put' or 'bite' and not lift out. Anchor dragging is the result of rope lines floating and lifting out the arms from their holding locations; thus, holding

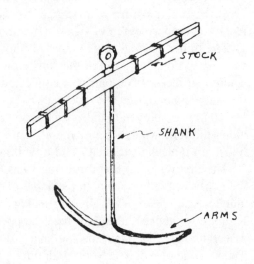

Fig. 1

power is proportional to the area of buried arm multiplied by the distance it is buried into the bottom. One of four components making up the load on an anchor is the wind pressure. Another component is the load due to current, equal to the resistance of the vessel travelling through water at the speed of the current. The third is the load due to surge while anchoring, and the fourth is the shock load due to the vessel's rising vertically on the sea, trying to lift the anchor.[20] These components can occur singly or in any combination. Any attempt to estimate the load to be resisted by these anchors would thus be wholly inadequate, since all of the factors are unknown for the early fifth century BC. Charles Chapman provides a table of suggested modern anchor weights (104), which for a storm anchor of a boat of 125 ft. would be 300 lbs. Another of his tables shows results of anchor-holding tests (104), with weights up to 31 lbs. Results varied from 9,600 lbs. in hard sand to 1,250 lbs. in very soft mud. These anchor weights are for the modern Danforth anchor and would be grossly inadequate for ancient anchors.

By placing the ships into prevailing winds, the exposed cross-sectional area above water was minimized. Also, anchoring 'into the current' helped to minimize the ships' resistance. Using mostly fifty-oared ships with lower profile and less draft was in-line with lightening the strain on the anchor cables.

The ships were lashed together to facilitate the laying of the anchors. First, the ship closest

[18] Casson, 54.

[19] J.G. Landels, *Engineering in the ancient world* (London 1978) 145, fig. 52.

[20] Chapman, 103.

to shore would be positioned and its anchors laid fore and aft. Then the next ship would be positioned alongside and lashed to the first one while the anchors from the second ship were placed in small boats and rowed to the appropriate locations fore and aft. The anchors would be lowered and the lines from the second ship pulled in until it was felt that the anchors dug in, a process still in use when many small boats wish to 'raft' together at one location. The lashing together served only the rafting process and would be of no structural significance once the bridge was completed. A solid line of ships was no doubt first laid in place to make the 'rope walk' as explained in B 6 above. After the cables were manufactured, ships could be removed as required for passage. Any lateral loads due to drifting at the passage site could have been addressed by extra lashings when conditions warranted. But it would seem probable that 'the narrow space' (B 5 above) would not be opened during unfavorable conditions.

4. The Roadway
The elements of the roadway are five: cables (six in number), planks, brushwood and earthen tread, palisades, plank joining concept.

Cables
(1) The cables 'of which a cubit weighed a talent' (A 6 above) can be configured using the following data: 1 cubit = 527 mm, 1 talent (Attic/Euboic) = 25.86 kg. = 57.01 lbs. (B 6 above). Thus, Herodotus' cables would have a wt/unit length = <u>32.97</u> lbs/ft which for a cable 1,500 m. long = <u>162,000</u> lbs. This includes water content as explained below. However, the weight stated in Herodotus was for rope as made *in situ*, which would include water content due to local humidity. A conservative estimate for such a marine location would be an 80% humidity level. At this level, water content of flax will equal 13% of dry measure.[21] Therefore,

$$1 \; talent \; = \; 57.01 \; lbs. \; = \; 113\% \; dry \; measure$$
$$and \; dry \; measure \; = \; \frac{32.97}{1.13} \; = \; \underline{29.176} \; lbs/ft$$

(2) Herodotus provides the unit weight of the cable. How do we determine its size? Using an analogy from the traditional art of rope-making, described in a manual dating to 1869,[22] we can make the following calculations, which are based on dry ropes. For the size of our cable we use: 'Rule for three-strand cable: to find the weight of 120 fathoms, square the size of the cable, and divide by 4.'[23]

$$Thus: \; \frac{(cable \; size)^2}{4} \; = \; X \; cwt. \, (long) \quad where \quad 1 \quad cwt. \; = \; 112 \; lbs.$$

Since our cable weighs 29.176 lbs/ft (dry), 120 fathoms weighs 187.56 cwt. Therefore, cable size = $[(4)(187.56)]^{\frac{1}{2}}$= 27.4 in. or approximately 27 in. *Herodotus' cables would thus be of a nominal circumference of 27" and a nominal diameter of 9"* (the rope-making industry uses 3

[21] Kutz, fig. 16.9.

[22] Chapman (n. 17) 6: 'This work has been written with the view of assisting the workman in obtaining a knowledge of the calculations necessary to the art of ropemaking; having in the course of my own practical employment, been frequently in want of such rules, and as often been disappointed when asking information of those it might have been expected from, I was in consequence, compelled to form rules to enable me to carry on the work and to answer questions put to me by the officers of the dockyards through the Lords of the Admiralty, and which were often very absurd; hence, the following rules and tables will be found chiefly to consist of those practical rules connected with the art of ropemaking.'

[23] Chapman (n. 17), 29-30.

as a conversion between circumference and diameter since a true cross section of a rope is not a true circle).

(3) For the tensile strength of our cable we use:
'Rule to calculate the tensile strength of a three-strand cable: square the size of the cable, and divide by 5.'[24]

$$Thus: \quad \frac{(cable\ size)^2}{5} \quad = \quad X\ tons\ (long) \qquad where\ 1\ ton\ =\ 2,240\ lbs.$$

$$Thus, \quad breaking\ strength \quad = \quad \frac{(27.4)^2}{5} \times 2,240 \quad = \quad 336,000\ lbs.$$

However, these rules reflect the use of Joseph Huddart's register plate and forming tube, invented in the 1790s. Their introduction doubled the strength of rope.[25] Therefore, dividing by two gives breaking strength = 336,000/2 = <u>168,000</u> lbs.

(4) The material about which Robert Chapman writes is hemp and our cable is flax. However, the density of hemp is exactly equal to that of flax,[26] resulting in the same weights.

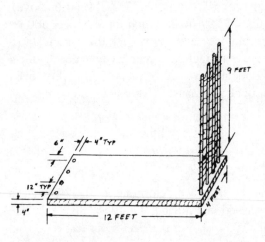

Fig. 2

Planks
The main bearing loads for traffic across the bridge were sustained by the planks cut from tree trunks. Hull planks of ships were made from fir, pine, cedar, and larch, but fir was the first choice.[27] It would follow that the first choice for roadway planks would also be fir. The width of planks taken from fir would be limited to about 4 ft. due to the natural size of the species. The length would be about 12 ft. (B 'Additional Comment' above). Thus, the roadway would be 12 ft. wide. The thickness of these planks would be in the order of 4 in.[28]

Brushwood and Earthen Tread. The brushwood is not described but can be envisioned to serve to span the gaps between planks, as well as a 'grid' to hold in place the layer of compacted earth laid over it.

Palisades. B 7 says 'the palisades were erected at the edges of the planks.' One configuration could be as shown in Fig. 2. Holes were drilled 4 in. from the edges at the spacing shown, with tree limbs of about 1 or 2 in. in diameter (at one end) thrust through the holes and lashed

---

[24] Chapman (n. 17), 31.

[25] Richard Holdworth and Brian Lavery, *The ropery visitor handbook* (Chatham [Kent] 1991) 12.

[26] Kutz, table 16.75.

[27] J.S. Morrison and J.F. Coates, *The Athenian trireme* (Cambridge 1986) 180.

[28] Ira Osborn Baker, *A treatise on roads and pavements* (New York 1908) 274: 'Plank roads were once somewhat common in the heavily timbered portion of the northern United States and of Canada. The first plank road on the continent was built in Canada in 1836... The method of construction most commonly followed is to lay down lengthwise of the road, two parallel rows of plank called sleepers or stringers, about 5 ft. apart between centers, and upon these to lay cross-planks 3 to 4 in. thick and 8 ft. long... The planks were often covered with gravel, sand, or loam to protect them from wear. ...when kept in repair, plank roads make a comparatively smooth roadway possessing some advantages for both heavy and light traffic...'

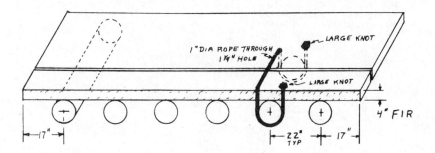

Fig. 3

together above and below the plank. Then smaller limb pieces with leaves were woven between the uprights, and additional brushy ferns added to make a solid screen 9 ft. tall.

Plank joining concept. B 7 says ' ... each plank being joined to its neighbour "at the top".' One configuration could be as shown in Fig. 3. Two holes of 1.25 in. diameter would be drilled at each cable location (adjacent to the cable and 4" from the plank edge), with a one inch diameter rope passed through one hole, down and round the cable. Coming up the other hole in the same plank and over to the next plank, it then passed down and around the cable, and up through the fourth hole. Finally, a large knot would be tied in one end, and after pulling tight (to draw the cable up against the planks) another large knot would be tied in the other end (just above the plank surface). This arrangement stitched the planks together at six places and secured them to the cables at either side of the 'joint'. While only one cross-link per location would have been achieved, the total of six 'stitches' would have provided about 12,000 lbs. of tension capacity.[29] This design has the advantage over a continuous stitching concept in providing independent backup capacity in case of failure at one location. One failure in a continuous lacing concept would result in total rupture of the joint.

5. Configuration of End Restraints

The revelation that rope was being made in place, across the rafts (serving as a ropewalk), allows the description of the terminals as 'spliced eyes'. These eyes retain 95% of the rope's original strength.[30] A 'spliced eye' can be made with any size opening allowing a wrought iron post to be placed through it. Herodotus mentions in i 68 the journey of Lichas that brought him to Tegea. Here he 'watched the forging of iron...'. Since Lichas lived during the reign of Croesus, we know wrought iron was being made *c.* 560-546 BC, which of course predates the building of the bridges at the Hellespont. The post could then be lashed to a team of horses and pulled as it was positioned into a stone-lined shaft. Any desired pre-tensioning could have been done by this process; however, from a load-carrying capacity standpoint, no large pre-tensioning was required—or desired. In fact, since positioning of the cable ends should have been accomplished before adding the planks, brush, earthen tread or palisade, significant tension would have been introduced with the addition of all that weight bringing the cable down to rest firmly on the raft of boats. The details could be as shown in Fig. 4. The wrought iron post would be sized to accommodate two parameters, structural capacity and space limitations. If we

---

[29] 1" dia. approximately 3" cir. Breaking strength = 4,032 lbs. (per Chapman [n. 17]). Total breaking strength per joint = $\frac{4,032 \times 6}{2}$ = 12,000 lbs.

[30] Chapman, 197.

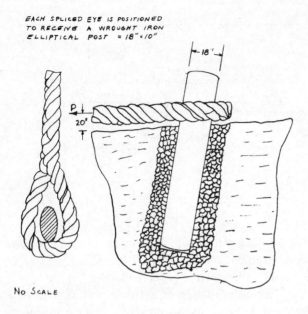

EACH SPLICED EYE IS POSITIONED
TO RECEIVE A WROUGHT IRON
ELLIPTICAL POST = 18"×10"

No Scale

Fig. 4

take the load 'P' of Fig. 4 to be that which ruptures the cable, and does not cause the post to fail or bend, we produce a configuration which retains the cable, and *not* the post, as the weak link. To that end we offer the elliptical shape 18 x 10 ins. The post would have been secured in a rock lined shaft to ensure the constraining moment of a cantilever beam. The maximum stress (Max s) would have been equal to the applied moment (M) divided by the section modulus (I/c) of a solid ellipse 18 by 10 ins.

$$Thus \quad Max \; s \; = \; \frac{M}{I/c} \; = \; \frac{168,000 \; lbs. \times 20''}{\frac{2862.8}{9''}} \; = \; 10,560 \; lbs. \; per \; sq. \; inch$$

Minimum stress to bend wrought iron = 25,000 lb. per sq. in.[31] Space requirements would be met by staggering the six posts. Then we would have the result shown in Fig. 5.

6. Bridge Analysis

Maximum Load Configuration. The maximum loading condition for a 13 ft. wide penteconter when being used as a bridge pontoon is made up of the following elements:

cables	13 x 32.97 *lbs/ft* x 6	2572
planks	13 x $\frac{4}{12}$ x 12 = 52.0 *ft*³ @ 39.96 *lbs/ft*³ [32]	2078
	(*Assume 13 ft. of solid board*)	
brushwood	(*Assume equal to* 1" *thick board*)	519

[31] *Marks standard handbook for mechanical engineers*[9] (New York 1987), table 5.1.1

[32] *Civil engineer's reference book*[4] (London 1989), table 31.6 'Timber properties'.

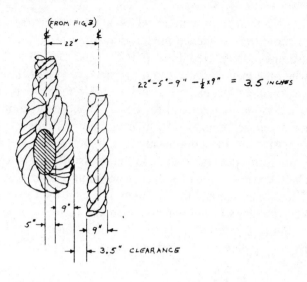

Fig. 5

earthen tread 13 x $\dfrac{3}{12}$ x 12 = 39.0 *ft*^{3} @ 125.0 *lbs/ft*^{3} [33]   4875

         (*Assume* 3" *of pressed loamy earth*)

palisades   13 x $\dfrac{2}{12}$ x 9 = 19.5 *ft*^{3} @ 39.96 *lbs/ft*^{3} 779

         (*Assume each side* = 1" *thick board*)   _____

         Total Dead Weight =   10823 *lbs*.

live load (*including dynamic loading* @ 2 *g's*)

         2 x 2 *abreast Nesaean horses* @ 1,000 *lbs*.   4000
         2 x 6 *men* (2 *ahead*, 2 *abreast*, 2 *behind*) @ 175 *lbs*.   2100

         Total Live Weight =   6100 *lbs*.

When the dead weight and the live weight are added together, the total maximum load on the penteconter is 16,923 lbs.

    The maximum loading condition for a 16 ft. wide trireme when being used as a bridge pontoon is the same as that for a penteconter per foot. But, instead of carrying only the 13 ft. loading of a penteconter, it carries the loading for its width of 16 ft. plus half the loading for the adjacent 16 ft. gap, or 24 ft. Supporting ramps would have been built in those locations where deck levels were uneven in order to assure uniform loadings. Thus the maximum load which a trireme has to carry is:

$$(\frac{24}{13} \times 16{,}923) \;=\; \underline{31{,}242} \; lbs.$$

[33] N.A. Lange, ed. *Handbook of chemistry*[6] (Sandusky, Ohio 1946) 1356.

Rather than attempting to calculate the capacity of these ships to sustain loading, it is possible to show from evidence in Herodotus that these maximum loads have been exceeded in actual use in antiquity. Herodotus (i 164.3) gives an idea of the capacity of a penteconter. In 540 BC, when the men of Phocaea on the coast of Asia Minor decided never to submit to Persia, 'they put on their penteconters their "children, women, all movable property" and some sacred objects, and they set sail for Chios.' Each penteconter was rowed by fifty oarsmen, and these men were accompanied by their families and possessions. If we assume that the average family consisted of the equivalent in weight to the weight of two and half men, and that the possessions plus the water and the foodstuffs for a voyage weighed half a man in each case, we shall arrive at a load for each penteconter, apart from the oarsmen, of the weight of 150 men. Thus, when we add the oarsmen, the total load is equivalent to 200 men. This is, of course, a very rough estimate, but it is adequate for our purpose. Additionally, each ship required basic 'running gear', i.e., oars, anchor lines, anchors, mooring lines, steering oars, a mast, sails, rigging, pulleys, etc. Thus weights for a penteconter in use:

crew (50) @ 150 lbs. ea.	7,500
load: weight of 150 men @ 150 lbs. ea.	22,500
oars 50 x 4.6 kg. [34]	500
anchor lines 6" cir, 2 lines, 200 ft. ea. [35]	500
anchors 2 @ 40 lbs.	80
mooring lines 4.5" cir, 2 lines, 100 ft. ea. [36]	140
steering oars (2) assume equal to 3 rowing oars, weight ea.	60
mast, sails, rigging, pulleys, etc.	500
penteconter calculated usage =	31,780 *lbs.*
(from p.103) maximum loading =	16,923 *lbs.*

Similarly, two other passages give the crew (vii 184.2) and fighting men (vi 15.1) numbers for a trireme in normal use. These, and the basic 'running gear' numbers provide weights for a trireme in use:

crew (170) @ 150 lbs. ea.	25,500
fighting men (40) @ 160 lbs. ea. (w/swords)	6,400
oars (170) x 4.6 kg.	1,720
anchors, anchor lines, mooring lines, steering oars,	
mast, sails, rigging, pulleys, etc. (same as penteconter)	1,280
trireme documented usage =	34,900 *lbs.*
(from p.103) maximum loading =	31,242 *lbs.*

Load Path Analysis. We consider now whether a whole bridge can sustain the total load, composed up of a vertical and a horizontal load.

Vertical: This component, distributed as a varying uniform load, produces reactions from ship buoyancy and, where the bridge is over land, the basic soil-bearing strength (Fig. 6).

Horizontal: A horizontal component also distributed as a varying uniform load is due to wind and water current forces. Reactions to these loads are from anchor line tensions and the holding

---

[34] J.F. Coates, S.K. Platis, and J.J. Shaw, *The trireme trials, 1988* (Oxford 1990) 52 describes advanced oar design weighing 4.6 kg. This figure is used both for the penteconter and the trireme oars.

[35] Casson, 250.

[36] Casson, 250.

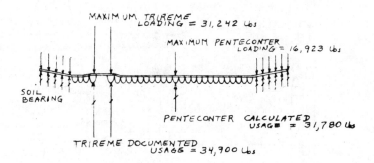

Fig. 6

power of the anchors. No reactions can be provided by the roadway cables.[37] (Fig. 7.) A secondary horizontal component, at right angles to the wind and current loads, is due to strain in the roadway cables as a result of ships moving up and down (due to wave action or local vertical loading). The resulting tension in the roadway cables is reacted through the end restraints (analysed on p. 102).

Category of Bridge. A simple analysis of the total dead weight of the roadway reveals further reasons for concluding that Xerxes' construction was a pontoon bridge.

$$Roadway \ length \ = \ 1,500 \ m. \times 3.28 \ ft/m. \ = \ 4,920 \ ft.$$

$$Total \ Dead \ Weight \ = \ \frac{10,823}{13} \ (p.103) \times 4,920 \ = \ \underline{4,096,000} \ lbs.$$

$$Total \ Breaking \ Strength \ of \ cables \ = \ 6 \times 168,000 \ (p.100) \ = \ \underline{1,008,000} \ lbs.$$

Modern day use of 'factors of safety' would dictate a minimum F.S.=5.0 and if human life were in danger, F.S.=10.0. The minimum F.S.=5.0 would reduce the total allowable working load, at each end, to

$$\frac{1,008,000}{5} \ = \ \underline{202,000} \ lbs.$$

Thus, the mere dead weight of the roadway is greater than the total capability of the cables, a characteristic of pontoon and *not* suspension bridges: the weight is simply too great to be suspended.[38]

7. Failure Analysis

The sequence in which elements of Xerxes' bridges failed can be envisioned as a reverse structural analysis of the assembly. That is to say, the weakest part will fail first and the strongest last. The loading condition will be a combination of the wind loads from the storm, creating direct horizontal loads and indirect vertical loads from wave action, and the dead weight loads of the bridge.

So let us visualize the scene. The wind is kicking up the water, causing waves of 6-8, maybe,

---

[37] If the roadway cables are attached to the boats (which they are not), the end restraint concept would be an inefficient manner to react what would then be additional tension in these cables. Perhaps they were attached in the first design of Herodotus vii 34 in which 'all' was lost. But they were not attached in the second design of Herodotus vii 36 so that the cables were still there in Herodotus ix 114. This allowed Oeobazus to have cable (at least pieces) to carry to Sestus.

[38] In a suspension bridge, half of the dead weight (2,048,000 lbs.), plus half of the live load (1,150,000 lbs.) would be supported (i.e., reacted) at each end. Since the present reconstruction allows for only 202,000 lbs. of allowable working load at each end, this is clearly *not* a suspension bridge.

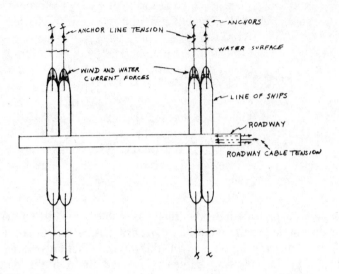

Fig. 7

10 ft. in height. The ships are bouncing up and down as well as against each other, all the while pulling at their anchors. The roadway dead weight is accelerated by the wave action and increases the downward thrust on the underlying ships. Rain may be pelting slantwise against the whole scene.

First, the palisades are blown away exposing the earthen tread to wind and rain. These forces soon scour the loamy earth away, attacking next the light underlay of brushwood, thus exposing the knots holding the walkway planks to wind-driven sand which cuts them like a knife. With no restraints to hold them in place, the planks become airborne 'missiles' weighing some 640 lbs. each with dynamic factors in excess of 5 g's. These planks randomly smash against the ships, acting with devastating effect. Even if the anchors held, the combination of flying planks, pounding wave action and adjacent ship-crunching would soon break up the formation and shatter the ships themselves. This would have left only the massive walkway cables still hanging together, provided they were not tied to the pontoon formation. However, the first set of bridges may have had their cables tied to the ships which would only serve to destroy them, as the cables would have been of smaller size which could not stand the vertical loading due to bouncing wave action. In the case of the second set of bridges, the exposed cables would not have experienced wind resistance forces large enough to rupture them (B 8 above).

No doubt, both cable size and anchor weights were increased by some significant amount as the new engineers tried to impress Xerxes with their improved bridge design. In fact, these are the only elements which could have been enlarged to increase the chances of survival.

D. Summary of the Main Arguments

We began with a close examination of the text of Herodotus, since it forms the basis of any reconstruction. It revealed the point that the cables of the first two bridges were destroyed. Twelve new cables, each 1,500 m. long, had to be provided. Where were they made? As a finished cable in humid conditions would have weighed not less than 162,000 lbs., it would have been laborious to manhandle and transport such a cable from Phoenicia, for instance, to Abydus. It was simpler to make it where it would be in use. It could have been made either on one shore, from which it would have to be hauled 1,500 m. to the other shore, or directly *in situ* on the pontoon bridge. A close look at Herodotus vii 36.8 and an understanding of how a cable is made (see C 1) enabled us to see that the cable-makers started on one shore ('from land') and worked on the pontoons 'extending while twisting on wooden donkeys (i.e. capstans) the cables' until they reached the other shore. The contemporary tenses (B 6) describe precisely the process of cable-making (C 1 'a number of strands are twisted together to make a rope'). No less important was the realisation that to 'extend and twist' a finished cable by force on capstans would damage the cable irreparably, thus ruling out the standard translation of vii 36.8, that of Rawlinson: 'they made the cables taut from the shore by the help of wooden capstans' (see B 6 and n. 16).

Once a cable was made from shore to shore, it had to be attached to land-piers or 'end restraints' (not described by Herodotus, but see B 6 and C 5). During the attaching process the slack of the cable had to be taken up, perhaps by the method suggested at the start of C 5, so that the cable was 'taut'. The cable's purpose, however, was not to act in suspension; for it could not carry even the total dead weight of the finished bridge. Rather it was, as Herodotus said, to form the basis of the roadway of wooden planking (vii 36.4 'arranged in order on top of the taut cables'; A 7 and B 7), in such a way that the cables not only held the roadway together but also provided the continuity and the elasticity which were needed in the gaps between pontoons (B 7).

The pontoon-bridges had to carry the entire weight of cables, roadway and traffic. Each pontoon, once it was manoeuvred into position, was anchored bow and stern with 'very long anchors' (A 5 and C 3); a study of ancient anchors and their holding power explains the expression 'very long' (C 3).

The above are the essential arguments. We have added the attendant circumstances, such as the configuration of the channel, the behaviour of the currents, and the character of the shores, which enable us to locate the bridge-ends. By far the most important gain is the demonstration in engineering terms that the bridges, which we have reconstructed in theory, would have worked in practice.[39]

N.G.L. HAMMOND
Clare College
Cambridge

L.J. ROSEMAN
University of Washington
Seattle

[39] We owe a special debt of gratitude to Professor Carol Thomas, whose enthusiastic interest and helpful comments have been an inspiration.

Journal of Hellenic Studies cxvi (1996) pp 108-118

THE INDEPENDENT HEROES OF THE *ILIAD*

MY objective in this paper is to consider the question of the mysteriousness or numinosity of the gods in the *Iliad* by examining first how heroes talk about and react to the gods, and second how Homer handles fate. My aim is to integrate the findings into a wider thesis about the *Iliad*'s narrative strategy.[1]

Griffin (1980) 152 discusses the mysteriousness and numinosity of Homeric gods, and cites *Il.* i 43-52, *Od.* iii 371-82, xix 33-42, saying 'It is perhaps worth emphasising that in each of these ... episodes, we see not only the god behaving like a real god, mysteriously, but also the characters who are present at the moment of revelation responding to it in what can only be called a religious way: adoration or reverent silence'. My point is very simple. This is not how the heroes themselves *talk* about the gods, nor (in the *Iliad* at any rate, I believe) is it how they *react* to them. To summarise my broad conclusions: when heroes talk about the gods, they talk of their power and their unpredictability. When they react to the gods, they do so as if they were reacting to very powerful humans, who may be friends or enemies. I see no indication anywhere in the *Iliad* of the heroes either talking about or reacting to the gods reverently, as if they regarded them as mysterious, numinous, venerable beings.[2] This, of course, is not to

---

[1] Two referees have acutely pointed out problems with the method. First, the work of Irene de Jong (1987) has blurred the crude distinction I wish to maintain between 'what humans say' and 'what the poet says'. Second, (here I quote the other referee) 'I would wish that the .. distinction between what "Homer" says and what "his heroes" say was qualified with reference to the variables of emphasis and projection ... sometimes it does not matter "who is talking" (because it hardly impinges on us). At other times it does impinge and it does matter'. To the first, I think I must say that if de Jong's work invalidates my thesis, so be it. I cannot see myself that it does. To the second, I think the weight of evidence for what I am arguing is so overwhelming as to override the 'variables of emphasis and projection' (which do, of course, exist). In other words, the heroes' view of the gods is so consistent throughout the poem that such variables, in this case, do not add up to enough to disturb the general thesis.

I refer to the following works by name and date: J.S. Clay, *The wrath of Athena* (Princeton 1983); I.J.F. de Jong, *Narrators and focalizers: the presentation of the story in the Iliad* (Amsterdam 1987); M.W. Edwards, *Homer, poet of the Iliad* (Johns Hopkins 1987); J. Griffin, *Homer on life and death* (Oxford 1980); A. Heubeck, S. West and J.B. Hainsworth, *A commentary on Homer's Odyssey vol. 1 introduction and books i-viii* (Clarendon 1988); J.B. Hainsworth, *The Iliad: a commentary vol. iii books 9-12* (Cambridge 1993); R. Janko, *The Iliad: a commentary vol. iv books 13-16* (Cambridge 1992); P.V. Jones, *Homer: Odyssey 1 and 2* (Aris and Phillips 1991); O. Jørgensen, 'Das Auftreten der Götter in den Büchern ι–μ der Odyssee', *Hermes* xxxix (1904) 357-82; G.S. Kirk, *The Iliad: a commentary vol. i books 1-4* (Cambridge 1985); G.S. Kirk, *The Iliad: a commentary vol. ii books 5-8* (Cambridge 1990); J.V. Morrison, *Homeric misdirection* (Ann Arbor 1992); M. Mueller, *The Iliad* (London 1984); S. Richardson, *The Homeric narrator* (Nashville 1990); T. Rihll, 'The power of the Homeric βασιλεῖς', in J. Pinsent and H.V. Hurt (eds), *Homer 1987* (Papers of the Third Greenbank Colloquium April 1987, *Liverpool Classical Papers* no.2), (Liverpool 1992) 39-50; R.B. Rutherford, 'Tragic form and feeling in the *Iliad*', *JHS* cii (1982) 145-60; A. E. Samuel, *The promise of the west* (Routledge 1988); S.L. Schein, *The mortal hero* (Berkeley 1984); M.S. Silk, *Homer: the Iliad* (Cambridge 1987); O.P. Taplin, *Homeric soundings* (Oxford 1992); W.G. Thalmann, *Conventions of form and thought in early Greek epic poetry* (Baltimore 1984); M.M. Willcock, *The Iliad of Homer books 1-12* (Macmillan 1978). All otherwise unmarked references are to the Oxford text of the *Iliad*. I am extremely grateful to Professor Alan Sommerstein and the *JHS* referees for their help, as I am to M.M. Willcock (University College London) and David West (University of Newcastle upon Tyne), who submitted an early draft of this paper to a searching ἔλεγχος, from which it emerged battered but considerably improved.

[2] The distinction that Homer maintains between his full, privileged understanding of events (expressed in the narrative) and human, partial understanding (expressed in what characters say) has been investigated by Jørgensen (1904), *cf.* Clay (1983) 1-25, Richardson (1990) 123-39, R.B. Rutherford, 'The philosophy of the Odyssey', *JHS* cvi (1986) 153 n. 43, M. Winterbottom, 'Speaking of the gods', *G&R* xxxvi no. 1 (1989) 33-41. *Cf.* the well-known phenomenon of human and divine proper names for the same thing (see e.g. Kirk [1985] on *Il.* i 403-4). de Jong (1987) 214 puts the case for the sort of analysis I wish to make as follows: 'when analysing divine interventions in the *Il.* one should distinguish systematically between the presentation and interpretation of NF₁ [i.e. the poet] and of the speaking characters. Differences between the two versions should not be ascribed, I think, to differences in religious belief or concepts between NF₁ and characters, but to a difference in narrative competence (the NF₁ is omniscient and knows more than the characters) or rhetorical situation' (here de Jong gives the example of Paris wishing to excuse his defeat vis-à-vis Helen). Taplin (1992) 129 says 'The Iliadic gods are a mixture of awesome

deny that when Homer as narrator describes the gods, he may invest them with these glamorous qualities.[3] But it is not the way his humans talk about them.

At the same time, I would like to raise a general question mark (no more) over the application of such terms as 'whim', 'the irrational', 'the inexplicable' to the heroes understanding of (that is, what the heroes say about) the gods. While the heroes are always saying the gods are unpredictable, I do not think it is nit-picking to assert that that is not the same as saying that they are whimsical or irrational.[4] The National Lottery and football pools are unpredictable, but they are not irrational, even if one fails to understand how they work.

I. TWO SCENES AT THE START OF THE *ILIAD*

At the start of the *Iliad*, Apollo inflicts a plague on the Greek camp for the insult done to his priest Chryses. Achilles knows plagues come from Apollo (i 64) and proposes action. Calchas confirms Apollo is angry and says Chryses' daughter must be returned (i 93-100). She is, with appropriate sacrifices (i 430-49), and Apollo is appeased (i 456-7). As a rational sequence of events in the eyes of those engaged in them, this is unimpeachable.[5] Everyone knows why the plague has happened. Appropriate action is taken and it ends. The god is seen as one who acts not randomly or mysteriously, but rationally. Humans therefore can analyse the problem correctly and come up with the solution. Indeed, we are close to magic here—'the art of influencing the course of events by compelling the agency of spiritual beings' (*SOED*)—only Homer suppresses the magical, and emphasises the rational. There is divine grandeur here, of course—Apollo's descent like night, the scenes of sacrifice, and so on. But such grandeur is evident in narrative, not speech.[6]

At i 188-222, Athena comes down from heaven at Hera's behest to prevent Achilles killing Agamemnon (i 195-6). As he is drawing his sword, she seizes him by the hair from behind (no one else sees this, Homer tells us - i 198). Achilles is amazed (he has just felt his hair pulled),[7]

---

power and quarrelsome pettiness, reflected in ethics by their mixture of roles as guarantors of justice and as amoral self-seekers'. The question I wish to clarify is 'in whose eyes?'

[3] Compare, for example, v 719-52, viii 41-77, xiii 17-31, xiv 346-51, xvi 431-61, 644-93, xvii 441-55, xviii 478-613 (and *cf.* Schein [1984] 51-2). See also e.g. oaths and sacrifice at n. 6, and the miracles on p.111. One may argue about the precise extent to which these passages demonstrate divine glamour and majesty (as a referee pointed out); but that humans never talk in these terms goes without saying.

[4] So, e.g. 'In the context of a society over which the Olympian gods rule, Achilles is pursuing an almost hopeless task...human success or failure can only be attributed to the whims or wills of the gods, fate, or both' (Samuel [1988] 45). '[The gods] function as a higher power, and provide an explanation of otherwise inexplicable events' (Edwards [1987] 125). 'For the human characters in the *Il.*, irrational evil comes from the gods' (Edwards [1987] 128, though he goes on to point out that for the poet, these evils are not irrational 'if one believe in gods like these'). I stress that these quotations are selected to serve my purpose: they are not supposed to characterise the whole picture of divine activity discussed in these works, which are extremely valuable and on which I shall draw in the course of this paper. I am obviously more in sympathy with e.g. Silk (1987) 30 and Mueller (1984) 125-33.

[5] Mueller (1984) 126 is aware of the reasonableness of the interaction between men and gods: when a god intervenes, 'the outcome is always an action that is perfectly intelligible in human terms.'

[6] Other sacrifices and oath-ceremonies are referred to with more or less elaboration at e.g. ii 305-7, 402-31, iii 268-301, iv 44-9, viii 548, ix 357, xi 726, 771, xxiv 33, 65-70. If I were to argue against my thesis, I would concentrate on passages like these, especially where the heroes call on the gods to witness oaths and curses. It is only here that I, at any rate, get any sense of the gods' numinous majesty expressed in a human's words, e.g. ii 402-18, iii 267-301, ix 453-7, 561-72, xix 257-68. Nevertheless, the ritual context of such passages is very strongly marked. This is special language for special events (*cf.* M. Leumann, *Homerische Wörter* [Basel 1950] 22-23). In Homer, such language is restricted to ritual occasions.

[7] A referee points out that Achilles' amazement may not be due to this, comparing e.g. iii 398 and iv 97 where the way the divinity looks to the human is enough to create θάμβος (*cf.* N.J. Richardson, *Homeric hymn to Demeter* [Oxford 1974] 188-90, though he does not deal with this passage). But at i 199, as the poet makes crystal clear, Achilles has not yet seen Athena because she approached him from behind. All he has done is felt her tugging his hair.

turns round and recognises the goddess by her glowing eyes (she is, after all, γλαυκῶπις)[8] (i 199-200). They discuss the situation, Achilles agrees to restrain himself in return for eventual compensation, replaces his sword, and Athena goes back to Olympus. Achilles' opening words to Athena hardly express reverent adoration: 'You see what Agamemnon has done to me? He'll pay for it'. He may have been amazed when he felt his hair being pulled, but no such feeling registers when he sees the goddess. He sheathes his sword only when Athena has given him a firm promise of compensation for Agamemnon's insult. This is not the attitude of a man who is overwhelmed by the divine presence. Nor does Athena speak like someone who is used to commanding men's unquestioning obedience: observe her polite αἴ κε πίθηαι (207) and πείθεο δ' ἡμῖν (214). As Willcock (1978) on i 207 remarks 'The goddess can advise but she does not compel: the decision and the responsibility remain with Achilles'.[9]

This scene is unquestionably impressive and thoroughly divine in character (those shining eyes at i 200). Griffin is surely right to reject the argument that the passage is 'little more than a figure of speech' for a change of heart in Achilles (Griffin [1980] 158-60). But what numinosity there is in the passage lies in the narrator's scene-setting, not in what his characters say.

It is remarkable, in fact, how characters respond when they come, or think they might have come, face-to-face with divinities: they might as well be facing very powerful humans. At iii 399-412 Helen with a passionate outburst refuses to do what Aphrodite has asked of her —even, surely ironically, addressing Aphrodite as δαιμονίη at 399 (see Kirk [1985] ad loc.). She has to be threatened into obeying (414-17). At v 180-91, Pandarus wonders whether it really is Diomedes he has been shooting at (181), or whether it is Diomedes protected by a god (185-6), or a god (183). From the way he talks, it seems all the same to him: his only reaction is to vow to smash his bow if ever he gets home (212-16). At v 433 Diomedes sees clearly that Apollo is protecting Aeneas, but still attacks him: he desists only when Apollo calls on him to retreat, which he does—a little (τυτθὸν ὀπίσσω—v 440-3). Griffin (1980) 155 is right to remark on the grandeur of Apollo's rebuke: my interest is in Diomedes' cool reaction. He is not even afraid of the god, merely careful to avoid (ἀλευόμενος) his wrath (cf. Silk [1987] 87). In v 596-606, Diomedes observes that Hector has Ares with him. He shivers and stops, baffled, like a man unable to cross a seething river, and then calls on the Greeks to retreat in orderly fashion—there is no taking on the gods in combat.[10] At v 800-824, Athena rebukes Diomedes for not being as good as his father Tydeus. Diomedes answers that he is merely following her instructions. See, for further examples, vii 43-53, xi 195-213, xiv 361-87, xv 236-62, xvi 513-31 (where Glaucus at least has the grace to recognise the god and rejoice [γήθησεν] when Apollo hears his prayer and heals his wound), xvii 326-431, xviii 169-201, xxi 284-300. Had these encounters not been with gods but with humans, there would have been nothing remarkable about the exchange of views expressed.[11]

---

[8]   If this is what γλαυκῶπις means: cf. e.g. Kirk (1985) on i 200.

[9]   A referee draws my attention to Zeus's 'compulsion' of Achilles at xxiv 116, expressed in the same way. This is how gods and humans frequently interact in the Il.. Rihll (1992) 46 argues strongly that power is negotiable in the Il.: 'neither Zeus nor Agamemnon have an unchallenged right to command' and need to adopt different tactics (from bluster to persuasion) to get their way.

[10]   A referee adds v 407, where Dione tells Aphrodite how foolish Diomedes is to fight the gods—that man does not live long—and vi 128-41, where Diomedes informs Glaucus that he will not fight with him if he is a god.

[11]   Even this analogy has its weaknesses. I can find, for example, only seven places where humans fear the gods (iii 418, v 827, 863, ix 244, xx 380, xxi 248, xxiv 170) and four where they fear Zeus's thunderbolt (vii 479, viii 77, 138, xvii 594-96). I discount xiii 624, xxiv 358, 689. As for humans fearing humans, I gave up counting when I reached fifty examples. Again, the heroes rarely acknowledge the gods even when their prayers are answered. They sometimes rejoice, like Glaucus at xvi 530-1 or Achilles at xxii 224 (though note that at xxii 393 Achilles claims the victory was all his doing), but more often than not they carry on without any acknowledgement at all, e.g. Ajax at xvii 645-55. A notable exception is x 570-1.

II. THREE MIRACLES

(*i*) iii 369-447: Aphrodite rescues Paris from death at Menelaus' hands, and carries him off to deposit him in Helen's bedroom. Aphrodite then summons Helen to join him. Menelaus searches in vain for his vanished opponent. The breaking of Paris's chin strap (iii 375) is assigned by the poet to Aphrodite but it is capable of a natural explanation and Menelaus is not surprised by it. He nonchalantly lobs the empty helmet into the crowd (iii 377-8), and turns to finish off his enemy (iii 379-80). It is at this moment that the miracle happens and Aphrodite wraps Paris in mist and whisks him away (iii 380-2).

Homer has described to us, his audience, a supernatural event. The question is: how do his characters respond to it? Paris makes no response at all. To judge from his words, no miracle has taken place. This is strange, since he was its beneficiary, and it was something to boast about when a god openly helped a hero (*cf.* e.g. xxii 270-1). Does the rather cryptic παρὰ γὰρ θεοί εἰσι καὶ ἡμῖν (440) constitute his reaction? Menelaus too expresses no surprise and makes no attempt to explain what has happened. Hector does not enlarge on the matter either at vi 326-31. In other words, the characters treat what is presented to us as a transparent miracle as if it were a given, a *datum* of human experience. They certainly do not speculate on the irrational or the inexplicable.

(*ii*) xx 321-52: Poseidon blinds Achilles, thoughtfully extracts Achilles' spear from Aeneas' shield and returns it to him (Achilles, of course, will need it when he meets Hector), and then hoists Aeneas up and away across the ranks to the edge of the fighting. Achilles angrily (ὀχθήσας) exclaims that he sees a μέγα θαῦμα because the spear lies on the ground but there is no Aeneas, but, unlike Menelaus, draws the right conclusion: the gods have intervened to save his opponent. 'What the hell', he concludes (ἐρρέτω): he won't be back in a hurry. One cannot say there is much 'adoration or reverent silence' here. Achilles is equally brusque with Apollo at xxii 20. Apollo has disguised himself as Agenor and led Achilles a merry dance. Apollo mockingly reveals himself and the furious Achilles says he would take his revenge on him, if he were able. This is the way a hero can, admittedly *in extremis*, address a god in the *Iliad*.[12]

(*iii*) xvi 786-867: Patroclus charges for the fourth time, and Apollo hits him. He knocks off his helmet, shatters his spear and breaks his corselet. Euphorbus stabs Patroclus as he tries to retreat, and Hector finishes Patroclus off. They exchange words before Patroclus dies.

As Griffin rightly says (Griffin [1980] 153), 'The combination of mystery, power, and effortlessness, marks this as a divine intervention': it is surely a scene unmatched in intensity, pathos and potency in the *Iliad*. Yet this transformation elicits no comment from any human actor. It might all be a mystery to us, but it is not to them. It is left to Patroclus to point out that (though he did not see them) divine agencies were involved: first, Zeus and Apollo, both of whom (he seems to think) stripped him of his armour (xvi 843-6); then fate and Apollo 'killed' me, he says (xvi 849, as do Achilles' horses at xix 411-14), and of men Euphorbus. That this is not what in fact happened (to be pedantic) is interesting. But then, how could Patroclus know? He was attacked *from behind* (xvi 79, *cf.* Athena's approach to Achilles from behind at i 197). But he has put two and two together (he had, after all, been warned that Apollo would attack him if he went too far—xvi 91-4, 288), and got it almost right: and by throwing in 'fate' and 'Zeus' too, he incidentally removes yet more glory from Hector.

---

[12] In the *Epic of Gilgamesh*, Enkidu makes the same sort of comment to the goddess Ishtar after he has slapped her in the face with the shoulder of the Bull of Heaven: 'If only I could get at you as that does, I would do the same to you myself' (VII v in *Myths from Mesopotamia*, tr. by S. Dalley [Oxford 1989]).

Patroclus, in other words, like any good historian, has given a rational account of what some might see as an irrational event. Indeed, as far as the humans' response goes, Apollo's intervention might never have happened. The whole episode is neither inexplicable nor mysterious nor irrational, to judge from the words of the speakers. Mueller (1984) 127, points out here that the 'violation of divine causality is emphasised'. By Homer, yes, but not by the characters.

For further miracles, see e.g. v 311-516, xv 355-66, xviii 205-6, xix 1-18,[13] 38-9, 352-4, 404-24, xx 441-6, xxi 221-382, 597, xxii 276-7, xxiii 184-191, xxiv 18-21, 416-23. It is superfluous to work through them all. These miracles are negotiated by the human actors without comment or with an offhandedness that would (one imagines) better characterise encounters between humans. It is almost as if the heroes expect the gods to intervene. We, of course, may feel the gods are using their superior force irrationally. It never crosses the heroes' minds to say that.

III. DIVINE POWER

I cannot find any speech by any human being in the *Iliad* which talks of the gods as mysterious beings. Humans talk in terms only of the gods' *power*—almost exclusively, their power to help them or hinder them, for which gods can be praised or blamed. For humans, gods are either on their side or against them. This increases the instability of human life, but it does not make it irrational or mysterious. There is nothing necessarily irrational or mysterious about superior force.

So, at viii 139-44, Nestor points out to Diomedes that Zeus gives victory to one man on one day, to another on another. Today, they are losing—so retreat (*cf.* xi 316- 19). At iv 160-8 and 235, Agamemnon is full of confidence that Zeus will help him to take Troy; but at ix 17-25, Agamemnon points out Zeus's power to do what he will: Zeus had agreed to let him take Troy, but he had deceived him (*cf.* Achilles at xix 270-5, blaming Zeus in similar terms). At xiv 69-73, Agamemnon contrasts the present, when Zeus helps the Trojans, with the past, when he helped the Greeks (*cf.* Ajax at xvi 119-21). At xv 490-3, Hector observes that Zeus can increase and diminish people's strength—and now he is diminishing the Greeks' (cf. Ajax at xvii 629-33 and Aeneas at xx 242-3). At xvii 176-8, Hector says that Zeus can drive a man into battle and on other occasions terrify him witless. At xxiii 546-7 Antilochus, thinking he is to be robbed of second prize in the chariot race, says Eumelus should have prayed to the gods (*sc.* to win). These sentiments could be duplicated many times.

Consider the evidence for prayer to the gods in the *Iliad*. I count thirty-four direct prayers for help.[14] All of them are utterly self-interested; all of them make specific requests for specific

---

[13] A referee rightly points out that the Myrmidons are afraid of the armour (xix 15). Here it is only Achilles who looks at it with pleasure. The referee adds xviii 205-6, but this is different. As far as Achilles is concerned, nothing miraculous is happening. Again, however dramatic the Trojan response to his appearance and shout, they do not acknowledge it as a miracle either.

[14] i 37 (Chryses to Apollo to punish the Greeks), i 407 (Achilles via Thetis to Zeus for glory), i 451 (Chryses to Apollo to end the plague), ii 412 (Agamemnon to Zeus to destroy Troy and Hector), iii 320 (the armies to Zeus over the outcome of the duel), iii 351 (Menelaus to Zeus to have revenge on Hector), iv 119 (Pandarus to Apollo to kill Menelaus), v 115 (Diomedes to Athena to kill Pandarus), vi 305 (Theano to Athena to kill Diomedes), vi 240 (Hector tells the women to pray to the immortals), vi 476 (Hector to Zeus concerning his son), vii 179 (Greek troops to Zeus, about the winner of the draw to fight Hector), vii 202 (Greek troops to Zeus that Ajax win), viii 242 (Agamemnon to Zeus that the Greeks be not destroyed), viii 346-7 (Greeks to all the gods under Hector's onslaught), viii 526 (Hector to Zeus and the other gods that he will rout the Greeks), ix 170 (Nestor to Zeus for his mercy), xi 183 (the embassy to Achilles, to Poseidon), xi 454 (Phoenix's father to the furies), xi 568 (Meleager's mother to Hades and Persephone), x 278 (Odysseus to Athena for glory), x 284 (Diomedes to Athena for protection), x 462 (Odysseus to Athena for guidance to the Thracian camp), xi 735 (Nestor and his men before battle, to Zeus and

action; most of them arise from life-or-death situations. None of them expresses to me any sense of adoration, reverence, numinosity, or mystery.[15]

While it is true that merely counting examples does not tell one much about the weight of importance an author attaches to any episode (there was, after all, only one Embassy to Achilles), it still strikes me as surprising that the heroes offer so few prayers to the gods in the course of the *Iliad*. There is so much they could seek divine aid for, but they never do unless life and death are at stake (or victory and defeat in games, virtually the same thing for these heroes), and they never express gratitude and rarely even acknowledge help received.[16] What is even more surprising, by contrast, is the number of times that the gods intervene on behalf of heroes without being invoked. This occurs far more frequently than the heroes' prayers to the gods. Consider, for example, the incessant uncalled-for interventions of Apollo, Athena, Poseidon and Zeus in v, xi-xv, and xvii in particular, as they intervene to support their favourites or advance their cause.

I have asserted that the heroes in the *Iliad* never talk in terms of divine mystery and numinosity. One cannot prove a negative. All one can do is to ask for counter examples. There are, for example, the three moral allegories of the *Iliad*. First, there is Phoenix's theological discussion of the Λιταί at ix 497-512. This says nothing more than that the gods respond to those who sacrifice to and supplicate them (as the Greeks well know—*cf.* the Chryses' episode in Book 1 already discussed). Far from wrapping the gods in mystery, Phoenix's aim is to explain graphically and with the utmost clarity how they work. Second, Agamemnon discusses ἄτη at great length at xix 86-138. His purpose is to move the blame for his clash with Achilles from his own shoulders onto Zeus's. This is a very practical argument, which does nothing to enhance our impression of the Greek leader. The 'mystery' of the gods is the last thing Agamemnon has in mind: his whole purpose, like Phoenix's, is to demonstrate the way they work, and why the quarrel with Achilles is not his fault. Third, Achilles reflects on Zeus's dispensation of good and evil at xxiv 525-33: to some he gives mixed good and evil, to others unmixed evil. This is part of Achilles' *consolatio* to Priam. Achilles uses it to show Priam that he has not (as he averred) lived a life of unmixed evil (xxiv 494-5), but one of mixed good and evil (543-9), just like Peleus (534-42). What strikes me is the clarity of Achilles' analysis. It does not read to me like the insight of a man who finds life an irrational mystery, lived at the mercy of numinous gods.[17]

Athena), xv 372 (Nestor to Zeus that the Greeks be not destroyed), xvi 233 (Achilles to Zeus for Patroclus' safety), xvi 514 (Glaucus to Apollo to heal his wound), xvii 45-6 (Menelaus to Zeus before attacking Euphorbus), xvii 498 (Automedon to Zeus for courage (?)), xvii 645 (Ajax to Zeus to shed light on the battlefield), xxiii 194 (Achilles to the winds to set Patroclus' pyre alight), xxiii 770 (Odysseus to Athena to give him speed), xxiii 871 (Meriones to Apollo to hit the target), xxiv 308 (Priam to Zeus to grant him an omen for a safe journey to Achilles).

[15] The same holds for prayers offered to Zeus to witness events or seal oaths (iii 276, 298, vii 76, 411, xix 259); 'statement' prayers, where a god is invoked, though not asked directly for help (e.g. iii 365, xii 164); and wishes (ii 371, iv 288, vii 132, x 329, xii 275, xvi 97, xvii 561, xviii 8, xxiii 650). See also n. 6 and Bremer (n. 16) on how comparatively ungrateful the heroes seem to be for the gods' help.

[16] See J.N. Bremer, *Greek religion* (Oxford 1994) 39.

[17] In n. 4, I disagreed with Edwards (1987) who suggested that the gods acted irrationally in men's eyes (though *cf.* Edwards (1987) 136, where he rightly says 'the poet needs to satisfy his audience's desire to find an order and rationality in human experience'). Achilles' speech here seems to me to support my disagreement. The rationality of the gods' intervention in human life, expressed in terms of (e.g.) *quid pro quo,* just deserts, or however it might otherwise be expressed, is simply not raised. Life, says Achilles, is not irrational. It is simply lived under divine control. In human eyes, then, the gods' acts may seem capricious or unpredictable—but that is not the same as irrational. Interestingly, the only time that the issue of human deserts is raised is in relation to τιμή, and there, of course, we are talking about human deserts in human eyes—a very different, and deeply contested, issue (as Taplin [1992] 50-1 rightly emphasises).

Nor does Achilles have anything more interesting to say about the relations of men and gods in his great speech in reply to Odysseus during the Embassy at ix 308-429. Here surely was the chance for a poet who was impressed by the mystery of the gods to raise the issues involved—after all, it is the *Iliad*'s greatest human dilemma. He does not take it: for it is, indeed, a *human* dilemma, related to human τιμή. So Achilles talks exclusively in human terms, with cursory references to sacrifice and gods' general oversight (357, 392) and nods in the direction of Zeus's power at ix 377 and 419-20 (I discuss Achilles' fate later on in this paper).

Finally, a general sweep through the poem. At various points in the *Iliad*, characters exclaim how much the gods help, love or honour someone. At others they pray warmly to them (e.g. x 277-95, xi 363-4). Paris praises the gifts of Aphrodite at iii 64. At iv 235 Agamemnon asserts Zeus will not give help to liars. At xiii 631-9, Menelaus acknowledges that Zeus is renowned for wisdom, but wonders whether this can be true since he is favouring the Trojans, and at xiii 730-4 the gods are credited by Poulydamas with giving men different gifts (*cf.* Diomedes at ix 37-9 on Zeus's gifts to Agamemnon—honour superior to anyone else's because he holds the σκῆπτρον, but no ἀλκή). The superiority of Zeus over men is acknowledged at e.g. xvii 176-8. I can do no better. If we are looking for signs of humans' belief in the mystery of the gods, they look pretty thin pickings to me.[18]

To summarise: the characters fully acknowledge the power of the gods and their extreme predictability in some cases, but unpredictability in others, but have nothing to say about numinosity, mysteriousness or reverence (*cf.* de Jong [1987] 228 'human characters...see what their human nature allows them to see'). These characteristics are reserved for the narrative. By the same token, I am not persuaded that the heroes have any problems with 'irrational' or 'inexplicable' gods. They simply find them more powerful, and willing to wield that power in any way they want to.

IV. FATE IN THE *ILIAD*

What, however, of fate? Here surely is a dark and numinous area, where humans grope for understanding in the face of an arbitrary and meaningless universe.

The facts about 'fate' in the *Iliad* can be briefly stated. Of the four most important words used to express the idea of fate in Homer, πότμος is always a synonym for death, μόρος always refers to death except in the phrase ὑπὲρ μόρον, μοῖρα (the most common word) always refers to death except in the phrases ὑπὲρ/κατὰ μοῖραν, and in a few places where it means 'share, portion, part' (x 253, xv 195, xvi 68, xix 256). [19] Only αἶσα (which also means 'share, portion' like μοῖρα) takes on any broader connotations of generalised 'fate' (e.g. v 209, xv 209, xvi 707). That said, the places where αἶσα is associated with 'death' easily outweigh the exceptions. As for the actual working of 'fate', it is made clear at xx 127-8 and xxiv 209 that it marks 'at a man's birth the circumstances, and especially the moment, of his death' (Hainsworth [1988] on *Od.* vii 196-8, which, however generalising it may look, must also be included if the analysis of 'fate' is correct; *cf.* Janko [1992] 5-6).[20] Even so, one's fate (i.e.

---

[18] Janet Watson points out to me by letter that only major Greek heroes (Achilles, Odysseus and Diomedes) converse with undisguised gods. Lesser heroes, she goes on, like the Aiantes, 'may be aware that a god has addressed them in the likeness of a mortal but do not know which one' (and she cites xiii 68-72). This observation seems to me at one with the general argument of this paper.

[19] The exceptions are xix 87 where Μοῖρα is associated with Zeus and the Erinyes, and xxvi 49 where Μοῖραι are said to give men an enduring heart. In these places it is clearly personified as a god. My analysis is rather different from that of Schein (1984) 62-63.

[20] A referee astutely points out that all these references are put in the mouths of the characters.

moment of death) is not necessarily invariable. It can be conditional on other circumstances, and consequently in those circumstances a man can even be said to be in control of his 'fate' (see Jones [1991] on *Od.* i 34).

Heroes in Homer acknowledge the existence of fate—since it effectively means 'death' they have little option—but do not live their lives oppressed by that knowledge. Thus Hector at vi 487-89 says that since everyone is born with an inescapable μοῖρα, he cannot die before his time comes.

In Achilles, however, Homer chooses to create a character who has, through his mother, unique and privileged access to the will of Zeus (xvii 409) and knows his fate from the very start of the *Iliad*. As early as i 352, he tells us that he will be short-lived (μινυνθάδιος). Further, his mother Thetis also informs him when he will die—shortly after he has killed Hector (xviii 96). Yet what is interesting about this is the lengths to which Homer goes to disguise the facts about Achilles' fate—or at least, to confuse them. Thus Thetis repeats her prophecy about Achilles' short life at i 417-18, and again at i 505-6. But this is contradicted by Achilles himself at ix 410-16, where he states unambiguously that Thetis told him he has two possible fates awaiting him: either he fights at Troy and dies young, or he goes home and lives to a ripe old age. Now, we know that he will return to the fighting, because Zeus prophesies it at viii 473-7: Hector, says Zeus, will not stop fighting till he has roused Achilles back into battle, when Patroclus is dead. But Achilles, (as far as we know by ix), does not know this: and it would be unthinkable for Achilles in ix to be lying, especially after what he says about liars (ix 312-4). It is, in fact, only in xviii that it is unambiguously revealed that Achilles' death will follow immediately he has killed Hector, and it is Thetis who reveals it (xviii 96, *cf.* xviii 98-9, xviii 329-32, xxi 110-13 etc.).

This lack of precise clarity about, indeed, often outright ignorance of, Achilles' fate is in fact a permanent feature of the narrative. At xvii 408-9, Homer reports that Achilles had often heard Thetis telling him of Zeus's will that he would not sack Troy either with Patroclus or without him (*cf.* Apollo at xvi 707-9). At xix 328-30, Achilles says that earlier he had hoped that he alone would die at Troy and Patroclus would return safe and sound to Phthia—as if he had known even before the Trojan War started that he would die at Troy. This sits oddly with xvii, and directly contradicts ix. At xxi 275-8, Achilles says his mother had told him he would die under Apollo's shafts at Troy. This is the first time we have heard this detail or that it was Thetis who told him. Or is this another of the things about the will of Zeus that Achilles says his mother used to tell him before he ever left for Troy (xvii 409)? At xxii 359-60, Hector adds further detail: Achilles will die at the Scaean gates and Paris as well as Apollo will be involved. The picture becomes finalised not through the mouth of Thetis, but of Achilles' dying enemy, to be further confirmed by the dead Patroclus in a dream at xxiii 80.

But this does not exhaust the cunning of Homer's method of dealing with fate, the future, or even the will of the gods (as Edwards [1987] 136 says: 'Fate is the will of the poet'). An inspection of the text reveals that the gods' knowledge too about fate can be as qualified and provisional as that of the humans. I take the fall of Troy and the death of Achilles as my examples.[21]

---

[21] See further S. West (1988) on *Od.* iv 379-81, who shows (with examples) that 'Homer's gods are omniscient in a rather limited sense'. Greek tragedy also manipulates fate inconsistently for, I would argue, a similar literary effect: *cf.* e.g. the oracles in Sophocles' *Trachiniae* and *Philoctetes* (see M. Davies, *Sophocles' Trachiniae* [Oxford 1991] 268-9). Homer deals with Patroclus' fate more consistently. At viii 477 Zeus announces it is ordained (θέσφατον) for him to die, and at xvii 268-73 movingly helps to protect him: he had not hated him while he was alive, comments Homer, impressing on us the needlessness of Patroclus' death. At xviii 9-11 Achilles tells us that he knew all along from his mother that 'the best of the Myrmidons' would die at Troy, which he now sees meant Patroclus. At xix 328-33, Achilles says he had hoped he alone would die at Troy and Patroclus would return.

First, the fall of Troy. It is not surprising that, despite the omens (for omens are slippery things), humans should wax optimistic (ii 330, iv 164-5, 237-9, vi 476-81), pessimistic (v 489, vi 447-9, ix 417-20) and uncertain (ii 252-3, 348-9, iii 92-4, iv 415-17, vi 526-9) about whether Troy will fall or not.[22] But that gods should do so comes as something of a surprise. Hera seems to envisage the possibility of the Greeks losing (ii 157-62, v 714-8). Zeus wonders whether to encourage friendship between the Greeks and Trojans (iv 16). Poseidon thinks Zeus might spare Troy (xv 212-17), while Zeus thinks Achilles may storm it ὑπέρμορον (xx 30) and Apollo is afraid it will be stormed that very day (xxi 516-17).

The certainty of the death of Achilles is also strangely elided in places. On the one hand, Thetis tells Hephaestus of it at xviii 440-1, and he responds sympathetically at xviii 464-7. At xix 408-17, Achilles' horses foresee his death. At xx 337 Poseidon says to Aeneas that he must keep clear of Achilles for the moment: only when Achilles is dead should he fight among the leaders again. At xxi 588-9, the Trojan Agenor foretells his death, and at xxii 359-60, on the point of his death, so does Hector.

Yet neither Zeus nor Hera says anything about Achilles' death at xviii 356-67, when the success of Hera's plan to ensure Greek victory is specifically under discussion. At xix 344-5, when Achilles has been grieving for Patroclus and thinking about his own death at Troy, Zeus suggests Athena comfort him for his grief but omits to say anything about his death. At xxi 216-17, the river god Scamander seems to think there is a possibility that Zeus has granted Achilles the power to take Troy, and at xxi 316-23 he says Achilles will be buried under sand and silt. At xxiii 150 and 244-8, where it seems that Achilles is announcing his death to everyone, no one responds.

I do not wish to make more of this than there actually is.[23] But the fact is that even on such an issue as the death of Achilles, Homer seems to go out of his way to muddy the waters, sometimes revealing the fact that it is fated and the gods know all about it, sometimes suppressing it or revealing that even the gods' knowledge is imperfect.

CONCLUSION

In this paper I have tried to develop two propositions. First, when Iliadic heroes talk about the gods, they do so as if they regarded the gods as no more than very powerful humans. They are forces that have to be taken into account, there are tried and tested methods of winning them to your side, and when they are appealed to, they can be both predictable and unpredictable in their responses. In heroes' eyes, gods are not mysterious or numinous or inexplicable or awesome. They pray to them in hard-nosed, self-interested terms. They express fear of gods far less frequently than they do of humans. Miracles are accepted almost as a *datum* of everyday human experience: life, after all, is full of surprises, some human, some divine.

Second, while there is no doubt that Troy is fated to fall and Achilles to die, the idea of fate is muffled by the poet. It looms large in certain contexts, only to be swept under the carpet in others. Even gods appear at times to be ignorant of its existence.

Homer is not a theologian. He is an epic poet. Gods and heroes are the engine of his poem, and he must develop a narrative strategy for their effective deployment. What, then, is the overall narrative strategy which Homer serves by articulating this picture of men, gods and fate? Broadly, it is a world which maintains a balance between free human activity and all-powerful

---

[22] Hainsworth (1993) on xii 237-43 points out that epic takes a rational view of omens, regarding them as confirmation or discouragement of decisions already taken, rather than allowing them to determine the action.

[23] On Homeric 'misdirection,' see Morrison (1992), *cf.* de Jong (1987) 68-81. Taplin (1992) 198 describes the changing revelations as 'the Homeric technique of increasing precision'.

divinities imposing their will on and constantly intervening in the cosmos, a world in which there is some sense of balance of forces between man, fate and the gods, where it is possible for men to play a full and free part.[24] Strictly, this world-view is irrational, of course. If gods are all-knowing and all-powerful, men cannot be free. But the conceit allows Homer to compose epic, and to have his cake and eat it, by juxtaposing the two worlds and focusing now on one, now on the other.[25]

This is not a new thesis, of course: Homer's rationalising tendency and the balance he maintains between human and divine responsibility are well recognised (see e.g. G.S. Kirk, *The songs of Homer* [Cambridge 1962] 380, Edwards [1987] 137, Silk [1987] 82, Kirk [1990] 1-14, Janko [1992] 1-7, Taplin [1992] 96 ff, 207 ff). But it is, I think, strengthened by this analysis which points up the strong sense of the independence of the human heroes. They feel no fear in front of gods. They summon the gods to help as little as possible. They are happy to accept divine assistance when it is offered, but give no sign of craving for it. Heroes, in other words, see gods as powers to be negotiated with only *in extremis*. Otherwise they see no reason to turn to them. Everyday issues of, for example, battle strategy and tactics and human man-management are never submitted to the gods for their involvement (only the Embassy to Achilles is—ix 172, 183-4—but that is not an everyday issue: it is one of life and death). These are matters for human discussion, for the Nestors, Odysseuses, Poulydamases and Hectors of this world, not the gods. When things go against them, it is accepted that this is the divine will and that is the end of the matter. Here we see that deep pessimism that runs through Greek literature as a whole, but also that desire to be free of divine control so characteristic of Ionian rationalism and later Greek thought (of which Homer is a more than merely temporal forerunner).

Now we can understand why Homer handles fate in the way that he does. As we have seen, Homer chose to elide and obscure it. His purpose surely was to heighten the sense that his heroes were independent human beings, making their own decisions.[26] This is why the prophecies of Thetis were revealed in the piecemeal and rather inconsistent way they were. Achilles must be seen to be acting as a free agent, otherwise the epic and Achilles' story would

---

[24] The efforts made by the gods constantly to thwart the will of Zeus (*cf.* viii 5-12) and divert the course of action so clearly predicted in places such as viii 473-7, xv 72-7 and xvii 596-614, and Zeus's own desire to change fate (e.g. xvi 431-61—admittedly fruitless, *cf.* xxii 167-85) add to this effect (in the *readers*' view) of the negotiability of existence. If the gods can play like this with the will of Zeus, and Zeus himself seems in theory able to change fate (*cf.* xvi 443=xxii 181), what price inevitable fate? How helpless are humans in its grasp? For the fluctuation of events in Homer, see Morrison (1992) 95.

[25] And, I would argue, accords with human experience. Many people feel that the decisions they take are entirely their own; but many of the same people at the same time look back over their lives and have the sense that God was guiding them. We are no nearer than Homer to solving the problem of divine omnipotence, free will and responsibility for action. In fact, Homer's solution (that both men and gods are 100% responsible) is remarkably appealing. *Cf.* Schein (1984) 58, Thalmann (1984) 85-6. R.Gaskin, 'Do Homeric heroes make real decisions?', *CQ* xl (1990) 1-15 (especially 6-7) is an excellent analysis of that particular problem, demonstrating conclusively that they do. This has important implications for the arguments about heroic freedom and independence in this paper.

In this respect, it is worth saying how useful a multiplicity of gods is to the poet (see further Edwards [1987] 121-42). This is the means of creating conflict in Olympus, which can be used to make sense of the swinging fortunes of men on earth (a device as old as Gilgamesh). The gods can contest among themselves the issue of their favourites (e.g. i 493-567, xiii 345-60, xv 89-238, xvi 444-9, xvi 354-67, xxiv 23-76 and the battle among the gods in xxi), and can deceive one another as they go about their business (*cf.* e.g. Apollo, learning late of Athena's schemes at x 515, and Poseidon's interventions and the deception of Zeus in xiii-xiv): see how dejected they are when they cannot intervene (xii 179-180). Men, in other words, have a chance. As they often say, the gods' favours constantly shift. Life would be intolerable if they did not.

[26] W. Schadewaldt in 'Die Entscheidung des Achilles' (*Von Homers Welt und Werk* [Leipzig 1965]) argues that in Achilles Homer created the first image of human freedom in the West. *Cf.* Rihll (1992) 50 '[Achilles] seeks his own freedom; freedom of action and freedom to live', and Gaskin (n. 25) 15. For the *Il.*'s human dimension, *cf.* de Jong (1987) 228: 'I submit that the *Il.* mainly presents a human vision of the events around Troy'.

become mere melodrama: mere Cyclic epic. As it is, it becomes tragic.[27]

Hector's speech at xxii 296-305 just about summarises everything this paper has been trying to say about men's responses to the gods. To Achilles' great delight (224), Athena has intervened to deceive Hector into standing and fighting (226-47); and she even returns Achilles' spear to him (276). Battle is joined, and Hector eventually realises he has been ruthlessly tricked. He analyses the situation perfectly (the gods are summoning me to death, 297), identifies the responsible god (Athena, 299), concludes that neither Zeus nor Apollo who once supported him continues to do so (correct, 301-3), says his μοῖρα now awaits him (it does, 303), and expresses the wish to die gloriously and do something for men in the future to hear about (304-5). Gods whimsical? Mysterious? Numinous? Inexplicable? Irrational? Not in Hector's book.[28]

P.V. JONES

University of Newcastle upon Tyne

[27] Janko (1992) 4 points out that Homer's handling has the effect of 'leaving an undefined area between free will and natural forces...Homer's characters are seen to suffer for their choices, which is clearly tragic, and yet the whole outcome seems to be beyond their individual control or even preordained, which is tragic in another way'. Exactly. *Cf.* Rutherford (1982), a richly rewarding article on tragic elements in the *Il.*. J. Griffin, 'The epic cycle and the uniqueness of Homer', *JHS* xcvii (1977) 39-53 and M. Davies, *The epic cycle* (Bristol 1989) between them draw out the contrasts between Homer and the Cyclic poets.

[28] In the light of this analysis, it is perhaps necessary to reassess some of the bolder generalisations about men and gods. Thalmann (1984), for example, talks of man being 'ultimately insignificant' (90), as does Schein (1984) 62. That is not the impression I get from the *Il.*, let alone from the *Od.*, and is certainly not the way the heroes view matters. Likewise, it is common to talk of the gods' combined triviality and grandeur (see e.g. Schein [1984] 52-3, Taplin n. 2 above). Since the heroes themselves never talk in these terms, the generalisation, I think, needs some refining.

Journal of Hellenic Studies cxvi (1996) pp 119-131

TORTURE AND RHETORIC IN ATHENS

IN a short article published one hundred years ago, J.W. Headlam presented the thesis that in Athenian law the function of the challenge to torture slaves was to propose an alternative method of trial outside the *dikastêrion*, a kind of ordeal.[1] The thesis met immediate opposition and—despite a brief rejoinder by Headlam to his first critic[2]—it has been rejected by those writing on Athenian law up to now,[3] including G. Thür, whose monograph is by far the most important work on the subject.[4] However, the significance of the issue compels us not to let it drop. For it touches not only upon the use of torture, which affects our understanding of the position of slaves, but also upon the Athenian rules of evidence, indeed, their entire method of dispute resolution. The purpose of the present paper is, first (I) to revive Headlam's thesis in a modified form and (II) to answer the criticisms against it. I shall argue that Headlam was essentially correct with regard to the judicial function of the challenge, but his association of it with the trial by ordeal was misplaced. Finally, (III) I shall touch upon the influence of rhetoricians in Athens, for they appear responsible for some of the disagreement.

I

In the surviving speeches of the Athenian orators there are many reports of challenges (*proklêseis*) to torture (*basanos*). The challenges were made generally before the dispute reached the *dikastêrion*, where the speeches are delivered. According to the usual report, a litigant proposed to his opponent to have a slave interrogated by torture: the owner would have brought the slave to his opponent for torture, but would have maintained a control over how it was done. The slave, the speaker argues, knows the truth of the disputed point, and torture, had it been applied, would have secured the truth.[5]

However, in almost all of the reports the challenge was refused, and in no reported case has a *basanos* actually been completed as the result of a challenge. In view of this evidence, Headlam asks the question, 'What happened if the challenge was accepted ... [and] the torture really came off?'[6] His answer is that a torture that was performed in these circumstances would resolve the dispute, that there would be no recourse then to a *dikastêrion*, and thus that there would then be no speeches to report a completed *basanos*. In fact, as Headlam knew, he was not the first to propose the thesis; in the second century AD, the lexicographer Pollux also said that the function of the challenge, whether to some defined oath or testimony or *basanos* or to something else of that sort, was the resolution of the suit.[7] Many cases were not so straightfor-

---

[1] J.W. Headlam, 'On the πρόκλησις εἰς βάσανον in Attic law', *CR* vii (1893) 1-5.

[2] See C.V. Thompson, 'Slave torture in Athens', *CR* viii (1894) 136 and Headlam 136-7.

[3] See e.g. R.J. Bonner, *Evidence in Athenian courts* (Chicago 1905) 72, J. Lipsius, *Das attische Recht und Rechtsverfahren* (Leipzig 1905-15) 889 n. 91, A.R.W. Harrison, *The law of Athens* ii (Oxford 1971) 147-50.

[4] G. Thür, *Beweisführung vor den Schwurgerichtshöfen Athens. Die Proklesis zur Basanos* (Vienna 1977). Thür's conclusions have been followed recently by M. Gagarin, 'The nature of proofs in Antiphon', *CP* lxxxv (1990) 22-32, and S. Todd, 'The purpose of evidence in Athenian courts', in *Nomos. Essays in Athenian law, politics and society*, P. Cartledge, P. Millet & S. Todd, eds. (Cambridge 1990) 19-40, esp. 34-5. Sympathy with the views of Headlam and those expressed here has now been expressed by the social historian, V. Hunter, *Policing Athens. Social control in the Attic lawsuits 420-320 BC* (Princeton 1994) 70-95.

[5] I am in complete agreement with Thür 181 when he argues that it was the function of the *basanos* either to affirm or to deny a statement formulated in the challenge. The torturer would not fish for new information.

[6] Headlam 1.

[7] Pollux vii 62: πρόκλησις δ' ἐστὶ λύσις τῆς δίκης ἐπί τινι ὡρισμένῳ ὅρκῳ ἢ μαρτυρίᾳ ἢ βασάνῳ ἢ ἄλλῳ τινὶ τοιούτῳ. The Suda, s.v., mentions private arbitration as well. *Cf.* Dem. xlv 15-16.

ward, for the statement of a slave might render only circumstantial evidence. Here the Athenian legal process gave protection to the slave (even if not intentionally). If a litigant wished to torture a slave with credibility, he had to make an agreement with his opponent and be willing to let the point, even the whole case, rest on the outcome. Sometimes this decision was a close call (see Dem. xxxvii 41). The mistake of many scholars, including Headlam, has been to emphasize the torture itself, while ignoring the challenge. Few would dispute that the Athenians agreed through challenges to end disputes by private arbitration or the swearing of prescribed oaths.[8] But the irrationality of resolving disputes by torturing a third party, as well as some obfuscated passages in the orators, has prevented Headlam's view from receiving wider acceptance.

The *basanos*-challenge functioned only for private disputes. Where state security was threatened, for instance in a case of treason, no private settlement was possible. On the other hand, in private disputes where exile or the death penalty was possible, for a homicide for instance, despite Thür's concerns,[9] it does not seem problematic that after privately surrendering the dispute through a *basanos* procedure an accused party would go into exile and leave the case judicially uncontested. Alternatively, if through the *basanos* he were shown to be innocent, the prosecutor would have little ground for continuing the prosecution. In either case, the validity of the *basanos* as a dispute-ending procedure would be guaranteed by sufficient witnesses from both sides.

Headlam offers several passages in support of his thesis; in each the *basanos* is portrayed as an alternative method of dispute resolution. In Isocrates' *Trapezeticus*, *basanos* and 'being put on trial' are pitted as alternatives: '(instead) he submitted both to being put on trial and to having the other accusations (made against him), so that there would be no *basanos* concerning this matter'.[10] In Lycurgus, the *basanos* is contrasted with the dicasts and so with the court, where, it is claimed, it is possible to mislead: 'What people was it impossible to lead astray through cleverness and the devices of the speech? According to nature, as you know, those tortured, the male and female slaves, were going to tell the entire truth concerning all the injustices'.[11] In [Dem.] xlvii, a suit for false testimony, acceptance of the *basanos* would involve release from the affair and the 'risk' from the dicasts: 'for while it was possible for them to be released of the matter and not to run the risk of coming before you by certifying in deed that the testimony was true, they have not been willing to surrender the person'.[12] In the *Tetralogies*, there is an informal challenge made before the court to let the case stand on an alibi that is to be supported by *basanoi*: 'for I surrender all of my male and female slaves for torture; and if I appear [as a result of the torture] on that night not to have been at home asleep or to have gone out somewhere, then I agree that I am a murderer'.[13]

In Dem. xxxvii 40-2 there is mention of an accepted challenge to torture that then broke down. But in section 40 the dispute-ending purpose of the *basanos* is clear: 'he read to me a great challenge demanding to have a slave tortured who, he claimed, knew these things and if

---

[8] See recently D.C. Mirhady, 'The Oath-Challenge in Athens', *CQ* xli (1991) 78-83.

[9] Thür 211-14.

[10] Isoc., *Trap.* xvii 55: ὑπέμεινε καὶ δίκας φεύγειν καὶ τὰς ἄλλας αἰτίας ἔχειν, ὥστε μηδεμίαν βάσανον περὶ τοῦ πράγματος τούτου γενέσθαι.

[11] Lyc., *Ev.* *Leocr.* i 32: τίνας ἀδύνατον ἦν τῇ δεινότητι καὶ ταῖς παρασκευαῖς ταῖς τοῦ λόγου παραγαγεῖν; κατὰ φύσιν τοίνυν βασανιζόμενοι πᾶσαν τὴν ἀλήθειαν περὶ πάντων τῶν ἀδικημάτων ἔμελλον φράσειν οἱ οἰκέται καὶ αἱ θεράπαιναι.

[12] [Dem.], *Ev.* xlvii 5: ἐξὸν γὰρ αὐτοῖς ἀπηλλάχθαι πραγμάτων καὶ μὴ κινδυνεύειν εἰσιόντας εἰς ὑμᾶς, ἔργῳ βεβαιώσαντας ὡς ἀληθής ἐστιν ἡ μαρτυρία, οὐκ ἠθελήκασι παραδοῦναι τὴν ἄνθρωπον.

[13] [Ant.], *Tetr.* i 4.8: πάντας παραδίδωμι βασανίσαι· καὶ ἐὰν μὴ φανῶ ταύτῃ τῇ νυκτὶ ἐν οἴκῳ καθεύδων ἢ ἐξελθών ποι, ὁμολογῶ φονεὺς εἶναι.

they were true, I should pay the statutory debt, and if they were false, the torturer Mnesikles would assess the value of the slave'.[14] In [Dem.] lix, a challenge expressly includes the condition that the litigant, Apollodorus, discontinue litigation if the *basanos* goes against him: 'and if it should appear from the torture that this man Stephanus had married a citizen wife, and that these children are his by another wife and not by Neaera, then I was willing to withdraw from the contest and not to pursue this charge'.[15] (The challenge is made so explicit because formally, as a *graphê*, the charge should not have been settled privately.) In Lysias vii the litigant indicates that whichever way the interrogation had turned out, the dispute would have been decided: 'for if (the slaves) said what this man wanted concerning me, it would not have been possible for me to make a defense, but if they did not agree with him, he was liable to no penalty'.[16] In *On the Embassy*, Aeschines challenges Demosthenes before the court and demands that the entire dispute be resolve by *basanoi*: 'if the slaves when tortured say that I slept away from my messmates, don't spare me, men of Athens, but rise up and kill me. But if you are disproved and lying, Demosthenes, then pay this sort of penalty'.[17] (It is a mock challenge, like *Tetr.* i 4.8, because the *basanos* cannot take place before the dicasts.)[18] In Dem. xxix, although many witnesses are offered on circumstantial points, the *basanos*-challenge relates to the point on which the whole case depends: 'since I knew that you would cast your votes concerning this issue, I thought it necessary to do nothing else before testing this man through a challenge'.[19] It could have carried the weight of the entire suit.

Thür raises the concern that in several speeches (e.g. Lys. iv 10-11, Is. viii 9 & 17 and Dem. xxx 26-7 & 35) the challenge deals with several questions and not simply the one that would decide the dispute.[20] However, it seems to me that in all of the passages every one of the questions could have decided the case by forcing an admission that would have been decisive. As Thür makes clear,[21] part of the preliminary strategy of a dispute was to elicit admissions (*homologiai*) on circumstantial issues. Regardless of the irrelevance of some point to the central issue, as may be the case in Dem. xxxvii 27, the parties could embarrass each other with the refused challenges. If a litigant knew his opponent would refuse the challenge anyway, why not offer to let the case depend on it?

Headlam bolsters his thesis by comparing the *basanos*-challenge to the oath-challenge, whose ·

---

[14] Dem., *Pant.* xxxvii 40: ἀναγιγώσκει μοι πρόκλησιν μακράν, ἀξιῶν, ὅν φησιν οἰκέτην ταῦτα συνειδέναι, βασανίζεσθαι, κἄν μὲν ᾖ ταῦτ' ἀληθῆ, τὴν δίκην ἀτίμητον ὀφλεῖν αὐτῷ. ἐὰν δὲ ψευδῆ, τὸν βασανιστὴν Μνησικλέα ἐπιγνώμον· εἶναι τῆς τιμῆς τοῦ παιδός.

[15] [Dem.]., *Neaera* lix 121: καὶ ἐὰν φαίνηται ἐκ τῆς βασάνου γήμας Στέφανος οὑτοσὶ ἀστὴν γυναῖκα, καὶ ὄντες αὐτῷ οἱ παῖδες οὗτοι ἐξ ἑτέρας γυναικὸς ἀστῆς καὶ μὴ Νεαίρας, ἤθελον ἀφίστασθαι τοῦ ἀγῶνος καὶ μὴ εἰσιέναι τὴν γραφὴν ταύτην.

[16] Lys., *Olive-Stump* vii 37: περὶ ἐμοῦ μὲν γὰρ εἰ ἔλεγον ἃ οὗτος ἐβούλετο, οὐδ' ἂν ἀπολογήσασθαί μοι ἐξεγένετο· τούτῳ δ' εἰ μὴ ὡμολόγουν, οὐδεμίᾳ ζημίᾳ ἔνοχος ἦν.

[17] Aesch., *Emb.* ii 127: κἂν βασανιζόμενοι φῶσιν ἀπόκοιτόν με τουτωνὶ πώποτε τῶν συσσίτων γεγονέναι, μὴ φείσησθέ μου, ὦ ἄνδρες Ἀθηναῖοι, ἀλλ' ἀναστάντες ἀποκτείνατε. ἐὰν δ' ἐξελεγχθῇς ψευδόμενος, Δημόσθενες, τοιαύτην δίκην δός.

[18] See Dem. xlv 16. *Cf.* Harrison 149 n. 4. Thür 190-2 is inclined to accept the legal, if not the practical possibility of a *basanos* before the dicasts in private disputes. In public disputes, moreover, where a whole day was allocated to the disputing positions, he sees the completion of Aeschines' challenge as more practically possible. I am more persuaded by Demosthenes's simple denial of the possibility in xlv 16. The rhetorical flash of Aeschines' challenge seems little diminished by the fact that its fulfilment was a legal impossibility. Andocides i 25-6 and 35 makes analogous mock challenges.

[19] Dem. *Aph.* 3 xxix 11: καὶ περὶ τούτου τὴν ψῆφον ὑμᾶς οἴσαντας ἐπιστάμενος, ᾠήθην δεῖν μηδὲν ἄλλο τούτου πρότερον ἢ τοῦτον προκαλούμενος ἐλέγξαι. See also xxix 38 and 51-3 and xxx 35.

[20] Thür 211-13.

[21] Thür 152-8.

function as an extra-judicial means of settling a dispute is supported by strong evidence.[22] But he also makes other remarks, and it is with them that I wish to take issue. First, he suggests that the *basanos* procedure was very rarely, if ever, used during the age of the orators.[23] About this view we do not have sufficient evidence. If it was used and if it always led to resolution of the dispute, we would not expect to see it mentioned in speeches before the *dikastêrion*, which was the court of last resort. (We do hear of one case, Dem. xxxix-xl, in which the less commonly mentioned oath-challenge was used to resolve a dispute.) Certainly the arguments we see concerning *basanos*, for and against, do not suggest that it is moribund or obsolete. Rather, they suggest the opposite: the great number of speeches that mention the possibility of slave torture suggests that its employment continued to be an actual possibility in many disputes. If the dicasts had not heard of its use in private disputes in fifty or more years, the challenge would have become a very transparent, and thus ineffective, tactic. I imagine that some forms of torture were used to settle disputes within an *oikos* with some regularity (see e.g. Lys. i 16, 18-19 and Dem. xlviii 16-18). and certainly torture, albeit different in function, continued in use where state security was in jeopardy (see Dem. xviii 133, Dein. i 63 and other passages cited by Thalheim in *RE* iii, 1 [1899] s.v. βάσανοι).

Headlam also wishes to liken the *basanos* to an 'ordeal'. He argues, 'if we knew more about the early history of Attic law, we should find that the effectiveness of the *basanos* depended very little on whether or not the man who was submitted to it knew anything at all about the matter on which he was questioned, and that it is really a vicarious ordeal, altered and wrested until it has become little distinguishable from ordinary evidence'.[24] Headlam is right that we know little of the early history of Attic law, but it is an integral part of the arguments that favour the *basanos* that they say that the slave 'knows the truth' of the matter.[25] It always appears as a way of eliciting truthful information, or, more precisely, of affirming or denying a proposed statement.[26]

II

Critics of Headlam want to make a distinction between those challenges that are to lead to resolution of a dispute—which all admit that there are—and those that simply have an evidentiary purpose. My view, like that of Pollux (see above, n. 7), is that they are all meant to lead to resolution, since that is the nature of the formal challenge. Criticism has centered on three points.[27] First, there are texts that appear to indicate that the results of *basanoi* could be employed before the *dikastêrion*. The *basanos*-challenge would then not be an alternative means of settling a dispute, but only a means for securing a piece of non-binding-evidence. Second, there are texts in which the *basanos* is compared to other forms of evidence that come before the courts, such as the testimony of free witnesses, with the implication that they share a similar status. Finally, there are texts according to which, it is claimed, the *basanoi*, had they taken place, would have come to court. All of these criticisms can be met.

---

[22] See Mirhady (n. 8) and Thür 205-6.

[23] The assumption that the *basanos* procedure was not employed during this period is shared by Thür, who makes that assumption the basis of his sixth chapter.

[24] Headlam 5.

[25] Thür 111-31 affirms the integral presence of the verb (συν)είδέναι in reference to the slaves.

[26] There are several passages in Attic literature in which a speaker expresses a willingness to undergo fire, voluntarily, in order to demonstrate good faith: Soph. *Ant.* 265-6, Xen., *Symp.* 4.16, Ar., *Lys.* 133 and Dem., *Conon* liv 40. But in these situations the pain to be endured is not meant to elicit any information or to act as a test. They also appear, accordingly, to illustrate something different from the mediaeval ordeal.

[27] I follow here the arguments of Thür 207-11.

In the first group there are nine texts. The first is Lys. vii 37: 'mind you, I was so solicitous because I thought that it was to my benefit that you learn the truth about the matter from *basanoi*, from testimonies and from sure signs'.[28] Here, as elsewhere, despite the most natural reading, the litigant means not that he would produce the *basanoi* themselves for the dicasts. Rather, he means only that he will produce the challenge to *basanoi* that he presented to his opponent. Since the opponent refused the challenge, the litigant feels justified in mentioning *basanoi* as if they had taken place and as if they had been in his favour, as is suggested by the reversal argument in vii 36: 'if I did not submit the people when Nicomachus was demanding them, I would appear to be conscious of my own guilt; accordingly, since he was not willing to accept [them] when I was submitting, it is right to form the same thought about him'.[29] In Isoc. xvii 54 there is also a suggestion that the dicasts should have the results of a *basanos* read before them: 'Pasion, since he knew these things, wished you to conjecture about the matter rather than to know clearly'.[30] The nature of this *basanos*-challenge as an alternative proposal is made clear in section 55 (see above, n. 10). The emphasis of the passage quoted here is that the dicasts decide by conjecture, not with clear knowledge. The words μᾶλλον ἢ σαφῶς εἰδέναι reveal a conceit: since they have no direct knowledge of a dispute, dicasts always decide by conjecture. The 'clear knowledge' stemming from a *basanos*—clear to both disputing parties as well as to other witnesses to the torture—would have obviated the need for the dicasts' decision. The more appropriate verb for the second-hand knowledge of the dicasts, as in Lys. vii 37, is πυθέσθαι.

[Dem.] xlvii 35 provides what might be seen to be the strongest evidence against Headlam: 'although I have demanded (this slave), I am not able to get her, so that you may learn the truth'.[31] However, in sections 7-8 it appears the *basanos* could have 'released' (ἀπηλλάχθαι) the allegedly false witnesses from the trial. Again, the speaker makes a presumptive point, as if the results of the *basanos* would have come before the dicasts, when in fact he can only refer to his own willingness for the procedure with the assumption—based on his opponents' refusal of the challenge—that the *basanos* would have been in his favour. Dem. xxix 11 (quoted above, n. 19) provides a clearer sense of how this presumptive argument is made. There the *elenchos*, the test, is achieved not by the *basanos* but by the challenge and its refusal. The implication is that through the refusal the opponent reveals that he knows he is in the wrong. In Dem. xxx 27 a similar scenario is described: 'since I wished to make these things clear to all of you, I deemed it right to disprove him'.[32] Demosthenes goes on to reveal that he challenged Onetor before witnesses, whereupon Onetor refused the *basanos* on one point and admitted to the other.[33]

In [Dem.] xlix 57 there is mention of a *basanos*-challenge over one of several points. Disagreement arises over the status of this point, had the *basanos* occurred. The key phrase is

---

[28] Lys., *Olive-Stump* vii 37: ἐγὼ τοίνυν εἰς τοῦτο προθυμίας ἀφικόμην, ἡγούμενος μετ' ἐμοῦ εἶναι καὶ ἐκ μαρτύρων καὶ ἐκ τεκμηρίων ὑμᾶς περὶ τοῦ πράγματος τἀληθῆ πυθέσθαι.

[29] vii 36: εἰ Νικομάχου ἐξαιτοῦντος τοὺς ἀνθρώπους μὴ παρεδίδουν, ἐδόκουν ἂν ἐμαυτῷ συνειδέναι· ἐπειδὴ τοίνυν ἐμοῦ παραδιδόντος οὗτος παραλαβεῖν οὐκ ἤθελε, δίκαιον καὶ περὶ τούτου τὴν αὐτὴν γνώμην σχεῖν. The 'reversal argument' (*hypothetische Rollentausch*) is common; it is discussed by Solmsen, *Antiphonstudien* (Berlin 1929) 10-14 and Thür 269-71.

[30] Isoc., *Trap.* xvii 54: ἃ οὗτος εἰδὼς ἠβουλήθη εἰκάζειν ὑμᾶς περὶ τοῦ πράγματος μᾶλλον ἢ σαφῶς εἰδέναι. See Thür 294-6.

[31] [Dem.], *Ev.* xlvii 35: ἐγὼ δὲ ἐξαιτῶν οὐ δύναμαι παραλαβεῖν, ἵν' ὑμεῖς τὴν ἀλήθειαν πύθησθε.

[32] Dem., *On.* I xxx 27: βουλόμενος δ' ἐμφανῆ ποιῆσαι ταῦτα πᾶσιν ὑμῖν, ἐξελέγχειν αὐτὸν ἠξίουν. *Cf.*, Dem. xlv 62.

[33] On such partial admissions and the procedural consequences of them, see Thür 152-8.

the following: 'and to exploit this sure sign before you that I am lying also with respect to the other matters'.[34] The 'sure sign' (τεκμήριον) is the unrealized eventuality that the *basanos* had gone against him. Thür argues that the passage can only be understood to mean that the *basanos* should serve both as a *Beweismittel* concerning the one point and as the basis for further conclusions, that is, whether or not the speaker is lying about other matters as well.[35] But 'that I am lying also with respect to other matters' can only mean that the speaker would have had to admit lying on the point tested by the *basanos*, if it had gone against him. Dem. xxxiii 13-14 shows it was possible to put aside some charges in a litigation through an accepted challenge: in that case it is an oath-challenge.

In [Dem.] lix 120 there is again reference to a challenge: 'I tendered him a challenge ... through which you might have known all the true facts'.[36] Thür puts emphasis on ὑμῖν ('for you') and argues that the *basanos* would come before the dicasts. But it is through the challenge (δι' ἧς), not the *basanos*, that Apollodorus proceeds to argue: 'and he himself will disprove himself because he is saying nothing sound after being unwilling to surrender the servants for torture'.[37] Lycurgus i 28 also mentions the dicasts' knowing the truth: 'I think that it is necessary that about such great matters you do not vote by conjecture, but by knowing the truth'.[38] In i 29 the source of 'the truth' is again revealed as his opponent's refusal of the challenge: 'for by fleeing the test by those who know, he has agreed that the charges are true'.[39] Finally, there is Lys. iv 11: 'Each of these points, as well as others, would have been nothing other than easy to make clear in other ways and especially by these means'.[40] Thür and many others translate τούτοις as *die Geschworenen*, the sworn judges ('make clear to these men'). But elsewhere in the speech the Areopagites, who are acting as judges, are always referred to in the second person. For this reason it seems better to translate the word as an instrumental dative referring to the *elenchoi*, that is, the *basanoi*. In iv 14 the test of the *basanos* and argumentation before the Areopagites appear as alternatives: 'he thought that after putting aside so accurate a test, it would be easy to deceive you'.[41] The test does not quite indicate that the *basanos* would have obviated an appearance before the Areopagus, but that is clearly the suggestion. Sections 12 and 17 of the speech give further indications of the decisiveness of the *basanos*.

The second group of texts shows the *basanos* compared to other forms of evidence, either as confirming them or opposing them.[42] In the first three the *basanos* is to serve as an *elenchos* for witnesses. First, Is. viii 10: 'since I wished in addition to the existing witnesses to have an *elenchos* done concerning them from *basanoi*—in order that you might believe them, not as (witnesses) who were yet to undergo an *elenchos*, but as having already undergone it concerning the matters about which they are testifying—I thought it right that they hand over their slave

---

[34] [Dem.], *Tim.* xlix 57: καὶ τεκμηρίῳ τούτῳ καταχρήσασθαι πρὸς ὑμᾶς, ὅτι ἐγὼ καὶ τἆλλα ψεύδομαι.

[35] Thür 208 n. 12.

[36] [Dem.], *Neaera* lix 120: πρόκλησιν αὐτὸν προὐκαλεσάμην...δι' ἧς ἐξῆν ὑμῖν πάντα τἀληθῆ εἰδέναι.

[37] [Dem.], *Neaera* lix 125: καὶ ἐξελέγξει αὐτὸς αὑτὸν ὅτι οὐδὲν ὑγιὲς λέγει, οὐκ ἐθελήσας παραδοῦναι εἰς βασάνους τὰς θεραπαίνας.

[38] Lyc., *Leocr.* i 28: οὐ γὰρ οἶμαι δεῖν ὑμᾶς ὑπὲρ τηλικούτων ἀδικημάτων εἰκάζοντας ἀλλὰ τὴν ἀλήθειαν εἰδότας ψηφίζεσθαι. Here the verb for the judges' 'knowing' is εἰδέναι since they can have direct knowledge of the refused challenge, which can be removed from the evidence jar and read aloud.

[39] i 29 ὁ γὰρ τὸν παρὰ τῶν συνειδότων ἔλεγχον φυγὼν ὡμολόγηκεν ἀληθῆ εἶναι τὰ εἰσηγγελμένα. *Cf.* i 35-6 and Thür 268-9.

[40] Lys., iv 11: τούτων καθ' ἓν ἕκαστον καὶ τῶν ἄλλων οὐδὲν ἦν ὅ τι οὐ ῥᾴδιον τοῖς τε ἄλλοις ἐμφανὲς καὶ τούτοις ποιῆσαι.

[41] iv 14: παραλιπὼν ἔλεγχον οὕτως ἀκριβῆ ἐξαπατήσειν ὑμᾶς ῥᾳδίως ᾠήθη.

[42] Thür 209; *cf.* 178-81.

women and men'.[43] As in several other passages, it is consistent with this text that the *elenchos* that was intended and that actually occurred derived not from *basanoi*—as is claimed—but from the challenge. The speaker goes on to note that his opponent has witnesses also, so the two groups of witnesses would cancel each other out. Whichever side loses could bring a *dikê pseudomarturiôn* against his opponent's witnesses, which would supply an *elenchos*, but only after the dicasts' decision. What the speaker argues in section 11 is that the dicasts must conclude from his opponent's refusal of the *basanos* that his witnesses are lying. The speaker's own witnesses have then, in a sense, already passed an *elenchos*, even if it is not in fact the one he implies. At viii 45 he refers back to the *basanoi* as if they had taken place. Lyc. i 28, discussed above (n. 28), presents a similar picture. According to the argument, the opponent who refuses to test the testimony of his witness through *basanos* admits that it is untrue. Is. vii 28 and fr. 23 Thalheim (= DH, *Is.* 12) illustrate the commonplace character of this argumentation. In both passages the *basanos* is initially mentioned as a support for witnesses that is purportedly analogous to the witnesses' support for the litigant's original statements. But when the speaker goes on to argue against the credibility of his opponent's statements, he can mention only the *refusal* of the *basanos*-challenge.[44]

Thür presents Dem. xlv 59 and lii 22 as similarly showing the speakers planning to refute a witness through a *basanos*. But in xlv 59 it is again not the *basanos* but the challenge that provides the refutation: '(the clerk) will read to you the challenge, from which you will catch them in the very act of false swearing'.[45] In lii 22 the refutation of witnesses through the *basanos* is mentioned as an unrealized possibility, for not even a *basanos*-challenge took place: 'they knew very well that there would be a test through torture of the slaves, if they told any such lie as this'.[46] The witnesses here did not in fact testify to the point about which a *basanos* might have taken place. The speaker claims that the possibility of a *basanos*-challenge dissuaded them.[47]

Two texts suggest that *basanoi* should buttress speeches. Demosthenes xxx 35 seems at first a clear case: 'so that there would be not only *logoi*, but also *basanoi* concerning these matters'.[48] But the *logoi* are not the speeches to be delivered before the court, but only preliminary discussions held before witnesses. Onetor, it is explained in the next section, was not willing at those discussions 'to have recourse' (καταφυγεῖν) to the precision of the *basanos*. Antiphon i 7 demonstrates how selective quotation can mislead. In Thür's (admittedly very rapid) critique of Headlam, only the following is quoted: 'if the slaves did not agree (that she is a murderer), he would have defended her with good knowledge'.[49] So much certainly speaks against the Headlam thesis, since the Greek word for 'defending' (ἀπολογέομαι) is the term used for making a defense in court. But what follows is left out: 'and his mother would have

[43] Is., *Ciron* viii 10: βουλόμενος οὖν πρὸς τοῖς ὑπάρχουσι μάρτυρσιν ἔλεγχον ἐκ βασάνων ποιήσασθαι περὶ αὐτῶν, ἵνα μᾶλλον αὐτοῖς πιστεύητε μὴ μέλλουσι δώσειν ἔλεγχον ἀλλ' ἤδη δεδωκόσι περὶ ὧν μαρτυροῦσι, τούτους ἠξίουν ἐκδοῦναι τὰς θεραπαίνας καὶ τοὺς οἰκέτας.

[44] Dem., *Aph.* 3 xxxix 21 also presents such a situation, but the argumentation is slightly different. In III, below, I shall discuss how Is. viii is notable for its confusion of the functions of *marturia* and *basanos*.

[45] Dem., *Steph.* I xlv 59: πρόκλησιν ὑμῖν ἀναγνώσεται, ἐξ ἧς τούτους τ' ἐπιορκοῦντας ἐπ' αὐτοφώρῳ λήψεσθε.

[46] [Dem.], *Call.* lii 22: εὖ εἰδότες ὅτι διὰ βασάνου ἐκ τῶν οἰκετῶν ὁ ἔλεγχος ἤδη ἔσοιτο, εἴ τι τοιοῦτο ψεύσοιντο.

[47] Thür 212 mentions three other passages that he says are predicated on the *Beweisfunktion* of the *basanos*, Isoc. xvii 54, Is. viii 10 and Dem. xxx 37. None of these affects Headlam's thesis in any way that has not already been dealt with. The parallel employment of the *basanos*-challenge and the oath-challenge in Dem. xxix 25 ff. underlines that the function of both challenges is the same, to propose an alternative means of settlement.

[48] Dem., *On* I xxx 35: ἵνα μὴ λόγοι μόνον, ἀλλὰ καὶ βάσανοι περὶ αὐτῶν γίγνοιντο.

[49] Ant., *Stepmother* i 7: μὴ γὰρ ὁμολογούντων τῶν ἀνδραπόδων οὗτος τ' εὖ εἰδὼς ἂν ἀπολογεῖτο...

been released from this charge'.[50] This subsequent wording clearly supports Headlam: if the tortured slaves had disagreed, the stepmother would have been off the hook legally. The prosecuting son could have continued to carry a grudge, but against that grudge his stepbrother would have had a vigorous reply (καὶ ἀντέσπευδε πρὸς ἐμέ).[51] A reason for confusion seems partly to be that two possibilities for torture are suggested: the defending son could have had the torture performed within the context of the challenge, or he could have performed it unilaterally, since he owned the slaves. If he had performed the torture unilaterally, the case might have proceeded and he might have claimed 'good knowledge'. But if the torture resulted from the challenge, his mother might have been freed of the trial.[52]

Lastly, there are texts in which it appears that evidence adduced in a *basanos* would come to a *dikastêrion*. In [Dem.] liii 22-4 there are counter-challenges to *basanoi*. The defendant in the *apographê*, Nicostratus, wishes the prosecutor, Apollodorus, to conduct *basanoi* on two slaves. But Apollodorus claims that the state owns the slaves and that he, as a private individual, cannot take responsibility for torturing them. According to his counter-challenge, the *basanos* should be conducted 'publicly' (δημοσίᾳ) by the Eleven. The evidence derived would then be produced before a *dikastêrion*. Headlam points out that what is suggested by Apollodorus is not the usual challenge, but the procedure to be followed where the state is itself one of the parties. However, Thür rejects the argumentation as highly suspect. Nicostratus, he argues, by agreeing to the public *basanos* would admit that the slaves belonged to the state and so concede the case. Perhaps that is true. Certainly Nicostratus would have argued along these lines, and Apollodorus was at any rate in no mood to achieve an extra-judicial settlement. But we really cannot say what rules there were regarding such situations, so that Thür's outright dismissal of Headlam's reading is not justified. What matters for the present is whether *basanoi* resulting from challenges resolved disputes or could serve merely as evidence. This text shows at most that *basanoi* conducted by the Eleven or some other delegated body could serve as evidence. Headlam's thesis, which concerns disputes between private parties, remains to that extent unshaken. Unlike private parties, where its interests were directly involved, the Athenian state seems not to have abrogated its decision-making prerogative to any arbitrary procedure. It selected officials to carry out the torture and have the results written down and sealed. On hearing the results of the *basanos*, the dicasts would have voted *however they saw fit*.[53] In general, I believe, the dicasts would have accepted the evidence of the *basanos*, conducted by the Eleven, as true (*cf.* And. i 64), but their voting might have included other considerations.

Dem. liv 27 is introduced with the suggestion that statements of slaves also are to be put into the evidence jars: 'they make a challenge—with a view to delay and preventing the evidence jars from being sealed—that they are willing to hand over their slaves concerning the assaults'.[54] Again it is not the *basanoi* that are to go into the evidence jars. Only the challenges, whose wording would have to be worked out in a time-consuming process, went into the collection.

---

[50] *ibid*: ...καὶ ἡ μήτηρ αὐτοῦ ἀπήλλακτο ἂν ταύτης τῆς αἰτίας. Thür quotes the passage fully several times elsewhere.

[51] This text suggests an interesting complication. The fact that there is more than one slave, as well as the fact that the verb used of the slaves' statements under torture is 'to agree' (ὁμολογέω), allows either that the slaves as a group would not have agreed with the prosecutor or that they would not have agreed with each other. Although in this case the first alternative is the only one possible, the second would clearly present difficulty for the Athenian view of torture.

[52] Thür 210 also mentions three texts in which he understands the terminological distinction between *marturia* and *basanos* to be blurred. They are [Dem.] xlvii 8, liii 22 and lix 122. The second is not problematic: the *marturia* is not identified with the *basanos* in liii 22. I shall discuss the other two in section III (nn. 75-6).

[53] [Dem.], *Nicostr.* liii 24: ἀκούσαντες ἐκ τούτων ἐψηφίσασθε ὁποῖόν τι ὑμῖν ἐδόκει.

[54] Dem., *Conon* liv 27: προκαλοῦνται ἐπὶ διακρούσει καὶ τῷ μὴ σημανθῆναι τοὺς ἐχίνους, ἐθέλειν ἐκδοῦναι περὶ τῶν πληγῶν παῖδας.

It appears that the slaves were not present at the arbitration and immediately available to be tortured, since, as the speaker alleges, time was taken even to write down their names.[55]

The result of the foregoing is that the criticisms levelled against Headlam's thesis are not insuperable: it is an economical way of dealing with the evidence, and there are no texts that cannot be adequately explained through it. Whether or not it was a procedure formally prescribed in Athenian law, the *basanos*-challenge appears to have been a traditional practice having *de facto* decisiveness for the parties. On the other hand, a key point of scholars like Thür, that the dicasts had the ability independently to evaluate the credibility of all forms of evidence that came before them (*freie Beweiswürdigung*) also appears confirmed. The *basanos* resulting from a challenge does not bind the dicasts since it never comes before them.[56]

In Ant. v a slave is tortured privately by the family of the murder victim and then killed. Euxitheos, the defendant, says to the prosecutors, 'you thought it right that [the dicasts] become judges of his words [under torture], while you yourselves became dicasts of his actions'.[57] The implication is that the prosecutors reversed their roles with the dicasts. Just as it was not the place of the prosecutors to judge and execute the slave for the murder of Herodes, it was not normally the place of the dicasts to assess the statements of a slave under torture. An owner was always free to torture his slaves and to report what was revealed in court, but such reports could scarcely have persuaded anyone but himself, since he had complete control over his slaves; they would have been almost useless before the dicasts.

The requirement of the Athenian·court that dicasts decide a case after only hearing brief presentations from the opposing sides entails that their judgements could only ever be based on opinion and conjecture, on at best second-hand information.[58] The litigants recognize that it would have been far better had they themselves—who had direct knowledge—resolved their dispute, or, alternatively, had they resolved it with the help of a private arbitrator, who would have had more intimate knowledge of the circumstances than the dicasts can achieve. Demosthenes xxvii l makes just this point: 'this man has fled those who have clear insight into our affairs determining anything about them, but has come to you, who have no accurate knowledge of our affairs'.[59] According to the Athenians, the *basanos*-challenge, like the private arbitration, afforded the opportunity to resolve the dispute based on 'accurate knowledge' or 'the entire truth'.[60] However, this view is not based on any division between 'technical' and 'non-technical' modes of argumentation, to which I shall return in the next section, or on a division between archaic and classical Athenian law. It is based on a recognition of the imperfect quality of the democratic *dikastêrion*, which lacked powers of independent investigation. A resolution of a dispute based on accurate knowledge had to stem from the resources of the parties themselves. The *basanos*, conducted through the agreement of both parties, represented one such resource.

---

[55] In [Dem.] xlvii 13-15 the speaker uses as evidence against the good faith of his opponent that, despite allegedly offering his slave for torture, he did not have her available immediately to hand over.

[56] Much of Thür's analysis of the tactical use of the *basanos*-challenge is unaffected by the correctness of Headlam's thesis. However, his hypotheses that in every case the challenge was only a trick and that the speeches we possess contain an unrepresentatively high number of *basanos*-challenges seem to me unnecessary.

[57] Ant., *Her.* v 47: καὶ τῶν μὲν ἄλλων λόγων τῶν ἐκείνου τουτουσὶ κριτὰς ἠξιώσατε γενέσθαι, τῶν δὲ ἔργων αὐτοὶ δικασταὶ ἐγένεσθε.

[58] See Thür 294-5.

[59] Dem., *Aph.* I xxvii 1: οὗτος τοὺς μὲν σαφῶς εἰδότας τὰ ἡμέτερ' ἔφυγε μηδὲν διαγνῶναι περὶ αὐτῶν, εἰς δ' ὑμᾶς τοὺς οὐδὲν τῶν ἡμετέρων ἀκριβῶς ἐπισταμένους ἐλήλυθεν. *Cf.* Dem. xlviii 40 and lv 35. On the role of the private arbitrators, see Thür 33 n. 36 and 228-31.

[60] Thür 294 gathers the relevant passages: Ant. vi 18, [Ant.], *Tetr.* i 4.8, Lys. vii 43, Isoc. xvii 54, Dem. xxx 35, Lycurgus i 28-9.

III

Now of course this is all rhetoric and the Orators were not serious in it.

Many legal scholars are tempted to dismiss the role of rhetoric as something extrinsic and bothersome to their study of legal procedures. Statements like Headlam's, above, are common in the literature. But it is my view that rhetoric is an essential part of ancient legal discourse and that an appreciation of it can be extremely helpful, even essential, for dealing with legal questions. In the period from which we have Athenian forensic writings, the late-fifth and fourth centuries BC, there were developments in two areas that greatly affected the rhetorical strategies used in litigation, including those directed toward the torture of slaves.

The first was the increasing use of written documents in court, which replaced the use of direct oral testimony. It is generally agreed that the transition to the use of written testimony was completed before Isaeus, perhaps by about 390 and at any rate not later than 378.[61] Accordingly, while the speeches of the earlier orators, Antiphon, Andocides, Lysias and Isocrates, employ oral testimony, those of Isaeus, Demosthenes, Lycurgus, Dinarchus, Demades and Hyperides use only written testimony. In the speeches themselves, this transition is most noticeable in that, in general, the speakers no longer say 'call the witnesses' but 'read the testimony'. In private suits, which came before a public arbitrator, written testimony may have been used right from the inception of public arbitration, about 403.[62] Certainly writing was used earlier, as is indicated at Ant. i 10, and the formulas by which evidence of various sorts was used did not change substantially. But the procedural changes made *c.* 380 must have forced a new examination of writing and written documents by those who were composing speeches to be used in court (*cf.* Dem. xlv 44-5).

The second development that affected rhetorical strategies resulted from the prodigious activity of the professional rhetoricians, both as speech writers and teachers. These rhetoricians served to canonize lines of argumentation in new ways. However, the process by which they did so could result in arguments based on an incomplete understanding of the legal procedure. As sophists, theirs was not a mode of thought that was informed simply by traditional conceptions or even by the law. The freedom with which they approached problems of law and legal procedure allowed them to see rationality in procedures where none existed, or where a quite different reasoning was at work. Our most direct evidence for the role of professional rhetoricians in categorizing forensic arguments consists of the accounts of Aristotle (*Rhet.* 1.15) and Anaximenes (*Rhet. Alex.* 14-17) on the *atechnoi pisteis*, the documentary evidence used in court. Rather than *atechnoi*, Anaximenes uses the term *epithetoi* ('supplementary') *pisteis*, which indicates that, like Aristotle, he sees them as somewhat extrinsic to the speech and the rhetorician's *technê*. These were the documents that could, for instance, be read aloud by the court secretary at the request of the speaker. Aristotle includes five sorts, laws, testimony of witnesses, contracts, *basanoi* and oaths, while Anaximenes has what he calls 'the opinion of the speaker' and then witnesses, *basanoi* and oaths.

Despite their superficial differences, both handbooks rely on a common precursor.[63] Although there are times when they differ in specific language, the arguments they recommend are essentially the same, the similarity being especially striking in the sections relating to *basanos*. Aristotle and Anaximenes composed their handbooks in the period 350-330 BC. If, as

---

[61] See Bonner 46-54 and G.M. Calhoun, 'Oral and written pleading in Athenian courts', *TAPA* i (1919) 177-93; *cf.* F. Pringsheim, 'The transition from witnessed to written transactions in Athens', in *Festg. Simonius* (1955) 287-97 and *Gesammelte Abhandlungen* (Heidelberg 1961) 2.401-9, and Thür 89-90.

[62] See R.J. Bonner, 'The institution of Athenian arbitrators', *CP* xi (1916) 191-5, and H.C. Harrell, *Public arbitration in Athenian law* (Columbia, MO 1936) 27-8.

[63] See D. Mirhady, 'Non-technical *pisteis* in Aristotle and Anaximenes', *AJP* cxii (1991) 5-28.

seems likely, the original handbook was composed specifically as a result of the changes made in judicial procedure that required the use of written testimony, about 378 BC, then it was probably written sometime between 378 and 360. That would put it one generation before the *technai* of Aristotle and Anaximenes.

However, the sequence in the handbooks 'laws, witnesses, *basanoi* and oaths' reveals an important difference between the judicial and rhetorical methods of categorization. In *Ath. Pol.* 53.2-3 it is said that the documents placed in the evidence jar after a public arbitration—which are the only ones that can be used before the court—are the 'laws, challenges and testimonies (of witnesses)'.[64] The rhetorical handbooks thus follow this judicial scheme, by including laws and witnesses, but they replace challenges with *basanoi* and oaths. Like the *Ath. Pol.*, the speeches of the orators give indications only for the court secretary to read challenges to *basanoi* and oaths, not *basanoi* or oaths directly. The substitution in the handbooks resulted perhaps from the economy of not having to deal with the challenge twice, first in terms of the *basanos* and then of the oath. In his treatment of oaths, Aristotle preserves the idea of the challenge, but in their treatments of the *basanos* both Aristotle and Anaximenes refrain from any suggestion of the challenge. On the other hand, as was observed throughout section II, the orators commonly speak of the *basanos* as if it had taken place, when in fact they can refer only to a challenge.

The consequences of the substitution, whatever its rationale, are more than superficial, for the handbooks take one further and very misleading step: with the procedural distinction of the challenge seemingly forgotten, they identify the *basanos* as a form of testimony (*marturia*). Aristotle calls *basanoi* a kind of testimony (μαρτυρίαι τινές), while Anaximenes calls a *basanos* 'an agreement of someone who knows, but is involuntary'; for him the only difference between a *marturia* and a *basanos* is whether the 'agreement' is voluntary or not.[65] Through this identification the rhetoricians put the *basanos* on a par with the testimony of free males. The identification comes easily to the modern perspective, as it must have to a sophist. Since we live in a slaveless society, we see little difference between the statement of a slave and that of a free person. Moreover, our difficulty in translating *basanos* adds to the confusion: the word is often rendered as 'the testimony of a slave under torture' and so the word 'testimony' is used of both *marturia* and *basanos*. The sophist must likewise have emphasized the parallel between the statements of free and slave involving 'those who know' the truth (οἱ συνειδότες). In Antiphon vi 22-5, where the speaker is emphasizing how he sought to settle his dispute amicably, there is close connection made between the two. But in Antiphon, unlike the handbooks, there is no confusion of *marturia* and *basanos*. In fact, in vi 25 Antiphon is at pains to emphasize the close parallel between *basanos* and oath.

If in the first part of this paper I had argued that Thür and the other legal scholars who have rejected Headlam's thesis are right and that the results of a *basanos* could come before a court, which would evaluate its credibility, then it would hardly matter that the handbooks identify it as a form of testimony. But if the *basanos* is actually an out of court means of settling a dispute, then what the handbooks say is quite misleading. The *marturia* and the *basanos* are in

---

[64] *Ath. Pol.* 53.3: οὐκ ἔξεστι δ' οὔτε νόμοις οὔτε προκλήσεσι οὔτε μαρτυρίαις ἀλλ' ἢ ταῖς παρὰ τοῦ διαιτητοῦ χρῆσθαι ταῖς εἰς τοὺς ἐχίνους ἐμβεβλημέναις. No particular weight should be put on the order. In 53.2 'laws' and 'testimonies' are reversed. *Cf.* Harpocration, s.v. διαιτηταί and *SIG*³ 953.20-3. Thür 132-48 argues in great detail against identifying the challenge as an *atechnos pistis* on the grounds that since its authenticity must be supported by *marturiai*, its evidentiary force is reducible to the *marturiai*. However, while it is correct not to make this identification—because the substitution made by the rhetoricians would cause us to label the *basanoi* and oaths as *atechnoi pisteis* twice—Aristotle supports the authenticity of contracts through *marturiai* and yet recognizes them as *atechnoi pisteis* (1376b2-5).

[65] Aristotle, *Rhet.* i 15 1376b31: αἱ δὲ βάσανοι μαρτυρίαι τινές εἰσι. Anaximenes, *Rhet. Alex.* 16.1: βάσανος δέ ἐστι μὲν ὁμολογία παρὰ συνειδότος, ἄκοντος δέ. Cf. *Rhet. Alex.* 36-18 and 31.

no way similar from a judicial point of view.[66] The *marturia* is the statement of a free male that is made in order to support the credibility of something said by the litigant in court. By making the statement, the man takes a share of the risk run by the litigant (*cf.* Arist. *Rhet.* 1.15 1376a8). The *basanos*, on the other hand, is an extra-judicial means of securing 'the truth' concerning a disputed point. Its function is to decide a dispute, just as would the decision of a private arbitrator or the agreed-upon swearing of an oath.

As was mentioned in section II, there are several texts in which speakers compare the *basanos* to the *marturia*.[67] Some understand the texts to be an indication of their judicially parallel status. However, they appear instead to indicate that the orators briefly took over a misleading step from the rhetoricians. In the speeches of Antiphon, Andocides and Lysias there is no suggestion that the *basanos* and the *marturia* are parallel. Isocrates (*c.* 393 BC), however, argues at one point that '[while the judges believe that] it is possible to suborn witnesses of things that have not occurred, *basanoi* demonstrate clearly which side is telling the truth'.[68] In so doing, he actually preserves the judicial distinction between the *basanos* and *marturia* since he does not quite suggest that they are parallel. At the same time he intimates a point of comparison. Isaeus (before 364) and Demosthenes (*c.* 363) take this point further. They connect another argument, which also appears in the handbooks, that the existence of a suit against false testimony (*dikê pseudomarturiôn*) implies the suspect nature of the *marturia* (cf. *Rhet.* i 151376a20-1, *Rhet. Alex.* 15.6) and argue as follows: 'you know that of those who have testified in the past some appeared not to testify truly, but none of those tortured has ever been proven to have said what was not true as a result of the tortures'.[69] This comparison is absurd from a judicial point of view, since slaves were tortured partly because they were not liable to prosecution for false testimony.[70] It was procedurally impossible for them to be caught saying what was untrue. One of the conditions necessary for an accepted *basanos*-challenge was that both parties believed the slave would tell the truth under torture.[71]

Another commonplace linking Isocrates, the rhetorical handbooks and Isaeus and Demosthenes is found in an argument used together with the identification of *basanos* and *marturia*. Isocrates says to the judges, 'I see that you think that concerning both private and public matters there is nothing more credible or truer than the *basanos*'.[72] Aristotle abbreviates the argument, but Anaximenes gives it in full: 'private people concerning the most serious matters and cities concerning the most important affairs take credence from *basanoi*'.[73] Isaeus

---

[66] See Thür 210 and Todd (n. 4) 27-31. See also G.R. Morrow, *Plato's law of slavery in its relation to Greek law* (Urbana 1939) 82 n. 48, on *Laws* 11.937b: 'Plato uses the word μαρτυρεῖν ... in its precise legal sense ... In the strict sense of the word neither the slave-informer nor the slave put to the torture could be called a μάρτυς'. *Cf.* [Ant.], *Tetr.* 1.2.7, 1.3.4 and 1.4.7, Lys., vii 37, Isoc., xxi 4, Dem., xxx 36, and Hyperides, fr. 5 Jensen.

[67] See Thür 209-10.

[68] Isoc., *Trap.* xvii 54: καὶ μάρτυρας μὲν ἡγουμένους οἷόν τ' εἶναι καὶ τῶν μὴ γενομένων παρασκευά–σασθαι, τὰς δὲ βασάνους φανερῶς ἐπιδεικνύναι, ὁπότεροι τἀληθῆ λέγουσιν.

[69] Isaeus, *Ciron* viii 12: σύνιστε γὰρ ὅτι τῶν μὲν μαρτυρησάντων ἤδη τινὲς ἔδοξαν οὐ τἀληθῆ μαρτυρῆσαι, τῶν δὲ βασανισθέντων οὐδένες πώποτε ἐξηλέγχθησαν ὡς οὐκ ἀληθῆ ἐκ τῶν βασάνων εἰπόντες. Dem. xxx 37 follows Isaeus almost verbatim.

[70] Plato, *Laws* xi 937a-b, allows slaves to testify (μαρτυρεῖν) and to speak in court only at trials for murder and only on the condition that they be made accountable through the *dikê pseudomarturiôn*. Attic law had no such provisions. Thür 309 calls the comparison of *basanos* and *marturia* hollow.

[71] *Cf.* Ant., *Stepmother* i 8, *Chor.* vi 25, Lyc., *Leocr.* i 29. Thür 227-34 points out that, in those disputes that refer explicitly to the dispute-ending quality of the *basanos*, the references to *aphesis* and *apallagê* correspond to the other methods of mutually ending disputes.

[72] Isoc., *Trap.* xvii 54: ὁρῶ δὲ καὶ ὑμᾶς καὶ περὶ τῶν ἰδίων καὶ περὶ τῶν δημοσίων οὐδὲν πιστότερον οὐδ' ἀληθέστερον βασάνου νομίζοντας.

[73] Arist., *Rhet.* i 15 1376b30-31: ἔχειν δὲ δοκοῦσι τὸ πιστόν. Anax., *Rhet.Alex.* 16.1: οἵ τε ἰδιῶται περὶ τῶν σπουδαιοτάτων καὶ αἱ πόλεις περὶ τῶν μεγίστων ἐκ βασάνων τὰς πίστεις λαμβάνουσι. *Cf.*, Lyc. 1.29.

(viii 12) and Demosthenes (xxx 37) rehearse nearly the same argument. Demosthenes' verbatim copying of Isaeus reflects a lack of intellectual commitment on the part of the young orator that may have guided Isaeus himself in this instance as well. It seems likely that Isocrates inspired this part of the original handbook, even if he did not have a role in writing it himself.[74] The comparison between the *basanos* and the *marturia*, which was irrelevant in terms of the law, was useful rhetorically. Isaeus and his student Demosthenes, who compose speeches only after all testimony is being committed to writing, appear to be influenced by the sort of handbook that inspired Aristotle. The chronology fits this pattern.

Basanos and *marturia* are directly identified in only two speeches. The first, [Dem.] xlvii, was composed *c.* 355, but the thrust of the argument, a paraphrase of the opponent, closely follows Isoc. xvii 54 with its suggestion of suborning witnesses: 'for [my opponent] said in the suit for assault that the witnesses who had been present and were testifying about what had happened—in writing according to the law—were false and had been suborned by me, but that the [slave] woman who had been present would speak the truth, testifying not in writing, but from the strongest testimony, while being tortured'.[75] The speaker reports a stock argument from the handbooks that his opponent (mis)used in order to deceive the judges in a previous suit (*cf.* xlvii 40). He reports the opponent's identification of the *basanos* as *marturia* ironically, since, even if this argument were persuasive at one time, it now appears a transparent deception as more importance is placed upon writing and conformity to the law. The irony suggests that this particular influence of the rhetoricians on the orators was short-lived. As influential (and misleading) as the passages that identify *basanos* as *marturia* have been for modern scholarship, they did not catch on among the orators. The only other occurrence [Dem.] lxix 122, is equivocal: '[Stephanus] might have made a demonstration from the most accurate testimony, by handing over these servants'.[76] Apollodorus is certainly referring to the *basanos*, but he also refers, metaphorically, to Stephanus' possible 'testimony' in simply acceding to the challenge and producing the servants (*cf.* Is. viii 14 for this metaphor of *marturia*.)

Since the rhetorical handbooks that we possess from the fourth century were composed after the speeches that survive, or at any rate after those who wrote the speeches were mature and unlikely to be interested in handbooks, it is often difficult to discern where systematic rhetorical thought has directly influenced the orators. But in the case of the *atechnoi pisteis*, where the general structure of what appears in our handbooks was probably already in circulation a generation before Aristotle composed his *Rhetoric*, it is plausible to search for such influences. Because the status accorded the *basanos* in the handbooks, as a form of *marturia*, differs so markedly from its judicial status, the influence of the handbooks becomes clearly apparent. It still remains to delve more deeply into the Athenian rationale for using torture as they did, but that must await another study.[77]

DAVID C. MIRHADY

University of Alberta
Edmonton, Canada

---

[74] See Plut. *Dem.* 5.5 and Mirhady, *'Pisteis'* (n. 63) 6-7.

[75] [Dem.], *Ev.* xlvii 8: ἔφη γὰρ ἐν τῇ δίκῃ τῆς αἰκείας τοὺς μὲν μάρτυρας τοὺς παραγενομένους καὶ μαρτυροῦντας τὰ γενόμενα ἐν γραμματείῳ κατὰ τὸν νόμον ψευδεῖς εἶναι καὶ ὑπ' ἐμοῦ παρεσκευασμένους, τὴν δ' ἄνθρωπον τὴν παραγενομένην ἐρεῖν τἀληθῆ, οὐκ ἐκ γραμματείου μαρτυροῦσαν, ἀλλ' ἐκ τῆς ἰσχυροτάτης μαρτυρίας, βασανιζομένην.

[76] [Dem.] lix 122 ἐξῆν αὐτῷ ἐκ τῆς ἀκριβεστάτης μαρτυρίας ἐπιδεῖξαι, παραδόντι τὰς θεραπαίνας ταύτας. *Cf.*, n. 36 above.

[77] For financial support I am indebted to the Social Sciences and Humanities Research Council of Canada and the Killam Memorial Trust. For helpful comments on earlier drafts, thanks are due to P. Harding, P. Kussmaul, E. Harris and, not least, G. Thür, as well as the readers for *JHS*. After completion of my paper, Professor Michael Gagarin kindly sent me his paper, 'The torture of slaves in Athenian law' *CP* xci (1996) 1-18; Professor Gagarin takes a position quite different from mine.

REPLY TO D. C. MIRHADY: TORTURE AND RHETORIC IN ATHENS

THE strong point of D. Mirhady's work (hereafter 'M.') lies in his interpretation of the rhetorical handbooks (*technai*). I agree in general with Part III, though admitting my lack of specialist knowledge in this field. To a large extent Part III confirms my observations on procedural law published in 1977 (*Beweisführung*, quoted supra n. 4). I approve of the opinion that, despite the use of written rather than oral testimony, the formulas, by which the evidence was used, did not change (M. after n. 62, see my recent article in: *Die athenische Demokratie*, ed. W. Eder [Stuttgart 1995], p. 329 f.). M. states an appealing hypothesis, that the introduction of written testimony did not so much change the procedure as provide the cause for a new handbook on rhetoric to be written, which he suggests was the common precursor to Aristotle and Anaximenes. The analysis of arguments brought forward for the rejection of the *basanos*-challenge proves to be important for the discussion of this special topic. To examine the lines of argumentation from Antiphon, Isocrates, Isaios and the early Demosthenes until [Dem.] xlviii 8 (which has to be taken ironically, n. 75) cannot be the task of a jurist; here we rely on interdisciplinary cooperation. Moreover, I have to acknowledge M.'s criticism in n. 64: without good reason I tried to exclude *proklesis* from the *atechnoi pisteis*. In 1977 I equated the *atechnoi pisteis* with judicial evidence in the modern sense (*Bew.* 147 f.; despite reservations p. 10 n. 4 and p. 316). Now I am convinced that the *atechnoi pisteis* must be considered from the rhetorical rather than the judicial point of view and have to be interpreted merely as written documents, for the reading of which the clepsydra in court was stopped. Of course, I too added challenges to those '*Prozeßurkunden*' (p. 148). Nevertheless my considerations p. 132-48 are still to be understood as follows (which will prove important in this discussion): the *proklesis*-document itself had no probative force whatsoever and the orators knew this well: ἅπαντα γὰρ ὅσα παρέχονται εἰς τὸ δικαστήριον προκαλούμενοι ἀλλήλους οἱ ἀντίδικοι διὰ μαρτυρίας παρέχονται. '*For all pieces of evidence which the parties to a suit bring before court when they tender challenges to one another, they bring in by means of depositions.*' ([Dem.] *Steph.* 2, xlvi 4). Those witnesses only testify that one of the litigant parties wanted to have a certain statement proved and the other rejected this challenge. The argument of a rejected *proklesis* is one of the classical tools of forensic oratory and its practical use should not be underestimated. It is this practical use that M. stresses, comparing Aristotle's *Ath.Pol.* 53,2-3 to *Rhet.* 1375a24. The enumeration 'laws, challenges and testimonies (of witnesses)' in *Ath.Pol.* points to the practical application of evidential documents, whereas the categorization 'laws, witnesses, *basanoi* and oaths' in the *Rhet.* has to be seen from the argumentative point of view, (I believe the contracts cited in *Rhet.* 1375a24 to be part of the testimonies in *Ath.Pol.*). Undoubtedly the *proklesis*, especially to *basanos*, forms the basis of artistically elaborate forensic argumentation. Undoubtedly the orators do call this challenge and not only the *basanos* '*elenchos*' (M. refers to Dem. *Aph.* 3 xxix 11 and *On.* 1 xxx 27). Still—in the strictly judicial sense—the piece of evidence is only the *basanos* correctly taken and confirmed to the court by witnesses.

Now we reach the main question that has been discussed for more than a century: is the testimony of a tortured slave, the *basanos*—which is often praised by the orators but apparently never used—to be considered a piece of evidence in Athenian procedural law or a means of settlement out of court, a trial by ordeal?

For what follows it might prove useful to repeat the principles of the *basanos*-procedure that are out of dispute. I refer to my resumé (*Bew.* p. 312-15) that has been summarized by M. Gagarin in his recent article (*CP* 91 [1996] 1-18). The procedure of the challenge to *basanos* was controlled by rules that apparently remained constant throughout the century of our evidence (*c.* 420-320). If a litigant wanted to use the testimony of servants, he first issued a challenge offering his own or requesting his opponent's slaves for interrogation; rarely slaves belonging to a third party were proposed (Ant. vi 23). The challenge would often give specific details about when and where the interrogation would occur and exactly what questions would be asked. The slave's testimony was limited to giving yes-or-no answers to the questions formulated in the challenge which was regularly written down and observed by witnesses. The other party could accept or reject the challenge, or accept it with modifications, or make a counter-challenge involving different slaves or different conditions. When the two parties had reached agreement, the slave was normally interrogated in the owner's presence by the litigant who was not his owner; occasionally a third party, referred to as βασανιστής, was chosen to conduct the interrogation (I am grateful to Prof. Gagarin for letting me use his manuscript). Herein we find a primitive mechanism of control: in the expectation that the slave will testify in favour of his master, the opponent is granted the right to conduct the torture and decide on its duration. Poor slave: if he sticks with his master, the physical pain will increase; if he switches sides, his master might take revenge later on. This dilemma was well known to the ancient orators (combine Anaxim. *Rhet. Alex.* 16,1 and 2; *Bew.* p. 195 f., p. 288 f.). Gagarin recently criticized this mechanism of control (*CP* 91 [1996] at n. 51-52): according to Dem. *Pant.* xxxvii 40-42 and Isoc. *Trap.* xvii 15-17 the owner could interrupt the interrogation at any time and withdraw his slave. Since the slave's answer never could satisfy both parties, the whole procedure thus proved worthless. Nevertheless, Gagarin fails to notice that in the texts he cites, the *basanos*-procedure has not yet started. When the owner had handed over his slave for torture (*para-* or *ekdidonai*, *Bew.* p. 166), he was not allowed to withdraw him arbitrarily (*Bew.* p. 190): it is out of the question that the legal conception of a procedure unanimously esteemed the highest form of proof in court should be undermined by such a defect. Therefore I cannot agree with Gagarin's explanation that the *basanos* formed a legitimate piece of evidence that was never used because of the room for disagreement on the procedure out of court. We have no evidence for a *basanos*-procedure having begun correctly that was sabotaged by one of the parties.

Do we now have to return to Headlam's thesis of the *basanos* being a trial by ordeal out of court rather than a piece of evidence? This thesis seemed to explain why there is no testimony delivered by a slave in the forensic speeches—and M. stresses exactly that point. In *Bew.* p. 205-14 (§13) I gathered all the texts opposing Headlam's theory that suggest that *basanos* was considered a piece of evidence. In Part II M. tries to disprove the conclusions I draw from these 'direct statements made by the orators' passing over the result of §14 (*Bew.* p. 214-32). Herein I discuss six texts, in which we find an expressively drawn up *basanos*-challenge regulating the way by which the slave's testimony could terminate litigation. This was never done by the act of interrogation or by arbitration but in an indirect way. A *basanos* comprising the intention of settling a dispute enacted a discharge (*aphesis*) or an agreement (*homologia*), whereas a simple *basanos* was used as a piece of evidence in court. (Todd [n. 4] p. 35 stated recently that a *basanos*, correctly completed, had 'compelling force' but in my opinion the Athenian *dikasterion*, which took its votes secretely, could not be bound by any evidence, see *Bew.* p. 151.) A party which had lost such a decisive *basanos*, would rate its chances poor in the future lawsuit—and would try to avoid it. The litigating parties would have a similar view of their chances regarding a *basanos* without the special clause (*Bew.* p. 232). This—hypothetically assumed—conduct of the litigants has to be clearly distinguished from the procedural consequences of the *basanos*.

Let us now consider M.'s arguments against my conclusions in *Bew.* §13. In a first group of nine texts the speakers want to persuade the dicasts of the fact that—by refusing the *basanos* - the opponent tries to suppress definite knowledge. Whether—in this connection—only the *basanos* or rather already the challenge are called *elenchos* does not matter from their point of view. The speakers—mentioning that the *basanos* could have released (ἀπηλλάχθαι) the opponent—describe the actual situation and not the legal consequences (for [Dem.] *Eu.* xlvii 5,7 and 9 see *Bew.* p. 222 f., p. 252-55). In Lys. *Tr.* iv 11 I would like to stress my conviction that τούτοις refers to the Areopagites. After the subjects bound to be confirmed by *basanos* were enumerated, the defendant addresses his opponents directly—consequently the judges are referred to in the third person. In the same way in Ant. *Her.* v 47 τουτουσί relates to the dicasts.

The second group of texts calling the *basanos*—or the challenge—*elenchos* for witnesses does not lead any further. Regarding their situation the speakers have to attach the same importance to a refused challenge as to a successful *basanos*. The texts M. has cited up to now often use 'good knowledge' (εὖ εἰδέναι) as an argument, e.g. Ant. *Stepmother* i 7. There we find 'the good knowledge' quoted from the oath of *diomosia* sworn by the defendant and her son. The same 'εἰδέναι' is used in the wording of testimony and for the regulation of the subject in the *basanos* (*Bew*. p. 130 f.). The defending step-brother's good knowledge in Ant. *Stepmother* i 7 relates to the act of *apologein* in a lawsuit that was—after an unsuccesssful *basanos*—*de lege* still possible for the plaintiff, although *de facto* there was no chance for him to win (ἀπήλλακτο, *Bew*. p. 222, 304.).

I do admit that it is often possible to explain the speaker's arguments based on the rejection of a challenge, as though it would have been possible to settle the dispute by the—now refused—*basanos*, without going to court. This exaggeration is due to the special situation. Dem. *Conon* liv 27-29, the last text of the third group (n. 54), is the best proof for the fact that according to the laws of procedure the *basanos* should be presented to the *dikasterion* together with all the other written documents. It was not a challenge to be worked out in an long-lasting process that might have delayed the sealing of the evidence jars. The *proklesis* was already drawn up (liv 29-31), and the names of the slaves had been written down (γράψαντες). Only the result of the torture, the *basanos*, was not yet in the *echinos*. As an exception to the rule, in this speech a speaker fought against an expected argument based on a challenge rejected by himself (liv 27, *Bew*. p. 252, 262). Although he did not dare to doubt the general probative force of the *basanos*, he constructed his arguments using the formalism of Athenian procedural law: the *basanos* does belong in the *echinos*!

Part I of M.'s article starts with a quotation from Pollux viii 62 (n. 7) that is of doubtful value. Lexicographers tend to generalize; of course challenges to an oath and to *basanos* with the intention of settling a dispute out of court existed—but also to simple *basanos*. I do not see how Pollux (or M.) imagines out of court termination of a dispute by means of *marturia* (testimony in court). Does he think of challenge to an oath sworn by the witness? This source is worthless because of its vagueness.

The great importance of the challenge—justly pointed out by M.—can be understood easily by correctly classifiying the *basanos* within procedural law, rather than by using Headlam's simplifying theory. Having reached agreement, both litigant parties co-operated in the *basanos*-procedure, so that the result—the testimony delivered by a slave—was theoretically of very high reputation. The *crux* is the agreement. Only a litigant confident in his advantage will enter into a *basanos* and in this case the opponent will try to avoid it. Without further exposition, I would like to presume that the *basanos* could only work in a system where the judicial magistrates had the possibility to force one litigant to enter into an action proposed by the opponent. If these conditions are assumed, *basanos* as well as a terminating oath can be called an ordeal (supposed in *Bew*. p. 307). In this sense, and restricted to the archaic period, but not 'to undergo fire' (n. 26) I take Headlam's observations for an important contribution. Considering democratic Athens there cannot have been coercion to the *basanos*. The testimony of a slave is a piece of evidence like many others. Left to the litigants, the elaborate bipartite procedure formed the legal basis for the risky game with the 'unacceptable challenge'. Still this 'game' often enough meant a fight for life.

I believe that the esteem for the *basanos* comes from an earlier period. The procedure is simple enough to appeal to every Athenian even without seeing it performed. Rejecting a challenge with unfavourable preconditions was natural. But why do we never read that a challenge that was accepted as fair by both litigants led to a *basanos*-procedure? The answer might be easy: masters and servants lived in different worlds. It was unworthy for an Athenian citizen to rely on the answer of a slave in an important matter. The epilogue to Lys. *Tr*. iv shows this mentality, although the passage does not refer directly to the *basanos* mentioned before (iv 19): ἀγανακτῶ δ', ὦ βουλή, εἰ διὰ πόρνην καὶ δούλην ἄνθρωπον περὶ τῶν μεγίστων εἰς κίνδυνον καθέστηκα, ... '*I am vexed, gentlemen, at finding myself in danger of losing what I value most on account of a harlot and a slave*'.

GERHARD THÜR

Graz

Journal of Hellenic Studies cxvi (1996) pp 135-151

THE REGAL IMAGE IN PLUTARCH'S *LIVES*

I. Physical Descriptions in Plutarchan Narrative*

THAT the physical description of a biographer's subject constitutes a natural and (one should think) necessary element of the genre seems an unremarkable premise on which to entertain a reading of Plutarch. In such chronicles of wasted time as we possess, after all, descriptions of the fair and the not-so-fair are hardly unusual, regardless of literary category. And, at least since the time of Leo, the prevailing scholarly assumption has been that Plutarch's *Lives* ordinarily include an account of the subject's appearance as a standard structural component of the biography—an idea still to be found in P. Stadter's magisterial commentary on the *Pericles*.[1] One ought perhaps to hesitate in speaking of generic requirements for Plutarchan biography, if only because we are now more than ever quite uncertain in which exact literary tradition our author is most appropriately situated, though it is fair (I think) to observe how commonly physical descriptions are to be found in the extant biographies of Cornelius Nepos and in Suetonius' *Lives of the Caesars*.[2] The narrative conventions of biography, one instinctively supposes, require a personal description. Moreover, the *eikonismos* (εἰκονισμός) was by Plutarch's day a staple of rhetorical technique, useful to encomium and invective alike, and regularly discussed in handbooks.[3] Literary and rhetorical expectations, then, tend to support Leo's proposition.

But, as Aristoula Georgiadou has pointed out, physical description is by no means a regular feature of Plutarchan biography.[4] Now, while my own reckoning diverges somewhat from Georgiadou's, and a few physical descriptions have been overlooked in her paper, none the less she is essentially correct to observe that in approximately forty percent of Plutarch's *Lives* the subject's appearance goes unrecorded.[5] Furthermore, several of Plutarch's descriptions are exceedingly brief, even by the standards of the *eikonismos*: Flamininus' appearance is simply φιλάνθρωπος; Themistocles' is simply heroic—although in each of these lives Plutarch alludes specifically to sculptural representations of their subjects. Marcellus is 'powerful in body with

* Versions of this paper were read at Siena and at Liverpool. I am grateful to both audiences for their patience and for their advice. Special thanks are owed to Jeri DeBrohun and Chris Pelling for their scrutiny of an earlier draft. Tim Duff was kind enough to lend me his copy of his Cambridge dissertation, *Signs of the soul: moralising in the parallel lives of Plutarch* (1994), which is soon to appear (in revised form) under the imprint of Oxford University Press. This final version incorporates some material that will appear in I. Gallo (ed.), *Teoria e prassi politica nelle opere di Plutarco. Atti del v convegno internazionale plutarcheo*. All references to Plutarch's *Lives* are to the Teubner editions of K. Ziegler.

[1] F. Leo, *Die griechisch-römische Biographie nach ihrer literarischen Form* (Leipzig 1901) 180 ff.; *cf.* P.A. Stadter, *A Commentary on Plutarch's Pericles* (Chapel Hill 1989) xxxiv.

[2] Genre: J. Geiger, *Cornelius Nepos and ancient political biography* (Stuttgart 1985); *cf.* J.L. Moles *CR* xxxix (1989) 229-34. Descriptions in Nepos and Suetonius: J. Couissin, *REL* xxxi (1953) 234-56; E.C. Evans, 'Physiognomics in the ancient world', *Transactions of the American Philosophical Society* lix (1960) 49 ff.

[3] G. Misener, *CPh* xix (1924) 97-123, is fundamental. Descriptive essays were part of the stock-in-trade of imperial sophists, *cf.* A.S. Pease, *CPh* xxi (1926) 27-42; C.P. Jones, *The Roman world of Dio Chrysostom* (Cambridge, Mass. 1978) 15.

[4] A. Georgiadou, 'Idealistic and realistic portraiture in the Lives of Plutarch', *ANRW* ii. 33. 6 (Berlin and New York 1992) 4616-623.

[5] Physical descriptions overlooked by Georgiadou: *Thes.* 5. 1; *Rom.* 3. 4-5; 6. 3; 7. 5 (see below); *Flam.* 5. 7. There are in some cases further instances in the *Lives* of a subject's description which are not noted in Georgiadou's article: e.g. *Sert.* 4. 3; *Pyrrh.* 24. 5; *Mar.* 34. 5; 43. 2. Such (venial) oversights (it must be said) constitute one of the common hazards faced by anyone studying so large a corpus as Plutarch's.

a hand forged to strike', whereas Coriolanus is merely 'strong'.[6] And it is hardly obvious exactly how one should receive what is more accurately designated as a non-description, such as the often cited representation of Marius at *Mar.* 2. 1: 'I have seen a marble statue of the appearance of Marius at Ravenna in Gaul; it very well conveys the harshness and bitterness which are ascribed to his *ethos*'. It too often passes unremarked that Marius's countenance is not actually described here, but rather his character.[7] The point of this is to notice not merely the occasionalness of physical description in the *Lives* generally, but to underline Plutarch's tendency to omit extended descriptions of his biographical subjects.

The relative infrequency of extended descriptions is remarkable in view of the factors which, in addition to the literary and rhetorical conventions just mentioned, ought to have prodded Plutarch toward the inclusion of descriptions in his *Lives*. Granted, most of Plutarch's subjects were amply represented in painting and sculpture, so that his contemporary readers will have possessed a satisfactory image of (say) Caesar's or Alexander's features when they began to unroll the relevant *Life*. Nevertheless, what most of all plants the expectation of physical description in the mind of Plutarch's reader, I should suppose, is the author's own intense and abundantly demonstrated interest in representing the *ethos* of his subject, a topic which invites a related interest in the subject's physiognomy.[8]

The notion that inner excellence is reflected in superficial beauty—as well as the reverse of that notion—was unquestionably a deep-seated habit of Greek thought, reflected in the perfection of Homer's gods and heroes—and the inferiority of Thersites—and the ubiquitous expression, καλοκάγαθός. Furthermore, the idea that physical appearance signified certain aspects of nature and character suffused Greek culture, though in various ways and with varying degrees of sophisticated reflection, from the vulgar popularity of the handsome[9] to the rather distasteful Greek disapproval of Oriental and barbarian physical traits[10] to the philosophical efforts in the Hippocratic corpus to explain the relationship between climate, physique and disposition.[11] The most extreme manifestation of this habit of mind is to be found in the writings of the physiognomists, scientists who explored in detail the relationship between the body and character—not for purposes of explanation (as Galen was to complain) but for diagnosis.[12] Few Greek or Roman authors emerge as strict physiognomists, but the proposition that a physiognomic consciousness pervaded Greco-Roman literature seems difficult to refute.

Physiognomic tendencies had their effect on Greek art as well, though not without some controversy. In his *Memorabilia* Xenophon represents Socrates and the painter Parrhasius debating whether it is possible for portraiture to imitate the *ethos* of the soul, an assertion

---

[6] *Flam.* 1. 1 (Flamininus' statue); 5. 7 (his appearance); *Them.* 22. 3; *Marc.* 1. 1; *Cor.* 2. 1. In each case, even the brief description provided by Plutarch plays into the thematic character of the life; for the latter two lives see esp. S. Swain, *JHS* cx (1990) 126-45, esp. 136-42.

[7] A realistic description of the overweight Marius comes at *Mar.* 34. 5, and at 43. 2 there is a (generalized) depiction of Marius' terrible visage.

[8] On the ethical purpose of the *Lives* see C.B.R. Pelling, *Plutarch, Life of Antony* (Cambridge 1988) 11 ff.; Stadter (n. 1) xxvi ff., T.E. Duff, *Signs of the Soul: Moralising in the Parallel Lives of Plutarch* (Diss. Cambridge, 1994) 2 ff., each with further literature.

[9] *Cf.* Plut. *Alc.* 16; *Pomp.* 2. 1.

[10] J. Jouanna *Ktema* vi (1981) 3-15; E. Hall, *Inventing the barbarian: Greek self-definition through tragedy* (Oxford 1989) 172 ff.

[11] An example would be the essay, [Hipp.] *De Aere Aquis Locis*; cf. Evans (n. 2) 17 ff.; W. Backhaus, *Hist.* xxv (1976) 170-85.

[12] In addition to the monograph by Evans (n. 2), see T.S. Barton, *Power and knowledge: astrology, physiognomics, and medicine under the Roman Empire* (Ann Arbor 1994) 95-131; M. Gleason, *Making Men: Sophists and self-presentation in ancient Rome* (Princeton 1995) esp. 55 ff.. Galen's complaint: Galen, *Mixt.* ii 6.

Parrhasius rejects by asking: 'But how could a thing be represented, Socrates, which has neither symmetry nor color ... and which, in fact, is not even visible?' (*Mem.* iii 10.3). Yet artists, especially artists of the Hellenistic age and later, claimed to employ not simply *mimesis* but a deeper intuitive insight, *phantasia* (φαντασία), which enabled them to portray dimensions of a subject that transcended mere physical appearance.[13] Hence the claim of Lysippus that, whereas others sculpted men 'as they were', he was able to represent them 'as they appeared'.[14] Plutarch was aware of the limitations of some artists, that not everyone could be a Lysippus: in his *De Fortuna Alexandri* (2.2 = *Mor.* 335B) Plutarch observes that 'Lysippus was the only one who revealed in bronze the *ethos* of Alexander and who at the same time expressed his virtue along with his form'. And in his explanation for composing a *Life of Lucullus* Plutarch remarks that 'since we believe that a portrait which reveals character and disposition (τὸ ἦθος καὶ τὸν τρόπον) is far more beautiful than one which merely copies form and feature, we shall incorporate this man's deeds into our parallel lives' *Cim.* 2. 2). Still, whatever the failings of various artists, the second century of our era was dense with paintings and statuary, coins and gems, all promulgating the likenesses of famous men, especially of past rulers and the current emperor, images which were wrought with the express intention of signifying one or several aspects of the ruler's character and which consequently required deciphering by the multiple constituencies of the viewing public.[15] The art of Plutarch's age, like its literature, encouraged the expectation that a biographer whose susceptibilities tended toward matters ethical would deal at least briefly with his subjects' physical appearance. And it must be observed that Plutarch himself draws the analogy between the artist's attempt to communicate his subject's *ethos* in the expression of the face (and especially in the eyes) and the biographer's intention that his own art will provide for each subject an image of his life.[16]

Nor should we forget that Plutarch lived at a time when interest in the science of physiognomy was at a peak.[17] His rough contemporary, the famous sophist Polemo of Laodicea, was an enthusiastic and influential student of physiognomy. Which is not to suggest that Plutarch was so much a child of his age that he could scarcely avoid being a strict physiognomist—a thing he certainly was not—but nor can we doubt that Plutarch was aware of the practices of the physiognomists or that he lived and wrote in an atmosphere heavy with what

[13] J.J. Pollitt, *The ancient view of Greek art* (New Haven 1974) 52 ff. and 293 ff. *Cf.* also *id.*, *The art of Rome, c. 753 BC-AD 337, sources and documents* (Cambridge 1983) 213 ff.

[14] Pliny, *N.H.* xxxiv 65: 'ab illis factos quales essent homines, a se quales uiderentur esse'. *Cf.* J.J. Pollitt, *Art in the Hellenistic Age* (Cambridge 1986) 47.

[15] Often a rather thorny matter owing to the problem of reallocation of statues: *cf.* Dio Chrysostom xxxi and Jones (n. 3) 28 ff. Reallocation also affected painting: Pliny, *N.H.* xxxv 94. That statues could be assumed to preserve an accurate likeness of their subjects (despite the problem of reallocation) was Plutarch's working principle, *cf.* A.E. Wardman, 'Description of personal appearance in Plutarch and Suetonius: the use of statues as evidence,' *CQ* xvii (1967) 414-20 and J. Buckler, 'Plutarch and autopsy', *ANRW* ii 33. 6 (1992) 4819 ff. and 4829 f., a view which obtains in modern scholarship as well, *cf.* G.M.A. Richter, *Greek Portraits* ii and iii (Brussels 1959-1960). The literary purposes to which statues were put by Plutarch are examined by J. Mossman, 'Plutarch's use of statues,' in M.A. Flower and M. Toher (eds.), *Georgica. Greek studies in honour of George Cawkwell*, *BICS* Suppl. lviii (London 1991) 98-119.

[16] Plut. *Alex.* 1. 3; *Cim.* 2. 3; *Per.* 2; *De Gen.* 1 = *Mor.* 575B-D; *cf.* F. Fuhrmann, *Les images de Plutarque* (Paris 1964) 47; Buckler (n. 15) 4789 f. and 4829 f.; Duff (n. 8) 4 ff.

[17] Evans (n. 2) 11 ff. On Polemo see W. Stegemann, *Antonius Polemon, der Hauptvertreter des zweiten Sophistik* (Stuttgart 1942); G.W. Bowersock, *Greek sophists in the Roman empire* (Oxford 1969) 20-25 and 120-23; (more generally) G. Anderson, *The Second sophistic: a cultural phenomenon in the Roman empire* (London 1993) 13-46; Gleason (n. 12) 21 ff.

I have already called a physiognomic consciousness.[18] This awareness, yet again, will have raised expectations of physical descriptions in Plutarch's work, even as it required the biographer to react to the prevailing tendency to associate external qualities with habits of character.

Plutarch's decision to eschew extended physical descriptions constitutes an issue both of literary style and of intellectual predisposition. To begin with the former, Plutarch must be said to be manipulating a narrative convention both when he omits extended descriptions and when, more rarely as we have seen, he includes one. For it was by no means the case that Plutarch was opposed to vividness (ἐνάργεια) in narrative. Quite the contrary: he regarded *enargeia* and even διάθεσις as high and admirable rhetorical virtues. Though Plutarch tended toward a Platonic suspicion of *mimesis* he was able none the less to acknowledge the aesthetic merits of a vivid text without thereby confusing graphic description for reliable history.[19] In the *Lives* Plutarch resorts to a great variety of narrative devices to portray the biographical subject: nearly every scene is composed with so much concentration on the actions, postures and manners of the protagonist that secondary figures are frequently occluded or ignored.[20] What rarely enters the picture is sheer physical description.

Consequently, in the context of Plutarchan biography, an extended description, especially in view of its marked quality, requires a critical response. The problem of description, that is, the contemplation of the nature of the relationship obtaining between (especially) set-piece descriptive passages and the actual telling of a story within a narrative, has increasingly become a topic of interest to students of classical literature.[21] The obvious focus of critical concern, it is fair to observe, has been the *ekphrasis* of poetry, and the current avenue of approach has been along narratological lines.[22] That such a tack is reasonable seems beyond question. The narratological studies of Gérard Genette and his successors have successfully established a vocabulary and a typology of techniques useful for isolating various modes of representation in narrative, though, as the continuing industry of literary theorists attests, the integration of narrative's many modes resists fully adequate articulation.[23] Descriptions, our concern here, can be understood variously as ornamental recreational pauses, as digressions challenging conventional ideas of literary unity and literary wholeness, or as discrete passages that inspire a need to integrate the description into the totality of the text.[24] Nor is this a problem confined to the study of poetry. Historiographers, too, have evinced an appreciation for this uneasy aspect of the texts which they must confront. While students of Plutarch's *Lives* have been for the most part blissfully unaffected by this literary-critical concern, it is clearly relevant to the study of

---

[18] Plutarch not a physiognomist: Wardman (n. 15) 414-20 (*cf.* 417: 'In all this Plutarch shows himself as a master of eclectic convenience'); Georgiadou (n. 4) 4623. Physiognomic expectations obtained in ancient drama as well: D. Wiles, *The masks of Menander* (Cambridge 1991) 152 ff.

[19] L. Van der Stockt, *Twinkling and twilight. Plutarch's reflections on literature* (Brussels 1992) 26-36.

[20] F. Frazier, 'Contributions à l'étude de la composition des "Vies" de Plutarque: 'l'élaboration des grandes scènes', *ANRW* ii 33. 6 (1992) 4493 ff. and 4506 ff.

[21] The bibliography is (of course) ponderous. Important modern contributions include: G. Genette, *Narrative discourse: an essay in method* trans. J.E. Lewin (Ithaca 1980); *id.*, *Figures of literary discourse* trans. A. Sheridan (New York 1982), esp. 127 ff.; J. Kittey, 'Descriptive Limits', *Yale French Studies* lxi (1981) 225-43; M. Bal, *Narratology, introduction to the theory of narrative* trans. C. van Boheemen (Toronto 1985). An excellent treatment, both theoretical and pragmatic, of this issue in Greco-Roman poetry is D.P. Fowler, 'Narrate and describe: the problem of Ekphrasis', *JRS* lxxxi (1991) 25-35 (Fowler provides a valuable bibliography of contemporary work at p. 25 n. 3).

[22] Genette, *Figures of literary discourse* (n. 21) 134; *cf.* Fowler (n. 21) 26; A. Laird, *JRS* lxxxiii (1993) 18 ff.

[23] P.J.M. Sturgress, *Narrativity: theory and practice* (Oxford 1992) 6 and 142 ff.

[24] Fowler (n. 21) 26-28.

ancient biography.[25] Granted that biographical (like purely historical) discourse is unlike pure fiction in important respects, it none the less tells a story by employing narrative techniques inviting literary analysis (however aware the critic must be of the genre's distinctive truth claims).[26]

Descriptive passages in Plutarch, if I may employ a crude functional distinction, fall into one of two sorts: one is the typical set-piece description, the *eikonismos*, coming near the beginning of the life and linked ordinarily with the subject's origins and early character; the other is more cunningly woven into the fabric of the story, where it is less ostensibly ornamental and operates more efficiently in the economy of the narrative. In both cases, as I hope to show, the physical description is integrated into the action, the themes and the lesson of the life.[27]

II. REGAL IMAGES

Let us turn now from matters of style. Philosophical suspicion of *mimesis*, whatever Plutarch's Platonist propensities, will hardly account for the rarity of physical descriptions that we have observed, since vividness represents a rhetorical virtue even for Plutarch—nor is *enargeia* a quality lacking in his *Lives*. It is not the representation of men, then, that troubles Plutarch, else he should not have become a biographer, nor does he shy from graphic narrative apart from treatments of personal appearance. Which makes it all the more intriguing that so many of Plutarch's physical descriptions are attached to the biographies of regal figures, an observation that brings us back to the physiognomic consciousness in view of the heavy significance of image in Greek philosophizing about monarchy.[28] It is from this perspective that Plutarch's intellectual predisposition can emerge into view. In what remains of this paper I should like to consider Plutarch's portrayal of kings, in order to illustrate the biographer's versatility in exploiting possibilities for integrating description into his narrative and in order to show how Plutarch's use of the image of the king underscores some of his own conceptions of monarchy, which diverge both from the vulgar tradition (as represented in the iconography of the plastic arts) and the philosophical tradition of kingship theory. It will become evident as we go along that Plutarch's dissatisfaction with traditional royal ideology is of a piece with his implied critique of the premises of the physiognomic consciousness.

But first a few comments on the ideology of monarchy. Kingship inspired in the Greeks a

---

[25] F.E. Brenk, 'Plutarch's Life "Markos Antonios": a literary and cultural study', *ANRW* ii 33. 6 (1992) 4402 ff. and 4420 ff.; Frazier (n. 20). See also A. Deremetz, 'Plutarque: Histoire de l'Origine et Genèse du Récit', *REG* ciii (1990/91) 54-78.

[26] *Cf.* Genette, *Fiction et diction* (Paris 1991), esp. ch. 3. Recent work that addresses (from varying perspectives) the literariness of biography includes: J.H. Anderson, *Biographical truth: the representation of historical persons in Tudor-Stuart writing* (New Haven 1984); P. Rose, 'Fact and Fiction in biography, in W*riting of women: essays in a renaissance* (Middletown 1985) 64-81; P.J. Eakin, *Fictions in autobiography: studies in the art of self-invention* (Princeton 1985); W.H. Epstein, *Recognizing biography* (Philadelphia 1987); P. Honan, *Authors' lives: on literary biography and the arts of language* (New York 1990). Very important for ancient historiography is the work of S. Hornblower in S. Hornblower (ed.), *Greek historiography* (Oxford 1994) 2 f. and 131 ff. (though Hornblower curiously refers to narratology as 'the new art' [p. 2] and as being 'in its infancy' [p. 166]).

[27] The two types outlined here should not be regarded as strict categories but rather as limits on a (not yet fully resolved) spectrum. *Lives* which present a typical *eikonismos*: *Cim.* 5. 3; *Per.* 3. 3; 5. 1; *Fab. Max.* 1. 4; *Sull.* 2. 1; *Demosth.* 4. 4-5; *Alex.* 4. 1-3; *Cat. Min.* 1. 3-5; *Ant.* 4. 1; *Pyrrh.* 3. 6-9 (but *cf.* 24. 5). *Lives* which display physical descriptions that are more functionally implicated in the text: *Thes.* 5. 1; *Alc.* 1. 4-8; 16. 3; *Lys.* 1. 1; *Ages.* 2. 3-4; *Cic.* 3. 7; *Caes.* 4. 5-9; 17. 2-3; *Sert.* 1. 8; 3. 1; 4. 3; *Eum.* 11. 3; *Agis* 4. 1. Less easy to decide are: *Them.* 22. 3; *Pomp.* 2. 1; *Phoc.* 5. 1; *Mar.* 2. 1; *Philop.* 2. 1-3; *Arat.* 3. 1-2. I have ignored *Cor.* 2. 1, *Marc.* 1. 1, and *Flam.* 5. 7 owing to their excessive brevity.

[28] Of the lives of kings, only *Numa*, *Cleomenes* (if that may be regarded as a separate biography) and *Artaxerxes* lack physical descriptions of their subjects.

vision, or rather visions, of the ideal monarch, a topic which has often attracted the attention of modern scholars.[29] Especially from the fourth century BC, prescriptions for the best kind of king are provided in abundance by philosophers and orators: he must possess every excellence, justice being the universally recognized *sine qua non* of the good ruler, and he ought to be superior in bodily appearance, like Isocrates' Evagoras (*Ev.* 22-23) or the ideal king of the neo-Pythagorean, Diotogenes, whatever his date.[30] It is worth observing that the idea of physiognomy was inherent in royal ideology from the start. The necessity of reinventing monarchy during the period of the 'successor kings' created an opportunity for artists and philosophers to explore the nature of the institution, one result of which is that Hellenistic monarchy remained the vehicle for the examination of the good ruler well into the empire, as the content of Dio Chrysostom's orations *Peri basileias* suffices to demonstrate (*Or.* i-iv).

Justice was important to the perfect king, but might—the capacity to win victories and to impose security—was crucial to his success. Consequently, an imposing physique which elicited awe, even outright fear, became an expectation of the good king both in the (explicit) opinion of intellectuals and in the view of ordinary subjects, as one can easily infer from extant royal portraits in sculpture and on coinage. The typical artistic representation of the Hellenistic king, a type which survived (though with decreasing frequency) well into the empire, is youthful, vigorous, strikingly handsome, and adorned with heroic and even divine attributes.[31] This corresponds all too neatly with the regal profile preserved in the surviving discourse of Diotogenes (*ap.* Stob. *Anth.* iv 7.62 = 266 ff. [Hense]):

> And besides issuing public decrees the good king should present to the state proper attitudes in body and mind. He should impersonate the statesman and have an appearance of practicality so as not to seem to the mob as either harsh or despicable, but at once pleasant and yet watchful from every angle. And he will succeed in this if first he make an impression of majesty by his appearance and utterances, and by his looking the part of a ruler; if secondly, he be gracious both in conversation and appearance, and in actual benefactions; and third, if he inspire fear in his subjects by his hatred of evil and by his punishments, by his speed of action and in general by his skill and industry in kingly duties. For majesty, a godlike thing, can make him admired and honored by the multitude; graciousness will make him popular and beloved; while the ability to inspire fear will make him terrible and unconquerable in his dealings with enemies, but magnanimous and trustworthy toward his friends. ... He must wrap himself about with such distinction and superiority in his appearance, in his thought life and reflections, and in the character of his soul, as well as in the actions, movements, and attitudes of his body. So will he succeed in putting into order those who look upon him, amazed at his majesty, at his self- control, and his fitness for distinction. For to look upon the good king ought to affect the souls of those who see him no less than a flute or harmony.[32]

The practical political dimension of the king's image must not be overlooked. Impressions mattered. As the thoroughly pragmatic Polybius tells us, Antiochus III judged Demetrius, the son of Euthydemus I of Bactria, 'worthy of kingship on account of his appearance, demeanour

---

[29] Fundamental is E.R. Goodenough, 'The political philosophy of Hellenistic kingship', *YCS* i (1928) 55-104. See also K. Scott, 'Plutarch and the ruler cult', *TAPhA* lx (1929) 117-35; G.F. Chesnut, *ANRW* ii. 16.2 (Berlin and New York 1978) 1310-32; A. Henrichs, *HSCPh* lxxxviii (1984) 139-58 (esp. 147 ff.); S.R.F. Price, *Rituals and power: the Roman imperial cult in Asia Minor* (Cambridge 1984); F.W. Walbank, 'Monarchies and Monarchic Ideas', in F.W. Walbank and A.E. Astin (eds.), *CAH*² vii. 1 (Cambridge 1984) 62-100; R.R.R. Smith, *Hellenistic royal portraits* (Oxford 1988) 49 ff.; S. Sherwin-White and A. Kuhrt, *From Samarkhand to Sardis: a new approach to the Seleucid empire* (Berkeley and Los Angeles 1993) 114-40; the essays by K. Bringman and L. Koenen in A. Bulloch, E.S. Gruen, A.A. Long, A. Stewart (eds.), *Images and Ideologies: self-definition in the Hellenistic world* (Berkeley and Los Angeles 1993) 7-24 and 25-115 respectively—all with further references.

[30] The importance of justice: Goodenough (n. 29) 57-79; Walbank (n. 29) 82 f. Diotogenes: Chesnut (n. 29) 1313 ff. (with discussion of the difficulties in dating). Diotogenes' views: Diotogenes *ap.* Stobaeus, *Anth.* iv 7. 61-2.

[31] Smith (n. 29) 46 ff.

[32] This translation is from Goodenough (n. 29) 71 f.

and bearing' (Polyb. xi 39).[33] The ideal king, then, ought in principle to incorporate his virtues, for reasons both philosophic and practical.

What is remarkable in view of the infrequency of extended physical descriptions in Plutarch's *Lives* generally is the fact that the image of the king does actually appear in most royal biographies. One might be tempted to assume that here at last our author has succumbed to the physiognomic sensibilities of his age and especially the weighty role of physiognomy in monarchical theory. Such an assumption would be erroneous, however, and, in order to make this clear, it is time now to turn from contexts to texts themselves. Which brings us to the regal image in two lives that I should like to examine with some care, the *Demetrius* and the *Romulus*.

III. DEMETRIUS

No physical description in Plutarch rivals in extent or detail that of Demetrius.[34] In the *Demetrius* the depiction of the king constitutes the sort of isolated segment one associates with the generic requirements of biography: it follows Plutarch's examination of Demetrius' origins and introduces an anecdote illustrating the intimacy that existed between Demetrius and Antigonus, itself a conspicuous theme of the *Life*. Like an *ekphrasis* in poetry, then, Plutarch's portrayal of the man who would be king has important implications for the remainder of the biography and for Demetrius' subsequent career; it begs for interpretation and remains a palpable reference for the interpretation of the biography:

> Demetrius was lesser in stature than his father, but he was tall none the less. In the appearance and beauty of his face he was astonishing and strange, so that none of the sculptors or painters achieved a likeness of him. For at once he had charm (χάρις) and gravity (βάρος) and the capacity to inspire awe (φόβος) and the freshness of youth (ὥρα)—and blended with his youth and impetuousness were a heroic appearance and a kingly majesty, all of which was hard to reproduce. His *ethos* was so fitted by nature as to inspire in men both fear and delight. For while he was a most agreeable companion and the most delicate of kings in the leisure devoted to drinking and luxury, he none the less had a most energetic and eager persistency in action. Wherefore he used to make Dionysus his pattern, more than any other deity, since this god was most terrible in waging war, and on the other hand most skilful, when war was over, in making peace minister to joy and pleasure. (*Dem.* 2. 2-3).

Here Plutarch has represented the ideal royal physique, corresponding perfectly both to the ideology of kingship purveyed in philosophical discourses and to the evidence of royal portraiture in the plastic arts, though it is worth observing Plutarch's insistence that the image he describes here could not be recuperated from an examination of art, an emphasis betraying at once the biographer's awareness of the difficulties faced by artists hoping to do more than fashion a mere likeness, as well as Plutarch's recourse to literary sources, in this instance to Hieronymus of Cardia.[35] Demetrius' *ethos* is embodied in a figure which boldly advertises his royal capacities, a glorious speciousness which the reader perhaps ought to read as ironic, owing to the proem of the work, which justifies the composition of the *Demetrius* on the grounds that 'great natures yield great evils as well as great virtues' (*Dem.* 1. 7) and which describes both Demetrius and Antony as blameworthy.[36] As one modern scholar has put it, 'Plutarch is setting

---

[33] *Cf.* Polyb. xxvii 12; xxx 18; xxxvi 15.

[34] Plut. *Dem.* 2. 2-3. The description of Antony in the parallel *Life*, *Ant.* 4. 1, in which Antony is assimilated to the image of Heracles (curiously categorized as 'realistic' by Georgiadou [n. 4] 4618), is similarly detailed. A recent, useful introduction to the *Demetrius* is O. Osvaldi and R. Scuderi, *Plutarco, vite parallele: Demetrio e Antonio* (Milan 1989) 35-93.

[35] J. Hornblower, *Hieronymus of Cardia* (Oxford 1981) 69; *cf.* Diod. Sic. xix 81. 4.

[36] *Dem.* 1. 7-9.

up his perfect Diadoch for his tragic reversal of fortune'.[37] Still, the impressive and extensive profile of Demetrius which Plutarch provides at this point in the biography at least raises the question whether his perfectly regal exterior signifies true regality or mere show. For at the start, as ch. 4 explains, Demetrius was by nature φιλάνθρωπος and inclined to justice.[38]

Indeed, the biography of Demetrius can scarcely escape becoming a commentary on Hellenistic kingship. As is well known, the diadem and the royal title were assumed by Antigonus in 306, after Demetrius' crushing defeat of Ptolemy at Salamis, a victory which established Antigonus' heir with the credentials critical for the assertion of a dynasty; immediately receiving the regal title, Antigonus sent a diadem to his son, whom he addressed as king. Thus was born the Hellenistic monarchy, imitated by the remaining successors, but invented, as it were, by Antigonus out of the martial successes of his son and out of their secure, stable relationship—the latter being an asset inimitable by Antigonus' rivals.[39]

Of these events Plutarch was well aware; indeed, he is a principal source for the modern historian. The process of the monarchy's reinvention after Alexander fascinates our author, who describes the flattering, despicable conduct of the Athenians in 307 when they hailed Demetrius as king (*Dem.* 10. 3) and elevated him nearly to the status of a god, an account in which reminiscences of the description of Demetrius can be detected: the image of the king is explicitly invoked at *Dem.* 10. 4-5, though from an oblique perspective and with greater conciseness ('They also decreed that the figures of Demetrius and Antigonus should be woven into the sacred robe of Athena, together with those of the other gods'); moreover, in ch. 12, we find the proposal that 'whenever Demetrius visited Athens he should be received with the same divine honors that were paid to Demeter and Dionysus' (*Dem.* 12. 1). In fact, the Athenians went so far as to rename the Dionysia as the Demetria (*Dem.* 12. 2).[40] But the image of the king is susceptible to cross-readings: the gods sent winds that tore to pieces the representation of Demetrius on Athena's robe, and frost forced the cancellation of the Demetria.[41]

Yet it is the investiture of 306 that most interests Plutarch, and he formulates the effect of the renewal of kingship in terms of an unfortunate costume change.[42] After citing the rush on the part of the other diadochs to imitate the Antigonids, Plutarch makes the observation: 'The assumption of these dignities meant something more than the mere addition of a name or a change in appearance. It stirred the spirits of these men, raised their ideas to a different plane' (*Dem.* 18. 5). The assumption of the monarchy introduced pride, self-importance, harshness and open autocracy; the successor-kings are compared to tragic actors who, though ordinary men, alter their deportment when they don regal robes for the stage.[43] Though possessed by nature of a genuinely royal presence, as we are told at the start, and naturally disposed to justice, Demetrius also participated—to his own disadvantage—in the charade of the new monarchy. That such was the case is made clear at *Dem.* 41 and following. There Demetrius is explicitly compared with actors, and his theatricality is criticized, along with his arrogance and his new

---

[37] Smith (n. 29) 52.

[38] *Dem.* 4. 1.

[39] R.A. Billows, *Antigonos the One-Eyed and the creation of the Hellenistic state* (Berkeley and Los Angeles 1990), 136 ff., esp. 155 ff. On the importance of the dynastic factor in Hellenistic kingship generally, see most recently Sherwin-White and Kuhrt (n. 29) 125 ff.

[40] The importance of Dionysus in royal portraiture: Smith (n. 29) 37 ff. It is unimportant to our purposes that Plutarch is historically inaccurate here, *cf.* Billows (n. 39) 150.

[41] *Dem.* 12. 2-7.

[42] *Dem.* 18.

[43] *Dem.* 18. 5.

unwillingness to dispense justice properly.[44]

Demetrius' conduct undermines his regal aspect, whereas we are told that the Macedonians came to admire Demetrius' rival, Pyrrhus, because only in his actions 'could they see an image of Alexander's courage' (*Dem.* 41. 5).[45] Not that courage is, in Plutarch's view, the chief glory of monarchy, a message he underscores in this *Life*:

> And indeed there is nothing that becomes a king so much as the task of dispensing justice. Ares, the god of war, is a tyrant, as Timotheus tells us, but Law, in Pindar's words, is the monarch of all things. Homer tells us that Zeus entrusts kings not with 'city-takers' or bronze-beaked ships, but with decrees of justice, which are to be protected and kept inviolate, and it is not the most warlike or unjust or murderous of kings but the most righteous to whom he gives the title of Zeus' confidant and disciple. Demetrius on the other hand took pleasure in being given a nickname which is the opposite of the one bestowed on the king of the gods, for Zeus is known as the protector of cities but Demetrius as the besieger. It is through such an attitude that naked power, if it lacks wisdom, allows evil actions to usurp the place of good, and glorious achievements to be associated with injustice (*Dem.* 42. 8-11).

Demetrius' nature and its handsome display become contemptible in the absence of a properly developed character. Lacking princely counsel, the dashing 'successor' doomed himself to failure and disgrace. For Demetrius there was to be no 'majesty though in ruin'.

IV. ROMULUS

The *Romulus* illustrates how Plutarchan descriptions can be more intimately involved in the movement of the narrative, what Genette has referred to as 'concurrence'.[46] In the *Romulus* Plutarch enjoyed a wider range for his literary invention. For, despite his hopeful wish that 'myth yield and be purified by reason and take on the appearance of history' (*Thes.* 1. 5), Plutarch cannot have failed to appreciate that the legendary quality of the lives of Theseus and Romulus introduced a certain poetic aspect to the biographer's art. Our awareness of the extent to which Plutarch succeeded in exploiting the literary possibilities of this *Life* has been enhanced by the recent work of A. Deremetz, who has demonstrated how Plutarch's narrative, through its juxtaposition of varying accounts of Rome's origins, requires the reader to rehearse the historiographical challenges facing the student of early Rome and, furthermore, that, in its preference for Greek accounts (chosen on grounds valid by Greek standards), the text both problematizes and affirms the role of Greek erudition in the recuperation of Roman history.[47] In short, Deremetz has made clear the extent to which narrative strategies are employed in the *Romulus* in order to deliver messages that are at once didactic and, from Plutarch's comprehensive perspective, philosophical. Plutarch's manipulation of focalization functions similarly in this *Life* to instruct the reader in the proper virtues of a king and on the discriminating appreciation of royal physiognomy.

---

[44] *Dem.* 41-42. Theatricality, of course, constitutes a criticism. Brenk (n. 25) 4364 has suggested that Plutarch's criticism of ruler cult may to some extent derive from the excesses of the Neronian period; if so, then the introduction of theatrical language in Plutarch's treatment of Demetrius carries additional significance (*cf.* Brenk, *op. cit.* 4356 f. and 4363).

[45] It may be, as Mossman (n. 15) 109 maintains, that εἴδωλον here suggests Pyrrhus' fundamental inferiority to Alexander, though the chief point is to criticize Demetrius. Elsewhere Mossman has perceptively if tentatively proposed reading the *Pyrrhus* and the *Demetrius* against the backdrop of the *Alexander* ('Plutarch, Pyrrhus, and Alexander,' in P.A. Stadter, *Plutarch and the historical tradition* [London 1992] 90-108, esp. 92 and 103 f.), a line of interpretation that merits further discussion for all the *Lives* of the 'successors'; *cf.* J.L. Moles, *CR* xliii (1993) 31.

[46] Genette, *Narrative discourse* (n. 21) 102. As an introduction to the *Romulus*, see C. Ampolo and M. Manfredini, *Plutarco: Le vite di Teseo e di Romolo* (Milan 1988) esp. vii-lxxxi.

[47] Deremetz (n. 25); on Plutarch's use of implicit moralism, see Duff (n. 8) 22 f..

At *Rom*. 3 and following, Plutarch reports the version of the origins and early career of Romulus and Remus that in his view enjoys the widest credence, in which account Romulus literally makes his first appearance along with his brother at *Rom*. 3. 4, when they are born to Ilia. The pair are described concisely and in a manner efficient to the advancement of the narrative: 'And she bore two sons who were extraordinary in size and beauty; for this reason Amulius was even more frightened and ordered a slave to take the boys and cast them away' (*Rom*. 3. 4-5). The description may adequately be categorized as ideal, reflecting the common if banal assumption that kings are (or certainly ought to be) big and beautiful. But is that all there is to Plutarch's treatment of the image of King Romulus?

The superior physique of the twins, indicative of their noble descent (from Numitor and ultimately Aeneas) and suggestive of their putative divine parentage (the legend of Mars' seduction of Ilia is recounted at *Rom*. 4. 2), constitutes from the perspective of the plot the immediate motivation for Amulius' deepened fear (*Rom*. 3. 5: δι' ὅ).[48] Thus we are presented with not only a representation of the twins' looks, but also an account of Amulius' reading of the significance of their looks. The narrative has suddenly shifted from an external focalization—an apparently neutral, objective description—to internal focalization: the character Amulius has become the percipient and it is his vision of the twins' physical attributes, which he correctly understands to signify their regal origin, that propels the story.[49] Royal beauty is polysemous, at once inspiring fear and delight, as was true of Demetrius' natural presence.

This initial description, after a digressive examination of variant accounts of the twins' origins, is essentially repeated at *Rom*. 6. 3, though here the twins' size and appearance are explicitly diagnosed for the reader by Plutarch ('The excellence of their bodies in size and appearance—even when they were infants—illustrated their nature'). Yet while their externals may demonstrate their *physis*, they are no precise guides to the *ethos* of either twin. For Plutarch immediately turns to the development of the two brothers, which is only to some degree—but by no means fully—prefigured in their childhood mould: 'And when they grew up, they were both courageous and manly, possessing minds that were inclined toward danger and a daring that was wholly unshakeable. But Romulus seemed to exercise his judgment more and to have a statesman's intelligence' (*Rom*. 6. 3). Thus the kingly features which frightened Amulius and reinforce for the reader the twins' regal essence are shown to be inadequate evidence for discerning their developed *ethos*. Unlike Amulius, whose construal of the twins' appearance was adequate for his own base purposes, the reader is instructed by Plutarch on the proper signification of the boys' superficial attributes.

This second description, which marks the conclusion of the digressive catalogue of variant origins, a common employment of ring composition in Plutarch,[50] might have been nothing more than a narrative pause allowing Plutarch to resume the thread of his narrative of the twins' adventures. But Plutarch makes it into a didactic passage which also introduces an exposition of character that elliptically transports our story from the twins' infancy to their young manhood.[51] The resumptive description, then, functions both to mark a section's conclusion

---

[48] The relationship between description and motivation in narrative: Bal (n. 21) 130.

[49] My use of the term 'focalization' (and related terms) derives from the treatment in Bal (n. 21) 104 ff., which, one should note, diverges significantly from the discussion in Genette, *Narrative discourse* (n. 21) 189 ff; *cf.* Genette, *Narrative discourse revisited* trans. J.E. Lewin (Ithaca 1988) 72 ff. See also the insightful article by Kittey (n. 21). The application of narratological technique to historical narrative is illustrated impresively by Hornblower, 'Narratology and Thucydides,' in Hornblower (n. 26) 131-66 (Hornblower tends to employ Genette's terminology).

[50] See the concise but excellent discussion in J.L. Moles, *Plutarch: the life of Cicero* (Warminster 1988) 11 and 13.

[51] See Genette, *Narrative discourse* (n. 21) 86 ff. for a discussion of narrative duration.

and to indicate the beginning of a distinctly new—and critical—stage in the twins' career.[52]

Plutarch's emphasis on physique through his twice repeated description of the infant twins may also be deemed proleptic, for, later in this *Life*, at *Rom.* 7, Remus' appearance plays an integral part in the reunion of the twins with their grandfather, himself the rightful king of Alba. Chapter 7 tells us how the herdsmen of Numitor fell upon Remus, who was taken prisoner and handed over by Amulius to Numitor for punishment. Numitor, however, 'was astonished at the young man's marked superiority in size and strength of body, and he perceived in Remus' countenance that the boldness and vigor of his soul could not be enslaved nor suffered from his present circumstances' (*Rom.* 7. 5). The portrait of Remus comes not as a decorative adornment to the tale but as an account of Numitor's own perception of the youth; the focalization is again internal, thereby revealing not only the vision of Remus but also elucidating the character of the observer, Numitor himself.[53] Numitor's reactions to the sight of Remus have double significance since, as Remus himself will inform his grandfather, the brothers are twins and therefore identical; the virtues of Remus' figure also belong to Romulus, who is not portrayed separately and redundantly by Plutarch.[54] This lends to the scene the presence of the absent Romulus. Numitor's insight into Remus' adult features contrasts sharply with Amulius' earlier fear of the infant pair. Numitor is a percipient who ought also to have been hostile and to have regarded Remus' grandness as menacing (though our expectations as readers familiar with the tale render Numitor's superiority to Amulius unsurprising), yet we find in him a cross-reading of Remus' looks that underscores the fundamental differences between the two brothers, Numitor and Amulius (differences greater than but also adumbrating those which must emerge between Romulus and Remus). Furthermore, Numitor, like a good Plutarchan, extends his curiosity beyond mere externals; he learns that Remus' deeds correspond to his looks.[55] This combined interest in appearances and actions instantiates the lesson presented earlier in Plutarch's second description of the twins.

Now properly informed, Numitor chances upon the truth of Remus' origins, though he does not reveal his discovery but instead makes further inquiries of his prisoner.[56] This time it is Remus' turn to read the signs of his captor's bearing; Numitor's gentle voice and philanthropic countenance inspire the young man with hope, out of which he declares, 'I will hide nothing from you, for you seem to be more kingly than Amulius', though this is not a conclusion Remus draws primarily from Numitor's physiognomy but rather from his conduct, as he goes on to say, 'for you listen and examine before you punish, while he surrenders men without a trial' (*Rom.* 7. 6). Once again, justice is the hallmark of the genuine monarch. And so begins the reuniting of Romulus and Remus with their proper—and royal—family.[57]

---

[52] On this technique in Plutarchan narrative, see Pelling (n. 8) 123.

[53] Bal (n. 21) 108.

[54] Remus stresses his twinship with Romulus at *Rom.* 7. 6. Remus' description, which applies as well to Romulus, is an example of what might be called 'iterative description', on which expression see Genette, *Narrative discourse* (n. 21) 99. Although mythical twins are frequently described as differing in some respect (e.g. Apollo and Artemis, the Dioscori, Heracles and Iphicles) and granted that δίδυμος admits of the same ambiguity as 'twin,' there is no reason to assume that Romulus and Remus were not identical, nor does Plutarch state or imply that they were not identical (except in matters of statesmanship). Iconographically, Remus' appearances are nearly always limited to the *Lupa Romana* or to scenes depicting the exposure of the infants, in which cases there is no real differentiation made between the twins; *cf.* J.P. Small, 'Romulus and Remus,' in *Lexicon Iconographicum Mythologiae Classicae* vii. 1 (Zurich and Munich 1994) 639-44.

[55] *Rom.* 7. 5. Plutarchan interlocutors often gaze at one another before they speak; *cf.* Frazier (n. 20) 4511.

[56] *Rom.* 7. 5.

[57] Similarly, in the parallel *Life*, Theseus' (concise) physical description (the shearing of his hair) marks the point when it is appropriate for him to learn his true identity, cf. *Thes.* 5. 1.

The image of the king in Plutarch's *Romulus* is at no point extraneous to the requirements of his biographical story. The three descriptive passages are thoroughly insinuated into the narrative, though their diegetic functions may vary. The reader, of course, finds a satisfactory representation of Romulus' beauty, obliquely provided through Numitor's inspection of his twin brother. Moreover, we find in Plutarch's treatment, both in his explicit commentary at *Rom.* 6. 3 and in the contrasting behavior of Amulius and Numitor—as well as in Remus' evaluation of his grandfather's royal nature—unmistakeable qualifications regarding the correct diagnosis of even a king's physiognomy. The multiple perceptions of the image of the king serve in themselves to illustrate the potential for misreadings when attention is directed too exclusively to externals.[58]

V. PLUTARCH AND THE REGAL IMAGE

Plutarch understood the polysemous quality of physical attributes at both the superficial and the moral levels. He begins his *Lysander* by referring to a statue standing within the treasury of the Acanthians at Delphi. Many viewers falsely identify the statue as Brasidas, 'but the portrait is of Lysander' (*Lys.* 1. 1). Plutarch then proceeds to describe the image as that of a traditional, old-fashioned Spartan sporting the beard and long hair of Lycurgan custom. He then adds that the lawgiver had established the habit of wearing long hair 'because it made the handsome more distinguished, the ugly more frightening' (*Lys.* 1. 3). As Stadter has demonstrated in a keenly perceptive article, the polysemous nature of this physical attribute, whose effect is formulated in terms that in Greek signify both appearance and character (καλός / αἰσχρός), renders Lysander's image a symbol of his own paradoxical life—he was in some respects exceedingly Spartan and yet in others quite un-Spartan.[59] This stance of uncertainty, which emerges in the *Sulla* (the life parallel to the *Lysander*) as well,[60] achieves a strong impression in the *Lysander* largely because Plutarch refuses to interpret explicitly the statue of Lysander which he has introduced as an emblem of the man's character and career (though of course we know that the portrait itself must be generically handsome, hence the false attribution to Brasidas). Plutarch finds less ambiguity when it comes to Philopoemen's appearance: 'he was not ugly, as some suppose; for a statue of him is still to be seen at Delphi'. But stories of Philopoemen's sordid looks persisted into the biographer's own day, for the last of the Greeks had an unfortunate penchant for less than fashionable dress. Still, the question of precisely how to interpret superficial appearance persists. For, when properly construed, Philopoemen's dress becomes a mark of his simplicity (ἀφέλεια), one of the man's indubitable virtues, whatever one takes to be Plutarch's ultimate judgment of Philopoemen.[61]

That physiognomic expectations can lead to interpretations of the regal image that are equivocal, to say the least, constitutes an obvious concern of the *Agesilaus-Pompey*. Although the Spartan king's deformity was familiar to his readers, Plutarch does not introduce it until he has related the quality of Agesilaus' character, a description that is embedded in a distinctly erotic context: while he was being trained in the traditional *agoge*, Agesilaus had as his *erastes*

---

[58] Plutarch's concept of *mimesis* requires a reader capable of perceiving—and appreciating—the intelligence manifested in the artistic representation; *cf.* Van der Stockt, *QUCC* xxxvi (1990) 23-31.

[59] P.A. Stadter, 'Paradoxical paradigms: Lysander and Sulla', in P.A. Stadter (ed.), *Plutarch and the historical tradition* (London 1992) 41-55.

[60] Cf. *Sull.* 2 and 6. 14 ff. See now, on the *Lysander-Sulla*, Duff (n. 8) 50 ff.

[61] That Philopoemen is portrayed by Plutarch as incorruptible and inclined to simplicity is the verdict of J.J. Walsh, *Philologus* cxxxvi (1992) 208-38, who none the less finds in this pair (*Philopoemen-Flamininus*) a harsher characterization of Philopoemen than does S. Swain, *ICS* xiii (1988) 335-47.

no less a figure than Lysander, who was smitten by the decency of the youth's nature,[62] a point Plutarch enlarges upon by delineating the various dimensions of Agesilaus' conduct, such as his keen ambition, his gentleness, his obedience and his intense sense of honor. Only then does the narrative mention Agesilaus' lameness, a physical defect that in Plutarch's account only heightens the appreciation on the part of others of the beauty of the Spartan's disposition, for down to his extreme old age Agesilaus' character rendered him more adorable (ἐρασμιώτερον) than even the handsome or the young.

What might appear a straightforward preference of excellence in character over excellence in body is somewhat tempered, however, when Plutarch concludes this section of his biography by alluding to the anecdote preserved by Theophrastus, according to whom Agesilaus' father was fined by the ephors for marrying a small woman, on the grounds that she would bear not kings but kinglets. The story possesses no real relevance to Agesilaus' deformity, but rather reinforces traditional physiognomic notions of the regal physique, and, unless Plutarch simply could not resist the ephors' *bon mot* the anecdote seems most of all to prepare the reader for the controversy of Diopeithes' oracle. For Agesilaus' elevation to the throne required that his claims be preferred to those of Leotychides, who Lysander insisted was a bastard.[63] Opposition to Agesilaus, in Plutarch's narrative, focuses on his lameness when Diopeithes reveals an oracle which he understands as proof that it is contrary to the gods' will that a cripple become king:

> Φράζεο δή, Σπάρτη, καίπερ μεγάλαυχος ἐοῦσα,
> μὴ σέθεν ἀρτίποδος βλάστῃ χωλὴ βασιλεία·
> δηρὸν γὰρ νοῦσοί σε κατασχήσουσιν ἄελπτοι
> φθισιβρότου τ' ἐπὶ κῦμα κυλινδόμενον πολέμοιο.

Bethink thee now, O Sparta, though thou art very glorious, lest from thee, sound of foot, there spring a maimed royalty; for long will unexpected toils oppress thee, and onward-rolling billows of man-destroying war.[64]

But Lysander interpreted χωλὴ βασιλεία not as a reference to anyone's superficial deformity but to the (alleged) illegitimate origins of Leotychides, whose investiture would, in Lysander's exegesis, yield a more profoundly 'maimed royalty' than that of the hobbling Agesilaus. Lysander's arguments won the day, but not to the satisfaction of Plutarch. In the *Synkrisis* (2. 1) Plutarch maintains that the Spartans could and should have found an heir who was alike of sound birth and of sound limb, an opinion suggesting that the author felt obliged to recognize the legitimacy of the oracle's admonition despite its physiognomic bias. Indeed, he faults Lysander for his obscurantist reading of the prophecy.[65] On the surface of things, though, Lysander's view of Agesilaus' deformity seems to have a properly Plutarchan appreciation of the superior significance attaching to actions rather than to mere appearance. Of course one might advance the observation that Lysander's reading of Agesilaus' looks is vitiated in the event by its corrupt motive, the impropriety of which is marked by the less than opaque quality of Diopeithes' oracle. But such an argument fails to explain entirely Plutarch's criticism of the Spartans' elevation to the throne of a physically unsound king. What persists is the impression that the physiognomic approach, while far from satisfactory, is nevertheless not wholly irrelevant to the institution of monarchy. In short, Plutarch tends to underscore the extent to which the ethical interpretation of physique must be problematic.

---

[62] *Ages.* 2. 1: Λύσανδρον ἔσχεν ἐραστήν, ἐκπλαγέντα τῷ κοσμίῳ τῆς φύσεως αὐτοῦ [viz. Agesilaus].

[63] Ample discussion of this (historical) event can be found in P. Cartledge, *Agesilaos and the crisis of Sparta* (Baltimore 1987) 112 ff.

[64] *Ages.* 3. 7, with B. Perrin's Loeb translation.

[65] *Synk. Ages.-Pomp.* 2. 1 (μὴ δι' Ἀγησίλαον ἐπεσκότησε τῷ χρησμῷ Λύσανδρος).

This complication can also be detected in Plutarch's treatment in this *Life* of the fact that Agesilaus forbade the rendering of his likeness in painting or in sculpture, a point introduced by the biographer as a qualification to his description of the king as small and unimposing. No motive for Agesilaus' decision receives mention, an omission which allows, if it does not actually encourage, the inference that it was embarrassment which prevented the king from permitting his image to be represented (despite Plutarch's undeniable stress on the healthy and easy sense of humor with which the king bore his deformity). That this is in fact the inference which Plutarch intended his reader to draw receives support from the observation that absent from the *Agesilaus* is one of the Spartan's best known apophthegms. In justifying his deathbed commandment against any fabricated likeness of himself, Agesilaus is said to have explained: 'For if I have done any noble work, that is my memorial; but if I have done nothing noble, then all the statues in the world, themselves the works of menial and worthless men, mean nothing'.[66] Such a sentiment—if expressed—would here have emphasized Agesilaus' superiority in virtue in despite of his inferiority in form. It can hardly be accidental that Plutarch, in inserting this information into his account of Agesilaus' youth' rather than that of his demise, removed the crucial *bon mot*. Indeed, if Plutarch had availed himself of the opportunity to include in this biography Agesilaus' alleged rejection of the Thasians' offer to grant him divine honors, then the king's avoidance of graven images might well have been implicated in the biographer's brief against the excesses of ruler cult.[67] Indications of such a connection, however, are wanting. In this instance, then, if Agesilaus' remarkable absence from the plastic arts serves deeper purposes in this passage, one must surely be to emphasize the king's problematic physique.

Agesilaus' looks, then, signify little (in Plutarch's view) as to the beauty of his character, nor do they hamper the benefits to his leadership capacities (of which Plutarch is quite respectful) wrought by his traditional Spartan education. Yet they are not wholly irrelevant to Agesilaus' kingliness: his smallness itself embodies a defect, and his lameness may reasonably be construed as vitiating his monarchy on religious grounds. And this remains true despite the man's glorious career. Plutarch's acknowledgement of the polysemous nature of the regal image, then, clearly punctuates physiognomy's problematic status: for the regal image to be appreciated correctly in each sighting, a detailed and thoroughly informed understanding of the sighting's context as well as an intense and thoughtful scrutiny are required.[68] Nothing could be further from the mechanical exercise of physiognomy advertised in the handbook of (e.g.) Polemo.[69]

Agesilaus' defective appearance contrasts markedly in this pairing with that of Pompey. Whereas the Spartan's manner compensated for his lameness and diminutive stature, the Roman's youthful good looks lent him an air of majesty; indeed, they 'pleaded for him before he spoke'.

From the start he had an appearance which in no small way made him popular with the people and pleaded for him before he spoke. For his loveliness was humanely dignified, and the prime of his youthful beauty at once made manifest the stateliness and the regal majesty of his *ethos*. And there was a certain unshakeable *anastole* of his hair and a softness of the contours of his face around his eyes, all of which produced a likeness—more talked about than apparent—to the statues of King Alexander (*Pomp*. 2. 1).

---

[66] *Apophth. Lac.* = *Mor.* 215A: εἰ γάρ τι καλὸν ἔργον πεποίηκα, τοῦτό μου μνημεῖον ἔσται· εἰ δὲ μή, οὐδ' οἱ πάντες ἀνδριάντες, βαναύσων καὶ οὐδενὸς ἀξίων ἔργα ὄντες. Essentially the same passage is found at *Reg. et Imp. Apophth.* 12 = *Mor.* 191D. *Cf.* Xen. *Ages.* 11. 7; Cic. *Fam.* v 12. 7; Dio Chrysostom xxxvii 43. It can be a mark of wisdom to avoid honorific statues: *Cat. Ma.* 19; *Mor.* 198E- F; 820B-C; *cf.* Mossman (n. 15) 113.

[67] *Apophth. Lac.* 25 = *Mor.* 210D. M. Flower, *CQ* xxxviii (1988) 123-34, has recently argued for the historical veracity of this event.

[68] One might compare Plutarch's similarly complex view of astronomical phenomena; *cf.* Duff (n. 8) 71 ff.

[69] Gleason (n. 12) 29 ff.

Pompey's physiognomy is unquestionably regal, but his actual similarity to the king *par excellence*, Alexander, is at once described in detail by Plutarch and discounted. Pompey, unlike Agesilaus, looks the part of a king, a role of course denied him by the realities of the Roman constitution but none the less a theme both of his actual career and his biographer's *Life*.[70] The correspondence between Plutarch's treatment of Pompey, which underscores not merely Pompey's kingly countenance but the importance of a majestic appearance as well, and that of Agesilaus is unmistakeable. The point, however, remains less obvious. The claims of physiognomy appear to possess greater legitimacy, at least in some respects, in this pair—though the obvious candidate for kingship (from the purely physical perspective) can only be said to be regal in a metaphorical sense.

The matching of Agesilaus with Pompey allowed Plutarch to introduce regal physiognomy into a non-regal life. That the manipulation of monarchical physiognomic expectations might provide a useful narrative strategy in formulating the *Life* of a pretender was not lost on the biographer, who employs the image of the ideal monarch yet again (and again with complications) in his *Eumenes*. Regal imagery, both in its marked absence and in its unmistakeable presence, constitutes an important compositional device in *Eumenes*, naturally enough in view of the man's actual manipulation of the royal mystique throughout his marvelously checkered diadochal career. Plutarch is quite plain in criticizing the destructive nature of Eumenes' φιλονεικία: Eumenes could have enjoyed high honor and secure prosperity as Antigonus' lieutenant (*Synk*. 2.1-2). But instead Eumenes, by protesting an unwavering loyalty to the Argead house, pursued an independent and rival policy in competition with the other successors. A pose of conspicuous fealty to Alexander's memory and to his legitimate heirs was Eumenes' means of securing the loyalty of his troops, and Plutarch's biography devotes considerable attention to this dimension of Eumenes' leadership—even at the expense of the Greek's actual (and considerable) military success.[71]

At *Eum*. 13 Plutarch indicates the favorable disposition of the Argead house toward Eumenes (whom it sees as the best counter against the burgeoning might of Antigonus): Olympias invited Eumenes to take charge of Alexander's son, while Philip Arrhidaeus sent him to fight Antigonus, an assignment that associated him with the commanders of the Silver Shields, Antigenes and Teutamus, men who envied Eumenes bitterly. In order to control these officers without outraging their Macedonian pride, Eumenes resorted to what Plutarch designates δεισιδαιμονία, superstition, by which he means the famous stratagem of the Tent of Alexander. Eumenes claimed to his officers that Alexander had appeared to him in a dream in which he promised that, if a tent were decorated in royal fashion with a throne placed within and if they should conduct their deliberations in that tent, then he would always be present to assist and bless their counsels. Antigenes and Teutamus embraced the revelation, which allowed Eumenes to command officers who credulously preferred the barest hints of Alexander's presence—for it was an empty throne that signified the great king—to the instructions of living Argeads or the directions of their gallant but Greek general. Plutarch's disapproval of Antigenes and Teutamus could not be more obvious, and the episode obviously adumbrates Eumenes' eventual betrayal at the hands of the venal Silver Shields.[72]

Alexander's empty throne constitutes a regal image meaningful only to Eumenes' jealous and superstitious officers, against which one may juxtapose the impression made by Eumenes'

[70] E.g. P. Greenhalgh, *Pompey, the Roman Alexander* (London 1980) 11 and 171 ff.

[71] A.B. Bosworth, 'History and artifice in Plutarch's *Eumenes*' in P.A. Stadter (ed.), *Plutarch and the historical tradition* (London 1992) 58, 63, 70.

[72] Tent of Alexander: *Eum*. 13. 4-5. Envy of Antigenes and Teutamus: *Eum*. 13. 3; 14. 1. Betrayal by Silver Shields: *Eum*. 17-18.

appearance during the siege of Nora:

> And his appearance was sweet—not at all like a warrior or someone tried with weapons—rather he was delicate and youthful; and with respect to his entire body he was perfectly proportioned as if he had been precisely assembled by art, with limbs that possessed astonishing symmetry (*Eum.* 11. 3).

This description derives from Hieronymus of Cardia, but the literary use to which it is put is Plutarch's own. In Nepos' *Eumenes* essentially the same description of the protagonist (in so far as the damaged text permits one to draw conclusions) comes in the recounting of Eumenes' exchange with Onomarchus when the former was Antigonus' prisoner. According to Diodorus' account, Eumenes was popular with his men at Nora because he shared their rations and was affable.[73] Plutarch employs Eumenes' shared table in order to lead into his physical description, a transition made by punning on the word ἡδύς, sweet. Eumenes clearly possesses the idealized royal physique of Hellenistic kingship: charming, handsome, youthful and perfectly proportioned.[74] His besieged troops take refreshment from his kingly presence—though Eumenes, despite his fierce ambitions, is forbidden any claim to royal station, a point driven home by the effectiveness of the Tent of Alexander in subsequent chapters. Here again it is difficult to miss Plutarch's critique of physiognomic expectations generally and, more specifically, of the specious obsessions of ruler cult, for the arrangement of these successive images—the regal Eumenes at Nora and the Tent of Alexander—enacts, both in the individual image and in their succession, an implicit argument.

The corresponding portrayal of Sertorius, it is perhaps worth noting, also strikes a (discordant) physiognomic note: the dashing general, Plutarch observes, retained only one eye, and such a condition (he jests) is a symptom indicating superior cunning and military capacity. There are few light moments in Plutarch's *Lives* and this one, which patently ridicules the physiognomic consciousness, is curiously blunt beside the more subtle use to which physiognomy is put in the *Eumenes*.[75]

Externals (by now it is unmistakeable) may mirror inner reality, or they may not. But in every case they are hazardous guides to character. Hence the biographer's distrust of external signs of regal excellence, which are all too liable to false readings. This is made abundantly clear in Plutarch's fragmentary *Ad Principem Ineruditum* (*Mor.* 779D ff.), a useful template for understanding the biographer's royal *Lives*. Here we learn that the good king must be the living Logos (ἔμψυχος λόγος)[76] and the champion of justice:

> Now justice is the aim and end of law, and law is the work of the ruler, and the ruler is the image of god who orders all things. Such a ruler needs no Pheidias nor Polycleitus nor Myron to model him, but by his virtue he forms himself in the likeness of god and thus creates a statue most delightful of all to behold and most worthy of divinity (*Princ. Inerud.* 3 = *Mor.* 780E).

This ruler is to be preferred to monarchs who, like unskillful sculptors, mistake the external signs of dignity and majesty for their substance,[77] or those who represent themselves in painting and sculpture with the attributes of the gods (a common practice in royal portrait-

---

[73] Nepos, *Eum.* 11. 5; Diod. Sic. xviii 42. 5.

[74] On the importance of symmetry, see Evans (n. 2) 53 f.

[75] *Sert.* 1. 8. *Cf.* C.F. Konrad, *Plutarch's Sertorius: a historical commentary* (Chapel Hill 1994) 31-33.

[76] *Princ. Inerud.* 3 = Mor. 780C.

[77] *Princ. Inerud.* 2 = Mor. 779F.

ure).[78] The image of the true king resides not in bronze or marble, but in action, in the execution of justice. This view of monarchy conforms with Plutarch's general concern with *ethos* and its proper development. Excellence lies in good character, which is in Plutarch's view only observable in the making of proper choices, in the performance of right actions.[79]

The theatricality of a Demetrius remains a sham even when the corrupted actor possesses a kingly disposition. And the intelligent percipient, like Numitor or Remus, will understand how much weight attaches to externals and how much to the evidence of deeds when estimating a man. Plutarch's *Lives* constitute the practical application of his own moral and political principles through the representation of men's actions in their historical context, by which means the biographer meant to provide an accurate and therefore instructive depiction of his subject. This is expressed with elegant conciseness in the introduction to the *Pericles*: 'What is beautiful and noble (τὸ καλόν) spontaneously drives us to itself and instills in us an immediate urge to action; it does not build character in the observer by means of representation (οὐ τῇ μιμήσει) but produces a moral purpose by means of the history of action (τῇ ἱστορίᾳ τοῦ ἔργου)'.[80]

That Plutarch's moral purposes underlie his literary choices has long been recognized. In the matter of physical descriptions, their common absence from his biographical narratives is by no means accidental; indeed, their omission or excessive conciseness represents a challenge to and a critique of prevailing literary and intellectual conventions. This at least seems the most obvious inference to be drawn from the uses to which he puts his extended descriptions in the regal biographies. There Plutarch's unmistakeable criticism of traditional royal ideology is sustained through a variety of stylistic techniques. Plutarch's literary exploitation of physical descriptions, whether as set-pieces or implicated throughout the narrative, reflects his conviction that externals are pale traces of inner reality.

W. JEFFREY TATUM

The Florida State University

---

[78] *Princ. Inerud.* 3 = Mor. 780F. On this practice in actual portraiture, see Smith (n. 26) 38 ff. See also Plut. *Praecepta Gerendae Reipublicae = Mor.* 820B-C, for Plutarch's recommendation that the statesman eschew the honor of a statue in favor of an inscription.

[79] Pelling, *ICS* xiii (1988) 257-74; *id.*, 'Childhood and personality in Greek biography', in Pelling (ed.), *Characterization and individuality in Greek literature* (Oxford 1990) 213-44. It scarcely need be said that in his emphasis on action as the proper sign of character Plutarch is part and parcel of traditional Greek thinking on this matter, *cf.* S. Halliwell, 'Traditional Greek conceptions of character', in Pelling, *op. cit.* 32-59. What distinguishes Plutarch is his cautious and explicit distrust (even distaste) for attending inordinately to the outward trappings of kingliness (or of excellence generally). One might compare his attitude toward feminine beauty at *Amat.* 23 = *Mor.* 769C-D.

[80] *Per.* 2. 4. The difficulties attending the proper interpretation of this sentence are discussed by Van der Stockt (n. 19) 32 ff.; *cf.* Stadter (n. 1) xxix-xxx.

NOTES

Veiling, αἰδώς, and a red-figure amphora by Phintias*

At p. 319 n. 203 of my recent book,[1] I discuss

the appearance of the letters ΑΙΔΟΣ ... designating the figure of Artemis on an Attic red-figure amphora (depicting the rape of Leto by Tityos) by Phintias (Louvre G42; ARV^2 23,1 [*Paralipomena* 323, *Addenda*[2] 154; see now also *LIMC* ii pl. 275, Apollon 1069, vi, Leto 34; PLATE I] ...). That this constitutes an association between the goddess and *aidôs* is the position of Kretschmer [*Die griechischen Vaseninschriften* (Gütersloh 1894) 197],[2] Norwood [*Essays on Euripidean drama* (Berkeley 1954) 76 n. 2], and Schefold [*Götter- und Heldensagen der Griechen in der spätarchaischen Kunst* (Munich 1978) 68].[3] Certainly analogous titles/epithets exist—the cult of Artemis Eukleia is discussed ... by Braund [*JHS* c (1980) 184-5],[4] and Schefold [(n. 3) 330 n. 152][5] points to a possible description of Artemis as Aretê on a black-figure neck amphora by the Antimenes Painter (Basel iii, 3; the figure so designated, however, is not certainly Artemis).[6] But the view of von Erffa [ΑΙΔΩΣ *und verwandte Begriffe, Philologus* Suppl. xxx. 2 (Leipzig 1937) 58] and F. Eckstein (in *LIMC* i.1, 352-3) that the letters are an abbreviation of the genitive *Artemidos* is not to be dismissed, notwithstanding Kretschmer's assurance [*Vaseninschriften* 197][7] that ΑΙΔΟΣ not [ΑΡΤΕ]ΜΙΔΟΣ is the correct reading (note that the vase also names Leto in the gen.).[8] An association of Artemis and *aidôs* makes sense, and a cult would not be impossible, but we should be wary of assuming either from such doubtful evidence.

* For assistance in the preparation of this note, I am indebted to: W.G. Arnott; H. Bernsdorff; D.H. Berry; F. Cairns; C.J. Classen; G. Davies; R. Hannah; Alexander von Humboldt Stiftung; Seminar für klassische Philologie and Institut für Archäologie (Göttingen); Department of Greek, Etruscan and Roman Antiquities, Musée du Louvre; A.H. Sommerstein; and two referees, one anonymous and one (C. Sourvinou-Inwood) not.

[1] *Aidôs* (Oxford 1993).
[2] *Cf.* E. Gerhard, *Auserlesene Vasenbilder* (Berlin 1840-58) i 81; J. Overbeck, *Griechische Kunstmythologie* (Leipzig 1871-89) iii 387.
[3] = *Gods and heroes in late archaic Greek art* (Eng. trans. Cambridge 1992) 71 (cited hereafter from trans.). *Cf.* A. Greifenhagen, 'Tityos', *Jb. Berl. Mus.* i (1959) 19; J. Hani in J. Duchemin (ed.), *Mythe et personnification* (Paris 1980) 105.
[4] On (Art.) Eukleia, see now *LIMC* ii.1, 677 (L. Kahil); H.A. Shapiro, *Personifications in Greek art* (Zürich 1993) 70-8.
[5] On *ABV* 269, 41 (*LIMC* ii pl. 553, Artemis 1300); *cf.* P.E. Arias and M. Hirmer, *A history of Greek vase painting* (rev. B. Shefton, London 1962) 318.
[6] Schefold (n. 3) 337 n. 353 also identifies as Arete the figure crowning Heracles on two vases described by J.D. Beazley (*AK* iv [1961] 56 no. 3, 57 no. 6).
[7] F. Hauser, in A. Furtwängler and K. Reichold, *Griechische Vasenmalerei* (Munich 1904-32) ii 273 n. 1, rejects the 'abbreviation' view, but interprets the letters as a slip for ᾿Αρτέμιδος; *cf.* H.R. Immerwahr, *Attic script* (Oxford 1990) 67. The hypothesis of M. Vickers and D. Gill, *Artful Crafts* (Oxford 1994)—that Attic painted pottery (including its inscriptions) imitates gold- and silverware—might explain *how* a slip was made (see esp. 164) but cannot prove *that* a slip was made.

The note does its job, after a fashion; but, in common with the works it cites (and most[9] other discussions of the scene) it overlooks the most obviously relevant detail in the image—that Leto is depicted as veiling (i.e. drawing her *himation* over) her head. This is a feature which this representation of the actual moment of the rape shares with several versions of its aftermath:[10] as Greifenhagen has shown,[11] the single female figure to whom Tityos clings, with whom he flees, or away from whom he falls when attacked by Apollo and/or Artemis must be Leto rather than Ge;[12] the once prevalent identification of the goddess with Ge rests on an illegitimate comparison with Antaeus' alleged need to maintain contact with his mother,[13] on a naive belief that a

[8] The complete list of inscriptions is: (A) ΧΑΙΡΕ ΚΑΙΡΕ (both horizontal, to left of Apollo) ΑΠΟΛΛΟΝ (vertical, to right of Ap.) ΛΕΤΟΥΣ (vert., to right of L.) ΧΑΙΡΕ (horiz., above Art.'s raised right hand) ΑΙΔΟΣ (vert., to right of Art.) (B) ΣΟΣΤΡΑΤΟΣ (horiz., above the two central figures) ΚΑΛΟΣ (horiz., at top right of scene) ΣΟΤΙΝΟΣ (vert., to right of figure on far left) ΧΑΡΕΣ (vert., to right of discus-thrower) ΧΑΙΡΕ (vert., between acontist's legs) ΔΕΜΟΣΤΡΑΤΕ (vert., to right of acontist) ΣΟΣΙΑΣ (vert., to right of spectator on far right); see Immerwahr (n. 7) 66-7. Sotinos and Sosias are the two older spectators; καλός goes with Sostratos and Demostratos is the recipient of the greeting; but it is unclear whether the discus-thrower is Sostratos or Chares, the acontist Chares or Demostratos; and neither χαῖρε nor καλός inscriptions need refer to individuals depicted on the vase. On A, the three χαῖρε inscriptions are most probably extra-iconic; given their position, it is unlikely that they and the other inscriptions are to be construed as one complete sentence ('Hail Apollo, son of Leto, hail Aidos!').
[9] But not all: see Roscher, *ML* v 1043 (O. Waser).
[10] Certainly London E 278 (*ARV*[2] 226, 2; *LIMC* vi pl. 133, Leto 36 = Apollon 1070 = Ge 43); Munich 2689 (*ARV*[2] 879, 2; *LIMC* ii pl. 275, Apollon 1071 = Ge 45 = Leto 45); Louvre G375 (*ARV*[2] 1032, 54; Leto designated Μέλουσα); a rf krater from the Loeb Collection (Munich, Loeb 472; J. Sieveking, *Bronzen, Terrakotten, Vasen der Sammlung Loeb* [Munich 1930] 61 and pl. 48, *LIMC* vi pl. 133, Leto 38 = Artemis 1368); perhaps also Berlin 1835 (*ABV* 286, 10: A. Furtwängler, *Beschreibung der Vasensammlung im Antiquarium* [Berlin 1885] 331-2); and possibly those canvassed in nn. 15-16 below). On an Argive-Corinthian shield-band relief of *c.* 540 in Basle (*LIMC* vi pl. 133, Leto 40) Leto draws her veil just as on the vases.
[11] (n. 3) 19-27; *cf.* P. Zancani Montuoro and U. Zanotti-Bianco, *Heraion alla Foce del Sele* (Rome 1951-4) ii 325-9, J. Henle, *Greek myths* (Bloomington 1974) 35-7.
[12] The interpretation which see Ge as practically a fixture in scenes of the pursuit/killing of Tityos goes back to Overbeck (n. 2) iii 383-90, and is well represented by the entries s.v. 'Tityos' in Roscher and *RE* (e.g. K. Scherling in *RE* vi A 1599: 'Wenn eine Frau neben T. oder zwischen ihm und Apollon steht, so ist es seine Mutter Ge'); despite rebuttal by Greifenhagen and Henle, it has some more recent adherents (e.g. G. Neumann, *Gesten und Gebärden in der griechischen Kunst* [Berlin 1965] 178 n. 127, 189 n. 280). See most recently M. Moore in *LIMC* iv.1, 175-6, L. Kahil, *ibid.* vi.1, 260.
[13] Greifenhagen (n. 3) 22, against (e.g.) Waser in Roscher, *ML* v 1047, Scherling in *RE* vi A 1602; the motif of Antaeus' need to maintain contact with Earth appears to be post-classical: see Gerhard (n. 2) ii 104; G. Oertel in Roscher, *ML* i 362; A. Furtwängler in Roscher, *ML* i 2208; E.N. Gardiner, *JHS* xxv (1905) 282-4; and R. Olmos/L.J. Balmaseda in *LIMC* i.1, 810-11.

figure who appears either to run away from Apollo or to stand between Apollo and his victim cannot be Apollo's own mother,[14] and on an assumption that the appearance of Ge (guaranteed by an inscription) on one particular rendering of the episode makes her presence a canonical element of the scene.[15] But in any depiction of the killing of Tityos featuring Apollo (or Apollo and Artemis), their victim, and a female figure, the economy of the scene demands that that figure be Leto.[16] The goddess featured in such scenes does not always veil, but does so often enough to make the veiling an aid to identification;[17] for the veiling of the head is a typical response of the recipient of unwanted erotic attentions.[18]

Veiling of the head in such circumstances clearly represents the victim's αἰδώς: covering one's head is a gesture which belongs in the general complex of associations between αἰδώς, the eyes, exposure and visibility.[19] Numerous passages make the connexion between αἰδώς and veiling explicit: in Euripides' *Hippolytus*, for example, the removal of Phaedra's headdress at 201-2, symbolizing the casting off of restraint which is apparent in her subsequent sublimated ravings, is answered by her desire to have her head covered again at 243, a desire which she explains with reference both to her αἰδώς at what she has said and to her wish to conceal her tears and the αἰσχύνη in her eyes (244-6).[20] This association between αἰδώς and the veil is also apparent in passages where the former is not mentioned: Penelope's repeated gesture,[21] for example, of drawing her κρήδεμνον across her face before entering the company of the suitors clearly belongs, as a precaution dictated by a woman's proper modesty, with her scrupulous care in ensuring that she is always flanked by two attendants.[22]

That an artistic representation of a woman veiling can be construed as a representation of αἰδώς is apparent from a passage in Pausanias' account of Laconia (iii 20.10-11):

> They say that the ἄγαλμα of Aidos, around thirty stades from the city, is a dedication of Icarius, and that it was created on the following account: when Icarius gave Penelope as wife to Odysseus, he tried to make Odysseus, too, settle in Lacedaemon, but when he failed in that, he then begged his daughter to stay behind, and as she set off for Ithaca he followed the chariot and kept pleading with her. For a while, Odysseus put up with this, but finally he told Penelope either to follow him willingly or choose her father and return to Lacedaemon. She, they say, made no reply, but veiled her head [ἐγκαλυψαμένης] in response to the question; Icarius, recognizing that she wished to leave with Odysseus, let her go, and dedicated the ἄγαλμα to Aidos; for this, they say, was the point on the journey that Penelope had reached when she veiled herself [ἐγκαλύψασθαι].

It is clear from the story that Pausanias relates that the ἄγαλμα portrayed a veiled woman (probably Penelope

---

[14] On one vase (New York 08.258.21, *ARV*[2] 1086, 1: *LIMC* ii pl. 275, Apollon 1072 = Leto 37) the figure depicted between Leto's children and Tityos in the pose supposedly typical of Ge is named as Leto.

[15] The presence of Ge in a version of the pursuit of Tityos is guaranteed by the inscription ΓΕ on a Tyrrhenian amphora in the Louvre (E 864, *ABV* 97, 33; *LIMC* ii pl. 274, Apollon 1066 = Ge 10); cf. Moore (n. 12) 175; n.b. Ge does not veil here. Two other vases (Tarquinia RC 1043 [*ABV* 97, 32; *LIMC* Ge 11 = Leto 42 = Niobidai 3], Villa Giulia, *ABV* 121, 6 [*LIMC* iv pl. 97 Ge 12 = Leto 34]) offer more than one female character (besides Art.), and so also permit an identification of Ge as a participant (cf. Moore, *loc. cit.*); in both, the central female figure, between pursuers and pursued, is veiling, and Greifenhagen ([n. 3] 11, 14) is prepared to allow that this is Ge rather than Leto. Leto's veiling, however, is more easily motivated than Ge's, and on the other vases depicting a veiled woman that figure is clearly Leto. But it is sufficient for our purposes that Leto's veiling should be a regular element of the scene, whereas the very presence of Ge is certain in only one example, and the possibility of her veiling highly uncertain.

[16] Henle (n. 11) 37. In only one case (a calyx krater by the Aegisthus Painter, Louvre G 164 [*ARV*[2] 504, 1; *LIMC* Ge 44 = Leto 44]) is there any difficulty in identifying a single veiled female as Leto (cf. Henle, 175-6 n. 7). The difficulty lies in the strange 'pin cushion' object attached to the figure's chest, into which Apollo has apparently shot his arrows; some see this as symbolic of the invulnerability of Ge (e.g. Waser in Roscher, *ML* v 1050), or of Apollo's arrows (untypically) falling to earth (E. Buschor in Furtwängler-Reichold [n. 7] iii 280); but the figure does veil, does stretch out her hand to Apollo, and her position in front of a palm suggests Leto or Artemis. Leto remains a strong possibility (so Greifenhagen [n. 3] 25-7) but the scene is enigmatic. See further A. Griffiths, *JHS* cvi (1986) 65 n. 37 and *BICS* xxxvii (1990) 131-3.

[17] Contrast Henle (n. 11) 37. The significance of Leto's veil is reflected in the detail given by Apollonius (i 759-62) and the Suda (s.v. 'Tityos'; iv 564-5 Adler), that Tityos dragged Leto by the καλύπτρη/κρήδεμνον. Cf. Zancani Montuoro and Zanotti-Bianco (n. 11) ii 326.

[18] See, e.g. Leningrad 709 (*ARV*[2] 487, 61; C. Sourvinou-Inwood, *'Reading' Greek culture* [Oxford 1991] pls 9-10); Leningrad 777 (*ARV*[2] 502, 11; Sourvinou-Inwood pl. 6); Madrid 11038 (*ARV*[2] 586, 46; K.J. Dover, *Greek homosexuality* [London 1978] R750); London E 64 (*ARV*[2] 455, 9); Paris, Petit Palais 316 (*ARV*[2] 639, 58).

[19] See Cairns (n. 1) 15, 98-9 n. 151, 158, 184, 217-18, 231, 292-3, 312, 352; also in *CQ* 46 (1996).

[20] Cf. *Her.* 1159-62, *IT* 372-6, *Or* 459-61 (Cairns [n. 1] 292-3), *Pho.* 1485-92; Pl. *Phdr.* 237a, Aeschin. i 26 (etc.); on veiling as stage business in tragedy see F.L. Shisler, *AJP* lxvi (1945) 385.

[21] *Od.* i 333-4, xvi 415-16, xviii 209-10, xxi 64-5; interpreted as a gesture of σωφροσύνη by Julian *Orat.* iii 127c-d (cf. H. F. North, *Sophrosyne* [Ithaca 1966] 308 n. 143).

[22] See M. Nagler, *Spontaneity and tradition* (Berkeley 1974) 44-72, 80, who also (47-9) notes the significance of the removal of the κρήδεμνον at *Il.* xxii 468-72, *Od.* vi 100 (cf. R. Seaford in T.H. Carpenter, C.A. Faraone [eds.], *Masks of Dionysus* [Princeton 1993] 177-21, id. *Reciprocity and ritual* [Oxford 1994] 333, 350-1). Contrast F. Studniczka, *Beiträge zur Geschichte der altgriechischen Tracht* (Vienna 1886) 125-7; H. Haakh, *Gymnasium* lxvi (1959) 374-80; and Neumann (n. 12) 179 n. 134, who believe that Penelope is unveiling herself in order to appear more attractive to the suitors. Cf. K. Friis Johansen, *The Attic grave reliefs of the classical period* (Copenhagen 1951) 41 n. 1, re sepulchral reliefs; C.M. Galt, *AJA* xxxv (1931) 373-93; also the summary of a paper by M.E. Mayo in *AJA* lxxvii (1973) 200, which appears to have argued that the drawing of the veil *always* represents unveiling (even in rape scenes). There need be no dispute that the gesture can be intended to) be attractive to men, since manifestations of αἰδώς (lowering the eyes, blushing, etc., as well as veiling) *were* attractive to men; cf. J.M. Redfield, *Arethusa* xv (1982) 196.

herself, rather than a personified Aidos);[23] the link between a woman's αἰδώς and her veiling, therefore, was so close that an artistic representation of the gesture could be construed as a representation of the quality itself.[24] Even more interesting, however, is the obvious fact that Pausanias' story is an *aition* of the veiling of the bride in the context of her wedding;[25] this, I think, makes it certain that we are not to think of the veiling of the bride as something distinct from veiling as a manifestation of αἰδώς. On vases, the veiling which signifies αἰδώς is not to be sharply distinguished from that which signifies 'marriage', for the latter is merely a ritualized form of a gesture which in everyday life might accompany a spontaneous emotional reaction or constitute a conventional way of displaying one's feminine virtue.[26]

Since there is very little indeed on veiling in the standard works on ancient gestures,[27] it is worth pausing to consider in what circumstances the covering of the head does and does not betoken αἰδώς. We have seen that the actual drawing of the veil, in the case of Penelope, of Leto, and of other victims of rape, can be a clear sign of αἰδώς; veiling in marriage, or veiling in abduction presented as marriage or marriage presented as abduction, also signifies αἰδώς.[28] The same gesture is found also in scenes in which the wife bids farewell to the departing warrior, where, far from being merely a gesture of 'greeting',[29] the tugging at the veil reminds us of the woman's marital status, indicates that her thoughts focus on her relationship with her husband, and promises fidelity in his absence. It is no coincidence that the drawing of the mantle before the face is the gesture most often chosen to represent the personified Pudicitia on imperial Roman coins,[30] nor is it fortuitous that Pudicitia seems to have been particularly associated with the *univira*.[31] The gesture in this latter case clearly conveys the same message as it does in the case of Penelope in the *Odyssey*. But the veil need not actually be drawn to indicate αἰδώς; in the iconography of the wedding, the head is veiled, but the veil is not necessarily drawn to

[23] *Cf.* F. Eckstein, *LIMC* i.1, 352; also R. Schulz, ΑΙΔΩΣ (Diss. Rostock 1910) 98-9; von Erffa, ΑΙΔΩΣ 57.

[24] *Cf.* the remark of Pliny (xxxv 63) that in his portrait of Penelope Zeuxis *pinxisse mores videtur* (cited by T.H. Carpenter, *Art and myth in ancient Greece* [London 1991] 235); Carpenter is no doubt right to say that Zeuxis depicted Penelope as in his fig. 347 (Chiusi 1831, *ARV²* 1300, 2); the pose of this seated, veiled Penelope is very similar to that of the Persepolis torso which Eckstein, *JDAI* lxxiv (1959) 137-57, *LIMC* i.1, 352-3 (pl. 270, Aidos 1 in *LIMC* i.2), regards as the Aidos/Penelope discussed by Pausanias; against this identification, see E. Langlotz, *JDAI* lxxvi (1961) 72-99; *cf.* W. Gauer, *JDAI* cv (1990) 31-65.

[25] On the wedding veil, see M.L. Cunningham, *BICS* xxxi (1984) 9-12; D. Armstrong and E.A. Ratchford, *BICS* xxxii (1985) 1-14; R. Seaford, *JHS* cvii (1987) 124-5; A. Carson in D.M. Halperin, J.J. Winkler, and F.I. Zeitlin (eds.), *Before sexuality* (Princeton 1990) 160-4; and J.H. Oakley, R.H. Sinos, *The wedding in ancient Athens* (Madison, Wis. 1993) *passim*, esp. 25-6, 30-2, 44.

[26] For Sourvinou-Inwood (n. 18) 69 the gesture of veiling is in itself polysemic, but in the particular context of erotic pursuits conveys an allusion to the marriage veil; this allusion is certainly present (for the representational schemes 'marriage' and 'abduction' constantly feed off each other in Greek art), but the basic reason why veiling is common to brides and to the objects of erotic pursuit (as well as to victims of rape, e.g. Leto) is that veiling typically expresses αἰδώς, and the normal focus of women's αἰδώς is sexual. For the bride's veiling as expression of her αἰδώς, see E. *IT* 372-6. There, Iphigeneia's αἰδώς is clearly a genuine emotional reaction; but it may be naive to assume that reflections of such anxiety in literature and myth are to be understood purely in terms of female psychology, for the bride's αἰδώς at leaving her father (as in the Pausanias passage) and at the thought of her future as a sexual being is also a valuable indication of her loyalty to her κύριος and of her innocence, and thus of her eligibility and promise as a wife; there may therefore have been a considerable element of cultural role-playing as well as of spontaneous emotion in her attitude. See I. Jenkins, *BICS* xxx (1983) 137-46; *cf.* Redfield (n. 22) 183-92; H. King in A. Cameron and A. Kuhrt (eds.), *Images of women in antiquity* (London 1983) 109-17; H.P. Foley, *Ritual irony* (Ithaca NY 1985) 86-9 etc.; Seaford (n. 25) 106-30, *JHS* cviii (1988) 118-24.

[27] C. Sittl, *Die Gebärden der Griechen und Römer* (Leipzig 1890), at least discusses veiling, sees the connexion with αἰδώς (84 and n. 7), and notes the iconographic link between wedding, abduction, and the 'marriage of death' (278-9), but his discussion is brief and unsystematic. In Neumann (n. 12) veiling receives no discussion in its own right, and *prima facie* similar poses involving the veiling of the head are distinguished on the most tenuous of criteria.

[28] For the interaction of 'marriage' and 'abduction' motifs, see (e.g.) the Meidias Painter's depiction of the rape of the Leucippides (London E 224, *ARV²* 1313, 5; L. Burn, *The Meidias painter* [Oxford 1987] 16-17, 25 and pls 1a, 2b-3, 4b-9b); Eriphyle is lifted aloft by Castor, who holds her exactly as Tityos does Leto on the Phintias vase (*cf.* n. 47 below), but the tugging at her veil is at once a spontaneous response to sexual outrage and a detail which recalls the wedding ceremony; the latter is yet more explicitly recalled in Polydeuces' use of a chariot to carry off Hilaeira (who also draws her veil). (On the chariot, *cf.* R. Lindner, *Der Raub der Persephone in der antiken Kunst* [Würzburg 1984]). *Cf.* Arezzo 1460, *ARV²* 1157, 25 (Pelops and Hippodameia), and depictions too numerous to list of the abduction and recovery of Helen in L. Ghali-Kahil, *Les Enlèvements et le retour d'Hélène* (Paris 1955) and *LIMC* iv pls 291-359 *passim* (*cf.* R. Rehm, *Marriage to death* [Princeton 1994] 39). On abduction/marriage, *cf.* A. van Gennep, *The rites of passage* (Eng. trans. London 1960) 123-9; T.B.L. Webster, *Potter and patron in classical Athens* (London 1972) 107; Jenkins (n. 26); Sourvinou-Inwood (n. 18) 65-70 and *passim*, ead. *BICS* xx (1973) 12-21; Rehm 36-40. The occurrence of the bridal gesture in other contexts suggestive of αἰδώς is reason to doubt the contention of Oakley and Sinos (n. 25) 30, 36, 44 that it always signifies unveiling in wedding iconography. Like Mayo (n. 22), they refer to 'the gesture known as the *anakalypsis*' (44); but no ancient author uses the term ἀνακάλυψις in the sense or the connexion they require.

[29] Haakh (n. 22) 375-6; see his pl. xv (= Munich 2415, *ARV²* 1143, 2; for the correct interpretation, see G. Davies, *Apollo* cxl no. 389 [July 1994] 6-7; *cf.* Würzburg 160, A. Rumpf, *Chalkidische Vasen* (Leipzig 1927) no. 14 pls 31-4.

[30] See R. Peter in Roscher, *ML* iii 3276-7; Langlotz (n. 24) 84-5; North (n. 21) 308-9; M. Grant, *Roman imperial money* (Amsterdam 1972 [¹ 1954]) 159-61.

[31] See Livy x 23, 3-10 (esp. 9); Festus p. 242, Paulus p. 243 Müller; *cf.* Peter in Roscher, *ML* iii 3277-9; G. Williams, *JRS* xlviii (1958) 23-4; N. Rudd, *Lines of enquiry* (Cambridge 1976) 42-3; Hani (n. 3) 107; E. D'Ambra, *MDAI(R)* xcviii (1991) 243-8, *Private lives, imperial virtues* (Princeton 1993) 36-9, 56-8, 79; G. Davies in E. Marshall, M. Harlow (eds.), *Messages from the past* (Exeter 1996).

cover the face;[32] equally, the heavily draped women and boys on vases indicate, by the mere fact of their covering themselves, their observance of the demands of αἰδώς/σωφροσύνη.[33] If there is a distinction to be drawn between the act of drawing the veil and the practice of covering the head, it is presumably not one between αἰδώς and not-αἰδώς, but between representations of occurrent and dispositional αἰδώς, πάθος and ἕξις.

Other representations of veiled figures may seem further removed from αἰδώς; Neumann, for example, considers that the veiled Penelope mentioned above (n. 24) portrays 'anxious expectancy' (banges Harren), and distinguishes this pose from others in which the veiled figure manifests grief, sorrow, resentment, or dejection.[34] But above all, Penelope is a heroine of conjugal αἰδώς; her attitude in the scene under discussion is certainly one of sad dejection, but the veiled head will also convey a message about her status as a married woman, her resistance to erotic attentions, and her loyalty. Equally, anger

and resentment clearly have a part to play in the motivation of Achilles (lamenting the loss of Briseis, rejecting the arguments of the ambassadors)[35] and Ajax (at the judgement of the arms)[36] as represented by vase-painters, but their veiling must also have something to do with their sense of humiliation and exposure to the ridicule of others. Perhaps the attitude in which veiling seems furthest removed from αἰδώς is that of grief; clearly, grief and αἰδώς have much in common—both are emotions in which one retreats into oneself and cuts oneself off from others, and both involve the sinking feeling of dejectedness which the Greeks called κατήφ–εια. This is as much as to suggest that veiling need not carry connotations of αἰδώς as such, but may be a symptom of something that αἰδώς shares with other emotions; yet in two ways, I think, the veiling which accompanies grief may have more to do with αἰδώς than that. First, where the veiled and grieving figure is a woman, veiling may suggest αἰδώς qua (wifely, motherly, daughterly, sisterly, etc.) loyalty to the deceased,[37] or, where the veiled figure is the deceased herself,[38] the αἰδώς which characterized the woman in life. More importantly, however, veiling as an accompaniment to any emotion may indicate a way of concealing emotion or coping with it with σωφροσύνη. Thus in the Homeric hymn to Demeter it is clear that Demeter veils her head and lowers her eyes as part of her grief at the loss of her daughter (40-2, 183, 194, 197), yet this is precisely the behaviour from which Metaneira construes αἰδώς at 213-15;[39] and passages in Homer and Euripides offer unequivocal examples of the αἰδώς which conceals or keeps private grief and other emotions.[40] Thus on works of art depicting veiled and grieving women, the veiling may be at once a manifestation of grief, a sign of a restrained and modest response

[32] Bf vases typically show the procession, with bride and groom in chariot, and the bride normally draws her mantle; on rf vases the bride is most often led, veiled but not veiling, χεῖρ' ἐπὶ καρπῷ; see Oakley and Sinos (n. 25) 26-34 (with ill.). Cf. veiling/χεῖρ' ἐπὶ καρπῷ motifs in the 'marriage of death' on Berlin 1902 (ABV 363, 37); Athens NM 1926 (ARV² 846, 193); also the grave relief of Myrrhine (Athens NM 4485; Friis Johansen [n. 22] fig. 82). Equally, some representations of Roman Pudicitia depict a veiled rather than a veiling woman; S.W. Stevenson, A dictionary of Roman coins (London 1964) 668. Some (quasi) wedding scenes are better understood as depicting unveiling rather than veiling (e.g. the Selinus metope showing Zeus and Hera: O. Benndorf, Die Metopen von Selinunt [Berlin 1873] 54-6 and pl. 8; cf. Hera and Zeus on the Parthenon frieze [K. Schefold, Die Göttersage in der klassischen und hellenistischen Kunst (Munich 1981) pl. 302], where Hera clearly is revealing her attractions to Zeus in what I.S. Mark [Hesperia liii (1984) 303-4] regards as an allusion to the ἀνακαλυπτήρια); but (a) unveiling implies previous veiling, to which αἰδώς is still relevant, and (b) this unveiling should not be assimilated to the modest gesture of drawing the himation across the face (see n. 22 above). (On the ἀνακαλυ–πτήρια, see J.H. Oakley, AA (1982) 113-18; R.F. Sutton in id. [ed.], Daidalikon: studies ... Schoder [Wauconda, Ill. 1989] 357-9; Oakley and Sinos [n. 25] 25-6, 30; Rehm [n. 28] 141-2.)

[33] On Mantelknaben and σωφροσύνη, see Sittl (n. 27) 7-8 (to his refs add Aeschin. i 26 [Athens], Xen. Lac. Pol. 3. 4 [Sparta]). Illustrations in Dover (n. 18) R637, 791, 851 (boys); 867 (woman); M.F. Kilmer, Greek erotica (London 1993) R196, 322, 576, 622.1 (boys), C1 (woman); cf. the muffled boy on Munich 2421 (ARV² 23, 7); cf. also the progressive unmuffling of the woman undergoing 'Bacchic initiation' (Florence 391, ARV² 769, 4; Oxford 1924.2, ARV² 865, 1; C. Bérard [et al.], A city of images [Eng. trans. Princeton 1988] figs 199-200); also the gesture of drawing the veil practised by women encountering strange men (Para. 73, 1 bis, Add.² 49; Würzburg 452 [ARV² 63, 6; LIMC i pl. 60, Achilleus 35]; London F 175 [A.D. Trendall, The red-figured vases of Lucania, Campania, and Sicily (Oxford 1967) 103 no. 539; LIMC iv pl. 304, Helene 73]; Bari 4394 [A.D. Trendall and A. Cambitoglou, The red-figured vases of Apulia (Oxford 1978-82) 17 no. 71, Ghali-Kahil (n. 28) pl. 29]); cf. the shy Maenad on Chiusi 1830, ARV² 975, 36. See in gen. Galt (n. 22).

[34] Op. cit. (n. 12) 134 (on the rf Pen.), 130-52 (in general), with figs 67-9, 71-2, 76. For Neumann these attitudes, in which veiling is a common factor, are distinguished by the position of the hands; but he cites no evidence to corroborate the fine nuances he assumes.

[35] London E 76 (ARV² 406, 1; LIMC iii pls 133, 136, Briseis 1, 14; Ach. veiled, Briseis veiled and led χεῖρ' ἐπὶ καρπῷ); Munich 8770 (Para. 341, Add.² 189; LIMC i pl. 104, Achilleus 445); London E 56 (ARV² 185, 39); cf. LIMC i, Achilleus 439-48, 452-3.

[36] Vienna 3695 (ARV² 429, 26; LIMC i pl. 243, Aias I 81); London E 69 (ARV² 369, 2; LIMC i pl. 244, Aias I 84).

[37] As in the mourning figures in the 'Penelope pose' in Langlotz (n. 24) figs 17-23; D.C. Kurtz and J. Boardman, Greek burial customs (London 1971) pl. 44; see also Friis Johansen (n. 22) 36-7 and fig. 18, figs 25, 79, 83; cf. the 'weeping women sarcophagus', R. Lullies and M. Hirmer, Greek sculpture (New York 1960) 89-90 and pls 207-9; also the female mourners of Memnon on the cup, Ferrara 44885 (ARV² 882, 35).

[38] As in the three examples in Haakh (n. 22) pls 16-18; cf. Friis Johansen (n. 22) figs 4, 6, 7, 10, 14, 21, 24, 67. On the deceased's veiling/unveiling, cf. Rehm (n. 28) 40 and n. 49.

[39] See Cairns (n. 1) 157-8, and contrast N.J. Richardson, The Homeric hymn to Demeter (Oxford 1974) ad. locc. Cf. the figure in the 'Penelope pose' from the 'Tomb of Persephone' at Vergina, identified as Demeter by M. Andronicos, Vergina (Athens 1987) 88-9 and fig. 48.

[40] See Od. viii 83-6 (Od. covers his face out of αἰδώς; cf. viii 532), xix 118-22 (cf. Il. xxiv 90-1); E. Her. 1162, 1200, Or. 280-2, IA 981-2. Thus even the veiling of Priam as he grieves for Hector on a Melian relief (Toronto 926.32, Carpenter [n. 24] fig. 319) may indicate an element of αἰδώς in the way that he copes with his emotions; cf. Achilles grieving for Patroclus on London E 363 (ARV² 586, 36, Carpenter fig. 313); on mourners' restraint on Attic white-ground lekythoi, see H.A. Shapiro, AJA xcv (1991) 652-3.

to grief, and a hint at the woman's possession of αἰδώς/ σωφροσύνη in a wider sense.

Even if this suggestion is unacceptable, it is undeniable that αἰδώς and veiling, and especially αἰδώς and the drawing of the *himation* across the face, are closely associated; and we have seen that the veiling of Leto is a recurrent feature in representations of her abduction. This makes it extremely unlikely that the appearance of the letters ΑΙΔΟΣ on the Phintias vase should have nothing to do with Leto's gesture. That the image has at its centre a female figure giving clear sign of her αἰδώς makes it distinctly improbable that the vase-painter should have used those letters purely as a deliberate abbreviation of the genitive Ἀρτέμιδος. And that an inscription is *verschrieben* is to be assumed only where it makes no obvious sense in context. Yet the precise significance of the word αἰδώς is still not entirely clear. Of the possible explanations the following seem least improbable:

(1) Λητοῦς αἰδώς is the title of the picture; this is the option favoured by Waser,[41] and is not as unlikely as it at first seems, given that there are vases on which inscriptions constitute titles.[42] One might argue that the two words are not particularly close, that they do look like identifications of the figures beside whom they are written, and that the genitive is most naturally taken, here as often elsewhere, as giving the character's name (sc. εἴδος).[43] This interpretation, however, might draw further support from the fact that on the other, non-mythological side of the vase, the words ΧΑΙΡΕ ΔΕΜ– ΟΣΤΡΑΤΕ, which obviously are to be construed together, are similarly written vertically and separated by (part of) one of the characters in the scene.

(2) Artemis is given the title Aidos, analogous to Artemis Eukleia and (the putative) Artemis Arete. Yet although Artemis is a figure with whom *ceteris paribus* αἰδώς might naturally be associated, it seems odd that attention should be drawn to *her* αἰδώς in a context where that of someone else is so clearly depicted. It is, of course, a requirement of αἰδώς that one should defend one's mother's honour, but this is a requirement which applies equally to Apollo. Leto clearly has a much stronger claim to αἰδώς in this scene, and it seems to me that only independent evidence (of which there is none)[44] for αἰδώς as a cult-title or epithet of Artemis would make this interpretation more likely than the previous.

Broadly, these are alternatives; other interpretations could only be refinements or combinations of the above.

[41] In Roscher, *ML* v 1043; *cf.* n. 9.
[42] See Kretschmer, *Vaseninschriften* 83; Immerwahr (n. 7) 112, 183-4.
[43] Vases regularly shift between the nom. and the gen. in naming figures (Kretschmer 137).
[44] The personification in E. *Hipp.* 78 (Aidos as Artemis' gardener; *cf.* Aidos as Athena's nurse, schol. vet. A. *PV* 12c Herington) does not prove that Artemis herself could be designated Aidos. Personification of αἰδώς on a vase (*cf.* the many similar cases in Shapiro [n. 4]) would not be impossible (though no example exists), but that is not what we have here, where the figure in question is clearly Artemis. (On personification of αἰδώς, see Hani [n. 3].)

(One might argue, for example, that αἰδώς could refer to Leto's veiling without having to be construed with the genitive, Λητοῦς, and some might be tempted to argue for a sophisticated pun in which ΑΙΔΟΣ both refers to Leto's gesture and designates Artemis.) On balance, and with some hesitation, I think Waser's straightforward explanation the most probable, but submit that, whatever sense we make of the inscriptions, the appearance of the letters ΑΙΔΟΣ cannot be irrelevant to the fact of Leto's veiling.

Thus we have gone some way towards understanding the significance of Phintias' depiction of the rape of Leto. But there is more to be said about the meaning of the scene, and about the relation between that scene and the overall decoration of the vase.[45]

First, the portrayal of the rape of Leto (a rarity, since normally it is the aftermath of the rape which is depicted) has much in common with other scenes of abduction; the basic pose, in which the abductor lifts his victim aloft is very common,[46] but, more particularly, the grip which Tityos employs is also a recurrent motif in such scenes.[47] This is a grip which is also found in other, quite different mythological scenes, especially featuring Heracles and Theseus,[48] but it is its appearance in numerous representations of the everyday techniques

[45] Here I build on the suggestion of R. Osborne, *Classical landscape with figures* (London 1987) 110-11, that the scenes on this amphora are related. For a suggestive approach to interaction between figure-scenes on vases, see F. Lissarrague in S. Goldhill and R. Osborne (eds.), *Art and text in ancient Greek culture* (Cambridge 1994) 12-27, esp. 18-19, 22-5.
[46] See (e.g.) Tityos and Leto themselves on a metope from the Heraion at Foce del Sele (Zancani Montuoro and Zanotti-Bianco [n. 11] ii 322-9 and pl. 93); *cf.* Theseus and Antiope (a) from the temple of Apollo at Eretria (F. Brommer, *Theseus* [Darmstadt 1982] pl. 19) and (b) on a rf cup in Oxford (1927.-4065, *ARV²* 62, 77).
[47] See Dover R750 (*cf.* n. 18 above); Castor and Eriphyle (*cf.* n. 28 above); Boreas and Oreithyia (Munich 2345, *ARV²* 496, 2; *LIMC* iii pl. 19, Boreas 626; *cf.* K. Neuser, *Anemoi* [Rome 1982] 30-87); Theseus and 'Corone' (Munich 2309, *ARV²* 27, 4); Peleus and Thetis (e.g. P. Jacobsthal, *Die melischen Reliefs* [Berlin 1931] no. 14 and pl. 8, no. 15 and fig. 2; vases: Boston 1972.850 [Carpenter (n. 24) fig. 287]; Munich 2619A [*ARV²* 146, 2]; Berlin 2279 [*ARV²* 115.2]; London, V&A 4807.1901 [*ARV²* 89, 14]; Villa Giulia 2491 [J.D. Beazley, *Etruscan vase painters* (Oxford 1947) 7, 80-4, pl. xx, 1]). See X. Krieger, *Der Kampf zwischen Peleus und Thetis in der griechischen Vasenmalerei* (Diss. Münster 1973 [1975]) 21, 25-43, 55-60, 66-74, 89-105, 113-21, with pls 2b-c, 3-4, 8b.
[48] Examples featuring Heracles now most conveniently in *LIMC*; see s.vv. 'Acheloos', 'Antaios I', 'Halios Geron', 'Herakles', 'Nereus'. *Cf.* R. Vollkommer, *Herakles in the art of classical Greece* (Oxford 1988). Theseus and Cercyon, see the Hephaesteum metope (Brommer [n. 46] pl. 7b); vases: London E 36 (*ARV²* 115, 3); London E 48 (*ARV²* 431, 47); Florence 91456 (*ARV²* 108, 27); Madrid 11265 (*ARV²* 1174, Aison 1); Louvre G 104 (*ARV²* 318, 1); Louvre G 195 (*ARV²* 381, 174). On wrestling/pankration techniques in mythological scenes, see E.N. Gardiner, *JHS* xxv (1905) 14, 282-4, xxvi (1906) 11-12, 15-18, *Athletics in the ancient world* (London 1930) 181, 205, 220; Schefold (n. 3) 71, 94, 138, 311; Brommer (n. 46) 19; M.B. Poliakoff, *Combat sports in the ancient world* (New Haven 1987) 136-9; on mythological paradigms for wrestling/athletics, see Webster (n. 28) 56, 62, 251, 260, 265.

of the palaestra which reveals its essential nature;[49] the grip is a visual metaphor from the world of wrestling and/or the pankration. Clearly, where Theseus and Heracles employ this grip, this belongs with their general presentation as paradigms of athletic prowess;[50] a similar allusion to youthful athleticism is apparent in Peleus' wrestling with Thetis and Atalanta. Equally clearly, however, Tityos is nobody's ideal athlete; but a paradigm may be negative as well as positive, and this is where the athletic scene on the other side of the vase comes in. One is already invited to consider the possibility of a relation between the two scenes by virtue of the compositional parallel; but the relation goes beyond the merely aesthetic. The athletes on side B are practising their skills in the proper context of the gymnasium, their youth and their beauty manifesting the admired ideal of athletic ἀρετή; their older companions watch with interest, but decorously.[51] The youths practise the javelin and the discus—not events in themselves, but part of the pentathlon.[52] These events, then, suggest combination with (and absence of) other events; on the other side of the vase we have a metaphor drawn from one of those events, indeed that in which the pentathlon actually culminated.[53] On the athletic side of the vase two pentathletic events are being pursued properly, on the mythological the techniques of the palaestra and the prowess which athletic training develops are being misused;[54] on the one side the pursuit of excellence by the youthful and the beautiful is presented for our delectation, while on the other a male athlete carries his desires beyond mortal limits.

There may be more: the athletes and their admirers on side B form two couples, distinguished by their being equipped with two pairs of matching garlands; the youths,

as any good reproduction will show, are luxuriating in the ἄνθος ἥβης, the first down of their beards sprouting on their cheeks; their ἐρασταί watch their naked exercise with interest (and no doubt more), but do not touch, whereas Tityos is a paradigm of excessive ἔρως,[55] embodying the familiar metaphor of sex as wrestling[56] in a hybristic, all too literal form. In short, the vase presents us with a juxtaposition of norm and transgression in two areas, that of sport and that of ἔρως, a juxtaposition which is effectively underlined by the contrast between the athletic scene, which depicts a natural and appropriate passage from youth to manhood, appropriate male interests, and a proper relationship between youthful (inferior) ἐρώμενος and older (superior) ἐραστής, and the mythological scene, which shows a mortal attempt to enter the sphere of the divine, manly pursuits being carried to excess, and an improper relationship between mortal (inferior) ὑβριστής and divine (superior) αἰδου-μένη.

These scenes and their juxtaposition are at home in the world of the symposium, a fact which is underlined by the vase's other inscriptions; χαῖρε (four times, once with specific addressee) is a typically sympotic imperative,[57] and the single kalos-inscription also places the vase in the pederastic milieu of the aristocratic symposium.[58] These inscriptions also fit well with the αἰδώς inscription, for αἰδώς is one of the canonical sympotic virtues, just as its negation, ὕβρις, is typically seen as a matter of sympotic excess.[59] It is perhaps not irrelevant that Leto and her children are commonly depicted as a threesome, enjoying the pleasures of music and festivity which are the mark of the perpetual felicity of the gods, to which mortals can only approximate in the transient atmosphere of the symposium;[60] it is this peace and harmony that are destroyed by the ὕβρις of Tityos, much as the χάρις, εὐνομία, and εὐφροσύνη of divine hospitality are shattered by the transgressions of Tantalus

[49] See (e.g.) Berlin 1853, CVA Berlin v, pl. 33.2; Vatican 414 (ABV 343, 3); bronze group, Walters Art Gallery, Baltimore 54.972 (Poliakoff fig. 32; cf. Gardiner, Athletics fig. 171; O. Tzachou-Alexandri, Mind and body [Athens 1988] pl. 165); Boston 01.8019 (ARV² 24, 11); Munich 1461 (Gardiner fig. 164).

[50] For literary parallels, see Pi. I. 3/4.61-73 (Her. and Antaeus; cf. N. 4.62-5, Peleus' wrestling with Thetis in an ode for a boy wrestler); B. 13. 46-57 (Her. and lion); B. 18. 26-7 (Thes. and Cercyon); S. Tr. 497-530 (Her. and Achelous; cf. Davies ad loc., and Gardiner JHS [1906] 16); Theocr. 25.262-71. For Plato (Leg. 796a), too, Antaeus and Cercyon are paradigmatic pankratiasts.

[51] One is himself stripped for exercise, the other an interested bystander (not a trainer; Arias-Hirmer [n. 5] 318).

[52] On the pentathlon, see Gardiner, Athletics (n. 48) 177-80; H.A. Harris, Greek athletes and athletics (London 1964) 77-80; id. Sport in Greece and Rome (London 1972) 33-9. The javelin, discus, and jump were peculiar to the pentathlon, and thus were used, singularly or in combination, to denote that event on Panathenaic amphoras (cf. Gardiner, Athletics 177; Webster [n. 28] 213; J. Neils et al., Goddess and polis [Princeton 1992] 35, 85-6, 205 n. 46). D.G. Kyle, Athletics in ancient Athens (Leiden 1987) 180-1, notes that the same pentathletic events also tend to be combined in generic 'palaestra' scenes.

[53] Cf. B. 9.30-9, where discus, javelin, and wrestling represent the pentathlon.

[54] The relation between the mythological and non-mythological sides of the vase thus bears comparison with those (contemporary) vases discussed by Webster (n. 28) 56, 251 which juxtapose athletic events and mythological paradigms of athletic events.

[55] Cf. Pi. P. 4.90-3.

[56] See (e.g.) A. Ag. 1206; S. frr. 618, 941.13 R (with Pearson ad locc.); Ar. Ach. 273-6, 994, Peace 896-9, Eccl. 259-61, 964-6; see J. Taillardat, Les Images d'Aristophane (Paris 1965) 336; J. Henderson, The maculate Muse (New Haven 1975) 156, 169-70; M.B. Poliakoff, Studies in the terminology of the Greek combat sports (Frankfurt 1986) 41-2, 101-36. Cf. Παλαιστώ (a hetaira) on a rf psykter, Leningrad 644 (ARV² 16, 15; Kretschmer, Vaseninschriften 209, Kilmer [n. 33] R20). N.b. the metaphorical use (Ar. Ach. 274; cf. Ael. Ep. Rust. 9, Straton, A.P. xii 206, 222, ps.-Luc. Asinus 10) of μέσον λαβεῖν/ἔχειν (vel sim.), i.e. Tityos' hold on Leto; see Gardiner (n. 48) JHS (1905) 24-6, 288, Athletics 191-2; Poliakoff, Studies 40-53.

[57] See Kretschmer, Vaseninschriften 195-6; F. Lissarrague, The aesthetics of the Greek banquet (Eng. trans. Princeton 1991) 60-7.

[58] See Webster (n. 28) 42-62 passim, Dover (n. 18) 117-19.

[59] On sympotic virtues and vices, see K. Bielohlawek, WS lviii (1940) 11-30; W.J. Slater, ICS vi (1981) 205-14; id. in O. Murray (ed.), Sympotica (Oxford 1990) 213-20; N.R.E. Fisher, Hybris (Warminster 1992) 71-2, 203-7, 218-19, 223-4, etc.

[60] See LIMC ii, Apollon 630-45b, 651a-54, Artemis 1105-23 (n.b. Leto [alone] is veiled on at least three of these [Apollo 651b, Artemis 1110, 1116]). Perhaps similarly, the 'relief of the gods', Brauron Mus. 1180 (L. Kahil in J.N. Coldstream and M.A.R. Colledge (eds.), XI international congress of classical archaeology [London 1978] 78 and pl. 32; LIMC ii Artemis 1225a) depicts a veiled Leto, matron of a divine family (Zeus, Apollo) greeting the arrival of Artemis.

in *Olympian* 1 and Ixion in *Pythian* 2. As does much archaic poetry, Phintias' vase, created for the enjoyment of symposiasts, embeds the general values of the aristocratic community in the specific context of the drinking party; and as in Pindar, the occasion of the symposium is used to set the heights of human πόνος, beauty, and ἀρετή against a negative mythological paradigm which emphasizes the limits of human striving.[61]

DOUGLAS L. CAIRNS

University of Leeds

[61] On the intersection of archaic poetry and vase-painting, see Lissarrague (n. 57) 123-39.

L'*ecphrasis* de la parole d'apparat dans l'*Electrum* et le *De domo* de Lucien, et la représentation des deux styles d'une esthétique inspirée de Pindare et de Platon*

Poésie d'apparat et de célébration, la lyrique de Pindare s'identifie à la préciosité d'un métal ou d'une pierre, et à l'art somptueux de l'orfèvrerie ou de l'architecture. Rivalisant avec elle, l'éloquence d'apparat[1] reprend et développe ces images à l'époque impériale, pour se représenter et exposer son esthétique, l'esthétique de la seconde sophistique, qui, inspirée de celle de Pindare et de Platon,[2] unit la fable et la vérité de l'ailleurs, l'illusion et la sagesse divine.

La démonstration d'une parole d'apparat, 'oratoire et persuasive',[3] s'appropriant la représentation éclatante et

* Cet article est la version augmentée, et pourvue de notes, des deux premières parties de la communication que j'ai présentée au colloque international sur la Lyrique antique de l'Université Charles de Gaulle—Lille III (juin 1993). La troisième partie, qui traite des *Ethiopiques* d'Héliodore, a paru, remaniée et pourvue de notes, dans *Poésie et Lyrique antiques*, Lille, 1996, 179-202.

** Les éditions utilisées, ainsi que les traductions, éventuellement modifiées, sont le plus souvent celles de la Collection des Universités de France. Mais pour Platon, j'ai utilisé aussi les traductions de la Bibliothèque de la Pléiade. Et pour le *Timée* et le *Critias*, j'ai consulté la traduction de L. Brisson avec la collaboration de M. Patillon, G.F. Flammarion, Paris, 1992. Pour Lucien, les références sont à l'édition des Oxford Classical Texts. La traduction de l'*Electrum* est redevable à celle de E. Chambry, coll. Garnier. Celles du *De domo* de Lucien et du *Peri Ideôn* d'Hermogène sont miennes.

[1] Voir Isocr., *Sur l'échange*, 166, citant Pindare, et se comparant à lui pour ses éloges d'Athènes.
[2] Pour l'influence de Pindare sur Platon: *Ion*, 534a-b; *Ménon*, 81b-c; et J. Duchemin, 'Platon et l'héritage de la poésie', in *R.E.G.* Lxviii (1955) 12-37. Voir aussi Aelius Aristide, *Défense de la rhétorique*, 109. Sur l'esthétique de la seconde sophistique héritière de l'art de Pindare et de Platon: M.M.J. Laplace, 'Eloquence et navigation à l'époque impériale', *Actes du XIe congrès de l'Association Guillaume Budé* (Paris 1985) t.I. 72-4. Pour l'importance des citations et références à Pindare chez Aelius Aristide, voir *Hymnes à Athéna*, 6; *à Zeus*, 22; 25; *à Dionysos*, 6; *Panégyrique au puits d'Asclépiéion*, 16; *Lalia à Asclépios*, 12; *Isthmique à Poséidon*, 25; *Dithyrambe aux Athéniens*, 25, 8.
[3] C'est l'une des définitions du véritable art de l'éloquence dans le *Phèdre*, 269 c-d.

précieuse des hymnes de Pindare, apparaît chez Lucien dans la *prolalia Electrum* et la *lalia De domo*.

Chez Lucien, comme chez Pindare, la somptuosité de la matière ou de l'édifice s'applique à une parole d'apparat rehaussée, directement ou indirectement, par des fables.

Pindare célèbre ainsi les exploits des Théandrides: 'Si tu me prescris encore, dit-il à Timasarque d'Egine, de dresser pour ton oncle maternel ... une stèle plus blanche que le marbre de Paros, sache que l'or qu'on passe au feu n'est plus que splendeur fulgurante, mais que l'hymne qui célèbre les grands exploits fait (τεύχει) d'un simple mortel l'égal des rois' (*Ném.*, IV 82-5).[4] Dans la VIIe *Néméenne*, dédiée à Sogénès d'Egine, Pindare compare au charme des fables d'Homère la préciosité de sa poésie: 'J'imagine que la renommée d'Ulysse a dépassé ses épreuves grâce au charme d'Homère. Car les fictions et la poésie au vol sublime lui ont donné je ne sais quel prestige: l'art nous dupe, en nous séduisant par des fables ... Au vainqueur ... je ne mets point de mauvaise grâce à payer mon tribut d'éloges. Tresser des fleurs en couronnes, tâche facile. Rejette-la! La Muse, elle, assemble l'or avec l'ivoire blanc et la fleur du lys qu'elle a soustraite à la rosée marine' (v. 20-79). L'hymne est comme un précieux collier, ou bracelet, fait d'or, d'ivoire et de corail.[5]

Pindare souligne le chatoiement trompeur de la fable éloignée de la vérité, quand il évoque, dans la Ière *Olympique*, un diadème d'or ciselé, serti de pierreries: 'Ah! le monde est plein de merveilles—et parfois aussi les dires des mortels vont au-delà du vrai (ὑπὲρ τὸν ἀλαθῆ λόγον): des fables (μῦθοι) ornées de chatoyantes fictions (δεδαιδαλμένοι ψεύδεσι ποικίλοις) nous illusionnent (ἐξαπατῶντι)' (v. 28-29). C'est à quoi Pindare renonce dans cette ode consacrée à Hiéron de Syracuse qui est elle-même présentée comme le joyau suprême, le pur éclat de l'or, parce qu'elle substitue à l'éclat d'une fable blasphématoire l'éclat divin d'une autre fable, véridique, en célébrant Pélops, dont l'arène d'Olympie immortalisa la gloire: 'Excellent bien que l'eau; mais l'or, étincelant comme une flamme qui s'allume dans la nuit, efface tous les trésors de la fière opulence, dit Pindare. Veux-tu chanter les jeux, ô mon âme? ne cherche pas, au ciel désert, quand le jour brille, un astre plus ardent que le Soleil, et n'espère pas célébrer une lice plus glorieuse qu'Olympie! De là part l'hymne que mille voix répètent' (*Olymp.*, I, 1-8). Après avoir évoqué le héros dont 's'éprit ... Poséidon, quand Clôthô le retira du bassin pur, l'épaule parée de l'éclat de l'ivoire' (*Olymp.*, I, 25-27), Pindare récuse cette tradition qui suppose que le corps de Pélops ait disparu dévoré par les dieux lors d'un festin offert par Tantale sur le Sipyle: 'L'homme ne doit attribuer aux dieux que de belles actions, dit-il: c'est la voie la plus sûre. Aussi, fils de Tantale, vais-je parler de toi autrement que mes devanciers: je dirai que, lorsque ton père, convive des dieux, leur offrant à son tour un banquet, les invita à la fête irréprochable du Sipyle ... ce jour-là, le Maître du trident splendide te ravit: l'amour avait dompté son coeur.

[4] Voir A. Puech, *Pindare. Néméennes*, C.U.F. (Paris 1923) 48, sur les critiques auxquelles Pindare répond dans la strophe V de cette ode: 'Ces critiques visaient sans doute le grand développement qu'il donne aux mythes'.
[5] Pour 'la fleur de lys soustraite à la rosée marine', j'adopte l'interprétation du scholiaste retenue par A. Puech, *op cit.*, 92 et 100.

Sur son char d'or il te transporta dans le palais céleste de Zeus souverain' (*Olymp.*, I, 35-43). Pindare concilie ainsi le charme de la fable et l'inspiration divine.[6]

Lucien, dans la *prolalia Electrum*, unit aussi la persuasion de la fable à la vérité de l'ailleurs, mais en contestant par la vérité toutes les fables de la poésie.[7] L'une des fables persuasives dont il invite à se déprendre est celle des larmes d'ambre versées par les peupliers des bords de l'Eridan déplorant la mort de Phaéthon: elle veut que les peupliers soient les soeurs du jeune homme métamorphosées en arbres à l'endroit où il était tombé. Lucien, après s'être assuré la connivence des auditeurs—ἠλέκτρου πέρι καὶ ὑμᾶς δηλαδὴ ὁ μῦθος πέπεικεν, dit-il (ch. 1)—raconte quel fut son 'espoir, en entendant les poètes chanter cette fable', s'il se trouvait 'un jour sur les bords de l'Eridan ... d'avoir de l'ambre (ἤλπιζον, εἴ ποτε γενοίμην ἐπὶ τῷ 'Ηριδανῷ,... ὡς ἤλεκτρον ἔχοιμι)' (ch. 1), et quelle fut sa déception: devant peu après descendre le cours de l'Eridan, il ne vit ni peupliers, ni ambre, et constata que les indigènes ignoraient même le nom de Phaéthon (ch. 2). Bien plus, lorsqu'il raconta la fable aux bâteliers de l'Eridan, ceux-ci s'exclamèrent: 'Qui t'a raconté cela ... quel illusionniste et diseur de fictions (ἀπατεὼν καὶ ψευδολόγος ἄνθρωπος)?' (ch. 3). Et ils lui montrèrent l'irréalisme de ce récit (ch. 3). 'Je gardai le silence, dit Lucien, honteux de m'être conduit comme un véritable enfant, en croyant (πιστεύσας) aux fictions incroyables (ἀπίθ- ανα ...ψευδομένοις) des poètes ... Je fus là détrompé d'un grand espoir (ἐλπίδος), et je m'en désolais comme si j'avais laissé échapper l'ambre de mes doigts; car je le façonnais déjà en cent objets divers à mon usage' (ch. 3).

Mettant en parallèle son éloquence avec l'antique poésie des fables, Lucien prévient ses auditeurs contre une pareille déception: 'On connaît souvent de telles désillusions, dit-il, quand on croit (πιστεύοντας) ceux qui exagèrent tout dans leurs récits. Aussi ai-je peur moi-même à présent qu'il n'en soit de même à mon égard, que vous, qui venez d'arriver et qui m'entendez pour la première fois, vous n'espériez (ἐλπίσαντες) trouver chez moi de l'ambre ... et que dans un moment, vous ne vous en alliez en vous moquant de ceux qui vous ont promis que mes discours contenaient beaucoup de trésors de ce genre. Je vous l'atteste, ni vous ni personne autre ne m'a entendu proférer de telles vanteries à mon propos. Vous pouvez en rencontrer d'autres, en grand nombre même ... qui distillent dans leur discours, non de l'ambre, mais de l'or même ... Mais mon discours, vous voyez déjà comme il est sans complication et sans fable (ἄμυθον), et il ne s'y ajoute pas de chant. Gardez-vous donc d'espérer (ἐλπίσας) trop de moi' (ch. 6).

Ces paroles rappellent celles d'Isocrate raillant les

premiers sophistes, leur prétention et leurs grandes promesses[8] démenties par leur pauvreté,[9] mais ambitionnant lui-même d'égaler par l'éloquence d'apparat la poésie chantée: 'Les poètes, écrit Isocrate ... ont la faculté de mettre les dieux en contact avec les hommes, de les faire dialoguer ...; et ils décrivent ces péripéties ... en parant leur poésie de tous les chatoiements du style. Les orateurs, au contraire, ne disposent d'aucune de ces facilités ... En outre, tandis que les uns écrivent toutes leurs oeuvres en s'aidant du mètre et du rythme, les autres n'ont en partage aucun de ces avantages dont le charme est pourtant si fort ... Cependant, la supériorité de la poésie, si grande soit-elle, ne doit pas nous faire hésiter' (*Evag.*, 9-11).[10] Héritier, lui aussi, de cette tradition, Aelius Aristide affirme même, dans l'introduction de *l'hymne à Sarapis*, que l'hymne en prose est supérieur à l'hymne poétique, parce qu'il ne recourt pas, pour louer les dieux, à des fables invraisemblables (*Disc.*, XLV, 1-13 Keil). Cependant, pas plus qu'Aelius Aristide,[11] Lucien ne renonce au charme de la fable. Pour l'intégrer à son discours, tout en se présentant comme un maître de vérité, et pour distiller l'ambre dans une prose simple, dépourvue de chant, et refusant la fable, Lucien s'inspire de Platon, et retourne le schéma de présentation de ses fables, pour illustrer une esthétique conforme à l'ideal défendu par cet émule d'Homère.[12]

L'espoir déçu de Lucien de posséder de l'ambre, dans *l'Electrum*, qui est semblable au rêve de richesse d'Adimante dans le *Navigium* (Πλοῖον ἢ Εὐχαί) du même sophiste,[13] est la contrepartie illusoire des fictions politiques et poétiques de Platon dans la *République* et les *Lois*. L'ambre que Lucien, revenu des bords de l'Eridan, croit lui échapper des mains, alors qu'il le façonnait déjà en cent objets divers à son usage—ἀνέπλαττον, dit-il (ch. 4)—est comme la richesse du rêveur Adimante, réplique amusée du poète et sage Socrate.[14] Adimante était tout

---

[6] Sans doute l'éclat de l'or dans la fable préférée par Pindare s'oppose-t-il à celui de l'ivoire dans l'autre fable, comme dans la représentation liminaire de l'hymne la splendeur de l'or contraste avec l'excellence de l'eau. D'autre part, le remplacement d'une fable impie par une fable respectueuse de la divinité est le fondement, de la *Palinodie* de Stésichore, dont le schéma est repris dans le *Phèdre*.

[7] Dans le *Gallus* de Lucien, le coq cite à Micylle les vers de Pindare, *Olymp.*, I, 1-2, comme décrivant exactement son rêve de richesse (ch. 7), avant de lui en montrer la vanité (ch. 28-33). Pour Lucien, l'édition utilisée est celle de M.D. Macleod, *Luciani opera*, 4 tomes (Oxford 1972-1987).

[8] Isocr., *Contre les sophistes*, 1, 16, 19, 21-22; *Eloge d'Hélène*, 1; *Busiris*, 4 (le terme dont Isocrate caractérise Polycratès μεγαλαυχούμενον, est celui que Lucien refuse pour lui-même, μεγαλαυχουμένου); *Sur l'échange*, 274.

[9] *Panégyr.*, 189.

[10] Voir aussi *Evagoras* 8, 11; *Sur l'échange*, 46-48.

[11] L. Pernot, 'Théorie et pratique de l'hymne en prose chez Aelius Aristide', in *Actes de XIe Congrès de l'Ass G. Budé*, t.II, 1985, 87.

[12] Pour la représentation, par Lucien, de sa dette envers Platon, philosophe et poète en prose (inspiré par Pindare): *Piscator*, 5-7. Sur les références de Lucien à Platon: J. Bompaire, *Lucien écrivain. Imitation et création* (Paris 1958) 143-44, 146, 149, 304-05, 307-14; G. Anderson, *Theme and variation in the second sophistic* (Leyde 1976) 6-8, 25, 29, 121-22, 155-56, 184. Pour la conscience que les critiques anciens avaient de la volonté de Platon de rivaliser avec Homère: Denys d'Halicarnasse, *Op. rhét.*, XI, 1, 12-13; Ps.-Longin, *Sur le sublime*, XII, 3-4.

[13] Pour la représentation à travers cette 'navigation' de l'esthétique de la second sophistique alliant l'art et l'inspiration divine; M.M.J. Laplace, *loc. cit.*, in *Actes du XIe Congrès de l'Ass. G. Budé*, t.II, 73.

[14] Voir M.M.J. Laplace, *loc. cit.*, *ibid.* En outre, selon l'habitude de Socrate (Aristoph., *Nuées*, 103, 363; Plat., *Banq.*, 174a, 220b' *Phèdr.*, 229a), Adimante va 'nu-pieds' (*Nav.*, 1). Comme Socrate (Aristoph., *Nuées*, 362; Plat. *Banq.*, 220b), Adimante est reconnaissable à sa démarche et à son manteau (*Nav.*, 10). Et son amour pour les jeunes gens (*Nav.*, 2, 18-19, 22) n'est pas moins célèbre que celui de Socrate (Plat., *Banq.*, 216d, 222b-223a; *Phèdr.*, 227c).

occupé de cette 'étrange pensée', lorsque Lykinos l'arrête et l'interroge: 'De quoi s'agit-il? Parle sans hésiter ...—J'ai honte de parler devant vous, répond Adimante. Tant ma méditation vous paraîtra être un enfantillage!' (*Nav.*, 11).[15] Pourtant, il raconte: 'Je me façonnais (ἀνεπλαττόμην) une sorte de richesse, ce que la majorité appelle une vaine félicité (κενὴν μακαρίαν) ... Si un dieu soudain me rendait maître de ce navire, quelle vie heureuse que la mienne! ... Et puis ... je m'étais déjà fait construire une maison bien située, un peu au-delà du Poecile. J'avais quitté la maison patern- elle près de l'Ilissos, et j'achetais serviteurs ... voitures et chevaux; et voilà que déjà même je naviguais ... Je regardais de loin vers le port, quand tu es survenu, Lykinos, tu as fait sombrer ma richesse et chavirer mon embarcation, alors qu'elle était si bien portée par le souffle favorable de mon souhait (εὐχῆς)' (*Nav.*, 12- 13).[16] La faveur de ses auditeurs soutient, au contraire, la théorie de Socrate sur la communauté des femmes et des enfants, bien qu'il ait commencé par souligner toutes 'les méfiances (ἀπιστίας)' qu'elle inspirait, et qu'il ait déclaré n'être 'pas persuadé lui-même' de 'savoir la vérité': 'J'hésite à aborder le sujet, de peur que mon discours ne paraisse être un pur souhait (εὐχή). —N'hés- ite pas', rétorque Glaucon (*Rép.*, V, 450c-d). Et Socrate développe cette partie de sa 'fable' politique—μυθολογ— οῦμεν, dit-il (*Rép.*, VI, 501e)—pour en affirmer, finale- ment, la 'vérité' (*Rép.*, VI, 502d).[17] Dans les *Lois*, l'Athénien est incité dans les mêmes termes à définir le modèle littéraire pour l'éducation de la jeunesse: 'Parle

sans hésiter aucunement', lui dit Clinias (*Lois*, VII, 811b-c). Et l'Athénien proclame que c'est le poème législatif qu'il compose (*Lois*, VII, 811c-e), avant de défier les poètes de tragédies qui demanderaient à entrer dans la cité future: 'Poètes vous êtes, poètes nous sommes aussi ... vos concurrents et vos compétiteurs, étant les auteurs du drame le plus beau, celui que seule une législation véridique est de nature à produire, ainsi que nous en avons, nous, l'espoir (ἐλπίς)' (*Lois*, VII, 817b-c).[18] Alors que le Socrate de la *République* et l'Athénien des *Lois* excluent de la cité idéale les fables des anciens poètes (*Rép.*, II, 377b-III, 398b; *Lois*, VII, 810b; 817c), parce qu'ils composent eux-mêmes des fables poétiques, philosophiques et politiques empreintes de vérité, Lucien dénonce l'illusion des antiques fables poétiques, pour avertir ses auditeurs qu'il n'est rien de plus précieux dans ses discours que son verbe, en dépit de sa simplicité.[19]

Mais à travers cette structure, où s'exprime la feinte modestie de Lucien, l'ambre de la fable apparaît dans son discours comme à travers un miroir, avec le charme de l'irréalité. Lucien le signifie lorsque, pour conclure, il invite ses auditeurs à 'ne pas ressembler à ceux qui voient les objets dans l'eau: ils pensent qu'ils sont aussi grands qu'ils leur apparaissent, vus d'en haut, alors que leur ombre s'élargit avec le reflet; puis, quand ils les retirent, ils sont dépités de les trouver beaucoup plus petits. Je vous en avertis donc à présent, dit-il: quand vous aurez vidé l'eau et découvert mes pensées, ne vous attendez pas à retirer rien de grand; autrement, n'accusez que vous de votre espoir (ἐλπίδος)' (ch. 6).[20]

Grâce à cette distanciation,[21] l'ambre de la fable apparaît avec l'attrait de l'irréalité, cependant qu'est révélée la vérité d'au-delà du miroir. Lucien illustre ainsi l'idéal platonicien selon lequel 'il n'existe pas d'art de la parole authentique qui ne soit attaché à la vérité' (*Phèdr.*, 260e). La vérité, Lucien la rapporte du pays des

[15] Μειρακιῶδες ὑμῖν δόξει τὸ φρόντισμα. Dans les *Nuées* d'Aristophane, les termes φροντιστής et φροντιστήριον désignent Socrate et son séjour (v. 4, 101, 128, 142, 181, 414, 456). Voir aussi Plat., *Apol.*, 18b, et, dans le *Banquet*, Socrate, invité d'Agathon, faussant compagnie à Aristodème pour s'abstraire dans sa réflexion comme dans 'un songe' (*Banq.*, 175e): Adimante, pendant la visite du navire de commerce, s'égare et perd ses amis (*Nav.*, 1-4), qui le retrouvent, perdu dans son souhait (*Nav.*, 11). D'autre part, chez Platon, c'est un cliché que les fables sont destinées aux enfants: *Prot.*, 320c; *Rép.*, II, 377a-c; *Polit.*, 268e; *Tim.*, 23b; *Crit.*, 112e. Voir aussi *Apol.*, 17c, Socrate se refusant à se présenter 'comme un enfant (μειρακίῳ) inventant (πλάττοντι) des histoires'.

[16] Ces thèmes sont explicités dans l'*Hermotimus*: 'Tu me parais ressembler à quelqu'un qui ... accuserait la fortune de ne pas pouvoir monter au ciel, dit Lykinos à Hermotime ... La cause du chagrin, c'est d'avoir espéré (ἠλπίκει) ... ou, si l'on ... s'est façonné (ἀναπλάσας) à soi-même un pareil songe (ὄναρ) ... de souhaiter sa réalisation (εὔχεται) ... Il en va de même pour ceux qui, en se façonnant à eux--mêmes la vaine félicité (τὴν κενὴν μακαρίαν...ἀναπλάττοντες) ... ont tous les honneurs que prodigue cette divinité qu'est le Souhait (Εὐχή)' (ch. 71).

[17] Voir aussi, dans la *République*, 'la fable' des guerriers autochtones, cette 'fiction phénicienne', dit Socrate, 'dont parlent les poètes, et dont ils nous ont persuadés, mais qui n'existe pas de notre temps, et dont je ne sais pas non plus s'il est possible qu'elle existe, à moins d'une patiente persuasion pour nous en persuader!' (*Rép.*, III, 414c-d). La présentation de cette fable est semblable: 'Comme tu as l'air d'hésiter à en parler, dit Glaucon—Quand j'aurai parlé, repartit Socrate, tu seras d'avis que, si j'hésite, c'est tout à fait à bon droit!—Parle et n'aie pas peur!' reprend Glaucon (*Rép.*, iII, 414c). Dans le *Navigium*, Adimante, après avoir été moqué par Lykinos, s'adonne à nouveau au plaisir onirique du souhait, en le partageant avec Timolaos et Samippe au long d'une promenade (ch. 16) qui rappelle celle des personnages des *Lois* de Platon.

[18] L'hésitation à s'exprimer est aussi manifestée par l'Athén- ien des *Lois* avant d'exposer ses conceptions sur l'éducation mathématique (*Lois*, VII, 818e-819a). Et la fausse hésitation est le préambule traditionnel des fables philosophiques inspirées de Platon, chez Plutarque (*De sera* 18, 516B; *De defect. orac.*, 21, 420E-421A), et chez Aelius Aristide (*Def. rhét.*, 394).

[19] L'analogie entre le narrateur de l'*Electrum* et le Socrate de Platon, dont il est la figure inversée, est confirmée par sa seconde désillusion. A défaut d'avoir recueilli de l'ambre, Lucien espère entendre sur les rives de l'Eridan les cygnes dont on dit que, 'parèdres d'Apollon', ils font entendre un chant mélodieux: voir *Phédon*, 84e-85a. Mais les bâteliers se rient à nouveau du Lucien: 'Des cygnes qui aient un chant plaisant et tel que tu dis, nous n'en avons même pas entendu en songe (οὐδὲ ὄναρ)' (ch. 5).

[20] Lucien, écrivain de la second sophistique, s'oppose aux premiers sophistes, tels que les représente Platon, *Soph.*, 239c- 240a: l'art du sophiste est appelé 'l'art des figures imaginaires', φανταστικὴν τεχνήν, et le sophiste est nommé 'créateur de simulacres', εἰδωλοποιόν, comme 'les simulacres qui apparais- sent sur les eaux et les miroirs'.

[21] Pour cette méthode de connaissance exacte, voir le *Pro imaginibus*, 12, cité par G. Anderson, *op cit.*, 122, qui considère justement cette opposition entre les deux visions, proche et lointaine, comme une variante du renversement de la représent- ation platonicienne des discours de Socrate, ridicules d'appar- ence, mais renfermant des images divines, dont il cite un exemple (*ibid.*) en *Lexiphanes*, 22. Un autre exemple est fourni par *Gallus*, 24.

fables, de la poésie et de l'imaginaire: elle atteste l'irréalité des fables, et la toute puissance de la parole et de sa persuasion.

Comprenant à la fois l'illusion et la vérité de la fable, la parole d'apparat de Lucien se représente dans l'*Electrum* comme une parole limpide[22] laissant voir en transparence l'ambre de la fable, un ambre grossi par cette transparence même.[23]

La *lalia De domo*, au contraire, contient une allégorie de la parole d'apparat où Lucien, exploitant les images par lesquelles Pindare identifie ses hymnes à des édifices, représente son discours d'éloge en prose comme une somptueuse demeure habitée par la Mémoire divine de la poésie.

L'image architecturale est l'une des images favorites de Pindare, qui en offre plusieurs variantes. Il compare la VIe *Pythique*, inaltérable au temps, au trésor de Delphes près duquel elle est chantée: 'Ecoutez, dit-il ...: nous labourons le champ des Grâces, en marchant vers le temple qui contient le nombril de la terrre ...; là, pour les Emménides fortunés, pour Agrigente sise auprès de son fleuve, pour Xénocrate enfin, s'élève le trésor des hymnes qu'ils ont mérités pour leur victoire pythique (Πυθιόνικος...ὕμνων θησαυρὸς... τετείχισται) ... Sa façade, illuminée d'une lumière pure, proclamera et fera redire par les hommes, ô Thrasybule, l'illustre victoire, commune à ton père et à sa famille, remportée à la course des quadriges' (*Pyth.*, VI, 1-18). La VIIe *Pythique* est assimilée au temple d'Apollon lui-même, rebâti grâce aux Alcméonides, ancêtres du vainqueur Mégaclès: 'Y-a-t-il un plus beau prélude que la grande cité d'Athènes pour jeter la base d'un chant (κρηπῖδ' ἀοιδᾶν) en l'honneur de la puissante famille des Alcméonides? demande Pindare ... Toutes les cités connaissent les concitoyens d'Erechthée qui, dans la divine Pythô, ont construit, Apollon, ta demeure admirable' (vv. 1-12). C'est à un somptueux édifice qu'est identifiée la VIe *Olympique* dédiée à Agésias de Syracuse: 'Pour soutenir le portique splendide, devant la demeure (θαλάμου), dressons des colonnes d'or; faisons comme si nous construisions un palais magnifique (θαητὸν μέγαρον). A l'oeuvre qui s'élève, il faut donner une façade qui brille au loin' (v. 1-4). Pindare

continue l'image quand, désireux de revenir aux origines de la famille d'Agésias, les Iamides, à l'Eurotas et à Pitané, pour une ample évocation des amours légendaires d'où naquit Iamos (v. 29-63), il invite le cocher à l'y conduire, avec les mules victorieuses: 'Devant elles, il le faut, ouvrons toutes grandes les portes de l'hymne (πύλας ὕμνων)' (v. 27-28). Mais Pindare assimile aussi les fastes de l'éloge à un bâtiment où la décoration murale s'ajoute à la magnificence architecturale: 'J'ai forgé, dit-il, une base en or pour mes chants sacrés (κεκρότηται χρυσέα κρηπὶς ἱεραῖσιν ἀοιδαῖς). Allons, bâtissons maintenant, chatoyant et sonore, un monument d'éloquence (τειχίζωμεν ἤδη ποικίλον | κόσμον αὐδάεντα λόγων)' (*Frag.* 194 Maehler).

Lucien, dans le *De domo*, reprend l'équivalence entre la parole d'éloge et un palais, ou un édifice aux parois ornées et multicolores, pour développer des correspondances entre la somptueuse demeure dont il est l'hôte, et le discours d'apparat qu'il y prononce en une prose 'poétique et chatoyante (ποικιλωτέρᾳ)', conforme à l'ambition d'Isocrate (*Sur l'échange*, 47), mais inspirée par l'oeuvre de Platon.

La représentation du principe de ces correspondances, le désir d'émulation de Lucien, et de ses effets dans le style de son discours d'apparat, est aussi influencée par Pindare. 'Qui, dit Lucien, voyant une demeure si grande en sa grandeur, si belle en sa beauté, si radieuse en sa luminosité, si éclatante d'or, et si fleurie de peintures, ne désirerait y prononcer des discours ... s'y illustrer ... et, autant que possible, participer lui-même de cette beauté?' (ch. 1). Saisi d'exaltation devant ces splendeurs visuelles, Lucien orateur se souvient de la profusion des images de la IXe *Olympique*, dédiée à Epharmostos d'Oponte: 'La flamme ardente de mes chants empourprera cette ville chérie, dit Pindare, et plus vite qu'un cheval généreux ou que le navire qui vole, je vais publier partout mon message, si le sort a bien voulu que ma main sache cultiver le jardin privilégié des Charites' (v. 21-27). Lucien reprend les deux comparaisons pour exprimer son désir d'émulation, et il exploite les deux métaphores pour en célébrer l'accomplissement par les qualités de sa prose d'apparat, fleurie et brillante. Ainsi, il compare l'attrait incitatif exercé sur l'orateur par un beau spectacle au plaisir que montre un cheval à courir sur une molle prairie inclinée—'s'adonnant entièrement à la course, il rivalise par la vitesse avec la beauté de la prairie' (ch 10)—puis à l'envie de naviguer qui s'empare d'un terrien, lorsqu'il regarde la voile d'un navire gonflée par le vent, ou le navire glissant sur les vagues (ch. 12). Non content de louer cette demeure par des expressions d'admiration, comme le fit le jeune Télémarque, ou même Homère, pour le palais de Ménélas et d'Hélène à Lacédémone, ou celui d'Alexandre à Troie,[24] Lucien va composer un éloge d'apparat en déployant les plus belles paroles devant le plus beau spectacle (ch. 3).

L'émulation, déjà, anime Pindare qui, dans un fragment partiellement restitué, se déclare incité par l'audition d'un poème à entonner sa propre ode: [κλύων]...-[ἐρεθίζ]ομαι πρὸς ἀοιδάν (*Frag. adesp.*, 2, 65-71 Puech). Mais, dans le *De domo*, c'est le spectacle de la beauté qui provoque l'éloquence, telle celle de Socrate

---

[22] L'image de l'eau a sans doute été influencée par la représentation traditionnelle de la parole comme flux, depuis Homère (*Il.*, I, 249), Hésiode (*Théog.*, 39-40, 95-6), Pindare (*Nem.*, VII, 12, 62-3; *Péan aux Delphiens*, 128-29). L'image est fréquente chez Platon (*Rép.*, VI, 492c; *Lois*, VI, 719c). Elle sert aussi à la critique littéraire. Dans le traité *Du sublime*, les écrivains sont identifiés soit à de petits cours d'eau 'transparents', soit à de grands fleuves, et même à l'Océan (35, 4). Du style 'simple' de Platon, Denys d'Halic. écrit qu'il est 'transparent comme le plus limpide (διαφανέστατα) des ruisseaux' (*Op. rhét.*, V, 5, 2 = XI, 2, 1), en évoquant la 'limpidité' des eaux de l'Illisos (*Phèdr.*, 229b: διαφανῆ). Voir aussi *Op. rhét.*, VI, 23, 2 et 20. Il représente, au contraire, le 'style élevé' de Platon comme le 'déploiement d'une vaine richesse de mots πλοῦτον ὀνομά-των...κενόν)' (*Op. rhét.*, V, 5, 5 - XI, 2, 1).

[23] C'est un mode d'amplification. Platon en attribue le principe à Tisias et à Gorgias: τὰ...σμικρὰ μεγάλα...φαίνεσθαι ποιοῦσι (*Phèdr.*, 267a). Isocrate considère que c'est l'une des manifestations du pouvoir de la parole: τοῖς μικροῖς περιθεῖναι μέγεθος (*Panég.*, 8). Et cette affirmation est pour l'auteur de traité *Du sublime* une preuve de la volonté d'Isocrate de 'tout amplifier par la parole' πάντα αὐξητικῶς...λέγειν (32, 2).

[24] Voir *De domo*, 3, 9, et *Od.*, IV, 43-47, 72-75' *Il.*, III, 421-23.

dans l'hymne à l'Amour du *Phèdre*.[25]

Car si, dans *l'Electrum*, Lucien se montre un parfait adepte du style 'simple', 'limpide' de Platon, vanté par Denys d'Halicarnasse,[26] dans le *De domo*, il illustre l'autre style distingué et critiqué par Denys d'Halicarnasse chez Platon, le style 'élevé', orné et poétique.[27]

L'image de ce style élevé est empruntée à Pindare et à Platon. Pindare termine la IIIe *Pythique* en évoquant la poésie d'Homère, sublime architecture: 'Si le dieu m'apporte la richesse charmante, j'ai l'espoir d'acquérir ... une gloire sublime (ὑψηλόν). Nestor et ... Sarpédon ... nous sont connus par les vers harmonieux qu'ont composés (ἅρμοσαν) de sages artisans (τέκτονες)' (v. 110-114).

[25] Voir *De domo*, 4, Lucien expliquant pourquoi, à son avis, la magnificence de la demeure exalte la pensée et éveille l'éloquence: 'Peut-être que de la beauté s'infuse (εἰσρεῖ) par les yeux jusque dans l'âme, et qu'en parure elle se renvoie à elle-même le langage'; et *Phèdr.*, 251b-c.

[26] *Op. rhét.*, V, 5, 2-3 = XI, 2, 1.

[27] *Op. rhét.*, V, 5, 4-6, 2 = XI, 2, 1; VI, 18, 14 (les erreurs de Platon sont dans le choix des mots). La beauté de la demeure pousse Lucien à retrouver quelque chose de la puissance de l'inspiration et du style de Platon dans le *Phèdre*, au lieu de s'en exaspérer comme Denys d'Halicarnasse, qui lui reproche le 'manque de mesure de son élan (ἅμετρον ὁρμήν) vers le beau langage' (*Op. rhét.*, V, 5, 4 = XI, 2, 1) (de même XI 2, 2); voir *Phèdr.*, 279a, Socrate regrettant qu'Isocrate n'ait pas été conduit par 'un élan tout divin (ὁρμὴ θειοτέρα)'. Comme, dans le *Phèdre*, Socrate prononçant deux discours sur l'amour, blâmable, puis digne d'éloge, Lucien oppose deux discours sur le spectacle de la beauté, propre à stimuler ou à paralyser la parole. Ce 'second discours', personnifié, est présenté par Lucien avec un détachement analogue au refus de Socrate d'assumer la paternité de son premier discours en l'attribuant à Phèdre (*Phèdr.*, 242d-e, 257b): φησὶν ὁ λόγος, dit Lucien (ch. 15) de ce discours, qu'il nomme ensuite ὁ ἀντίδικος (ch. 17) (de même ch. 32). Et de même que Socrate intègre dans l'hymne à l'Amour, pour en montrer la défaite, une représentation de l'outrance du désir (*Phedr.*, 253d-254e), dont son premier discours racontait la domination et les méfaits, Lucien intègre à son discours d'éloge le discours qui en nie la possibilité (ch. 14-20), pour faire ressortir l'audace de son entreprise (ch. 21), et accroître son renom d'orateur auprès de ses auditeurs (ch. 32). Mais chez Lucien, l'opposition entre les deux discours, sous la fiction du débat judiciare (ch. 15, 32), apparaît comme un débat intérieur à l'orateur entre l'exaltation devant la beauté (ch. 4) et la peur de prononcer un éloge qui lui soit inférieur (ch. 7). Et c'est aussi un débat sur les pouvoirs respectifs du spectacle et de la parole. Or le 'second discours' est présenté dans le cadre judiciaire où étaient prononcés les discours du logographe Lysias; le témoin qu'il cite, Hérodote, est loué pars Denys d'Halicarnasse pour les mêmes 'grâces' du style, naturelles et simples (*Op. rhét.*, VI, 3, 13-18) que Lysias (*Op. rhét.*, iI, 10, 3-12); et Denys d'Halicarnasse rapporte, en exemple, le passage de l'histoire de Candaule et de Gygès d'où est tirée la formule citée par le 'second discours' de Lucien sur le crédit plus grand accordé aux yeux qu'aux oreilles (Hdt., I, 8 = D.H., *Op. rhét.*, VI, 3, 15 = Lucien, *De domo*, 20) (ainsi se comprend ce que G. Anderson, *op cit.*, 182, nomme 'Herodotus' surprise appearance'). Le discours prédominant de Lucien apparaît donc comme une défense et illustration du style des discours qui, dans le *Phèdre*, sont opposés au discours de Lysias (voir *Phèdr.*, 257a: l'ironie de Socrate sur le prétendu caractère poétique du discours de Lysias). J. Bompaire, *op cit.*, étudiant les auteurs modèles de Lucien, remarque (145) qu'il ne fait 'aucun éloge de Lysias'.

Dans le *Timée*, Platon assimile la fable de la création de l'univers à un édifice et à un corps humain: 'Maintenant que, tels les matériaux devant les artisans (τέκτοσιν), devant nous se trouvent les genres de causes dont nous devons confectionner le reste de ce discours, retournons brièvement au début, et à cette fable, tâchons dès lors d'ajouter une fin et une tête (κεφαλήν) qui soient en harmonie (ἁρμόττουσαν) avec ce qui précède' (*Tim.*, 69a-b).

Pour caractériser la beauté de ce style élevé, d'apparat, Lucien représente les fleurs et l'éclat de la poésie. C'est ainsi que, dans la IXe *Olympique*, Pindare célèbre, après 'le jardin .. des Charites, 'les fleurs des hymnes (ἄνθεα δ' ὕμνων)' (v. 48). De la VIe *Olympique*, présentée, en prélude, comme un édifice, il dit, en finale, qu'elle est 'la fleur charmante de (ses) hymnes (ὕμνων– ...εὐτερπὲς ἄνθος)' (v. 105). Et dans le fragment du *Dithyrambe pour les Athéniens* transmis par Denys d'Halicarnasse,[28] Pindare se représente offrant aux Olympiens 'ces chants que l'on cueille au printemps (τῶν τ' ἐαριδρόπων ἀοιδᾶν) ... lorsque ... la végétation ... amène le printemps parfumé' (*Dithyr.*, IV, Fr. 75, 6-15 Maehler).

Dans le *De domo*, tout n'est qu'images, de la peinture ou de l'éloquence. Lucien commence par louer la décoration qui l'entoure, 'les fresques des murs, la beauté de leurs couleurs, l'éclat, la précision, la vérité de chacune d'elles,' comparables 'à une vue de printemps et à une prairie bien fleurie' (ch. 9). Leur beauté est impérissable: ce sont là 'printemps (ἔαρ) éternel, prairie (λειμών) inaltérable, et floraison (ἄνθος) immortelle, car seule la vue les atteint et cueille (δρεπομένης) le plaisir du regard' (Ch. 9). Lucien compare ensuite son désir de parler dans ce décor (ch. 10) au plaisir que prend le paon à 'venir, au début du printemps, sur une prairie, lorsque les fleurs apparaissent ... en quelque sorte plus fleuries et d'une teinte plus pure; alors, le paon, étalant son plumage ... et faisant la roue, déploie ses fleurs et le printemps de son plumage (ἐπιδείκνυται τὰ ἄνθη τὰ αὐτοῦ καὶ τὸ ἔαρ τῶν πτερῶν), comme si la prairie l'invitait à la rivalité' (ch. 11).[29] Qu'à travers cette comparaison, image de son éloquence 'fleurie'– (ἀνθηρός)[30]–Lucien se révèle imitateur de la prose poétique de Platon influencé par Pindare est prouvé par les déclarations de Parrhèsiadès à Platon dans le *Pisca-*

[28] *Op. rhét.*, VI, 22, 11.

[29] De même, dans le roman d'Achille Tatius, Clitophon voulant séduire Leucippé par un discours 'panégyrique' composé de fables à l'éloge du pouvoir de l'Amour (I, 17-18) se comporte comme le paon qui, sur la prairie du parc, 'déploie la prairie' fleurie 'de son plumage' devant la paonne (I, 16); et Leucippé répond à ce discours en chantant des images de la poésie épique et lyrique (II, 1): M.M.J. Leplace, *Recherches sur le roman d'Achille Tatios, Leucippé et Clitophon*, thèse de doctorat d'État dactyl., Paris-X, 1988, t,II, 216-32.

[30] Voir *De domo*, 1: οἶκον...γράφαις ἀνθηρότατον. Pour l'emploi de ce terme dans la critique stylistique: Denys d'Halicarnasse, *Op. rhét.*, V, 18, 7; VI, 22, 6; *De audiendo*, 8 (les effets 'dramatiques et panégyriques' des sophistes, pareils à ceux du théâtre et de la lyrique, sont opposés au style de Lysias, ch. 9). Voir aussi l'emploi de εὐανθής: εἰ μὲν εὐανθές τι εἴη τὸ δηλούμενον, εὐανθῆ καὶ τὴν φράσιν εἶναι (Théon. *Progymn.*, 11 - II, 119, 31-120 Sp.).

tor:[31] 'Les choses mêmes que je dis, où les ai-je prises, sinon chez vous, butinant vos fleurs comme une abeille,[32] pour les présenter aux hommes (ἀπανθισάμενος ἐπιδείκνυμαι)? Les hommes louent chaque fleur, et reconnaissent où, chez qui, et comment je l'ai choisie; et, à les entendre, ils admirent mon florilège, mais, en vérité, c'est vous et votre prairie (λειμῶνα) qu'ils admirent, vous qui avez produit des fleurs aux teintes si chatoyantes et multiformes que, quand on sait les choisir, les disposer et les harmoniser, elles ne détonnent (ἀπᾴδειν) pas l'une par rapport à l'autre' (ch. 6).

Dans le *De domo*, Lucien associe à l'image des fleurs de la poésie celle de son éclat, en soulignant que le brillant chatoiement de sa prose d'apparat est le chatoiement non pas seulement d'un style, mais aussi d'une culture.[33] En effet, lorsqu'il loue 'les parties élevées (ὑψηλά) et supérieures de la demeure' (ch. 9), son plafond, il décrit l'effet de la luminosité solaire sur cette surface dorée selon un schéma qu'il reprend pour le plumage du paon embelli par les rayons solaires, avant de l'appliquer à sa parole prenant pour sujets les fables peintes sur les murs. La plafond doré, d'abord comparé au ciel étoilé, constellé de 'fleurs de feu (ἀνθῶν τῷ πυρί)' (ch. 8), est ensuite représenté éclairé par le soleil: 'Il colore toute la salle de son rougeoiment; car lorsque la lumière solaire ... l'atteint, et se mêle à l'or, ils étincellent d'un commun éclat (κοινόν τι ἀπαστράπτουσι), et le rougeoiement de l'or brille d'une clarté redoublée (διπλασίαν τοῦ ἐρυθήματος ἐκφαίνουσι τὴν αἴθριαν)' (ch. 8). De même, les 'fleurs' du plumage du paon brillent au soleil 'd'un éclat plus merveilleux': 'son plumage, dit Lucien, prend une autre parure (μετακοσμεῖται) sous la lumière solaire' (ch. 11).[34]

C'est ainsi que la prose de Lucien reçoit son éclat poétique des fables qu'elle décrit sur les murs. Eprise de 'sujets si beaux et si chatoyants (ποικίλας τὰς ὑποθέσεις)', elle ne saurait manquer de les dépeindre. 'Car la précision de leur art et l'utilité de leurs histoires, jointe à leur ancienneté, sont vraiment attrayantes et réclament des spectateurs cultivés (πεπαιδευμένων) ... Eh bien, dit Lucien, à moi de vous les peindre (γράψωμαι) de mon mieux par le langage. Vous prendrez plaisir, je pense, à l'audition de ce qui émerveille votre regard. Et peut-être me louerez-vous ... d'avoir redoublé (διπλασιάσαντα) votre plaisir. Mais, voyez la difficulté et l'audace de l'entreprise: composer tant d'images (εἰκόνας) sans couleurs (χρωμάτων), ni formes (σχημάτων), ni espace; car la peinture du langage est en quelque

sorte dépouillée (ψιλὴ γάρ τις ἡ γραφὴ τῶν λόγων)' (ch. 21).[35]

Dans cette définition de son discours, Lucien transpose à la dualité entre peinture murale et peinture oratoire la distinction entre poésie et prose, et signifie son intention de réaliser, par la description de fresques, le projet d'Isocrate et de Platon d'une prose poétique. Car si l'exaltation de l'entreprise rappelle les fières déclarations d'Isocrate,[36] l'emploi de l'adjectif ψιλός appartient à la tradition platonicienne de caractérisation de la prose, par contraste avec la poésie. Dans le *Ménexène*, l'art de la prose d'éloge est désigné par l'expression λόγῳ ψιλῷ κοσμεῖν (293c), et opposé à celui des hymnes poétiques: ἐν μουσικῇ ὑμνήσαντες (239d). Dans le *Phèdre*, l'opposition subsiste, alors que tout langage littéraire est compris sous l'acception générique de 'poésie': ποίησιν ψιλὴν ἢ ἐν ᾠδῇ (278c). Et Aristide Quintilien la reprend dans les mêmes termes: ποίησις...διὰ ψιλῶν...λέξεως (*De musica*, II, 63); ἐν ψιλῇ ποιήσει (*De musica*, II, 67). Tel est le dépouillement de la prose désignée par Lucien comme une sorte de peinture abstraite et incolore.[37] Elle l'incite à la même

---

[31] Bien, que, en *Pisc.*, 5, l'interlocuteur de Parrhèsiadès soit 'le philosophe' selon tous les Mss, et en *Pisc.*, 7 'le philosophe' ou 'les philosophes' selon les Mss les plus anciens, et 'Platon' seulement dans les Mss plus récents (voir éd. de Macleod), si la leçon des *recentiores* ne transmet pas le texte originel, elle en explicite du moins le sens.

[32] Voir *Plat., Ion*, 534a-b.

[33] Cette exigence est formulée dès le début: *De domo*, 2.

[34] J. Bompaire, *op. cit.*, 718-19, comparant è l'*ecphrasis* du paon dans l'*Olympicos* de Dion de Pruse celle du *De domo* de Lucien, écrit: 'Vraie symphonie de couleurs et de reflets, qu'on ne retrouve pas chez les autres écrivains'. Voir aussi V. Andò, *Luciano critico d'arte* (Palerme 1975) 63-4.

[35] Comme le terme εἰκών (voir *infra.*, n 37), les termes χρῶμα et σχῆμα appartiennent à la fois au vocabulaire des arts plastiques et à celui de la critique littéraire. Pour χρῶμα, voir Denys d'Halicarnasse, *Op. rhét.*, IV, 4, 1-2, VI, 24, 11 (avec énumération de différentes 'couleurs' du style de Thucydide); VII, 42, 4 (voir aussi Lucien, *Quom. hist. conscr.*, 23: χρή...τὰ πάντα...ὁμόχροα εἶναι καὶ συνᾳδὸν τῇ κεφαλῇ τὸ ἄλλο σῶμα). Pour σχῆμα, voir Denys d'Halicarnasse, *Op. rhét.*, VI, 8, 1, 19, 13; et G. Aujac, *Denys d'Halicarnasse. La composition stylistique* C.U.F. (Paris 1981) 86 n.1 et 165 n. 2. Sur 'le nom, imitation comme la peinture', mais s'addressant à l'ouïe, tandis que la peinture s'addresse à la vue, et sur la comparaison entre les images représentées par les noms et les phrases du discours au moyen de lettres et les images peintes produites par 'des couleurs et des formes (χρώματά τε καὶ σχήματα)': Plat., *Crat.*, 430e-431c.

[36] Voir *supra*, 2-3.

[37] Cette définition est une variante de la formule attribuée à Simonide, que Plutarque rappelle après avoir indiqué 'que la parole est un art d'imitation ... qui fait, pendant à la peinture (ἀντίστροφος τῇ ζωγραφίᾳ) ... La poésie est une peinture parlante, et la peinture une poésie silencieuse' (*De aud. poet.*, 3, 17E-F) (voir aussi Plut., *De ad. et am.*, 588; *Quaest. conu.*, 748A; *De glor. Ath.*, 346F). Cette formule, dont Plutarque écrit qu'elle était 'rebattue' (*De aud. poet.*, 17F), est l'une des bases structurelles des romans de Longus, Achille Tatius et Héliodore. Longus présente son écrit comme le pendant d'une belle image peinte, qui attire les spectateurs: εἰκόνος γραφήν...ἰδόντα με... πόθος ἔσχεν ἀντιγράψαι τῇ γραφῇ (*Prooem.*, 1). Chez Achille Tatius, où le récit de Clitophon fait pendant à la description du tableau de l'enlèvement d'Europe (I, 1, 1-3, 1), l'allusion à la formule apparaît, à l'intérieur du récit de Clitophon, quand est repris le schéma d'un récit corrélatif d'une description de peinture (V, 3, 4-5, 9). Mais cette peinture, qui est celle du 'viol de Philomèle ... et de la mutilation de sa langue' par Térée (V, 3, 4), et qui montre le voile brodé par Philomèle (V, 3, 5-7: τὴν τοῦ πέπλου γραφήν), représente l'envers du schéma initial (et de sa signification d'une fin heureuse): κείρει τῆς φωνῆς τὸ ἄνθος...ἡ...Φιλομήλας τέχνη σιωπῶσαν εὕρηκε φωνήν, explique Clitophon à Leucippé (V, 5, 4). Selon un agencement différent, Héliodore offre aussi trois modalités, intérieures l'une à l'autre, de l'équivalence entre art graphique et récit. L'histoire de Chariclée et de Théagène est conforme à la fable peinte d'Andromède et de Persée, mais ce tableau est décrit sur une bande brodée par

'audace' que Platon célébrant par un 'hymne' 'l'espace supra-céleste' occupé par 'la réalité essentielle, sans couleur ni forme (ἀχρώματός τε καὶ ἀσχημάτος) ... qui ne peut être contemplée que par l'intellect' (*Phèdr.*, 247c).

En effet, pour donner à sa prose formes et éclat, Lucien constuit, à l'image de la somptueuse demeure ensoleillée dans laquelle il parle, un discours descriptif et chatoyant d'images (εἰκόνες) poétiques et mythologiques,[38] dont les modèles sont à la fois 'l'hymne mythologique' du *Phèdre*[39] et les hymnes de Pindare, que Denys d'Halicarnasse oppose fallacieusement aux 'dithyrambes' du *Phèdre*, en citant l'invocation au Soleil d'un *Péan pour les Thébains*.[40] Car si Lucien, en décrivant les fresques murales (ch. 22-31), évoque, tel Pindare, d'antiques histoires légendaires, et non des images allégoriques, comme celle de l'attelage ailé de l'âme dans le *Phèdre*,[41] il affirme aussi l'esthétique de la seconde sophistique, et son adhésion à l'éloquence inspirée du *Phèdre*, en défendant le style 'élevé' (ὑψη–λός) de Platon. Contredisant Denys d'Halicarnasse, qui reproche à ce style ses 'allégories ... dépourvues de mesure' et ses 'figures poétiques', et qui le caractérise comme 'tempétueux'–χειμάζεται περὶ τὴν τροπικὴν φράσιν (*Op. rhét.*, V, 5, 5-6)—Lucien illustre les images printanières que Denys d'Halicarnasse réserve au style 'simple' du début du *Phèdre*—μεστὸν ὥρας ἄνθος...· ὥσπερ ἀπὸ τῶν εὐωδεστάτων λειμώνων (*Op. rhét.*, V, 5, 3; 7, 2)—dans une allégorie du discours d'apparat dont le cadre raffiné est opposé à la simplicité du paysage du *Phèdre*, et dont la résonance poétique et divine contraste avec la clameur répondant aux discours des sophistes réprouvés dans la *République* de Platon.

la mère de Chariclée, Persinna (IV, 8, 3-5); et le dénouement heureux de l'histoire de Chariclée permet que les inscriptions brodées sur la bande avec cette description (IV, 8, 8: τὰ τῆς γραφῆς) ne restent pas 'muettes': ταυτά σοι διείλεγμαι τὸ γράμμα διάκονον εὐραμένη...τάχα μὲν κωφά...τάχα δὲ καὶ εἰς ὀφελός ποτε ἤξοντα, a écrit Persinna (IV, 8, 8). En outre, le récit par Calasiris des aventures de Chariclée et de Théagène équivaut à une bague au chaton d'améthyste gravée.

[38] Sur le caractère 'poétique' de la 'comparaison' (εἰκών) dans le langage: Aristote. *Rhét.*, III, 4, 1406b, 20-25; III, 10, 1410b, 16. Pour l'analogie entre l'image mythologique et l'image peinte: ὅταν εἰκάζῃ τις κακῶς τῷ λόγῳ περὶ θεῶν τε καὶ ἡρώων οἷοί εἰσιν, ὥσπερ γραφεὺς μηδὲν ἐοικότα γράφων (Plat., *Rép.*, II, 377e). Pour l'analogie entre les différentes variétés de stylistique et les différents mélanges de couleurs utilisés par les peintres: Denys d'Halicarnasse, *Op. rhét.*, VI, 21, 1-2; entre l'interaction dans le discours du sublime et du pathétique et des figures (σχήματα) et la répartition de la lumière et de l'ombre dans un tableau: *Du sublime*, 17, 2-3; entre l'emploi de la fable mythologique dans un récit et l'emploi de la couleur en peinture: Plut., *De aud. poet.*, 2, 94B. J. Bompaire, *op cit.*, 715-17, montre comment Lucien fait percevoir le dessin des fresques; et V. Andò, *op cit.*, 63, souligne les notations de couleur.

[39] *Phèdr.*, 265c: μυθικόν τινα ὕμνον.

[40] *Op. rhét.*, V, 7, 7: 'Là, il n'y a nulle allégorie, comme chez Platon', conclut Denys d'Halicarnasse, en oubliant les nombreuses images, métaphores et comparaisons, de la poésie de Pindare.

[41] En fait, Platon désigne successivement cette image par la notion d'εἰκών (*Phèdr.*, 246a) et par le terme μῦθον (*Phèdr.*, 253c); voir Théon, *Progymn.*, 3 = II, 72, 27 Sp: Μῦθός ἐστι λόγος ψευδὴς εἰκονίζων ἀλήθειαν.

Telles sont, en effet, les deux références, l'une explicite, l'autre implicite, par rapport auxquelles Lucien compose son allégorie de la parole d'apparat, d'inspiration divine.

Pour Socrate, dans la *République*, les sophistes étaient les corrupteurs de l'éducation et de la culture, 'lorsque la multitude compacte, venue siéger à l'assemblée, au tribunal, au théâtre, ou au camp ... accueillait avec une clameur multiple, tantôt par le blâme, tantôt par l'éloge, tout ce qui se disait ou se faisait ... tandis que les rochers du lieu où ils se trouvaient leur renvoyaient la clameur redoublée par l'écho (ἐπηχοῦντες διπλάσιον θόρυβον) du blâme et de l'éloge' (*Rép.*, VI, 492b-c).[42] Mais dans le *Phèdre*, 'il suffit à Socrate, dit Lucien, d'un platane ... d'une pelouse ... et d'une source limpide non loin de l'Ilissos: assis là ... il invoquait les Muses, certain qu'elles viendraient prendre part aux discours sur l'amour, et il n'avait pas honte, lui, un vieillard, d'inviter des jeunes filles à chanter avec lui des amours de jeunes garçons. Dans un si bel endroit, continue Lucien, admiratif du cadre de son éloquence, ne pouvons-nous penser qu'elles viennent d'elles-mêmes, sans être invitées?' (ch. 4).

De fait, la somptueuse demeure qui accueille la louange de Lucien lui 'répond doucement en écho (συνεπηχῶν), comme les antres ... Ainsi, dit-il, les cimes des monts accompagnent de sons de flûte les airs de flûte des bergers ... Mais les profanes croient qu'une jeune fille donne la réplique (ἀμειβομένην) aux chanteurs ... et parle de l'intérieur des rochers' (ch. 3). Pour cette demeure à l'acoustique merveilleuse, dont le plafond doré est, en outre, assimilé à une tête au beau visage (ch. 8), Lucien préfère évoquer, plutôt que la nymphe Écho, l'image d'un personnage 'savant (εὐμα–θής), qui écoute, loue l'orateur, et lui renvoie, en échange de ses paroles, une création non dépourvue de poésie (ἀντίδοσιν οὐκ ἄμουσον ποιούμενος πρὸς αὐτά)' (ch. 3),[43] puis celle d'une femme chaste et belle, élégamment et sobrement parée (ch. 7). De sorte qu'est suggérée pour cette demeure naturellement familière aux Muses la figure de leur mère, Mnèmosynè, la Mémoire divine personnifiée.

Or Lucien se représente pareil à ce personnage, lorsqu'il s'oppose aux profanes qui, dans une telle demeure, se contentent de regarder, 'sans pouvoir prononcer des paroles dignes de ce qu'ils regardent'; 'c'est, dit-il, manquer grandement de sens du beau et, en outre, de don poétique (ἀμουσία), que ... de rester étranger aux plus belles choses ... Celui qui voit les belles choses en homme cultivé (μετὰ παιδείας) ... ne saurait accepter d'être le spectateur muet de la beauté; il tentera, autant que possible, de donner, par la parole, la réplique au spectacle (λόγῳ ἀμείψασθαι τὴν θέαν). Et la réplique (ἀμοιβή) ne sera pas seulement l'éloge de la maison ...; convoquer les plus belles paroles pour y donner une

[42] La critique est reprise dans les *Lois*, IX, 876b, mais sans l'image de l'écho.

[43] La formule combine, semble-t-il, à la référence au discours *Sur l'échange d'Isocrate* (περὶ τῆς ἀντιδόσεως), comparé à une oeuvre plastique, statue ou peinture (ch. 2), et désigné 'comme une image (εἰκών) de la pensée et de la vie' d'Isocrate (ch. 7), le souvenir de l'ordre reçu en rêve par Socrate: μουσικὴν ποίει (Plat., *Phèd.*, 60e). Et l'évocation élogieuse de l'écho est inspirée d'Homère: δώματα ἠχήεντα (Od.,IV,72)~ἠχήεντι οἴκῳ (*De domo*, 16).

démonstration d'éloquence (τοὺς βελτίστους συγκαλέ–σαντα λόγων ἐπίδειξιν ποιήσασθαι) constituera aussi une partie de l'éloge' (ch. 2-3). Telle est la 'réplique' que l'éloquence de Lucien donne au spectacle de cette demeure: elle s'en fait l'écho dans un discours d'apparat qui 'redouble (διπλασιάσαντα) le plaisir' des spectateurs (ch. 21)[44] par l'éloge des beautés, et par la description des images plastiques ornant les murs, fresques (ch. 22-25; 27-31), ou statue (ch. 26), dont les fables poétiques, d'Euripide et de Sophocle notamment, sont 'l'archétype' (ch. 23). Le discours d'apparat de Lucien est donc à l'image de cette demeure: il est habité par les Muses, il est comme la Mémoire de la poésie. Cette demeure, figure de Mnèmosynè, est ainsi l'allégorie de la parole d'apparat de Lucien: en la décrivant, il présente une *ecphrasis* de son esthétique littéraire.

Habitée par l'inspiration divine de la poésie, et admirable tant par 'l'harmonie' de ses dimensions (ch. 6: τὸ...εὔρυθμον) que par 'la juste mesure' de ses dorures (ch. 7: τὸ τοῦ χρυσοῦ ἐς τὸ εὐπρεπὲς σύμμετρον), cette belle et plaisante demeure se différencie de la simple beauté d'un platane ombreux (ch. 5), mais aussi de la magnificence insolente du palais des Arsacides, où 'ni la mesure ni l'harmonie (ἢ τὸ σύμμετρον ἢ τὸ εὔρυθμον) ... n'étaient associées aux dorures (ch. 5).[45] Or ces deux sortes de séjour sont comparées par Lucien à deux types féminins, celui de la femme belle de sa beauté naturelle (ch. 15), et celui de la courtisane privée du beauté, mais couverte de bijoux (ch. 7), qui correspondent aux représentations que Denys d'Halicarnasse donne de 'la Muse attique', servie par Lysias, et de 'la Muse d'Asie' (*Op. rhét.*, I, 1-2), dont il découvre déjà les défauts chez Gorgias et dans les 'dithyrambes' de Platon (*Op. rhét.*, II, 3, 3-4). Il apparaît donc que, dans le *De domo*, Lucien, 'ami du beau' et 'amoureux de la parfaite élégance' (ch. 2), reprend, contre Denys d'Halicarnasse défenseur de Lysias, le débat oratoire du *Phèdre*,[46] et montre son adhésion à l'esthétique de l'hymne à l'Amour,[47] en s'inspirant, non sans humour,

de Pindare pour l'illustrer.[48]

A l'image de la somptueuse demeure par laquelle elle se décrit, la parole d'apparat de Lucien, émule de celles de Pindare et de Platon, est un éloge habité par les Muses, et agrémenté par l'or et les fleurs de la poésie.

Traduisant la double fascination de l'illusion et de la vérité, la parole d'apparat de Lucien se représente soit comme une parole limpide qui fait miroiter, attirant et irréel, l'ambre de la fable, soit comme un édifice élevé et harmonieux, paré du chatoiement des fleurs de la poésie et de la fable, et habité par les Muses et la Mémoire divine. Dans l'éloquence d'apparat de Lucien, le style simple et le style élevé de Platon, distingués par la critique de Denys d'Halicarnasse, deviennent des représentations imagées qui témoignent doublement de l'admiration de Lucien pour une esthétique inspirée des hymnes de Pindare. Dans l'*Electrum*, Lucien ajoute à la Muse attique le charme du rêve; dans le *De domo*, il exalte une Muse d'Asie harmonieuse.[49]

MARIE MARCELLE JEANINE LAPLACE
Université de Bretagne Occidentale

---

[44] Cité *supra*. p. 163; voir aussi *De domo*, 4 (cité *supra*, n. 25) et 13: le langage est la parure de la beauté visuelle.

[45] Voir Plat., *Critias*, 116d: chez les Atlantes, le temple élevé de Poséidon possède la mesure et l'harmonie des dimensions (ὕψος...σύμμετρον). 'mais il a une sorte de beauté barbare'.

[46] Denys d'Halic., *Op. rhét.*, XI, 1-14 indique que sa méthode de critique littéraire, fondée sur la comparaison, est imitée du *Phèdre*. De même, Plutarque recommande, pour juger un conférencier, la méthode de la comparaison, en citant pour modèle Platon dans le *Phèdre* (*De aud.*, 5, 40D-E).

[47] 'Le second discours', qui interrompt le discours d'*ecphrasis* (ch. 14), et lui cède ensuite la parole (ch. 21), le dote par antiphrase d'un pouvoir d'attraction magique ou divin en évoquant, à la manière de Platon dans l'*Ion* (533b-c), Démodocos, Phémios, Thamyris, Amphion et Orphée, seuls capables, à son avis, de distraire la pensée d'un tel spectacle (ch. 18), puis en opposant à la beauté pétrifiante des Gorgones le charme enjôleur des mélodies des Sirènes (ch. 19). Mais, au lieu de prétendre contrarier l'attrait exercé par la beauté, le discours d'*ecphrasis* se propose d'en 'redoubler' le plaisir et le pouvoir d'attraction (ch. 10: ἐπαγωγότατον γάρ τι ἡ ὄψις τῶν καλῶν; ch.21: ἐπαγωγόν), à moins qu'inversement, les auditeurs, partisans du 'second discours', ne décident d'écouter la parole d'*ecphrasis* 'en fermant les yeux' (ch. 32).

[48] Denys d'Halicarnasse cite la formule de Pindare (*fr.* 159 Maehler) 'le temps, meilleur sauveur des justes', pour se féliciter de l'honneur retrouvé de 'l'antique et chaste rhétorique', originaire d'Attique, dont Lysias est le parangon, et du discrédit de l'autre, la rhétorique venue d'Asie, 'jeune et insensée' (*Op. rhét.*, I, 2, 1-2), dont Gorgias fait entendre des sons 'bien proches du dithyrambe' (*Op. rhét.*, II, 3, 4), comme Platon qui avoue ce défaut (*Op. rhét.*, V, 6, 3-5; 7, 5-7). Près de deux siècles plus tard, Lucien de Samosate se représente, dans le *De domo*, pareil à Pindare, poète du *Dithyrambe pour les Athéniens* (voir *supra*, p. 161).

[49] Racontant la panégyrie de Delphes, Calasiris dit, que 'l'oeil dédaignait de voir, tant l'ouïe était charmée', que les spectateurs étaient 'comme attirés par l'écho du chant' des jeunes filles thessaliennes, mais que l'apparition des éphèbes à cheval 'démontra qu'un beau spectacle l'emporte sur toute audition' (III, 3, 1). Pourtant, en Egypte, loin de Delphes, Calasiris réussit, par sa description, à rendre cette panégyrie présente pour Cnémon, et à réaliser ainsi le projet que Lucien exprime à la fin du *De domo* (ch. 32; voir *supra*, n. 47), en souhaitant que ses auditeurs ferment les yeux pour l'écouter. En effet, Cnémon trouve le récit de Calasiris 'captivant' comme le chant des Sirènes: σειρήνειον (V, 1, 4). Pour l'éloquence de Calasiris reflet de celle d'Héliodore: M.M.J. Laplace, 'Les *Éthiopiques* d'Héliodore, ou la genèse d'un panégyrique de l'Amour', in *R.E.A.* xciv (1992) 200-1, 226-28. Voir aussi Thyamis persuadé par les paroles trompeuses de Chariclée: ὥσπερ τινὸς σειρῆνος κεκηλημένος (I, 23 2).

Evans, Mackenzie, and the history
of the Palace at Knossos*

At Knossos Mackenzie seems again to have performed the duties that we would now designate as those of the site supervisor. But the exact nature of his responsibilities, the limits of his authority and the personal relationship between him and Evans are something of an enigma. The problem has important scientific implications in view of the controversy that has developed since 1962 about the dependability of some aspects of Evans's publications. The conundrum, in short, concerns the exact roles that the two men played in the gradual evolution of theories from the moment of discovery of crucial evidence until the final arguments and conclusions appeared in definitive publications. (W.A. McDonald and C.G. Thomas, *Progress into the past: the rediscovery of Mycenaean civilisation* [2nd ed., Bloomington and Indiana 1990] 119).

... Evans in an eloquent passage towards the end of his first report for the year 1900 makes it quite clear that he regarded the pithoi in the South Propylaion (B) as belonging to the same fire-destroyed palace as the pithoi in the West Magazines (C) and the Linear B tablets. This rather suggests that it was Mackenzie and not Evans who evolved the theory of the 'Reoccupation' in the first instance. If so, he convinced Evans. (Sinclair Hood, '"Last palace" and "reoccupation" at Knossos', *Kadmos* iv [1965] 18)

Duncan Mackenzie (1861-1934) is usually remembered as Sir Arthur Evans' loyal assistant or 'site supervisor' and author of the 'Day-books of the excavations at Knossos'—the only continuous and systematic record of the excavations of this site. Little attention has been paid to his contribution to Minoan and Aegean scholarship, largely because he published very little, but also because, as Evans's employee, he was destined to remain in the background.[1] However, his unpublished 'Day-books of the excavations at Knossos' and his correspondence with Evans show that crucial ideas or interpretations of the archaeology of Knossos did originate from Mackenzie. These sources provide much evidence upon the complex relationship between the two scholars, and show how Mackenzie's influence upon Evans ranged from pottery analysis and classification, to stratigraphy and architecture, to Minoan religion, and to racial and anthropological issues typical of much of nineteenth- and early twentieth century archaeology.

This note is concerned with one particularly revealing document, a letter from Mackenzie to Evans of 1901, now kept in the Evans Archive of the Ashmolean Museum, Oxford, which clarifies the 'enigma' of Mackenzie's relationship with Evans and his role in the 'evolution of theories' about Knossos (the full text is printed below). It is just one example of how Mackenzie influenced Evans, but it is important because it concerns the history of Knossos, and, consequently, the history of the whole Aegean, particularly in the Late Bronze Age. This letter demonstrates beyond reasonable doubt that it was Mackenzie 'who evolved the theory of the "Reoccupation" in the first instance', as suggested by Hood in 1965.

The letter, dated 5th February 1901, was sent by Mackenzie to Evans from Rome, where he normally resided between 1900 and 1910 when not at Knossos or engaged in other archaeological activities. The letter consists of two parts: the main text and a long 'Post Scriptum'. The structure of the letter itself is intriguing. The main text deals with practical matters such as photography of site and finds, problems with Cretan workmen, Mackenzie's salary, his precarious financial situation (and dependence on Evans), accommodation in Crete, etc. Particularly touching is the passage in which Mackenzie reports that one of the workmen had been wrongly accused of theft: 'There is one thing I have on my conscience about Themistocles. The twelve tins of Asparagus were found and he was most seriously anxious that you should know.'[2] But the letter contains some fundamental observations of an archaeological character, which have significant implications for the history of Knossos and of Aegean scholarship. These are confined to the 'Post Scriptum', almost as if Mackenzie had been diffident to criticise Evans.

In this 'Post Scriptum', Mackenzie outlined the main phases in the history of the Palace at Knossos as summarised below:

1. A 'Kamarais' Palace, (Old Palace phase).
2. A 'Mycenaean Palace' (Neopalatial phase).
3. A period of 'decline' ('reoccupation' phase).[3]

---

* I should like to thank Sinclair Hood and Jeremy Johns for reading a draft of this note and encouraging me to publish it; Alistair Bain Mackenzie, for allowing me to use and quote from his uncle's letters; Michael Vickers, the Visitors of the Ashmolean Museum and the Evans Trust for allowing me to study and quote from Mackenzie's 'Day-books' and Evans's 'Notebooks' of the excavations at Knossos. All quotations from Mackenzie's 1900 'Day-book' refer to the inked version.

[1] See, e.g., S. Horwitz, *The find of a lifetime* (London 1981) 105: 'Hired as an assistant, Mackenzie was destined to remain in second place...'. D. Levi, *Festós e la civiltà minoica* I (Rome 1976) 8: '...unico archeologo di professione, esperto e accurato-durante tutti gli anni delle spettacolari scoperte del Palazzo minoico...'. Colin Renfrew, in his introduction to his transcription of Mackenzie's 'Day-books of the excavations at Phylakopi' describes them as 'outstanding examples of systematic archaeological reasoning, produced at a time when scientific principles of excavation had not yet been established. Duncan Mackenzie was one of the very first scientific workers in the Aegean, and his Day-books have therefore a considerable historical value, which I believe would alone warrant their duplication'. Copies of this transcription are in the libraries of the British School at Athens, the Museum of Classical Archaeology, Cambridge, and the University of Cincinnati. There is no complete transcription of the 'Day-books of the excavations at Knossos'. N. Momigliano, 'Duncan Mackenzie: a cautious canny Highlander', in C. Morris (ed.), *Klados: essays in honour of J.N. Coldstream* (London 1994)163-70, is a short biographical note containing a bibliography of published works by Mackenzie.

[2] We can trace the history of the twelve tins of asparagus one year back. The invoice from the Junior Army and Navy Stores listing the twelve tins, dated 9 February 1900, is still kept among the Evans Archive papers in the Ashmolean Museum.

[3] Mackenzie also mentions a much later phase represented by structural remains over part of the West Magazines, probably what was later identified as a Greek temple (S. Hood and W. Taylor, *The Bronze Age palace at Knossos* [London 1981] no. 62, with references).

The opening phrase of the 'Post Scriptum' ('As regards the question ...') suggests that Mackenzie is answering a query from Evans, which in turn must have been prompted by a previous letter from Mackenzie, now lost, in which he must have pointed out a discrepancy between his and Evans's views of the main phases in the history of the Palace.[4] Although not stated explicitly, the discrepancy clearly concerned the existence of a phase of 'decline', i.e. the 'reoccupation'. As Hood pointed out in 1965, in his 'Day-book of the excavations at Knossos' for 1900, Mackenzie had clearly foreshadowed the 'reoccupation' theory, describing a 'somewhat later floor-level' which belonged 'to a period when the palace was no longer inhabited as such'. Evans, on the contrary, in the report published in the *Annual of the British School at Athens* gives the clear impression that the building which he had excavated during the first season was destroyed at one time and showed no sign of later use.[5] The discrepancy between these two views is clarified and underlined by Mackenzie's letter.[6]

This letter, together with Mackenzie's 'Day-book' for 1900, demonstrates that it was he who first envisaged the 'reoccupation', and—more important—he who first had the idea that this was of non-palatial and decadent character. It is this idea—expressed explicitly for the first time in the letter published here—that has the greatest historical implications. For if the reoccupation represented a period of decadence, it followed that the Linear B tablets could not be assigned to this phase. If Mackenzie had based his interpretation precisely upon the observation that no tablets were found associated with the latest stratigraphical levels, then one of the most hotly debated problems in Aegean archaeology would have never arisen. But this is not the case. From Mackenzie's 1900 'Day-book' and from his letter of February 1900 we can see that his 'non-palatial' interpretation was based essentially upon observations concerning later structures in the West Magazines (where indeed tablets were found in 1900),[7] in the North West Portico,[8] and in the South Propylaeum.[9] After the second excavation season, the purely subjective notion that the pottery later called LM III A and B was somewhat decadent was added to the 'reoccupation' theory.[10] It appears that Mackenzie found it difficult to accept that the Linear B tablets, the most explicit symbols of high civilisation, could be associated with a phase in the life of the palace which, because of its architecture and pottery, he perceived as a 'period of decline'. One wonders whether the problem of the date of the Linear B tablets from Knossos does not originate in part precisely from Mackenzie's desire to separate the tablets from a phase that he considered decadent.

We may or may not agree with Mackenzie's interpretation of the non-palatial character of the reoccupation.[11] It is not the aim of this note to argue for or against this view, nor to trace the various stages in the evolution of the 'reoccupation' theory, but simply to show that it was Mackenzie who first provided a clear description of the main phases of the history of the Palace at Knossos, and who proposed an interpretation of the character of the 'reoccupation' which has important implications for the history of the whole Aegean in the Late Bronze Age.

It is both fascinating and terrifying to see in Mackenzie's letter the main stages of the history of Knossos already crystallised in outline by February 1901, after a single season of excavation. From the moment in which Mackenzie convinced Evans of the 'reoccupation' and of its non-palatial character, until the late 1950s-early 1960s, no scholar challenged this reconstruction of the

---

[4] Indeed, another passage in the main text ('About the proposal ... I made to you in my letter before last ...') shows that this letter was preceded by at least two which are now, unfortunately, lost, probably written between September 1900 and January 1901.

[5] S. Hood, '"Last palace" and "Reoccupation" at Knossos', *Kadmos* iv (1965) 17-18. *Cf.* Mackenzie's 1900 'Day-book', *passim* (especially entries for Thursday 5 April, Friday 13 April) and A.J. Evans, 'Knossos. I. The Palace', *BSA* vi (1899-1900) 3-70, especially 63-66. See also E. Hallager, *The Mycenaean palace at Knossos. Evidence for final destruction in the III B period* (Stockholm 1977) 15-16.

[6] Although Mackenzie did not use the word 'reoccupation' itself in his 1900 'Day-book', nor in the letter published here, it is clear that this is what he meant.

[7] See Mackenzie's 1901 letter: 'the wall going across the long corridor between the 2nd and 3rd galleries...'. '2nd and 3rd' is likely to be a mistake for '3rd and 4th galleries', for this must be a reference to the wall described in Mackenzie's 1900 'Day-12 book' (27 April) as follows (my italics): 'The gallery—3—opening out W from this, where several fragments of inscription tablets were previously found has a doorway 2.29 wide and the N jamb of the gallery has just appeared behind *a later wall which had been apparently built up for dwelling purposes and in order to close up the wide passage N-wards*, at a time when the palace must have already fallen into ruins but previous to the erection of the wall which appear next the

surface above the walls of 1, 2, 3, 5 [The Greek Temple: see n. 3 above].' Mackenzie's 1900 'Day-book' also provides a sketch of the wall blocking the long Corridor (entry for 18 April, sketch no. 26), reproduced in Hallager (n. 6) 36 fig. 19. Evans in his 1900 'Notebook' also refers to a wall between Magazines 3 and 4 (quoted in Hallager, *ibid.*).

[8] The 'N Propylaea' in Mackenzie's letter. The later structures must be the wall which blocked the eastern door-jambs on the south side of the North West Portico, and the wall to the west of the door-jambs: see Mackenzie's 1900 'Day-book', entries for 23 and 26 May and sketches no. 60 and 62; A.J. Evans, *BSA* vi (1899-1900) 46 and *The Palace Minos* III (London 1930) 37 note 1. See also J. Raison, *Le palais du second millénaire à Knossos I: le quartier nord* (Paris 1988), chp. V, especially 193-196, with quotations from Mackenzie's 'Day-book'.

[9] For the South Propylaeum see Mackenzie's 1900 'Day-book' (5 April): 'It is important to notice that the bases of the pithoi 3, 4, 5 came about .30 [m.] higher than the level of the adjacent cement-flooring. Also wall 4 is quite clearly later construction. The pithoi taken in connection with this wall and in this position so near the important looking column-bases would seem to belong to a period when the palace was no longer inhabited as such.' See also Hood and Taylor (n. 3) no. 32, with references. It is well known that in his 1900 'Daybook' Mackenzie described a few areas where Linear B tablets were found associated with pottery later assigned to the 'reoccupation': see, e.g. L.R. Palmer, 'The find places of the Knossos tablets' in L.R. Palmer and J. Boardman, *On the Knossos tablets* (Oxford 1963) 115-16, and 121 (North Entrance Passage).

[10] Hallager (n. 5) 16; Hood (n. 5) 18 and especially 28-32; M.R. Popham, 'The Palace of Knossos: its destruction and reoccupation reconsidered', *Kadmos* v (1966) 21.

[11] As pointed out by Hood (n. 5) 27, some of the problems with the reoccupation theory 'would be removed if it could be assumed that the "reoccupation" was "palatial" in character'.

history of the Palace at Knossos, which is still accepted by many scholars.[12]

134 Via Monte Giordano,
Rome.
5th Feb. 1901.

Dear Evans,

I write you once more before leaving. As regards Papadakis I had it in my mind to mention to you, in the last letter I should write before leaving, that he spoke to me before I left Crete asking me to recommend his services to you. He also told me he could do all the photographing we required provided there were lenses for general views and for details. He says he knows how to photograph potsherds etc. from above, having, indeed, he says, done all that sort of thing for the Greek Archaeological Society. I shall make a search for him at once on arriving in Crete. While we are on photographing might I suggest that you should also take a Kodak with the largest size of plate for taking instant- pictures of bits of excavations such as might illustrate interesting stages in operations, and might I also suggest that I should be free to use such Kodak.

Another thing I should like taken would be the day-book of last year's excavation. I shall have much to add to it from time to time in the way of notes which can be written on the blank right-hand pages.

There is one thing I have on my conscience about Themistocles. The twelve tins of Asparagus were found and he was most seriously anxious that you should know.

I shall at once look out for suitable houses on my arrival at Candia for you to select from when you come yourself. The house where the things are will do me quite well on my arrival.

About the proposal for more work I made to you in my letter before last I quite agree with what you say about the unremunerative character of much archaeological work. I, however, did not look at the matter at all from that point of view, and in view of the expenses you have had already in connection with Knossos I only feel that if it were possible I should much rather give my services for nothing. As it is I should be perfectly content if I were able to subsist without difficulties for the whole of the period between excavations. If there were work I should not expect to be payed at the same rate as at Knossos where I at present have £15 a month and expenses. I have not liked to mention any sum yet £10 a month for four extra months' work, without any expenses of course, would be sufficient and would not be a grievous addition to what I receive already provided there is a generous response to your appeal for funds.

I must say when I think of those I am only sorry I cannot contribute anything instead of bothering you thus.

One great difficulty of working at Knossos is the extreme unhealthiness of the district. Study of the

building would mean that. As [sic] much as possible must be done before the bad season comes on.

Hoping to meet you soon in Crete, I am,

very truly yours,
Duncan Mackenzie

As regards the question of periods at Knossos I must say that from the time evidence was forthcoming I always believed:-

(1) that the main constructions such as the 'Council-chamber', the 'Procession-corridor' and the Magazines belonged, as construction, to the last Mycenaean period, the decorations belonging to the same general period as the walls and the evidence of the pottery—in every case Mycenaean where the evidence could be tested through the presence of underlying pavements or well-marked floor-levels—fully confirming the same general conclusion. Holding to this fact as central it seemed to me:-

(2) that there was evidence of later Mycenaean occupation represented by the existence of the pithoi with their raised floor-level and the adjacent wall in the S portico, the wall going across the long corridor between the 2nd and 3rd galleries and the structures superimposed upon the low doorjambs of the N propylaea. A second period of much later occupation seems to be represented by the 'free stone' doorjambs near the surface forming superstructures to the *gypsum* doorjambs of the galleries 1 and 2. But as these constructions are as yet very obscure they may be as evidence for the present be [sic] left out of account.

In the course of the season it became more and more clear that the structures belonging to the main building represented by the Magazines, the 'Council Chamber' and the 'Procession-corridor' *gave evidence of a reuse of blocks from a previous building*. Of these blocks one in the long corridor, I think, and one in the S wall of the 'bath' has signs. Other reused blocks are apparent in the E wall of the S portico in the substructures between the column-base of the same portico and elsewhere. It seemed to me

(3) that these blocks, and the previous building indicated by them must represent the 'Kamarais' palace of Knossos. In agreement with this view is the discovery we made of Kamarais ware beneath the floor-level of the Mycenaean palace. The typical large 'Kamarais' vase with small ones inside it was found *below* the floor-level of the 2nd gallery and although this magazine had no pavement, the vase itself was broken away all round the shoulder either simply through its proximity to the floor-level or through the levelling process connected with the laying out of the ground-plan of the Mycenaean palace.

We have then in chronological order evidence of

I. A 'Kamarais' palace of which we have found occasional gypsum blocks sometimes with signs reused in later construction as well as corresponding 'Kamarais' ware underneath the Mycenaean floorlevel but as yet no trace of *construction* in situ which could be identified as belonging to this 'Kamarais' palace. Much of this 'Kamarais' construction must have disappeared when the area was levelled out for the

---

[12] In *BSA* xi (1904-5) 16 and in the first volume of *Scripta Minoa* (1909) 53-5, Evans maintained that Linear B continued to be used in the 'reoccupation' period, but he retracted this statement quite emphatically in *Palace of Minos* iv (1935) 737-8.

foundations and floors of the Mycenaean palace, for in the 'clay area' N of the S portico we find Mycenaean construction immediately above Neolithic deposit. It must be born in mind, however, that we have as yet excavated very little beneath the Mycenaean floor-level. This previous building would correspond to the 'Kamarais' palace at Phaestos.

II. A Mycenaean palace with 'Council Chamber', magazines and 'Procession-corridor'. The construction has almost everywhere on its gypsum blocks signs like the 'Kamarais' ones, but the construction itself, apart from the occasional *reuse* of 'Kamarais' blocks, is Mycenaean, by which I mean that it belongs to the same general period as the typical Mycenaean ware found in the Magazines and elsewhere.

III. Later constructions belonging to the periods of decline.

It has to be noticed in favour of my views
(1) That the 'Kamarais' ware was found not on but below the Mycenaean floor-level.
(2) That pictographic signs like those of Phaestos were, as a matter of fact, found at Knossos on bed blocks built into Mycenaean construction. These signs must accordingly be earlier, factually, than those on the fresh gypsum blocks of the Mycenaean construction. On the other hand these latter signs do not require to indicate a 'Kamarais' period for the walls since similar signs occur on pictographic inscriptions contemporarily with those of the great 'linear' class. Both classes of inscriptions are in turn contemporary with the Mycenaean ware of the magazines.

D.M.K.

NICOLETTA MOMIGLIANO
Balliol College, Oxford/University of Bradford

Piglets again*

In a note to volume cxi of this journal,[1] I observed that the word δελφάκιον, although a diminutive, did not at all periods describe a piglet. In the classical period, it seems to have meant a small but not necessarily immature pig; in Hellenistic Delos and in Egypt, a pig full-grown or nearly so, apparently synonymous with the non-diminutive δέλφαξ; then by the first post-Christian century the term δελφάκιον came indeed to mean 'piglet', a meaning previously expressed by χοῖρος.

I was not able to give a certain meaning either for δέλφαξ or for δελφάκιον, and my difficulty was complicated by the fact that other words referred to piglets (χοῖροι), sows (ὕες), and boars (κάπροι). I did, however, make two suggestions: a δελφάκιον was either 'an adolescent, if the term is properly applied to swine',

* An earlier version of this paper was presented at the twenty-third annual convention of the Society for the Promotion of Classical Studies in Israel held in Be'er Sheva on May 26, 1994.

[1] 'When is a Piglet not a Piglet?', *JHS* cxi (1991), 208-9.

or else a castrated animal. It appears, thanks to the helpful correspondence of Professor Dwora Gilula of the Hebrew University, Professor W. Clarysse of Leuven and Dr David Bain of Manchester, that there is more to be said on the subject, and a better reason can now be suggested for the changes in meaning.

Before we can speak of a δελφάκιον, we shall have to define its parent word, δέλφαξ. A δέλφαξ is surely not a castrated anything at all. Athenaeus collected a number of examples of this word both in the masculine and in the feminine,[2] and indeed etymologists both ancient and modern have suggested that it is derived from the word δελφύς, 'uterus',[3] which would make the feminine meaning the original one. This etymology should now be abandoned,[4] but it is certain that a δέλφαξ can be feminine, and hence cannot be castrated.

What is a δέλφαξ? Despite my hesitancy, it does indeed appear to be an adolescent. Aristophanes of Byzantium, as Eustathius quoted him, was quite clear:

τῶν συῶν οἱ μὲν τέλειοι καὶ ἐνόρχαι κάπροι· οἱ δὲ πίονες αὐτῶν σίαλοι· ἡ δὲ θήλεια σῦς μόνον. Ἱππῶναξ δὲ [fr.103.11 West] γρόμφιν λέγει, εἴτε καθόλου πᾶσαν ὗν δηλῶν, εἴτε τὴν παλαιὰν τῇ ἡλικίᾳ. τὰ δὲ νέα, δέλφακες μὲν τὰ πεπηγότα πως ἤδη τοῖς σώμασι, τὰ δὲ ἔτι ἀπαλὰ καὶ ἔνικμα χοῖροι.[5]

For Aristophanes the grammarian, a pig was a δέλφαξ when it had 'already become somewhat firm[6] in [its] body'. Some moderns[7] have taken sexual maturity to be the dividing line between χοῖρος and δέλφαξ, and the

[2] Athenaeus, *Deipnosophistae* ix 374 d-375 b and xiv 656 f-657 a.

[3] *Ibid.*, ix 375 a; *cf.* P. Chantraine, *Dictionnaire étymologique de la langue grecque* i (Paris 1968) 261, and H. Frisk, *Griechisches Etymologisches Wörterbuch* i (Heidelberg 1960-1970) 362.

[4] The root of δέλφαξ is certainly the Indo-European g^{w}elbh-, g^{w}olbh-, which is also the root of the English calf (so correctly E. Klein, *A comprehensive etymological dictionary of the English language* i [Amsterdam 1966] 223). The semantic field with which this root is associated appears to include other forms of swollen flesh besides the womb. The calf of the leg, *pace* Klein *ibid.*, is from the same root: *cf.* O.J. Sadovszky, 'The reconstruction of IE *pisko and the extension of its semantic sphere', *Journal of Indo-European Studies* i (1973) 81-100, for the surprising but well-attested semantic connection between the calf of the leg and fish roe. Suetonius, *Galba* 3.1 tells us that the Gauls called a very fat person (*praepinguis*) *galba*, and this, too, will have come from the same root: so E. Partridge, *Origins: a short etymological dictionary of modern English* (London 1958) 71, who writes that 'the basic idea in IE is app(arently) a "swelling of the body"'. This being the case, it needs no special explanation why a pig of either sex should be called δέλφαξ, a 'swell'. I owe this note to the learned comments of Dr. Daniel Gershenson and Professor David Weissert; my thanks to both.

[5] A. Nauck, *Aristophanis Byzantii, Grammatici Alexandrini, Fragmenta* (Halle 1848, reprinted Hildesheim 1963), chapter IV (Λέξεις), fragment III, 101-2, quoting Eustathius' comment on Hom. *Od.* xiv 80-2, = Ar. Byz. *fr.* 169 Slater.

[6] See *LSJ* s.v. πήγνυμι III, from Aelian and Galen.

[7] Chantraine (n. 3): 'il désigne une jeune bête, mais apte à la réproduction', G.P. Shipp, *Modern Greek evidence for the ancient Greek vocabulary* (Sydney 1979) 209 follows him: 'a young but sexually mature animal.'

hapax δελφακουμένα in the *Acharnians*[8] seems indeed to point in that direction. It is undoubtedly sex that interests Aristophanes the comedian (here as elsewhere), but it does not necessarily follow that it was sexual maturity that defined a δέλφαξ; for that matter, there is no compelling reason to presume that there was a single standard definition. In modern American usage the term *heifer* signifies to some a cow that has given birth only once, to others a young cow that has never given birth. G.P. Shipp, in his survey of modern Greek terms, found the Bovan term Δerfáci (= δελφάκιον) to refer to a 'year old pig'.[9]

It will now be clear to us why the diminutive did not, at least in Athens, refer to a suckling-pig: the diminutive suffix could not negate entirely the meaning of the root noun. For an English parallel we might take a word like *girlie*, whose diminutive suffix may indicate either affection or contempt, but does not turn a girl into a baby.[10] On Delos, as mentioned in my previous article, the diminutive seems to have taken over the semantic field entirely. A δελφάκιον is an adolescent pig, and the word δέλφαξ is not attested at all.

Age may not be the essential variable here. English, with its characteristic wealth of vocabulary, distinguishes swine (a general term); pigs (usually those breeds raised for eating); piglets (new-born); boars (male); sows (female); hogs (usually pigs of some maturity; *Webster's Third International* gives 120 pounds as a minimum); barrows (male pigs castrated before maturity); gilts (females that have not borne, or have borne only one litter); porkers (young pigs fattened for the table) and shoats (young hogs of either sex, especially less than one year old)[11]. Various modifiers offer more precision: brood-sow (one kept for raising piglets), lard-hog (raised for its fat), bacon-hog (raised for cured meat).

In Greek papyri of third- and second-century Egypt, we find δέλφακες in various contexts. Sometimes they are opposed to χοιρίδια[12] or χοιροδέλφακες;[13] that opposition surely distinguishes the adolescents from the babies. The same may be true when they are distinguished from ἱερεῖα, sacrifices, if the custom was (as in certain cases it certainly was)[14] to offer piglets to the gods.[15] The most common distinction, however, seems to be between δέλφακες and τοκάδες, brood-sows.[16] The author of one papyrus says that he has 'one brood-sow, her five δέλφακες, and two barrows'; the latter will have been castrated pigs being kept and fattened ('the labouring man's pig is his bank', as one author puts it).[17] In this period, it would appear that the Greeks in Egypt continued to use the term δέλφαξ for a pig larger than a χοῖρος but still clearly distinguished from those swine raised into old age for breeding or fattening.

It may be that not every language had distinguished the age of swine with the same precision. An Egyptian demotic papyrus from 229 BCE notes *rr*, a pig; *išw.t*, a sow; *še*, a boar; and *tlpgs*, a previously unknown word that can only be the Greek δέλφαξ. The original editor could not imagine what a *tlpgs* might be;[18] Prof. Clarysse, who did recognize it,[19] was not able to say what was left after pigs, sows, and boars had been excluded. From what has preceded, we have, of course, no hesitation in identifying a *tlpgs* as a partially grown pig. I think, moreover, that it should not be difficult to guess why a Greek term was used. Demotic, I suspect, had not distinguished among swine with the same precision that Greek used. There surely were δέλφακες in Egypt, and the conquering Greeks will have considered them a different kind of animal, not quite a piglet and not quite a pig. The Egyptians had to register them in some way, and they had nothing better to call them than *tlpgs*.

The interesting thing is that the distinction does not seem to have been maintained in Egypt. The word δέλφαξ, and more commonly the diminutive δελφάκιον, reappears in late papyri, but it does not seem to be distinguished from other pigs by age; it is simply a pig. The imported distinction between χοῖροι and δέλφακες, so clear in the papyri of the generations immediately after Alexander's conquest, did not last. There is no doubt that the Greeks of Egypt could distinguish a suckling-pig from a year-old specimen, but where the distinction was immaterial, their language did not make it. The identification of a pig as adolescent, once so essential a part of a Greek's perception that the conquered Egyptians had imported it, was no longer part of his pig-view. It may have been the older Egyptian vagueness that reasserted itself, or perhaps changing circumstances of their lives made distinctions among

---

[8] Ar. *Ach.* 786.

[9] Shipp (n. 7).

[10] I do not, offhand, find an English equivalent in the masculine, presumably because *boy* does not lend itself to the addition of *-y*; but Yiddish offers us the term *bocher'l*, where the diminutive suffix *-l* may indicate affection towards or contempt for the adolescent *bocher*, but does not change his age. English-speaking Jews of Yiddish background use the hybrid word *boychik* in the same sense. The case of μεῖραξ, an adolescent girl, whose diminutive μειράκιον denotes an adolescent boy, was mentioned in my previous article.

[11] This last term is the one chosen for δέλφαξ by C.B. Gulick in the Loeb *Athenaeus* ix 374 d-375 b; in xiv 656 f-657 a, on the other hand, where Athenaeus is not distinguishing various words for pigs, Gulick contents himself with more pedestrian terms such as sow and pig.

[12] *PCair.* 59346 line 20, *cf.* lines 24, 28.

[13] *PCair.* 59274, where the δέλφακες are explicitly called μεγάλοι by comparison. In the second century of the current era, on the other hand, when the word χοῖρος had come to be a general term for 'pig', SB IV 7469 spoke of a τελεία ('full-grown') χοιροδέλφαξ.

[14] The sanctuary at Delos was purified every month with a χοῖρος; δελφάκια, on the other hand, were sacrificed to three gods at the annual Posideia (IG xi 2 and *Ins. Dél., passim*).

[15] One might, of course, take the ἱερεῖα to be ritually perfect (i.e., unblemished) animals, but the contexts do not suggest any such distinction: *PCair.* 59310 complains that a swineherd has run away while in debt for a certain number of ἱερεῖα and another number of δελφάκια. *PCair.* 59769 mentions pigs in three categories: ἱερεῖα, δέλφακες, and ἄρσενες.

[16] *PTebt.* 883, *PCair.* 59312 and 59349, *PLond.* 2186, *PSI* IV 379 B, line 22.

[17] R. Wallace in *Encyclopedia Britannica*[11] xxi 595.

[18] *PLille* III 99

[19] W. Clarysse, 'Greek Loan-Words in Demotic', in S.P. Vleeming, ed., *Aspects of Demotic lexicography* (Leuven 1987) 22 n. 71. The original editor, F. de Cenival, has since agreed to Professor Clarysse's interpretation (personal correspondence of Professor Clarysse).

pigs less familiar or less important to most Greek-speakers. I suspect, however, that the blurring of the distinctiveness of the word δέλφαξ was driven by a broader semantic change.

Homer had called a sheep ὄϊς and a pig ὗς. Various phonetic developments, however, combined to erase the distinction between the two words. The first two vowels of ὄϊς coalesced into a diphthong; by the classical period, ὄϊς had disappeared from Attic prose, replaced by the unambiguous πρόβατον. As time went on, the rough breathing dropped out of some dialects, and eventually all; the diphthong οι and the vowel υ became indistinguishable, so that the Byzantines called the υ by its now familiar name upsilon (υ ψιλόν) to distinguish it from its diphthongal homonym. These developments are hard to date precisely, but the last of them seems to have taken place by the second century of this era.[20] Once this happened, ὗς was no longer a suitable general term for a pig. Even though the word ὄϊς was not in use, it remained as a poetic term. Children still learned to read from Homer, and the term ὗς will have been inconvenient once the homonymy was complete.

Its place was taken by χοῖρος, as has long been recognized, and now for the first time the term χοῖρος designated a pig of any age rather than a suckling. Δέλφαξ, for its part, seems also to have ceased to carry the same implication of adolescence that it had once borne. Perhaps, as suggested above, it was foreign influence or a different life-style that had caused the change. Equally likely, however, is that it was only now that the change in χοῖρος caused the change in δέλφαξ: once the former was not necessarily young, the loss of the semantic contrast meant that the latter was not necessarily older. It was in this situation that the diminutive δελφάκιον, freed of its adolescent connotation, came to denote a piglet.

We can now follow the history of our words with more precision than we had previously offered. A δέλφαξ in the classical period was a pig neither new-born nor old; its diminutive form δελφάκιον carried the usual meanings of diminutives, but did not reduce it to a piglet. This distinction may have been without parallel in the native Egyptian speech, if its appearance as a Demotic loan-word is significant. Eventually the term δέλφαξ and its diminutive lost their force as being specifically adolescent pigs. This may have occurred early as a result of foreign influence or increased urbanization, or later because of the loss of the opposition to χοῖρος. It was thus either a cause or an effect of the change in δέλφαξ that when phonetic developments caused ὗς to drop from use and χοῖρος to take its place as the usual term for swine, the diminutive δελφάκιον finally came to mean what we once thought it had always meant, a suckling-pig.

The perceptive reader will note the significant variation of an apparently straightforward term over a relatively short period of linguistic time. I leave it to that perceptive reader to decide how sweeping will be his conclusion about the sandy foundations of our semantic speculations over the vaster ages.

Bar Ilan University   DAVID SCHAPS

[20] W.S. Allen, *Vox Graeca*[3] (Cambridge 1987) 53, 81 n. 51.

Fifth century chronology and the Coinage Decree*

The debate over the chronology of the history of Athens in the fifth century BC has entered a new phase recently with the publication by Mortimer Chambers and his colleagues of physical evidence that seems to confirm Harold Mattingly's view[1] that a crucial inscription bearing three-bar sigmas and tailed rhos (*IG* i³ 11) was cut during the archonship of Antiphon in 418/7, and not during that of Habron in 458/7 as was generally thought.[2] This development has not been greeted with universal approval, however, and A.S. Henry, for one, has been unwilling to accept what is by any standards a radical shift.[3] His arguments have, though, been more than adequately countered by Chambers,[4] and the judgement of Jacques Tréheux remains as true now as it did in 1991: 'La mesure des intervalles entre les lettres, la superposition des photographies multiples et, surtout, le bombardement du marbre par un rayon laser ont prouvé (les photographies en couleur A et B ne permettent pas d'en douter) qu'il fallait lire et rétablir ʼΑντ]–ιφ͂ον (*a.* 418/7).'[5] Many competent scholars have already been convinced, and 'waverers will surely have to come round in the end'.[6]

There is an important issue at stake here (and one that is not unconnected with further chronological shifts that might be made at an earlier period). The position has never been better put than by Russell Meiggs who, although he favoured the earlier, higher, chronology, knew very much what was involved:

The main evidence for the *history* of the Athenian Empire (as distinct from an analysis of its character in the period covered by Thucydides and Aristophanes) comes from a long series of inscriptions, the most important of which are not explicitly dated. From the literary evidence (if Plutarch is dismissed as

* Acknowledgements: Thanks are due to Ernst Badian, Mortimer Chambers, David Gill, Stefan Karwiese, the late D.M. Lewis, Harold Mattingly, Wolfgang Schuller and *JHS*'s anonymous readers for, in various measure, advice, assistance and criticism in the preparation of this note.

[1] First expressed in his 'The growth of Athenian imperialism', *Historia* xii (1963) 257-73.
[2] M.H. Chambers, R. Gallucci, and P. Spanos, 'Athens' alliance with Egesta in the year of Antiphon', in I. Worthington (ed.), *Acta of the University of New England International Seminar on Greek and Latin Epigraphy* (Bonn, 1990) 38-63; also published in *ZPE* lxxxiii (1990) 38-63; M.H. Chambers, 'Photographic enhancement and a Greek inscription', *CJ* lxxxviii (1992/3) 25-31. For a survey of other readings, see G. Németh, 'Was sieht ein Epigraphiker?', *Acta Classica Univ. Scient. Debrecen.* xxvii (1991) 9-14.
[3] A. Henry, 'Through a laser beam darkly: space age technology and the Egesta Decree (*IG* I³ 11)', *ZPE* xci (1992) 137-46.
[4] M.H. Chambers, 'The archon's name in the Athens-Egesta alliance (IG I³ 11)', *ZPE* xcviii (1993) 171-4; *idem*, 'Reading illegible Greek inscriptions: Athens and Egesta', *Thetis, Mannheimer Beiträge zur klassischen Archäologie und Geschichte Griechenlands und Zyperns* i (1994) 49-52, pl. 5.
[5] J. Tréheux, 'Bulletin épigraphique: Attique', *REG* civ (1991) 469.
[6] H.B. Mattingly, 'Epigraphy and the Athenian empire', *Historia* xli (1992) 129.

unreliable) two views of the empire, each coherent, are tenable: (1) that strong imperialism developed only after the death of Pericles and is to be primarily associated with the rise of Cleon and his successors; (2) that the vital steps from Alliance to Empire were taken in the early forties. It is no exaggeration to say that the answer to these questions depends primarily on whether criteria based on letter forms (especially but not solely sigma), first formulated in the late nineteenth century, are still valid. A History of the Athenian Empire which ignored this question should have no authority.[7]

An important element in the debate has been the date of the Coinage, or (better) Standards, Decree which imposed the use of Athenian weights and measures on the tributary allies. One school has favoured c. 449 BC for this development,[8] while another would see it as having occurred in the 420s,[9] or even later (the decree seems to be alluded to at Aristophanes, *Birds* 1040 ff. [414 BC]). Recently, Mattingly has produced what would appear to be confirmation of a late date for this measure, in the form of the text of the Standards Decree found at Hamaxitus in the Troad.[10] Since Hamaxitus did not become part of the Athenian empire until after the Mytilenean revolt in 427 (Thuc. 3.50.3), it is unlikely that the decree was promulgated before then.[11] Only the possibility that new members of the empire had to erect copies of the Decree on entry[12] stands in the way of a wholly watertight case for a late date. A point that Mattingly made to meet this possible objection repays further study.

One of the copies of the Standards Decree was found on Cos, and Mattingly notes that in the spring of 431 'the island paid only part of its tribute and the anomalous amount in Attic currency (3 T. 4,465 dr.) suggests at least partial payment in non-Attic silver'.[13] If so, it is either the case that the Coans disregarded the terms of the Standards Decree, or that the Decree had not yet been passed. The likely sums involved will be discussed below, but they need to be seen against a wider background.

Anomalous weights occur quite frequently in the literary and epigraphic record relating to gold and silver vessels, and these can often be interpreted as the restate-

ment of an amount actually paid in non-Attic currency, struck on Persian standards. This is scarcely surprising given the immense size of the Persian Empire compared with that of the Athenian. Anomalous gold weights can regularly be interpreted in terms of darics, and silver in terms of *sigloi*. Evidence from hoards seems to show that silver *sigloi* might acceptably weigh between 5.40 and 5.67 grams. (*Sigloi* were in fact struck on two weight standards: an earlier one which ranged between c. 5.20 and 5.49 grams and a later, heavier standard of between c. 5.40 and 5.67 grams).[14] Anomalous weights in the sources can often be read as, for want of a better term, 'round' weights in another standard. Thus, the fourth-century Demosthenic speech *Against Timotheus* refers to 'two *phialai* of Lycian workmanship' which were in dispute. The plaintiff's father persuaded an associate 'to accept the value of the *phialai*, as much as their weight amounted to, which was two hundred and thirty-seven drachmae';[15] 237 drachmae equals 180 *sigloi* whose average weight is 5.66 grams. In the same speech, we hear of a loan for 'thirteen hundred and fifty-one drachmae and two obols';[16] a sum which equals 1,025 *sigloi* at 5.67 grams (assuming in both cases a drachma of 4.30 grams).

Moreover, the weights of vessels dedicated in the Parthenon are given in Attic drachms in both 'round' and 'anomalous' figures.[17] The latter may be easily read in terms of darics and *sigloi*. A set of seven *phialai* said to weigh 643 dr. 2 obols, for example, converts to 500 *sigloi* at 5.53 grams. Of the silver vessels whose complete weights are preserved, just over 20 kg were made to the Attic standard, and nearly 40 kg to the Persian.[18] These were dedicated between 434/3 and 414/3 BC. We cannot know, however, where or when they were made, and so this evidence is of little direct relevance to the date of the Standards Decree.

Nor can we be certain when the objects were made that are mentioned in an inventory drawn up in 429/8 BC of silver items in the keeping of the treasurers of the Other Gods at Athens (*IG* i[3] 383). Very few complete weights survive on this list, but among those that do are those of some large amounts of silver belonging to different Athenian cult-centres (Table 1), most of them 'anomalous'. While little can be done with the silver *phialai* of Hera or the silver of Datyllos,[19] the figures for

[7] R. Meiggs, 'The dating of fifth-century Attic inscriptions', *JHS* lxxxvi (1966) 98.

[8] e.g. *ATL* ii. D 14; R. Meiggs and D.M. Lewis, *A selection of Greek historical inscriptions*, 2nd edn (Oxford 1988) No. 45.

[9] M.N. Tod, review of *ATL* in *JHS* lxix (1949) 105; H.B. Mattingly, 'The Athenian Coinage Decree', *Historia* x (1961) 148-88; E. Erxleben, 'Das Münzgesetz des delisch-attischen Seebundes', *Archiv für Papyrusforschung* xix (1969) 91-139; xx (1970) 66-132; xxi (1971) 145-162.

[10] E. Schwertheim, 'Ein Dekretfragment aus dem 5. Jh. v. Chr. aus Hamaxitus,' *VI. Araştırma Sonuçları Toplantısı* (1988), 283-5.

[11] H.B. Mattingly, 'New light on the Athenian Standards Decree (*ATL* II, D 14)', *Klio* lxxv (1993) 99-102.

[12] *Cf.* D.M. Lewis, 'The Athenian Coinage Decree', in I. Carradice (ed.), *Coinage and administration in the Athenian and Persian empires* (The Ninth Oxford Symposium on Coinage and Monetary History: B.A.R. International Series 343) (Oxford 1987) 56.

[13] Mattingly (n. 11) 102.

[14] S.P. Noe 'Two hoards of Persian sigloi', *NNM* cxxxvi (1956) 42; cf. A.S. Hemmy, 'The weight standards of ancient Greece and Persia', *Iraq* v (1938) 65-81. S. Karwiese, 'Zur Metrologie der persischen Sigloi', *Res Orientales* v (1993) 46-9 argues for an 'ideal weight' for the heavier *siglos* of 5.574 grams related to a gold daric of 8.3611 grams. While the underlying principle is sound, these figures may be on the low side: see M. Vickers, 'Metrological reflections: Attic, Hellenistic, Parthian and Sasanian gold and silver plate', *Studia Iranica* xxiv (1995) 169-70.

[15] [Dem.] xlix.32.

[16] [Dem.] xlix.6.

[17] W.E. Thompson in *IG* i[3] pp. 318, 331-2.

[18] M. Vickers, 'Golden Greece: relative values, minae and temple inventories', *AJA* xciv (1990) 613-25; M. Vickers and D.W.J. Gill, *Artful crafts: ancient Greek silverware and pottery* (Oxford 1994).

[19] Although Stefan Karwiese kindly points out that they may be the equivalents of 666.66 *sigloi* (at 5.55 grams) and 266.66 *sigloi* (at 5.58 grams) respectively.

Table 1: Objects in the Temple of the Other Gods at Athens

Line number/objects	Wt in Attic drachmas	Wt in grams	*Sigloi*	Weight of *sigloi*
65 silver *phialai* of Hera in Xypetos Dionysou	860 dr. 1 ob.			
68-71 4 *karchesia*	4395 dr. 1 ob	18899.27	**3,333.33**	5.67
72-3 silver of Ge Olympia	494 dr.	2124.20	**375**	5.66
74-5 silver of Theseus	4270 dr.	18361.00	**3,250**	5.65
76-7 silver of Datyllos	346 dr.			
78-9 Silver of Olympian Zeus	5931 dr.	25503.30	**4,500**	5.67

(*IG* i³ 383, 65-79)

some of the other properties can easily be read in Persian terms. The four *karchesia* weighing one-third of ten thousand *sigloi* and the silver of Olympian Zeus weighing 4,500 *sigloi* are especially suggestive,[20] and in the present context the fact that they seem to come in at 5.67 grams to the *siglos* suggests that the silverware in question was probably new (in that it would appear not to have lost weight through wear). The silver of Ge Olympia weighing 375 *sigloi* and that of Theseus weighing 3,250 reinforce this picture. The objects could, of course, have been made some decades earlier, but the conjunction of so much silver (nearly 65 kg) in Athenian shrines apparently made on an alien standard suggests that the Standards Decree was not yet in force.[21]

There is an extraordinary congruence at the higher end of the bracket for the later *siglos* weight which should override any reservations arising from the fact that, given the tolerances involved with more worn coin, it is an easy matter to find 'round' *siglos* approximations for most 'odd' figures in the tribute lists. The *sigloi* postulated for the 4 *karchesia*, for the silver of Olympian Zeus, and for the 1,351 dr. 2 obols in the speech *Against Timotheus*, work out at 5.6698, 5.6674, and 5.6690 grams. Not only does this imply highly accurate systems of acertaining weights at the period, but that 4.30 grams was the conventional weight of the drachma.[22] The best physical evidence we have is in the form of an Achaemenid stone weight found at Persepolis in 1939. 'Slightly chipped', it weighs 9.95 kilos and is

inscribed '120 karsha' in Old Persian[23] and '20 mina' in Babylonian.[24] 9.95 kilos would produce 1800 units of 5.53 grams. A loss of 250 grams (or a quarter of one per cent) would give 1800 *sigloi* at 5.666. By contrast, the lower limit is much looser, but this is to be expected in that there would have been a good deal of variation in the amount of wear that coins received in use. There is contemporary evidence for this in Xenophon's formula of five Attic drachms for four *sigloi*,[25] which can only relate to worn coins, not new ones.

The possible use of the Persian standard in the anomalous figures in the Athenian tribute lists has already been invoked, but not perhaps to the extent that it should. S.K. Eddy saw evidence for the use of electrum coinage (which was not affected by the standards legislation) for payment of the tribute in figures divisible by 24,[26] but D.M. Lewis felt that many of the 'anomalous' figures, several of those divisible by 24 included, could be more easily read in terms of silver coinages. He did not publish his own calculations, finding that his arithmetic 'was getting fancier and fancier'.[27] There are undoubted snares along the way, generated in large part by the fact that, since both the Attic and Persian standard were ultimately derived from the Babylonian, there are inevitable correlations between the one and the other. Thus, for example, 1.5, 3 and 7.5 Attic talents would equal 7,000, 14,000 and 35,000 *sigloi* all at 5.53 grams. There is therefore a possibility of apparent relationships even when they may never have been present in the first place, and what follows should be treated with appropriate caution.

[20] M. Vickers, 'The metrology of gold and silver plate in classical Greece', *The Economics of Cult in the Ancient Greek World*, *Boreas* (Uppsala) xxi (1992) 53-72.

[21] Vickers (n. 17); *idem*, 'Metrological reflections; the Georgian dimension', in the *Proceedings of the 7th Vani Symposium 1994* (forthcoming).

[22] I am grateful to one of *JHS*'s anonymous referees for having noted this.

[23] R.G. Kent, *Old Persian* (New Haven 1950) 114, 157 (Wc).

[24] E.F. Schmidt, *The Treasury of Persepolis and other discoveries in the homeland of the Achaemenians* (*OIC* xxi [Chicago 1939]) 62-3, fig. 43.

[25] Xen. *Anab*. i.5.6.

[26] S.K. Eddy, 'Some irregular amounts of Athenian tribute', *AJP* xciv (1973) 47-70.

[27] Lewis (n. 12) 62.

Eddy only touched on the possibility of some tribute payments having been made in Persian silver. The examples he cites are of the dynast Sambactys who paid 6,400 dr. in 453, and of two Carian towns, Euromus and Casolaba, which paid annual tributes of 2,500 dr., the former between 449 and 439 and the latter between 453 and about 446. 'At 4.3 grams apiece', Eddy writes, '6,400 drachms weigh 27,520 grams. Reckoning an average siglus at 5.5 grams, this is the weight of exactly 5,004'.[28] He is probably correct in his assumption that Sambactys made his payment with 5,000 Persian *sigloi* —at 5.504 grams to the *siglos*. It is less likely, however, that the payments made by Euromus and Casolaba were made in this way, for the figure of 2,500 dr. or 25 *minae* is in any case a round figure.

Eddy believed in an early date for the Standards Decree, and this, coupled with his primary interest in payments in electrum coinage, perhaps caused him to overlook other possible payments in Persian silver coins. Mattingly quite properly drew attention to the payment made by Cos in 431 of 3 talents 4,465 dr., suggesting that it implied 'at least partial payment in non-Attic silver'. 4,465 dr. indeed makes for 3,500 *sigloi* at 5.49 grams, but the whole tribute payment as recorded happens to equal 17,500 *sigloi* at 5.52 grams—which may point to the whole amount having been paid in *sigloi*. There are other cases of the same kind. Abydus paid 5 T. 3,260 dr. in 429: the equivalent of 26,000 *sigloi* at 5.50 grams. In 444, Abydus had paid 4 T. 315 dr.: 19,000 *sigloi*, also at 5.50 grams. Their payment of 4 T. 2,260 dr. in 453 may have been made with 20,000 *sigloi* at 5.64 grams; if so, with less worn coin.[29]

Cyzicus, whose coinage was of electrum, might well be expected to have paid its tribute in that metal. If this were the case, we might expect it to show in sums divisible by 24. While Cyzicus' tribute for 428 (8 T. 1,680 dr.) does make for 2,070 electrum staters (49,680 divided by 24), the 8 T. 3,500 dr. paid in 429 is not thus divisible; it does, however, produce 40,000 *sigloi* at 5.54 grams. Then, Byzantium's payments in 429 and 428 of 21 T. 4,740 dr. and 15 T. 90 dr. (neither divisible by 24) give 100,000 and 70,000 *sigloi* (at 5.62 and 5.53 grams respectively).[30] Such large 'round' figures as 40,000, 100,000 and 70,000 are especially significant in the present context.

This note has dealt with only a few of the suggestive figures in the Tribute Lists (and there may well be other explanations), but their consistency perhaps implies that on the whole payments were made in *sigloi* rather than a mixture of currencies. The pattern exists throughout the tribute lists, from the earliest entries, and may well reflect the Persian practice on which the Athenian was based. If the existence of anomalous figures in the later entries also reflects a historical reality in which large tribute payments were made in Persian coin in the late 430s and early 420s, they would go some way towards explaining why a Standards Decree was introduced a few years later, for it would certainly have been administratively more convenient to have payments made in a uniform coinage.[31] In addition, to oust Persian coinage altogether from the cities of the Athenian empire would have made a loud symbolic statement about the New World Order. One might guess that this occurred at the time of the major, and harsh, re-assessment of 425/4.[32]

Do these considerations simply reinforce the case consistently argued by Mattingly that 'strong imperialism developed only after the death of Pericles and is to be primarily associated with the rise of Cleon and his successors', or are matters more complex? Clearly, the 'law' that three-barred sigma disappeared from public inscriptions after 446 BC should now go out of the window, and dating by letter forms (or 'intuitive decadology') with it, but the fact that a three-barred sigma might occur after 420 does not necessarily mean that other examples are commensurately late. Each document will have to be examined in its own context. Much the same holds good with the non-inscribed material culture of Athens. The 'shift akin to a landslide'[33] on the epigraphic front should have implications for the chronology of pottery, sculpture and other arts currently based on the views of the late E. Langlotz,[34] but there is no predicting where things will end up.

MICHAEL VICKERS

Ashmolean Museum, Oxford

[28] Eddy (n. 19) 54.

[29] The tribute figures are most conveniently given in R. Meiggs, *The Athenian empire* (Oxford 1972) 538-61.

[30] By contrast, the 'anomalous' (H.B. Mattingly, 'The Athenian Coinage Decree and the assertion of empire', in Carradice [n. 12] 65) tribute payments made by Thracian Berge in 451, 446 and 434-31 may well have been made in Cyzicene staters, for 2880, 3240 and 3120 dr. are all divisible by 24, and produce 120, 135 and 130 staters respectively.

[31] *Cf.* Lewis (n. 12) 62.

[32] On which see M. Ostwald, *From popular sovereignty to the sovereignty of law: law, society and politics in fifth-century Athens* (Berkeley and Los Angeles 1986) 293; M. Vickers, *Pericles on stage: political comedy in Aristophanes' earlier plays* (Austin, Tx. 1995).

[33] Chambers (n. 4) 52.

[34] E. Langlotz, *Zur Zeitbestimmung der strengrotfigurigen Vasenmalerei und der gleichzeitigen Plastik* (Leipzig, 1920), based in turn on the work of Ludwig Ross and Franz Studniczka: see E.D. Francis, *Image and idea in fifth century Greece: art and literature after the Persian wars* (London, 1990) 107-111.

NOTICES OF BOOKS

ERBSE (H.) **Studien zum Verständnis Herodots.** Berlin: de Gruyter, 1992. Pp. xiii + 198. DM 120.

PRITCHETT (W.K.) **The liar school of Herodotus.** Amsterdam: Gieben, 1993. Pp. v + 359. Fl. 110.

ROLLINGER (R.) **Herodots babylonischer Logos: eine kritische Untersuchung der Glaubwürdigkeitsdiskussion an Hand ausgewählter Beispiele.** Innsbruck: Univ. Inst. für Sprachwissenschaft, 1993. Pp. 249. Ös. 640.

When Alexander the Great was in India, Nearchus says, they saw no actual specimens of Herodotus' gold-digging ants, but plenty of their skins were brought to the camp, and they looked like the skins of panthers (Nearchus *FGH* 133, F 8). Were Herodotus' notorious ants the product of garbled fact, Herodotean invention, literary construct, or a wild jumble of legend and travellers' tales?

The works reviewed here approach Herodotus' *Histories* from different angles and divergent scholarly traditions, yet are in essence all grappling with this central problem of Herodotean scholarship, that of his credibility, and the status of the author implied by his far-fetched tales of the wondrous or schematized folktales. Rollinger presents a meticulous study of the Babylonian logos, with a very welcome knowledge of recent work on Persia and Persian sources. The two more general studies of Herodotus by Erbse and Pritchett devote much attention to the presence or absence of deliberate 'fiction' in Herodotus, with the accusation that he was a 'liar' or that the *Histories* were a kind of '*Schwindel-Literatur*'. Both mount a spirited defence of Herodotus as a historian and pursuer of *historie*. Pritchett does this throughout his openly polemical work; Erbse more towards the end (Part II, Ch. 5, and conclusion), the more surprisingly since much of his earlier discussion of '*Novellen*' and '*Anekdoten*' argued that Herodotus had invented some of the best known and most loved of his tales. Otherwise they complement each other exactly. For while P. is concerned primarily with the material or legendary content of Herodotus within the wider context of fifth century Greek culture and knowledge of the *oikumene* at the time, E. gives us a subtle literary treatment of the *Histories,* emphasizing the internal construction of the text, the internal significance of each tale, but in a world in which, it would seem, literary texts only speak or refer to other literary texts. However, E. grapples with a very real problem in Herodotean interpretation, how Herodotus could have picked out from a melting pot of folktales, oral traditions, literary 'novellas', a selection which so fitted into his *Histories* that they could represent his overall moral or political views. How can we reconcile his acquisition of raw oral traditions or folktales, with the way they create such powerful recurrent images in his *Histories*?

P.'s aim is a sustained, outspoken, often frankly acerbic attack, chapter by chapter, on the representatives of what he calls the 'liar school', Detlev Fehling being the main villain and ringleader, who suggested in conclusion 'the extreme possibility that [Herodotus] never left his native Greece',[1] with S. West, F. Hartog and Armayor following closely. P.'s fluent irritation mounts in this long, immensely erudite, and often repetitive book. Much of the text consists of extensive quotation of the most offending passages of the 'liar school', and longer full quotations from alternative authorities. The tone, style and structure will put off many readers; but that would be a pity. For in this compendious book, there is much of importance for any one interested in current controversies about the reliability of the *Histories*; also somewhat buried, but with cumulative force, are important methodological points. His main method of attack is to show that Fehling (*et al.*) is insufficiently cognisant of the nature of the Greek world, of the areas on its edge (Scythia and Egypt especially), and the extent of its interaction with them. P.'s extraordinarily wide knowledge of geography, topography and archaeology is trained upon example after example of Fehling's 'Demonstrably false source-citations' in Herodotus, with massive bibliography, to show that the arguments were based on insufficient grasp of current archaeological knowledge, or an over-limited view of what the Greeks *could* have believed about the way the world worked (*cf.* in particular his discussions of origin-traditions, 34 ff.; the stelai of Sesostris, 106 ff.; Scythian strategy, 198 ff.; Herodotean inscriptions, Ch. 3). Lest it be feared that this involves reiteration of dolphin stories, P. goes far beyond *realia* to remind us again and again of the wealth of traditions, cult-tales, folk-tales and myths in existence in the Greek world, of which only a portion have entered our surviving literature. Fehling assumed that a story could have only one place of origin:[2] 'whoever adopts Fehling's premises is endorsing the position that all 'stories', or what others call folktales, sagas or myths, ... are but fabrications by the writer in whose work the tale first appears' (P., 24-5; *cf.* 49).

But in any case, P.'s method of attack by adducing archaeological evidence, topography etc. in support of Herodotus has some validity here precisely because it answers in the same terms the method used by Fehling to prove the falsity of Herodotus' source-citations. For Fehling, Herodotus' remarks about an event or place are measured against what we know he should have seen, or against what we know is plausible. When Herodotus can be caught out, then his 'source-citations', are, it is argued, proved fictional, and much of what he claims to have seen, as inventions of his own. As P. points out, such an approach seems impervious to the difficulties for a Greek (or anyone else, for that matter) in understanding another culture; or in recording each detail (or each detail we might think should be given), in a world without libraries, instant reference books to check where memory fails, guide books to remind one of place names, scientifically accurate maps. A hurried chapter on later travellers and travel literature (a topic which deserves development) suggested further exploration of

---

[1] D. Fehling, *Herodotus and his 'Sources'. Citation, Invention and Narrative Art* (Leeds 1989): translation and revision of *Die Quellenangaben bei Herodot* (Berlin 1971).

[2] See Fehling, 21-22.

the realms of the irrational and the credulous, and may be closer to the French structuralist approach than he would admit. Intriguing comparisons are provided throughout with the later observations of Pausanias (but then Fehling thinks, as he has to, that Pausanias was simply copying Herodotus); or with later geographical or scientific writers: 'We may poke fun at his geography and his concept of the *oikumene*, until we read the Alexandrian historians, Eratosthenes and Strabo' (264f.).

Fehling and his followers do indeed often approach Herodotus from the point of view of 20th century scholarly rationalism. P.'s recurrent demand is to avoid anachronistic assumptions in interpreting Herodotus, and to allow more room for the 'irrational' in the classical world (e.g. 17, 80, 106). He uses this point devastatingly. We may also remember that Fehling's main argument was aimed at Herodotus' 'source citations' (*Quellenangaben*: not 'sources' as the English version somewhat misleadingly renders the German title). Yet it is far from clear, as Marincola has pointed out, and as Erbse endorses,[3] that when Herodotus says 'as the Corinthians say', he is actually intending to give a 'source-citation' in the formal sense, as Fehling takes it. The combination of these different arguments, along with the initial review of Cobet's[4], make Fehling's arguments (first published in 1971) seem over formalistic, a criticism of E.'s, and in the 1990s, when so much has changed in the study of the classical world, depressingly over-rationalistic.

Whilst one has a clear sense in P. of the problems Herodotus had in grappling with a half-known *oikumene*, a wide variety of peoples, and a past mistily preserved in contradictory myths and traditions, there is little on the creation of the *Histories* as a literary work; nor on how, precisely, such sources might have been inserted or manipulated for the purposes of the *Histories*. Here E. offers a detailed, interesting and meticulous analysis of the text. Part I examines the '*Anekdoten*' and '*Novellen*', moving through from Gyges the Lydian, to Themistocles. Part II deals with '*Exkursen*', but objecting to the over-formalistic approach, argues plausibly for the integral role of the excursuses, whether geographical or ethnographic, to the main historical aims of the *Histories*. More strikingly, E. also argues that the method of the excursus was taken from Homer: this then broadens into the claim, mainly adumbrated in the conclusion, that just as the main aim of the *Histories*, in arresting oblivion and preserving fame, is Homeric, so the narrative technique in its basic sense is essentially Homeric. In order to preserve the past, Herodotus has to make it 'narratable' (*erzählbar*): this point, which only emerges fully in the Conclusion, leads from E.'s analysis of individual tales in Part I. It leads also to his final conclusion that the *Histories* are historical—rather than 'pseudo-*historie*'—if only we avoid modern and anachronistic ideas about historiography (see 186 f.). This briefly discussed claim might seen unexceptional, were it not that Part I has argued that many of the best known tales in Herodotus were pure Herodotean 'inventions'. We are back again to invention in Herodotus but in a quite different context from that of Fehling.[5]

Much hinges on the nature and extent of oral traditions (folktales, or any other traditions) in Herodotus' time, and on the way he incorporated them into his narrative. Unfortunately E. only confronts this head-on in general terms in the conclusion, and one must piece together the train of argument from earlier individual analyses (and often from the small-print insets). He puts his finger on a real and fascinating problem, and one not often enough brought out explicit, how the author who is making use of oral tales, folktales or anecdotes, for his own narrative, actually alters, selects or otherwise manipulates them to form a coherent presentation. E. wishes to stress more than others the extent to which Herodotus organized his material freely (e.g. 185). As he points out, very plausibly, Herodotus did not just 'write down what was said', certainly not *everything* that was said.[6] That would indeed court the risk simply of making a confused heap of contradictory information, which is evidently not the case. The coherence of theme and moral running through the stories of Solon and Croesus, Cleobis and Biton, Tellos, etc. in Book I for instance, suggest anything but an unselected collection of 'raw' oral traditions. The motif of the 'warner' from Herodotus' Solon or Croesus to Demaratus, or most striking, the nature of their warnings, surely belong to Herodotus' own narrative creation rather than possible traditions he collected. But when we look in depth at E.'s analysis of the short stories (whether we call them anecdotes, folktales or novellas), there seems to be considerable tension, unresolved, between the idea that Herodotus 'ordered' or rearranged traditions, and the idea that he invented a story wholesale and from scratch.

The main impulse for E.'s suspicions is when an apparently traditional tale in the *Histories* coincides with or reinforces Herodotus' understanding of the subject, or fits perfectly with his 'teleology'; but in fact criteria vary. The following are suggested inventions: the Tellos story (I 30), as part of the Solonian moralizing about Croisos' wealth which fits so perfectly with the later disaster (14); the whole Atys-Adrastos narrative (I 34-45), created and designed by Herodotus from two far blander facts (17); the anecdote about Harpagos' plot with Cyrus (I 123.1) and the trick with the hare (38), because it is unlikely and because the trick is reminiscent of Histiaeus' trick involving the shaven head (V 53.3); the anecdote about Cyrus giving the Persians alternate days of hard work and then feasting (I 125 f.), invented to show Cyrus' cleverness, organizational capacities, so as to give a kind of history lesson (39-40); the vivid episode in which Cambyses taunts the Egyptian king Psammenitus by sending out in rags before him members of his family, many Egyptians, and finally the old friend now a beggar (III 14), invented apparently because of the tragic treatment and the impossibility that Herodotus could have heard this story from anyone (49). It is Herodotus who added the significant detail that Cambyses wounded the Apis bull in the thigh (III 29), so as to connect it better with Cambyses' own fatal injury in the same part of the anatomy (III 64.3, where

---

[3] J. Marincola, *Arethusa* 20 (1987), 26-32, and 126; Erbse 76 n. 6.

[4] J. Cobet, review of Fehling, *Gnomon* 46 (1974), 737-46.

[5] Erbse is critical of Fehling's approach, esp. his treatment of monuments: Pt.II, ch. 4.

[6] Point well made by S. Flory, *The Archaic Smile of Herodotus* (Detroit 1987) ch. 2.

the coincidence is pointed out); as also the oracle at Buto itself (III 64), part of Herodotus' teleology. Various anecdotes about Darius make a coherent picture of the king: following Köhnken, E. thinks the story of Oebares, the trusty groom whose trick enables Darius to win the kingship, is invented (along with the relief and inscription: III 85-88), on the grounds that there are no oriental parallels to the relief and inscription (but see P., 173 ff. for a series of possibilities), and because it creates the sort of image of Darius that Herodotus wishes to convey (60-62); the story of the Paeonians (V 12-14), to explain a historical event and to point up Darius' character as the shopkeeper king (62-3); also the tale of Darius opening Nitocris' tomb (I 187), to show Darius' temperament (63). Similarly with the apparently unintelligible behaviour of the Scythians in their symbolic reply to Darius (IV 131 f.) and in the episode of the hare which interests the Scythian host more than the advancing Persians (IV 134): 'even as a fiction they are significant and meaningful', expressing something very true about the Persian expedition (65-7). The various anecdotes about Xerxes' hubristic and naive confidence are Herodotean—his designs on the river at Tempe (VII 129-30), his ungoverned lashing of the Hellespont (VII 35). Though it is astounding that the latter in particular could only have entered Greece only via Herodotus, E., avoiding Fehling's mere scepticism (85-88), suggests that such invented anecdotes are connected with Xerxes because they illustrate a historical truth about his character (91-2).

An unlikely tale which reflects Herodotus' ideas about human fate and insecurity is invented by him for that end, using 'anecdotal' or freely invented details: the story of Polycrates' experiment with the ring and Amasis' reaction (III 41-43) is invented also because it is so unlikely and 'perplexing' that it cannot be true (96). The equally memorable tale of the youthful and risky trick of the later Alexander I of Macedon against the Persian embassy (V 17-22) is invented because the story is implausible and allows Herodotus to treat the king as consistently pro-Greek at heart (99 ff., esp. 101-4). Irony is also a criterion for fiction in the case of Psammetichus' experiment to find the oldest language (II 2-3) (Part I, ch. 8).

But something is awry here. So many different criteria offered for Herodotean invention invite scepticism and one longs for more explicit and sustained discussion of the concepts and processes involved. E.'s view would make Herodotus (at least for parts of the *Histories*) the most remarkable teller and brilliant inventor of cautionary and moralizing tales. Perhaps—an arresting vision which takes to its furthest extent the implication of the interplay of motifs and repetition of themes often noted by Herodotean specialists.[7] E. offers this as a speculative and tentative study. But there are considerable difficulties which seem to require further refinement.

Often the reason for invoking an invention is that a tale is implausible: but E. might apply his distrust of

anachronistic views of history to criteria for implausibility. Often such Herodotean 'inventions' are replicated, or have elements replicated, in folktales from all over the world. But E. takes motif-recurrence within Herodotus to be a sign that it is Herodotus who is transferring them freely (e.g. 38; or 183: motifs belong to Herodotus' personal storytelling rather than to the original stories). How do we know when Herodotus is using a highly traditional motif on his own account, or simply stressing the motif as it has been conveyed within a traditional folktale? E. is generally unwilling to entertain the possibility that other tales and traditions might have been available beyond those we happen to know about from Greek literature (he is also reluctant to see any role for such stories in political propaganda (*cf.* Alexander I of Macedon), or for particular political groups). Herodotus would thus be working in a world narrowly limited in its traditions and popular tales: the enterprising and committed 'story-teller' must preserve this horribly shrinking and slight past by adding new and memorable anecdotes (*cf.* 91-2), developing his image of the past from the slight remnants and then elaborating gloriously in what (I suppose) might be the manner of the oral epic poet (a comparison not made by E.). Yet as we see from Xenophanes (fr. 22), or Ion of Chios, there were plenty of informal occasions when Greeks told each other stories of the past or boasted of their own exploits, and plenty of more formal means for the past to be celebrated, however misleadingly (e.g. festivals, cults, victory celebrations, etc.). E. has an interesting discussion in the case of Arion of possible traditions which might lie behind Herodotus (154, a more subtle reading than Fehling's), but if here, why not elsewhere?

These are important questions, but more subtle differentiation concerning the nature of folktales or oral traditions seems needed. No reference is made here to the vast mass of recent work on folktales, or to any of the important work of anthropologists on oral traditions of all kinds who have dealt with many problems very relevant to this discussion;[8] nor to recent work on oral traditions in the Greek world.[9] One wonders if discussion can really progress further in this difficult area without at least some attempt to look at what sort of possibilities might be suggested from outside the discipline.

A case in point is the problem familiar to anthropologists working on oral traditions in the field, or on collected oral traditions, that the very process of recording a tale may affect the content: with the best will in the world to record accurately, the external, foreign observer may end up giving an alien order and sense to a mass of traditions which may have been contradictory and irreconcilable precisely because they were all remembered in their separate social context as separate

---

[7] E.g. the recent study by Flory *op. cit.*; also A. Griffiths, 'Democedes of Croton: a Greek doctor at Darius' court,' *Achaemenid History II. The Greek Sources,* ed. H. Sancisi-Weerdenburg and A. Kuhrt (Leiden 1987), 37-51.

[8] See especially Jan Vansina, *Oral Tradition as History* (London and Nairobi 1985); *Oral Tradition. A Study in Historical Methodology* (Harmondsworth 1973; Fr. ed. 1961); D.P. Henige, *Oral Historiography* (London 1982); *The Chronology of Oral Tradition. Quest for a Chimera* (Oxford 1974).

[9] R. Thomas, *Oral Tradition and Written Record in Classical Athens* (Cambridge 1989); J.A.S. Evans, *Herodotus Explorer of the Past* (Princeton 1991), ch. 3, 'Oral tradition in Herodotus'; O. Murray, 'Herodotus and oral history', in *Achaemenid History II. The Greek Sources* (1987) (as n. 7 above), 93-115; J. Gould, *Herodotus* (London 1989).

entities corresponding to the needs or rivalries of, say, different families. The fact that the anthropologist may have made something new in collecting, sifting, and making sense of such different versions does not necessary mean either that such oral traditions do not exist, or that the anthropologists have 'invented' those oral traditions in the usual sense of that word. E. sometimes seems to conflate the arranging and rearranging of traditional tales with the invention of them. Similarly, it would be a strangely romantic view of oral traditions to think that they had to be plausible or historically true to be traditional tales (cf. Polycrates' ring). It also seems odd to attribute such an 'implausible' tale instead to the pen of a sophisticated writer like Herodotus (and if to Herodotus, why not to Plato, who recounts a folktale about Gyges (Rep. 359c ff.)?), when what gave that tale currency in the first place was probably precisely that it was traditional.

There remains the forceful point about Herodotus' masterly organization in weaving such tales into the grand structure of the narrative. I remain unconvinced by E.'s final arguments that the very coherence of such tales within the narrative is part of the historian's invention and attempt to make the past 'narratable', for it involves an image of traditional tales which is again too simple. For example, to suggest that Herodotus invented entirely Xerxes' hubristic actions implies that there were no stories or rumours about Xerxes' tyrant-like behaviour circulating 30 or 40 years after his defeat; that Herodotus decided in his own mind but with no clear examples to back him up that such was Xerxes' character, and then had to invent stories to illustrate it. This *reductio ad absurdum* lies in a sphere and period where there is no difficulty in accepting that plenty of Greeks knew tales, apocryphal or not, of Xerxes' overbearing behaviour (cf. *Persai*).[10] The fact that the tale of Thrasyboulos' silent advice to a fellow tyrant occurs within the speech of Sosikles in Herodotus' narrative (V 92; 184), does not imply that such an excellent anti-tyrant tale could have had no provenance or use elsewhere.

A coherent image or moral message in Herodotus' traditional tales might be the result of Herodotus' selectivity (provided one admits he had tales to select from), and some rearrangement of emphasis, perhaps even invention; but it may also be part of the character of a great many folktales and traditional tales.[11] E. leans much on the point that Herodotus had to make his enquiries 'narratable': but one should add that any tradition, any traditional tale, story or anecdote will have been narratable already in some way, or important in some form to its audience, otherwise it would not have been retold or remembered. Oral traditions all over the world have a tendency to become rapidly reshaped so that they correspond to some element of the past which is crucial to the present, and there is little indication to suggest that ancient Greece was any different in this respect. Given this tendency for such tales to bear slanted

moral, religious or political meanings (cf. the various traditions alive in Athens about its liberation from tyranny; or Herodotus' disrespect for the only family tradition he mentioned explicitly, V 57.1), one can perhaps be less struck by the appearance of a moral coherence in some of Herodotus' early tales. He may well have shaped them further, for any retelling may reshape, but why could the traditions about Solon, or Croesus, or any connected with Delphi, not already have a religious and moral weight before Herodotus wrote them down? It would be precisely this moral bearing and narratability which ensured their preservation and retelling.

One may not agree with all the connecting threads, but this is an important and thought-provoking analysis of Herodotus' anecdotes and tales which goes beyond the mere attribution of authorial invention to find a role consistent with Herodotus' painstaking enquiries in the rest of the *Histories*. As P. stresses, Herodotus of all writers needs to be interpreted in the wider cultural context of the time. The question remains what that is.

ROSALIND THOMAS

Royal Holloway,
University of London

---

[10] Cf. E. Hall, *Inventing the Barbarian* (Oxford 1989), ch. 2.
[11] See Flory *op. cit.* (1987) for discussion of folktales with opposing morals. One hint of contradictory versions within in the *Histories* occurs at I 91, the oracle to Croesus, not entirely consistent with the earlier Gyges story (discussed by Erbse, 6).

REVIEW ARTICLE II: APOLLONIUS RHODIUS

APOLLONIUS RHODIUS, *Argonautica*. **Jason and the Golden Fleece.** Tr. and comm. R. Hunter. Oxford UP, 1993. Pp. xxxvi + 175. £25.

CLAUSS (J.J.) **The best of the Argonauts: the redefinition of the epic hero in Book I of Apollonius' *Argonautica*.** Berkeley: U of California P, 1993. Pp. xviii + 238. $35.

THIEL (K.) **Erzählung und Beschreibung in den *Argonautika* des Apollonios Rhodios: ein Beitrag zur Poetik des hellenistischen Epos.** Stuttgart: Steiner, 1993. Pp. xi + 263. DM 96.

DRÄGER (P.) *Argo pasimelousa*: **der Argonautenmythos in der griechischen und römischen Literatur. I: Theos aitios.** Stuttgart: Steiner, 1993. Pp. x + 400. DM 136.

There has been a latter-day surge of interest in the *Argonautica* of Apollonius Rhodius, as is evidenced by the ever-lengthening bookshop shelf-space devoted to studies of this particular epic poem. It is really only within the past seven or eight years that Apollonius has emerged from the Stygian gloom of critical neglect; quite apart from any other reasons, the continuing fascination with all things Alexandrian and with anything even remotely connected with narratology means that Apollonius Rhodius is now, as never before, *seriously* trendy. The *Argonautica* is a Janus-type poem, looking back to Homer, but at the same time pointing the way towards the achievements of Latin epic. As such, the attention which it is now receiving is as necessary as it is welcome.

It happens that the four books reviewed in this article approach the complexities of Apollonius' poem from very different standpoints. One is a translation into

English of the poem, one involves the tracing of a particular theme in the opening book, one presents an analysis of narrative technique, the fourth a broader discussion of literary treatments of the Argonautic myth. None of these books is without its merits and, considered as a group, they constitute a useful sample of the current (healthier) state of Apollonian studies. The translation will be discussed in a moment; but the least to be said in general terms about the other three critical works is that, directly or indirectly, they (re)assert the *Argonautica*'s eminent status in the development of ancient epic by emphasizing three important points, respectively: the undoubted refashioning of the concept of the epic hero on the part of Apollonius; the equally undoubted importance of this text for the study of (epic) narrative; the skill of the Alexandrian poet in manipulating the mythical tradition.

But I begin, appropriately, with a look at a new translation of Apollonius' epic. It is a truth universally acknowledged that there has not been an English translation of the *Argonautica* which has done justice to the quality of the poem. Hunter's stated intention in offering his new prose version is to bring the epic of Apollonius Rhodius within the reach of a wider readership in a manner consonant with 'both the stylistic variety of the poem and the fact that all of it is written in a language very far from the everyday'. H. criticizes his own efforts in advance, warning the reader to expect a translation which scores for being *utile* rather than *dulce*. In fact, such reservations prove groundless, and H.'s translation succeeds admirably in being sensitive both to the needs of a Greek learner who is grappling with the original and to the exigencies of fluent English. In maintaining this balancing-act he manages not to stray from the spirit and content of the Greek. A case in point comes early on in Book I of the *Argonautica*, in the description of the first launch of Argo by means of a specially constructed slipway. The original Greek text is full of technical detail and descriptions of complex manoeuvres executed by the Argonauts. But this episode is no pedantic display of engineering knowledge on the part of Apollonius; rather the poet's aim (immediately after the awkward question of leadership of the expedition has been decided) is to emphasize how quickly the crew of the Argo learn to work in harmony, by this means pointing up just how much the success of the mission depends on concerted rather than individual action. The Greek vocabulary at this point in the poem would present difficulties for any translator, as is evidenced by Seaton's stilted rendition of 1.371-77:

And they quickly dug a trench as wide as the space the ship covered, and at the prow as far into the sea as it would run when drawn down by their hands. And they ever dug deeper in front of the stem, and in the furrow laid polished rollers; and inclined the ship down upon the first rollers, that so she might glide and be borne on by them.

The superior smoothness and readability of H.'s version of the same lines is immediately apparent:

Then they quickly dug out a channel wide enough for the ship, leading from the prow down to the sea; along this their arms would pull the ship, and as they

proceeded they hollowed it out to a depth lower than the bottom of the keel. In this channel they placed polished rollers, and then manoeuvred the ship onto the topmost rollers, facing down to the sea, so that it could be transported by sliding over them.

H. is no less adept at translating passages where the Greek *text* itself is uncertain. A prime example of this can be found in Book 2, in the beautiful simile describing the swift movement of Athena (541-48). There is more than one textual crux in these lines, but H.'s version is entirely persuasive:

As when a man who wanders far from his own land—as indeed we wretched men often do wander, and no land seems distant, but all paths are spread before us—can picture his own home, and as he sees in a flash the path there over land and sea, his thoughts dart quickly and his eyes grasp one place after another, just so did the daughter of Zeus swiftly leap down and place her feet on the Thynian coast of the Inhospitable Sea.

There are many other aspects of H.'s translation which could be highlighted here; suffice to say that the translator shows himself equal to the challenges posed by Apollonius' variegated style and subject-matter. This is one instance where familiarity does not breed contempt—at all times H. treats the original with the respect it deserves. His version is accompanied by detailed notes and an index, together with a clear, concise introduction to the poem and its place in the Alexandrian tradition. Lecturers planning a Classics-in-translation course for Greek epic need look no further than this volume for an accessible translation which will stimulate student interest and imagination. This book will be the standard English-language translation of Apollonius' *Argonautica* for many years to come.

Clauss' book was a dissertation in a previous incarnation; the present work is a 'thoroughly reconceived and rewritten version' of an earlier study of allusion and narrative style in *Argonautica I*, a thesis which will be familiar to anyone who has done research on Apollonius. The revision of the original is indeed considerable, and now the emphasis is placed less on questions of narrative technique than on the greater issue of definition of the Hellenistic hero. In this book C. presents a sequential reading of the episodes of Book I, pointing out how the text explores and qualifies the tension between two constructs of epic hero, 'the man of skill' and 'the man of strength': which of these two models is better equipped to cope with the vagaries of the Argo voyage? The argument exists on a lower level between, for instance, the two latecomers to Pagasae, Acastus and Argus, and between Idmon and Idas on the night before the voyage. Nonetheless it is, of course, between Jason and Heracles that the tension is greatest, beginning from the moment when Jason asks the crew to choose a leader and they plump for ... Heracles. But it is ultimately Jason, the man with the 'passive style' and the diplomatic skills to unite a disparate bunch, a leader who is a more realistic Alexandrian-type of hero, 'a totally dependent man of limited skills', who proves to be the best of the Argonauts.

Although heroic excellence is the main theme of his

book, C. might have done better to choose a different title. *The best of the Argonauts* encourages the reader to anticipate a bargain-basement, derivative version of Nagy's study of Homer. C.'s book, however, does not need to invoke such an illustrious predecessor; like the *Argonautica* itself it is quite capable of standing on its own merits. There are many highlights here; C.'s discussion of the Catalogue of Argonauts and the inherent antithesis between Orpheus and Heracles is finely judged (and completely convincing), as is his handling of the Lemnian episode in Ch. 6. Also worth noting are his comments (196 ff.) on the reactions of the Argonauts after they realise that they have left Heracles behind at Mysia. This is a defining moment for the Argonautic expedition and C.'s close analysis serves to underline the fact that, paradoxically, it is Jason's aloofness from the action which best qualifies him for the active role of leader.

On the debit side, C. manifests an occasional tendency towards over-reading. His interpretation of the crucial Iphias scene, whereby Jason 'coldly' leaves behind 'a woman who has apparently outlasted any importance or usefulness she may have had' (95), seems to me to be decidedly slanted (surely προθέοντος ὁμίλου) at line 314 indicates that it is the press of the crowd, as much as anything, which separates them?), while the effort to read into the launch of the Argo a complex set of allusions to the *Homeric Hymn to Hermes* smacks of special pleading. But the major criticism to be levelled at his work is one of which C. himself is already aware, namely that it is confined to the first book of the poem. C. defends the scope of his study on the basis of the 'unity and integrity' of Book 1, with its linear development of the theme of the 'best' hero. I would be willing to accept this, except that the issue of heroic behaviour is not *resolved* at the end of Book 1, nor the question of the efficacy of brawn versus brain. Even the most catatonic of readers will notice that the conflict between skill (civilization) and strength (barbarity) is a major theme throughout the Bebrycian episode of Book 2, where Amycus and Polydeuces engage in a grim David-and-Goliath struggle, yet this episode receives but a brief mention on 34, a mention which even in itself is outside C.'s professed remit. And, to ask the obvious question, *what about Medea*? If the best of the Argonauts is a 'man of skill' (in diplomacy), what does it mean when the climax of the poem is an episode where a *woman* temporarily turns him into a 'man of strength' for the purposes of yoking the fire-breathing bulls and slaying the dragon's teeth warriors? C.'s analysis of Book 1, admirable though it undoubtedly is, screams out loud for elaboration in the context of the poem as a whole, not least because such elaboration would inevitably involve modification of his thesis.

I have said enough, however, about what is missing from C.'s book; what *is* between the covers is well worth reading. C. has performed a valuable service in refocussing attention on one of the lesser-known parts of Apollonius' poem, and his work will deservedly reach a wide audience.

Thiel's book (originally a dissertation from Trier) deals, as its title suggests, with narrative technique in Apollonius. The device of *ecphrasis* is given primary attention and, as a prelude to his work, T. begins with a survey of ancient and modern opinions on the nature of *ecphrasis*. Starting with the ancient rhetoricians, T.'s *Ekphrasisbegriff* follows through to Lessing and beyond, even managing to include René Magritte and his dubious pipe. The general thrust of this section of the book appears to run along the lines of 'although nobody knows what they are on about when they talk about *ecphrasis*, we may as well go ahead and have a look at a few, anyway'. Though this is a major comfort to those of us who have to struggle through the complexities of academic narrative-speak for a living, it is not the most promising way in which to commence a book on the subject.

Having identified the critical uncertainty pertaining to his topic, T. makes the deliberate decision to analyse descriptive passages in Apollonius according to a distinction set out by Heinze in his *Virgils epische Technik*. In a brief section towards the end of that work Heinze made some brief comments on poetic description in Virgilian epic, in which the following sentence was, in T.'s view, crucial:

> Das gemeinsame aller Arten von Beschreibung ist, dass dabei die fortschreitende Handlung stockt; der Leser bleibt stehen und beschaut ein Bild in allen seinen Einzelheiten.

T. categorises the Apollonian descriptions which he chooses to analyse on the basis of whether or not 'die Handlung stockt'. Two basic types are therefore created, by means of which T. can classify his thirty-four excerpts: those in which the narrative stands still (Type B) and those in which it does not (Type A). A third category (Type AB) proves necessary, to cover the grey area of descriptions which also serve to carry the narrative forward. In his analysis of all these passages T. proceeds under the following headings: 'Struktur nach der äusseren Form'; 'Struktur nach dem Inhalt'; 'Struktur nach der Schilderungstechnik'; 'Metrische Strukturierung'; 'Struktur nach der Sprache'; 'Funcktion des Exkurses'; 'Wie Realistisch ist der Exkurs?'; 'Geschehen und Zeit innerhalb des Exkurses'.

It will immediately be seen from the above that T. cannot be accused of being 'discursive' in his approach, and some readers will no doubt be dismayed by the clinical rigidity of the book's programme, and its scientific treatment of a subject which is, by its nature, difficult to pin down. It is worth looking beyond this, however, as students of Apollonius will find considerable worthwhile material here, and also learn much about Apollonian narrative style. For example, T.'s lengthy discussion of the 'Jason's Cloak' *ecphrasis* has pertinent comments to make on the different narrative techniques employed by Apollonius in this description. I especially liked his discussion of 'Aphrodite and the Shield of Ares', the *omphalos* of the *ecphrasis*, which T. treats as a display of *Erosmacht*, a *Bild im Bild* in which the epic language used is strikingly different from what precedes it. (It is a feature of T.'s work that his linguistic analyses of all these Apollonian excerpts and their relationship to epic models is particularly detailed.) He discusses the second Apollonian 'cloak-description'—the garment used by Medea to lure Apsyrtus to his death—in the light of the earlier *ecphrasis*, to good effect: 'die erste ist δίδαγμα, Lehrmittel, die zweite θελκτήριον, Lockmittel' (105). Other passages subjected to close scrutiny include the 'description of Aeetes' palace' from Book 3, and the 'launching of the Argo' and the 'song of Orpheus' from Book 1.

T.'s work is not without its drawbacks, however. One is relatively minor, but extremely irritating: the book itself suffers from a bad dose of wordprocessor-itis. Someone obviously thought it a good idea to divide the text into subsection piled upon subsection, to mix up upper and lower case, to go from **bold** type to normal to *italics* **and back again** at will, occasionally to alter font size and spacing for no apparent reason. They were wrong.

The second problem is less trivial. The author is well versed in German scholarship on his subject, but seems to have ignored/be unaware of many relevant works written in other languages. To give but a few examples, in a study whose principal tool of analysis depends upon the notion of narrative pause, it is bizarre that there is no reference to Genette. Moving closer to home, despite T.'s manifold sections on (pictorial) realism in Apollonius, he displays no consciousness of Zanker's *Realism in Alexandrian poetry*. Third, it is a mistake to offer to study of narrative technique in the *Argonautica* without some acknowledgement of Fusillo's work in this area. In the light of lapses such as these, my endorsement of T.'s book must remain qualified.

This brings me, finally, to Dräger's volume (another dissertation from Trier), which is quite up-front as to the scholarship which it tends to ignore. Here is presented a study of the Argo myth in Greek and Latin literature. It becomes obvious as early as 7 that D. has a very specific methodology in mind:

In m.E. der Klassichen Philologie erlaubter Beschränkung bleiben—auch in den darauffolgenden Kapiteln —'moderne' Betrachtungsweisen des Mythos wie die von Ethnologie (bzw. social anthropology), (Tiefen-) Psychologie/Psychoanalyse, Funktionalismus, Strukturalismus etc. grundsätzlich ganz ausser Betracht.

It is refreshing to come across a critic who is willing to avoid beating about the bushes, but I must confess to reservations concerning the desirability of going at said undergrowth with a chainsaw.

D.'s survey of the Argonautic myth breaks down into four main parts; the first section deals with the Homeric/early versions of the myth; the second (and longest) section discusses Pindar's *Pythian 4*; the third focuses upon Apollonius, while the fourth section takes a brief look at Valerius Flaccus. The whole is accompanied by extensive footnotes and bibliography. D.'s work is less all-embracing than it might seem, however—the present volume concentrates on the pre-voyage section of the myth, i.e. the motivation behind the Argo quest. In the Apollonius section this leads him to go through the poem's prologue with a fine toothcomb, pointing out 'problems' (how, for instance, does Jason *know* when Pelias' feast is due to take place?), differences in approach from Pindar (Apollonius is less concerned with the throne-robbing origins of Pelias' reign), and how Apollonius highlights the theme of *göttliche Rache* on Hera's part (as implied by the prologue and, again, in Book 3). Another (controversial) motivation for the voyage is the anger of Zeus, which is not mentioned until much later in the poem. Here D.

discusses in detail the relevant passages (2.1192-95 and 3.333-39), as well as the textual crux of line 2.1146 (exactly *whose* idea is it that the ram should be sacrificed?).

The above will give some idea as to the content of D.'s book. His aim, in the case of Apollonius, is to show how the poet engages in an Alexandrian process of mythical contamination, being willing, whenever appropriate for his purposes, to bypass Pindar and adapt material from earlier versions of the myth. It cannot, of course, be denied that Apollonius is also highly original, particularly in the psychological portrayal of the heroine in Book 3. This last may not exactly be news to us but surprisingly enough (given the over-elaborate footnoting), this book is by no means pedestrian. D. is adept at analysing the various strands of the myth and the concluding section, a synthesis of the different angles from which the poets surveyed tackle the Argonautic myth (including a potted version of a 'pre-Homeric *Argonautica*'), is perhaps the most useful. Occasionally D. is prone to flights of fancy, such as the entertaining assertion that Phrixus' body is actually rolled up in the Golden Fleece as it hangs on the tree, a suggestion to which the only appropriate response is, er, no. D.'s book is not the last word on Argonautic myth, but it does push the arguments forward. For the immediate future, those shelves in the bookshop seem likely to creak still further.

R.J. CLARE

University of Leeds

REVIEW ARTICLE III: BIBLIOGRAPHICAL DATABASES

MALITZ (J.) **Gnomon bibliographische Datenbank: internationales Informationssystem für die klassische Altertumswissenschaft.** München: Beck, [1994]. 10 disks and reference manual (loose-leaf). Initial price: DM 498 (DM 398 for subscribers to *Gnomon*); subscription price (annual up-date): DM 298.

Progetto Ἡρακλῆς: **banca-dati bibliografici del mondo antico.** Release 1.2. Roma: "L'Erma" di Bretschneider, [1994]. 2 disks and reference manual (loose-leaf). Initial price: L 220,000 (individuals), L 315,000 (institutions); subscription price (2 issues p.a.): L 140,000 (individuals), L 200,000 (institutions).

Bibliographical databases for classical studies seem to be like London buses in the old joke: nothing for ages, and then they all come at once. There are five sources known to me which are available or have been announced at the time of completing this review (February 1996): apart from the two under consideration, these are the *Database of Classical Bibliography* (the CD-ROM version of *L'Année philologique*, issued initially in July 1995), and the *Bibliographia Graeca & Latina* (recently announced, and also to be on CD-ROM). I have included an outline description of the remaining source, *Dyabola: electronic subject catalogues of publi-*

	Dyabola	Gnomon	Herakles
System	MS-DOS comp.	MS-DOS comp.	MS-DOS comp.
Version	4.0 or higher	3.3 or higher	3.3 or higher
RAM	640 Kb	384 Kb	1 Mb
Free hard disk space	150 Mb	65 Mb	20 Mb
Data source	CD-ROM	Disk (9)	Disk (1)
Operating languages	E/F/G/I	E/G	E/F/G/I
Subject range	Archaeology/art	All	Emphasis on archaeology/art
Year range	1956-	1925- (but see review)	1992- (but see review)
Search methods	Fields (8)	Fields (5) or descriptors from thesaurus or free text (see review)	Fields (5)
Subject retrieval	DAI subj. headings	Thesaurus	Own classification
Boolean operators	Yes	Yes	Limited (see review)
Save search option	Yes	Yes	No
Printing	Yes	Yes	Limited (see review)
Downloading	Yes	Yes	No
Updating	Annual	Annual	Semi-annual

cations on history of art and the ancient world.[1] Although *Dyabola* has not so far been submitted for review, I have been able to consult it at the Institute of Classical Studies;[2] it was the earliest of the five databases to become available, and shares a subject emphasis with *Progetto* Ἡρακλῆς (*Herakles*).

The three sources have distinct origins: *Dyabola* corresponds to the subject catalogue of the library of the Deutsches Archäologisches Institut (DAI) in Rome (1956-), together with those of the Römisch-Germanische Kommission in Frankfurt (1992-) and the DAI in Madrid (1991-); *Gnomon* is based on the reviews in or quarterly supplements to that journal; *Herakles* is the database of the bookseller and publisher "L'Erma" di Bretschneider. Specification details and technical requirements for the three sources may be summarised in tabular form as shown above. All the databases will run on a 286 processor, although a 486 is recommended (and was used for this review).

Gnomon
The review copy supplied was the first instalment, issued in 1994; it contains 120,371 records. There has since been a further instalment in the same form, and it has been announced that a CD-ROM version will become available later in 1996. In addition, a version of the current database from 1990 onwards has been available on the Internet since January 1996 (http://sokrates.ku-eichstaett.de/Gnomon/). For the purposes of this review, which must be considered against this evolving background, I shall discuss the first instalment and the initial Internet version.

In the introductory section of the manual, the range of the database is explained as being based on volumes 1-63 inclusive of *Gnomon*, for the years 1925-1993. It consists of bibliographical records for all the book reviews in these volumes, supplemented by those for the Personalnachrichten and Nekrologe sections. The bibliographical appendix (Bibliographische Beilage) which appears in every other issue of the journal is included, however, only from 1990 onwards. To compensate for this, there are other additional sources of data. First, it is claimed that eleven journal titles (*AU, A&A, Chiron, CQ, G&R, Gymnasium, Hermes, Historia, JHS, JRS, ZPE*) have been completely indexed. Second, the reviews from 1987 onwards in *JHS, JRS* and a further four journals (*AAHG, AJA, CR, GGA*) are included. Third, some journals not previously indexed in the Bibliographische Beilage are apparently included (although neither the German nor English version of the manual is specific on this point), and there are a few older defunct journals (*Neue Jahrbücher für das klassische Altertum* together with its successors for 1898-1942 and *Die Antike* for 1925-1944 are cited). Fourth, the database contains references from some more general journals which include regular publications of relevance to classical studies; the titles cited are *Archiv für Kulturgeschichte, Geschichte in Wissenschaft und Unterricht, Historische Zeitschrift, Saeculum* and *Universitas*. In addition (and not mentioned in this introduction), the database contains a large number of entries for articles from standard encyclopaedias, such as the *OCD*, and collected works of scholarship (*ANRW* and *CAH*). I am surprised that some of these were considered a priority, although *ANRW* in particular is useful.

The installation procedure is clearly explained. During this procedure (which took about 22 minutes rather than the 30-40 suggested in the manual), the datafiles are compressed from the required maximum of 65 Mb to about 50 Mb. In order to activate the Lidos

[1] CD-ROM/program: instalment 3. Ennepetal: Biering & Brinkmann, [1995]; manual: third edition. Ennepetal: Biering & Brinkmann, [1992]. Initial price for Frankfurt, Madrid and Rome databases: DM 4642; subscription price (annual update): DM 418. Prices exclude VAT. Networking is allowed at no extra cost within a single library, institute or department. The Frankfurt and Madrid databases are also available on disks.

[2] I am grateful to the Library staff at the Institute of Classical Studies/Joint Library, and in particular to Mrs S. Willetts, for help in the preparation of this review.

bibliographic software program which is used to run the database from the C:\GNOMON subdirectory, it is necessary to enter the command Lidos l=e (or Lidos f l=e, if a colour monitor is used), but this command line can be installed from one of the batchfiles, so that the program can be run directly without the need to quit from Windows to DOS first.

The database is organized into fifteen fields (*Autor*; *Co-Autor*; *Jahr*; *Titel*; *Textfeld* [title keywords]; *Ort*; *Verlag*; *Zeitschrift* [journal titles]; *Sammelwerk* [titles of anthologies or collected studies]; *Reihentitel* [publisher's series title, sometimes abbreviated]; *Band* [volume number]; *Heft* [part number]; *Seiten*; Art [type of publication, such as monograph or review]; *Deskriptoren* [subject or general keywords, contained in the thesaurus of the database]). Of these fifteen, five can be searched separately: author (or co-author—no distinction is made between the two fields in this type of search), year of publication (in conjunction with author searches or separately), title keyword, journal title, or anthologies. This method of seaching is one of three; the other two are searching on subject or generic keywords, using the thesaurus, or free text searching, using specified fields or the whole database. For obvious reasons, the last method is much the slowest although most searches took less than two minutes to perform; naturally, less specific searches will be slower to run.

The Lidos program bears the copyright dates 1987-1989. This is antique in software terms; nothing wrong with that, necessarily, as long as it performs adequately. Unfortunately, the program is—it seems to me—user-hostile. It depends upon the operation of function keys throughout, the meaning of which changes from one part of the program to another. There are no on-screen help facilities. Instead, some sample tasks (23 in all) have been added which can be used to learn the program initially. But this is hardly an adequate substitute; in the middle of a search, surely the user should not be expected to fumble around in the manual (not indexed) to find the relevant example (identified only as AUFTR_01-23), call this up and then return to the search. Admittedly, function keys F7 and F8 allow such examples to be retrieved or stored fairly easily, but new filenames should be chosen, as otherwise the guidance offered by the manual will be lost if the examples are overwritten.

Even basic operations involve multiple function key sequences. Before anything can be done, it is necessary to press F1, type Archiv, press Return twice to get past the password screen, then F1 again. Only then is the basic menu screen reached. Thereafter one presses F3 (retrieval) and F2 (new search) and arrives, somewhat exhausted, at the search menu. The default search is by author; to activate one of the other separate types of search described above F10 must be pressed; F3 and F4 switch to descriptor or to free text searching, respectively.

A few conventions need to be observed in searching. An author's name or initial should be followed by a full stop, for example, to allow for searching on different forms (no standardisation has been attempted). Despite the layout, which allows for the entry of a range of terms from ... to ..., it is not necessary to enter a second term.[3]

[3] For some reason, it is not possible to use the tab key to move from one line in this and similar display screens to the next.

For title keyword searching, because of the haphazard way in which such keywords have been provided—generally in German or Latin, but often not at all—it may be useful first to experiment generally on a particular part of the alphabet, as the manual suggests, to obtain some idea of how useful such searches are likely to be.

The program is versatile in allowing different fields or types of search to be combined, but complicated searches are likely to try the user's patience on occasion; this is particularly true of descriptor searches which make use of the hierarchical thesaurus. The full subject thesaurus (in German—an English version is promised for subsequent releases) can be printed out in its hierarchical or alphabetical form, but as it contains over 3000 keywords, the former will run to about 60 pages and the latter double this number. In fact, the thesaurus can be consulted quite easily on screen. The problem lies in selecting terms to form a search strategy, since the hierarchical structure can be elaborate (under the descriptor *Vergilius poeta* there is a lower level for individual works, and a further level for individual books, for example). To select all the relevant descriptors, it is necessary to invoke a direction operator (in this instance, 'down'); failure to do so can lead to significant shortfalls in the search result. Searching by year, within descriptor searches, is also cumbersome, since it is not possible to search on a range of years just by entering 1988-1992, for example. Each year is entered separately into the thesaurus, and it is necessary to generate a search statement in the form (1988 or 1989 ... or 1992). Even for the example given in the manual, all articles in *ZPE* from the years 1991-1993, more than 20 key-strokes are necessary and it would be easy to exceed this number. Though the manual does not suggest it, there is an easier way to perform this type of search by using the periodical title search and then refining this by year, when a range can be specified; the speed of searching is slower, but at least there is a chance at the end that the user may still remember the reason for doing the search in the first place.

Free text searching is less problematic, except for the need to specify the field label (such as r for Reihentitel) and to enter any word between two full stops. The use of the Boolean operators is complicated, unnecessarily, by the different treatment of the 'not' operator, which has to be entered separately in a statement of the form 'and not'.

Once a search has been carried out, the result can be displayed on screen in short or full form, sorted according to the default method (author then year) or customised by specifying up to five of the different fields (in ascending or descending order), stored internally, printed or downloaded. The manual does not suggest any limit on the number of searches that can be stored; presumably this is dependent, to some extent, on the size of the result. Sorting is quick and seems to be performed accurately, allowing for the general caveat about incomplete fields which I shall discuss below. Because of the extended field structure, it is not possible for the full record display to be accommodated on a single screen, although the display area can be enlarged by pressing the Escape key. A feature of the program which may be useful is its ability to combine different search results, to compare them for common references, or to separate them by displaying those references unique to each result. Printing involves some preparation: the appropriate print driver must be specified (a list of those supported by the program is given in appendix 2 of the manual), together with the print format (four are given in default settings, which can be modified) and the printer port; once set, these remain in operation until further modified. It is possible to print the result of a whole search file or to select individual entries by means of the lightbar and F7 (single document printing). In the latter case, when printing has finished, it is necessary to cancel the print command (F8 followed by F5), otherwise the program will not close down.

It is perhaps inevitable that mistakes will find their way into a database in its earlier stages, and this version of the *Gnomon Datenbank* has its fair share. There are a few duplicate or inconsistent entries, and mistransliterations from the Greek, but the most frequent cause for complaint is the incorrect or incomplete entry of bibliographical data. A few examples. First, incorrect data entry has led to mistakes in authors' names such as Aadlders for Aalders, Row for Rowe, and the confusion of Mac and Mc, an old favourite. Second, review citations. In these, the author of the work reviewed is entered in the co-author field (and is distinguished by the addition of a preceding quotation mark); such authors are therefore searchable separately. In too many instances, however, this information is missing, with the result that an author search will fail to find reviews of particular works.[4] Third, given the elaborate field structure for each record, it is regrettable that this structure is so often ignored in the entry of data. One might not perhaps want to search very often for books issued by a particular publisher within a specified period, but the database theoretically allows this and ought to retrieve an accurate result. In practice, however, the place and publisher (and sometimes even the date) are frequently lumped together into the place of publication field. In some instances, this sort of information strays elsewhere, with bizarre results: a fictitious journal with the title *Oxford* has been created as a result of the place of publication ending up in the periodical title field—perhaps a drawback of a database which uses the same template for different publication types. Other examples: periodical references can be confused, with volume and page numbers appearing together, or page numbers cited incompletely, even when *Gnomon* in its printed version records them complete. My impression is that data entry needs much firmer editorial checking and control.

I have referred in passing to some shortcomings in the instruction manual, including the lack of an index. There are some places where the information is simply incomplete or confusing. On p. 18, *Textfeld* is omitted from the list of possible searches. P. 24 mentions descriptor searches, but provides no cross-reference to the section which describes them. One of the operators (#poly) is not explained at all, nor is the differential treatment of the Boolean operator 'not' (*cf.* 43). Under descriptor searching, the user is not told that F5 (select by name) must be pressed first if it is necessary to return

one stage, as the F1 key is deactivated in this part of the program. Worst of all is the section on downloading (67) which instructs the user to return to the main menu (rather than the search menu) and then omits the crucial instruction to press F7 (print command) followed by Return.

The Internet site for *Gnomon* is not actually the first for bibliography in classics, since the useful TOCS-IN resource (at Toronto) has been in operation for some time. It differs in two important respects from the disk version, in that it covers the period from 1990 onwards only, and also allows the user to browse through the contents of individual issues of *Gnomon*. At the time of completing this review, only those for 1995 onwards were available, but it is intended to make the future contents sections available in advance of the print version. In addition to these *Inhaltsverzeichnisse*, the site offers three other search options: *Thesaurussuche, Thesaurusanzeige, Volltextsuche*. The first of these allows keywords to be entered and matched against sections of the thesaurus (divided into twenty-five broad subject terms, from *Archäologie* to *Zeitschriften*). In the second option, a similar section of the thesaurus is selected first, and then the search is refined by alphabetical index keys; this will result in an alphabetical display of the relevant thesaurus section, with each entry forming a hypertext link to the relevant data. An example of this would be the selection of classical authors beginning with the letter C. The third option allows for searching on up to four specified fields (author, year, title keyword, thesaurus entry) or a combination of these. Boolean operators for 'and' or 'or' are available. It would be premature to judge the effectiveness of the database in this form from the comparatively small amount of data available (reviews cited from *Gnomon, CR, JHS, JRS*), but it does seem to me to have an advantage over the disk version in providing a simpler approach to descriptor searching.

Herakles

The database was supplied for review initially in its original version (1.0) and the publisher kindly provided an update (1.2) on request. The main differences between the two versions are the speed of operation (the newer version is claimed to be nearly twice as fast) and number of entries (3439 in the first version, 9795 in the second). The data are taken from the publisher's *Bollettino novità*, the first instalment including entries from number 44 (1992), the update those from 44 to 47 (1992-1994). Other differences include the introduction of word truncation and enhanced scrolling.

Installation is reasonably straightforward, following the instructions given in the manual. The original installation of version 1.0 took nine minutes; that of the update, however, took the best part of an hour, most of which was spent in rebuilding the search indexes. The operating language can be changed within each session by the use of function keys (F6 for English), or the configuration can be changed permanently from the maintenance section of the program. Searching is also straightforward, and the program as a whole is not troublesome to use; function keys, for example, have the same significance throughout, unlike *Gnomon*. This is, however, a reflection of the fact that there is only a limited amount which can be done with the database.

---

[4] An alternative means of finding such reviews would be to use a descriptor search on the term *Rezensionen* and to combine this with a free text search on the title field.

The basic menu has four options: book search, display orders, maintenance (which includes options for backup and data acquisition, for updates), quit.

In the first of these, the default option is to search by title. The entry of an initial word or partial word prompts a title index display, through which it is possible to move using arrow or page up/down keys. A new search can be started from within the index by typing another word. The other search options are activated by the F3 key (limit setting); these options are authors/editors, classification, year of publication, words from any field in the 'bibliographical file' (keywords), or no limit. The author and classification options open similar index displays, whereas the year option offers the possibility of searching before, after or in a given year, or between two chosen years. The keyword option allows the entry of any single term from the bibliographical file; the option 'none' removes any set limits. A warning shows on the screen display when a limit is in operation. The classification scheme uses three separate levels: chronological (6 subdivisions), subject (25) and publication type (14). These may be joined together, so that it is possible to limit searching to monographs on ceramics from the classical period, for example; one or more levels may be left unspecified, to expand the search to all monographs on ceramics, or all publications on ceramics. The different search options may be combined (author and year, classification and year, or author, keyword and year), but it is not possible to search for more than one author or keyword at a time.

Once a title has been selected, the relevant data are displayed. The upper half of the screen display shows the code number (to be used for ordering), numeric classification, year of publication, title, classification in words, author and/or editor; the lower half (the 'bibliographical file') repeats the title, with added subtitle, series (if any), edition (other than the first), date of publication, source (the relevant *Bollettino novità* number) and price in Lire. Place of publication and publisher information is excluded; this reflects the commercial origin of the database, but makes it of less value as a bibliographical tool.

There are some limitations which should be noted. First, a search under classification by chronological period alone reveals that fewer than half of the entries (4588 out of 9795) are specific to the broad period designation for the Classical Period. Additional references are to be found in the Prehistory and General subdivisions, but even so the total cannot be much more than 50% of the database. Second, it is perhaps inevitable that the subject classification (with only twenty-five headings) is insufficiently comprehensive; if one wanted information on temples, for example, it would be difficult to isolate the relevant entries from other works on architecture, unless the word 'temple' or its equivalent in another language was present in the title, and thus retrievable through keyword searching on the bibliographical file. Third, as in the case of the *Gnomon* database, no attempt has been made to bring the different forms used for headings—particularly those for classical authors—into a standard form, and they reflect what is found on the title page. Accordingly, four separate forms are used for Aristotle, and, because of the limitation on multiple searches of the same field and on truncation noted above, four separate searches are

therefore necessary to retrieve all the information. Fourth, it is not possible to download information to a disk file (although it can be stored internally), and the printed output is limited to records which have been selected for order, and which are therefore printed out in the form of dated orders addressed to "L'Erma" di Bretschneider.

The instruction manual is generally clear and concise; the Italian- and English-language versions are printed on facing pages, so that the occasional obscurity in English may be clarified by reference to the Italian. It lacks an index, but includes useful information on the structure of the database, including the classification, and details of ordering procedures.

Dyabola

Only a brief description can be included here. The database may be installed from the program disk or from the CD-ROM, and there are separate instructions for network installation. The program will support the modern Greek alphabet and an extended character set for European languages. Although it operates in English, French, German or Italian, some features (such as keywords) are not fully available in all four languages. An aspect which may be useful for libraries is the option of including local data, such as shelf marks/call numbers, which can be used as a search option. The other seven options are subject, keyword (for subjects), author, title, series, periodicals, or any part of the title. It is not possible to perform a free text search on any part of the database as it is in *Gnomon*, but the results of different types of search can be combined.

Subject searching is possible in accordance with the structured subject headings (similar in concept to the *Gnomon* hierarchical thesaurus); there are 35 terms at the initial level, and at this and subsequent levels, an asterisk against the reference number for each heading indicates that further subdivisions are available. In some instances, links to keywords are provided: examples of this are the general subdivisions 'other themes' under 'iconography' and 'sites' under 'topography'. Keyword searching is applicable to classical names (geographical, historical or mythological) and to modern place names (for conference venues) or personal names (Festschrift recipients). For author searches, it is sufficient to enter the initial letters of the surname (as in *Herakles*) and an alphabetical list is displayed; titles and series are listed similarly, but are truncated. Searching for periodicals is possible either by entering the standard abbreviation or the full title. The last option, searching for any part of the title, involves an additional stage for specifying the level of searching ('exact spelling', for example).

The user is always prompted to give the search result file a name, and to specify whether the whole chronological range of the database, or selected years only, should be searched. Information is shown on the screen in the form of display windows. The result files from successive searches are displayed in a window to the right of the screen. Individual references are displayed in another window to the left. It is possible to call up information to enhance the bibliographical data on display: for collections of articles in book form the contents can be displayed; abbreviated journal references can be expanded; the full range of subject headings for each title, or book reviews, or corporate bodies (for conferences) can also be retrieved in this way. It is possible to print individual references directly from the display screen (as in *Gnomon*).

Searches may be combined by using the 'tools' option from the main menu screen; they can be saved, reloaded and modified. For printing an Epson LQ-mode dot matrix (or fully compatible) printer is specified; for use with other printers, the results must be downloaded and this will result in the loss of the extended character set.

Conclusion and summary
Both the databases reviewed have points in their favour; neither is ideal. With *Gnomon* I have the feeling that a potentially useful database is struggling to escape from an operating program which hinders it at nearly every stage; and that the standard of accuracy is not what users have come to expect from the valuable printed bibliographies in the journal source. The instruction manual is inadequate. Nonetheless, the product has some helpful features, allows quick (if not straightforward) searching, and is reasonably priced for libraries and departments. I suspect that the annual subscription price is a little high for many individuals; they may be better advised to wait a little longer in order to compare the CD-ROM version (and to compare that with the *Database of Classical Bibliography*), or to watch the development of the Internet site, if their main interest is in current bibliography. *Herakles* is straightforward to use, but limited both in its scope other than as a general bibliography of art or archaeology and in the use which can be made of it. It may be convenient for libraries or individuals who regularly order books from "L'Erma" di Bretschneider. For scholars working in the areas of classical art or archaeology access to *Dyabola* is likely to prove more attractive, by reason of its much greater scope and versatility; but the cost is correspondingly much higher.[5]

                                                      G.H. WHITAKER
Glasgow University Library

[5] Libraries planning to order any database product, but particularly CD-ROM sources, will know that it is necessary to consult technical staff on the requirements for installing and running these; the same applies to departments or to individuals. As libraries now find, the purchase of such products entails a continuing need to invest in hardware or software upgrades; again, the same applies to departments or to individuals.

GILL (C.) and WISEMAN (T.P.) *Ed.* **Lies and fiction in the ancient world.** U of Exeter P, 1993. Pp. xviii + 263. £26.50.

When the Muses met Hesiod on Mount Helicon they told him that they knew how to say many false things that are like the truth, but also how to tell the truth when they wished: ἴδμεν ψεύδεα πολλὰ λέγειν ἐτύμοισιν ὁμοῖα, / ἴδμεν δ' εὖτ' ἐθέλωμεν ἀληθέα γηρύσασθαι (*Theog.* 27-8). What do they mean by this enigmatic statement, and how are we to interpret the words ψεύδεα...ἐτύμοισιν ὁμοῖα? Do they mean that they know how to tell lies which poets (and their listeners) believe to be true, or do they imply that they

can inspire utterances which are neither true, nor false, but in some sense fictional? Here we are confronted with the key problem which this collection of essays sets out to explore: how far did ancient authors distinguish between lies and fiction, and when, if at all, did the ancient world develop a concept of fiction which corresponds to the modern understanding of the term?

E.L. Bowie's opening chapter considers the question in relation to early Greek poetry. Against the view that the archaic poets saw themselves primarily as preservers of society's collective memory whose function was to transmit traditional truths, B. argues that already in the early period there are indications that poets were well aware of their powers of invention. In the *Odyssey* Odysseus' lying tales are likened to the plausible ψεύδεα of a poet in words which resemble those of Hesiod's Muses (*Od.* 19.203). The self-reflexive nature of the poem, with its bard-like hero and its emphasis on story-telling, suggests that the *Odyssey* poet himself was not unconscious of the fictional status of his own composition. Later, in Stesichorus' *Palinode*, we have a clear case of a poet who explicitly presents his own made-up version of a traditional legend. And further evidence for the development of an interest in the fictional potential of poetic discourse is provided by the various first person statements of the 'lyric I' in archaic Greek poetry.

The following chapter by Christopher Gill, 'Plato on falsehood—not fiction', appears to come to the opposite conclusion. G. points out that we do not need the concept of fiction in order to make sense of Plato's critique of poetry, and he regards Plato's lack of interest in the lies/fiction distinction as symptomatic of Greek culture as a whole, which places greater emphasis on the ethical value of fictional statements, than on the nature of their reality. Whilst he argues convincingly that Plato's treatment of myth, both his own and that of the poets, centres on ethical issues rather than on questions of fictionality, Plato's practice of drawing attention to the ambiguous truth status of his own myths, and sometimes indeed of his own dialogues, positively invites speculation about the role of fiction in his writing.

Issues of fact, fiction and falsehood in ancient historiography are the focus of J.L. Moles' chapter on 'Truth and untruth in Herodotus and Thucydides'. M.'s detailed analysis of the prefaces of these two authors shows how they present themselves as inheritors of the epic tradition in their task of commemorating the deeds of the past, and as innovators in their search to express the truth about events in a way that distinguishes them from their poetic predecessors. But the differing notions of historical truth which emerge from their writings involve no clear cut distinction between fact and fiction, a theme which is further explored by Peter Wiseman in his discussion of the criticisms levelled against 'lying historians' in the Hellenistic and Roman world. From a modern perspective the techniques of rhetoric, drama and imaginative discourse employed by ancient historians at times seem more akin to those of the historical novelist than the historian proper. But does it therefore follow that the conception of truth in ancient historiography is significantly different from our own?

The question of how far the concept of fiction was developed in antiquity becomes most pressing in relation to the ancient novel, a genre of literature which we would regard as purely fictional. The narrative strategies used by these writers and the reading practices which they imply, perceptively analysed by Andrew Laird and J.R. Morgan, suggest a sophisticated awareness of the way in which fiction works. Yet ancient critics never mention the novel, nor do we find any recognition of fiction as a literary genre in ancient critical theory. Why this should be so remains a puzzling question. Undoubtedly the priorities of ancient criticism reflect a world in which literature is viewed as a means of conveying shared ethical values. But this predominantly ethical focus does not preclude an interest in the nature of fictional discourse. If the range of ideas developed by ancient writers does not precisely correspond to modern categories, that is hardly surprising: as Michael Wood and D.C. Feeney argue, the boundaries between fact, fiction and falsehood are culturally determined and change over time. This book explores the varying ways in which these categories were constructed in the ancient world, and in the process raises important questions about the definition of fiction in contemporary culture.

PENELOPE MURRAY
University of Warwick

PRATT (L.H.) **Lying and poetry from Homer to Pindar: falsehood and deception in archaic Greek poetics.** Ann Arbor; U of Michigan P, 1993. Pp. ix + 180.

This lucid and intelligent book investigates the relationship between poets and liars in early Greek poetry, and challenges the assumption that there was no concept of poetic fiction in the archaic world. Recent scholarship has emphasised the commemorative function of poetry in the oral culture of early Greece, attaching particular significance to the poet's claim to tell the truth. But Louise Pratt argues that this commitment to truth does not preclude an awareness of the poet as an artificer and shaper of fictions: indeed the agonal context of poetic performance in early Greece encouraged poets to produce competing versions of the truth, so that one poet's truth could easily become another poet's lie (witness the *Homeric Hymn to Dionysus*, 1-8 or Stesichorus' *Palinode*). And once we are faced with the possibility that poets lie, how do we know that this particular poet's version of the truth is true? The truth claims of poets are thus much more ambiguous than they first appear.

Furthermore, we need to distinguish between different types of poetic truth, and in particular between factual truth and what one might call wisdom or general truths. The claim that the poet preserves accurate factual information about the past (as implied e.g. by the invocation to the Muses before the catalogue of ships at *Il.* 2.484) is distinct from the view of the poet as an authority on ethical matters that we find in Hesiod or Solon, and from the concern of encomiastic poets such as Bacchylides and Pindar to establish the validity and appropriateness of the praises which they offer their patrons. P. argues that in all these cases the truth claims of poets refer to the particular contexts in which they

are embedded, rather than to the nature of poetic narrative in general, and therefore should not be regarded as evidence for a generic association between poetry and truth. When poets do speak about the function of poetry in general, it is pleasure rather than truth which is emphasised.

P.'s insistence on the importance of the connection between poetry and lying in early Greek culture is hardly controversial, and most people would agree that poets, at least from the *Odyssey* onwards, were well aware of their ability to craft and fashion their narratives. But does this amount to an appreciation of the fictionality of poetic discourse? Indeed can we speak of a notion of fiction as opposed to lies when the Greek language itself did not distinguish between these categories? P. finds evidence for an idea of fiction in the value attached to certain kinds of lying and deception in archaic Greek poetry, arguing that when the authors of e.g. the *Odyssey* or the Homeric *Hymn to Hermes* create affinities between poets and liars, and celebrate the positive qualities of the latter, these authors are affirming the fictionality of their own poetry. Certainly Odysseus' capacity to charm and persuade his audience into believing that what he says is true, regardless of its veracity, raises the (for us) important question of what it means to believe in fictional stories, but was this a central issue for Homer and his audience?

I agree with P. that there are indications in early Greek poetry of an appreciation of what we would call fictionality, but what is less clear is the extent to which the fact/fiction distinction mattered at this period. Like Gill in the volume reviewed above, P. emphasises the ethical focus of ancient poetics: when Plato criticises poets for telling ψεύδεα what concerns him is not the fact that their stories are false as narratives, but rather that they convey the wrong ethical messages, and in this respect at least, Plato is not untypical. Whether we should regard these ψεύδεα as 'lies' or 'fiction' remains an open question. The problem of where to draw the boundaries between these categories is no doubt a modern preoccupation rather than an ancient one; but, as this book shows, many of the issues which arise in modern discussions of the nature of poetic fiction are prefigured in the connection between poetry and lying developed by the early poets of archaic Greece.

PENELOPE MURRAY
University of Warwick

KAHANE (A.) **The interpretation of order: a study in the poetics of Homeric repetition.** Oxford UP, 1994. Pp. xi + 190. £25.

Ever since its inception the oral-traditional approach to Homeric diction has been taken (not altogether justly) to undercut a literary approach to the Homeric style. The harder the Parryism the deeper seemed to be the undercutting and the deeper the sensitive reader's resentment, especially where it was felt that the placing of words owed more to art than to formular composition. There is no simple, or single, model of the Homeric style. So much is now clear. The enterprise on which Kahane is embarked rests more easily on Visser's model (*Homer-ische Versifikations-technik* [Frankfurt 1988]), operating with a key element (which may be a word) that determines the remainder of the phrase and/or sentence, than on any model that assigns priority to formulae.

It is often the case that sense-units (formulae) and metrical units (cola) coincide or, as K. prefers to put it, the patterns of word-ends and sense-pauses within the hexameter converge, but not infrequently the sense-units, even traditional sense-units, override caesurae and line-ends. Can anyone be deaf to the effect of enjambement? Or to the smooth flow engendered by coincidence of sense and colon? Or to the disturbed harmony in the verses of an impassioned speaker? K. has only to point out this obvious fact at the beginning of this important monograph to establish the point: even in the hardest version of Parryism that anyone would nowadays dare to maintain there is room for the placing of words itself to be part of the meaning of the poetry. Nor would anyone dispute, or summon theory to justify, the suggestion that it is the conformity of the initial placing of μῆνιν (Achilles' μῆνις) at *Il.* 19.75 that echoes the placing of μῆνιν at *Il.* 1.1 and adds meaning to the later use—and would make the addition of a complement (οὐλομένην) otiose.

The realisation of such effects depends on the 'phonostyle', by which K. means that the effect is latent, waiting for the skilled reciter or the sensitive inner ear. How much is latent? K. argues that the programmatic use of μῆνιν, in that case and in that position, at *Il.* 1.1 must be an instance of 'pattern-deixis' and 'anaphora' (in the linguistic sense), that is to say, accusative μῆνιν is 'marked' from that point as an allusion to the thematic wrath of the *Iliad*. And sure enough it is on the poet's mind, with six occurrences out of nine in that case and position against none in the *Odyssey*. How does this work for the first word of the *Odyssey*? Odyssean ἄνδρα has a certain liking for the initial position (11 times out of 32 occurrences), but unlike μῆνιν, ἄνδρα is not a distinctive word. Can the marking be strong enough to evoke *Od.* 1.1 every time? As a test I suggest the translation 'hero' for initial ἄνδρα. There is a possible enhancement of meaning in nine instances—but not at *Od.* 22.32 where ἄνδρα κατακτεῖ-ναι is a formula displaced from the verse-end by the form of the infinitive.

The central point of K.'s methodology is that the marking is achieved by position in the verse, and it is a point with which many will take issue. Position in the verse is also position in a sentence, an ambiguity that is often concealed by the coincident boundaries of verse and sentence in Homeric style. How crucial is this ambiguity is apparent when the formula 'marked *versus* unmarked' is applied to the placing of names in the vocative. K. posits a neutral or default position, at the head of the *verse*, on the assumption that the point of the vocative is merely to draw the addressee's attention; a medial or terminal position is then 'marked' and acquires significance. In the most general way the function of the vocative is to establish a rapport between speaker and addressee. It is therefore placed early in the *sentence*, if the speaker has no ulterior motivation, especially in formal discourse, e.g. *Il.* 9.308. (In familiar, or would-be familiar, discourse it may yield the

initial position, for example, to an imperative or an interrogative word, e.g. *Il.* 9.225.) Since the Homeric habit is to begin direct discourse with a new verse the vocative falls also at or near the beginning of the verse. But the initial position is assertive; the deferential Phoenix, *Il.* 9.434, therefore postpones his address, *cf.* the ingratiating addresses at 485 and 494, while the urgent appeals at 496 and 513 bring the vocative forward. Achilles and Odysseus, however, are often final in the vocative whatever the nuance. Metre plays its part here, of course, but K.'s concern (as he reiterates) is with effects not causes. Is the effect of the final placing to create a marked form, the mark of a mighty hero?

A final placing is characteristic on a crude count of the personal name as subject. Statistics, of course, are always misleading! It is a mere slip that K. counts 23 final occurrences of Νέστωρ as 61% of a total of 50 (the correct ciphers are 36 out of 59, which gives indeed 61%). However, 22 of the final occurrences are occasioned by the formular verses that introduce speech or resume the narrative after it. The residue, 14 final occurrences out of 37 or 38%, is less impressively verse-final. Whatever the cause the effect, K. argues, is that the final placing of personal names in such archetypal epic verses as τὸν δ' ἀπαμειβόμενος... characterizes them as heroes. The boy Telemakhos and the despicable suitors, Antinoos and Eurumakhos, of course, do not enjoy this metrical advantage.

This is a clearly reasoned and thought-provoking book. K. does not claim proof for his theses, except insofar as the enhanced appreciation of students of Homer is a proof. It does not matter that K. is sometimes over-indulgent towards the interpretative power of his method; his monograph is an important demonstration that the oil and vinegar of formular composition and literary intention are after all perfectly compatible.

J.B. HAINSWORTH

New College, Oxford

STANLEY (K.) **The shield of Homer: narrative structure in the *Iliad*.** Princeton UP, 1993. Pp. xii + 470. £30.

This book is perhaps more accurately described by its subtitle, *Narrative structure in the Iliad*. Stanley's basic thesis appears to be that there were two 'Homers' responsible for the text of the *Iliad*, a 'founder' and an 'expositor'. The former stands for the epic as established by eighth century oral tradition, the latter (i.e. the version of the poem which we possess) a calculated, detailed, revision and restructuring of the poem, which happened during the sixth century. This revision took place in a literary context. 'To the temporal aspect of oral epic was gradually joined that of literary space and thus of literary form, with extension and further fixation of meaning through the recoding devices we have seen in our poet's rearrangements, expansions, and recontextualizations of earlier material' (296).

In support of this thesis S. offers an exhaustive, book-by-book, structural analysis of the entire poem. His method is to conduct a survey of ring-composition within (sections of) individual books and groups of books, with all of the expected consequences and conclusions to be drawn from the identification of such structures. His overall aim is to uncover the imprint of a master-editor and, to this end, many diagrams are provided. The scholarship which S. brings to bear on such a task is formidable: the reader will find notes and bibliography totalling 150 pages for a main text which is less than 300 pages in length. S. is at his best in his analysis of those sections of the text which are, by their very nature, rigidly structured, namely the *Shield* and *Catalogue of ships*. In the course of his larger analysis he also makes useful observations on, *inter alia*, the *Doloneia*, the chthonic aspects of Book 24, and the question of book-divisions in the poem. Lastly, as one would expect, his grasp of issues pertaining to oral-formulaic theory is not to be surpassed.

My reservations about this book concern the methodology. There is, of course, a myriad of ways in which the Homeric texts may be approached but, notwithstanding the general principle of each to his own taste, I suspect that many readers will find the detail of S.'s project somewhat arid and unappealing. In effect, S. analyses the *Iliad* as if it were a work of narrative science rather than treating it as a work of narrative art. In this regard it is interesting that the author, in his own defence, quotes Schlegel on p. 38:

But it is no less necessary to be able to abstract from all the details, to have a loose general concept of the work, survey it *en bloc*, and grasp it as a whole, perceive even its most hidden parts, and make connections between the most remote corners. We must rise above our own affection for the work, and in our thoughts be able to destroy what we adore; otherwise, whatever our talents, we would lack a sense of the whole.

Even leaving aside the issue of methodology, however, S.'s Casaubon-like search for the key to all narrative structure in the *Iliad*, while throwing up some interesting ideas, inflicts upon the reader schemes of such structural complexity that, at times, his book becomes, to all intents and purposes, unreadable. Admittedly it is not necessarily the easiest of critical tasks to present detailed formulaic analyses of the Homeric texts in a user-friendly format, but S. in striving to prove his thesis runs the risk of crushing it beneath the dead hand of his diagrammatic systems. *The Shield of Homer* has some worthwhile points to make, but it is a moot point whether the average reader will be willing to devote the time necessary in order to decipher them.

R.J. CLARE

University of Leeds

YAMAGATA (N.) **Homeric morality.** Leiden, Brill, 1993. Pp. xiv + 261. Fl. 25.

This book (originally a London University doctoral thesis) is divided into two parts, the first (Chs. I-VI) dealing with 'Morality of the Homeric gods', the second, and somewhat longer (Chs. VII-XI), with 'Morality of Homeric man'. 'No attempt is made to distinguish the Iliadic and Odyssean moralities. This does not presuppose, however, that Homeric morality is uniform throughout the two epics, but merely reflects the fact that Homer *was* treated as a unity by later Greeks' (XI). Ch. I, 'Moral functions attributed to the gods', concludes (21) that while '[p]ious Homeric men seem to believe in the gods' morality', in fact 'the gods' moral functions do not meet much of human expectation'. Four 'possible cases of the gods' moral concern' (*ibid.*) then receive detailed consideration in a chapter apiece: the fall of Troy; the death of the Suitors; Phoenix's remarks about *Litai* at *Il.* 9.502 ff.; and the reference to Zeus' wrath against unrighteous judges at *Il.* 16.384 ff. Ch. VI, 'Divine anger and morality', argues that what determines the gods' reaction to human conduct is above all their sense of *moira* and concern for *time*, and reaches the following general conclusion: 'The gods do have some sense of morality, but its focus is always on [*moira*]. Unless what [*moira*] bids coincides with the moral virtue of men, the gods do not behave as, or rather they do not appear to be, defenders of human morality'. (101) The first two chapters of Part Two, 'Fate, gods and men' and 'Honour and revenge', pick up and develop the themes of ch. VI; ch. IX, 'Forces that restrain human behaviour', examines the terms *erinus, nemesis, aidos, sebas*, and *eleos*; ch. X, 'Good and bad', *inter alia* the terms *arete, agathos, esthlos, aristos*, and *kakos*; and ch. XI, 'Seemly and unseemly', the terms *kalos* and *aischros*. A concluding chapter summarizes the argument of the book as a whole, and sums up its conclusions thus: 'Homeric morality consists of two major sub-categories, divine morality based on [*moira*], and human morality based on [*themis*] and [*dike*]. The latter is further divided into morality in peace among one's friends and that in war among one's enemies. However, there is one ... element which overrides the boundary between men and gods, and that between friends and enemies, namely, [*eleos*], which is an outstanding characteristic of Homer and is completely absent in Hesiod' (243). There follow a Bibliography, a General Index, and an Index of Passages Cited (which seems in fact to be an index of passages quoted). Greek, of which there is, understandably, a lot, is rarely translated and never transliterated; there are real footnotes.

Yamagata is of course engaging in a long-standing debate; indeed, she sees her book as having 'turned out to be a sustained critique' of two major contributions to that debate, Adkins' *Merit and responsibility* and Lloyd-Jones' *The justice of Zeus* (XI). If what Y. herself has to offer is a good deal less incisive and coherent than it might have been, this is above all because, rather surprisingly, Y. takes the term 'morality' so much for granted that, far from discussing how she proposes to use it, she nowhere makes clear what precisely she takes it to mean. Moreover, Y. seems to me generally not very subtle in her approach to religious commitment, and sometimes rather mechanical in her handling of particular passages of what are, after all, *poems*. The point, and presentation, of the various lexical investigations in Part Two are not always entirely clear; thus on 226 Y. lists, in no particular order that I could discern, some sixty 'material objects' characterized by Homer as *kalos*.

It is wholly unsurprising that a book written in (generally serviceable) English by a Japanese scholar, and published in the Netherlands, should be pervasively marred by infelicities of expression; it is though a pity, and the result is in places not merely irritation, but confusion.

R.I. WINTON

University of Nottingham

ZANKER (G.) **The heart of Achilles: characterization and personal ethics in the *Iliad*.** Ann Arbor: U of Michigan P, 1994. Pp. viii + 174. $34.50.

Graham Zanker sets out to explain the social and ethical system that motivates Iliadic warriors to co-operate with each other, and then to understand Achilles' behaviour in the light of that code. The first part of the argument is filtered through reactions to other scholars' work, especially A.W.H. Adkins' *Merit and responsibility* (1960). Z. challenges 'the Adkinsian analysis' (28), according to which Iliadic society is driven above all by the selfish imperative of the need for τιμή and κλέος, on the grounds that he can show us that warriors are also liable to act from purely emotional motives. This leads to the main treatment. At the dramatic date of the *Iliad*, when the Achaeans in particular have been 'brutalised' by nine years of war, the tension between the two motives for action produces personal folly and social breakdown. Achilles and Hector are parallel examples of this, because each acts destructively out of too great desire for personal τιμή above the common good. Achilles was mild and gentle before his quarrel with Agamemnon, but he endangers the Achaeans' safety when he abandons them in order to requite Agamemnon's insult; Hector, correspondingly, is motivated at first by the need to protect city and family, but at the end he hastens his people's end by throwing his life away because he fears loss of τιμή if he avoids Achilles. However, when Achilles returns to the fray he is no longer motivated by τιμή, whose value as a social ideal he has rejected in his conversation with the Embassy. What drives him now is affective emotion—desire to avenge his friend and sate his anger, and above all the certainty that his own death is approaching. In turn this mood heightens into the savagery of his treatment of Hector, but the other side of his new sympathy with his emotions appears when he shows mercy and generosity to Priam. All this goes to show that the pursuit of honour and fame is not everything, and that Homeric heroes are also capable of love, hate and pure generosity.

So stated, this is reasonable enough, but there is much that worries me in the way the argument is presented. I cannot grasp the basis of Z.'s methodology. He wants to give us 'a text-based reading' (43-5), but although there is much detailed summary of relevant passages there is often surprisingly little discussion of the words of the text beyond paraphrases. The trouble is that such an approach can easily slip into subjectivity unless it is provided with some external sounding-board, whether from comparative anthropology or Greek cultural history or close grappling with the Homeric vocabulary. I will restrict myself to one example (47-9). To show that the Achaeans have turned to 'excessively cruel reactions' and abandoned the normal values of

warrior ethics, Z. cites the episode (6.37-65) where Agamemnon advises Menelaus not to accept a ransom from the Trojan Adrestus, who is clasping his knees as a suppliant, and tells his brother that no Trojan should be spared, 'not even the boy-child carried in his mother's womb'. What Z. does not mention is that Homer describes Agamemnon here as αἴσιμα παρειπών (6.62). On a straightforward reading, something is αἴσιμος if it is in accord with αἶσα, with the proper order or limit of things: if this is right, then Homer is telling us straight out that Menelaus does not breach any fixed norms of behaviour by killing the suppliant as he does. Z. has not simply overlooked these words, because in a very different context fifty pages later he cites them in a footnote. There he lists a number of discussions of them, all of which interpret αἴσιμα παρειπών in contradictory ways. One of these discussions (S. Goldhill, *Hermes* 118 [1990] 373-6) suggests that the advice is αἴσιμα because it will bring about Adrestus' death, his αἴσιμον ἦμαρ, which at a pinch would allow Z. to interpret Agamemnon's speech in the way he does; but its argument is very subtle and difficult, and if Z. has decided to follow it he ought to tell us so in his interpretation of the passage itself. That he declines to face the word there is an indication, I think, of the impulse that drives his whole study: an honest desire to find a fixed moral code in Homer that enjoins mercy and condemns vindictive anger. Z. has to argue that this code is established in the background of the Iliadic world but has been temporarily distorted at the time of the action. But indications of the existence of this code are very hard to locate, so that Z. has to return repeatedly to a very few examples of past acts of generosity referred to in the poem—notably the fact that Achilles ransomed Lycaon and did not mistreat the body of Eetion after killing him (see 21.34-48, 6.415-420). After reading the book twice I cannot believe that the argument holds water, if only because Z. has not produced a convincing explanation as to where this code is supposed to have existed—in the poet's mind, in the ethics of his audience, in other epic poems before the *Iliad*, or somewhere else under the sun. It remains possible for the reader to object that there is no reason to believe that military ethics are any more rigidly encoded in the invented world of Greek epic than in a real-life social milieu.

MICHAEL CLARKE

University of Manchester

AUSTIN (N.) **Helen of Troy and her shameless phantom.** Ithaca: Cornell UP, 1994. Pp. xiv + 223. £24.95.

Few things in Greek literature are as strange as Stesichorus' *Palinode*, the story that Helen never went to Troy and that the war was fought around an empty phantom, an εἴδωλον (frr. 192-3 Page). In this vigorous study Norman Austin fits that poem into a sequence of shifting images of Helen extending from the *Iliad* and *Odyssey* to Euripides' *Helen*. The central point is that throughout the tradition Helen embraces two conflicting identities: on the one hand the familiar arch-adulteress and on the other a fully-fledged goddess worshipped in numerous regional cults. The successive versions of her story make sense of this ambiguity in changing ways.

A. finds traces of Helen's divinity already in the *Odyssey*, not only in her mysterious powers with drugs and mimicry but also in the implication that it is through her that Menelaus will become immortal (οὕνεκ' ἔχεις Ἑλένην καί σφιν γαμβρὸς Διός ἐσσι, 4.569). In the *Iliad*, however, she is reduced to a cipher as Aphrodite's creature and the embodiment of compulsive sexuality. From the Helen who is both prize and spectator of the heroes' duel in the *Teichoscopia* (3.121 ff.) A. moves ingeniously to Sappho (fr. 16 Lobel-Page), where the situation is reversed. Just as Sappho values her beloved above all the pomp of armies, so Helen chose Paris above home and family and the best of husbands: here Helen presides over a contest where she is not the prize but the judge. A. isolates a nice textual problem concealed in Page's edition in *Lyrica Graeca Selecta* (Oxford 1968):

> ...ἀ γὰρ πόλυ περσκέθοισα 6
> κάλλος [ἀνθ]ρώπων Ἐλένα [τὸ]ν ἄνδρα
> τὸν [πανάρ]ιστον
> καλλ[ίποι]σ' ἔβα' ς Τροΐαν πλέοι[σα...

περσκέθοισα is explained as a scribal error for περσ–χέθοισα, so Helen is 'far excelling human beauty'. But in the papyrus only περσκ is legible at the end of l.6, and the shreds of the line-end give equal grounds for reading, περσκοπεῖσα, with Helen 'surveying all the beauty of mortals' and choosing Paris. This gives a stronger sense in the context and supports A.'s emphasis on Helen's free choice of lover; it seems to be through modesty that he holds back (58) from definitely proposing it against Page's reading. περσκοπεῖσα was read by Hunt in the original edition of the papyrus, and J.U. Powell's emendation to περσκέθοισα seems to have been motivated by nothing but Edwardian sensibility (*CQ* 9 [1915] 142-3). A.'s sensitive discussion is a reminder that textual criticism should be the servant of literary understanding rather than the reverse.

The core of the book, however, is A.'s analysis of the *Palinode* itself. He argues—convincingly in my view—that the effect of the εἴδωλον story was to harmonise local and Panhellenic traditions, reconciling the Iliadic Helen with the goddess who was worshipped in Stesichorus' native Sicily as well as in the more famous cult at Sparta. If the woman who burnt a thousand ships becomes an empty image, the reputation of the divine Helen is restored untarnished, and the tragedy of the Trojan war gains in starkness in one direction while being undermined in another. Inevitably A. can only guess at the relationship of this version to those of Herodotus (2.112-20) and of Euripides in the *Helen*. When Herodotus proposes that Paris left Helen in Egypt, and that the Greeks must have disbelieved the Trojans when they said they did not have her (2.120), it is easy to suppose (as I did before reading this book) that he is giving us the *Palinode* story with the fantastic part ironed out. However, A. holds that Stesichorus cannot have brought Helen to Egypt with Paris, since Plato's legend about the writing of the *Palinode* (*Phaedrus* 243a2-b7) implies that it must have completely exonerated her from blame. If Stesichorus' Helen had accom-

panied Paris as far as Egypt he would still have made her an adulteress. Consequently, A. argues that Herodotus introduced the theory that Helen stayed in Egypt, killing two birds with one stone by accounting for the mysterious cult of Aphrodite the Stranger at Memphis (112.2) and also explaining why the Trojans did not save their city from destruction by returning her to the Greeks. Euripides then borrowed from Herodotus as well as Stesichorus to invent his own version, where the εἴδωλον has been substituted at the very start of the affair and she herself has been moved to Egypt by Hera at the same moment (summarised, *Helen* 22-51).

Inevitably this is mostly guesswork, and it would be churlish to try to pick holes in A.'s careful reconstruction. Throughout, however, I was troubled by a more serious issue, namely A.'s assessment of the kind of creativity Stesichorus was engaged in when he used the motif of the εἴδωλον. The pivotal word in this book is 'revisionism': Stesichorus is seen as subversive of a fixed Homeric tradition, undermining it with the new intellectual freedom of the age of Ionian philosophy. A. even draws a parallel between Stesichorus reducing Helen of Troy to an εἴδωλον and Xenophanes reducing the traditional gods to empty idols (111-13). It seems to me that this misses the point that the device of substitution by an εἴδωλον is thoroughly traditional in itself. In epic there are two especially close parallels. In the *Iliad* Aphrodite whisks Aeneas from the battlefield and removes him to the Trojan citadel, letting the battle continue around the empty phantom (5.445-53), and in the Nekuia an εἴδωλον is introduced to explain how Heracles is visible in Hades when other myths tell of his translation to immortality on Olympus (11.601-4). A. is swayed by analyst criticism of a rather circular kind to suspect that these passages are additions originating in Stesichorus' own time (see 4 n. 2, 110-11). But is there any internal reason to exclude these passages from the original corpus of Homer? A. does not mention the εἴδωλον that Athena substitutes for Penelope's sister when sending her a dream (4.795-839), an episode whose authenticity is doubted by no-one, and it is doubly puzzling that he also seems (105-10) to accept the antiquity of the Hesiodic story that Iphimede (= Iphigeneia) was replaced by an εἴδωλον at Aulis (*Catalogue of women*, fr. 23a M-W; he does not discuss Endymion, fr. 260 M-W). If we allow the phantoms of Aeneas and Heracles to Homer, they can be seen as exactly prescribing the motif and story-pattern that Stesichorus used. From the first passage comes the image of the warriors raging around an empty phantom, from the second comes the use of an εἴδωλον to reconcile an epic story with a cultic myth. If this is right, it was *within* the Homeric ambit that Stesichorus found the materials for his new story, in much the same way as Pindar invokes the existing tradition about Ganymede to give shape to his retelling of the story of Tantalus and Pelops (*Olympian* 1.43). I suspect that in terms of its mythical grammar and vocabulary Stesichorus' 'revisionism' was less radical and less opposed to the traditions of Homeric narrative than A. suggests; but it is always easy to cast cold water on ideas as adventurous and thought-provoking as those in this book.

MICHAEL CLARKE
University of Manchester

Poiss (T.) **Momente der Einheit: Interpretationen zu Pindars Epinikion und Hölderlins *Andenken*.** Vienna: Österreichischen Akad. der Wissenschaften, 1993. Pp. 257.

Poiss skips from theme to theme in this book rather like Pindar himself in his odes, but underlying his researches is the familiar question, 'Wherein lies the unity of a Pindaric ode?'. We are given running commentaries on ten odes (*O*. 4, 11, 12, 14; *P*. 3, 4; *N*. 1, 2, 7, 9) and on the Hölderlin poem, complete with texts and translations (except in the case of *P*. 4). P. is a thoughtful and well-read critic, and one of the virtues of his piecemeal approach is that it acknowledges the heterogeneity of the odes and that different odes cohere in different ways. The thrust of his work is to remind us that much of Pindar's theme-jumping is contrived rather than spontaneous, designed to give the odes a pleasurable dynamic and dramatic quality and, if we look beneath the surface, to create correspondences and reinforce ideas; in sum, it is just when Pindar seems to be most unstructured that he is being most unifying: ἁρμονίη ἀφανὴς φανερῆς κρείττων.

Some examples: *N*. 2 curiously ends ἀδυμελεῖ δ' ἐξάρχετε φωνᾷ. What is this singing that is to begin? P. rightly takes the imperative not as pointing beyond the ode itself to further singing but as comparable to one of Pindar's many self-fulfilling uses of the future tense, 'begin with sweet voice' being substituted for e.g. 'continue to sing with sweet voice' for the sake of a thematic link-up with the start of the poem (ὅθεν περ καὶ ᾿Ομηρίδαι...ἄρχονται 1-3), and to reinforce the message of lines 6-12 that the victor has returned to the victorious ways begun by his ancestors. *O*. 14 is mainly an invocation of the Graces worshipped at Orchomenus, the victor's city; but towards the end of the poem Pindar orders Echo to report the news of the victory to the victor's dead father in Hades. But what seems like a change of theme is, P. convincingly suggests, not so; the link is the 'charm of song' theme, which has been latent in the poem from the start: the sweet news to be conveyed by Echo comes from the Graces themselves (σὺν γὰρ ὔμμιν τά τερπνά καὶ / τὰ γλυκέ' ἄνεται πάντα βροτοῖς, 5-6). And in *O*. 11 P. not implausibly sees the ode's last sentence (τὸ γὰρ ἐμφυὲς οὔτ' αἴθων ἀλώ-πηξ / οὔτ' ἐρίβρομοι λέοντες διαλλάξαιντο ἦθος, 19-20) as alluding to the enduring qualities of not only the recently mentioned Epizephyrian Locrians but also Pindar and his poetry, thus returning us to the theme of 4-6 in the first strophe and to the equation of poet and victor enigmatically expressed in line 10 (ἐκ θεοῦ δ' ἀνὴρ σοφαῖς ἀνθεῖ πραπίδεσσιν ὁμοίως).

So, seemingly disparate elements in Pindar's odes are unified, not in a superficial way through e.g. repetition of words or recurrent imagery, but at a deeper level; and what seems to be discrete *Momente* are in reality parts of an *Einheit*. In the penultimate section of the book P. shows that this way of looking at poetry works also for Friedrich Hölderlin's *Andenken*, sixty lines of reminiscences of Bordeaux composed at the beginning of the nineteenth century, a poem with affinities to *P*. 3 and whose meaning (like that of most poems) is greater than the sum of its parts.

P. is always penetrating, often original; one hopes that he will apply his approach to other Pindaric odes.

STEPHEN INSTONE
University College London

HEDREEN (G.M.) **Silens in Attic black-figure vase-painting: myth and performance.** Ann Arbor: U of Michigan P, 1992. Pp. x + 219 + ill. $39.50.

Satyrs (or silens, as Hedreen wishes us to call them) are a constant source of investigation, whether in literature or art. Euripides' *Cyclops* has been much examined recently with editions and productions, Sophocles' *Ichneutai* has been given an afterlife in Tony Harrison's *The Trackers of Oxyrhynchus*. In the field of art we have been asked to consider why satyrs are good to represent, and new vase finds continue to add to the list of possible illustrations of satyr-plays. H. takes a different line. He would have us consider how far back in time we can take the satyr-plays (or performances), i.e. can we get behind Pratinas in the late sixth century, was he the first known writer of satyr-plays or was he the first to write words for performance, what of satyrs in Dionysiac festival entertainments earlier in the century?

In order to do this, H. has had to look very closely at the many Attic black-figure vase scenes that include satyrs in their compositions. This involves looking at their general relation to Dionysos and to the nymphs (not maenads—see H., *JHS* 1994) that have a part to play in the company. He shows that the iconography of black-figure is different from that of the later red-figure and also more limited. H. takes as a basic tenet that the black-figure scenes are narrative, not symbolic, and so the satyrs, whether with Dionysos, accompanying the return of Hephaistos, involved in the Ariadne story or in any other association, should always be understood as part of a narrative (however scant the evidence for a story may be). So the questions arise: what are they doing in these stories, why in these and no others, is it possible that they are part of a performance, even in the middle of the sixth century, and how might one decide?

H. looks closely at the stories and takes a different line from Carpenter (*Dionysian imagery in archaic Greek art*, 1986) who studied the images pragmatically and refused to take to more than modest flight. In chs. I, II and III H. allows himself to speculate and to press into service small details in the images in an attempt to construct more imaginative narratives, coming to the conclusion that the island of Naxos can be shown to figure prominently in the myths, with a vineyard, a fabulous wine fountain, a spring where silens and nymphs met, etc. H. sees this 'Naxian cycle' as linked to the Athenian wine festivals of the Anthesteria and the Oschophoria.

In the second half of his thesis (chs. IV, V and VI), H. explores the relationship of these early satyr myths to the practice of dressing up and performing in honour of Dionysos. What H. is concerned to prove is the falsity of the premise that 'all scenes of silens predating 520 BC were based on myth, nondramatic poetry, or fantasy, but not on satyric performances' (116). In order to do this, H. discusses the costume of the satyrs and shows how in later vase-painting costume is not a wholly necessary prerequisite for presenting satyrs in performance, so he maintains (perhaps illogically) that undressed satyrs may be 'performing' in the earlier sixth century. An interesting point that H. makes is that the 'regimentation' of satyrs should be taken to indicate performance—satyrs are not so easily given to that form of group activity in 'real life'. So black-figure vases are combed for costume (present or absent), the aulos-accompaniment and regimentation, and H. demonstrates that on that basis satyric performances can be traced back into the first half of the sixth century, right to the earliest instances of satyrs in imagery. So 520 BC may still represent a pivotal date for the start of satyr-plays and still be connected with Pratinas, but prior to that date there were satyr performances which consisted of choral dancing with men dressed up as satyrs (and maybe as nymphs as well) to sing and dance the stories of Dionysos, with, it is suggested, non-choral elements as a possibility.

With the publication of this book, it will be necessary to rethink, even if not rewrite, the beginnings of Athenian drama. It is still difficult to imagine what these early performances looked or sounded like, but H. has certainly given us food for thought on the subject. Nor is the book confined, as its title forecasts, to Attic black-figure; H. considers Laconian, Corinthian, Boeotian, 'Chalcidian', East Greek as well as Attic red-figure. It is a rich presentation with detailed information on the literary and artistic evidence, and a good sprinkling of vase illustrations.

B.A. SPARKES

University of Southampton

THIEL (R.) **Chor und tragische Handlung im 'Agamemnon' des Aischylos. (Beiträge zur Altertumskunde, 35.)** Stuttgart: Teubner, 1993. Pp. xxiii + 468. DM 128.

Although this very large book is concerned primarily with the role of the Chorus in *Agamemnon*, Thiel recognises (146, 157) that the choral utterances can hardly be considered in isolation from their context, and he provides a long discussion of the third episode, and in particular of the 'carpet'-scene, in which the Chorus plays no part at all. His intention, as announced at the beginning, is to demonstrate that the Chorus is not simply the mouthpiece or instrument of the poet, but a consistent *dramatis persona*, all of whose utterances, in both lyric and dialogue passages, are to be interpreted in terms of its knowledge at the various stages of the play—a doubtless correct view which is, I think, more widely held than he suggests. In fact for much of the book we lose sight of this question, while T. concentrates on his exhaustive analysis of every choral passage in turn, with the parodos alone receiving 133 pages including a full text, *apparatus criticus*, and German facing translation. It is not clear to me why T. found it necessary to provide this for the parodos (but not for the other choral odes), and then to repeat some of the translation at appropriate points in the discussion.

T.'s other principal concern is with the personality and responsibility of Agamemnon. In his discussion of the parodos he concludes that there was no insoluble dilemma for Agamemnon at Aulis. Agamemnon simply makes the wrong choice because in his passionate desire for the expedition he becomes incapable of calculating carefully the consequences of his decision, and fails to recognise that the means (the sacrifice of Iphigeneia) are disproportionate to the end. Zeus does not command the expedition, but, because Paris deserves to be punished, merely guarantees its success should Agamemnon proceed with it, and Artemis does not demand the sacrifice: rather she makes it a condition of Agamemnon's success, in the hope that he will recognise that the cost is too high and will therefore abandon the expedition. Thus T. happily (60-1; but see also 389) eliminates the 'insoluble theological problems' of a situation in which the gods ensure that Agamemnon will be guilty whatever he decides to do. Not everyone will accept that this is a desirable simplification. For anyone who takes this line the problem is that three times (59, 61, 111) the Chorus says explicitly that Zeus *sends* the avengers, and T. does not convince me that this gives Agamemnon a right, but not a duty, or that the Chorus here is merely trying to reassure itself that the expedition was justified, and will therefore be successful. And, as for Agamemnon's supposed passion for the war, he makes too much of 48, 122-4, 230. For the 'carpet'-scene T. presents a similar interpretation. Agamemnon knows that σωφροσ–ύνη should prevent him from walking on the fabrics, but he allows himself to abandon his principles at the decisive moment, because he really wants this demonstration of his glory and success. Again he makes the wrong choice, because he is led to do what under other circumstances he would not have done, forgetting the danger inherent in his action. In this respect he is closer to Page's Agamemnon than to Fraenkel's, but for T. he is not an arrogant despot or a *hybristes*: rather he is to be seen as a good and god-fearing king, who falls victim to a *hamartia* in the Aristotelian sense. He could have acted otherwise, and so he must be held responsible. The rest of the trilogy is rarely mentioned, but it would be interesting to know if T. would want to explain Orestes' responsibility along similar lines.

One may question many of T.'s conclusions, and feel that he is too dependent on H. Neitzel, seventeen of whose articles appear in the Bibliography. It is surprising that he finds no underlying anxiety in the second stasimon. While it is true that the Chorus's reflections on *hybris* are ostensibly prompted by the fate of Paris and Troy, is the audience not expected to relate them also to Agamemnon, who is already waiting to make his dramatic entrance and to be greeted by the Chorus as πτολίπορθος (783)? But the strength of this book lies in its careful, thorough, and often sensitive detailed analysis, and in its criticism of others' views. Good examples are his treatment of the Cassandra-scene (the Chorus eventually comes to understand and to believe her prophecy of her own death, and to understand, but not to believe, her prophecy of Agamemnon's death), of the stichomythia between Agamemnon and Clytaemestra at 931-43, weakened only, I think, by an improbable interpretation of the MSS reading at 934), and of 1331-43. No future writer on the play can afford to ignore the book.

I could wish only that T. had presented his arguments a little more concisely and with less repetition (by contrast, his treatment of the Chorus's behaviour during Agamemnon's murder is disappointingly short). There is too much, often inconclusive, discussion of textual problems (the attempt to allow the lengthening of a short final syllable at 741, 768, 1470 is quite unconvincing). Do we really need nine pages on the difficult φέρει φέροντ' at 1562? The final chapter, entitled *Zusammenfassung* (421-56), is a repetition, rather than a summary, of everything that has gone before.

A.F. GARVIE

University of Glasgow

KNOEPFLER (D.) **Les Imagiers de l'Orestie. Milles ans d'art autour d'un mythe grec.** Zurich: Akanthus, 1993. Pp. 112 + ill. SFr. 65.

This admirable small book is described as the catalogue of an exhibition of some twenty vases from collections in Switzerland, France and Austria illustrating the *Oresteia* story, which formed part of the contribution of the museum and the University of Neuchâtel to the 700th anniversary celebrations of the Swiss Confederation in 1991. Rather unusually, it was published nearly two years after the original exhibition closed, to accompany a revived but reduced version at Bulle in 1993. The reason for this retrospective publication lies partly in the success of the show, partly in the lack of readily accessible yet comprehensive overview of the iconography of the story for the whole of its life, from Homer and before down to the Romans and beyond, for this work even touches on the Byzantine view of the *Oresteia*.

The book is in fact not an exhibition catalogue at all. It has its intellectual origins in a seminar of the University of Neuchâtel. Although the exhibition was restricted to vases in collections that are readily accessible to a Swiss university—and it is only possible to find which vases had a place in the exhibition from Knoepfler's introductory remarks—the book has become a far more comprehensive pictorial summary of the *Oresteia* as a whole. It is however almost entirely secondary, for K. does not regard himself as a classical archaeologist, and claims only to have been drawn into compiling the catalogue with reluctance: his usual pastures are epigraphic rather than iconographic. He relies very heavily though not exclusively on *LIMC*, and the bibliography for most pieces is very properly restricted to the *LIMC* references. But his book is accessible in a way that *LIMC* cannot be (and is not intended to be), and therein lies its great value, along with K.'s clear text and sympathetic descriptions, and the high quality of the illustrations and indeed of the overall production: every piece is photographed in black and white, and selected pieces, particularly from southern Italy, are shown in colour as well.

Such a book must restrict itself in its selection of pieces: despite its small size nearly all the usual repertoire is there, including some new pieces such as the Aegisthus Painter's krater in the Getty Museum and a recently discovered Cretan relief pithos fragment which

if it does depict the Death of Clytemnestra (I think it does) is very important as the first sure illustration of this scene before the later fifth century. Some unexpected pieces appear, such as the relief from Samothrace depicting Agamemnon, Talthybios and Epeios, new to me, which is included because of the light it throws on the herald's role. With space at a premium, it is curious that K. includes a few pieces over whose identity he is himself in doubt, and one can of course grumble at some of the omissions, which occasionally lead the author to some false conclusions—by leaving out the Jahn Painter's amphora in Philadelphia showing the death of Aegisthus K. ends up with a distorted picture of the Etruscan interest in the story, as well as of some of the implications of its late appearance in Athenian art, to which he very rightly draws attention in other respects.

There are a few other occasions where K. is perhaps led astray by his lack of first-hand acquaintance with the pieces he describes. For example, like many others before him, he uses the Gortyn pinax of the Death of Agamemnon as evidence for the early appearance of the 'net-cloak' in which Agamemnon is entrapped, but like them he has not studied the piece properly and seen that what appears to be a piece of cloth over the victim's head is merely a 'double-exposure' caused by slipping in the mould (later he too fails to distinguish between Aeschylus' use of the net as a simile and the cloak as a stage-prop). He reproduces Fittschen's reconstruction of the marvellous bronze mitra from Olympia depicting a young warrior in lion-head headgear approaching an enthroned woman without indicating clearly on the drawing that the woman on the left—'Electra', crucial to the interpretation—is purely hypothetical.

The book is divided into five main sections: the 'Prehistory of the *Oresteia*', 'Texts and monuments of the Archaic period', the 'Precursors of Aeschylus', the 'Aeschylean *Oresteia*', and the '*Oresteia* in Etruria and the Roman world', ending with a short concluding survey of the thousand years before the Renaissance during which the story was seemingly forgotten. Generally pieces are described chronologically within these sections, but this rule is not invariable, which can be confusing for those trying to follow the iconographic trail: the significance of the appearance of the lyre in the death of Aegisthus, and the link with the Orpheus iconography, is thereby all but lost.

There are very few misprints and technical blemishes: I sympathize with K. in his confusion over the order of my many initials (82, 84—elsewhere he gets them right!), and it is unfortunate that he has apparently followed a misprint introduced by Aris and Phillips into my own disastrous book in making Proteus' account of Agamemnon's fate begin at *Od.* iv 521 instead of 512 (19); the village in Cheshire after which the Apulian vase-painter is named is Tarporley, not Tarpoley; and Aeschylus himself would have found wry humour in the omission of the connecting line between Atreus and his progeny in the genealogical table on 13!

Yet these are minor cavils. There is a great deal that is good about this book. Although he only has space to touch on it, K. handles the political dimension sensitively, and he firmly and correctly detaches the Dokimasia Painter's krater from Aeschylus. The picture-story of the *Oresteia* has, rather surprisingly, never had the benefit of a brief, sympathetic and well-produced overview like this. Other iconographic surveys of the story, though much more detailed and comprehensive, have restricted themselves to the Archaic period or to the vases of southern Italy, and for that reason alone this book deserves a place not only in every university library but in the hands of all students of the *Oresteia* story. At this time when students are increasingly reluctant to read in languages other than their own, the author and his publishers would do well to consider translations at least into English and German.

One question still puzzles me, however: why K. chose to call the book and the exhibition before it, 'Les Imagiers de l'Orestie': an *imagier* is a painter of popular pictures, as indeed a vase-painter must have been, yet the focus throughout is almost always on the pictures rather than on the artists themselves.

A.J.N.W. PRAG

The Manchester Museum

PORTER (J.R.) **Studies in Euripides' Orestes**. (*Mnemosyne* Suppl. 128) Leiden: Brill, 1994. Pp. xiii + 364. Fl. 170, $109.75.

These studies have a clearly stated programme: to contest interpretations of *Orestes* variously founded in the conviction of Orestes' 'criminal insanity and moral folly', and the 'irony ... central to such interpretations' (43, 45).

Ch. 2 'General interpretation' follows a survey of the play's critical history. It concludes (97): '*Orestes* presents the picture of a world gone bizarrely awry, where the hero's expectations are constantly raised only to be cruelly dashed ... The resulting tensions and frustrations eventually lead Orestes to lash out in a manner reminiscent of Euripides' earlier tragic victims, but with an important difference. For in this case the sense of chaos and confusion that occasionally attends such revolts expands to envelop the last four hundred lines of the play ... Eventually the stress will become so great that it strains the boundaries of tragic convention itself until, in the end, the tragic potential of Orestes' predicament becomes lost amid the moral, political, and situational chaos of the late Euripidean stage'. We are left wondering whether we are to be edified, entertained or merely baffled by all this 'chaos' with 'loss of tragic potential' or whether it is the (perverse? unintended?) consequence of a dramatic art over which the dramatist has lost control.

Four further chapters offer supporting analysis of 'The Agon' (491-541, 544-604, 640-79), 'The Phrygian messenger', '*Orestes* 1503-36', 'The *Exodos*'. Of the eight appendices some are πάρεργα (1. 'A pro-satyric *Orestes*?', against C.W. Müller; 5. on 536-7 = 625-6, 6-8. on 544-50, 585-90 and 1344 ff.), but three are directly germane: 2. 'Madness and ΣΥΝΕΣΙΣ in *Orestes*'; 3. '*Orestes* 819-24 and the Second stasimon'; 4. 'Euripides and Thucydides 3.82-83'. The book ends with an immense and up-to-date Bibliography, 'Passages cited from *Orestes*' and 'Select Index.'

Ch. 1 is usefully comprehensive, but culpably misstates (42) what my commentary has propounded as the primary idea of the play: *not* 'Euripides' invention of the new and audacious attack on Helen, around which he crafts a suitable plot'; rather, his invention of a brilliantly ingenious plot *paradoxically culminating in Helen's apotheosis* (foreshadowed in *Helen*). Inadequate attention to the actual τέλος of the play vitiates also Ch. 6, and indeed the 'General Interpretation' in whose 'Conclusion' Helen has no place.

Much indeed of Ch. 2 is persuasive, on the sympathy generated by lines 1-469, on the shocking effect of Menelaus' betrayal and on 'the psychopathology of moral outrage' as a feature of this and other Euripidean plots (notably *Medea* and *Hecuba*). But eyebrows rise at the 'essentially innocent' hero (innocent of matricide?) 'unjustly condemned by the corrupt whim of the Argive mob' ... 'the vicious excesses that characterize the urban mob' (75). Even the naive and partisan narrator of 866 ff. (his loyalties are explicit, and it is *not* 'contrary to convention' that a messenger's report should display partisanship) does not allude to 'corruption' or 'vicious excesses'. The proceedings in the (partly epic-toned) ἀγορᾶς κύκλος are orderly, and different views are freely expressed. It is not surprising that the proposal of the admired αὐτουργός to crown Orestes as a benefactor does not prevail. One can properly pity a matricide, but only a god can (narrowly) exonerate him.

The Second Stasimon, preceding the assembly-trial, is literally central in the play; and it is confessedly 'a stumbling-block—P. deserves credit for honesty in highlighting it in Appendix 3—that the otherwise sympathetic chorus in 819 ff. appear to be condemning Orestes in extremely hostile terms as guilty of ἀσέβεια and παράνοια. After justly impugning all versions of the text, P. concludes: 'given these difficulties, and in view of the fact that the line clearly has suffered at the hands of later interpolators, 823 should be printed: †τὸ δ' αὖ κακουργεῖν† ἀσέβεια ποικίλα'. By all means obelise; but it is vain to shelter here behind 'interpolators'. The metre is well-preserved, and it is certain that *something* is here condemned as 'impious madness', shortly before matricide is declared to be the greatest, if also the most pitiable, νόσος (831 ff.). If the hostile terms are not aimed at Orestes himself, the target can only be persons who perversely regard matricide (as described in 819-22) as 'good' and/or 'fine'. This surely has a bearing on how we are to listen to the narration of the assembly-trial. [I hope to pursue elsewhere what we might now read in 823.]

Ch. 3 is good on forensic and supplicatory *topoi*, less so on how, with what purpose *and effect*, they are deployed. P. demonstrates that Orestes' ἀπολογία and ἱκεσία are in line with accepted strategies; but 544-604 remains ill-judged (by Orestes) in reply to 491-541, in that it explicitly *increases Tyndareus' anger* (607 ff.), and must have been composed by Euripides, in line with his plot, with that effect in mind. The rest of the book similarly contains much of value, while not seldom inviting disagreements.

Since the Preface concedes 'numerous ironies' in the play and 'irony' is prominent (negatively) in P.'s programme, it is a defect that 'irony' does not feature in the Index. One would have welcomed also some focus on 'paradox' and 'ambivalence' (the latter recurrent in the thematic epithet τλήμων, also absent from the Index).

In sum this is a solid, if overlong and in part blinkered, contribution to study of this much-studied play; in general well written (but P. is too fond of the adjective 'feckless' with an ill-defined range of meaning), and well proof-read (but 72 and 108 n. 24 repeatedly offer οὐκ (sic) ἑκόντες and οὐχ (sic) ἄκοντες).

C.W. WILLINK

Highgate, London

SCHWINDT (J.P.) **Das Motiv der "Tagesspanne": ein Beitrag zur Ästhetik der Zeitgestaltung im griechisch-römischen Drama**. Paderborn: F. Schöningh, 1994. Pp. 232. DM 44.

'Die Aufhellung des Handlungsgefüges (sc. eines Dramas), soweit es vermöge seiner zeitlichen Ordnung als Spannungsgefüge organisiert ist, insonderheit der Nachweis motivischen Gebrauches der 'Tagesspanne' als der dominierenden Zeitstrecke im Drama' (19) bildet den Schwerpunkt der Bonner, von O. Zwierlein angeregten Dissertation. Der Autor kann sich dabei auf mehrere Arbeiten des 19. Jahrunderts stützen (14, n. 5-8). Das wesentlich Neue von Schwindts Arbeit besteht darin, daß es ihm nicht darum geht, den berühmten Aristotelischen Satz, die Tragödie—im Gegensatz zum Epos—'versuche, möglichst in einem Sonnenumlauf sich abzuwickeln' (Poetik 1449b 12 f.) an den Texten der erhaltenen antiken Dramen positivistisch nachzuprüfen; vielmehr will S. die dramaturgische Funktion des 'Motivs der Tagesspanne' erhellen. Daß er angesichts der Fülle des Materials selektiv vorgeht und sich auf exemplarische Interpretationen beschränkt, ist zwar verständlich, aber trotzdem bedauerlich. Von Aischylos fehlen Cho. und Eum., von Sophokles Phil. und O. C.; Euripides ist mit 9 Stücken aus allen Schaffensperioden vertreten (Alc., Med., Hipp., Andr., Her., I.T., Or.). Daß S. auch die in der Autorschaft umstrittenen Stücke, (Aesch.) P.V. und (Eur.) Rhes. einbezieht, ist zwar verdienstvoll, angesichts der knappen Seite jedoch, die er P. V. widmet (44), hätte er auf dieses Stück jedenfalls auch verzichten können, zumal es zu seiner Fragestellung nichts beiträgt. Insgesamt erbringen jedoch die Abschnitte zu den griechischen Tragikern sehr schöne Detailinterpretationen und gelungene Beobachtungen zum Text (Soph. O.R. 1213 [61], 1524-30 [n. 166], El. 278 [n. 176], Eur. Med. 335f. [n. 220]) und zur Exegese einzelner Partien (oft steckt ein ganzer Schatz an Erklärungen in den Fußnoten, vgl. z.B. zu Aesch. Ag. auf 37-40). Häufig gelingt es S. den Zusammenhang zwischen der Zeitverwendung und der Gesamtkonzeption der Stücke überzeugend zu klären (insbesondere zur Bedeutung des 'Entscheidungstags' bei Soph.). Besonders hervorzuheben sind die Gegenüberstellungen, die S. zwischen den griechischen Originalen und den senecanischen Stücken vornimmt (Ag. 41 ff., Ps.-Sen. H. O. 55ff., Oed. 63 ff., Med. 89 ff., H.F. 111 ff., Phaedr. 122 ff.). Hier kann S. in überzeugender Weise durch die Darstellung der 'Zeitverwendung' bzw. des 'chronodramatischen Raums' (so S.s Neologismus 17) Wertvolles zum Unterschied zwischen griechischem und römischem Drama herausarbeiten und die Besonderheiten der senecanischen Dramaturgie herausstellen. Auf

eine Fehlinterpretation zu Sen. Med. 25 f. (93) sei hingewiesen: Medea wünscht mit dem Satz *parta iam, parta ultio est: / peperi* nicht, daß Jason 'von eigener Kinder Hand die Rache erleide', sondern sie deutet damit an, daß sie durch die Ermordung ihrer gemeinsamen Kinder Jason am meisten treffen könne (vgl. auch V. 40 *per viscera ipsa quaere supplicio viam*).

Wie S. bei der Auswahl der Komödien im 2. Teil seiner Arbeit verfahren ist, ist nicht ganz einsichtig (Men. Dysk.; Ter. Andr.; Plaut., Poen., Pseud., Pers., Most., Merc., Bacch.) (vgl. zur Begründung 22 f.). Vor allem enttäuscht, daß er sich in dem abschließenden Motivindex (188 ff.) allein auf die griechische Tragödie beschränkt. Der Hinweis auf die 'unlängst begonnene monumentale Kritik und Exegese des Komikers' Plautus durch O. Zwierlein, nach deren Abschluß man den römischen Komiker in Reinform, 'befreit von den Wucherungen einer entzündeten Phantasie', und in einem 'bündigeren Konversationstone', in 'gerafftrer Szenenführung' und in einer 'stärkeren chronodramatischen Konzentration' endlich vorliegen habe (23), dürfte eigentlich nicht genügen, um die Vielzahl methodischer Probleme, die mit der 'Plautusfrage' verbunden ist, vom Tisch zu wischen.

Der weitgesteckte Rahmen von S.s Arbeit läßt natürlich kaum zu, die Sekundärliteratur umfassend zu berücksichtigen. Es stört jedoch, wenn zu den Suppl. des Aischylos mit Bestimmtheit gesagt wird, sie seien das 1. Stück der Danaiden-Trilogie, ohne daß darauf hingewiesen wird, daß diese communis opinio in den letzten Jahren stark erschüttert wurde (vgl. M. Sicherl, *MH* 43 [1986] 81-110; die Arbeiten von W. Rösler, *RhM* 136 [1993] 1-22 und A.H. Sommerstein, *DRAMA* 3 [1995] 111-133 konnten S. noch nicht bekannt sein).

S.s Buch ist insgesamt als eine solide Motivuntersuchung zur griechisch-römischen *Tragödie* zu betrachten, deren Wert durch den Motivindex unterstrichen wird. Der Untertitel des Buches jedoch 'ein Beitrag zur Ästhetik der Zeitgestaltung im griechisch-römischen Drama' verspricht mehr, als die Untersuchung erbringt (oder auch aufgrund des Themas erbringen kann). Dazu hätte der Autor in höherem Maße auf die theoretische Diskussion—vor allem in der Einleitung—Rücksicht nehmen müssen (vgl. z.B. die Skizzierung der Problematik in M. Pfister, *Das Drama* [München 1977] 359 ff.). Abschließend möchte ich doch noch darauf hinweisen, daß die Lektüre der Arbeit häufig etwas unerfreulich wird: Der Autor befleißigt sich eines übertrieben antiquierten, manieristischen Stils, der keineswegs zur Klarheit der Darstellung beiträgt und oft Gefahr läuft, Stilblüten hervorzubringen. Störend ist auch die gewisse Überheblichkeit, mit der der Autor sich mit konträren Positionen auseinandersetzt bzw. über sie hinweggeht (z.B. 73 n. 171).

BERNHARD ZIMMERMANN

Düsseldorf

ARISTOPHANES: *Thesmophoriazusae*. Ed., tr., and comm. A.H. Sommerstein. Warminster: Aris & Phillips, 1994. Pp. xii + 242. £35 (£14.95, paper).

The latest volume in Professor Sommerstein's Aristophanes series, giving this comedy a much-needed modern commentary, is well up to his usual high standard. It fulfils the hope expressed in the Preface, that the enjoyment felt in working on this play, which was 'more ... than (with) any of the previous volumes', will be shared by the reader.

Because *Thesmophoriazusae*, apart from four papyrus fragments totalling *c.* one hundred lines, survives only in the Ravenna codex and its Munich copy, with many mis-spellings and wrong word-divisions as well as occasional more serious corruptions and the special problem of the Scythian's barbarous Greek, an editor must decide how many small corrections to record. S. has gone for fullness: his apparatus for *Thes.* is one hundred lines longer than that for the corresponding number of lines in *Lys.*, and is printed continuously in a separate section, between text and commentary. Although it is useful to have R systematically reported, those interested in textual points may find it inconvenient to keep turning to pp. 139-56, even if the usual format might have given some pages as much apparatus as text.

S.'s text and apparatus are naturally indebted to the conjecture-hunting and editorial labours of Colin Austin (C.A.), as reported especially in C.A.'s two articles on the text in *Dodoni* 16 (1987) and 19 (1990); e.g. at 702 both follow Hamaker in combining Bentley's and Porson's conjectures, and at 967 C.A.'s ὡς πρὸς is preferred to Enger's ὡς ἐπ'; at 495 S.'s attribution of deletion of τοῦ to Bentley, not Biset as in C.A., is presumably mistaken; conversely, at 138 S. like C.A. restores R.'s λύρα, but unlike him sees this as a different instrument from the βάρβιτος of 137. But S. often adopts a different text from C.A.; perhaps preferable are e.g. S.'s adoption at 80 of Nauck's ἐπείπερ ἐστι (even if Callimachus' explanation in the scholia is right, to have both τρίτη and ἡ Μέση is improbably tautologous), and at 710-11 his deletion of ἥκεις[2] with Meineke (the idiom of euphemistic reticence cited as parallel by C.A. seems inappropriate here); at 952 μολεῖν, conjectured for R.'s μέλλειν by Casaubon and Anon. Parisinus, seems better than Zanetti's μέλειν; at 1214 Gannon's ἐπίτρεκ' (= Att. ἐπίτρεχ'), 'run after', fits the action better than R.'s ἀπότρεκ'. Less convincing divergences from C.A. are e.g. at 23 adopting Reiske's ἐξεύροις (but Euripides has already discovered this, as Sandbach noted), and at 1018-19 pedantically altering Mitsdörffer's αὐτὰς to αὐταῖς, because 'an echo is never so clear and sharp as the original sound'. At 910 S.'s text prints with daggers, presumably by an oversight, the impossible ἰφύων but his translation, 'that sailcloth', implies C.A.'s excellent ἱστίων, commended in the commentary alongside Grégoire's ἀμφίων.

The translation is predictably accurate, and the barbarity of the Archer's Greek clearly explained and turned into equally defective but clear English. The commentary fits an impressive amount of essential information into eighty-one pages, but it is a pity that space limits leave so many details of Ar.'s extensive structural as well as textual distortions in parodying Euripides' *Helen* to be inferred from a table listing the corresponding line-numbers with Euripides' speaker-attributions added. On Ar.'s own plot-structure, there is an admirable note at 1160-1226 on the dramatic superfluity of hoodwinking the Archer, but in the first scene

no comment on the lack of any motive for Euripides' bringing Inlaw to the interview with Agathon; from 208-14 it is clear that substituting him for Agathon is not Euripides' idea, but Inlaw's own. On staging, S. accepts (on 295) Wilamowitz's identification of the Kritylla (898) who guards Inlaw as the priestess of the Thesmophoroi, who also earlier recites all the lines assigned by R to 'Herald'; but although giving the priestess the question at 759 suits the comic stereotype of religious official alert for perquisites, the wording of 762-3 implies that Kritylla has recently entered, and an absence from the scene, unmotivated for the priestess, suggests that Kritylla may rather be the second speaker of the debate, now returned from delivering her garlands, whose allegation about Inlaw's intentions (893-4) is then not 'lying' (Sommerstein) but ignorance due to absence. More convincing to the reviewer are the notes on 1009-14 and 1098 on staging the flying 'Perseus', and on 1056-97 rejecting the ancient idea that Euripides plays Echo; but at 96 and 265 there is a strange silence about Agathon's use of the *ekkyklema*.

Of the sprinkling of misprints noted, the only serious one is ἔχεις for ἔχῃς in the text at 602; on 4, line 7, a presumably incomplete alteration has produced 'he' where the sense requires 'Euripides'.

NAN V. DUNBAR

Somerville College, Oxford

ZAGAGI (N.) **The comedy of Menander: convention, variation and originality.** London: Duckworth, 1994. Pp. 210. £35.

Menander—author of 'puffball plays' (see Peter Green, *Alexander to Actium: the Hellenistic age* [1990] 67), soap-opera scriptwriter or literary ancestor of Molière and Shakespeare? Menandrian studies have expanded beyond enthusiasts' dreams in recent years, with the sands of Egypt continuing to reveal new and exciting fragments. And yet Menander continues also to divide scholars into polarities of admiration or derision. This important new synthesis by Netta Zagagi, which examines the surviving texts sympathetically and in depth, is therefore very welcome. Z. shows convincingly that (34) 'Menander takes the banal situation out of its traditional, vulgar context and transfers it to another, higher plane—that of serious consideration of human relationships'.

Z. does not attempt a general survey of all aspects of Menandrian comedy (Preface), but the book is instead a literary analysis of the texts. She demonstrates (ch. 1) how convention is exploited to weave each time a traditional 'New' Comedy, but one with a recognisably *new* pattern, usefully comparing (16) the way in which fans of twentieth century Westerns expect as a starting point for their entertainment a canvas of familiar elements. Z. deals well (ch. 2) with Menander's clever use of tragedy and economy of detail; she touches also on his techniques of characterization, demonstrating in particular how probable audience expectation is overturned. The likely effects for the performance as a whole of the diminishing role of the chorus are interestingly examined (ch. 3); note, for instance, her suggestion (81) that at the end of Act II of *Epitrepontes* the interlude contributes to Onesimos' characterization as a procrastinator. Motifs, particularly *unfulfilled* motifs used as comic devices, are clearly identified and analysed (ch. 4). In the course of detailed studies of the *Dyskolos* and the *Samia*, she makes some good points about character and the importance of looking at the plays as social comedies (ch. 5); see, for instance, on *Samia* (119): 'it is Demeas the *father, head of the oikos* whom we encounter on this first appearance, not Demeas the lover ...', and for *Dyskolos* her analysis (97) of Sostratos' meeting with Knemon's unchaperoned (free-born) daughter at the well. She also addresses thoroughly the question of the part played by the divinities of the prologues.

Much modern writing on the theory of comedy is often disappointingly dull, as somehow with analysis the jokes, the gestures and the atmosphere of the live performance tend to disappear. Even so, some such discussion would seem to be essential in any study of Menander—but at 57 ff., Z. avoids describing in any detail the different kinds of comedy she claims are to be found in his plays, and refers, for example, to 'the farcical element of the cook' at *Samia* 357 ff., and, elsewhere to Menander's 'controlled use ... of the elements of farce' (58), without seeking to define her terms further. The selection of valuable examples given of how social history might be used to study the plays could have been expanded to include, for instance, a fuller discussion of rape and seduction, the peg for many New Comedy plots.

Although Z. deliberately avoids any in-depth discussion of stage production, some reference to the exciting discoveries of masks and actor figurines from Lipari might have been appropriate: see David Wiles', *The masks of Menander: sign and meaning in Greek and Roman performance* (1991), with, for detail, L. Bernabò Brea, *Menandro e il teatro greco nelle terracotte liparesi* (1981), and, now, J.R. Green and Eric W. Handley, *Images of the Greek theatre* (1995), and the magnificent J.R. Green and A. Seeberg (eds.), *Monuments illustrating New Comedy, 2v., 3rd. ed.*, revised and enlarged (1995) = *BICS supplement* 50. Some more scholarship in this rapidly expanding field was too new to be included: discussion of the effect of the 'tragic' recognition scene in the *Perikeiromene* should now take account of the fact that it was accompanied by music (see M. Huys in *ZPE* 99 [1993] 30-32); more mysteriously, David Konstan's excellent articles and essays on *Epitrepontes, Perikeiromene* and *Samia* now available in revised form in *Greek comedy and ideology* (1995), do not appear in the bibliography, which is otherwise full and wide-ranging.

Z. refers to 'a long and difficult period of writing'—all too common for many academics today, particularly women. But the result—careful and thorough—has been worth the wait. This book should be on the shelves of anyone *seriously* interested in New Comedy and fourth century BC Greece.

ANGELA M. HEAP

University College London

WORTHINGTON (I.) *Ed.* **Persuasion: Greek rhetoric in action**. London and New York: Routledge, 1994. Pp. xi + 277. £37.50 (£12.99, paper).

The twelve essays in this collection are divided into three parts, entitled *Communicating, Applications* and *Contexts*. This order enables them to conform to a broadly chronological plan. The first essay, 'From orality to rhetoric: an intellectual transformation', by Carol G. Thomas and Edward Kent Webb, examines the importance of rhetoric before it was formalised. It traces the teaching of oratory through early poetry to the supposed contributions of Corax and Tisias. Their connection with *orthoepeia* (13) is, however, unattested, and that of Gorgias with *kairos* (not *to kairon* [14]), is mentioned by Dion. Hal. (*CV* 12) only to say that he wrote nothing of note about it. The proposition that 'orality was the first component of rhetoric' (16) might have been better formulated to emphasise its historical meaning. But the essay is useful for its survey of early sources. Christopher Carey, 'Rhetorical means of persuasion', performs a valuable service in showing how practising orators bettered the theorists. He deals both with general topics such as *pathos* and *topoi* proper. In discussing the presentation of the greed-motive exposed in Lysias 12.19, he could have pointed up its political significance—that the Thirty were less ideological than purely materialistic. But he is signally successful in cramming a lot of material into his allotted space, and the effect is a compendious digest of *materia rhetorica*. In his essay, 'Probability and persuasion: Plato and early Greek rhetoric', Michael Gagarin explains clearly the reasons for Plato's hostility, but he also reconsiders the much-examined passages in *Phaedrus* and Aristotle *Rhetoric* about the nature and scope of *eikos*-argument, and discusses examples of it in the Antiphontean *Tetralogies* and *Murder of Herodes*. He rightly warns against assuming from their wide use that Plato was correct in asserting that probability argument was routinely preferred to direct evidence. David Cohen's, 'Classical rhetoric and modern theories of discourse' is a survey of contemporary literary thought in relation to rhetoric, and in particular how 'rhetoric' has come to include every conceivable means of communication.

The first of the four essays in *Part II: Applications*, Josiah Ober's 'Power and oratory in democratic Athens: Demosthenes 21, against Meidias', focuses on the immediate subject (not mentioning, for example, Plato *Gorgias*). He sees 'dicanic oratory' as 'among the primary instruments whereby the power of the individual Athenian was tested against the power of the demos' (86). Preliminaries are somewhat prolonged, and in the space he leaves himself he might have devoted less time to the question of whether the speech was actually delivered. It is to be assumed that the essay went to press before the author could read the arguments ably deployed by MacDowell (*Commentary* [1990] 25-28). The next essay, 'History and oratorical exploitation' by Ian Worthington, refers to recent work on the use of historical *paradeigmata* in oratory, but not to Jost's fundamental work. His special interest in 'ring-composition' does not advance the main discussion: one would readily agree with his statement 'The implications of ring-composition in oratory cannot be underrated' (116), but unfortunately I think he meant to write *should* rather than *cannot*, or *overrated* rather than *underrated*. All too often, the ring breaks or is obscure. This is not to say, however, that orators do not frequently conclude with a summary affirmation of their opening statement, but an imposed overall symmetry leads only to distortion. Edward M. Harris, 'Law and oratory', aims to mitigate the harsh verdict traditionally passed on Athenian juries and show that they usually respected the law, so that scope for rhetoric was to be found mainly in cases where the facts were in dispute or the law as applied to them was unclear. The law about the crowning of magistrates, central to the celebrated showdown between Demosthenes and Aeschines, may fall into this category. Harris contends strongly that Demosthenes had the better case, but the latter's rhetoric, rather than Aeschines' presentation(s) of the law, may yet betray the weakness of his case. Peter Toohey's, 'Epic and rhetoric' finds rhetorical structure in the speeches of Homer's heroes, with *paradeigmata* playing a central role, but other features of rhetorical *partitio* are also present. Victor Bers, 'Tragedy and rhetoric' makes a similar contribution to an even more thoroughly explored field, but interestingly calls attention to the consequences of the contemporaneity of drama and the new genre of oratory, which include a two-way influence. Philip Harding's excellent 'Comedy and rhetoric' concentrates on one-way influence, and avoids the danger of narrowing the discussion down to comic abuse and invective by choosing for analysis orations in which the touch is light. Of these Lysias 24 is perhaps the most intriguing, and H.'s suggestion of a *mundus perversus* might have led him to the conclusion, for which I hope to argue elsewhere, that this speech, like Gorgias *Helen*, is a *paignion* (Dion. Hal. *Lys* 3 [..μετὰ παιδιᾶς ἔγραψεν]). No less impressive is Stephen Halliwell's, 'Philosophy and rhetoric', in which, among other difficult exercises, he examines the extent to which Aristotle in the *Rhetoric* tried to meet the objections raised by Plato in the *Phaedrus*. In the final essay, the second contribution by the editor, 'The Canon of the ten Attic orators' is seen as a 'destructive compilation' (245) which may have consigned many worthy orators to oblivion, even (fruitless speculation?) one or more superior to Demosthenes (249). W.'s conclusion that the 'prime suspect' (255) was Caecilius of Caleacte is neither original nor supported by new arguments. Signs of haste in composition include Thuc. 8.61.1 for 8.68.1 (246), a sentence without a main verb: 'A disaster not only for the orators affected but also for posterity in that we have no real knowledge of other orators and their talents'; and something amiss in the sentence 'Attic oratory declined before the so-called 'Asianic' trend, and (*which*?) was not to be effectively challenged until the Augustan age'. Nevertheless, his own energies as compiler of this volume are to be commended: it will be instructive and stimulating to those wishing to approach oratory from a variety of literary standpoints.

S. USHER

Royal Holloway, University of London

HOLZBERG (N.) **The ancient novel: an introduction**. Tr. C. Jackson-Holzberg. London and New York: Routledge, 1995. Pp. ix + 129. £30 (£8.99, paper).
O'SULLIVAN (J.N.) **Xenophon of Ephesus: his compositional technique and the birth of the novel.** Berlin and New York: de Gruyter, 1995. Pp. x + 215. DM 140.

One does not need to work with the Greek novels for long before sensing something odd about the *Ephesiaka*. Its structure is more blatantly episodic, its narration more short-breathed, its texture less permeated by literary allusion, and its prose style simpler and more repetitive than those of its fellows. Hitherto these oddities have tended to be attributed either to ineptitude on the part of its obviously pseudonymous author, or, following an influential article by K. Bürger ('Zu Xenophon von Ephesus', *Hermes* 27 [1892] 36-67), to a putative epitomisation of a fuller and more satisfactory original. James O'Sullivan develops a different approach in this lucidly argued study. Stripped down his case goes like this:

(1) The conventional dating of the novel to the second century is based on inadequate evidence, and there is nothing to disqualify the idea that Xenophon rather than Chariton is the earliest novelist known to us.

(2) Minute analysis of the text reveals it to be permeated by formulae of phraseology and sterotypical scene-construction.

(3) Analogy with Homeric epic and Irish tales suggests that this is characteristic of oral compositions.

(4) Bürger's epitome theory and that of R. Merkelbach (now abandoned: *Roman und Mysterium in der Antike* (Munich and Berlin 1962) 91-113) that what we have is an originally Isiac text worked over by a 'Heliosredaktor' both fail to recognise the special nature of the text, and fall because those sections of the novel which supposedly betray the hand of epitomator or redactor in fact display the same formulaic characteristics as the rest.

(5) Comparison with Chariton confirms that Xenophon's technique is vastly the more formulaic, and thus closer to its roots in oral storytelling; in passages where one writer seems to be using the other, Chariton is the more likely to be the borrower.

If all this is correct, the consequences are obviously of the first importance. Not only are the apparent oddities of the *Ephesiaka* explained and much of the aesthetic criticism levelled against it seen to have been misconceived, but also current orthodoxies on the genesis and history of the novel as a form are called into question. Rather than being a literary creation, directed from the beginning at more or less the same educated minority of the Hellenistic population that read the rest of Greek literature, the novel will have emerged from a now disappeared pool of popular oral storytelling, and its subsequent history thus represent a progressive domestication by the reading classes, with a chasm reopened between the genuinely popular novels of Xenophon and Chariton, and the 'sophistic' works of Longos, Achilleus Tatios and Heliodoros.

O'S.'s case is cogently presented, and demands the attention of anyone interested in Greek fiction. The thesis of the orality of the early novel is not new in itself (*cf.* S. Trenkner, *The Greek novella in the Classical period* [Cambridge 1958] 178-86; T. Hägg, 'Orality, literacy, and the readership of the early Greek novels' in R. Eriksen [ed.], *Contexts of pre-novel narrative* [Berlin and New York 1994] 47-80), but it has never before been underpinned in such meticulous and forceful detail. The following comments dwell on nodal points where it seems to me that O'S.'s argument might be uncoupled, but most of its constituent elements can stand alone and in themselves compel reassessment of widely held positions.

(1) O'S. is absolutely right to highlight the flimsy basis of the second-century dating. This resides on a reference to an eirenarch, an office first attested in an inscription of 116/17. The inscription refers to the post *en passant* as if familiar, and Xenophon's character is designated not by the title but by a periphrasis that does not necessarily denote formal office. This does not, however, establish the earlier dating, which rests only on O'S.'s reconstruction of literary history.

(2) Detailed textual analysis lies at the heart of the book, and there can be no doubt that O'S. has conclusively documented Xenophon's tendency to work with repetitions of a restricted vocabulary and a limited number of narrative building blocks. To call these phenomena 'formulae', however, already interprets their function, a question O'S.'s working definition as 'repeated word-group' (19) begs. Many of the verbal repetitions involve colourless key-words and are not exact; even where they are, they *may* just be the most natural way for a stylistically colour-blind author to express a recurrent idea. The 'formulaic' scenes are certainly striking, but readers of Jeffrey Archer will be only too aware that sterotyped plotting can betoken poverty of imagination as well as oral composition. It is a question of degree, involving inevitably subjective judgement. In any case, the 'formulaic' scenes constitute only a fraction of the whole: the *Ephesiaka* is not itself a fully oral text but a transitional one 'with an oral background' (99).

(3) The use of formula in Homeric epic is closely tied to metre: hence the appearance of Irish prose tales in the argument, as a possibly more exact analogy. I find this evidence difficult to control. Oral poetry tends to be formulaic, but formulae are not necessarily a proof of orality. The colourful formulae in the Irish tales *may* be as much a product of their 'jocose/burlesque tone' (75) as a tool of oral composition, in which case the argument for X.'s orality is seriously dented. Compare, on the other hand, Hägg's analysis of the use of retrospective summary and prospective headings as directed at listeners rather than readers.

(4) Oral prose narrative (i.e. folk tale) generally works less with formulae repeated within each telling than with basic story-types that underlie a multiplicity of different stories. That is to say, the formulae belong at the level of the whole tradition rather than the individual narrative. We obviously know very little of the content and style of oral popular storytelling in antiquity, but no evidence suggests that any oral storyteller ever produced a unitary narrative of the length and complexity of the *Ephesiaka*, episodic though it is. For what the observation is worth, Xenophon's motif-repertoire has much more in common with the later literary romances than it

does with any recorded corpus of folk tale. I should not want to exclude the possibility that the *Ephesiaka* is an orally (or aurally: this is Hägg's point) organised trope, how typical we cannot tell, of a fundamentally literary subject-matter and story-type.

(5) Bürger takes a serious knock. His attempt to identify precisely the work of his epitomator is effectively demolished. And yet there remains a sense, inevitably subjective, not just that the text is thin, but that it repeatedly goes out of its way to create opportunities which it does not pursue, that in places it preserves only an outline of something much richer. There is obviously a way in which this sort of reduction would exaggerate the formulaic feel of a narrative, pruning out the unessential details that individualise structurally similar episodes, and preserving a higher proportion of neutral summative vocabulary. In a context like this we need to think more flexibly about terms like 'author' and 'redactor'. Our *Ephesiaka* may be just one—and not the most impressive—version of a fluid *texte vivant* (like, for instance, the *Historia Apollonii Regis Tyri*). Or it may have been prepared by someone as the basis for a kind of performed reading that allowed for improvisatory expansion. Only the discovery of a papyrus that could be convincingly linked with the *Ephesiaka*—as the 'Antheia' fragment (*PSI* 726) unfortunately cannot—would cast some light on the history of the novel before it found its way into its solitary and quirky surviving manuscript. It may turn out that after all the Souda's infamous reference to an *Ephesiaka* in ten, not five, books is more than a simple mistake.

Niklas Holzberg's superb introduction to the novels appeared in German in 1986, (*cf.* the review by K. Dowden in *CR* 38 [1988] 57-9), and this English translation preserves its sterling virtues of accuracy, clarity, brevity and level-headedness. All that needs to be said now is that there is simply no better book in any language to put in the hands of a student (or colleague) venturing into the field of ancient fiction for the first time. H. has kept abreast of developments in the nine years since first publication. Apart from updating an already first-rate bibliography, the text incorporates a number of revisions. Most notable is the additional space allowed to some of the 'fringe' material, on which H. and his students have been particularly active in the interim; thus there is a whole new section (19-21) on the *Briefroman*, while the *Aesop Romance* and the Trojan War narratives of Dictys and Dares receive more sympathetic treatment. Among other details, H. has beaten a quiet retreat on the suggestion that pseudonyms may conceal female authors of the novel. He responds to the *Zeitgeist* by dropping the fear of nuclear holocaust as a modern motive for taking to escapist fiction, but I am rather sorry (given my initials) to have lost the reference to *Dallas* in the opening paragraph!

In their very different ways, these two excellent books confirm that the novels have entered the mainstream of classical scholarship. Each makes a valuable contribution.

J.R. MORGAN

University of Wales, Swansea

GOLDHILL (S.) **Foucault's virginity: ancient erotic fiction and the history of sexuality.** Cambridge UP, 1995. Pp. xiii + 194. £30 (£9.95, paper).

Know a book by its index: adultery, bondage, brothels, desire, fantasy, Halperin, Hexter, kissing, male bleeding, masturbation, menstruation, orgasm, penetration, pleasure, rape, violence, Winkler, Zeitlin; know it by 'some critics' opinions' on the cover: 'a corrective supplement to Foucault's work on sexuality in the ancient world ... a valuable contribution to the cultural history of desire' (Tanner), 'acumen, wit, and bravura ... his own sparkling intellect' (Zeitlin). Certainly, this is a book to be to read and to be read in one go. It is exciting and enjoyable. It does say new things, but it also repackages many old ones. It is sharp and perceptive, but also at times surprisingly pedestrian. And there is rather too much ego and phallogocentrism in Goldhill's swipes at Foucault.

That mainstream Hellenists are turning their attention to later Greek literature is extremely welcome. G. brings with him an immense knowledge of classical Greek poetry. At the same time, though he may be quite at home with the politics and culture of fifth century Athens, he knows little of the historical and social background of Greek novelistic fiction and its congeners. The point may or may not be pedantic; but it offers a clue to his interpretative strategy, especially his presentation of himself as a simple 'reader', because the 'historical import' and 'sociological perspective' of the texts he has 'mobilized' (Longus, Achilles Tatius, [Lucian] *Erôtes*, Plutarch's *Eroticus*, Dio's *Euboicus*) cannot be constructed 'from the present state of knowledge of the[ir] dates, place, and cultural milieu' (110). There is some truth in this; on the other hand, far more is known about the culture and society that produced second sophistic literature, including novelistic fiction, than is known about that of archaic and classical Greece.

So, G. concentrates on how his texts describe 'discursive space as a site of engagement and negotiation rather than simply as messages and lessons' (161). In *The care of the Self* Foucault had fastened upon them too readily as illustrations of sexual morality and had failed to note the problematization they present us with. In this regard G. engages particularly well with Achilles Tatius' *Leucippe and Clitophon* (66-102). This text is a gigantic exploration of coming to terms with self and sexual/emotional conduct. It is, as G. stresses, an amusing, even funny novel and deliberately challenges the boundaries set by 'the *sophia* of the period' (93). But this phrase has implications. The *sophia* (if it is right to use the word) of this period is as rule-bound as any could be. True, the wider the territory encompassed by rules, the greater the potential for transgressing them. But challenge is not the same as transgression. G. acknowledges this in the context of his first chapter discussion of Longus' *Daphnis and Chloe*, where he quite rightly points out that Winkler's belief in the insubordination this text offered patriarchal control cannot be sustained (39: it is 'an ironic manipulation of *and within* the terms of patriarchal narrative'). Challenges often work out to be remarkably validating exercises. In the case of Chariton's *Chaereas and Callirhoe* G. has a good discussion of what marriage means in a novel where the husband batters a pregnant wife and the wife takes for a while a second husband (127-32). But the author himself tells us that his final chapter will (in Reardon's translation) 'prove very agreeable to its readers: it cleanses away the grim events of the earlier ones. There will be no more pirates or slavery or lawsuits or fighting or suicide or wars or conquests; now there will be lawful love and sanctioned marriage' (8.1.4).

Negotiation, breakdown, rupture are traced by G. also in Plutarch and Dio. 'Few would accuse [Dio] of sharing the sly knowingness of Achilles Tatius' (123); yet he too is 'straining at the assumptions of civic morality' (126). But, again, it would be better to situate Dio *within* normative morality *precisely because* he strains at it. Thus his profound aversion to homosexuality (stemming according to John Moles from 'an incident in the showers at Prusa') is extreme but can be understood against the elite pagan ethics of this period and their denial of intellectual credibility to relationships other than those leading to 'lawful love and sanctioned marriage'. No-one, including Foucault, has ever suggested that these ethics were not debated and not found difficult. In sum, though I agree with G. that a text like Plutarch's *Eroticus* is a prime example of 'discursive space' (161), it and its fellows also reveal what is truly significant: the space—however it is used—is now open.

S.C.R. SWAIN

University of Warwick

HOPKINSON (N.) *Ed.* **Studies in the *Dionysiaca* of Nonnus**. Cambridge: The Cambridge Philological Society, 1994. Pp. iii + 187.
HOPKINSON (N.) *Ed. and comm.* **Greek poetry of the Imperial period: an anthology**. Cambridge UP, 1994. Pp. xiii + 224. £37.50 (£15.95, paper).

The *Dionysiaca* of Nonnus is the longest surviving poetical work from antiquity. Yet, it has been much neglected. Dating from about the middle of the fifth century AD it is usually considered too late by classicists and too early by Byzantinists. Readers have been put off too by its baroque features—its extraordinary lush language, its almost endlessly twisting plot, its obscure mythological digressions, its hero's fantastic exploits. However, in more recent decades interest in the poem has grown. Two valuable tools were provided with Keydell's text of 1959 and Peek's *Lexikon* of 1968-75. The publication of the Budé edition (begun in 1976 and still continuing) and of various articles by two Budé editors (Vian and Chuvin) has given a special impetus to Nonnian studies.

Studies in the Dionysiaca of Nonnus is part of this recent development. It consists of seven articles, all by different contributors, three of whom have already edited one or more of the Budé volumes. One of the three is Hopkinson himself, who has also written the introduction. There he stresses both the traditional and the contemporary in the *Dionysiaca*. The first five essays deal with the former aspect of the work (though in the fourth this is more implicit than explicit and is not the author's main concern), the last two with the latter.

The first essay, 'Nonnus and Homer', by H. gives a fascinating insight into the complexity of Nonnus' attitude to his great model. Homer is a 'poetic father' to Nonnus, 'ally and rival, inspiration and threat' (33, 11), and the way Nonnus' admiration and competitiveness interact and affect his poem is convincingly worked out under a variety of headings and in considerable detail. H. sums it up thus: 'In striving to emulate yet to escape, to be like yet unlike Homer, [Nonnus] works within that blend of imitation and anxiety, obedience and rebellion, which so often distinguish the offspring of famous fathers' (32). (*Cf.* Harold Bloom's theory that a writer is in a sort of oedipal competition with his predecessor and that this finally leads him to attempt to depose his 'father' by surpassing him.)

The second essay, 'Nonnus and Hellenistic poetry', by A. Hollis concentrates on the Alexandrian features of the *Dionysiaca*. As more fragments of Hellenistic poetry come to light, it is becoming increasingly clear that Nonnus had strong roots in that poetry. His imitation and adaptation of it under different headings is well discussed here. Hollis in his final paragraph (58-9) uses the evidence of Hellenistic sources to offer an appealing argument to support the view that Nonnus was the common author of the *Dionysiaca* and the *Paraphrase of St John's Gospel*. In the third essay, 'The pastoral mode in the *Dionysiaca*', B. Harries shows how pastoral themes and motifs are exploited by Nonnus: these are fused with and then absorbed by corresponding Bacchic ones as the poem progresses and Dionysus becomes dominant. The fourth essay, 'Dionysus in the Indian War: a contribution to a study of the structure of the *Dionysiaca*', by F. Vian is particularly valuable. It helps the reader to see and understand the underlying pattern beneath the bewildering innumerable surface episodes of the poem and especially of the *Indiad* (Books 13-40).

M. Whitby in her essay, 'From Moschus to Nonnus: the evolution of the Nonnian style', goes further than Wifstrand to trace as far as Nonnus the development of late epic style through six extant (and four fragmentary) epics. She confirms that Nonnus was less original in form than might *prima facie* seem the case. Her article (the longest in the book) illuminates the outstanding features of Nonnian style while it conveniently brings together much valuable but diffuse research on the epic between Moschus and Nonnus. Her arguments are based on a close examination of the texts and are backed by a wealth of evidence much of it statistical (some her own, some taken from others). Although the technical parts of her paper do not make for easy reading, W. makes an important contribution to our understanding of late epic.

The sixth essay, 'Dionysus as an epic hero', by G. Bowersock attempts to answer the obvious question: why should a fifth century AD poet write forty-eight books of epic with a pagan god as hero? Bowersock, having traced the development and exploitation of Dionysus' image through history, uses the evidence of art and literature to make the lucid and attractive argument that in Nonnus' time Dionysus had 'become, for pagans and Christians alike, a powerful universal-ising god of salvation' (162).

In the final essay, 'Local traditions and classical mythology in the *Dionysiaca*', P. Chuvin also sees

contemporary influence at work. He argues that Nonnus' topography/mythology was much more detailed for some cities (e.g. Tyre and Beirut) than for others (e.g. Gaza and Antioch), simply because Nonnus had more infor-mation available on the former than the latter. The reason was that the former (much more than the latter) had kept alive an interest in their local pagan traditions, that their knowledge of these was available to the wandering poets from whom they commissioned *patria*-poems, and that these poems in turn were important sources for Nonnus for this antique lore. And Dionysus' enemies, the Indians, Chuvin sees as a metaphor for the Sassanid Persians who were a constant threat to the Empire on the east.

Taken together these essays help us to get a deeper appreciation of Nonnus' multifaceted genius and point to areas which will repay much future research. Yet, clearly some of the papers have a more central concern than others. Hence one might question the sequence in which they are arranged. The fundamental issue treated in Bowersock's essay suggests that it be better placed first, followed perhaps by Vian's very helpful contribution on structure. The more specialised papers (led by H.'s own on the Homeric relationship) could then follow. And the book would, I think, be better rounded off with one additional essay. W. rightly refers to the 'Nonnian revolution' (114). One consequence of Nonnus' modern-ist tendency was that later authors found him irresistibly fascinating and so his influence on them was great—the poets of the *Cycle* of Agathias being a case in point. Yet, there is very little on this here. Perhaps it may come at a later date? For a second collection from H. and his collaborators (including an essay on the beauty and power of Nonnus' poetry ?) would be very valuable.

Meanwhile *Studies in the Dionysiaca of Nonnus* in spite of these minor criticisms is to be warmly wel-comed. Hitherto there has been no one good general book in English on the subject. This work, although relatively slight in appearance and not written specifi-cally to fill that need, does in fact go a good way towards doing so. It is, moreover, (apart from a few trivial misprints) carefully proofread and, it would seem, error free. (However, reference to Beckby's *Anthologia Graeca* should be to the 2nd revised edition, 1967-68; and *A. P.* 5.224 [quoted 51] may not be quite the bland epigram it appears, v. *RE* XIV [1] 772).

H. is also the editor of *Greek poetry of the Imperial period*. This comprises selections from the *Anacreontea*, Mesomedes, the *Greek anthology*, Quintus Smyrnaeus, Nonnus, Musaeus (the entire *Hero and Leander*), Oppian, [Oppian], [Manetho], [Orpheus] and Babrius. In his preface H. says his 'aim ... is to provide guidance along some of the little known by-ways of Imperial Greek poetry', and when this is taken in conjunction with the purpose of the series to which the work belongs—that of providing 'sound, well edited texts for school and university use'—H. can be said to have succeeded admirably.

His Introduction though brief provides a lucid informative survey of the political, educational, cultural and religious background of the poems. The extracts chosen are suitably representative. From the *Anthology* e.g., we get a little lumber, one or two jewels and the rest from in between. (However, in that section the sequence of epigrams in a couple of categories is puzzling, being neither chronological nor in line with *A.P.*). The decision to print the attractive *Hero and Leander* in its entirety is particularly laudable. The texts with limited *apparatus criticus* are based on available editions. The Commentary is excellent for its size and scope. It provides essential information on genres, poets and poems as well as a meticulous line by line annotation which excludes little of importance from its scrutiny. It ranges from the basic to the advanced, is up-to-date, balanced and full of good sense. One of its special merits is its illuminating store of references and quotations drawn mainly from the genres to which the texts belong. Throughout H. writes with a welcome avoidance of critical jargon. At one point, however, he chooses (one presumes with a smile) what is obsolete: '[Babrius]... was the first to fabulate choriambically' (207). And he allows himself one aside: 'Less superstitious members of the public have learnt with indignation and astonishment that on matters of national importance astrologers have recently been consulted by an American president, an Indian prime minister and a British princess' (206).

Very occasionally, however, the exigencies of the series to which the work belongs forces excessive brevity. The serious student would surely welcome the inclusion of (for example) the following: a reference to the standard article on the sneeze omen (A.S. Pease, 'The Omen of Sneezing', *CP* VI [1911], 429-43: 100); an explanatory source for the grammatical terms 'a-grade', 'o-grade' and 'zero-grade' (111); a comment on the preferred reading (with anastrophe/tmesis) at Quint. Smyrn. 10.466 (119); something a little fuller and clearer on the 'Nonnian School' (86, 137, 140-1) or on the resemblance between the *Halieutica* and the writing of Stoics like Seneca and Lucan (186).

H.'s fairness to differing points of view permeates the commentary and is apparent both in his scrupulous presentation of the evidence and in his evenhandedness in reaching conclusions. Indeed, if anything he is too fair, for on rare occasions one would like him to tip the scales decisively one way or the other. A good example of this occurs in his treatment of *A.P.* 5.225.6 (21, 90). There he rightly prints the MSS reading, but, not certain of its correctness, sees some merit in Alan Cameron's emendation. Yet, the latter is (in this reader's opinion) entirely unnecessary. Not only does it damage (as H. notes) the parallel with the Telephus theme, but it introduces an elision carefully avoided elsewhere by the poet. More importantly though, it takes no account of the fact that beauty as a missile had a long tradition among the erotic writers (cf. e.g. Nonn. *D.* 29.40). The text as it stands is metrically sound, makes good sense ('end my desire with your beauty, as you hit <me with your beauty>'), and should surely not be tampered with.

The work is carefully proofed. Only one slip is worth noting: on 196 *ad* Opp. *Hal.* 5. 660 the reference should be to *Hom. Hymn to Apollo* 186 (not 86). A couple of errors caught the eye. Stephanus not Jacobs was the source for 'the most likely' emendation at *A.P.* 11.408.1 (22, 92). And 'Silentiarius' was hardly Paul's 'surname' (85), merely the title of his office.

These, however, are small points and do not in any serious way diminish one's admiration for this fine edition. Filling an obvious gap, it is particularly suitable for a specialism in traditional undergraduate courses or within taught M.A. programmes. For its timely publication now, as Greek poetry of the Imperial period attracts increasing interest, both editor and publishers deserve our gratitude.

JOHN A. MADDEN

University College, Galway

BOWDEN (E.) **Cybele the Axe-Goddess: alliterative verse, Linear B relationships and cult ritual of the Phaistos Disc.** Amsterdam: Gieben, 1992. Pp. xvii + 286.

Bowden claims to have found 'previously undiscovered alliterative verse forms in the Phaistos Disc text. The alliteration, plus a substantial number of similarities to Linear B signs, enables half of the disc's pictograms to be acrophonically identified. Plausible transliterations of the remainder then allow a phonetic transliteration of the text to be written, ... provisionally read as Greek, ... [and] related to the cult of Cybele ... in a totemistic Achaean horse pastoralist cult ...'

B. is not only an anthropologist but also a statistician. He should therefore understand probability. Nevertheless his results are highly improbable. For example Side A, words 7-11, are transliterated *pe.ro.no IQ^U-S.po.ro ku.pu.phu IQ^U-S.o.da.phu pe.o(s).lu.the*, interpreted as περονῶ ἸqᵘϜῶς πῶλον κοπίφι· Ἰqᵘέως αὐδάφι παὸς λυθείη. and translated 'I pierce the Horseman's foal with knives; by the Horseman's utterances may the brother-in-law be loosed (in death)'.

The implausibilities of the Greek will be obvious to readers of this journal. The anthropology is precarious. B. stresses the human sacrifice, yet this is his only textual evidence. If one interpreted πέος instead of παός it would be equally good evidence for circumcision! Even the proposed values are unsatisfactory. Why is αυ rendered by *o* when there is both an *a* and a *u* series? Why are two separate signs deciphered as *pe*? (And the full picture is worse—eight such superfluous homophones but twenty-seven values left without a sign.)

B. seems unconscious of these credibility gaps. He uses his statistical skill on outlying matters—to argue (interestingly) for a full repertoire of about sixty signs for the disc's syllabary instead of the fifty-five currently assumed, to suggest that the sign-set for Side B is different from that for Side A, and to assure us that a kind of visual punning (where the sense of a word is reinforced by the pictorial relevance of the signs chosen to spell it) occurs with a frequency 'far beyond the limits of random statistical probability' (139). But what we never get is reassurance on the validity of the core reasoning.

B.'s starting point is the discovery of a pattern that manifests itself at each seventh sign. This is achieved by a method he calls autocorrelation, but special pleading is involved at every turn. The pattern only applies to parts of the inscription. The incised stroke is counted in the same way as the impressed characters. On two or three occasions the omission of a syllable is assumed, and once two syllables have to be crowded into the space of one. B.'s next step is to take this pattern as evidence of alliteration, and so perhaps of Indo-European, since in Indo-European alliteration is both widespread and early. Another chain of reasoning now carries him to his decipherment. The Phaistos Disc signs must be acrophonic. Therefore identifying a sign from its appearance and matching it to a known word of Indo-European root will give its phonetic value. Thus Sign 1, 'walking man', is deciphered as *pe* (*cf.* Greek πεζός Latin *pes*, etc.). The results are confirmed in some twenty instances by an apparent Linear B derivative (e.g. Sign 8, 'gloved hand' = *no* cf. Greek νωμάω 'handle'(!) > Lin. B. 52 *no*). But the identification on which B. rests most weight is that of the head-dress on Sign 2 of the Disc. He sees this in terms of a horse's mane and not as a Medinet-Habu style plumage. This gives him a phonetic value *i* (from ἵππος), a p-alliterative theme for the metrical part of the inscription and a horse totem cult as a major feature of the society. He calls the identification and its consequences 'a credible ethno-linguistic hypothesis' (29). Maybe it is. But credible does not mean probable, let alone true. If it did, each suspect in a detective story would be the murderer!

So what are the chances? Is the hepta-syllabic pattern genuine and is it alliterative? Must alliteration mean Indo-European? How likely is the 'acrophonic principle' considering that in the vast majority of phonetic scripts whose history is known the signs are not acrophonic but borrowed? If we rate these probabilities at a quarter, a half, and a third respectively (which is being charitable), then the *initial odds* against B.'s conclusions are twenty-four to one. We must still judge whether the Greek, the anthropology, and the grammatology are in themselves likely or unlikely.

The verdict is beyond reasonable doubt. Not deciphered.

MAURICE POPE

Oxford

AUBENQUE (P.) and TORDESILLAS (A.) *Ed.* **Aristote politique: études sur la *Politique* d'Aristote**. Paris: Presses Universitaires de France, 1993. Pp. ix + 552. Fr. 498.

This substantial volume contains twenty-two papers by a cadre of leading scholars, including Enrico Berti, Geoffrey Lloyd and Wolfgang Kullmann as well as its distinguished editor, Pierre Aubenque. Most of the papers are either new or substantially revised. Unlike many such productions in the world of Anglo-Saxon publishing, this volume contains much genuinely novel material—and at a very reasonable price.

The papers are arranged in four groups. The first is devoted to the main theme of Aristotle's *Politics*—the state and membership of it. Secondly, there is a group of papers on 'anthropology'; this means the study of individual human nature insofar as it bears on the individual's social identity. There follows, thirdly, a weighty group of essays on the general theme of Democracy and *Logos*; and the fourth group considers some aspects of the influence and afterlife of the *Politics*. All of this is supplemented by thorough indexes of pass-

ages—in Aristotle and other ancient authors—, of proper names, and of topics.

The range and focus of the collection is exemplary. Almost all of the main themes and arguments of the *Politics* are discussed. A critic who was determined to cavil might question the fairly scant treatment of revolution (στάσις) and Book E. He might also question the preferred place accorded to democracy in the discussion of particular forms of political organisation. To be sure, democracy is the perspective from which we, in our current historical situation, must assess Aristotle's work. But that does not mean that we have to process that assessment as democrats; and that is just as well, since Aristotle's own preferences between different forms of constitution were much more finely nuanced than would be permitted by modern political orthodoxy.

There is an implicit answer to such criticism in the organisation and content of the third main section of the collection. What is the significance of λόγος in Aristotle's discussion of politics? Does this idea justify the preference accorded to democracy by those who comment on Aristotle in this section? A number of the essays, notably those by A. and Michel Narcy, emphasise Aristotle's respect for democracy as a system of government, by contrast with his philosophical predecessors, especially Plato. Both recognise, of course, that Aristotle reserves the name 'democracy' for a perverted constitutional form; his favoured form of rule by the many is called by the suggestively opaque name of 'constitution' (πολιτεία).

Nonetheless both find support, particularly in *Politics* Γ 11, for the substantive claim that the numerical scale of democratic (however named) government provides, in itself, political merits; the bigger the better, is the main argument of this intriguing chapter. Narcy couples this claim with a challenging presentation of Aristotle as umpire in the dispute between Socrates and Protagoras in Plato's eponymous dialogue. Aristotle shows how real expertise—or knowledge—is not incompatible with respect for democracy. The key to such a reconciliation, he argues, lies in the distinction between the good person and the good citizen—a distinction which is far from being merely analytic; for merit as a citizen derives from the merit of the city (or constitution), and the latter form of merit logically requires supplementation from the nature of the constitution itself. All such subtleties were missed by Socrates with his context-free probings into the nature of human merit.

The focus on democracy, which these and other contributors adopt, is made the more plausible by some seminal remarks in *Politics* A 2 concerning human nature and λόγος. It is a distinctive property of humans to possess λόγος; and in A 2 Aristotle uses this point as a premiss to promote an argument for the conclusion that living in a political context is essential to the achievement of a good human life. The rational and linguistic capacities of human beings entail that in this case, more than in that of any other living kind, the good life is the good *communal* life.

But what, more exactly, is the significance of λόγος? The essays of Rüdiger Bubner and Barbara Cassin very usefully explore two different answers to this question. B. contends that in this context λόγος clearly means 'language'. The unique linguistic abilities of human beings give them access to such notions as the *useful* and the *fine*; and these ideas are unavailable to any other communitarian creatures which, however superficially similar in social arrangements, lack the human power of communication. The language-generated facility supplies, in turn, the intersubjective awareness of shared ends which results in the specifically human form of community. As he puts it, 'Sans *polis*, pas de fonction du *logos*, et sans *logos*, pas de politique'.

For Barbara Cassin, by contrast, the primary function of Aristotle's discussion of λόγος is to highlight a contrast between the rational nature of humans and the irrationality of other creatures, with particular emphasis on the intuitive grasp of first principles (νοῦς). She distinguishes Aristotle's ideas from those of his sophistic predecessors precisely because in his treatment, unlike theirs, the notion of λόγος encompasses the rational content of utterances rather than the utterances themselves.

One might question whether some elements of each of B.'s and C.'s cases are constructed on the basis of a false antithesis, perhaps to add dramatic quality to their presentation. Nonetheless the inclusion of these two essays in this central section of the collection does serve to underpin the claim, which is implicit in the editor's title for the whole section, that human beings' unique possession of rational communication lends support to the thesis that democracy is valuable as a form of government.

Therefore Aristotle may take his place among those philosophers for whom a grasp of the importance of language as a social phenomenon carries as an entailment a particular left-of-centre stance in politics. He would stand in company with Locke, Wittgenstein and Putnam, but arguably not with Nietzsche, Mill or Russell. A.'s well edited volume will have value in stimulating reflections on such matters and on much else besides.

J.D.G. EVANS

Queen's University of Belfast

LAKS (A.) and SCHOFIELD (M.) *Ed.* **Justice and generosity: studies in Hellenistic social and political philosophy**. (Symposium Hellenisticum 6). Cambridge UP, 1994. Pp. ix + 304. £40.

Although its name fails the test of strict alliteration, this volume otherwise upholds the high standards of its five illustrious predecessors (*Doubt and dogmatism, The norms of nature*, et al.). It too celebrates the vitality of Hellenistic thought. And it should be particularly welcome to readers of this journal, because its topics come closer to the concerns of general classicists. Earlier volumes have provided feasts for the philosopher; here there is also abundance for historians and sociologists. There is also more to interest Latinists.

In essays of any philosophical merit there will be much to disagree with; I found much in most of the nine chapters. Since brevity precludes articulate disagreement, a brief *précis* of each piece will be of more service.

In the first essay, D. Hahm takes us around the Polybian *anakuklôsis* once again, making the case for its coherence. His integration of the *akmê*-model with the

cycle is convincing; his account of the psychological factors underpinning the cycle is at least a plausible candidate for what Polybius had in mind. H.'s aim throughout is to vindicate, and in this he succeeds; Polybius comes off looking like a philosophically-minded historian whose views should be of interest to both disciplines.

J.-L. Ferrary discusses Cicero's politics in his *Republic* and *Laws*, and in particular the figure of the *optimus civis* as it functioned in his theorizing about the Roman constitution. There are useful discussions of the content of missing books, of Cicero's debts to Plato, and of the psychology of the *Republic*. F. does prove his point, that the figure of the statesman played an important role in these writings, but no more definite thesis seems to be on offer.

J. Annas examines the Stoicism in accounts of Peripatetic politics by Antiochus and Arius Didymus, arguing that it is not the result of doxographical carelessness, but rather a conscious attempt to modernize Aristotle so as to incorporate the successful aspects of Stoicism. She concludes that the attempt fails to produce a viable hybrid, because Stoicism has made fundamental ethical advances that cannot be integrated into the Peripatos. Anyone persuaded by her recent book on ethics will find this piece equally convincing.

C. Natali surveys discussions of the *tekhnê oikonomikê*—including little-read stretches of ps.-Aristotle, Philodemus, and the Pythagoreans—in order to ascertain the 'theoretical field' of ancient economics. Income and expenditures did form one topic, but equally important were human affairs within the *oikos*—the right relation between master and slave, husband and wife, and parents and child (although '*peri tekhnôn*', the title of Stobaeus IV.18, does *not* mean 'about children', 100). Neither deep nor insightful, but a useful overview of unfamiliar territory.

J.L. Moles discusses the Cynics. There are political treatises from Cynic pens, but most of this material is late, eclectic and 'soft', i.e. non-Diogenic. The 'hard' Cynicism of Diogenes replaces conventional politics with the life of the Cynic; 'the Cynic state', M. writes, 'is the 'state' of being a Cynic'. But even this rejection, he argues, constitutes a contribution to political theorizing. A good chronological collection of material, and some good points on Diogenes.

A. Alberti's study of the Epicurean theory of law and justice shows how the two notions were distinguished. Law derives from utility, justice from a contract in the realm of utility; neither is analytically connected to the other. Like utility, both have some degree of objectivity and some degree of relativity to context. This is the strongest piece in the volume, and the best work on the subject to date; I look forward to arguing with it and assigning it to students.

M. Schofield makes a valuable contribution to a debate about Stoic ethical theory. A current revisionist fashion argues against the view that Stoic ethics depends on theology, emphasizing parallel discussions which seem to ground ethics in non-theological common conceptions, or human rationality, or *oikeiôsis*. S. suggests that the two approaches are related as the *gnôrimôteron hêmin* and the *gnôrimôteron phusei*; the individual may approach ethics in the non-theological way, but full understanding will require theology. An important step in the right direction.

A.A. Long presents an excellent adjunct to studies of the philosophical antecedents of Cicero's *De Officiis*, by showing how it was also influenced by historical events and personal motivations detailed in the letters and speeches. The concern with property rights and the correct desire for *gloria* reflects Cicero's meditations on the degeneration of the Roman honour-code into the power-mad free for all of the 40s. A model application of non-philosophical considerations to the illumination of a philosophical text.

In the last chapter, B. Inwood explores Seneca's treatment in the *De Beneficiis* of Stoic paradoxes about giving and receiving. Seneca attempts to apply rigorous and sometimes counter-intuitive ethical principles to the concrete demands of gratitude and reciprocity in Roman society. I. judges the reconciliation of pure theory and practical concerns successful, and suggests that such integration may have characterized Stoic philosophy from the start. A valuable essay with implications for the interpretation of all periods of Stoicism.

To sum up: a fine collection of essays with particularly strong pieces from Hahm, Annas, Schofield, Long and Inwood, and a new state of the art from Alberti.

Editorial errors in the volume are few: on 32 fn. 41 read 'hostility or' for 'hostility of'; 112 '*diexodois*' for '*diedoxois*'; 107 fn 38 'temperance' for 'temperament'; 271 Grilli (1971) read 'Rivista' for 'Revista'.

T. BRENNAN

King's College London

PLUTARCH **Plutarque: Oeuvres Morales XII.2. Opinions des philosophes.** Ed., tr., and comm. G. Lachenaud. Paris: Les Belles Lettres (Budé), 1993. Pp. 475. Fr. 335.

PLUTARCH **Selected essays and dialogues.** Tr. D.A. Russell. Oxford UP, 1993. Pp. xxx + 431. £7.99.

These two books are intended for quite different readerships, but share one admirable characteristic: both maintain the highest standards of scholarship.

Lachenaud has performed an extremely useful service in producing this meticulous edition of the Ps-Plutarchan *De placitis philosophorum*. He provides a thorough introduction which deals clearly with the transmission of the text, the place of the work in the history of doxography, and the methods of analysis employed in it, ending with a synoptic table to assist the reader in assessing the relationship of the *De placitis* to other doxographical works. The Greek text and French translation are accompanied not only by an *apparatus* and a list of testimonia, but also by foot-notes and extensive end-notes. L. is very widely read, and both introduction and notes display formidable learning. In particular, he makes good use of his knowledge of the Arabic tradition (discussed in the introduction, 10-15). The Arabic sources regularly provide attractive alternative readings, for example at 889C (on which see 250-1) and 907D (on which see 305). There is much interesting information in all parts of the book, and it is clear that any student of doxography will need to consult this edition regularly.

More readily accessible, but no less scholarly, is Russell's new translation in the *World's Classics* series. This is designed to complement rather than replace the recent volume of selected *Moralia* published by Penguin, and since only three out of a substantial total of seventeen essays coincide, this intention is fulfilled. It is an admirable volume in every way. The selection of essays is designed to convey the variety of the *Moralia* (see the introduction, xiii-xiv), and succeeds in doing so. The introduction glows with quiet wit and elegance, and simultaneously welcomes the general reader with a portrait of a humane and attractive author, and impresses the specialist with its range of insights and its scholarship. A feature of the book is the care which has been taken with its organization: a comprehensive list of all the essays is given, with the titles in transliterated Greek, Latin and English, and brief comments, indicating spuriousness or incompleteness. The conflicting conventions by which the *Moralia* are cited are explained. Each essay is given a brief preface to itself, and is annotated with end-notes, supplemented by a separate list of the Sources of Quotations and a Glossary of Proper Names, which includes cross-references to the *Oxford Companion to Classical Literature*.

The translation is elegant and supple throughout, a pleasure to read. Needless to say, the notes display much learning, and, which is rarer, an excellent sense of what the general reader is likely to be looking for: particularly interesting are the comments on the use made of Plutarch by later authors (introduction x-xii, and notes on e.g. 373, 375, and 381).

Scholarship on the *Moralia* is being well-served, therefore, and it is to be hoped that the appearance of these two very different, but very valuable, books will encourage more publication on these fascinating and varied texts.

JUDITH MOSSMAN

Trinity College Dublin

NARBONNE (J.-M.) *Ed., tr., and comm.* **Plotin. Les deux matières: Ennéade II.4 [12].** Paris: Vrin, 1993. Pp. 378. Fr. 235.

This book is far more than a text, translation and commentary on *Ennead* II.4. In fact the introduction of some two hundred and seventy pages forms the substantial part of the volume. Narbonne begins with a discussion of the status of the One and the attempts of later neoplatonists, particularly Damascius, to resolve some of the apparent contradictions of Plotinus' treatment of the One. Although some of this discussion may at first seem somewhat removed from the subject of matter there are important links of both cause and of analogy between the highest and the lowest factors in the Neoplatonic hierarchy. N. also argues that our understanding of the otherness of the One is to be closely allied to our understanding of the otherness that is matter.

Of the two types of matter which form the subject of Plotinus' treatise Intelligible matter is the one that has provided the most difficulty for interpreters of Plotinus. While some commentators have described the notion as totally alien to Plotinus' metaphysics (Merlan) and have even argued that he eventually rejected the notion (Heinemann), nearly all (apart from Faust and Buchner) find it embarrassing in some way. N. vigorously, and in my view correctly, rejects the extreme views of Heinemann and Merlan in arguing that the theory is linked closely with the main structural dynamics of Plotinus' metaphysical system in which each Hypostasis is produced by its prior as an unformed power (equivalent to intelligible matter) which in returning on and contemplating its prior is perfected. He is still however worried about the apparent inconsistency of maintaining what looks like potentiality in the Intelligible world, of movement from one state to another, which is incompatible with its unity, stability and eternity. To an extent he counters this by reading back the same problems and tensions in Plato and Aristotle. These comparisons are new and useful. It is essential to question the consistency of Plotinus' ideas in this way. But while it may be comforting to think that Plotinus is in good company in facing (and not necessarily solving) the same problems as his predecessors, N. is sometimes over-sensitive to 'contradictions' in the *Enneads*. There is no need, for example, to see a contradiction (78) between matter as causal unity (II.4.4,4; 15-16) and matter as 'otherness' (II.4.5,28) since matter is not identified as otherness but the latter is said to be the ἀρχή of matter. This is then consistent with II.4.16,1 f. where Plotinus denies that matter is otherness but accepts that it is an aspect of it. N. sometimes looks for a greater degree of uniformity than we need expect. Should one explanation of the relationship of Nous to its objects be *traduisible* (69) into another? The most we need expect of different explanatory concepts, analogies or images is that they are not inconsistent with each other in essentials; for Plotinus employs a variety of expositions either to enlarge our understanding of a basic metaphysical principle or to observe it from a different perspective in another context.

Plotinus' theory of sensible matter presents equally baffling if different problems. The consensus view that matter is created (either by soul or by the One) was disturbed by Schwyzer who argued for uncreated matter, a view to which Armstrong inclines. The issue is important since matter is the source of evil and in any case an uncreated matter might puncture the monism of the system. N. presents in a systematic way the texts which would support these conflicting views. His own view is that Plotinus was uncertain and did not wish to commit himself either way. More perceptively he rejects the black and white notion of either created or uncreated as deceptive. After carefully reviewing all the texts which can be adduced to support the claim that matter is produced by soul he rightly concludes that most of them are doubtful or even point to the opposite. Nor is the case any stronger for the One or Intellect. The one indubitable text which supports a created matter (I.8[51]7, 16-23) occurs in a late treatise concerned primarily with the source of evil. Paradoxically, N. argues, in facing up to the problem of evil, whose source is matter, he is forced to recognise it as more than the mere privation of everything and to give it a positive force as an ἀρχή, but at the same time avoid such clear cut dualism by asserting its dependency, in fact on soul. He is thus compelled by the strongly

ethical element of the metaphysical discussion to avoid the indecisiveness of his earlier considerations. Although I find it hard to agree with all of N.'s interpretations of passages dealing with soul's relation to matter, there is sufficient lack of clarity in Plotinus' thought to support N.'s thesis and his interpretation of the role and significance of I.8 is convincingly argued. But N. does not seem to have made it clear why Plotinus decides in I.8 to have soul rather than the One engender matter and the important text VI.3.7, which might support the latter, is held back to the end of the argument. More consideration might also have been given to the difficulties to Plotinus caused by the concept of matter as privation; for how can what-is-not be created? Did Plotinus have a final view?

This is a thoughtful and comprehensive exposition and analysis of some central Plotinian issues, a volume which will be immensely useful for its detailed documentation and interpretations even if some of N.'s bolder analyses may not gain immediate acceptance in their entirety.

ANDREW SMITH

University College Dublin

SCHUBERT (C.), BRODERSEN (K.) and HUTTNER (U.) *Ed.* **Rom und der griechische Osten. Festschrift für Hatto H. Schmitt zum 65. Geburtstag.** Stuttgart: Steiner, 1995. Pp. xii + 375 + ill. DM 148.

This is a weighty *Festschrift*: nearly four hundred closely printed and densely documented pages of scholarship, which make few concessions to a wider readership. The title implies a hope that the contributions share a common focus, but many of the papers have no obvious connection with relations between Rome and the Greek world. In general they reflect Schmitt's own wide interests in ancient history and historiography, but the result, as always with *Festschriften*, is a miscellany.

Coherence would have emerged more clearly if the the papers had not been arranged in random, (almost in alphabetical), order. In fact there is a reasonably close-knit group of papers on the philosophy of history and historical theory: F.G. Maier on 'Endzeit und Historie', W. Beierwaltes, contrasting Hegel with Plato; Ch. Schubert, on Polybian and earlier theories of mixed and balanced constitutional systems; *F. Walbank comparing the experiences of Polybius and Josephus as they came to terms with Roman power as defeated expatriates; *A. Winterling, arguing that Aristotle in the *Politics* paid little detailed attention to inter-state relations in the Greek world not because they were unimportant, but precisely because they were the most important destabilising factor in Greek politics, a fact recognised in much historical analysis today; and H. Beister on pragmatic historical writing, essentially a commentary on Polybius. 9.1.2-2.6.

The other studies lean heavily towards political and diplomatic history, and in general have a rather old-fashioned feel to them. There are three weighty papers on earlier Greek history: an important one by *D. Kienast on the role of Delphi in the great Persian war; a confusing one by E. Bloedow on Alexander burning

Persepolis; and a thorough study of the Italic league in the fourth century BC by R. Werner. The largest group of papers is concerned with Rome and the eastern Mediterranean in the middle to late Republic: J.-G. Dieter, splicing together thoughts on oracles and letters as forms of resistance to Roman influence in the East; C. Leidl, laboriously demonstrating the fictitious nature of Hannibal's letter to the Athenians, which requested that Carthaginian deeds be celebrated by Greek writers (P. Hamb. 129); three papers largely concerned with Pyrrhus, by S. Lücke (unconvincing on a detail of his numismatic propaganda), J. Seibert (on the reality or otherwise of Roman fears of invasion from the East during the third and second centuries BC), and *W. Suerbaum (fundamental on the speech delivered by Ap. Claudius Caecus in 280/79 against the eastern threat); N. Mantel on the treaty between Philip V and Hannibal and Livy's perception of the continuity between the second Macedonian and second Punic wars; L.-M. Günther arguing from a reappraisal of the monumental column at Delphi which carried his statue, that L. Aemilius Paullus showed no special philhellenic instincts, but those of a victorious general; H. Wild speculating in detail on the political situation at Rome in 197, when T. Quinctius Flamininus was elected consul; and two straightforward, but thorough reappraisals of regional history in relation to Rome, by H. Nottmeyer on the Achaian League, and S. Kreuter on Crete. Three papers focus on the origins and early years of the principate: *U. Huttner's usefully shows the propaganda value to Antonius of his supposed descent from the Heraklidai (Plutarch, *Ant.* 4.2); *T. Scheer writes an excellent commentary on *Res Gestae* 24, to show that, despite this profession to the contrary, Octavian behaved like any other Roman victor in the East in removing treasures and art works from Greek sanctuaries; and W. Jakob-Sonnabend pleads on unconvincing grounds (the favourable geographical situation of the island) that Tiberius' withdrawal to Rhodes was a political gamble that failed.

The remaining papers do not fit so easily into any scheme. Two are from jurists: G. Thür, on the late third century BC treaty betwen Stymphalos and Demetrias (Sikyon); and D. Nörr, who identifies the *xenokritai* of an imperial inscription from Lycia as Roman *recuperatores* acting for the Roman provincial governor. W. Günther publishes a fragmentary proxeny decree from the Ionian city of Myus; *J. Nollé contributes an extremely illuminating paper on the way in which Roman colonies and Greek cities continued to present themselves as 'allies' of Rome in the eastern wars of the third century AD; E. Simon publishes a togate Palmyrene portrait of the early third century; and K. Brodersen shows that the alleged twelfth century Byzantine geographical writings of Nikephoros Blemmyes are in fact compilations of an unknown western author of the sixteenth century. Last but not least, the only 'literary' study is a masterly essay on history and fiction by *N. Holzberg, wearing his learning lightly, which offers a typological classification of the forms of ancient fiction, corresponding to Macrobius' commmentary on Cicero. *Somn. Scip.* 1.2.7-8, and concentrates especially on the novels and letters which aspired to historical verisimilitude, διηγήματα πλασματικά, explaining the basis of their appeal to an ancient readership .

All the papers are presented with a high degree of professional competence, and specialists should not overlook those which are relevant to their own interests. The asterisks in my text indicate those with good claims on a wider readership.

STEPHEN MITCHELL

University of Wales, Swansea

MEISSNER (B.) **Historiker zwischen Polis und Königshof: Studien zur Stellung der Geschichtsschreiber in der griechischen Gesellschaft in spätklassischer und frühhellenistischer Zeit.** Göttingen: Vandenhoeck & Ruprecht, 1992. Pp. ix + 605. DM 150.

Meissner's meticulous study, outgrowth of a Heidelberg dissertation, studies the social position of 'historians' from the time of Xenophon to about 250 BC. The book, in five parts, covers (1) their origins and education, (2) their professions and occupations, (3) their political activity, (4) their military service, and (5) their ties with royal courts.

To write 'historians' may be to go too far, but as M. stresses there was no recognised profession (in a modern sense) of historiography in this (or any other) period of antiquity, nor were those who wrote history the product of any special training. Not surprisingly, therefore, M.'s investigation of social origins reveals that those who wrote Greek history after, as before, Thucydides overwhelmingly derived from the upper-class literati of the poleis. If anything, the social prerequisites for historiography narrowed further in the period examined, since one of the hallmarks of these classes was increasingly an expensive education under sophists and philosophers, whose milieu remained polis-based, since the royal courts never developed educational institutions of their own (for all that a Callisthenes might give impromptu instruction to Alexander's 'royal pages'). 'Historians', therefore, at one level were no more or less than part of the highly-ramified world of the Greek literati and intellectuals in this period and, in a sense, to treat them separately, as M. does, is to run the risk of creating a category which contemporaries only rarely, if ever, perceived as separate.

The big development of the age, one which no doubt helps to explain its historiographical productivity, was the emergence of Greco-Macedonian monarchy as the dominant state-form of the times. The new literary opportunities thus presented were not lost on Greeks who could wield the pen, and history-writing became one of the services which Greeks could offer a ruler in return for material reward. The way to court tended to depend on the same network of personal contacts which brought upper-class Greeks from the poleis into royal service in other capacities, above all as recruits to the circle of royal friends as soldiers and men of affairs. Indeed, to write history was, for many, a subordinate aspect of a political or military career under one or more rulers, as in the case of Alexander-historians such as Nearchus or Hieronymus, chronicler of the Successors.

The prizes for literary activity under royal patronage are obvious. M. stresses that there were also risks—if only to the liver, toping playing a large part in court life.

Aristippus of Cyrene was notorious for winning drinking contests at the court of Dionysus I. There was also the issue of honour. Court-historians were a byword among the ancients for the sacrifice of personal autonomy for gain, and even Callisthenes, apparently an intellectual of real integrity, was unable to escape the charge of 'flattery'. Again, here the larger context is the stigma of dependency and parasitism which, as Gabriel Herman has shown, their (envious?) fellow-citizens attached to Greeks who successfully entered royal service. But the rewards, well-treated by M., were too great for this to be a real obstacle: as well as money, there was the higher standard of living in a royal palace, and the possibility of a larger role in affairs (e.g. Persaeus of Citium, who ended up as Antigonid commander at Corinth), or, at the least, of some courtly intrigue.

M. rightly notes the role of historians in royal propaganda. But the low opinion in which court historians were held raises the question—hard to answer, since so little survives—of how much real impact their products had. At any rate, the most widely-read Alexander-history in the Hellenistic age was probably the more critical account of Cleitarchus, who is not known to have enjoyed royal patronage; nor, presumably, did the anonymous authors of the Hellenistic tracts providing the seeds of the Greek Alexander Romance.

There is, indeed, a danger of overstating the contemporary significance of historians *qua* historians in this period. Insofar as they could act as influential go-betweens between their cities and the kings, they did so as well-connected, upper-class Greeks—compare Callias of Sphettus, e.g., who is not noted as a history-writer, however. In this sense M.'s book is in danger of falling into the same trap as some older work on the Greek sophists in the Roman empire: like the sophists, M.'s historians, if they had influence, wielded it chiefly as paid-up members of the polis- and royal élites, not because they happened also to write some history.

A.J.S. SPAWFORTH
University of Newcastle-upon-Tyne

FLOWER (M.A.) **Theopompus of Chios: history and rhetoric in the fourth century** BC. Oxford UP, 1994. Pp. xii + 252. £30.

Theopompus' work challenges an historical mind: it is fragmentarily preserved, ambivalent in political orientation, and somewhere in between history and rhetoric; it has been called a 'work without parallel', both approvingly (Wilamowitz) and disapprovingly (Lane Fox). Flower's monograph is the second within three years, which suggests that something new may have to be said about this much underrated (or over-rated) author.

In the Introduction F. proposes that Theopompus' work can only be properly understood if he is not taken as either orator, or philosopher or historian (2 ff.). Moreover, a proper picture of Theopompus can only emerge if the surviving fragments are studied in the literary context in which they survived (7).

In chapters on life and work F. dates the publication of the *Philippica* to shortly before Theopompus' expulsion from Chios in 323 BC, the *Hellenica* before 343 BC, and his birth before 378 BC. With Shrimpton (*Theopompus the Historian*, 1991), furthermore, he rejects the idea that Theopompus wrote the *Hellenica Oxyrhynchia*, but he is sensibly careful not to suggest an alternative author (27 f.).

In subsequent chapters F. dismisses a series of mistaken allegations of the nature of Theopompus' work. First, he argues that Isocrates was not Theopompus' teacher, nor did he teach him the writing of 'rhetorical history'. Stylistic similarity was hardly enough evidence for a teacher-pupil relationship. Speusippus and Porphyry, moreover, simply inferred from Theopompus' proclaimed enmity against Plato that he belonged to Isocrates' school (52-7). Exploring then Theopompus' moral, political and philosophical directions, F. finds them well in line with conservative positions current at the time. Theopompus was not an original thinker, and neither did he have a distinct political vision, nor follow a particular philosophical school (e.g. 97; *cf.* 146). It was his moral assumptions that made him adopt certain positions such as an admiration for Lysander and Agesilaus and a rejection of Philip's politics (*cf.* 83). Why did Theopompus choose Philip as the central figure of an extensive historiographical work given that the extant fragments display nothing but moral contempt for his behaviour? F. comes to the conclusion that although not admiring him, he saw in him the major causative force of the events of his time (115). Moral decay as an explanation for historical events was a common theme in the historiography of the late Roman Republic and it should be accepted equally as a theme in fourth century historical writing (130). Moreover, personal motivation, whatever its moral quality, was a perceived key to understanding the historical process since Herodotus. Having thus endowed Theopompus with the credentials of an historian, F. attempts to place him in an historical tradition. Because of the extensive use of excurses and digressions, Herodotus, rather than Thucydides, is suggested as the most influential model (160-5). New was Theopompus, particular interest in luxury (*truphê*) as an explanation for historical change, which had a strong, though not lasting, influence on subsequent historians (most notably Timaeus, Duris and Phylarchus, *cf.* 166-68). In conclusion F. argues that Theopompus' rhetorical ambitions did not detain him from historical accuracy. Rhetoric could be used either as a means or as an end, and one should ask whether 'objective recording of ascertainable facts' (184) was sacrificed to rhetoric as an end in itself. Although the extant verbatim fragments, mainly preserved by Athenaeus, did display a certain hyperbolic style, testimonies about his work as a whole suggested, rather, that he employed different rhetorical strategies for different types of narrative (187).

F.'s book offers discussion and correction of earlier scholarship without, however, suggesting a genuinely new approach. Points of detail are convincingly argued, and the method of reading fragments in their literary contexts proves to be helpful for isolating Theopompus' voice from the argumentative context in which it is preserved (e.g. F 27 = Polyb. 8. 9. 1-4, (98-104); F 381 = Strab. I.2.35 (33)). Yet little advance is made in the question of the relationship between history and rhetoric.

The promising proposition to read Theopompus as a representative of a complex intellectual environment in which professional distinctions between historian, orator and philosopher could no longer easily be drawn (2), is never put into practice. F. is anxious to 'remove Theopompus from the shadow of Isocrates', but a closer look at the way Isocrates straddles generic boundaries would have led to a better appreciation of the interdependence of rhetoric, historiography and morality in Theopompus (*cf.* Y.L. Too, *The Rhetoric of Identity in Isocrates: Text, Power, Pedagogy* [1995]). The distinction between history and oratory, let alone rhetoric, was never as clearly defined as F. wants it to be (e.g. 184-6). The possibility that Theopompus participated in reassessing their relationship is never considered. The particularly valuable F 25, in which Theopompus praises the unprecedented union of the two in his own person, would have been a starting point, but is barely discussed by F.

Anyone who wishes to use Theopompus as an historical source will read F.'s book with profit; the one who is interested in the relationship between history and rhetoric in the fourth century BC will be disappointed.

SITTA VON REDEN

University of Bristol

HORNBLOWER (S.) *Ed.* **Greek historiography**. Oxford UP, 1994. Pp. xii + 286. £35.

This book is a sign of the increasing interest in historiography, which progressively is becoming a subject in itself. Until recently historians of antiquity or other periods were considered either as sources for reconstructing the historical past or from an aesthetic point of view, which explains the neglect of some very important authors. The present volume is the result of a series of lectures delivered in the University of Oxford in 1991.

The editor has had the excellent idea of writing an extensive introduction as the first chapter (1-72) to summarise the contents of the different chapters (1-7), the text of each lecture. Next, Hornblower has produced a short history, which he calls 'story', of Greek historiography in order to fill the gaps among the following chapters as well as to interrelate them. H. offers interesting reflections on the division in books of the historians (16-17). Very rightly he has introduced the figure of the *historiographer* as different from that of the *historian* (12, 24), and he cleverly distinguishes *History* 'as a way of looking at the past' from *Historiography*, 'which is the work of fallible human beings with often strong political and other beliefs, cannot help but manipulate the past' (38). H. devotes a section to intertextuality and Greek historians, in which he introduces the idea of intertextuality to explain the relations among the different historians and their relations with other sorts of authors (54).

The second chapter, 'Historical explanation: Polybius and his predecessors' (73-90) is by P. Derow. He considers Polybius as part of a process, in which his predecessors are, Hecataeus, Herodotus and Thucydides. This is a short, but very good paper on a key figure of historical explanation who following Thucydides' in-

sight introduced the categories of αἰτία, πρόφασις, and ἀρχή. D. has adduced plenty of texts in support of his thesis.

The third chapter, 'Herodotus and religion' (91-106) by J. Gould, is an approach to this historian from the standpoint of modern religiosity, which is very much in the line of today's approach to ancient authors.

The fourth chapter, 'Herodotus on Alexander I of Macedon: a study in some subtle silences' (107-30) by E. Badian, is a deep analysis on a fashionable subject: what has been omitted by historians in their narratives. There is an appendix on Amyntas and Elimeia (127-30).

In the fifth chapter, 'Narratology and narrative techniques in Thucydides' (131-66) H. introduces into historiography the notion of narratology: 'the theory that deals with the general principles underlying narrative texts' (131). He has been stimulated by W. Booth, *The rhetoric of fiction* (Harmondsworth 1983²) and by G. Genette, *Narrative discourse* (Oxford 1980) and *Fiction and diction* (Paris 1991), as well as by M. Bal, *Narratology: introduction to the theory of narrative* (Toronto 1985).

In the sixth chapter, 'The world of Theophrastus' (167-91), P.M. Fraser deals with botany in this author, confining himself to the Middle East and Italy. It is a very highly specialised paper.

In the seventh chapter, 'The tradition about the first Sacred War' (193-212), J.K. Davies has produced a fine analysis with an appendix of 'Some basic texts' (206-10) and a bibliography (211-2).

In the eighth chapter, 'Diodorus and his sources: conformity and creativity' (213-32), K.S. Sacks argues in favour of the fact that Diodorus of Sicily does not follow his sources with servility and stresses his hostility towards Rome, a power that he saw through the eyes of a provincial. This paper reflects the approach which S. has adopted in his book *Diodorus Siculus and the first century BC* (Princeton 1990).

In the ninth chapter, 'Symbol of unity? The Persian-wars tradition in the Roman empire' (233-47), A. Spawforth studies the Parthenon inscriptions, Persians and Parthians in Imperial ideology, and subject Greeks and the Persian wars. His approach has the merit of having related literary sources to inscriptions very well.

This book is tremendously stimulating and a companion volume for Roman historiography would be welcome. The work ends by a well chosen bibliography (249-69) and a useful index (271-86).

The impression that one obtains from reading this book is of the modernity of the authors' approaches, and of how much there is still to do in the field of ancient historiography. The editor of the volume has introduced some important points in the field, e.g. intertextuality, narratology. Several chapters of the book show what could be profitably undertaken in the relation of historiography to other subjects: religion, natural sciences, epigraphy. The same applies to other disciplines such as philosophy, numismatics and so on. Moreover, the outlook of ancient historians in their social and political contexts could form the basis of a systematic study of Greek and Roman historiography.

J.M. ALONSO-NÚÑEZ

Madrid

DICKINSON (O.T.P.K.) **The Aegean Bronze Age**. Cambridge UP, 1994. Pp. xxii + 342 + ill. £40 (£17.95, paper).

The simple title of this medium-sized and moderately priced volume, unencumbered by any qualifying subtitle, immediately suggests an introductory handbook. This impression is reinforced by the author's contention in the very first sentence of his preface that 'this book is intended to be a general introduction to the Aegean Bronze Age'. For those of us who regularly teach survey courses in Aegean archaeology and for more than fifteen years have been in search of a text that is more up-to-date than E. Vermeule's, *Greece in the Bronze Age* (1964, 1972), more detailed than P. Warren's, *The Aegean civilizations* (1975), more archaeological in its approach than S. Hood's, *The arts of prehistoric Greece* (1978, 1988), and more comprehensive in its coverage than the numerous texts devoted to single Aegean prehistoric cultures, Dickinson's survey would appear to be an answer to a prayer. Unfortunately, despite the fact that it is as up-to-date, detailed, and archaeological in its orientation as can reasonably be expected, this book will not serve as a satisfactory introductory text for two very basic reasons: first, it effectively *assumes* prior knowledge of the principal sites, monuments, and artifactual forms of the Aegean Bronze Age rather than serving as a genuine introduction to them; and secondly, the book's organization according to spheres of cultural activity (with chapter titles such as 'Settlement and Economy', 'Arts and Crafts', 'Burial Customs', 'Trade', 'Exchange and Overseas Contact' and 'Religion') makes its use in a course organized according to the principal chronological and regional subdivisions of the Aegean Bronze Age both unnecessarily and undesirably complicated. Such considerations would make the 1989 survey by R. Treuil, P. Darcque, J.-C. Poursat, and G. Touchais entitled *Les Civilisations égéennes* preferable as an introductory text, were it not for the fact that the latter is available only in French and lacks sufficient illustrations.

Whatever its inadequacies as an introductory text, however, D.'s text is an excellent handbook for anyone having some familiarity with Aegean prehistory. His suggestion in the opening section on 'Terminology and chronology' (9-22) to divide the two millennia of the Bronze Age into five pan-Aegean historical periods pegged to the rise and fall of the region's palatial societies (Fig. 1.2; Prepalatial, First Palace, Second Palace, Third Palace, and Postpalatial) has much to recommend it. His brief summary of the region's environment and natural resources (23-29) is as good a piece of concentrated reading on this subject as exists anywhere. His survey of the Stone Age prelude to the Aegean Bronze Age (30-44) is equally effective, though this now needs to be supplemented by Demoule's and Perlès' recent overview of the Greek Neolithic in the *Journal of World Prehistory* 7 (1993) 355-416. An informative series of maps showing the principal sites in specific regions during particular intervals of time provides far better coverage of this kind than in any other existing text. The bibliography, though explicitly keyed to titles that provide coverage of previous discussion and that will be most accessible to an English-

speaking readership (hence the disproportionately small number of titles in Greek, Italian, and even German), is unusually rich and up-to-date (as of mid-1992). And last, but certainly not least, the topical coverage of the Bronze Age Aegean itself is comprehensive in its breadth, although it must often cut corners in terms of depth.

Though topical coverage may be relatively complete, spatial coverage is clearly not. D. notes in his preface that he will limit his survey to the Minoan, Cycladic, and Helladic cultural spheres, so that the extreme north of the Aegean is perhaps understandably excluded. But since the south-west Anatolian littoral is no less Minoan or Mycenaean than coastal Thessaly or the north-western Peloponnese in the Late Bronze Age, surely it should merit inclusion. The absence of any mention of the Trojan War also comes as a surprise. The simple fact is that a basic handbook entitled *The Aegean Bronze Age* should not omit consideration of the eastern and northern portions of this region.

D.'s decision to employ topics rather than periods and regions as the organizational backbone of his text requires him to postpone consideration of major historical questions until his final chapter (295-309). As were his highly compressed but both rich and readable introductory sections, this concluding 'semi-historical narrative' is a fine piece of writing that should become mandatory reading in any course that includes a component on Greek prehistory. Though it claims to focus on the how's and why's of the rise and fall of Aegean palatial societies as well as on their legacy to subsequent Greek culture, this essay in fact addresses a much wider range of issues, including some that have just emerged as central scholarly concerns within the past decade (e.g. the missing ruler in Aegean pictorial art). The single major theory to have appeared so recently as to have escaped critical assessment here is R. Drews' 1993 hypothesis that the collapse of Mycenaean palatial culture may have resulted from a fundamental change in the nature of warfare.

As D. sagely observes, synthetic works in a branch of archaeology as subject to change from new discoveries as is Aegean prehistory must inevitably be progress reports rather than 'final' publications. The discovery of Linear B tablets in an unmistakable LM IIIB context at Chania, one of them written by a hand considered by some also to be represented at Knossos, has shown that at least some of the Knossos tablets are very likely to date from the thirteenth century BC and that the palace there continued to function as an administrative centre well over a century after its partial destruction in the early fourteenth century (*Kadmos* 31 [1992] 61-87; *BCH* 117 [1993] 19-33; *Minos* 27-28 [1995] 261-81). The compromise position in favour of a single destruction in the later fourteenth century advocated by D. (21-22) thus seems as unnecessary as it is improbable. The date of the Theran eruption is on the point of being much more precisely identified by P. Kuniholm, S. Manning, and their collaborators with the aid of dendrochronological data from Anatolia. Extensive programmes of trace element analysis by neutron activation of later Mycenaean pottery by two teams based at the University of Heidelberg and Manchester University have made it possible to discriminate between the products of individual

Pelponnesian centres and are thus dramatically improving the precision with which some aspects of Mycenaean trade can be studied. Geomorphological studies by E. Zangger of individual sites are showing how dramatically different prehistoric landscapes may have been, especially in coastal locations (*JFA* 18 [1991] 1-15; *AJA* 98 (1994) 189-212; *OpAth* 20 (1994) 221-39). And the discovery of Minoan palatial buildings and 'villas' proceeds apace, with the result that D.'s Fig. 4.22 requires some modifications: Kommos and Petras both need to be upgraded to the rank of 'major centres', Mochlos has become the site of a 'villa', and the altogether new site of Galatas some 15 km south-east of Archanes should be added as a palace.

In view of the discipline being surveyed and the format of the publication, this book is necessarily inadequate as either a final publication or an introductory text. On the other hand, as a summary of the present state of scholarship on the Aegean Bronze Age, D. has provided an unusually comprehensive and up-to-date synthesis of a body of data that is rapidly becoming too large for any one individual to be able to control with authority. In exhibiting such control, he provides numerous insights into this era and its remains that will be of interest to all levels of readership from the intermediate student to the specialist professional.

JEREMY RUTTER

Dartmouth College

LAVELLE (B.M.) **The sorrow and the pity: a prolegomenon to a history of Athens under the Peisistratids, c. 560-510** BC (*Historia* Einzelschr. 80). Stuttgart: Steiner, 1993. Pp. 147. DM 58.

Although 'a true history of the tyranny is, quite simply, beyond possibility' (10) Lavelle is engaged on a 'history' of Peisistratid Athens (130) and the present work is the result of what was originally intended as an introductory chapter growing to a disproportionate size. Its central proposition, that the historical record about the Peisistratid tyranny is characterised by the lacunae and manipulations of revisionism, is not one which most readers will find unfamiliar or surprising. (After all, Thucydides already sounded off about the myth of the tyrannicides, and the conflict between alleged perpetual Alcmeonid exile and the inscription showing Cleisthenes as eponymous archon under Hippias is notorious.) Nor is the idea that the tyranny produced stability and prosperity exactly *recherché*. For L., however, most moderns (though he only cites Berve) are still deluded into believing Athens under the Peisistratids to have been a captive nation, oppressed by dictators. He therefore sets out to redress the balance. Insofar as there is anything distinctive about this enterprise it is partly (i) an insistence that all surviving information about the Peisistratids derives from fifth century Athens and that 'the Athenians' have a collective responsibility for establishing and denaturing the historical record (which is not to say that all Athenians always say the same things), but most obviously (ii) the claim that the phenomenon can be illuminated by comparison with the

creation of Myth of Resistance in post-1945 France. (The book takes its title from *Le Chagrin et la Pitié*, the 1971 Marcel Ophuls film which, on an epic scale, relentlessly exposed evidence for widespread tacit collaboration.)

Of these propositions the first merely makes explicit what most students of Athenian political history probably take for granted, and there is no harm in that. The French comparison is trickier ground. If it has any real worth (and the rarity with which reference is made to the matter outside 16-22 makes one wonder) it should involve a claim that it was not the distaste of good democrats for tyrannical government but collective guilt at collaboration with tyranny which led to fifth century Athenian lies about Peisistratus. But is this true?

The French and Athenian cases are certainly not altogether similar.

(a) L. writes over thirty pages on the Genesis of the Athenian Myth of Resistance, but Athens actually produces no myth of collective resistance. Leipsydrion was a factionally celebrated failure, and the Tyrannicide Myth is much more about how Liberation was achieved (one designed to claim maximum *Athenian* credit for it) than about general attitudes to the tyranny during its course. (In L.'s view it did not even acquire the elaboration of claiming that Athenians were disarmed and therefore unable to act against tyrants until well into the fifth century when people started telling the 'true' story.)

(b) L. argues that Athenians tolerated Peisistratids in their midst until after 496 (Hipparchus' archonship). Then in 493-487 things changed. The failed Ionian Revolt and events surrounding Marathon prompted execration of the whole family because of its treacherous collusion with the Persians. A two decade delay before revisionist guilt set in has no analogue in France. Here there was certainly *an* historical perspective (defeat and occupation was the latest item in a long history of Franco-German conflict), but there were immediate reasons for revisionism: if France was to claim parity with the other victor powers she had to construct a history of internal resistance which, added to the small but ideologically vital Free French contribution to military liberation, could save her from being merely patronized—necessary *inter alia* to help overcome disgust at having been worsted by Germans. The implication of L.'s comparison is that the Athenians felt neither patronized nor guilty in 510. That they did not feel guilt would presumably be due to their not thinking Peisistratid rule so bad that collusion with it was embarrassing. That, of course, is what L. would expect, and it would also leave them more likely to feel annoyed at than patronized by Spartan interference.

But L. does not really spell out why a 1945-style reaction of guilty revisionism was required twenty years later. The grave Persian threat explains, perhaps justifies, furious anger at and complete execration of the Peisistratids *en masse*. But why guilt? Perhaps an answer can be found by attending rather more to the Athenian decision to enter and then abandon the Ionian Revolt—the miscalculation that caused Athens to be targeted by Darius in the first palace (and gave Hippias the opportunity to attempt a violent come-back). Consequent recriminations might be an environment in which critics of those who exposed Athens to restoration of a retrospectively criticised tyranny could find themselves being told that they or their ancestors had not seemed particularly anti-tyrannical at the time of Peisistratus and Hippias. This would certainly help produce the political blood-letting of the 480s, but would it produce collective guilt? And is not the invention of the tyrannicide myth in any case more to do with uneasy relations with Sparta?

I append a few more specific observations.

(a) The misrepresentation of which Athenian tradition is accused is rather odd since it largely avoids attributing tyrannical behaviour to the tyrants. (True, the murder of Hipparchus supposedly prompted a nasty interlude, but the mythical version *ex hypothesi* did not admit that interlude.) Fifth century Athenians are supposed to have taken refuge in representing their ancestors as stupid enough to be outwitted by a recidivist would-be tyrant about whom tales of brutality and perversion were then *not* invented. (The irregular sexual union with Megacles' daughter will have struck most Athenians as a joke against Megacles, not a proof of Peisistratus' deviant character.) This is a peculiar form for a *guilty* reaction to take. (Of course, part of the trouble may be that the mainline 'official' version is badly attested in its own right: we have to deduce the tyrannicide myth from a statue group and the implicit or explicit denials of Herodotus and Thucydides and we see Alcmeonid manipulations more clearly than 'popular' ones. But L. does not allow himself this way out, for he regards the general silence about events during, as distinct from at the start and end of, the tyranny as a reliable datum from which the fact of revisionism can be inferred.)

(b) According to L. (69 f.) Thucydides lacked evidence to prove that Hippias was *the* tyrant as is shown by methodological weakness of his deductive proof (based on likelihood that P. would have appointed the oldest son, which Thuc. thinks he can demonstrate was Hippias). Is this such a bad piece of deduction? What does L. think would count as the sort of information likely ever to exist from a largely pre-documentary society which would have enabled Thuc. to prove the point to L.'s satisfaction?

(c) 109 f.: the *epikouroi* of Hdt. 1.64 are not foreign mercenaries but foreign allies (possibly true) and the bodyguards of Thuc. 6.56-7 must be Athenians, for which *cf.* Antiphon fr. 1, Ar. *Kn.* 448 (but *pace* L. not *Lys.* 665 f.). But under any scenario there will be *some* pro-Peisistratid Athenians: the fact that 'undesirables' (Antiphon, Cleon-Paphlagon—who *is* of course 'foreign') are accused of being, or being descended from, tyrant's *doruphoroi* establishes nothing interesting.

(d) 32: L. apparently believes at one and the same time that Hippias wanted restoration to Athens and that Athens in 490 faced complete annihilation. How so?

(e) 45 f. might make more of the irony of the construction of Theseus as political totem of Athenian democracy when it had arguably been the Peisistratid period which turned him into a specifically Athenian hero in the first place.

(f) 94 n. 23: L. attacks the view of Fornara and Samons that 'Alcmeonid' views could be heard in Athenian barbershops. But this cannot be entirely right. He fails to allow for something at least implicit in his own presentation, namely that different parts of society could collude in face-saving representations.

(g) L. on one hand notes representations of Pericles as a new Peisistratos (while saying nothing about equations of empire and tyranny—a serious shortcoming), yet finds something substantial in the Aristophanic view that Cleon's talk of tyrannical conspiracies contrasted with fifty years in which the word tyranny was hardly heard (125).

(h) L. (98 n. 35) argues that Diakria was not Athenian before 546, and then uses this fact to underline his claim that the overall story about Peisistratus' attempts to get tyranny is incredible. Why can the apparent marginalisation of Diakria not itself be due to deformation? One could make the same point against L.'s conclusion that Megacles was involved in Peisistratus' First Tyranny (his ground being that P. could only have won a body-guard from the assembly if one of the other faction leaders swung his chaps' votes behind him)—all the 'facts' here are part of an in itself coherent 'story', and if we start (as L. does) saying that the whole fake wound story is a *topos*, we are not entitled to regard anything that goes with it as worth building on.

CHRISTOPHER TUPLIN

University of Liverpool

POWELL (A.) and HODKINSON (S.) *Ed.* **The shadow of Sparta.** London: Routledge, 1994. Pp. vii + 408. £35.
MALKIN (I.) **Myth and territory in the Spartan Mediterranean.** Cambridge UP, 1994. Pp. xviii + 278. £37.50.

When the sun finally sets on Lakonian studies as a privileged domain within a non-Athenocentric Greek history, the long shadow that Sparta has cast on both ancient and modern historiography will inevitably fade with it. Happily, while that shadow is still lengthening the reservoir of further enquiry has not yet been entirely exhausted. The loosely defined aims of the volume edited by Powell and Hodkinson are 'to cast light both on non-Spartan thought and on Spartan practice' and 'to examine possible effects of images of Sparta, whether realistic or not, upon the thought of non-Spartan Greeks' (vii). Within this broad canvas, the ten contributors embrace a variety of approaches and themes which spans literature, philosophy and history.

Unlike Powell's earlier and more thematically-based collection of *Lakonika* (*Classical Sparta* [London 1989]), the majority of the contributions in this volume confine themselves to discussing individual authors, and particularly their attitudes towards Sparta. Thus William Poole, in a cautious and judicious survey of Euripidean tragedy, sees the anti-Spartan invective that issues from the mouths of both protagonists and choruses as a vehicle for the tragedian's own embitterment, while David Harvey—after a couple of slightly dubious leers to 'the lads in the gallery' (35, 38)—constructs a plausible argument for Aristophanes' latent sympathies towards Sparta, engendered perhaps by his Kimonian outlook. Xenophon's sympathies towards Sparta are well known, but in an essay challenging the view that the portrayal of Persia in the *Kyropaidia* is simply an allegorical depiction of Sparta, Christopher Tuplin maintains that the historian was capable of a more discriminating, detached and perhaps even critical outlook towards the state that took him under its wing. Any ambivalence in Isokrates' attitudes towards Sparta in the *Panathenaikos* is dispelled by Vivienne Gray, who makes a forceful case for viewing the infuriatingly involuted epilogue as a reinforcement, rather than deconstruction, of the criticisms expressed earlier in the work. G. also considers the important question of possible Lakonian—or at least Lakonising—elements within Isokrates' audience, and this issue is resumed by P., this time for Plato's *Laws*. P. infers that Lakonians were prominent in the author's mind as a potential audience not only from the evident distinctiveness of the *Laws* within the Platonic corpus, but also from the clear influence of Spartan institutions, religion, narrative techniques and modes of persuasion upon the work. By presenting the Spartans with the image of an ideal society with which they could already find some degree of communion, Plato fulfils the role of a second Tyrtaios in providing a new set of *nomoi* to remedy Sparta's ills.

Plato's criticisms of Sparta were inherited by Aristotle, and Eckhart Schütrumpf contrasts Aristotle's critique (*Politics* 2.9) of the flaws endemic in the Spartan constitution from the outset with the heuristic concept of moral decline favoured by Xenophon and Ephoros. This is a theme which is also taken up in the broader analyses of Nick Fisher, whose examination of public attitudes towards Sparta in the fourth century highlights the enduring fascination that a now-enfeebled Sparta continued to hold for the Athenians, and of Stephen Hodkinson, who focuses on the role of wealth in Spartan discourse and the proverbial disdain for sumptuary display supposedly held by earlier generations of Spartan citizens. H. attributes the creation of this *topos* to external influences operative towards the end of the fifth century—partly the upsurge in philosophical speculation and partly the increasing disenchantment of the Athenian élite—but he also tentatively suggests that the denouncement of the corrupting influence of coined money found in Diodoros (and, we assume, Ephoros) may derive from the pamphlet allegedly written by the Spartan king, Pausanias, during his exile after 395 BC.

The two remaining contributions concentrate more on the testimony of historians. In describing the battle of Plataia in 479 BC, Herodotos (9.54) reports that in Athenian experience, the Spartans tended to think one thing, but say another. Nevertheless, as Alfred Bradford points out, the theme of Lakonian duplicity does not emerge in any of Herodotos' extended portrayals of individual Spartans (Kleomenes, Leonidas, Pausanias). In this sense, a clear departure is marked by the creation of this duplicitous stereotype in authors such as Euripides, Aristophanes and particularly Thucydides, whose concern was to endow his characters with complete and coherent psychological profiles which conformed to imputed ethnic traits. Michael Whitby's target is the view—now virtually (though not entirely) *de rigueur* among ancient historians—that the whole edifice of the Spartan system was founded on the anxiety of helot insurrection and the repression which this fear occasioned. Reviewing the evidence, Whitby argues that in fact the Spartans regarded the helots as more of a facility than a hindrance.

There is much of interest here: ancient historians will find W.'s synthesis of previous work in the area extremely useful, while G.'s discussion (and rejection) of the authority of 'reader-reception' and polysemic reading in antiquity is an important contribution to the field of ancient rhetoric. It is, however, disappointing that although many of the authors correctly identify the role of outsiders in the creation of the *mirage spartiate* during the fourth century, there is no systematic discussion of Herodotos' earlier role in presenting Sparta as a paradigm of alterity. Not only (as Paul Cartledge has observed) is Sparta the only Greek state which attracts the ethnographic treatment that Herodotos normally reserves for *barbaroi*, but an explicit opposition between Sparta and Athens is introduced into the opening sections of the *Histories* (1.56-68), where the well-governed Dorian city of Sparta, founded by immigrant Greeks, is contrasted with the tyrannically-governed Ionian city of Athens, founded by indigenous Pelasgians.

A far more serious failing of this volume is its lack of cohesion—something which invariably characterises the whole *genre* of edited volumes. There are a number of themes which run throughout the collection - notably Spartan duplicity, the artificial creation of a gulf between the idealised past and the corrupt present of Sparta, and the role of Lakonisers in Athenian ideology—yet such is the general lack of engagement between the individual contributions that one wonders whether it was simply cynical irony that attributed the term 'colloquium' to the forum at which they were first aired. These problems could have been partially remedied by a more intrusive editorial intervention: greater cross-referencing would have been desirable, while the absence of an introduction which might have served to frame the succeeding papers is particularly serious.

The title of Irad Malkin's monograph might seem astonishing at first sight, especially to those accustomed to think of Sparta as 'a land-locked, introverted, xenophobic city, disclaiming commerce, money, and the sea' (8). In fact, as M. demonstrates with his customary eloquence, Sparta was enmeshed in a discursive network of foundation legends and legitimation myths which created—in conceptual terms, at any rate—a 'Spartan Mediterranean'. The foundation of Taras (traditional date 706 BC) and of Herakleia Trachinia (426 BC) are familiar episodes in the story of Spartan expansion, but at one time or another cities as far apart as Kroton, Lokroi, Kythera, Melos, Thera, Gortyn, Lyktos, Polyrrhenia and Knidos all claimed a Spartan heritage (or did they have it foisted upon them?), and beyond these were the granddaughter colonies such as Cyrene, founded by Thera and linked to both her metropolis and her grand-metropolis through the shared cult of Apollo Karneios. At the centre of this Mediterranean-wide imagined community lay Sparta, itself considered to be a colonial foundation of the Dorians and the descendants of Herakles.

The creation of 'charter myths', which justify present anomalies by reference to an invented past, constitutes one of the ways in which Greek cities could articulate territorial claims and rights of conquest. Thus the Dorian claims to the Peloponnese derived from the fact that Zeus had promised it as a gift to the Herakleidai (ch. 1), while Battos' right to rule at Cyrene was guaranteed by the clod of Libyan soil that had been given to his mythical ancestor, Euphemos, by a son of Poseidon (ch. 6). Far more innovative, however, is M.'s emphasis on 'precedent-setting' myths. Unlike charter myths, these are generally elaborated before—rather than after—the event and express territorial aspirations rather than retrospective legitimation. Particularly useful from this point of view was the *nostos* tradition, found in a succession of authors from Homer onwards, which recounted the involuntary wanderings of Menelaos on his return from Troy (ch. 2). Thus Homer's description (*Od.* 4.85-91) of Menelaos' visit to Libya could be employed as a precedent for settlement, opening up Libyan territory for those Therans who were to follow in the footsteps of their mythical Spartan ancestor. Indeed, M. tentatively suggests that the localisation of the 'Port of Menelaos' on the Libyan coast may represent the territorial aspirations of the future Greek colonists of Cyrene during the precolonial period when they occupied the offshore island of Plataia. Post-Homeric authors (notably Lykophron, though the tradition could be earlier) had Menelaos blown off course to the Italian peninsula and M. sees in Menelaos' disembarkation at Cape Lakinion another mythical antecedent which served to open up Krotoniate territory for eventual Spartan settlement. Similarly, deducing that the localisation at Irasa of the mythical struggle between Herakles and Antaios predates Cyrenean annexation of this part of Libya, M. argues that its function can hardly be a *post eventum* justification for conquest but instead anticipates eventual territorial expansion on the part of Cyrene.

M.'s decision to adopt a *polis*-oriented approach is dictated by his concern with the *historical role* of myths rather than with 'myth' *per se* (8). Nevertheless this inevitably excludes other ramified appeals and claims within colonial relationships. It is, for example, entirely feasible that the legend of Menelaos' disembarkation at Cape Lakinion serves as a validation myth, opening up Krotoniate territory to colonisation. Nevertheless, while Menelaos was undoubtedly a Lakonian hero, he was also an Achaian hero (the Achaians were considered to have occupied Argos and Sparta prior to the arrival of the Dorians) and I see no compelling reason to privilege the story of the Lakonian foundation of Kroton (63-64) over the better established Achaian origins of the city that are presented by Herodotos (8.47) and Antiochos of Syracuse (*FGrH* 555.10), especially since the Spartan pedigree is only explicitly attested for the first time in Pausanias (3.3.1).

M. emphasises the important historical function that myths serve in articulating attitudes. Nevertheless, while espousing enthusiastically an *histoire de mentalité*, M. is reluctant to abandon entirely *histoire événementielle* (thus the historicity of the Dorian invasion is defended on the basis of the long-term persistence of the myth concerning the return of the Herakleidai). Theoretically, there need be no contradiction between these two approaches—social reality both structures and is structured by *mentalité*—but their juxtaposition in this book leads to a certain ambiguity. For instance, in discussing the supposed Spartan foundations of Aegean islands such as Melos, Thera or Krete, M. maintains that the

reality of an original Spartan colonisation is irrelevant to the perceptions that were held by these settlements in the Archaic and Classical periods (67). Yet he immediately qualifies this statement by suggesting that the origin and persistence of these perceptions argue for their veracity and ends up by proposing a 'true' reconstruction in which the integration of Amyklai into the Spartan state created a category of excluded Lakonians who colonised Melos, Thera, Krete and Knidos in the mid-eighth century (113). Ironically, in order to retain Spartan agency within this reconstruction, M. is forced to reject the Thucydidean date for the Lakonian colonisation of Melos (1116 BC) and to appeal to the archaeological record which demonstrates no stable settlement patterns before the last third of the eighth century. Yet at Gortyn (which M. considers to have been colonised in the same wave) the settlement evidence is considerably earlier. Admittedly, the seemingly unbroken sequence down into the seventh century at Gortyn cannot exclude Spartan infiltration into a pre-existing settlement, but if we are to regard the Spartans as archaeologically invisible then we can hardly appeal to the material record in dating their supposed arrival on Melos. The example demonstrates the danger in attempting to ground what may be originally independent discursive appeals to a Spartan heritage within a 'real' and 'integrated' historical past.

Indeed, M.'s self-professed positivism can occasionally lead to some rather uncritical conclusions. In describing the abortive colonisation attempts on the part of Dorieus (the half-brother of the Spartan king, Kleomenes), M. argues that the (non-Delphic) oracle authorising the Libyan venture must be a genuine response rather than a *post eventum* invention, since the colony failed after only two years (198). Yet there are other explanations—we cannot, for example, rule out the possibility that the whole story of Dorieus' preparations was a piece of Delphic propaganda, invented after the failure of the colony to advertise the dire consequences that befall those who set out without obtaining the official Pythian seal of approval. Again, M. seems inclined to accept the historical existence of Phalanthos, one of the traditional founders of Taras (132-33, 142). However, in marked contrast to other *oikistai*, Phalanthos was to have no tomb or even a cenotaph in the Tarantine *agora* (though it should be noted that archaeologically speaking, there are as yet very few places where an *agora* can be dated back to the earliest years of a colony). Justin's explanation for the absence of a tomb—namely, that Phalanthos had died in exile among the Brentesians and been cremated so that only his ashes could be returned to Taras and scattered over the *agora*—seems a little too convenient and surely invites scepticism rather than credulity.

For all that, this is a wide-ranging, intellectually stimulating and scholarly book which makes an important contribution to the cognitive history of Greek antiquity. Ultimately, the judicious and disciplined analysis of myths as historical formulations of a Spartan self-concept represents a more fruitful approach to the Lakonian past than undue reliance on the refracted perceptions of Athenian writers.

JONATHAN M. HALL

University of Chicago

GABRIELSEN (V.) **Financing the Athenian fleet: public taxation and social relations**. Baltimore and London: Johns Hopkins UP, 1994. Pp. xvii + 306. £37.

Although the Athenian trierarchy has been dealt with in a number of social, economic and naval histories, monographical treatment has long been awaited. Gabrielsen has filled this gap with a study that is well researched, clearly and persuasively argued, and above all highly readable. Not only do we now have a third monograph on a key institution of Athens—after Rhodes, *The Athenian boule* (1972) and Hansen's *The Athenian Assembly in the age of Demosthenes* (1987)—but progress is also achieved by the fact that the political importance of a non-constitutional institution has been fully recognised. The trierarchy lies at the interface of political, economic and naval history and highlights how the three were inseparably linked in classical Athens. As G. himself maintains, it gives access to the important question of the attitude of democracy towards its wealthy citizens and of their changing role in the course of the fifth and fourth centuries (4, 8). Although G. does not offer radically new views, some of his observations have important implications. No serious student of fifth and fourth century Athenian history will be able to pass by this book.

In Part I ('The origins of the Athenian trierarchy') G. argues against both the view that the *naucrariai* were the antecedants of the trierarchy and the view that Themistocles founded the trierarchy in 483/2. Although the *naucrariai* obviously held financial duties in sixth century Athens, nothing suggested that these included the construction and maintenance of ships. He rightly rejects etymological arguments as well as the evidence from lexicographers (21-22). There was also no indication that Themistocles introduced the trierarchy together with his naval programme. Rather, 'a gradual increase in the number of public vessels to be commanded by individuals other than the traditional proprietors of ships began to give shape to a new duty that required a well defined set of rules' (34). The trierarchy, like the choregia, stood in the tradition of aristocratic funding of public projects (350).

In Part II, dealing with the financial and demographic scope of the trierarchy, G. stresses the flexibility of the system. Both eligibility and outlay were relative, taking into account changes of fortune and individual social ambition. Rejecting the view that there was a liturgical census, he argues, like Davies (*APF*), that the upper and lower limits of property qualification were highly flexible, depending on the number of trierarchs available, their willingness to spend and overspend, the internal political situation, and the state's own liquidity. Yet against Davies he suggests that even estates worth 1 tal. 2000 dr. (Is. 5.35-6) could at times be eligible (52). Further important arguments in this section include (a) that it was property that carried liability, rather than people (66); (b) that there were no liturgical registers before 358/7 (73 ff.); and (c) that the major problem the trierarchy faced at the time of the early naval records was manpower shortage and shortage of equipment (82 f.). All this points to a system that did, and had to, combine voluntarism and compulsion (72). Although it worked not without internal tensions (e.g. *antidosis*

procedures, withdrawal from service, embezzlement of equipment), its flexibility ensured that there was always a sufficient number of trierarchs available (221).

Part III focuses on the actual costs accruing. G. argues that the general tendency of Athenian trierarchic politics was to privatise naval costs (117 ff.). In principle, the state financed ship building, equipment and the salary (*misthos*) of the rowers, whereas the trierarchs paid for food (*trophê*), bonuses (*epiphorai*) and maintenance of ships. Yet the division was by no means clear-cut, since on the one hand the state salary to soldiers decreased when public wealth declined, and on the other trierarchs created financial incentives for able crew. Trierarchic costs thus varied immensely according to the state's economic situation, its ability to obtain money from *eisphora* payments, and the triearch's ambition (118-25). G. rightly emphasises, however, that trierarchs never built ships on private expense. Naval *epidoseis* referred to payments on equipment and crew, but not to the donation of ships (201 ff.).

Increasing shortage of people able or willing to serve and, due to embezzlement and damage, increasing shortage of equipment called for reforms in the mid-fourth century (Part IV). The symmories founded in 358/7 were, as G. argues against Ruschenbusch and Mossé, distinguished from those organised for the collection of *eisphora* (183 ff.). G. assesses the total of trierarchs over a period of three years at 1200 (177), so that each symmory included sixty men, serving either as active trierarchs or *synteleis*, or both. The function of the symmories was to structure trierarchic service more efficiently, to relieve the shortage of equipment by the introduction of financial contributions only (*synteleia*), and to recover naval debts (*cf.* 224 f.). Further reforms in 340 aimed at a fairer distribution of financial burdens among the twelve hundred by 'adding up' partial financial contributions made in the form of syntrierarchies and *synteleis*. Against Rhodes (*AJAH* 7 [1982]), G. argues that in 340 neither the number of trierarchs nor that of the symmories were reduced (211 f.). The book finishes off with an assessment of the participation of trierarchs in active politics (213-17), which unfortunately is based on rather poor statistical grounds.

G. has succeeded in demonstrating how the trierarchy continuously operated on traditional ethics of generosity and political pressure, on the state's careful handling of voluntarism and compulsion—which says much about Athenian internal politics in general. Less satisfactory is G.'s tendency to represent problems and tensions arising from the trierarchy, both within the liturgy—paying class and between them and the rest of Athenians, as matters easily solved by legal compulsion and administrative reforms. Only when the public negotiation of taxation and power is understood as a continuous process does the specific relationship between wealth and democracy come into focus. Despite its perhaps at times too legalistic perspective, G.'s book is a very useful one.

SITTA VON REDEN

University of Bristol

WORLEY (L.J.) **Hippeis: the cavalry of ancient Greece**. Boulder: Westview P, 1994. Pp. xiii + 241 + ill. £24.95.

Until relatively recently the cavalry of ancient Greece was neglected in favour of the hoplite. This has to some extent warped our understanding of ancient warfare—as can be seen in V.D. Hanson's *The western way of war* (New York 1983) and J. Keegan's *A history of warfare* (London 1993). However, the last ten years has seen a timely renewal of interest in the cavalry and Worley's book (part of Westview's History and Warfare series), is the third on this topic since 1988. The first was Glenn R. Bugh's *The horsemen of Athens* (Princeton 1988), the second my own *The cavalry of classical Greece* (Oxford 1993).

W.'s stated aim in writing is to redress the lack of attention paid to ancient Greek cavalry and in particular to its military aspects. Following an introduction which argues this, he covers chronologically the history of Greek cavalry from Mycenae to Alexander (the Hellenistic cavalries are not included). The chapters are: 'The Mycenaean mounted warrior', 'Greek cavalry in the Archaic period', 'Greek cavalry in the Periclean age', 'Greek cavalry in the Peloponnesian War', 'Greek cavalry in the fourth century BC', and 'The cavalry of Philip II and Alexander III'. A short conclusion sums up his central thesis, that the cavalry played a more important role on the battlefield than is usually realised.

The chapters vary considerably both in content and length. The first two, for example (14 and 32 pp. respectively) concentrate on establishing the existence and organization of cavalry during the Mycenaean and Archaic periods. The second of these also contains a substantial digression on the Assyrian cavalry. The remaining chapters focus more on the battlefield employment of the cavalry. In fact, much of the last two chapters is devoted to detailed battlefield description. 'Greek cavalry in the fourth century BC' (30 pp.) begins with a discussion of cavalry in Asia Minor (including that of the Ten Thousand) and of Xenophon's works on cavalry organization and equipment. Almost half of it, though, examines two battles—Leuktra and Mantineia. Similarly, after a brief discussion of the history and organization of the Macedonian cavalry (including the battle against Bardylis), over half of the short (16 pp.) chapter 'The cavalry of Philip II and Alexander III', is devoted to Chaironeia and Issos.

The book is fluently written, easy to read, and provides a solid general introduction to the military history of ancient Greek cavalry. The maps and illustrations are clear and useful. One of the strongest aspects of the book is W.'s ability to sum up his arguments clearly and concisely at the start and end of each chapter. As a fairly general work it seems best suited to senior secondary school students and junior undergraduates.

However, because the book is very readable, the unwary could easily fall victim to its relatively uncritical use of the evidence (especially the artistic material) and the tendencies to gloss over debate and to state theory as fact. For example, W. accepts (136-9) that Xenophon's recommendations on cavalry formations and equipment apply to Agesilaos' mercenary cavalry because 'it seems almost certain that Xenophon played a major role in [their] organization and training'. This is possible, but there is no ancient evidence for it and, earlier (74-5), W. accepted that these same descriptions applied to the Athenian cavalry. That Xenophon's works make recommendations and do not necessarily describe existing practice fails to emerge from W.'s discussion. Similarly, there is little evidence for the cavalry organization and formations of many *poleis*, so any reconstructions are necessarily rather speculative, but W. often rather incautiously puts his forward as definite. A number of names and titles are also consistently misspelled—'Spartulos' for 'Spartolus', 'enomotachos' for 'enomotarchos', 'Tolimedes' for 'Tolmides', and 'Campanian cavalry' for 'Companion cavalry'.

The book basically narrates the history of Greek cavalry from Mycenae to Alexander, with appropriate analysis inserted on the way. This essentially duplicates Bugh's method in the military sections of *The horsemen of Athens*. W. is less focussed on Athens, spends more time on the earlier periods, and provides rather more detailed analysis of fourth century battles. Otherwise, those familiar with Bugh's work will not find a vast amount which is new—especially in the chapters 'Greek cavalry in the Periclean age' and 'Greek cavalry in the Peloponnesian War'.

This chronological emphasis has also resulted in gaps in the treatment of important topics. It is not made clear, for example, what weaponry was carried by the various cavalries at different times and there is no attempt to define 'shock tactic', nor to discuss how it could work. This leads to some vagueness, and occasional inconsistency. For instance, Athenian cavalry is described as 'heavy' cavalry (70) and, later on, as being equipped with javelins (77); the Boiotian arm is equipped with javelins (62) but is earlier assumed to be capable of employing 'the direct assault or shock tactic' (55).

In short, the book has good features and W. also correctly identified a gap which at that time existed in the literature. However, his chronological approach is rather limiting and his evidence and argument need to be treated with caution.

I.G. SPENCE

University of New England, Australia

BALTRUSCH (E.) **Symmachie und Spondai: Untersuchungen zum griechischen Völkerrecht der archaischen und klassichen Zeit (8.-5. Jahrhundert v. Chr.).** Berlin and New York: de Gruyter, 1994. Pp. xi + 274. DM 188.

Here is a book best read back to front. Not only is the conclusion easily the clearest and most engaging exposition of what the book has been all about, but the author actually postpones until the end such preliminaries as a survey of past scholarship (189-91) and cautionary remarks about the interpretation of Greek terminology (200-5). At the beginning, we are offered instead only the most perfunctory page-and-a-half of introduction before being plunged into a discussion of symmachies (Part I). These military alliances, we are told, could be concluded only after the establishment of another, much older type of agreement, the *spondai*, discussion of which is reserved for later (Part II). Dealing first with what, historically and institutionally, comes first presumably seemed too obvious to Baltrusch, but it would have helped make his argument less convoluted and repetitive. For all its frequent summaries and elaborate hierarchy of subdivisions (see 130-1, for example, for sub-sub-sub section II.2.B.b.β.ββ), the book is feebly organized.

In spite of this, it emerges that B. is embarked upon quite an interesting enterprise, which is to reconstruct changing patterns of interstate relations from Homer to the end of the Peloponnesian War. During the eighth century, he argues, communities were related to one another, not by collective ties, but by personal bonds of marriage, kinship, guest-friendship, or *Gefolgschaft* among their leading families. There was neither room nor need for specifically military alliances. In war, leaders might arrange, by means of *spondai*, brief interruptions of the fighting, but *spondai* could not bring wars to an end; only a decisive military result or the establishment of friendship could achieve that. From the seventh century onwards, we begin to find collective ties between communities as such being created. Symmachies were developed to establish such links, while *spondai* became longer-term arrangements, suspending hostilities for so long that they in effect became a means of making peace. Gradually, as the network of relations between *poleis* grew ever more intricate, and as Athenian imperialism broke the mould altogether, the terms of alliances and treaties grew more complex and more concerned to safeguard the political status of the less powerful. By the time of the Peloponnesian War, the system could no longer ensure any stability in international relations, and by the beginning of the fourth century, the creation of a new kind of international order was underway.

In all this, the treatment of *spondai* is coherent and largely plausible. I cannot agree, though, that in origin and essence the term meant a guarantee of safety from violent assault (99, 101, 125, 202). The Homeric evidence cited shows that *spondai* could apply to a variety of promises and agreements, provided these were made binding by a libation to the gods. Nor is B. likely to persuade many that the famous treaty between Chalkis and Eretria not to use long-range missiles against one another was misunderstood by our sources and was intended to regulate, not the whole conduct of war, but only a single, final duel (109-11). Yet in general, this, the longest part of the work, contains a good deal of worthwhile comment.

The treatment of alliances has its moments, too, but is on balance unconvincing. Wholly inadequate is the sketchy treatment of 'personal' international relations in Homer, which cites hardly any evidence and no literature more recent than 1914 (4-5). It is, moreover, quite at odds with B.'s own subsequent—rather good—account of the roles of community and state in Homer (92-9). Several key assertions about the nature of symmachies seem questionable. However often it is reiterated, there is no apparent foundation for the claim that the clause stipulating that both parties should have 'the same friend and foe' was always aimed at one particular enemy. The corollary assumption that Spartan treaties were always

concluded against the enemy within—the helots—is implausible (11, 17-18, 29, 40). It is said that the 'friend and foe' clause was sworn unilaterally by the party accepting alliance, while the party actively seeking it promised assistance in different terms (often agreeing 'to follow wherever they might be led', 18-19, 58, 66). Furthermore, it is claimed that, in the complex world of the late fifth century, the 'friend and foe' clause was replaced by a more restricted one, merely promising assistance 'if anyone should invade the territory' of the ally (68-82). I fail to see how either view is compatible with the acknowledged fact that the 'friend and foe' clause features, alongside a promise to follow where the ally leads, in the terms of alliance imposed by Sparta as late as 404 and 379 BC (23-4, 26).

Without modification, then, B.'s picture of historical development cannot stand. Yet his study deserves serious attention, dealing as it does with an important subject, to which it applies considerable scholarship. Tellingly, B. never feels the need to explain the abbreviation 'StV II', ubiquitous in the footnotes. No doubt, like an academic Alexander, he sleeps with Bengtson's *Staatsverträge* under his pillow.

HANS VAN WEES

University College London

HUNTER (V.J.) **Policing Athens: social control in the Attic lawsuits, 420-320 BC** Princeton UP, 1994. Pp. xv + 303. £25.

Virginia Hunter, previously best known for her provocative treatments of Thucydides and Herodotus, has in recent years been working on the orators and comedy as sources for the legal and social history of the classical Athenian community. This book, developing from preliminary articles on widows, women's property-ownership, and gossip, much of which appears reworked here, is a substantial and often very illuminating analysis of many aspects of Athenian familial and social life and the related operations, formal and less formal, of the legal system; it is likely to be followed by a further study, concentrating on the role of state officials and the penal system in regulating behaviour. One of the most notable, and largely successful, aspects of this work is H.'s judicious use of comparative material, methods and models, both from anthropological studies, largely of the supposed 'Mediterranean' societies, and from historical work on pre-industrial societies; particularly interesting, I thought, were the use of material from eighteenth and early nineteenth century England to illustrate systems of voluntary prosecution, from early modern Spain to illustrate arbitration procedures, and from the Americas to speculate about methods of control over slaves.

'Policing' and 'social control' are interpreted very broadly: the book is as much about the dynamics of relationships inside households and in kin and social networks as about legal processes within the community. Thus in ch. 1 H. focuses on husband-wife relations, and emphasises the flexibility of the institution of the *kyrieia*—not only changing over time, e.g. from father to husband to son, but on occasions at least varying at the same time according to role. She suggests plausibly that a wife might, if appealing to her natal kin for protection against her husband, be acting in recognition of their residual, and renewable, *kyrieia*, while she might also prefer another male (or males) than her husband, or in addition to him, to act for her legally (the case rests especially on Isaeus 7 and 11, where Wyse, perhaps rashly, argued that plural *kyrioi*, where a husband was alive, were mere rhetoric). She also supports the lines (taken, recently, in various forms by Foxhall, Harris, Brock and others), that women's work, their 'ownership' of land, slaves and money, e.g. through dowries, and their general informal influence within households, were all phenomena which it would be dangerous to underestimate. It is clear that her main aim here is to emphasise the elements of mutual interaction and female influence underplayed in traditional accounts; but it remains a little odd, given the proper attention paid elsewhere in the book to violence between citizens, to slave-owners' use of brute force to control slaves, and to the ideological importance of the inviolability of the citizen body, that no attention is paid to the strong probability that householders exercised control over wives and daughters through orders, threats and beatings; nor does she ask how men may have conceptualised the differences in respect of bodily punishments between slaves, children (also of course *paides*) and adult free women. There is some relevant evidence, e.g. from drama (Ar. *Lys.* 510 ff., Eur. *Med.* 241-3), and it seems well worth asking what it suggests, and why there is not more.

The chapter on disputes within kin has an admirable focus on the role of arbitration, both private and public, as a very important way in which the community sought to settle disputes through non-violent self-help and widespread participation, avoiding full legal actions. H.'s attempts at reconstruction of their procedures and styles are valuable; perhaps she might have emphasised even more the likely confusions, delays and abuses possible (*cf.* above all Dem. 21.83 ff.). Perhaps rightly, she explores the possibility that much of the time, although naturally invisible in detail to us, depending as we do for our information on speeches delivered in court, such practices, the widespread participation they involved, and the emphasis on resolution and equity rather than strict law, may have worked well enough. Throughout, H.'s analysis, rather like Ober's recent work, focuses on cohesive community practices, discourse and spirit, operated by relatively large numbers of male citizens who had some resources, awareness of procedures, and networks of kin and friends; but, as she emphasizes on the very last page, other analyses, based more on differences of class and status, could produce a more complex and less optimistic picture.

Much in the book (above all ch. 6) focuses on issues of bodily punishment or maltreatment and the free-slave distinction, whether inside the household, or through the legal system. Material, both Greek and comparative, is collected on the private 'punishment' of slaves, and a tentative conclusion reached that while whipping was certainly systematic, and the type of offenses and types of whippings inflicted seem broadly comparable between Greece and the Americas, the absence, in Greek texts containing advice on slave-management, of the elaborately calculated scales of appropriate punishments found in American handbooks may be significant, and explained by the relatively small, largely domestic, scale of operations. But one might wonder how far such a conclusion is justified, given the brevity of the treatment of slave-management even in Xenophon's and Pseudo-Aristotle's treatises and their moral agendas; they do not read as realistic, detailed and practical advice. As with wife-beating, a systematically harsh reality may only very rarely surface into the sort of texts we have; on the other hand, H. puts together well some neglected evidence from various cities for the 'mill/correction house' for seriously troublesome slaves, and finds appropriate analogies elsewhere.

On the equally important question of judicial slave torture, H.'s discussion seems inconsistent and ultimately unsatisfying. On 70-1, and again on 90, H. appears to accept the traditional view that slave-torture very rarely (if ever) occurred, as those challenged always refused, whether because they feared what might be said, or because they were reluctant to entrust the case to a slave or to let a valuable slave be damaged. At the same time she argues that the possibility that slaves might give evidence against their masters was a significant element of social control; the more since, as she observes in a useful discussion, slaves went about everywhere, often ignored, in houses and streets. In Appendix I to ch. 3, however, H. accepts Headlam's view, recently reasserted by Mirhardy (*CQ* 41 [1991] 78 ff.), that challenges to slave-torture may have been not so infrequent, despite the fact that in all our forensic examples the challenge was denied, because where it did take place it was decisive, and the case would not have come to court. Hence the 'deterrent value' of slave information may have been the greater. Their case rests on Aristotle *Rhetoric* 1377a 1 ff. on the oath-challenges, and on a brief remark of Pollux (8.62); the arguments are complex and controversial, and it is not enough for H. merely to declare Mirhardy's case 'incontrovertible' (93), especially since neither addresses the various forensic passages which have seemed to most to assert that evidence acquired under torture could in principle be presented as (very strong) evidence at a jury-trial.

There are other places where one wished for more, for example on the ideological problems involved in the Athenian use of slaves, some of them ostentatiously barbarian slaves (the Scythian archers), as 'police', admittedly in strictly limited roles; none the less, armed with bows and whips, they could be charged by councillors or other magistrates to control or discipline citizens (H. describes their activities in a number of places, esp. 145-9, but her only explanation for their use of weapons against citizens, as an anachronistic survival from the archaic period, does not convince, 243 n. 53). But the book contains a great many valuable and convincing discussions, and overall makes another substantial contribution to our understanding of how Athenian society and laws worked; it also shows in an exemplary manner how cautious use of comparative material can shed light in many a dark corner of our evidence and of Athenian life.

NICK FISHER

University of Wales, Cardiff

MAASS (M.) **Das antike Delphi: Orakel, Schätze und Monumente**. Darmstadt: Wissenschaftliche Buchgesellschaft, 1993. Pp. ix + 319 + ill. DM 64.

A monograph on Delphi—is that really needed? Are there not enough of them already? No, a check in the bibliography shows that monographs on the subject are very few and that there seems to be nothing comparable. So this new book is certainly to be greeted with gratitude.

To start from the last chapter there is a short but concise exposé on the research history of the site, from the discovery by Cyriac of Ancona in 1438 to the denomination 'archaeological area' in 1972, the salvation from the construction of an aluminium factory in 1986 and the entering into UNESCO's list of cultural inheritance in 1988. A special reference is made to the regrettable controversy concerning the research and publication of the inscriptions at the turn of the century.

There is an introductory chapter on the landscape and the environment giving a survey of the Corycan cave, the stone-working in the environment, and valuable notices on geology and botanics. A survey of earthquakes and important travellers, both ancient and modern, is also given.

In the historical chapter, Maass stresses that the 'first holy war' of 595-585 was not called holy but should be called Kirrhan or Crisean, and that the first holy war should be the one of 457 (on p. 4, however, a line of holy wars from the sixth to the third century is mentioned), further that it is as controversial whether the Persians sacked Delphi in 480 as how far the Celts reached in 278, that Delphi had its own coinage in classical times, and that Delphi avoided being compromised in the Perseus war. Augustus had the Amphiktyoni reorganised by inserting Nicopolis and erasing the obsolete Dolopians from it. The role of Plutarch, and the later history of Delphi with its confusion with Amphissa and the lacunae in its history in Late Antiquity, are also mentioned.

The chapter on the oracle naturally deals with many controversial points. It is uncertain whether there was any oracle before Apollo and whether the references to Pytho (as the site was called until the fifth century) in Homer can be trusted. Concerning the references to oracular guiding for colonies M. stresses that already the earliest colonies have a cult of Apollon Archegetes which points to the genuineness of the tradition. Concerning the emanations from the rock—considered geologically impossible—which guided the Pythia, M. considers them spiritual, not chemical. We get references to catalogues of oracular responses (already from 200 BC) and modern lists of attempts at bribing the oracle.

The book has about a hundred photographs, some of them in colour, of good quality and well chosen and variegated. On the other hand, there are few drawings (except some reproduced from illustrations by early travellers). The plans are few but almost sufficient (I should like to see a plan of the vicinity, too). There is an extensive section of notes and a seemingly vast bibliography, but a closer study of the notes shows that numerous works mentioned in the notes are not included in the bibliography, which could thus in fact be much

longer. There is also a well chosen glossary of terms; on the other hand there is unfortunately no index of any sort.

Half of the book is dedicated to the large chapter on the sanctuary itself, including sections on the temple, the treasuries and other buildings, the votives and the dedications. It is a thorough description including many photographs of objects in the museum (on which there is no separate section).

The chapter on the sanctuary at Marmaria is of course much shorter but informative of how little we know about it. The description of Pausanias is not of much help, and we are not informed of the function of the tholos, not even by Vitruvius, although he tells us that its architect wrote a book on it. And we do not know the function of the Mycenaean idols on the spot (which are numerous also in the sanctuary itself).

Finally the chapter on the feasts and their sites is rather short. We are informed that the Pythian games existed already before 582 BC and that there were also other games like the Soteria. We get information on the functionaries, the authors of winners' lists and the scanty information of participation by women. The stadion and the theatre and their history are also described, but nothing is said about the undiscovered hippodrome, which is supposed to have been situated in the valley below. The gymnasion, on the other hand, is found included in the chapter on the town, springs, fortifications, necropoleis, Christian monuments, and mosaics.

The book is well produced and almost without misprints (there is of course the all too common Flaminius for Flamininus, s.v. Chamoux in the bibliography).

PAAVO ROOS

University of Lund

HAMILTON (R.) **Choes and Anthesteria: Athenian iconography and ritual**. Ann Arbor: U of Michigan P, 1992. Pp. xv + 250 + ill. $37.50.

To those who have used it, van Hoorn's *Choes and Anthesteria* of 1951 is both a blessing and a curse: a blessing because it contains such a wealth of photographs (what Hamilton calls 'a convenient assemblage of illustrations', 210), a curse because the journey from photographs to text is maddeningly circuitous, and the text itself is not closely argued. H. shares van Hoorn's title but adopts a much more rigorous approach to the testimonia and a more methodical way of dealing with the images.

H.'s purpose is, as far as possible, to judge the testimonia separately from the images. The testimonia are treated first, and H. has quite rightly chosen to use English translations in the running text and to list the eighty-one items in Greek in an appendix (149-71). He is sharp with earlier scholars who have mixed text and image in an uneasy mélange to create a cumulative fiction; H. quotes Burkert's synthesis of the official, public celebration of the Anthesteria (1-2) only to pick it to pieces in the following pages. He adopts a minimalist attitude to the evidence: 'Applying even the least stringent standards, we can put aside almost half of the testimonia' (59). The three-day festival in February (the Pithoigia, the Choes and the Chytroi) is in H.'s view a fiction. The Pithoigia may not even be classical at all, the Choes is well evidenced but has had extraneous elements added to it by modern scholars, and the Chytroi, which involves another deity (Hermes, not Dionysos), may have taken place on the same day as the Choes. Many elements that earlier scholars had crowded into a three-day festival are rejected: holy marriage, mummers, *katagogia*, emphasis on three-year old children; but H. highlights choral performances, public sacrifice, etc. Central to the Choes was what H. calls the chugging contest, followed by private parties; for non-Americans, 'chugging' means downing your drink in one, in this case directly from the jug.

In the next chapter H. rejects the evidence of the large choes as irrelevant and narrows the study down to the small ones (15 cm and below) but is unwilling to connect any of the small ones with official celebrations, He also shows that the small choes are not primarily grave goods (as has been suggested), and where they are found in graves, size and iconography are shown not to be related to the age of the recipient. H. also suggests that the narrow chronological range of production (*c.* 420-390 BC) should gives us pause (81, n. 48)—the small jugs were the fashion of a generation.

H. now stops being negative and in Ch. 4 he looks in a new way at the small choes and their iconography. Statistics rule, with Appendix 3 (175-208) as a useful database. H. has worked out a tableau, a set of coded elements: naked boy; table or stool; chous; cart or roller; cake; grapes; a pet animal. 'There is no one element that never appears with another. Conversely there is no one element that *always* appears with another' (99). To qualify as an illustration of the tableau a chous must show two or more elements. In the following chapter H. proceeds to demonstrate the meaning of the tableau. He isolates four groups: naked crawler with amulets; pet/grapes/band/other; wreathed chous; cake/table/cat/stoop (*sic*—stool?). After a discussion of these H. concludes 'Naked child is to (unseen) dressed adult as grapes are to contest wine. The cake-laden table and chous represent the contest for which the naked child is not yet ready; rather the child belongs with his friends and pets playing with the carts which will some day be Choes wagons and with the grapes that will eventually become the wine, just as he will eventually (we hope) grow up to take part in the Choes contest.' (117). On 121 H. concludes that all small choes were gifts; the ones referring to the Choes contest were gifts given at that time, the other tableau choes may also have been gifts at Choes-time but the non-tableau small choes were purchased and given at other times.

The final chapter points to the wider implications of the approach for the study of religious iconography. Three issues are highlighted: the distinctiveness of the group; the meaning offered by internal analysis of the iconography; the relationship between that iconography and the testimonia. H. applies the method adopted for the choes to four other groups (krateriskoi; Panathenaic amphorae; Lenaia vases; sacrifice scenes) and assesses the closeness of the identity of each group based on the headings of shape, iconography, testimonia, date, function, findspot, size. In comparison the 'tableau'

choes fare well as a distinctive group.

This is a serious attempt to make sense of a complex subject; it takes us further than any previous treatment. H. has shown that the method of dealing with material that includes testimonia and image must be treated with particular care. The statistical analysis of the iconography is ingenious but perhaps needs finer tuning. Those students without access to van Hoorn are at a disadvantage, as H. has been stingy with illustrations and cavalier with those he includes. Only fifteen choes are shown, and there is no discernible pattern behind the order of their placing. No help is given in moving from pictures to text. Though much emphasis is placed on comparative sizes in the text, it is sad to see no measurements given for the illustrations and no attempt made to keep to a consistent scale (fig. 1 is reduced from 23 cm to 15 cm on the plate; fig. 4 is enlarged from 11 cm to 14 cm, etc).

B.A. SPARKES

University of Southampton

ROSIVACH (V.J.) **The system of public sacrifice in fourth-century Athens**. Atlanta: Scholars P, 1994. Pp. x + 171. $29.95 ($19.95, paper).

The Athenian *demos*, its critics asserted, spent most of the year feasting at public expense. In this valuable study, Rosivach seeks first, with due reservations about the possibility of precision, to quantify that proposition; he goes on to consider how the provision of so many animals fitted into the rural economy of Attica, and finally asks what resources the various bodies concerned (primarily the *polis* and the demes) used in order to meet their sacrificial expenditure. He concludes that in the fourth century the city distributed meat to all its members who cared to attend on not less than sixteen occasions annually, an average deme on about twenty occasions. Animals were not bred primarily for sacrifice but for their other uses; sheep were probably supplied to the sub-groups such as demes by group members at a traditional price, whereas more of a market existed in cattle. The city financed the 'additional' sacrifices that involved large scale meat distribution from general revenue, only the more modest 'ancestral' sacrifices from specific sources (above all rental income); the demes by contrast relied principally on rental income, supplemented by the *philotimia* of individuals, for all their sacrifices. The monograph is short and unpretentious, but consistently informative and interesting on a wide range of topics (the lack of an index is very regrettable). R. makes good use of recent work on such subjects as Greek stockrearing and the 'group solidarity' financial arrangements of the sub-sections of Attic society. Let me highlight too an ingenious argument (84-88) that Greek gourmet cooking exploited only those parts of the animal that were unsuitable for consumption on the spot at a sacrificial feast (whence he concludes that there can have been no trade in '*mageiros*-sacrificed' or 'sacrificed but then sold' joints); also a discussion of Greek age-terms for animals, with special reference to teeth and the term λειπογνώμων (148-53).

If I go on to register some doubts and disagreements,

it is not at all with an intent to devalue R.'s work. He assumes throughout that there existed a firm distinction between 'traditional' and 'additional' (i.e. post-Solonian) sacrifices, and that the two categories were treated financially in quite different ways. It is, of course, clear that publicly financed sacrifices on the grand scale attested by the Lycurgan skin sale receipts only grew up after Solon. But the distinction between 'traditional' and 'additional' sacrifices is surely a product of 'good old days' rhetoric, not accounting practice (cf. J. Yuan's comments in Bryn Mawr Classical Review [1994] 5.19). To which category should the Panathenaea belong? To 'additional', according to R., because we believe the festival to have been reorganised c. 566 and because it involved mass sacrifices. But whether we choose to associate the Panathenaea more closely with Cecrops or Erichthonius or Theseus, on any plausible guess about Athenian perceptions it must surely count as 'traditional'. R. argues, on the basis of a phrase of Isocrates which was already variously explained in antiquity (7.29), that the ancestral sacrifices were financed, in the fourth century, from rental income (so Didymus ap. Harpocr. *s.v.* ἀπὸ μισθωμάτων). But in its context θύειν ἀπὸ μισθωμάτων must refer to a kind of pinchbeck celebration, and it is much easier to see how 'sacrificing by contract, farming out sacrifices' (so Hesych. and *Anecd. Bekk.* 1.207 *s.v.* ἀπὸ μισθωμάτων θύειν) might have acquired such a connotation than how 'sacrificing from rental income' might have done. (For the practice of leasing contracts for the provision of sacrificial victims and other items see Sokolowski, *LSCG* 65.64-73, 98.2-20, 166.21-23, 167.5-7, *LSA* 32.59-61; *cf.* from Athens *LSCG* 33.27-28). R.'s argument about the frequency of deme sacrifice depends on the assumption that all the offerings listed in the calendars except those of young animals were intended, in principle at least, to feed all eligible demesmen. He may be right; but I would not myself care to invite three hundred people to a barbecue with no more than a single pre-modern sheep to divide among them. (The animal offered to demesmen in Men. *Sik.* 184 is a βοῦς, though comic grumbling reduces it to a λεπτὸν βοΐδι–ον.) Comparative evidence would doubtless help to make judgement in this area a little less subjective. Rather more is known about tribal feasts than R. mentions (see P. Schmitt Pantel, *La cité au banquet* [Rome 1992] 121-31); and to get a picture of the variety of forms of communal feasting one should also remember those festivals such as the *Diasia* at which numerous sacrifices were performed, but at the expense as it seems of demes or individuals rather than of the state.

I end with some details. 23 n. 40: R. takes the specification πρατόν in the Thorikos calendar to mean 'sold', which he rightly finds puzzling. But according to the usual principle for such formations (*cf.* W.S. Barrett's note on Eur. *Hipp.* 677-79, and e.g. πλωτός, navigable) it may also mean 'which may be sold'. 58 n. 127 and passim: *IG* II² 47 belongs to the second quarter of the fourth century, not its beginning (see S.B. Aleshire, *Asklepios at Athens* [Amsterdam 1991] 244-46). 164: a little information from an unpublished inscription concerning a further cult tax is now available in M. Faraguna, *Atene nell' età di Alessandro* [Rome 1992] 345. Finally, it might have been worth mentioning

Photius β 246 (and parallel texts) βουτρόφους· τάξις, ὥς φασι, τὶς ἱερωσύνης ἡ τρέφουσα τοὺς βοῦς, ὥστε θύεσθαι δημοσίᾳ, though one must certainly allow that the office need not be Athenian.

R.C.T. PARKER

Oriel College, Oxford.

PERPILLOU-THOMAS (F.) **Fêtes d'Egypte ptolémaïque et romaine d'après la documentation papyrologique grecque**. Louvain: Studia Hellenistica, 1993. Pp. xxix + 293. Fr. b. 1600.

This volume is a revision of a doctoral thesis presented by the late Françoise Perpillou at the University of Rouen in 1991. It is divided into two parts. The first lists, with extensive discussion, private festivals, mainly *rites de passage*, 'social' festivals which were celebrations related to the establishing of status within communities, religious festivals, and royal or imperial festivals. There is also a brief discussion of the various calendars in use during the period. Part two lists and discusses items used during festivals, the financing of festivals, payments made and taxes charged at festivals, and attitudes towards festivals. Many of these chapters are catalogues and discussions of the various attestations, normally arranged alphabetically, an . arrangement P. excuses as being 'least bad' and reflects the impossibility of imposing adequate categories on the disparate material discussed here. The format reflects the problems of working on this area. Although temple archives obviously provide a considerable number of attestations and are particularly useful when discussing the materials used in the celebration of festivals, many of the references to festivals are drawn from material disparate in period, type, and provenance. There are considerable difficulties in simply collating all the Greek and Demotic material, especially when translation or inaccurate transliteration may obscure congruities. P.'s grappling with these problems results in a rather technical survey of festivals and one wishes for a greater level of synthesis of the points that emerge from the survey.

The survey brings us only a little closer to understanding the experience of individual participants in the festivals or of the general population and there is little discussion of the relative importance of festivals. P., however, presents material concerning the distributions at festivals that could further investigation of the issue of popular involvement. Distributions of beer, wine and food to workers, the giving of presents and other signs of popular participation show that some festivals at least were celebrated by more than the priestly elite. Many of the listed festivals were publicly administered, through the temples or the city authorities, and it is this aspect of festivals that the papyri are best suited to illuminate. However, our literary sources and some of the material collected here show a level of popular participation in Egyptian festivals sufficient to confirm that some were important forms of communal expression. In addition, the presumed ethnicity of the various attested participants demonstrates that seemingly Egyptian festivals were celebrated by Greeks or Romans, further eroding any residual belief in firm ethnic and cultural boundaries in Ptolemaic and Roman Egypt.

The festivals listed display a mix of traditional Egyptian, Greek and Roman influences on Egyptian cultural life in this period. Most notable is the considerable impact of Greek religion. One expects that the Greek papyri would attest some Greek festivals and that the Greek immigrant communities would have celebrated their own festivals, but we see here a more fundamental integration of the cultures. The evidence appears to show the transference and integration of Greek festivals into the traditional Egyptian religious calendar and is not merely a matter of Greek nomenclature masking essential continuity.

The Roman impact on the festival calendar was slight by comparison. The major Roman contribution was in municipal festivals and in the development and imposition of the imperial cult. Although these will have had an impact on other festivals, P. is probably right to regard these as different in type and to discuss them in a separate section.

The second part of the work is perhaps less immediately illuminating. The list of materials used during festivals holds few surprises since most of the goods were commonly used in the religious practices of many Mediterranean regions, though the extensive use of aromatics suggests that Egyptian festivals may have had a stronger olfactory element. Nevertheless, we can see changes even here. Roses became an important item in the celebration of festivals and may have been adopted in the worship of Isis, though P. is perhaps overly cautious here. There was also a notable use of pigs as sacrificial animals though they were only rarely used in the Pharaonic period.

Overall, P. presents us with a picture of complexity. The material shows chronological and regional variations which may or may not correspond to real differences in religious practice. There were both clear continuities and changes in Egyptian festivals but the significance of these is difficult to assess. Some may relate to the impact of Ptolemaic rule in Egypt but sufficient evidence is here collected to suggest that some of the changes were internal developments. The subtleties of interaction are demonstrated by the syncretic idenitfication of Souchos, a crocodile god, with Kronos in the South Fayum so that a statue of Souchos could carry a dedicatory inscription to Kronos. The blurring of distinctions so evident here can be seen in many other areas of Egyptian and Greek religion, be it the numerous terracottas of deities from Egypt or the export of Isis, Osiris and Hermes-Thoth to the Mediterranean. P.'s study is a valuable contribution to the study of religion in Egypt which will be a useful work of reference for the scholar interested in religion and for the general papyrologist. Her study demonstrates the need for a more extensive investigation of Egyptian religion using literary, papyrological and the archaeological material. Such a study would hopefully bring into clearer focus the chronological, cultural and regional variations emerging here.

R. ALSTON

Royal Holloway, University of London

GAGOS (T.) and VAN MINNEN (P.) **Settling a dispute: towards a legal anthropology of late antique Egypt.** Ann Arbor: U of Michigan P, 1994. Pp. x + 150 + ill. £35 (£18, paper).

This volume announces a new series of Michigan publications of ancient texts. The authors have the entirely laudable aim of making their text, an agreement from Aphrodito in Upper Egypt which probably dates to AD 537, available to those outside the discipline of papyrology. The introduction provides a full context for the text and is a useful, if basic, introduction to the Aphrodito archives. The commentary is exceptionally full. The volume seems in some ways a model presentation of a document, though one wonders whether a rather repetitive text of 116 lines justifies a publication of 150 pages and I rather fear that publication of papyri would virtually cease if this was adopted as a new standard for publication. Some sections of the introduction and commentary are unnecessarily lengthy while the benefits of having two versions of the Greek text are unclear.

The text is an almost complete agreement of 116 lines concerning land near the village of Aphrodito which was sold even though it had been used as collateral on a loan. All the parties to the original agreement had died and both the property and the debt had passed to the next generation. The issue was complicated by the fact that the debt had passed to the son of the original owners of the property while the property itself had passed to his nephews and nieces. The nephews and nieces promptly sold the property without taking account of the debt. This agreement was between the new owners and the son. The son paid the debt and acknowledged the new owners' rights over the property in perpetuity at some (excessive) length. In return, the current owners paid a sum of money to the son, as the son acknowledged several times in the course of the text. The agreement was brought about through the representations of the head of the village and the intervention of certain 'good friends' of the parties.

The major interest of the authors is in the role of mediation in resolving the dispute. To widen the context, they provide brief descriptions of many of the texts from Late Roman Egypt which attest mediation. They note the increased attestation of mediation and arbitration in this period and that the official courts are rarely attested. Since we do not have the detailed ethnographic data for Egypt concerning the process of dispute resolution, they apply models from elsewhere to explain the process and the forces that shaped the eventual settlement. These models stress the role of social pressures in securing a settlement and that any settlement would be likely to reflect the unequal status of the participants. Gagos and van Minnen note the complexities of the process and the pressures which would encourage the socially weaker party to seek a resolution of the dispute at local levels before it became an official matter (when it would be judged in courts where the more socially powerful might be able to exert more influence), though they underestimate the social pressures on the powerful to preserve order and to be seen to be generous rather than oppressive and the probable reluctance of the powerful to see the dispute taken beyond the confines of the community.

All the parallel examples refer to arbitration and mediation in Late Antique Egypt and G. and M. note that such activities are far more frequently attested than in the Roman period, though it is to be noted that there is considerable evidence of the use of such methods of dispute resolution in Ptolemaic Egypt. It is not immediately obvious why there should be this chronological pattern. Since G. and M. propose a model which sees such dispute resolution as deeply embedded within the social structure, are we to see this as evidence for a radical change in either legal practice or social structure between the Roman and Late Antique periods? The wider implications of their model are not adequately discussed.

This brings us to the fundamental and related issue as to whether this form of dispute resolution is similar in type to that in other more modern societies. G. and M. quote an example from modern Crete of, in fact, a failure to abide by the customs of dispute resolution. The case involved sheep stealing. If the dispute had followed established custom, the proposed mediation would have involved the policeman, who was bringing the case, the shepherd accused of stealing the sheep, and two mediators from the local village. The mediation would have taken place at the shepherd's hut, on the side of a mountain. Our case involves a complex dispute over a point of law, the rights of ownership of the purchasers of a property on which there was a lien, and the obligations of the person who had inherited the original debt. The resolution of the dispute took place not in Aphrodito before the assembled elders of the village, but in the courthouse in Antinoopolis. There are similarities between the cases, but also obvious and fundamental differences.

Anthropological models of dispute resolution drawn from Egypt in later periods or from other areas stress the importance of mediation in healing breaches in the community and in preventing external authorities becoming involved. Yet, in some of the listed disputes, very public disputes were not resolved, nor was there much attempt to resolve them for some time. Some dispute resolutions occur, either metaphorically or literally, at the doors of the court. This may attest a reluctance to go to the expense and trust to the uncertainty of the formal legal process, but also shows that the Law and legal process actually had a prominent part to play in these Late Antique dispute resolutions: they were not just about competing social status and the harmony of a community. G. and M. rightly place dispute resolution in a social context and state the 'we do not believe that even the strictest form of dispute settlement ... was effective only because of the legal formulas included in the settlement document', but this is not to stay that the legal formulations were unimportant. This text is a legal document, clearly intended to be legally enforceable and although the substance of the settlement is made clear fairly quickly, the terms are repeated in various forms intended to provide for every conceivable eventuality, such as the continuation of the dispute, changes in law, or imperial edicts. By emphasising particular anthropological models, G. and M. risk undervaluing the legalism of this document, itself an important sociological feature, and by creating a dichotomy between societies which practise arbitration and those which more readily turn to more formal court procedures, they grossly oversimplify dispute resolution procedures. In many systems, ancient and modern, both informal and formal arbitration may co-exist with highly developed and frequently used official courts. It seems inconceivable that a society that relied almost solely on communal dispute resolution enforced by communal and social pressures could produce a text such as this.

R. ALSTON

Royal Holloway, University of London

FELDMAN (L.H.) **Jew and gentile in the ancient world: attitudes and interactions from Alexander to Justinian.** Princeton UP, 1993. Pp. xii + 679. $59.50.

This is easily the fullest account of the relationship in the ancient world between Judaism and the various cultures it encountered both at home and in the Diaspora. The first two chapters examine this encounter in Israel and abroad; there follows three chapters on prejudice against Judaism (playing down the degree of gentile hostility), balanced by three more on the attractions of Judaism for gentiles (less effective: a long analysis, for instance, of Josephus' portrayal of Moses [243-285], does nothing to demonstrate whether Moses proved an attraction to gentiles or not). Finally we reach what is in many ways the heart of the book, a study of the success of Jewish proselytism stretching into the fifth century AD (chs. 9-11). The author's range and learning are admirable. There is a huge amount of material discussed, extensive bibliography, and in general much that impresses. It is a large and important book on a large and important subject.

But *caveat lector*! The tone is at times pronouncedly polemical, and Feldman has a number of axes to grind (rather than conclusions to present that result from a neutral interpretation of the evidence). Indeed the work has a purpose that goes beyond the purely scholarly: it is a rousing assertion of Jewish strength, designed to refute the 'lachrymose' conception of Jewish history, that sees the Jews purely as victims of gentile oppression and hate. Such a negative approach was never convincing, in view of the evident vitality and vibrancy of ancient Judaism, but F. overplays his hand: almost every interpretation, even in the smallest of matters, is made to redound to the credit of Judaism. In my opinion, this weakens the often strong case he has.

His starting point is frustratingly contentious: in view of the evident hostility against Judaism in antiquity, how is it that the Jews managed to win so many adherents, whether as sympathizers or converts? This begs the huge and disputed question of the nature and extent of Jewish proselytism: we have to accept the assumption of massive Jewish success in winning converts and supporters, until the subject is treated in chs. 9-11. And even there, one crucial element in the equation, high Jewish population figures, is accepted with almost no critical analysis: there is only the briefest nod at demographic discussion (555-556 n. 20), and mostly we find an uncritical acceptance of Baron's completely hypothetical estimates, which posit 150,000 Jews in 586 BC and possibly eight million by the first century AD. Without large-scale conversion to Judaism, how else can you explain the huge increase in numbers? There has been a great deal of discussion on this subject recently, and there are other explanations. I find Goodman's *Mission and Conversion* preferable, but F. makes his case vigorously. It contains much that is interesting and helpful (see, for instance, his discussion in ch. 11 of Roman imperial legislation and Christianity's response to Judaism), but also much that is disputable. The inscriptions from Aphrodisias, for instance (362-369), are undoubtedly dramatic, but apart from the general information that there were good relations between Jews and gentiles in Asia Minor, I am not sure they tell us anything very specific: we do not really learn about the mechanisms of the relationship, and we do not know to what extent, if any, God-fearers adopted Jewish practices or beliefs. And in the matter of Christian legislation against proselytism and intermarriage of Jew and Christian (387 ff.), I am not convinced that the explanation is that Christianity was worriedly looking over its shoulder at the growing success of Judaism. In the admittedly different circumstances of modern Ireland the Catholic church has made life very awkward for those wishing to contract 'mixed' marriages, until recently extracting a promise from both partners to bring up the children as Catholics. This has nothing to do with fear of Protestant competition, but exemplifies rather a sort of Catholic triumphalist authoritarianism; perhaps it was this sort of attitude which lay behind the aggressiveness of fourth and fifth century Christianity.

While constantly upbeat, F. is not immune to adopting 'lachrymose' positions himself, or at least, the rhetoric of lachrymose positions. Ancient authors who have anything adverse to say about Judaism invariably attract emotively hostile descriptions. Lysimachus is never just Lysimachus; he is always 'the Alexandrian anti-Jewish bigot Lysimachus', or 'the fiercely anti-Jewish Lysimachus', or 'that arch-Jew-baiter Lysimachus'. Similarly with 'the arch-anti-Jewish bigot, Apollonius Molon', or 'one of the most vicious Jew-baiters of them all, Tacitus'. Anyone who ever crosses the Jews must be a 'Jew-hater'. Three Old Testament examples are listed on 84-85: the king of Egypt who declares 'Behold the people of Israel are too many and too mighty for us'; Amalek and his attack on the Israelites; and Haman's vendetta against Mordechai. You might think from the language that bigotry is everywhere, and that everyone has it in for the Jews (see the title of ch. 3, 'Official Anti-Jewish Bigotry'), but in fact much of this is rhetoric, and F.'s conclusions often argue convincingly in the opposite direction. For instance, he rightly concludes (in ch. 3, in spite of the title) that official prejudice against the Jews was not a significant feature of governmental policy in Hellenistic and early imperial times; he provides a convincing corrective to the notion of Tacitus as unequivocally hostile in all respects to Judaism (184-196); he shows that the Biblical incidents mentioned above are not really examples of Jew-hatred at all, rather of fear; and from Stern's collection of Greek and Latin sources on the Jews he interestingly counts 18% favourable, 59% neutral and only 23% overtly hostile (123-125).

Ch. 1 represents a full, and in many ways healthy,

retreat from Hengel, even if, as almost everywhere in the book, the case is overstated. The extent of Greek language and influence is constantly played down, as if it somehow casts aspersions on Judaism to accept that Daniel and Ben Sira, for example, might owe something to Greek thought, or that some Palestinian Jews spoke Greek. And in reverse, something like Josephus' story of Pythagoras' indebtedness to Judaism is accepted fully (201-202), even though it is blatantly apologetic, and later writers like Origen and Antonius Diogenes do nothing to make it more credible. In the *Cambridge History of Judaism* Hengel speaks of the encounter between ancient Palestinian Judaism and what he calls the *superior* (my italics) Hellenistic culture. It is this sort of attitude that forms a call to arms for F., who, rightly in my opinion, would not regard Judaism as inferior at all. I find his overall picture of a dynamic, confident and fundamentally Jewish Judaism convincing, but would have serious trouble with a great many of his particular arguments.

BRIAN MCGING

Trinity College Dublin

GARLAND (R.) **The eye of the beholder: deformity and disability in the Graeco-Roman world**. London: Duckworth, 1995. Pp. xviii + 222. £35.

Robert Garland's latest contribution to the study of ancient social life may be seen as part of the growing corpus of work which elevates the human body in antiquity as a theoretical space. The study of dysfunctional bodies clearly has an important part in this fashionable field of scholarship. In the last decade or so Peter Brown, Helen King, Danielle Gourevitch, Aline Rousselle and other scholars have highlighted particular moments of somatic divergence in ancient society, but G. is the first to attempt a synoptic study of 'deformity and disability in the Graeco-Roman world', which is the subtitle of his book. Indeed, G. takes a refreshingly broad view of what constitutes the Graeco-Roman world, and this reviewer was pleased to see that he includes evidence from times and places often considered marginal to it, such as Egypt. He cites an impressively wide range of classical literary sources, often rather obscure ones of which it is useful to be aware. His word picture is illustrated by an equally wide range of sixty-four plates, which run from pharaonic human remains, numerous vase paintings and Hellenistic terracottas to contemporary images from the American trash press. There is certainly much to praise in having all this evidence for deformity and disability so easily accessible in one book.

How successful G. has been at melding all this diverse information into a coherent whole is another matter. In the preface (which starts off with a rather sententious quote from Derrida), Garland says that his aim is 'to distinguish between species-related behaviour on the one hand and its culturally specific manifestations on the other' (xii), hence his utilisation of material relating to disability from all over human history. However, G. is not always very careful about using these cross-cultural parallels. Take, for example, his discussion of the iconography of the Egyptian pharaoh Akhenaten (108). Later on in his reign, this pharaoh is depicted with certain feminising physical characteristics, such as a broad pelvis, fleshy breasts and full thighs. G. is quite right to point out that such a representational mode poses a number of interesting questions for the historian of the body. But his solution is that these conventions are to be taken at face value as representing a physical reality, and that the pharaoh was afflicted with the endocrinal condition known as Fröhlich's syndrome, which can cause these bodily changes. This notion has long been dismissed by Egyptologists, and Akhenaten is actually represented as a Nile god, fertility personified, rather than as a deformed individual, which would be unthinkable within Egyptian notions of royal iconographic decorum. I do not necessarily criticise G. for being unaware of a specialised area of scholarship well outside his normal field of research. What I do find problematic is an approach that can sacrifice historical accuracy and cultural specificity for the sake of painting a fictive broader picture. G. could have made exactly the same point about the difficulty of interpreting images of somatic otherness by using iconographic evidence from a period about which he was better informed.

Other aspects of G.'s general approach to his spectrum of evidence are problematic, too. Consider the large visual section of the book. The numerous illustrations, from ancient bronze figurines of dwarves and leptoi to exploitative features from recent National Enquirers ('Incredible Crab People have claws for feet!'), imply an essentialist view of disabled people: there they always were, from antiquity to the present day. But who were 'they', and how did 'they' experience physical dysfunction? G. opines that for the social historian of antiquity, a 'rich understanding of the plight of the disabled...is necessarily predicated upon a rich empathy' (xi). Yet this 'rich empathy' is not easy to find in the text, and sometimes G.'s attempts to embody the lived experience of disability verge on the offensive. For instance, on 114 G. discusses a group of Hellenistic miniature terracotta heads (plates 33, 36-37, 61) showing individuals with slack, open mouths and rather desperate expressions. He comments that 'some convey malignity, others rage helplessly against existence itself or gaze benightedly at unseen terrors, still others...merely testify to the pathos of brainlessness. These in brief are the social rejects of any and every culture, whose descendants may be seen wandering aimlessly along the corridors of any modern mental institution.' I wonder what representatives of disability rights associations and the staff of psychiatric wards would think of this characterisation of their clients.

All in all, then, this book is an opportunity missed. G. might have been far more successful had a more culturally specific approach been adopted: if, for instance, he had limited himself to sources from Greece or Rome alone. By assembling but not rigorously analysing his wide-ranging evidence, G. has constructed a falsely monolithic view of deformity and disability in the ancient world which takes little account of real individuals and their responses to dysfunction. He presents 'disability' as an essentialist category which binds people across spatial and temporal boundaries. But perhaps the biggest omission is that no significant

account is taken of the actual physical remains of deformed and disabled people. While paying lip service to being empathetic, G. actually undermines the emotive and experiential dimension of disability in antiquity.

DOMINIC MONTSERRAT
University of Warwick

TÖLLE-KASTENBEIN (R.) **Das archaische Wasserleitungsnetz für Athen**. Mainz: Zabern, 1994. Pp. iv + 120 + ill. DM 39.80.

The two elements of the building programme of the Pisistratid tyrants of Athens widely remembered are the plan to build a great temple to Zeus Olympios (started indeed, but abandoned, unfinished, on their overthrow in 510 BC), and some improvement in the water-supply system of the city, at least partially completed; Thucydides, born at most sixty years after their fall, associated (II.15.5) with the tyrants the Enneakrounos fountain-house fed by the Kallirhoe spring, which he implies lay in the south-east of the city, perhaps near the Ilissos. Pausanias some six hundred years later identified a fountain-house near the Agora by that name (I.14.1). However, Athens (unlike Megara and Samos) lacks any real literary record of its water-supply system in classical times, basic though it was to the citizens' well-being: an underground and invisible network of pipelines, once in place, is easily taken for granted and never mentioned. That system has received some detailed, if sometimes desultory, attention in modern times. In this splendid, and splendidly illustrated, volume, Renate Tölle-Kastenbein has pulled together a great deal of pre-existing information to give a comprehensive and detailed account of the fresh drinking-water supply system of late-archaic and classical Athens. She draws on a wide range of published and unpublished material: the vital initial exploratory fieldwork of Ziller in the foothills of Hymettus and the Ilissos valley in the 1870s, the survey-work of Curtius and Kaupert (*Karten von Attika*) and Milchoefer's commentary, Dörpfeld's extensive and carefully recorded excavations south and west of the Acropolis and Areopagus in the 1890s, Gräber's and Judeich's studies of Athenian topography, and the information gathered by Greek, American, and German excavators within the city in the vicinity of the Acropolis, and in the Agora, Kerameikos, and Academy areas. She builds up an impressive picture of the extensive network of tunnels and pipelines (some 15 km in overall length) and the fountain-houses which these served. The distant source was the catchment area of the Ilissos, a hollow on the seaward slope of Hymettus (where, east and uphill of Ag. Ioannis Theologos, some ancient foundations and a rock-cut basin noted in the 1870s may have marked the ultimate source). From there a deep-laid terracotta pipeline led down the Ilissos valley, first along its south then its north side for some 8 km, to a fork east of the Acropolis; one branch led south of the Acropolis (with two superimposed pipeline tunnels and a later loop along part of this stretch) west towards the Pnyx; another led north-west towards the Agora (and its archaic South-East Fountain-house). To that basic network, further extensions were added from time to time, new branches, loops in the course of repair-work, and new fountain-houses. The evidence of chance finds made during rescue excavations (reported in *Arch. Deltion*) has been incorporated in this survey, but the rapid build-up of post-war Athens, and the sheer costs and dangers of deep excavation made test-trenching to check and supplement earlier discoveries impractical. However parallels from Megara, Samos and elsewhere are adduced and the illustrative evidence of pottery exploited to help interpret and date the Athenian evidence (terracotta pipes laid underground can have a long life and are not in themselves easily dateable). T.-K. recognised three main building phases: (i) a late archaic foundation of the main network; (ii) extensions and repairs in the fifth century BC; (iii) further extensions and renovations in the fourth century; and then local repairs in the imperial Roman period. T.-K.'s first chapter (5-28) deals with the routes of the main-feed pipeline and its supplementary branches; her second (29-45) with building techniques; her third (46-72) with the classification of the terracotta pipes; and her fourth (73-87) with the fountain-houses. Ch. 5 (88-100) reviews, with photographs and tabular analysis, those Athenian black-figured pots, mostly hydrias and mostly from Italian find-spots, which illustrate, even 'advertise', these new Athenian amenities, the fountain-houses. Ch. 6 (101-5) interprets the chronology: Phase I was started by Hippias before 510 BC, but finished in the years after his expulsion; Phase II covered renewal of the network after 480 BC and extensions to the Kerameikos, to a new Dipylon fountain-house after 460 BC, further repairs after 450 BC, and a later extension to the south-west; and Phase III involved extensions and repairs, 350-325 BC with a rebuild of the Dipylon fountain-house, 307-304 BC. Short appendices deal with the Dörpfeld excavation diaries of 1892-97, the geological nature of the Hymettus catchment area, and the probable capacity of the whole network. Excellent photographs, diagrams and folded plans enrich a well-balanced, well presented text.

JOHN ELLIS JONES
University of Wales, Bangor

SHEPHERD (R.) **Ancient mining**. London and New York: Elsevier, 1993. Pp. xv + 494. £69.

This is supposedly a comprehensive account of mining in classical antiquity. Shepherd planned a sequel to his *Prehistoric mining and allied industries* (1980), originally aimed to cover both mining and metallurgy, but confined himself to mining, yet referring often to smelteries, ingots etc. as proof of local mining. S. combines ancient literary allusions, cited by author and mostly by book and chapter, with modern accounts, cited by author and year only, which makes checking difficult. A preface on scope and methods is followed by two chapters on ancient practice (46 pp.) and administration and labour (22 pp.), then by a regional survey with a chapter on Greece (67 pp.), seven on the Roman empire (Gaul and the Rhineland getting 17 pp., Britain 141 pp. with 22 pp. on coal), and a final chapter on quarries and building stone, with appendices, bibliography (19 pp.) and indices to end. Clearly an ambitious if derivative project, laborious in every way.

Parturiunt montes. The result is not an authoritative survey, rather a ragbag of fascinating gobbets (e.g. nice to be reminded, 59, 335-7, of the stamped copper ingot from near 'Caerhyn', omitted in RCAM Caerns I; but surely one, not two?). The book is often misleading and confusing; it is not up-to-date in its sources, it misquotes, includes misunderstood material, contradictory accounts without attempt at resolution, and careless errors. All the worse because it was published for the Institution of Mining and Metallurgy (as if it were a summary of the latest research, which it certainly is not), and at a price (£69) which makes it poor value for money.

To set the context S. works in much, indeed too much, potted history, mostly inoffensive if repetitive, but often wrong, naive or inane. S. attributes (98, 100) Xerxes' defeat entirely to the Athenians and the battles of Salamis and Plataea both to 480 BC. Populonia was destroyed by Sulla in the third century BC (143). Coins were found representing Flavian emperors up to the third century AD (180). All small beer. 'The wheel was probably invented as early as the fourth century BC. The ancient Britons used wheeled chariots in battle and prehistoric man right back to the Neolithic period had knowledge of the wheel' (43). The Etruscans conquered Italy 600-524 BC, and were expelled from Rome in 510 BC (136); *after* their defeat in Italy they *began* to exploit rich iron deposits on Elba and probably copper and tin on the mainland (142), yet the peak period of mining in Tuscany was *c.* 1000 BC (143), except that Etruscans may have been mining *iron* near the Alps 'as early as 2700 BC' (145). One hardly blinks at Thermistocles, Brasides, Ordovicea, and the emperors Antonius Pius, Magnentias, Valentinus, Valentian, and Engenius.

As for modern sources, S. culls from many, often 'antiquarian' and obscure works, but not many recent reports. His preface cites Ardaillon's *Les Mines de Laurion dans l'antiquité* of 1897 and Ramin's *La Technique minière et métallurgie des anciens* of 1977 as essential works; only later (95-6) does he note his debt also to Oliver Davies' *Roman mines in Europe* (1935) and J.F. Healy's *Mining and metallurgy in the Greek and Roman world* (1978). His long bibliography lacks important works of the 1980-90 period, e.g. Conophagos' *Le Laurium antique* (1980) and the Belgian series of *Thorikos* reports. So, while including Lewis and Jones' *JRS* 1970 article on Roman gold-mining in Spain, S. omits Jones' *JRS* 1980 article on Rio Tinto, not to mention Domerque's *Les Mines de la péninsula ibérique dans l'antiquité romain* of 1990. Did S. lay the groundwork alongside his 1980 book on prehistoric mining, adding some top-up later?

On technical and scientific points also S. is sometimes shaky. He overemphasizes (25-29) the dangers of vertical and lateral pressures, real enough in deep coal measures, but hardly so in ancient metal-mine galleries in harder rocks. Noting Gale's work on lead isotopes (125) he slackly refers to 'isotope analyses of high antimony content'. He cites James' radiocarbon date for copper mining near Llandudno once (280) as *c.* 2700 BC and again (328) as *c.* 2700 BP (both wrongly, as the publication cited, 461, records it as 2940 ± 80 BP).

As regards Greece in particular, S. often betrays his unfamiliarity with the ground and recent researches (apart from Siphnos). He notes (89) that in Laurion mines, pillars of 'inferior ore, i.e. less than 8% silver' were left as underground supports: anything like 8% silver content would be extremely rich and extremely rare, anywhere. Discussing methods of lighting inside Laurion mines, he cites (90) the (late Roman) lamps found in the Vari cave excavations of 1900 (when indeed Vari was just a village of 'some thirty houses'!) rather than, say, the classical lamps from Thorikos studied by Blondé in *Misc. Graeca* 6, 1983. He omits reference to the only excavation to date of a Laurion gallery, discussed in *Thorikos* vols. 8 and 9, published 1983 and 1990. Describing ore-treatment at Laurion washeries, he states (91) that crushed ore was *'thrown on to* the table at the point where the water was fed in' (an idea not much supported nowadays), while his own borrowed fig. 18 overleaf includes those riffled sluices proposed by Conophagos, and mentioned by Healy (145). Further on (423) he discusses the bluish-grey marble of Hymettus, south-west of Athens, next the marble of Agrileza, and then adds: 'also in Attica were the quarries of Imettos near the west coast', seemingly unaware that Hymettus and Imettos are variants of the same name.

JOHN ELLIS JONES

University of Wales, Bangor

Proceedings of the International Symposium Cyprus in the 11th century BC ... Nicosia 30-31 October, 1993. Ed. V. Karageorghis. Nicosia: A.G. Leventis Foundation, 1994. Pp. xvi + 247. £C20.

In contrast to the saturation coverage which the thirteenth and twelfth centuries BC in the eastern Mediterranean have received in recent archaeological congresses and publications, the eleventh century BC has on the whole been benignly neglected. This does less than justice to its pivotal importance. It represents the transition between the end of the Late Bronze Age, itself the culmination of civilisation in the ancient Levant in the third and second millennia BC, and the beginning of the so-called Dark Age, whose hallmark, iron, may have ushered in the new era but did not instantly endow it with the trappings of recognisable progress. Indeed the Dark Age is unquestionably a misnomer, for there is ample evidence at this time for the continuity and development of material culture and most importantly the seeds of the changes that would grow into the Classical world of which Western civilisation is the ultimate heir.

In devoting an entire symposium to the period between 1100 and 1000 BC the organisers, represented by Professor Karageorghis, had the intention of bringing together a number of younger scholars, as well as members of the older generation, to explore the 'tangible evidence for a number of political and cultural changes in the island which predestined its evolution during the first millennium BC, in fact down to the present day' (xi). Central to their enquiry were the beginnings of the Hellenisation of Cypriote society, which up until that point in time had retained a largely indigenous character, despite the extensive commercial relations which grew up during the Late Cypriote I and II periods. To this end invitees presented papers predominantly concerned with archaeological, art historical and topographical subjects, examining evidence for contacts and influences from western Asia as well as from the Aegean and focusing on the implications of the data for the 'ethnogenesis' of Cyprus.

While the time-span covered by the symposium in absolute terms is correspondingly finite, the relative chronology of the period is less clear to the reader of these proceedings and is nowhere tabulated so as to facilitate ready comprehension. K. equates 1200 BC with the start of Late Cypriote IIIA (2) but does not indicate where he considers 1100 BC or 1000 BC to lie. Other participants are equally imprecise. Sheratt places Cypro-Geometric IA-B in the 11th-10th centuries BC (71) while Vanschoonwinkel schematically ends Late Cypriote IIIA at 1120-1100 BC, IIIB at 1050 BC and Cypro-Geometric IA at 1000 BC (110). Catling addresses the relative and absolute chronologies more explicitly, ending Late Cypriote IIIA at perhaps *c.* 1125 BC and IIIB *c.* 1050 BC (134) but only Iacovou specifically identifies the 'two distinct and quite separate cultural phases' encompassed by the eleventh century BC, Late Cypriote IIIB (*c.* 1125-1050 BC) and Cypro-Geometric IA (*c* 1050-1000 BC) (149).

As is common to all symposia, the papers vary considerably in length, content and critical apparatus, but adhere to the basic theme and draw on the wealth of material now available for study. It is therefore most appropriate that the first substantive contribution, by Deger-Jalkotzy, deals with the earliest testimony for the use of the Greek language in Cyprus. She concludes that the evidence for the development of the dialects of Greek 'no longer supports the still widely believed idea that immediately after the catastrophies (*sic*) of the Mycenaean palaces their inhabitants partly fled to Arcadia while others sought refuge in Cyprus' (41) and that 'the establishment of Cypriot speaking Greeks (*sic*) on Cyprus seems to have taken place on the eve, or even on the dawn, of the eleventh century BC' (24). Drawing on similar evidence, Vanschoonwinkel is equally measured in his observations, for he discounts the thesis of a Greek colonisation of Cyprus, arguing for the gradual immigration of Greek speaking peoples who by the end of the eleventh century BC had effectively brought about the Hellenisation of the island (126).

Most of the other contributors are also circumspect in their interpretation of the data at their disposal. Apart from the papers by Mazar, who deals essentially with another kind of 'ethnogenesis', and by Bikai, who philosophises about the Phoenicians in Cyprus, the rest tend to concentrate on objects, motifs and sites from Cyprus and place them in a wider archaeological context with a view to determining the extent to which the evidence allows deductions to be made about the geopolitical configuration of the island in the eleventh century BC. The material assembled attests to lively metallurgical, ceramic and commercial activity in the island at this time and to a diversity of Aegean and West-

ern Asiatic traits in the excavated remains. The significance of these findings for the incipient Hellenisation of
Cyprus is thoughtfully considered not only by Deger-
Jalkotzy and Vanschoonwinkel but by Catling and
Coldstream, though it is most evocatively expressed by
Yon, who argues that after the upheavals of the twelfth
century BC, stability returned to Cyprus, which came
together again with 'un nouveau visage culturel, à la fois
solidement ancré dans son terroir et les forces naturelles
des montagnes et des activités agricoles, et d'autre part
tributaire aussi d'une origine lointaine, avec laquelle la
mer le maintient en contact' (198).

The volume has been handsomely produced by the
A.G. Leventis Foundation. Contributions were made in
Greek, English and French, with all papers in Greek
translated into English and all English and French
papers followed by Greek summaries. Illustrations and
bibliographies accompany each article, and there is no
general index. Editorially and typographically the text
maintains the high standard we have come to expect
from K., who has added to our knowledge of Cypriote
history at the end of the second millennium BC a substantial work of lasting value. May we now look forward to the symposium he has foreshadowed on the long
and complex process of Hellenisation of the island (7)?

R.S. MERRILLEES

GUIDI (A.) **La necropoli veiente dei Quattro Fontanili
nel quadro della fase recente della prima età del
ferro italiana**. Florence: Olschki, 1993. Pp. 124. L
55,000.

It is a truth universally acknowledged, that a reliably
excavated and properly published Italian Iron Age
cemetery must be in want of a seriation chart of tombs
and artefact types (see further *JRA* 7 [1994] 303-16).
The slim volume under review—forty of its 124 pages
are wholly devoted to figures and tables—represents the
third major assault of this kind on the Quattro Fontanili
cemetery at Veii in Southern Etruria: 651 Villanovan
graves excavated in twenty-one campaigns between
1960 and 1972 and published in seven issues (and more
than a thousand pages) of *NSc* between 1963 and 1976.
Although Guidi's work is certainly not without interest
and even merit, more happened since its presentation as
a postgraduate thesis in 1985 than he was able to take
into account by mid-1991 (the date of his *Premessa*; and
see 7, n. 7). For this and other reasons, I do not find his
book quite as original and instructive for the 1990s as
the articles of his two distinguished predecessors were
for the 1960s and the 1980s: J. Close-Brooks, *NSc*
(1965) 53-64 with *StEtr* xxxv (1967) 323-29 = D. and
F.R. Ridgway, eds., *Italy before the Romans* (London
1979) 95-113; J. Toms, *AIONArchStAnt* viii (1986) 41-
97. G. himself claims (17) that, unlike theirs, his
seriation uses *all* the artefact types—at any rate in the
second and better represented phase with which he is
primarily concerned, and which corresponds (on anybody's chronology) to most of the eighth century BC.
Personally, I can see no particular virtue in this: inevi-

tably and obviously, some types last for a long time, and
their inclusion in the *trattamento informatico* can thus
actually distort the evidence provided by other types for
the short-term stylistic change on which meaningful
seriation depends. First principles are all very well, but
the specialists for whom G. is writing already 'know' a
great deal about Villanovan material, and have done
since Montelius' time.

At all events, G.'s results confirm much that had
previously been established by Close-Brooks and Toms
in the matter of cemetery growth (outwards from the
middle) and the possible existence of family groups (78;
cf. Toms *op. cit.* 72-73). Then, following a comparative
study of the sequences available from Latium vetus and
Pontecagnano to the south and from Bologna to the
north, he proposes (99-100) an absolute chronology for
the years between *c.* 800 and *c.* 720 that has three
phases (IIA, *c.* 800/790-*c.* 760; IIB, *c.* 760-*c.* 730; IIC, *c.*
730-*c.* 720) where Close-Brooks had two (IIA, *c.* 800-*c.*
760; IIB, *c.* 760-*c.* 720).

It is not until the fifth and final chapter (101-20) that
we find something relatively new: an attempt to extract
some kind of social structure from the funerary data
around the time of the first contacts with the Greek
world represented by the Euboean skyphos types for
which Quattro Fontanili is justly famous. Sensibly, G.
elects to examine the state of his evidence at three
stages ('before', 'during' and 'after'), corresponding to
early IIA, later IIA with early IIB, and later IIB with
IIC—and hence for all practical purposes to the first,
second and third quarters of the eighth century. The
picture of an increasingly complex social structure that
(perhaps predictably) emerges stands or falls on the
choice of indicators and on the weight that is assigned
to them, subjects that require comment on a scale that is
not possible here (but compare now the investigation of
Orientalizing patterns of organization and funerary
customs conducted at Pontecagnano by M. Cuozzo, *J.
European Archaeology* 2:2 [1994] 263-98). One observation, however, struck me as particularly interesting for
non-combatants. It is contained in the last sentence in
the book: 'the fact that precisely at the moment of
greatest social complexity the need was felt to keep an
ideal link with the cultural models and usages of the past
... seems to be an important sign of continuity between
the aristocratic *gentes* and the leading [*egemoni*] social
groups of the first Villanovan phase' (120). This is a lot
to base on the rite and contents of the two richest graves
(both of *cavalieri*) encountered at Quattro Fontanili in
the third quarter of the eighth century, Z 15A (*NSc*
[1965] 171-82) and AA 1 (*NSc* [1970] 296-308), and on
the deposition of numerous pottery *rocchetti* (spools) in
contemporary rich female burials. But, given what we
already know, it is not too much: and it is also a timely
and most effective reminder that, these days, 'Hellenizat-
ion of the barbarians' is not even half the story at Veii
or anywhere else in Tyrrhenia.

DAVID RIDGWAY

University of Edinburgh

JAMESON (M.H.), RUNNELS (C.N.) and VAN ANDEL (T.)
A Greek countryside: the southern Argolid from prehistory to the present day. Stanford UP, 1994. Pp. xviii + 654 + ill. £84.95.

A Greek countryside is the long-awaited report on more than thirty years of research in the southern Argolid, though its general results have been available in semi-popular form since the publication of *Beyond the Acropolis* by van Andel and Runnels in 1987. The detail is in the volume under review. The authors see the book as 'a contribution to the study of how people have lived in Greece from their first comings to the present day' (2), but they set out with two specific aims. The first is to present the archaeology and history of the southern Argolid in its environment, while the second is to offer 'an interpretation of the long, if patchy, record of human interaction with the environment in this area' (v). The authors go on to justify their essentially holistic approach and the need to see the Argolid in a wider context (10-12). Their ambitions are thus considerable.

The approach is more conventional. After setting out the background to the project in terms of local studies in Greece, the authors move into a general topographical description of the study area and outline its settlement history. The second chapter pulls together all the available literary, epigraphic and archaeological information for the historical period into a summary of the area's economic, social, and political development down to the present day. These overviews are followed by three substantive chapters of interpretation.

Ch. 3 outlines how the history of the landscape was studied. The land was seen in terms of the changing resource options available to its inhabitants, whilst the approach integrated environmental and archaeological research. Terrain, climate and vegetation are described and change in each is explored. However, the most important section is the discussion of late Quaternary erosion, alluviation and soil formation. This should be read by all undertaking similar research in Greece and elsewhere in the Mediterranean region. Also of particular value is the discussion of shorelines and coasts in relation to global and regional change.

Ch. 4 is devoted to the archaeological survey of the southern Argolid, but it also contains a valuable contribution to the debate about the definition of sites and site forming processes (221-24). The overall approach is set out and evaluated with great care so that future researchers can learn from the Argolid Project. Site functions and settlement patterns are outlined in the text and displayed in useful period tables and maps, though more information might have been squeezed from the data if some simple statistical tests had been employed. Appendix A contains the full register of 328 sites. The resources available to the inhabitants of the region at different periods are described in ch. 5 which also includes a 'somewhat encyclopedic review' (260) of the possible ways in which they might have been exploited, using modern ethnographic data as the interpretative basis. Thus hunting and gathering are considered, as well as cultivation and pastoralism, mining and quarrying, and the various ways in which the sea was exploited. Throughout the supportive capacity of the local economy is assessed in relation to changing

external contacts. At the end of the chapter, the question is raised as to how typical or different the study area is in the diachronic experience of Greece.

The grand synthesis of all the Project's information and the authors' interpretations is attempted in ch. 6. All the environmental possibilities are brought together and examined in conjunction with the socio-economic processes leading to particular levels of resource exploitation. Interaction and mutual feedback are stressed. The causes of the population fluctuations suggested by the settlement data are explored in the wider context of the Aegean and the Mediterranean. Most of the chapter, however, is devoted to following themes of land, land use and settlement through time and to bringing out how phases of expansion and contraction, intensification and retrenchment, alternated with each other. The treatment, however, is by chronological period, starting with the Palaeolithic Age and working through the Bronze Age (early, middle, late) into the Early Iron Age and Archaic Period, through the Classical, Hellenistic and Roman Periods into a medieval period defined as lasting from the mid-seventh to the end of the seventeenth century and concluding with the Early Modern and Modern periods. Something more imaginative might have been tried.

However, it would be wrong to finish on a carping note. The book is a splendid achievement. The text is clear, the illustrations are plentiful and apt. A vast amount of information is made available, not just about the Argolid, and the reader is skilfully guided through it. There are seven appendices, a rich bibliography and a sensible index. The methodological sections are exemplary and other researchers will read them with profit. The whole volume demonstrates the value of landscape as the focus for study and the benefits which accrue from collaborative research.

M. WAGSTAFF

University of Southampton

VICKERS (M.) and GILL (D.) **Artful crafts: ancient Greek silverware and pottery**. Oxford UP, 1994. Pp. xiii + 255. £40.

In discussions following the appearance of this book, my pupils Ruth Lindner and Matthias Steinhart contributed much to the following review.

We are grateful to Vickers and Gill, who help us to strengthen our love for Greek pottery. For a modern lover of art, the material does not matter: thus a drawing consisting only of pencil lines on paper may be a superb work of art. Mr Bareiss, a well-known collector of Greek pottery, told me that he had once collected modern drawings until he became aware of the masterly graphic art on Greek clay pots. Surely he was not influenced by the pottery fever of the eighteenth or nineteenth century, which is well described in ch. 1 of V.&G., but used his own eyes.

The neo-classical 'cult of simplicity' (1-32) had its ancient origin, I think, in Latin authors, because in Roman religion certain cult vessels had to be of clay, e.g. the *simpuvium Numae* in the cult of Vesta (Zwierlein-Diehl in *Tainia, Fest. R. Hampe* [1980] 405-22). These *simpuvia*—made of *impasto* or *bucchero*—had the shape of *kyathoi*. Attic *kyathoi* found in Etruscan graves show by their peculiarities that Attic potters would imitate *bucchero* vessels to suit the demands of the export market rather than because they were metal (although *bucchero* is of course connected with metal in shape [117 fig. 5.10]). In addition, *kyathoi* are symposion vessels. People in antiquity liked long symposia and cool wine; fired clay is porous, and earthenware filled with water and/or wine keeps the liquid cool and makes it even cooler through evaporation. The latter does not apply to silver or gold, and in this respect *hydriai*, mixing bowls, *oinochoai*, *kyathoi* and *kylikes* made of clay added more to the sense of well-being at symposia than metal vessels. For this reason we find clay cups even in Macedonian palaces. V.&G. would answer that the slaves drank from them, but their masters also liked to drink cool wine. On the other hand, in the northern Black Sea area or near the sources of the Seine, where the climate was quite different, wine remained cool enough in vessels of bronze, silver and gold.

Ch. 2 (33-54) deals with the high prices for plate in antiquity in comparison with the low prices for clay vessels, in order to show that pottery was of very little value. V.&G. pretend that we know a lot about ancient prices, but I should like to quote B.A. Sparkes, *Greek pottery: an introduction* (1991) 129: 'It is not easy to speak of vase prices with any confidence'. In fifth century Athens a mason or a sailor could earn one drachma (= 6 obols) a day; thus the price of two or three drachmas for a red-figure hydria is comparatively high (*cf.* Sparkes, *op. cit.* 120). In the *Kaminos*, 'Homer' wishes the potters to sell much in the market-place and the streets, and to gain great profit, *Homeri opera* V [OCT] 212).

Sparkes also wrote a review of V.&G. (*Antiquity* 69 [1995] 619-21) in which he criticizes especially ch. 3 (55-76) because V.&G. 'pluck statements out of context'. This is also the case in other chapters. Thus V.&G. cite the golden *phiale* at the beginning of Pindar's *Olympian* 7 twice (4, 43), but never the metal (I think golden) *depas* of Achilles in *Iliad* 16.225 ff., from which the hero only poured wine when praying to Zeus. These two passages have in common that a golden bowl, 'the peak of possessions', was used only in special cases, not at random. Furthermore, Pindar is also quoted in ch. 4 (78, 102), but never his *fr.* 124 Snell, the *enkomion* sent to the Deinomenid Thrasyboulos. Here the poet speaks of '*kylikes* from Athens' used in the symposia of the tyrant at Akragas. Of course V.&G. would interpret this as referring to gold or silver cups, but Pindar does not say so, and his poem belongs to the heyday of the Attic clay *kylix*. Its special elegance, e.g. that of the Brygos cup in Würzburg's Martin-von-Wagner-Museum, could not be attained by hammering silver or gold, but only by a quickly turning wheel and the potter's hands. That cup-*skyphoi* and 'acrocups' have their silver pendants we learn from figs. 5.11-5.13; the shape of the Brygos cup, however, does not have such pendants. Clay is plastic by nature, metal is not. And fired clay—as we have seen—keeps the wine cooler than does metal.

In ch. 5, 'The influence of precious materials' (105-53), we are given a good survey of this phenomenon from prehistoric times onwards. For V.&G., the prototype is always metal or ivory, but I should like to question this. For example, the shape of the *kantharos* (frontispiece) has so many prehistoric earthenware forerunners in Troy and elsewhere that the golden *kantharoi* from shaft grave IV at Mycenae and Kalamata (Hampe-Simon, *The birth of Greek art*, fig. 113) are surely precious exceptions—like the above quoted *depas* of Achilles—and do not belong to 'normal' sets. Of course there are many examples of pottery copying plate throughout the centuries, but V.&G. neglect the proper development of those 'copies'. A potter can take over the shape and peculiarity of a metal vessel, but afterwards the clay product has a career *sui generis*.

In addition, we do not have many incised silver vessels, and V.&G. give plausible reasons for this, but I doubt that incisions in metal like figs. 5.20 and 5.22-5.24 are really better works of art than red-figure masterpieces. The authors do not give illustrations of the latter, but prefer to illustrate the work of *banausoi* like Oikopheles (157, fig. 6.1) who was 'ein rückständiger Dorftöpfer' (Pfuhl, *MuZ* I 253). In any case, we can learn from catalogues such as C. Vermeule, *Geek and Roman sculpture in gold and silver in the Museum of Fine Arts, Boston* (1974) that gold-and silversmiths, if compared with potters, are not always the better artists. I doubt 'that no-one in antiquity would have understood' this (83).

V.&G.'s book shows throughout a tendency to diminish Beazley's achievement. They show another 'Way Forward' in ch. 7 (191-204), a way which is gone by many archaeologists today. In spite of this, Beazley's lists remain fundamental also for entirely new approaches. V.&G. think the same: 'Beazley's framework of attributions can be an important starting point for research on Greek pottery' (193). But why must they write in a warning tone about his predilections—the Berlin Painter and so on (4 f., 82 f.)? We all have predilections, V.&G. too, and they are not the worst of us. I fear the two authors have a Beazley syndrome, and this makes their comments sometimes tendentious where they should be grateful to a scholar who has helped us so much in understanding—with our mind which is, of course, different from the mind of two and a half millennia ago—ancient pottery.

ERIKA SIMON

Würzburg

CORPUS VASORUM ANTIQUORUM. Italia LXVIII. Gioia del Colle, Museo archeologico nazionale, I. By A. Cancio. Rome: L'Erma di Bretschneider, 1995. Pp. 35 + ill. L230,000.

The archaeological museum at Gioia del Colle was founded in 1977 to accommodate the finds from excavations at the important site of Monte Sannace. The present volume of the *CVA*, the first to be devoted to this museum, publishes a selection of complete vases and fragments, in all fifty-nine pieces, mainly of the sixth and fifth centuries, including native Peucetian wares (pls. 1-20), imported Attic black-figure (pls. 21-26) and red-figure (pls. 27-33, 36-37, 39), and Early South Italian red-figure (pls. 34-35, 38?, 40). The catalogue is prefaced by a short discussion of the types of pottery as they are represented at Monte Sannace and elsewhere in Apulia.

While one can only welcome the publication of material from a significant, but perhaps less well-known, museum, the usefulness of the present work is, unfortunately, reduced by two problems. In the first place, the author has not stated clearly what criteria were used in the selection of the material. All the pottery comes from the excavations of 1957-61 or 1976-83 at Monte Sannace, some vases from the acropolis, others from the settlement, many from the tombs, but there is no discussion, or even an index, of the archaeological contexts, which is particularly disappointing for vases that served as grave-offerings. In fact, the format of the *CVA* is not intended for the presentation of such excavation material. And it is particularly hard to understand the reason for this volume, when one soon discovers that some of the pieces have already been adequately published in earlier comprehensive reports on the excavations at Monte Sannace, to one of which the author herself made a major contribution. Indeed, sometimes the earlier publication is more informative: for example, in the case of the fragment on pl. 3, 1, the original publication gives the diameter of the lip, a drawing of the upper surface of the lip, and a profile; and pl. 3, 2 is hardly comprehensible without recourse to the drawing and profile supplied in the original publication. In these circumstances, it would perhaps have been more useful to have concentrated upon one class of pottery (for example, the local matt-painted Peucetian ware), incorporating a discussion of its presence at the site, or alternately to have kept to unpublished material.

The second problem involves the description and attribution of the black-and red-figure pottery. Not only are the descriptions not as accurate as one would like, but the attributions are not always reliable. For example, the fragments illustrated on pls. 36-37, and 39 are all misidentified as Lucanian or Apulian, when they are clearly Attic.

The illustrations are generally of reasonable quality, but the printing of the photographs is not always as clear as it could be. The layout is sometimes wasteful, and the figured fragments are not always posed correctly.

Given that there are only forty plates and thirty-three pages of text (including introduction, bibliography and indexes), this volume of the *CVA* hardly represents value for money.

I append a few detailed comments:

Pl. 11, 3 and 4. These have been switched. 3 is *Monte Sannace*, pls. 178 and 214, 2.

Pls. 21-22. The first Amazon must be moving to the left, looking back; the second does not hold a 'scudo a pelta' but a 'Boeotian' shield. Is the charioteer on side B really an Amazon, and not a male in long white garment?

Pl. 23. The description is incomplete, and the fragments should have been rearranged in their proper sequence for photography (and could have been printed on a larger scale).

Pl. 24, 1. 'Overlap' decoration; the two draped figures are male.

Pl. 24, 3. Again the fragments have been wrongly composed.

Pl. 25. Each of the draped males wears a himation but not a chlamys.

Pl. 28. Details 4 and 5 have been printed in reverse. The left-hand figure on the reverse is a woman, holding a sceptre.

Pl. 29. The left-hand woman holds clappers (*krotala*), not a 'black ribbon'.

Pl. 31. The 'four vertical lines' represent a torch held by the woman. The helmeted figure is probably a mortal warrior, not a divinity.

Pl. 34-35. This bell-krater is not by the Amykos Painter, but by the Pisticci Painter. The vase is, in fact, listed by Trendall, *LCS* 21, no. 47.

Pl. 37, 1. Not Apulian, by the Painter of the Berlin Dancing Girl, but Attic, by the Painter of Louvre G 456 (attribution by Adrienne Lezzi-Hafter).

Pl. 37, 2-3. Also Attic, a fine early work by the Painter of Louvre G 456 (Adrienne Lezzi-Hafter). About 450-440. What is the subject of the picture on the outside? The running male seems to have something around his lower leg. The head and torso on MG 350 belong to the second figure from the left on MG 349.

Pl. 39, 1-3. Not Lucanian, of the Intermediate Group, but Attic, about 440-430.

Pl. 39, 4-6. Not Apulian of the first quarter of the fourth century, but Attic about 440-430. Same cup as pl. 39, 1-3?

Pl. 40. The two fragmentary cups on this plate are by the same painter: Early Apulian, in the vicinity of the Anabates Painter, to judge from the draped male on the outside. Why was the outside of pl. 30, 1 not illustrated?

IAN MCPHEE

La Trobe University

BYRNE (M.) **The Greek Geometric warrior figurine: interpretation and origin**. Louvain and Providence RI: Collège Érasme and Brown U, 1991. Pp. 256. Fr. b. 2,800.

This informative and well illustrated book seeks to examine the reason for the widespread use of the warrior motif during the Geometric period, attempt its interpretation, and determine its origin. As the bulk of the material evidence for this study if confined to Olympia and Delphi, both centres of Panhellenic importance, Byrne wisely concentrates his efforts upon the relevant anthropomorphic votive figurines from these two sites.

B. argues that the armed male terracotta figurines and the majority of the bronze series of armed male figures from Olympia represent Zeus. Initially, the author bases his argument upon Pausanias' (5.17.1) sighting of a 'crude' statue of Zeus in the Temple of Hera, together with that of Hera, which was standing, bearded and wearing a helmet; most of the terracotta and bronze series are standing and armed, the majority are wearing helmets, a few are bearded. Furthermore, B. sees in these early armed figurines the prototype for the later Zeus stereotype, i.e. bearded and standing, and armed with a thunderbolt. He rightly points out that Zeus in Homer is 'arbiter of war, to whom warriors pray for victory' (28), although his claim that there is a 'special connection between Zeus and armour' because of the great quantity of votive arms and armour unearthed at Olympia is, perhaps, a little wide of the mark (29). Admittedly Olympia houses an unparalleled collection of arms and armour, but this may be due to the simple fact that pieces of armour, having been thrown out, were reutilized as filling-material for the artificial banks of Stadium III, while others were used to help shore up the banks of the Kladeos. When, according to Polybios (5.8.9), the Macedonian soldiery of Philip V sacked Thermon, they took down no less than fifteen thousand suits of armour which had been dedicated to Apollo in the stoas there. Those they did not keep for themselves in exchange for their own battered armour, they melted down. The association between Zeus and war, which B. does indeed cover in a later section of his book, is better confirmed by the god's close affinities with the Semitic Baal and Anatolian Teshub. Both these Near Eastern gods are thunderers and rain-makers, reside on mountain-tops, and are represented as bearded, armed and striding in a smiting posture. Both are also associated with the bull, and with a female partner.

Delphi's armed figurines demonstrate that the motif of the armed male was not exclusive to Zeus. As these votive figurines postdate the earliest series found at Olympia, B. suggests that Delphi borrowed the motif—which, by the beginning of the eighth century BC, was fully developed, i.e. full warrior position with the right arm raised, bored for a spear, left forearm extended forward, bored for a shield (or, as I would suggest in Apollo's case, an arrow)—from Olympia. In the *Iliad*, for example, the arrows of Apollo signify pestilence, and B. points to the Canaanite smiting god Reshef who as a plague god shoots firebrands; in Ugarit and on Cyprus he is called Reshef of the Arrow. The author notes further examples of the armed Apollo figure from Thermon, perhaps Kalopodi and, of course, Amyklai (though he fails to mention the identical colossus of Apollo at Thornax attested by Herodotus [1.69] and Pausanias [3.10.8]).

Other Geometric sites considered for evidence to support the existence of an armed divinity include Dodona, Tegea, Samos, Lindos, Athens, Sparta and Argos. Argos, for instance, shows up a predominance of armed horsemen in its male series of figurines and, interestingly, this reminds us of Aristotle's comment (*Pol.* 1297b 16-9) that mounted warriors dominated the warfare of early Greek communities at the time of the disappearance of kingship and the transition to aristocratic rule. Despite the fact that these sites offer fewer examples of the armed male figurine, the evidence offered is important as it does confirm the interpretation of an armed Zeus at Olympia and an armed Apollo at Delphi.

Although Baal and Reshef were, iconographically and functionally, closely akin to Zeus and Apollo, B. rigorously pursues the idea that the adoption of the armed warrior motif in mainland Greece was not due to direct influence from the Near East but was borrowed from Crete. He stresses that Cretan characteristics, such as symmetrical arm and leg position, the πέτασος headdress, and beaky type of facial modelling, are to be found in several of the figurines from Olympia and Delphi. B. also points to the close association of both

Zeus and Apollo with Crete, and that between the second and first millennium BC an armed male divinity was clearly worshipped on the island; this cult goes back at least to the MM III, before the importation of Near Eastern armed figurines into the Aegean area, with a fully-developed smiting gesture appearing in Minoan and Mycenaean iconography as early as LM IA. The emphasis on the theme of the armed male is also apparent when the author considers Cypriot material, and he postulates that Cyprus was perhaps the point of transfer of the motif from the Near East.

For the ancient Greeks there was no single and exclusive god of war. True, we are accustomed to view Ares as such—he is the ultimate personification of the lust for battle—but Ares does side with the ultimate losers of the Trojan War. In the *Iliad*, for instance, we read that Hector promises to dedicate the armour of his opponent to Apollo, and Odysseus hands over Dolon's fur cap, bow and spear to Athena (7.8.1-3; 10.458-64). In particular, no less dreadful upon the field of battle are Zeus the Leader, Zeus Victorious and Zeus of the Rout, and it is hardly surprising, therefore, to witness the power of the strongest of Olympian gods manifesting itself in a martial context. This shift from the prehistoric cult of the all important female divinity (the Great Mother), who was invariably accompanied by a less important male partner (the Young God), to the cult of a male who is potent in warfare, as B. cogently sums up, coincides with the shift from a predominantly pastoral society with primary needs based on preservation and continuation of livestock, to a more urbanized community with primary needs of protection of the city and its wealth. Religion, says B., adapts to changing circumstances and the threat of war appears to have favoured the growth in importance of a male war god.

NIC FIELDS

Athens

KOTANSKY (R.) **Greek magical amulets: the inscribed gold, silver, copper, and bronze lamellae. Part I: published texts of known provenance (*Pap. Colon. XXII.1*).** Opladen: Westdeutscher Verlag, 1994. Pp. xxx + 415 + ill.

Original ancient Greek magical texts come down to us mostly on papyri, gemstones, the thin sheets of precious metal known as phylacteries (φυλακτήρια), and lead tablets. To scholars at the Institut für Altertumskunde at Cologne we owe the major ongoing work in establishing the texts of the magical papyri (Robert W. Daniel and Franco Maltomini, *Supplementum magicum I-II* [= *Pap. Colon.* XVI. 1-2, Opladen 1990-92], which includes eighty-four papyri, two phylacteries, fourteen curse tablets, and an inscribed haematite falcon; Daniel, *Two Greek magical papyri in the National Museum of Antiquities in Leiden, a photographic edition of J 384 and J 395* [= *Pap. Colon.* XIX, Opladen 1991]), the gemstones (Erika Zwierlein-Diehl, *Magische Amulette und andere Gemmen des Instituts für Altertumskunde der Universität zu Köln* [= *Pap. Colon.* XX, Opladen 1992]), and now the phylacteries. On these last, Roy Kotansky, who completed the present book while a Humboldt

Fellow under the direction of Reinhold Merkelbach, has long established himself as the world's expert.

He presents here sixty-seven phylacteries that range chronologically from the first century BC through the fifth or sixth century of our era and geographically from Yorkshire to the Crimean peninsula and Nubia. The book in fact includes sixty-nine tablets, but the two somewhat more monumental bronze examples (K.'s *11a, b*) are texts available for public reading and not phylacteries, properly speaking. As for the selection, we may wonder why, if texts with only *charaktêres* are admitted, the examples from War Kabūd in Luristan (L. Vanden Berghe, *Iranica Antiqua* 9 [1972] 10-12, Pl. II-V), important not least because they have a recorded excavation context, are not: their routine *charaktêres* are no less or more Greek than those from Yorkshire (*1*). An interesting Greek and Aramaic phylactery from Tell el-Amarna is excluded (p. xix) because of its Aramaic, yet this does not count against 56, from Haifa with its five lines of Aramaic plus eleven of Greek. And where is the splendid phylactery from Amorgos (Th. Homolle, *BCH* [1901] 430-56) that exorcises a tumour in the name of God who 'through his son illuminated Jerusalem and through Michael and Gabriel slew the twelve-headed dragon'? Or the example from Rome (W. Froehner, *Bulletin de la Société des Antiquaires de Normandie* 4 [1866-67] 217-31; *Sur une amulette basilidienne inédite du Musée Napoléon* [Caen 1869]; G. Pelliccioni, *Atti e memorie delle RR. deputazioni di storia patria per le provincie dell'Emilia* n.s. 5.2 [1880] 177-201) with its early mention of Solomon's pact with the demons? K. may have good reasons for excluding these texts, but he leaves us to guess what they are. Is this fair play in a corpus?

Despite the title of the volume, many of the texts are Latin or consist of magical *charaktêres* that need not imply Greek. It is instructive to compare, statistically, the papyri and ostraca of *Suppl. Mag.*, which divide themselves into two basic types, formularies (31) and 'effective' texts (47). Of these latter, the average length is 13.2 lines; the average for phylacteries, 11.6 lines. (One of K.'s phylacteries, *52*, with its 121 lines, rather skews the averages. I have excluded it in calculations.) The average 'effective' magical papyrus or ostracon, if we use *Suppl. Mag.* as a base, has 9.6 lines in a language that can be read (Greek, Latin); for K.'s phylacteries, the figure is 5.1. We may speculate that if phylactery texts are generally shorter, it is because gold and silver were much more expensive than papyrus and potsherds. And we may guess that if phylactery texts have a higher percentage of *charaktêres*, magical vocables, and the like, it is because such 'fromage mystique' was designed to appeal to the 'upmarket' buyer or at least to part the fool the sooner from his money. A great number of the texts that K. has collected consist solely or largely of these outlandish and apparently meaningless vocables. Their Egyptian and Semitic roots are important evidence, however, of how cross-cultural the ancient magical *koinê* was. Where K., with his knowledge of Semitic languages, excels is in his analyses of these vocables. His notes on them will be a boon to all who seriously study this part of Mediterranean culture.

The book began life as a doctoral thesis, supervised by Hans-Dieter Betz, for the Divinity School of the University of Chicago. K. claims that 'any resemblance between the thesis and the present corpus now proves almost impossible to descry', but the reader will soon discover that the content remains largely unsublimated. The result is disappointing but often richly rewarding. There is little sense of what is worth commenting on in a corpus, or of where innovation does violence to a text; nor do we find what we might expect, a full record of previous readings and scholarship. I think in particular of the notes to *52*; it is admittedly the longest of the texts, but does it require thirty-one pages? On line 100, for example, K. writes that 'the references refer to poisoning, erotic love-potions, or both', whatever this may mean. The words in question, μήτε ἐν βρώσει μήτε ἐν πόσει, are too straightforward for comment. Nor do I see why in a corpus we need two pages explaining the word βασιλίζων at *36*.18-19. Again, comparison with the 'effective' texts of *Suppl. Mag.* is instructive: each of their 620 lines gets about a quarter of a page of treatment; each of the 766 lines (again, I exclude *52*) of K.'s phylacteries gets about half a page. Some years ago Louis Robert (*Hellenica, recueil d'épigraphie, de numismatique, et d'antiquités grecs* [Paris 1960]) wrote an especially fierce review of a Leiden dissertation whose author published it as a book before sufficiently editing it. Virtually all his criticisms would apply here, but I would add what Robert did not, that the advisers and editors are at least as much to blame as the author himself.

Lemmata consist of bibliographies (alas, in no consistent order), texts if the phylacteries are legible, translations if there is anything translatable, and commentaries. A photograph or a drawing, the latter usually K.'s own, accompanies almost every text. K. has no doubt seen many of the tablets himself, but only three of his own drawings (*3, 51, 62*) does he claim to have made from the original; the rest are 'from photos' or 'after' an earlier editor; two (*56, 58*), puzzlingly, are 'after Kotansky', who himself was responsible for previous editions. If K. had told which tablets he had actually seen, we could more easily evaluate his drawings and transcriptions, for photographs are not always reliable, and clearly his eye is that of the master when he reads from autopsy.

The Greek of phylacteries is often corrupt and bristles with difficulties. *11*, a charm from Avignon against hailstones, begins ΘΩΣΟΥΔΕΡΚΥΩ / ΑΛΩΗ / ΝΟΥΜΙΧ–ΩΝ / ΘΕΙ. K. presents an interesting argument that this is a corruption of *Il.* 5.89 f., ἰσχανόωσαν / οὔτ᾽ ἄρα ἕρκεα ἴσχει ἀλωάων ἐριθηλέων, from the description of how Diomedes swept like a rainstorm across the plain. His notes to *32* offer an unexpected gift to Septuagint studies, the identification of a new witness to the Aquilan text of Deut. 32.1-3, embedded in lines previously unread. His text of *58* is a triumph.

Several of his interpretations, admit, I think, of improvements. *23*, for example, its text consisting of magical *charaktêres* plus Ιαω Αθων / Ιω Ιω, K. calls a 'Totenpass' because it was found in a burial. Especially because of the naming of Yahweh here, this identification requires more support. Burials have produced several phylacteries whose owners used them during their lifetimes, e.g. *19* (against elephantiasis), *31* (against eye ailments), *36* (against witchcraft), *41* (for general welfare of the household). That a phylactery was found in a burial therefore does not imply any intended use in the underworld. It is not even certain that the well-known gold tablet (27) from a Roman grave, with its late mangling of 'Orphic' verses, was not worn in the deceased's lifetime simply as an amulet.

Of 28 I myself, at *AJA* 89 (1985) 162-67, gave a tracing and a text, from autopsy:

Αἰωνεργέτα κύριε
Σάραπι, δὸς νείκην
κατὰ τῶν ὑπογεγραμ–
[μένων.............]

'Creator of eternity, Lord Sarapis, give victory over the underinscribed ...'. The hand is firm and confident, the letters regularly spaced. J. Gw. Griffiths, *ibid.*, 167 f., pointed out that the first word, hitherto unattested in Greek, is in fact a translation of an Egyptian term. On the tablet, there is a vertical crease about four letters away from the left-hand edge; it has produced a diamond-shaped wrinkle between κατὰ and τῶν in line 3. K., evidently relying on a photograph, draws and interprets the wrinkle as a deliberate mark and prints κατὰ ὀ(νομάτων). We may pass over the fact that the abbreviation in the one instance that K. cites, *Suppl. Mag.* II 94 ii 24, is not ο but ō, but is it likely that such a good scribe would have misunderstood any such abbreviation in his model and then tucked it up under the arm of another letter? K. in his commentary prints 'Αἰωνεργέτα (?)' and suggests Αἰὼν <εὐ>εργέτα, nowhere mentioning Griffiths' Egyptian antecedent of the new epithet.

36 opens, according to K., ἐγώ εἰμι ὁ μέγας ὁ ἐν οὐ/ρανῷ καθήμενος, / τὸ μολὸν κύτος ὅλου / τοῦ κόσμου, 'I am the Great One who sits in heaven <upon> the moving vault of the whole cosmos'. There is no '<upon>' in the Greek, and μολόν can hardly mean 'moving' here. It is better to assume a scribal corruption from a model that had τὸ μόνον κῦρος 'the sole governing force'. What follows is almost surely corrupt: σάον ὄνομα Μιαρσαυ, 'the sure name (is) Miarsau' in K.'s translation. Farther down, K. translates καὶ εἴ τίς με ἀδικήσι ἐπέκινα ἀπόστρεψον as 'and if anyone shall injure me henceforth, turn (him) away'. Better: 'and turn away whoever shall injure me on the other side'—i.e. turn away supernatural visitors. The next phrase shifts to mischief at the hands of humans: μήτε με φάρμακον ἀδικήσι. (Reference to Griffiths, *CPh* 48 [1953] 145-54, could have eliminated most of the six-page excursus on the expression 'King of Kings'.)

Of 40, which begins with an invocation of Aphrodite's name, K.'s text and translation of lines 7-12 run ποιήσαται ἐπίχαρειν (for –ριν), εὐοδίαν πᾶσιν ἀνθρώποις κὲ γυνεξί, μάλιστα δὲ πρὸς ὃν θέλι αὐτή 'make favour, success with all men and women, but particularly with him whom (she) herself wishes'. The word ἐπίχαρις, which K. assumes to be a noun, is an adjective. M. Siebourg, *BonnJbb* 103 (1898) 134, whose text K. does not quote, recognized that we have here the proper name Euodia; otherwise there is nothing for αὐτή to refer to. Better (in normalised spelling): either ποιήσατε ἐπίχαριν Εὐοδίαν 'make E. pleasing'; *cf. Cyran.* 87.59 Kaim. ποιεῖ δὲ καὶ ἐπίχαριν τὸν φορ–οῦντα.

We can expect at least one more volume, K. tells us,

and eventually a general introduction to the subject. I hope that he and his editors will read and take to heart that severe review of Robert's. If they do, the whole, I am confident, will be a solider monument that will long outlast any of the ἀγωνίσματα ἐς τὸ παραχρῆμα ἀκούειν of writers on ancient magic who have not touched and felt such texts as these.

DAVID R. JORDAN
Canadian Archaeological Institute at Athens
American School of Classical Studies at Athens

TRAILL (D.) **Schliemann of Troy: treasure and deceit.** London: John Murray, 1995. Pp. xiv + 365 + ill.

David Traill's detailed account of Heinrich Schliemann's archaeological career is at last with us. T. has published the most painstaking research into the life of the 'Father of Mycenaean archaeology' since Ernst Meyer's monumental *Heinrich Schliemann: Kaufman und Forscher*, published in 1969. Precisely because of this, his book—for the present reviewer at least—is in some respects a disturbing example of biographical methodology. In the name of 'truth' (13) and a compilation of moral precepts that would make even St Paul blush with envy, Heinrich Schliemann is given the proverbial 'works' by a scholar who still has not sufficiently defined what it is he wants to *tell* us, as opposed to *prove*. Is this a biography or a show trial?

Perhaps the book's title says it all. This tome is a *summa* of what T. calls the 'new, sceptical view of Schliemann' (10) that saw its first dramatic epiphany on 6 January, 1972, in William Calder III's (in)famous lecture at Mecklenburg where Schliemann was likened to a psychopath. The new book, and the 'school', appears to be mostly concerned with investigating the inconsistencies between Schliemann's autobiography, letters and texts on the one hand, and the 'truth' on the other. These having been established to the satisfaction of the author, certain episodes in Schliemann's archaeological career are scrutinised; it would seem that this is the book's main purpose. Priam's Treasure, the treasure from the Mycenae shaft graves, and other finds: where, when and how were they found? Are some pieces nineteenth-century fakes? For 'With an individual like Schliemann, we need always to be on our guard' (7). It is insinuatingly stated that 'as recently as the early 1980s, archaeologists maintained that Schliemann's archaeological work remained uncontaminated by this kind of behaviour [bribing and fraud]' (6). But then T. on the next page states: '... there is no doubt that for the most part Schliemann's archaeological reports are reliable. Later archaeologists have shown that the picture of sites presented by Schliemann's excavations is accurate' (7).

I leave it to the archaeologists to review his assessment of the Troy and Mycenae treasures. It should be noted, however, that T.'s well-known allegations that items in the Athens Archaeological Museum from the Mycenae excavations, including the famous death mask 'of Agamemnon', are nineteenth century fakes is presented as if it were a view held by many scholars (3: 'It has long been suggested ...') rather than his own cherished theory. Not a single reference, incidentally, is made—even in the bibliography!—to the important works by Edmund F. Bloedow on this and related subjects (chiefly 'Schliemann at Mycenae', *Echos du Monde Classique/Classical Views* XXXIII n.s. 8 (1989) 147-65, written in collaboration with S. Noyes-Roberts and D. Smulders, where T.'s Mycenae theories are roundly refuted.)

Here, I want to discuss T.'s biographical methodology as concerns the first four chapters of the book (childhood up to 1868), a period which I and my colleague Dr Mark Lehrer have been working on for some years for a book on Schliemann's 'conversion' to archaeology.

No biographer would deny Schliemann's penchant to inflate his self-image. T. himself actually admits this (4) but on the same page he states that 'Scholars have not been immune to the spell [of Schliemann's autobiography] ... It is scarcely surprising if many should find the recent revelations unwelcome.' (4). He continues: 'Clearly, if we want to penetrate the cocoon of myth woven by Schliemann and his biographers we need to adopt a more critical attitude to Schliemann's statements about himself than has hitherto been customary.' (4). This, of course, ignores the manner in which human autobiography develops over time. T. confines himself to comparing and scrutinising letters, diaries, and published documents in a magnificent example of detective work, but very little else.

The book's air of objectivity and scholarly aloofness masks the fact that much of what T. has to say reflects his own at times eccentric opinions. And when the myriad occurrences of words such as 'probably', 'perhaps', 'undoubtedly' and 'unquestionably' are taken into account, cracks appear in his conclusions. Innuendo is used with such dexterity that it seduces the unsuspecting reader (including many reviewers of this book, who seem to have taken its findings at face value). For instance, see T.'s extraordinary effort to explain S.'s academic interests prior to 1868 (31). (Please note the present reviewer's italics).

On 14 February [1866] he wrote to her [his first Russian wife, Katerina]: 'Every evening I go to the theatres or to scholarly lectures ... and I could tell you stories for ten years without wearing you out'. There is a touch of pathos in this letter or rather *what seems to lie behind it*. He is *clearly* doing the best to make himself and his mode of life in Paris sound appealing. *Given* that his cultural activities were designed to meet with Katerina's approval, it *seems likely* that his *sudden* interest in cultural self-improvement in 1856 was *also* intended to please her. *If so, then* the crucial conversion from merchant to archaeologist ... between 1856 and 1870 *may* have found its *original* impetus in the impossible task of pleasing a woman who despised him. *It is* in this tragic irony, not in the trumpery of the 'childhood dream', that the real romance of Schliemann's life resides.

'A masterpiece'! A = B, so therefore C must lead to D, and E is thus an emphatic 'It is ...' This is sloppy historical methodology. T. has the advantage of knowing his extensive material, but he gives the impression of cutting

and pasting it to suit his various arguments. Only when one actually sits with Schliemann's letters and diaries does it become clear that T.'s image of his subject's life is not always as clear as he would have us think.

One of the book's leitmotifs is that Schliemann's childhood 'dream of Troy' is a hoax. Nowhere does Schliemann give any indication, prior to 1868, that he *specifically* wanted to excavate Troy. This is, as far as we know, true. But then T. also attempts to diminish Schliemann's interest in Greece and things Greek prior to 1868, the year of his first visit to the Troad. Schliemann is said to have learnt Greek simply to do transactions with Greek businessmen in Russia (25), and was an autodidact just to impress his first wife (*supra*). On 26, we read that for Schliemann Greece was just another 'warm spot ... The mood [of the letters] in fact has much in common with that of today's northern European flipping through a travel brochure towards the end of another dreary winter ...'

There are, in fact, quite a number of letters and drafts in Schliemann's language exercise book—many in Greek—dating to between 1856 and 1868 that indicate that Greece and things Greek, ancient and modern (as opposed to a *specific* intention to excavate Troy), were not simply a whim in Schliemann's pre-1868 career. Why has T. not addressed these letters, some of which were used by Emil Ludwig, and will be reused—along with unpublished material—by Lehrer and myself in our forthcoming book? Why has so much material been suppressed or overlooked by one of the only persons on the planet who *must have read it*? On 27, for example, T. quotes a passage in Schliemann's language exercise book from July 1856: 'I think Greece will be of great interest to me and I will stay there ... and then see the Pyramids ...' etc. T. comments: 'Here again there is no indication that a visit to Greece might be the fulfilment of a childhood dream, no sign of a specific interest in Homeric sites or even in archaeology, and no mention at all of Troy'. Fair enough. But why has T. failed to mentioned the unpublished passage (translated here from the Greek, courtesy of the Gennadeion) in the same book where Schliemann states:

> I yearn to travel and visit Greece. Until now, I never enjoyed or was satisfied with my travels, always being caught up in business matters ... Now I can travel for other purposes involved with my beloved sciences, and in particular with philology ... I plan to go to Greece and Egypt with Homer and Thucydides in hand, and visit Ithaca, the Peloponnese, the plain of Troy, the Skamander where Achilles fought ... and the other worthy ruins of antiquity—of which there are now only paltry remains. (Draft, from before 9.1.1858, of a letter dispatched on that date to Carl Andress. This section does not appear in full in the final letter.)

Is this just more mendacity and day-dreaming? Of course, it would be naïve to indulge in using quotes such as these as any form of 'evidence' (e.g. of a wish to excavate Troy). But that is not the point. They exist, and the biographer has to look into the context in which they exist; how they could come to be stated in the first place. The very few of these texts that have been used by T. are fobbed off in footnotes, where he does not mention having seen the originals, but only cites secondary sources: e.g. ch. 2, n. 11, 13, 44, 48, 63-65 etc. Ironically, this methodology is precisely that that T. accuses Ernst Meyer of having used, in favour of the latter's hero (9)!

An analysis of the intricate manner in which T. fashions his prose and selects his facts to back up his thesis would take up a volume. I feel obliged to state that his methodology is in itself as worthy of suspicion as any mask from Mycenae or trinket from Troy. For instance, in 1866 Schliemann wrote to his uncle and cousin that he intended to visit Troy after visiting the Black Sea. T. then states darkly: 'In the end he did not go so far south' (30). Why does he not also state that Schliemann writes in his 1866 diary (Gennadeion, A10, p. 46, September 5) that he had not been given a passport due to problems with St Petersburg, and this hindered his plans? Tricks like this abound.

Perhaps in the final analysis we cannot confine ourselves to facts and dates and letters and diaries. T.'s book suffers from a fundamental inability to grasp the importance of the human experience, to understand that meaning is far more important than the register of mundane tabulated facts. When Schliemann uncovered Priam's Treasure, and claimed that his wife was next to him at the time, the most important fact for the biographer is that Schliemann *wanted* her there at the time, at a crucial point in his life. So what if she were not really there? Pedantic footnotes of this nature make interesting reading buried at the back of a book but the real purpose of biography is to delve into the meaning of a person's life with tools of research that can help us rise above the empirical record of events.

Much of the fictional in Schliemann's life is probably the most important *fact* of his life. The dream of Troy may not exactly have happened as Schliemann said it did. But the dream is eminently capable of serving as a way into the mind of a complex human being with exceptional gifts of insight, whose life was expressed in a web of simile that at times merged into metaphor, to become *reality*.

But T. retorts in the finest empirical tradition, 'Fiction should be treated as fiction. Why then do biographers of Schliemann present his childhood conversation with his father as biographical fact?' (6). T. has not even paused to reconsider his method. The supreme goals of truth and (oddly enough) impartiality are paramount for him. But what is truth? And who is going to play God in defining it especially when it comes to biography? The rather Victorian set of values used to shore up T.'s arguments has nothing to do with what modern biographical research is all about. Why, when it comes to biography, should we treat the character of a 'fictitious' book differently from a 'real' historical figure? These are, I feel, fundamental questions that we should all be thinking about.

DAVID TURNER

British School at Athens

SCHREINER (P.) **Byzanz**. Rev. ed. Munich: Oldenbourg, 1994. Pp. xvi + 260. DM 38.

In common with all good things Byzantine, Schreiner's *Byzanz* comes in three parts: a basic chronological exposition of the Byzantine experience; a discussion of basic problems and directions in research in the field, and an extensive bibliography of primary and secondary sources.

The stated purpose of the series is to provide a helpmeet for historians, whether teachers or students, working in adjacent periods or territories, who require some guidance through unknown territory. Furthermore, the authors of individual volumes have been encouraged to present their material so that it may be used with profit by the non-specialist (v).

Given this aim, S.'s *Byzanz* is a remarkable achievement. In two hundred and sixty pages, he provides a chronological survey of ninety-eight pages; a survey of the major questions and problems of research in seventy-five pages; six pages of bibliography of primary sources; forty pages of bibliography of the secondary literature; one page of commonly encountered journal abbreviations; two pages of ruler lists; eight pages of simplified dynastic family trees; five pages of basic chronology; two maps; an index of places and objects; and finally an index of authors. In this structured fashion (aided by marginal keywords for each paragraph), S.'s *Byzanz* does indeed provide a clear guide to the world of Byzantium, but I was struck by the lack of illustrations in a work that discusses material evidence.

In the first edition (1985) introduction, reprinted here, S. describes his main goal as giving factual information about the Byzantine state in all its manifestations (xiii). After marking the boundaries, Schreiner gives a political history in twenty-five pages. Economic and social history is covered by coinage and its debasement; taxation; the relationship of persons to the land and between the powerful (*dynatoi*) and those tied to the land (*paroikoi*); the institutions of *charistike* and *pronoia*; and then matters of urban development, including social mobility, *demes*, guilds, the *eparch*, trade and price controls. Relief comes in the form of ten pages on government (46-56) and eleven on constitutional history (56-67). A section on the Church and Monasticism (68-81) follows, before attention turns to cultural and spiritual life (82-98). Language (82) is immediately followed by literature (83-91) which leads into education, its content, format, availability and the relationship between monasticism and learning (*Bildung*). Art history (94-97) and music (97-98) are then dealt with.

Treating problems and research, S. stresses the interdisciplinary nature of Byzantine Studies, uniting history, philology and literature, art history and archaeology. The section '*Forschungsgeschichte*' (99-104) is to my mind the reason that native English speakers should turn to this book. This five page section provides a summary of the historiography of Byzantine Studies. From Wolf, through the works of DuCange, Mabillon and de Montfaucon to Jean Bolland and the *Acta Sanctorum*, the survey moves on to cover the nineteenth century and then a nation by nation roster in the twentieth century. S. gives a useful history of the development of the subject and a thumbnail sketch of who does what where.

Dealing with the various aspects of research, there is a tendency for it to become a mere listing. Ancillary disciplines are followed by specialist areas, followed by links to other subjects: like Anna Komnene faced with the theology of Maximos Confessor, one's head begins to spin! Methodological problems follow: the loss of sources (113-17) and the role of Byzantine rhetoric and its impact on the utility ('*Informationswert*') of our sources and the implications for our understanding (117-19). New areas of research are identified: emperor, state and church (153-59); freedom and dependency (159-66); literature and its readership (166-71). Works published in the ten years since the first edition are mentioned and indications given of developing trends.

Like this book, my conclusion has three points. It is a pity there is no mention of the application of new computer technologies to research. Secondly, by transliterating Greek terms, the work is made more accessible to the non-specialist, but a certain inconsistency in the treatment of terminology (whether the Greek is followed or precedes its German equivalent) may cause problems for the non-specialist reading the book in a foreign language. These criticisms aside, however, S.'s *Byzanz* achieves its aim admirably. The section on the history and development of Byzantine Studies by itself is reason enough for non-native readers of German to turn to it.

DION C. SMYTHE

King's College London

KONDIS (B.) and MANDA (E.) **The Greek minority in Albania: a documentary record (1921-1993)**. Thessalonika: Institute of Balkan Studies, 1994. Pp. 130.

A central dimension to the tragic crisis that has overtaken the Balkans in the last five years has been the inability of most Balkan states to find a *modus vivendi* for the significant minorities living within their borders. In a sense, in the old Yugoslavia, virtually everybody was a minority of some kind, either in relation to the old Yugoslav state, or one of the component republics. This situation led to the retention of historic grievances as part of the normal contemporary political discourse and the endless repetition of old ethnic conflicts.

In the surrounding states, such as Bulgaria, Romania and Albania, there are also large minorities, but so far at least, the ruins of settled political life in the region left by fifty years of communism and now war and political turmoil have not led to outbreaks of widespread violence. But among these numerous groups, the Greek minority in southern Albania has one of the most sensitive positions, and tension over its human rights problems and political grievances has led to a marked deterioration of bilateral relations between Greece and Albania. The problems of the minority have been closely linked since the end of communism in 1991 with the wider question of Albanian mass emigration into Greece.

In this volume, Professor Basil Kondis of the Institute of Balkan Studies in Thessalonika, and his collaborator, Eleftheria Manda have assembled a useful collection of documents that sets out the main events that have affected the minority since the foundation of the modern Albanian state during the First World War, after the original declaration of independence by Ishmail Kemal Bey at Vlora in 1912. It is, in the main, a depressing story, with a Greek community of perhaps 75,000 people in the southern part of Albania with great historic and cultural traditions, remarkable music and songs especially, being continually buffeted by political extremists of all kinds, on both sides, and clerical irridentists. After the carnage in northern Epirus described so graphically by the French war correspondent Rene Puaux in his book *The sorrows of Epirus*, there seemed to be some hope that the post-1921 period might lead to better things, but on the whole these hopes were disappointed. It bears out the contemporary Balkans, where in many situations if you think of the worst thing that can possibly happen, that is what usually transpires.

The 1920s were a period of some progress, with the establishment of a rudimentary education system in the Greek language, and relative inter-communal peace, but the border issue was never really settled, with many Greeks unable to accept the decisions of the Boundary Commissioners and the 1913 Protocol of Florence that established the modern boundary of the Albanian state. To this day, the Greek Foreign Ministry has refused to mark it clearly with boundary posts. On the Albanian side, the minority were always seen as a Trojan horse that could lead to an attempted Greek take-over of the country, and the rhetoric of some elements in the Greek Right and the Church did little to calm these fears.

After the overthrow of the Fan Noli government by Ahmet Zogu, later King Zog, an increasingly nationalist and aggressive atmosphere prevailed in Tirana. Greek education was closed down in the early 1930s, and many priests were either expelled or imprisoned, sometimes in mental institutions. Wartime saw some improvement, with Greeks playing a leading part in the anti-Axis struggle but the Greek community was split between those who favoured the communist Partisans, led by Enver, Hoxha, and the Right wing Northern Epirus Liberation Front. The latter was destroyed in vicious fighting by the Axis occupiers and Albanian Balli Kombetar nationalists in 1943, leaving the field open to the communists to take over the leadership of the Greek minority with ease after 1945.

There is much for historians to learn about these events, in particular if the promised opening of the archives in Tirana actually takes place. This volume of documents is a good start, and will help educate English-language readers. The sections on the inter-war problems of the coastal communities around Himara is particularly valuable.

A fuller introduction would have been helpful, including something to give the student of the subject a better idea of the background about bitter controversy on archaeological and ancient history that is an important part in both the Greek minority and Albanian political identities in the region.

JAMES PETTIFER

St Antony's College, Oxford

BOOKS RECEIVED

ADAMS (J.N.) **Pelagonius and the Latin veterinary terminology in the Roman Empire.** (Studies in Ancient Medicine 11.) Leiden: Brill, 1995. Pp. viii + 695. Fl.342, $195.50.

AILIANOS (K.I.) **Mia prooptike symmachias Ellados-Avstro-oungarias choris Epavrio, 1883-1887.** Thessaloniki: Institute for Balkan Studies, 1994. Pp. 154. 9607387058.

ALCHEMISTS. *Les Alchimistes grecs.***4.1.** *Zosime de Panopolis. Mémoires authentiques.* Ed. and tr. M. Mertens. Paris: Les Belles Lettres (Budé), 1995. Pp. clxxii + 299, ill. Fr. 395. 2251004483.

ALCOCK (S.E.) **Graecia capta. The landscapes of Roman Greece.** Cambridge UP, 1993. Pp. xxi + 307, ill. £40 (£14.95, paper). 0521401097 (hb); 0521568-196 (pb).

ALEXIOU (E.) **Ruhm und Ehre. Studien zu Begriffen, Werten und Motivierung bei Isokrates.** (Bibliothek der klassischen Altertumswissenschaften, Neue Folge 2, Bd. 93.) Heidelberg: Winter, 1995. Pp. 272. DM 98. 3825302946.

ALGRA (K.A.) **Concepts of space in Greek thought.** (Philosophia antiqua 65.) Leiden: Brill, 1995. Pp. 365. Fl. 145, $ 83.00. 9004101721.

ALLES (G.D.) **The *Iliad*, the *Ramayana*, and the work of religion. Failed persuasion and religious mystification.** University Park, Pa.: Pennsylvania State UP, 1994. Pp. viii + 207. £27.00, $30.00 (£14.50, $15.95 (pbk.). 0271013192 (hb); 0271013206 (pb).

ALONSO TRONCOSO (V.) **El comercio griego arcaico. Historiografia de las cuatro ultimas decadas, 1954-1993.** La Coruña: Gaesa, 1994. Pp. 157. 8460517764.

ALVIS (J.) **Divine purpose and heroic response in Homer and Virgil. The political plan of Zeus.** Lanham, MD: Rowman and Littlefield, 1995. Pp. x + 269. $58.50 ($21.95, paper). 0847680142 (hb); 0847680150 (pb).

AMATO (E.) **Studi su Favorino. Le orazioni pseudo-crisostomiche.** Salerno: Edisud, 1995. Pp. xvi + 164, ill. L 29,000. 8885224555.

AMBAGLIO (D.) **La biblioteca storica di Diodoro Siculo.** Problemi e metodo. (Biblioteca di Athenaeum 28.) Como: New Press, 1995. Pp. 176. L 40,000.

AMELING (W.), BRINGMANN (K.) and SCHMIDT-DOUNAS (B.) **Schenkungen hellenistischer Herrscher an griechische Städte und Heiligtümer. Teil 1. Zeugnisse und Kommentare.** Berlin: Akademie Verlag, 1995. Pp. xi + 592, ill. DM 398. 3050022744.

AMOURETTI (M.-CL.) and VILLARD (P.) *Ed.* Eukrata. **Mélanges offerts à Claude Vatin.** (Travaux du Centre Camille Jullian 17.) Aix-en-Provence: Publications de l'Université de Provence, 1994. Pp. 210. Fr. 210. 2853993469.

ANCONA (R.) **Time and the erotic in Horace's *Odes*.** Durham, N.C./London: Duke UP, 1994. Pp. x + 186. £37.95. 0822314762.

ANDERSEN (O.) and DICKIE (M.) *Ed.* **Homer's world. Fiction, tradition, reality.** (Papers from the Norwegian Institute at Athens 3.) Bergen: Norwegian Institute at Athens, 1995. Pp. 173. 8299141192.

ANDERSON (W.D.) **Music and musicians in ancient Greece.** Ithaca, N.Y./London: Cornell UP, 1994. Pp. xiii + 248. £27.50. 0801430836 (hb), 0801430305 (pb).

ANDOCIDES: **Works.** Ed., tr. and comm. M. Edwards. Warminster: Aris & Phillips, 1995. Pp. viii + 216. £35 (£14.95, paper). 0856685275 (hb), 0856685283 (pb).

ANDREAE (B.) and others **Museo Chiaramonti.** (Bildkatalog der Skulpturen des Vatikanischen Museums 1) Berlin: de Gruyter, 1995. 3 vols, pp. xiii + 146, 1106, ill. DM 840. 3110138999.

ANGOLD (M.) **Church and society in Byzantium under the Comneni, 1081-1261.** Cambridge UP, 1995. Pp. xvi + 604. £60. 0521264324.

ANTONACCIO (C.M.) **An archaeology of ancestors. Tomb cult and hero cult in early Greece.** Lanham, Md.: Rowman & Littlefield, 1995. Pp. xiv + 295. $39.50 ($17.95, paper). 0847679411 (hb), 0847679-42X (pb).

ARENA (R.) *Ed.* **Iscrizioni greche arcaiche di Sicilia e Magna Grecia. 3. Iscrizioni delle colonie euboiche.** Pisa: Nistri Lischi, 1994. Pp. 136, ill. L 25.000.

ARISTOPHANES: *Birds.* Ed. N. Dunbar. Oxford UP, 1995. Pp. xvii + 782. £65. 0198149344.

ARISTOPHANES: *Las nubes, Las ranas, Pluto.* Ed. and tr. F.R. Adrados and J.R. Somolinos. Madrid: Catedra, 1995. Pp. 263, ill. 8437613671.

ARISTOTLE: **Aristotle. Selections.** Tr. T. Irwin and G. Fine. Indianapolis: Hackett, 1995. Pp. xxiii + 627. £32.50 (£15.95, paper). 0915145685 (hb), 091514-5677 (pb).

ARISTOTLE: **Il trattato sul cosmo per Alessandro attribuito ad Aristotele.** Ed, tr. and comm. G. Reale and A.P. Bos. (Pubblicazioni del Centro di Ricerche di Metafisica. Temi metafisici e problemi del pensiero antico. Studi e testi 42.) Milan: Vita e Pensiero, 1995. Pp. 534. L 55,000. 8834308212.

ARISTOTLE: *Poetics* (ed. and tr. S. Halliwell), [LONGINUS]: *On the sublime* (ed. and tr. W. Hamilton Fyfe, rev. D. Russell), DEMETRIUS: *On style* (ed. and tr. D.C. Innes). Cambs, Mass./London: Harvard UP (Loeb), 1995. Pp. 533. £11.95. 0674995635.

ARISTOTLE: *Politics*, **Books 1-2.** Tr. and comm. T.J. Saunders. Oxford UP, 1995. Pp. xvi + 194. £30 (£9.99, paper). 019824892X (hb), 0198248946 (pb).

ARISTOTLE: *Politics*, **Books 3-4.** Tr. and comm. R. Robinson, rev. D. Keyt. Oxford UP, 1995. Pp. xxx + 155. £25 (£9.99, paper). 0198235917 (hb), 0198235-925 (pb).

ARISTOTLE: *Politics*. Tr. E. Barker, rev. R.F. Stalley. Oxford UP, 1995. Pp. xlvii + 423. £6.99 (paper). 0192831097.

ARRIAN: *Periple du Pont-Euxin*. Ed. and tr. A. Silberman. Paris: Les Belles Lettres (Budé), 1995. Pp. xlvii + 69. Fr. 225. 2251004467.

ARRIGHETTI (G.) *Ed.* **Poesia greca.** (Biblioteca di studi antichi 72. Ricerche di filologia classica 4.) Pisa: Giardini, 1993. Pp. 279.

ATIK (N.) **Die Keramik aus den sudThermen von Perge.** (Istanbuler Mitteilungen Beiheft 40.) Tubingen: E. Wasmuth, 1995. Pp. xx + 211, ill. 3803017-394.

ATKINSON (J.E.) **A commentary on Q. Curtius Rufus'** *Historiae Alexandri Magni*, **Books 5 to 7.2.** (Acta Classica Supplementum 1.) Amsterdam: Hakkert, 1994. Pp. iv + 284. SwFr. 90. 9025610374.

AVRAMEA (A.) and others **Thrace.** Tr. A. Doumas. Athens: Idea, 1994. Pp. 411, ill. 9608560918.

AZARA (P.) **La imagen y el olvido. El arte como engano en la filosofia de Platon.** (La Biblioteca Azul Serie Memor 8.) Madrid: Ediciones Siruela, 1995. Pp. 249, ill. 8478442677.

BAGNALL (R.S.) **Reading papyri, writing ancient history.** London/New York: Routledge, 1995. Pp. viii + 145, ill. £35 (£9.99, paper). 0415093767 (hb), 0415093775 (pb).

BARBANERA (M.) **Il guerriero di Agrigento. Una probabile scultura frontonale del museo di Agrigento e alcune questioni di archeologia ''siceliota''.** (Studia archaeologica 77.) Rome: ''L'Erma'' di Bretschneider, 1995. Pp. 101, ill. L 150,000. 887062-904X.

BARBER (R.) **Greece.** (Blue Guides, ed. 6). London: A & C Black/New York: W W Norton, 1995. Pp. 768, ill. £16.99 (paper). 0393312739 (USA), 071363250X (UK).

BARNES (J.) *Ed.* **The Cambridge companion to Aristotle.** Cambridge UP, 1995. Pp. xxv + 404. £40 (£17.95, paper). 0521411335 (hb), 0521422949 (pb).

BARNES (T.D.) *Ed.* **The sciences in Greco-roman society.** (Apeiron 27, 4.) Edmonton, Alta.: Academic Printing and Publishing, 1994. Pp. 125, ill. $54.95 ($19.95, paper). 0920980600 (hb), 0920980619 (pb).

BARRINGER (J.M.) **Divine escorts. Nereids in archaic and classical Greek art.** Ann Arbor: U Michigan P, 1995. Pp. xx + 276, ill. $52.50. 047210-4187.

BATCHELDER (A.G.) **The seal of Orestes. Self-reference and authority in Sophocles'** *Electra.* Lanham, Md.: Rowman & Littlefield, 1995. Pp. xii + 163. $52.50 ($21.95, paper). 084767990X (hb), 0847679-918 (pbk.).

BATTEZZATO (L.) **Il monologo nel teatro di Euripide.** (Pubblicazioni della classe di lettere e filosofia, Scuola Normale Superiore, Pisa 14.) Pisa: Scuola Normale Superiore, 1995. Pp. 210. 8876420398.

BEARD (M.) and HENDERSON (J.) **Classics. A very short introduction.** Oxford UP, 1995. Pp. 136, ill. £4.99. 0192853139.

BECKER (A.S.) **The shield of Achilles and the poetics of ekphrasis.** Lanham, Md.: Rowman & Littlefield, 1995. Pp. xii + 191. $52.50 ($21.95, paper). 084767-9977 (hb), 0847679985 (pb).

BEHRENDS (O.) and SELLERT (W.) *Ed.* **Nomos und Gesetz. Ursprunge und Wirkungen des griechischen Gesetzesdenkens. 6. Symposion der Kommission ''Die Funktion des Gesetzes in Geschichte und Gegenwart''.** (Abhandlungen der Akademie der Wissenschaften in Göttingen, Philologisch-historische Klasse Folge 3, 209.) Göttingen: Vandenhoeck & Ruprecht, 1995. Pp. 261. DM 124. 3525825978.

BELL (R.E.) **Women of classical mythology. A biographical dictionary.** New York: Oxford UP, 1993. Pp. xii + 462. £9.99. 0195079779.

BELLI PASQUA (R.) **Sculture di età romana in ''basalto''.** (Xenia antiqua monografie 2.) Rome: ''L'Erma'' di Bretschneider, 1995. Pp. 163, ill. L 200,000. 887062885X.

BENAKI MUSEUM. **Thymiama ste mneme tes Laskarinas Boura.** Athens: Benaki Museum, 1994. Pp. xviii + 368 in 2 vols, ill. 9608516021.

BERGENGRUEN (W.), SCHAFER (W.) and MAYER-ECKHARDT (V.) **Novellen um Winckelmann.** (Beiträge der Winckelmann-Gesellschaft 20.) Mainz: von Zabern, 1993. Pp. 256. DM 35. 3805315899.

BERGGREEN (B.) and MARINATOS (N.) *Ed.* **Greece and Gender.** (Papers from the Norwegian Institute at Athens 2.) Bergen: Norwegian Institute at Athens, 1995. Pp. 184, ill. 8291626006.

BERTI (F.) and GUZZO (P.G.) *Ed.* **Spina. Storia di una città tra greci e etruschi.** Ferrara: Comitato Ferrara Arte, 1993. Pp. xv + 380, ill. L 85,000.

BETTS (G.) *Tr.* **Three medieval Greek romances. Velthandros and Chrysandza, Kallimachos and Chrysorroi, Livistros and Rodamni.** (Garland Library of Medieval Literature 98, Series B.) New York/London: Garland Publishing, 1995. Pp. xli + 192. $35. 0815312792.

BIANCO (E.) **Atene ''come il sole.'' L'imperialismo ateniese del v secolo a.c. nella storia e oratoria politica attica.** (Fonti e studi di storia antica 2.) Alessandria: Edizioni Dell'Orso, 1994. Pp. ix + 196. L 25,000. 8876941835.

BIELMAN (A.) **Retour à la liberté. Libération et sauvetage des prisonniers en Grèce ancienne. Recueil d'inscriptions honorant des sauveteurs et analyse critique.** (Etudes epigraphiques 1.) Paris: De Boccard (for École Française d'Athènes & Université de Lausanne), 1994. Pp. xxvii + 367, ill. 2869580673.

BILLOWS (R.A.) **Kings and colonists. Aspects of Macedonian imperialism.** (Columbia studies in the classical tradition 22.) Leiden: Brill, 1995. Pp. xv + 240, ill. Fl. 125, $71.50. 9004101772.

BIRASCHI (A.M.) *Ed.* **Strabone e la Grecia.** Naples: Edizioni Scientifiche Italiane, 1994. Pp. 247. L 33,000. 8871048113.

BJORK (C.) **Early pottery in Greece. A technological and functional analysis of the evidence from neolithic Achilleion, Thessaly.** (Studies in Mediterranean Archaeology 115.) Jonsered: Astrom, 1995. Pp. ix + 172, ill. 9170810915.

BLOK (J.H.) **The early Amazons. Modern and ancient perspectives on a persistent myth.** (Religions in the Graeco-Roman world 120.) Leiden: Brill, 1995. Pp. xxiii + 473. Fl. 228, $130.50. 9004100776.

BLUNDELL (S.) **Women in ancient Greece.** London: British Museum P, 1995. Pp. 224, ill. 0714112968.

BOARDMAN (J.) **The diffusion of classical art in antiquity.** London: Thames & Hudson: 1994. Pp. 352, ill. £34. 0500236968.

BOARDMAN (J.) **Greek sculpture. The late classical period and sculpture in colonies and overseas. A handbook.** London: Thames & Hudson, 1995. Pp. 248, ill. £6.95. 0500202850.

BOLDRINI (S.) **Le ceramiche ioniche.** (Gravisca: scavi nel santuario greco 4.) Bari: Edipuglia, 1994. Pp. 281, ill. L 130,000. 8872281156.

BOMMELAER (J.-F.) and DES COURTILS (J.) **La Salle hypostyle d'Argos.** (Etudes Peloponnesiennes 10.) Paris: de Boccard, 1994. Pp. 72, ill. 2869580711.

BORN (H.) and HANSEN (S.) **Frühgriechische Bronzehelme.** (Sammlung Axel Guttmann 3.) Mainz am Rhein: Sammlung Guttmann/von Zabern, 1994. Pp. 167, ill. DM 128. 3805316658.

BOSWORTH (A.B.) **A historical commentary on Arrian's** *History of Alexander*. **Vol.2. Commentary on books IV-V.** Oxford UP, 1995. Pp. xviii + 382, ill. £45. 0198148291.

BOURRIOT (F.) **Kalos kagathos - kalokagathia. D'un terme de propagande de sophistes à une notion sociale et philosophique. Étude d'histoire athénienne.** (Spudasmata 58.) Hildesheim: Olms, 1995. 2 vols, pp. v + 626, vi + 654. DM 128 (per vol.). 3487100002 (set), 3487100010 (v.1), 3487100029 (v.2).

BOWDEN (E.) **Cybele the axe-goddess. Alliterative verse, Linear B relationships and cult ritual of the Phaistos disc.** Amsterdam: Gieben, 1992. Pp. xviii + 286, ill. Fl. 60. 9050630812.

BOWERSOCK (G.W.) **Fiction as history. Nero to Julian.** (Sather Classical Lectures 58.) Berkeley: U California P, 1994. Pp. xiv + 181. $30. 0520088247.

BRACCESI (L.) **Poesia e memoria. Nuove proiezioni dell'antico.** (L'eredità dell'antico passato e presente 4.) Rome: "L'Erma" di Bretschneider, 1995. Pp. ix + 197. L 45,000. 8870628841.

BRAHMS (T.) **Archaismus. Untersuchungen zu Funktion und Bedeutung archaistischer Kunst in der Klassik und im Hellenismus.** (Europäische Hochschulschriften Reihe XXXVIII, Archäologie 53.) Frankfurt am Main: Lang, 1994. Pp. 452, ill. £46, DM 118. 3631478062.

BRAUDEL (F.) **A history of civilizations.** Tr. R. Mayne. London: Penguin Books, 1995. Pp. xl + 600. £8.99. 0140124896.

BREUER (C.) **Reliefs und Epigramme griechischer Privatgrabmäler. Zeugnisse bürgerlichen Selbstverstandnisses vom 4. bis 2. Jahrhundert v. Chr.** Cologne: Bohlau Verlag, 1995. Pp. 151, ill. DM 148. 3412158933.

BRIANT (P.) and LEVEQUE (P.) *Ed.* **Le Monde grec aux temps classiques. 1. Le Ve siècle.** Paris: Presses Universitaires de France, 1995. Pp. lv + 456. Fr. 198. 2130466125.

BRINKMANN (V.) **Beobachtungen zum formalen Aufbau und zum Sinngehalt der Friese des Siphnierschatzhauses.** (Studien zur antiken Malerei und Farbgebung 1.) Munich: Biering & Brinkmann, 1994. Pp. 192, ill. DM 158. 3930609002.

BRISSON (L.) **Le Même et l'autre dans la structure ontologique du** *Timée* **de Platon. Un commentaire systématique du** *Timée* **de Platon.** Ed. 2. (International Plato Studies 2.) Sankt Augustin: Academia Verlag, 1994. Pp. 611. DM 128. 3883456330.

BRISSON (L.) **Orphée et l'orphisme dans l'antiquité gréco-romaine.** Aldershot: Variorum/Brookfield, Vt.: Ashgate, 1995. Pp. viii + 301. £49.50. 0860784533.

BROWN (J.P.) **Israel and Hellas.** (Beihefte zur Zeitschrift für die Alttestamentliche Wissenschaft 231.) Berlin: de Gruyter, 1995. Pp. xxii + 407. DM 178. 3110142333.

BRUER (S.-G.) **Die Wirkung Winckelmanns in der deutschen klassischen Archäologie des 19. Jahrhunderts.** (Abhandlungen der Geistes- und Sozialwissenschaftlichen Klasse/Akademie der Wissenschaften und der Literatur 1994, 3.) Mainz: Akademie der Wissenschaften und der Literatur/Stuttgart: Steiner, 1994. Pp. 246. DM 89. 3515065415.

BRUYN (O. de) **La Compétence de l'Aréopage en matière de procès publics des origines de la polis athénienne à la conquête romaine de la Grèce (vers 700-146 avant J.-C.).** (Historia Einzelschriften 90.) Stuttgart: Steiner, 1995. Pp. 226. DM 80. 35150-66543.

BUITRON-OLIVER (D.) **Douris. A master-painter of Athenian red-figure vases.** (Forschungen zur antiken Keramik II. Reihe Kerameus 9.) Mainz am Rhein: von Zabern, 1995. Pp. xi + 115, ill. DM 198. 38053-13578.

BURTON (J.B.) **Theocritus's urban mimes. Mobility, gender and patronage.** (Hellenistic culture and society 19.) Berkeley: U California P, 1995. Pp. viii+ 298. £32, $40. 0520088581.

CABANES (P.) **Le Monde hellénistique de la mort d'Alexandre à la paix d'Apamée, 323-188.** Paris: Seuil, 1995. Pp. 276, ill. 2020131307.

CALAME (C.) **The craft of poetic speech in ancient Greece.** Tr. J. Orion. Ithaca: Cornell UP, 1995. Pp. xviii,+ 220. £31.50 (£12.50, paper). 0801427436 (hb), 0801480221 (pb).

CAMERON (A.) **Callimachus and his critics.** Princeton UP, 1995. Pp. xiv + 534. £37.50. 0691043671.

CAMPS-GASET (M.) **L'Année des Grecs. La Fête et le mythe.** (Annales litteraires de l'Université de Bésançon 530.) Paris: Les Belles Lettres, 1994. Pp. 193. 2251605304.

CAPDEVILLE (G.) **Volcanus. Recherches comparatistes sur les origines du culte de Vulcain.** (Bibliothèque des Écoles Françaises d'Athènes et de Rome 288.) Rome: École Française de Rome, 1995. Pp. vii + 519, ill. 2728302723.

CARGILL (J.) **Athenian settlements of the fourth century B.C.** (Mnemosyne Supplement 145.) Leiden: 1995. Pp. xxvii + 487 ill. Fl. 250, $143. 9004099913.

CARRADICE (I.A.) **Greek coins.** London: British Museum P, 1995. Pp. 112, ill. £9.99. 0714122106.

CARTER (J.B.) and MORRIS (S.P.) *Ed.* **The ages of Homer. A tribute to Emily Townsend Vermeule.** Austin: U of Texas P, 1995. Pp. xvii + 542 + ill. $40.

CASTRIOTA (D.) **The Ara Pacis Augustae and the imagery of abundance in later Greek and early Roman imperial art.** Princeton UP, 1995. Pp. xviii + 253, ill. 0691037159.

CERASUOLO (S.) *Ed.* **Mathesis e philia. Studi in onore di Marcello Gigante.** Naples: Dipartimento di Filologia Classica dell'Università degli Studi di Napoli Federico II, 1995. Pp. 555, ill.

CHARITON: *Chaereas and Callirrhoe.* Ed. and tr. G.P. Goold. Cambridge, Mass./London: Harvard UP (Loeb), 1995. Pp. viii + 425. £11.95. 0674995309.

CITTI (V.) **Eschilo e la lexis tragica.** (Lexis Supplemento 2.) Amsterdam: Hakkert, 1994. Pp. 209. 9025610706.

CLACKSON (J.) **The linguistic relationship between Armenian and Greek.** (Publications of the Philological Society 30.) Oxford: Blackwell, 1994. Pp. x + 272. £19.95. 0631191976

CLAIRMONT (C.W.) **Classical Attic tombstones. Supplementary volume.** Kilchberg: Akanthus, 1995. Pp. 174. 3905083094.

CLEARY (J.J.) **Aristotle and mathematics. Aporetic method in cosmology and metaphysics.** (Philosophia antiqua 67.) Leiden: E.J. Brill, 1995. Pp. xxxvi + 558. 004101594.

COHEN (B.) *Ed.* **The distaff side. Representing the female in Homer's** *Odyssey***.** New York: Oxford UP, 1995. Pp. xviii + 229, ill. £30 (£15.99, paper). 0195086821 (hb), 019508683X (pb).

COHEN (D.J.) **Law, violence and community in classical Athens.** Cambridge UP, 1995. Pp. xii + 214. £35 (£12.95, paper). 0521381673 (hb), 0521388-376 (pb).

COHEN (M.), CURD (P.) and REEVE (C.D.C.) *Ed.* **Readings in ancient Greek philosophy from Thales to Aristotle.** Indianapolis: Hackett , 1995. Pp. xiii + 786. £32.50 (£18.95, paper). 0872203131 (hb), 0872203123 (pb).

COLEMAN (J.) **Against the state. Studies in sedition and rebellion.** London: Penguin/BBC, 1995. Pp. ix + 229. £6.99. 0140248161.

COMOTH (K.) **Rekonstruktionen zum delphischen Epsilon und gnostischen Gamma.** Heidelberg: Winter, 1995. Pp. 27, ill. DM 15. 3825303276.

CONRAD (L.I.) and others **The Western medical tradition, 800 BC to AD 1800.** Cambridge UP, 1995. Pp. xiv + 556, ill. £60 (£24.95, paper). 05213-81355 (hb), 0521475643 (pb).

CORPUS VASORUM ANTIQUORUM 66. 4. Frankfurt am Main, Universität und Liebieghaus. Ed. S. Mayer-Emmerling and U. Vedder. Munich: C.H. Beck, 1994. Pp. 141, ill. DM 148. 340638949X.

CORPUS VASORUM ANTIQUORUM 68. 1. Gioia del Colle - Museo archeologico nazionale. Ed. A. Ciancio. Rome: "L'Erma" di Bretschneider, 1995. Pp. 34, ill. L 250,000. 8870628868.

CORPUS VASORUM ANTIQUORUM 69.5. Museo nazionale di Napoli. Raccolta cumana. Ed. N.V. Mele. Rome: "L'Erma" di Bretschneider, 1995. Pp. 56, ill. L 450,000. 887062899X.

CORPUS VASORUM ANTIQUORUM. SWEDEN 4.2. Medelhavmuseet and Nationalmuseum, Stockholm. Ed. C. Gillis and others. Stockholm: Kungl. Vitterhets Historie och Antikvitets Akademien, 1995. Pp. 88, ill. SwKr. 260. 9174022547.

COURT (B.) **Die dramatische Technik des Aischylos.** (Beiträge zur Altertumskunde 53.) Stuttgart/Leipzig: Teubner, 1994. Pp. 330. DM 110. 3519076020.

COURTNEY (E.E.) **Musa lapidaria. A selection of Latin verse inscriptions.** (American classical studies 36.) Atlanta, Ga.: Scholars Press, 1995. Pp. x + 457, ill. $41.95 ($27.95, paper). 0788501410 (hb), 07885-01429 (pb).

CRIELAARD (J.P.) *Ed.* **Homeric questions. Essays in philology, ancient history and archaeology, including the papers of a conference organized by the Netherlands Institute at Athens (15 May 1993).** (Publications of the Netherlands Institute at Athens 2.) Amsterdam: J.C. Gieben, 1995. Pp. xii + 316, ill. Fl. 140. 9050630952.

CROTONE e la sua storia tra iv e iii secolo a.C. Naples: Università degli studi di Napoli "Federico II", Dipartimento di discipline storiche, Centro di studi per la Magna Grecia, 1993. Pp. 291, ill. L 60.000.

CROTTY (K.) **The poetics of supplication. Homer's** *Iliad* **and** *Odyssey***.** Ithaca, N.Y./London: Cornell UP, 1994. Pp. xiii + 240. £29.95. 0801429986.

CSAPO (E.) and SLATER (W.J.) **The context of ancient drama.** Ann Arbor: U Michigan P, 1995. Pp. xv + 435. £34 (£16.95, paper). 0472105450 (hb), 0472082752 (pb).

CURTY (O.) **Les Parentés légendaires entre cités grecques. Catalogue raisonné des inscriptions contenant le terme "sungeneia" et analyse critique.** (Hautes Études du Monde Gréco-romain 20.) Geneva: Librairie Droz, 1995. Pp. xvi + 284. 2600000666.

CUVIGNY (H.), HUSSEIN (A.) and WAGNER (G.) **Les Ostraca grecs d'Ain Waqfa (Oasis de Kharga).** (Documents de fouilles/Institut Français d'Archéologie Orientale du Caire 30.) Cairo: Institut Français d'Archéologie Orientale 1993. Pp. 91, ill. 2724701-437.

CUVIGNY (H.) **Papyrus Graux ii (P. Graux 9 a 29).** (Hautes Études du Monde Gréco-romain 19.) Geneva: Librairie Droz/Paris: Librairie Champion, 1995. Pp. 92, ill. 2600000410.

CYRINO (M.S.) **In Pandora's jar. Lovesickness in early Greek poetry.** Lanham, Md.: UP of America, 1995. Pp. ix + 197. $39.50. 0819197521.

DALBY (A.) **Siren feasts. A history of food and gastronomy in Greece.** London/New York: Routledge, 1995. Pp. xv + 320, ill. £35. 0415116201.

DALCHER (K.) **Studia Ietina. 6. Das Peristylhaus 1 von Iaitas. Architektur und Baugeschichte.** Zürich: Archäologisches Institut der Universität Zürich, 1994. Pp. 183, ill. Sw.Fr. 150. 390509908X.

DANFORTH (L.M.) **The Macedonian conflict. Ethnic nationalism in a transnational world.** Princeton UP, 1995. Pp. xvi + 273, ill. £27.50. 0691043574.

DATSOULE-STAURIDE (A.) **Glypta apo tin Thyreatida.** Athens, 1993. Pp. 61, ill.

DAVIDS (A.) *Ed.* **The Empress Theophano. Byzantium and the West at the turn of the first millennium.** Cambridge UP, 1995. Pp. xvi + 344, ill. £40. 0521452961.

DAVIES (W.V.) and SCHOFIELD (L.) *Ed.* **Egypt, the Aegean and the Levant. Interconnections in the second millennium B.C.** London: British Museum P, 1995. Pp. viii + 156, ill. £25. 0714109878.

DELAVAUD-ROUX (M.-H.) **Les Danses armées en Grèce antique.** Aix-en-Provence: Publications de l'Université de Provence, 1993. Pp. 210, ill. Fr. 140. 285399323X.

DELAVAUD-ROUX (M.-H.) **Les Danses pacifiques en Grèce antique.** Aix-en-Provence: Publications de l'Université de Provence, 1994. Pp. 237, ill. Fr. 160. 2853993450.

DEMING (W.) **Paul on marriage and celibacy. The hellenistic background of 1 Corinthians 7.** (Society for New Testament Studies Monographs 83.) Cambridge UP, 1995. Pp. xiv + 265. £35. 0521472849.

DENCH (E.) **From barbarians to new men. Greek, Roman and modern perceptions of peoples of the central Apennines.** Oxford UP, 1995. Pp. xiii + 255. £32.50. 0198150210.

DES COURTILS (J.) and MORETTILES (J.-C.) **Grands ateliers d'architecture dans le monde égéen du VIe siècle av. J.-C. Actes du colloque d'Istanbul, 23-25 mai 1991.** (Varia Anatolica 3.) Paris: De Boccard (for Institut Français d'Études Anatoliennes d'Istanbul), 1993. Pp. 278, ill. 2906053309.

DEVINE (A.M.) and STEPHENS (L.D.) **The prosody of Greek speech.** New York: Oxford UP, 1994. Pp. xvii + 565. £35. 0195085469.

Diethnes symposio vyzantini Makedonia, 324-1430 m.Ch. Thessaloniki, 29-31 oktobriou 1992. (Makedoniki Vivliothiki 82). Thessaloniki: Society for Macedonian Studies, 1995. Pp. 392, ill. 9607265238.

DIEZ DE VELASCO (F.) **Los caminos de la muerte. Religión, rito e iconografia del paso al mas en la Grecia antigua.** (Coleccion Paradigmas 8.) Madrid: Editorial Trotta, 1995. Pp. 198, ill. 8481640166.

DIK (H.) **Word order in ancient Greek. A pragmatic account of word order variation in Herodotus.** (Amsterdam studies in classical philology 5.) Amsterdam: Gieben, 1995. Pp. xii + 294. Fl. 135. 9050634-575.

DILCHER (R.R.) **Studies in Heraclitus.** (Spudasmata 56.) Hildesheim: Olms, 1995. Pp. 207. DM 44.80. 3487099861.

DILLERY (J.) **Xenophon and the history of his times.** London/New York: Routledge, 1995. Pp. xii + 337. £40. 041509139X.

DIXSAUT (M.) **Le Naturel philosophe. Essai sur les dialogues de Platon.** Paris: Les Belles Lettres/Vrin, 1985, repr. 1994. Pp. 423. Fr. 198. 2251326146 (Les Belles Lettres), 2711612112 (Vrin).

DODD (C.H.) **The Cyprus issue. A current perspective.** Ed. 2. Huntingdon: Eothen Press, 1995. Pp. vi + 37. £4.95. 0906719356.

DONDER (H.) and VOGELE (H.) **Katalog der Sammlung antiker Kleinkunst des archäologischen Instituts der Universität Heidelberg. Bd. 3. Teil 2. Die Fibeln.** Mainz am Rhein: von Zabern, 1994 Pp. ix + 147, ill. DM 98. 3805315376.

DOUKELLIS (P.N.) and MENDONI (L.G.) **Ed.** **Structures rurales et sociétés antiques. Actes du colloque de Corfou (14-16 mai 1992).** (Centre de Recherches d'Histoire Ancienne 126.) Paris: Les Belles Lettres, 1994. Pp. 491, ill. 2251605088.

DOXIADIS (E.) **The mysterious Fayum portraits. Faces from ancient Egypt.** London: Thames & Hudson, 1995. Pp. 247, ill. £48. 0810933314.

DRAGER (P.) **Stilistische Untersuchungen zu Pherekydes von Athen. Ein Beitrag zur altesten ionischen Prosa.** (Palingenesia 52.) Stuttgart: Steiner, 1995. Pp. vii + 98. DM 56. 3515066764. DM 56.

DREHER (M.) **Hegemon und Symmachoi. Untersuchungen zum zweiten athenischen Seebund.** (Untersuchungen zur antiken Literatur und Geschichte 46.) Berlin/New York: de Gruyter, 1995. Pp. xi + 316, ill. DM 198. 3110144441.

DUCAT (J.) **Les Pénestes de Thessalie.** (Annales littéraires de l'Université de Bésançon 512. Centre de Recherches d'Histoire Ancienne 128.) Paris: Les Belles Lettres, 1994. Pp. 135. 2251605126.

DUCHEMIN (J.) and DEFORGE (B.) **Mythes grecs et sources orientales.** Paris: Les Belles Lettres, 1995. Pp. xv + 349. Fr. 175. 2251324224.

DUCHENE (H.) **L'Or de Troie, ou le rêve de Schliemann.** Paris: Gallimard, 1995. Pp. 144, ill. Fr. 82. 2070533107.

DUKE MUSEUM OF ART. **A generation of antiquities. The Duke classical collection, 1964-1994. Duke Museum of Art, 20 January-26 March 1995.** Durham, N.C.: Greek, Roman, and Byzantine Studies, 1994. Pp. x + 86, ill.

DUTTENHOFER (R.) *Ed.* **Ptolemaische Urkunden aus der heidelberger Papyrus-Sammlung (P. Heid. vi).** (Veroffentlichungen aus der Heidelberger Papyrus-Sammlung n.F., 7.) Heidelberg: Winter, 1994. Pp. xxi + 199, ill. DM 130. 3825301435.

DZIELSKA (M.) **Hypatia of Alexandria.** Tr. F. Lyra. (Revealing antiquity 8.) Cambridge, Mass.: Harvard UP, 1995. Pp. ix + 157. £23.95. 0674437756.

EBERT (T.) **Sokrates als Pythagoreer und die Anamnesis in Platons Phaidon.** (Abhandlungen der Geistes- und Sozialwissenschaftlichen Klasse 1994, 13.) Mainz: Akademie der Wissenschaften und der Literatur/Stuttgart: F. Steiner, 1994. Pp. 106. DM 49. 3515066527.

EITELJORG (H.) **The entrance to the Athenian Acropolis before Mnesicles.** (AIA monograph, new series 1.) Dubuque, Iowa: Kendall/Hunt Publ. Co., 1995. Pp. xvi + 146, ill. $40. 0840393911.

ELSNER (J.) **Art and the Roman viewer. The transformation of art from the pagan world to Christianity.** Cambridge UP, 1995. Pp. xxvi +375. £40. 0521453542.

ENDRESS (G.) and GUTAS (D.) *Ed.* **A Greek and Arabic lexicon. Materials for a dictionary of the mediaeval translations from Greek into Arabic. Fasc.1.** (Handbuch der Orientalistik 1. Der Nahe und Mittlere Osten 11.) Leiden/New York: E.J. Brill, 1992. Fl. 80, $45.75. 9004094946

ERATOSTHENES: **Die Erigone des Eratosthenes.** Ed. and comm. A. Rosokoki. (Bibliothek der klassischen Altertumswissenschaften Neue Folge 2. Reihe 94.) Heidelberg: Winter, 1995. Pp. 140, ill. DM 74. 3825302997.

ERLER (M.) and others **Grundriss der Geschichte der Philosophie begründet von Friedrich Ueberweg. Die Philosophie der Antike. 4. Die hellenistische Philosophie.** Basel: Schwabe & Co, 1994. Pp. xxvii + 1272 in 2 vols. Sw.Fr. 290, DM 248. 3796509304.

ESLER (P.F.) *Ed.* **Modelling early Christianity. Social-scientific studies of the New Testament in its context.** London/New York: Routledge, 1995. Pp. xv + 349. £45 (£14.99, paper). 041512980x (hb), 04151-29818 (pb).

ESPEJO MURIEL (C.) **Grecia sobre los ritos y las fiestas.** Ed. 2. (Biblioteca de estudios clasicos 4.) Granada: Universidad de Granada, 1995. Pp. xv + 195. 8433810995.

ESPOSITO (A.M.) and DE TOMMASO (G.) **Museo Archeologico Nazionale di Firenze. Antiquarium. Vasi attici.** Florence: Edizioni Il Ponte, 1993. Pp. 102, ill. L 18,000.

ESTIOT (S.) **Ripostiglio della Venèra Nuovo. Catalogo illustrato. Vol. 2/1. Aureliano.** Rome: "L'Erma" di Bretschneider, 1995. Pp. 270, ill. L 250,000. 887062-8922.

EURIPIDES: *Andromache.* Ed., tr. and comm. M. Lloyd. Warminster: Aris & Phillips, 1994. Pp. xxviii + 178. £35 (£14.95, paper). 0856686239 (hb), 0856686247 (pb).

EURIPIDES: *Bacchae.* Tr. and comm. R.E. Meagher. Wauconda, Ill.: Bolchazy-Carducci Publishers, 1995. Pp. vi + 97. $6. 0865162859.

EURIPIDES: **Selected fragmentary plays, Vol. 1.** *Telephus, Cretans, Stheneboea, Bellerophon, Cresphontes, Erechtheus, Phaethon, Wise Melanippe, Captive Melanippe.* Ed., tr. and comm. C. Collard, M.J. Cropp and K.H. Lee. Warminster: Aris & Phillips, 1995. Pp. viii + 280. £35 (£14.95, paper). 0856686182 (hb), 0856686190 (pb).

EURIPIDES: *Suppliant Women.* Tr. R. Warren and S. Scully. New York: Oxford UP, 1995. Pp. x + 82. $7.95. 019504553X.

EURIPIDES: **Tragedias 3.** *Medea, Hipolito.* Ed. and tr. F.R. Adrados and L.A. de Cuenca. Madrid: Consejo Superior de Investigaciones Cientificas, 1995. Pp. xxxvi + 147. Ptas 2884. 8400075161.

EVELY (D.), HUGHES-BROCK (H.) and MOMIGLIANO (N.) *Ed.* **Knossos. A labyrinth of history papers presented in honour of Sinclair Hood.** London: British School at Athens/Oxford: Oxbow Books (distributor), 1994. Pp. xxv + 210, ill. £18. 0904887154 m.

FAUTH (W.) **Helios megistos. Zur synkretistischen Theologie der Spätantike.** (Religions in the Graeco--Roman world 125.) Leiden/New York: Brill, 1995. Pp. xxxiii + 268. Fl. 145, $83. 9004101942.

FEJFER (J.) *Ed.* **Ancient Akamas. Vol. 1, Settlement and environment.** Aarhus UP, 1995. Pp. 199, ill. £40, DKr. 318, $53. 8772884819 (v.1); 8772886811 (set).

FERBER (R.) **Zenons Paradoxien der Bewegung und die Struktur von Raum und Zeit.** Ed. 2. Stuttgart: Steiner, 1995. Pp. vii + 124. DM 56. 3515067035.

FERRARI (F.) **L'alfabeto delle Muse. Storia e testi della letteratura greca.** Bologna: Cappelli, 1995. 3 vols, pp. 611, 710, 805. L 41,000; 46,000; 49,000. 8837907397 (v.1), 8837907400 (v.2), 8837907419 (v.3).

FIGAL (G.) **Sokrates.** Munich: Beck, 1995. Pp. 144, ill. DM 19.80. 3406346421.

FITTON (J.L.) **The discovery of the Greek Bronze Age.** London: British Museum P, 1995. Pp. 212, ill. £25. 0714112984.

FLANNERY (K.L.) **Ways into the logic of Alexander of Aphrodisias.** (Philosophia antiqua 62.) Leiden: Brill, 1995. Pp. xxiv + 170. Fl. 120, $86.75. 9004099980.

FLINTERMAN (J.-J.) **Power, paideia & Pythagoreanism. Greek identity, conceptions of the relationship between philosophers and monarchs and political ideas in Philostratus'** *Life of Apollonius.* (Dutch Monographs on Ancient History and Archaeology 13.) Amsterdam: Gieben, 1995. Pp. ix + 276. Fl. 125. 905063236X.

FLOURENTZOS (P.) **Odegos Eparchiakou Mouseiou Larnakas.** Nicosia: Department of Antiquities, 1995. Pp. vi + 76, ill. 9963364217.

FONTAINE (P.F.M.) **The light and the dark. A cultural history of dualism. Vol. 8. Gnostic dualism in Asia Minor during the first centuries A.D. 1.** Amsterdam: Gieben, 1993. Pp. xlv + 339. Fl. 90. 9050630936.

FONTAINE (P.F.M.) **The light and the dark. A cultural history of dualism. Vol. 9. Gnostic dualism in Asia Minor during the first centuries A.D. 2.** Amsterdam: Gieben, 1994. Pp. xlix + 305. Fl. 90. 9050633463.

FORNARA (C.W.) **Die Fragmente der griechischen Historiker. Teil 3. Geschichte von Städten und Volkern (Horographie und Ethnographie), C. Fascicle 1. Commentary on nos. 608a-608.** Leiden: Brill, 1994. Pp. ii + 113, ill. Fl. 80, $45.75. 9004099751.

FORTASSIER (P.) **Le Spondaique expressif dans l'***Iliade* et dans l'*Odyssee.* (Bibliothèque d'Études Classiques 5.) Louvain/Paris: Peeters, 1995. Pp. 194. Fr. b. 1000. 9068317512 (Peeters Leuven), 2877232-76X (Peeters France).

FRANCIS (J.A.) **Subversive virtue. Asceticism and authority in the second-century pagan world.** University Park, Pa.: Pennsylvania State UP, 1995. Pp. xviii + 222. £29.50. 0271013044.

FRANK (M.) **Seneca's** *Phoenissae.* **Introduction and commentary.** (Mnemosyne Supplement 138.) Leiden: Brill, 1995. Pp. xvii + 268. Fl. 125, $71.50. 9004097767.

FREUDENTHAL (G.) **Aristotle's theory of material substance. Heat and pneuma, form and soul.** Oxford UP, 1995. Pp. xii + 235. £30. 0198240937.

FRONTISI-DUCROUX (F.) **Du masque au visage. Aspects de l'identité en Grèce ancienne.** Paris: Flammarion, 1995. Pp. 191, ill. Fr. 180. 2080126296.

FURTWANGLER (A.), SCHNAPP (A.) and others **Eleutherna. Tomeas 2. 2. Ena ellenistiko spiti ("spiti a").** Rethymno: Panepistemio Kretes, Tomeas Archaiologias kai Istorias tes Technes, 1994. Pp. 229, ill. 9608546834.

GAGARIN (M.) and WOODRUFF (P.) *Ed. and tr.* **Early Greek political thought from Homer to the Sophists.** Cambridge UP, 1995. Pp. lvi + 324. £40 (£14.95, paper). 0521431921 (hb), 0521437687 (pb).

GAGOS (T.) and VAN MINNEN (P.) **Settling a dispute. Toward a legal anthropology of late antique Egypt.** (New texts from ancient cultures 1.) Ann Arbor: U Michigan P, 1994. Pp. x + 150, ill. £35.60 (£18, paper). 0472095900 (hb), 0472065904 (pb).

GALLO (I.) *Ed.* **Seconda miscellanea filologica.** (Quaderni del Dipartimento di Scienze dell'Antichità/Università degli Studi di Salerno 17.) Naples: Arte Tipografica, 1995. Pp. 302. L 35,000.

GALEN: *L'Âme et ses passions. Les Passions et les erreurs de l'âme. Les Facultés de l'âme suivent les temperaments du corps.* Tr. and comm. V. Barras, T. Birchler, A.-F. Morand. Paris: Les Belles Lettres, 1995. Pp. lviii + 157. Fr. 130. 2251339264.

GARDINER (R.) *Ed.* **The age of the galley. Mediterranean oared vessels since pre-classical times.** London: Conway Maritime P, 1995. Pp. 256. £28.

GARLAND (R.S.J.) **The eye of the beholder. Deformity and disability in the Graeco-Roman world.** London: Duckworth, 1995. Pp. xviii + 222, ill. £35. 0715626515.

GARRISON (E.P.) **Groaning tears. Ethical and dramatic aspects of suicide in Greek tragedy.** (Mnemosyne Supplement 147.) Leiden: Brill, 1995. Pp. x + 210. Fl. 110, $63. 9004102418.

GARVER (E.) **Aristotle's** *Rhetoric.* **An art of character.** U Chicago P, 1994. Pp. xii + 325. £43.25 (£15.25, paper). 0226284247 (hb), 0226284255 (pb).

GASPARRI (F.) **Introduction à l'histoire de l'écriture.** Turnhout: Brepols, 1994. Pp. 239, ill. 2503503942.

GEHRKE (H.-J.) **Rechtskodifizierung und soziale Normen im interkulturellen Vergleich.** (ScriptOralia 66 Reihe A, Altertumswissenschaftliche Reihe 15.) Tübingen: Narr, 1994. Pp. 183. DM 96. 3823345567.

GENTILI (B.) **Poesia e pubblico nella Grecia antica da Omero al V secolo.** Ed. 3. Rome: Laterza, 1995. Pp. viii + 426. L 45,000. 8842047244.

GIANNANTONI (G.) and others **La tradizione socratica. Seminario di studi.** (Memorie dell'Istituto Italiano per gli studi filosofici 25.) Naples: Bibliopolis, 1995. Pp. 158. L 35,000. 8870883531.

GIANNOTTA (M.) and others **La decifrazione del Cario. Atti del primo simposio internazionale, Roma, 3-4 maggio 1993.** Rome: Consiglio Nazionale delle Ricerche, 1994. Pp. 253, ill. L 50,000, $50. 8880800051.

GIGANTE (M.) **Philodemus in Italy. The books from Herculaneum.** Tr. D. Obbink. Ann Arbor: U Michigan P, 1995. Pp. xiv + 153, ill. $32.50. 0472105698 m.

GILL (C.) **Greek Thought.** (Greece & Rome New Surveys in the Classics 25.) Oxford UP for the Classical Association, 1995. Pp. 103. 0199220743.

GILLIS (C.), RISBERG (C.) and SJOBERG (B.) *Ed.* **Trade and production in premonetary Greece: aspects of trade. Proceedings of the third International Workshop, Athens 1993.** (Studies in Mediterranean Archaeology and Literature Pocket-book 134.) Jonsered: Astrom, 1995. Pp. 157, ill. 9170811024.

GIUDICE (F.), TUSA (S.) and TUSA (V.) **La collezione archeologica del Banco di Sicilia.** Palermo: Edizioni Guida, 1992. 2 vols, ill. 8885900143.

GLAD (C.E.) **Paul and Philodemus. Adaptability in Epicurean and early Christian psychagogy.** (Supplements to Novum Testamentum 81.) Leiden/New York: Brill, 1995. Pp. xiv + 414. Fl. 205, $117.25. 9004100679.

GOLAN (D.) **The *res graecae* in Polybius. Four studies.** (Biblioteca di Athenaeum 27.) Como: Edizioni New Press, 1995. Pp. 138. L 30,000.

GOLDHILL (S.) **Foucault's virginity. Ancient erotic fiction and the history of sexuality.** Cambridge UP, 1995. Pp. xiii + 194. £30 (£9.95, paper). 0521473721 (hb), 0521479347 (pb).

GOMEZ-LOBO (A.) **The foundations of Socratic ethics.** Indianapolis/Cambridge: Hacket, 1994. Pp. v + 149. 0872201740 (hb), 0872202364 (pb).

GORANSSON (T.) **Albinus, Alcinous, Arius Didymus.** (Studia Graeca et Latina Gothoburgensia 61.) Goteborg: Acta Universitatis Gothoburgensis, 1995. Pp. 257. SwKr. 200. 9173462829.

GRANT (M.) **Art in the Roman Empire.** London/New York: Routledge, 1995. Pp. xxii + 146, ill. £25. 0415120314 m.

GRANT (M.) **Greek and Roman historians. Information and misinformation.** London/New York: Routledge, 1995. Pp. xii + 172. £35 (£10.99, paper). 0415117690 (hb), 0415117704 (pb).

GRECO (G.) and KRINZINGER (F.) *Ed.* **Velia. Studi e ricerche.** Modena: Franco Cosimo Panini, 1994. Pp. 183, ill. L 60,000. 8876863087.

GREEN (J.R.) and HANDLEY (E.) **Images of the Greek theatre.** London: British Museum P, 1995. Pp. 127, ill. £9.99. 0714122076.

GREEN (J.R.) **Theatre in ancient Greek society.** London/New York: Routledge, 1994. Pp. xxii + 234, ill. £40. 041504751X.

GREGORY OF CORINTH: **Exegesi al Canone giambico per la Pentecoste attribuito a Giovanni Damasceno.** Ed. and tr. F. Montana. (Biblioteca di studi antichi 76.) Pisa: Giardini, 1995. Pp. lxxiii + 95, ill. 8842700061.

GRIFFITHS (A.) *Ed.* **Stage directions. Essays in ancient drama in honour of E.W. Handley.** (Bulletin of the Institute of Classical Studies Supplement 66.) London: Institute of Classical Studies, 1995. Pp. vii + 160, ill. £25. 0900587776.

GRUBBS (J.E.) **Law and family in late antiquity. The emperor Constantine's marriage legislation.** Oxford UP, 1995. Pp. x + 390. £37.50. 0198147686.

GUIDA (P.C.) and FLOREANO (E.) *Ed.* **Mnemeion. Ricordo triestino di Doro Levi. Atti della giornata di studio (Trieste, 16 maggio 1992).** (Studi e ricerche di protostoria mediterranea 3.) Rome: Quasar, 1995. Pp. 199, ill. L 60,000. 8871400801.

GUNTHER (H.-C.) **The manuscripts and the transmission of the Paleologan scholia on the Euripidean triad.** (Hermes Einzelschriften 68.) Stuttgart: Steiner, 1995. Pp. 329, ill. DM 120. 3515065911.

HABICHT (C.) **Athen. Die Geschichte der Stadt in hellenistischer Zeit.** Munich: Beck, 1995. Pp. 406. DM 78. 3406397581.

HADOT (P.) **Philosophy as a way of life. Spiritual exercises from Socrates to Foucault.** Ed. A.I. Davdson, tr. M. Chase. Oxford/New York: Blackwell, 1995. Pp. viii + 309. £45 (£15.99, paper). 0631180-32x (hb), 0631180338 (pb).

HAGG (R.) *Ed.* **Ancient Greek cult practice from the epigraphical evidence. Proceedings of the Second International Seminar on Ancient Greek Cult, organized by the Swedish Institute at Athens, 22-24 November 1991.** Stockholm: Svenska Institutet i Athen/Jonsered (distributor: Astrom), 1994. Pp. 184. SwKr. 250. 9179160298.

HANSEN (M.H.) **The trial of Sokrates from the Athenian point of view.** (Historisk-filosofiske Meddelelser [Kongelige Danske Videnskabernes Selskab] 71.) Copenhagen: Munksgaard, 1995. Pp. 36. DKr. 60. 8773042668.

HANSEN (M.H.) *Ed.* **Sources for the ancient Greek city-state. Symposium August 24-27, 1994.** (Historisk-filosofiske Meddelelser [Kongelige Danske Videnskabernes Selskab] 72. Acts of the Copenhagen Polis Centre 2.) Copenhagen: Munksgaard, 1995. Pp. 376, ill. DKr. 450. 8773042676.

HANSEN (M.H.) and RAAFLAUB (K.) *Ed.* **Studies in the ancient Greek polis.** (Papers from the Copenhagen Polis Centre 2. Historia Einzelschriften 95.) Stuttgart: Steiner, 1995. Pp. 376, ill. DM 68. 3515067590.

HARRIS (D.) **The treasures of the Parthenon and Erechtheion.** Oxford UP, 1995. Pp. xiv + 306, ill. £55. 0198149409 m.

HARRIS (E.M.) **Aeschines and Athenian politics.** New York: Oxford UP, 1995. Pp. x + 233. £35. 01950-82850.

HATZOPOULOS (M.B.) **Cultes et rites de passage en Macédoine.** (Meletemata 19.) Athens: Centre de Recherches de l'Antiquité Grecque et Romaine, FNRS, 1994. Pp. 169, ill. Fr. 290. 9607094867.

HAVELOCK (C.M.) **The Aphrodite of Knidos and her successors. A historical review of the female nude in Greek art.** Ann Arbor: U Michigan P, 1995. Pp. xii + 158, ill. £35.60. 047210585X.

HAWLEY (R.) and LEVICK (B.) *Ed.* **Women in antiquity. New assessments.** London/New York: Routledge, 1995. Pp. xix + 271. £35 (£12.99, paper). 0415113687 (hb), 0415113695 (pb).

HAYES (J.W.) **Greek and Greek-style painted and plain pottery in the Royal Ontario Museum, excluding black-figure and red-figure vases.** Toronto: Royal Ontario Museum, 1992. Pp. xv + 223, ill. C$95. 0888543980.

HEATH (M.) **Hermogenes, *On Issues*. Strategies of argument in later Greek rhetoric.** Oxford UP, 1995. Pp. ix + 274. £40. 0198149824.

HEIDEN (J.) **Die Tondächer von Olympia.** (Olympische Forschungen 24.) Berlin/New York: de Gruyter, 1995. Pp. xiv + 242, ill. DM 340. 3110143747.

HEINAMAN (R.) **Aristotle and moral realism.** London: UCL Press, 1995. Pp. vii + 239. £35. 1857283392.

HELD (G.F.) **Aristotle's teleological theory of tragedy and epic.** (Bibliothek der klassischen Altertumswissenschaften Neue Folge 2. Reihe 95.) Heidelberg: Winter, 1995. Pp. x + 162. DM 48. 3825303004.

HELLY (B.) **L'État thessalien. Aleuas le Roux, les tetrades et les tagoi.** (Collection de la Maison de l'Orient Mediterranéen 25. Série épigraphique 2.) Lyon: Maison de l'Orient Mediterranéen, 1995. Pp. 384, ill. Fr. 210. 2903264171.

HENIG (M.), SCARISBRICK (D.) and WHITING (M.) **Classical gems. Ancient and modern intaglios and cameos in the Fitzwilliam Museum, Cambridge.** Cambridge UP, 1994. Pp. xxx + 538. £125. 052123901X.

HENRY (M.M.) **Prisoner of history. Aspasia of Miletus and her biographical tradition.** New York: Oxford UP, 1995. Pp. 201, ill. £22.50. 0195087127.

HIGBIE (C.) **Heroes' names, Homeric identities.** (A. B. Lord Studies in Oral Tradition 10.) New York/London: Garland Publishing, 1995. Pp. xi + 223. $34. 0824072707.

HIGBY (G.) and STROUD (E.C.) *Ed.* **The history of pharmacy. A selected annotated bibliography.** (Bibliographies on the History of Science and Technology 25.) New York/London: Garland Publishing, 1995. Pp. xi + 321, ill. $50. 0824097688.

HILLGRUBER (M.) **Die pseudoplutarchische Schrift De Homero. Teil 1 Einleitung und Kommentar zu den Kapiteln 1-73.** (Beiträge zur Altertumskunde 57.) Stuttgart/Leipzig: Teubner, 1994. Pp. ix + 190. DM 64. 3519076063.

HIMMELMANN (N.) **Antike zwischen Kommerz und Wissenschaft. 25 Jahre Erwerbungen für das Akademische Kunstmuseum Bonn.** Opladen: Westdeutscher Verlag, 1994. Pp. 40, ill. DM 16. 3531073265.

HOFF (R. von den) **Philosophenporträts des Fruh- und Hochhellenismus.** Munich: Biering & Brinkmann, 1994. Pp. 209, ill. DM 189. 3930609010.

HOMER: *Iliad* Book 9. Ed. and comm. J. Griffin. Oxford UP, 1995. Pp. vii + 152. £25 (£8.99, paper). 0198140789 (hb), 0198141300 (pb).

HOMER: *Odyssey*. Vol. 1. Books 1-12. Ed. and tr. A.T. Murray; rev. G.E. Dimock. Cambridge, Mass/London: Harvard UP (Loeb), 1995. Pp. viii + 481. £11.95. 0674995619.

HOMER: *Odyssey*. **Vol. 2. Books 13-24.** Ed. and tr. A.T. Murray; rev. G.E. Dimock. Cambridge, Mass/London: Harvard UP (Loeb), 1995. Pp. 467. £11.95. 0674995619.

HOPWOOD (K.) **Ancient Greece and Rome. A bibliographical guide.** Manchester UP, 1995. Pp. xiv + 450. £50. 0719024013.

HOSE (M.) **Drama und Gesellschaft. Studien zur dramatischen Produktion in Athen am Ende des 5. Jahrhunderts.** (Drama: Beiträge zum antiken Drama und seiner Rezeption 3.) Stuttgart: M & P Verlag für Wissenschaft und Forschung, 1995. Pp. 214. DM 45. 3476451445.

HOWGEGO (C.) **Ancient history from coins.** London/New York: Routledge, 1995. Pp. xvi + 176, ill. £35 (£10.99, paper). 0415089921 (hb), 041508993 (pb).

IHM (S.) *Ed. and comm.* **Der Traktat *Peri ton iobolon therion kai deleterion pharmakon* des sog. Aelius Promotus.** (Serta Graeca 4.) Wiesbaden: Ludwig Reichert, 1995. Pp. x + 169, ill. DM 78. 3882268220.

INNES (D.), HINE (H.) and PELLING (C.) *Ed.* **Ethics and Rhetoric. Classical essays for Donald Russell on his seventy-fifth birthday.** Oxford UP, 1995. Pp. xvi + 378. £45. 019814962x.

IPLIKCIOGLU (B.), CELGIN (G.) and CELGIN (A.V.) **Epigraphische Forschungen in Termessos und seinem Territorium. 2.** (Sitzungsberichte der Österreichische Akademie der Wissenschaften. Philosophisch-historische Klasse 583. Veröffentlichungen der Kleinasiatischen Kommission 2.) Vienna: Österreichische Akademie der Wissenschaften, 1992. Pp. 45, ill. 3700119518.

IRWIN (T.) **Plato's ethics.** New York: Oxford UP, 1995. Pp. xx + 436. £40 (£14.99, paper). 0195086449 (hb), 0195086457 (pb).

J.A.C.T. **An independent study guide to *Reading Greek*.** Cambridge UP, 1995. Pp. xi + 346. £14.95. 0521478634.

JAMES (P.) **The sunken kingdom. The Atlantis mystery solved.** London: Jonathan Cape, 1995. Pp. xiii + 338, ill. £18.99. 0224038109.

JAMESON (M.H.), RUNNELS (C.H.) and VAN ANDEL (T.H.) **A Greek countryside. The southern Argolid from prehistory to the present day.** Stanford UP, 1994. Pp. xviii + 654, ill. £84.95. 0804716080.

JANAWAY (C.) **Images of excellence. Plato's critique of the arts.** Oxford UP, 1995. Pp. x + 226. £30. 0198240074.

JARVA (E.) **Archaiologia. On archaic Greek body armour.** (Studia archaeologica septentrionalia 3.) Rovaniemi: Pohjois-Suomen Historiallinen Yhdistys/Societas Historica Finlandiae Septentrionalis, 1995. Pp. 176. FM 240. 9529888031.

JENKINS (I.) **Archaeologists and aesthetes in the sculpture galleries of the British Museum 1800-1939.** London: British Museum P, 1992. Pp. 264, ill. £25. 0714112992.

JOCELYN (H.D.) *Ed.* **Tria lustra. Essays and notes presented to John Pinsent, founder and editor of**

Liverpool Classical Monthly, **by some of its contributors on the occasion of the 150th issue.** (Liverpool Classical Papers 3.) Liverpool: Liverpool Classical Monthly, 1993. Pp. xii + 353. £35. 1871245206.

JUSTINUS: **Epitome of the** *Philippic History* **of Pompeius Trogus.** Tr. J.C. Yardley; comm. R. Develin. (American Philological Association Classical Resources 3.) Atlanta, Ga: Scholars Press, 1994. Pp. xii + 337. $44.95 ($29.94, paper). 1555409504 (hb), 1555409512 (pb).

KARAGEORGHIS (V.) *Ed.* **Proceedings of the International Symposium 'Cyprus in the 11th century B.C. ...'** Nicosia 30-31 October, 1993. Nicosia: A.G. Leventis Foundation, 1994. Pp. xvi + 247. £C 20. 9963560210.

KARAGEORGHIS (V.) and HERMARY (A.) *Ed.* **Chypre au coeur des civilisations mediterranéennes.** (Dossiers d'archéologie 205.) Dijon: Dossiers d'Archéologie, 1995. Pp. 136, ill. Fr. 68.

KARAGEORGHIS (V.) **The coroplastic art of ancient Cyprus. 4. The cypro-archaic period. Small male figurines.** Nicosia: A. G. Leventis Foundation, 1995. Pp. xiii + 175, ill. £C 30. 9963560229.

KARAMOUTSOU-TEZA (S.) **E chronographia tes pentekontaetias. Symvole sten istoria tes periodou 479-431 p.ch. A'. Apo te sesto os ten ekstrateia ton athenaion sten aigypto.** Ioannina: Panepistemion Ioanninon, 1994. Pp. 137. 960220740X.

KARWIESE (S.) **Gross ist die Artemis von Ephesos. Die Geschichte einer der grossen Städte der Antike.** Vienna: Phoibos Verlag, 1995. Pp. 184, ill. öS 462, DM 66, $46. 3901232052.

KEIZER (H.M.), J.M. BREMER and RUIGH (C.J.) **Indices in Eustathii archiepiscopi Thessalonicensis commentarios ad Homeri Iliadem pertinentes ad fidem codicis Laurentiani editos a Marchino van der Valk.** Leiden: Brill, 1995. Pp. xix + 656. Fl. 270, $154.50. 9004103279.

KELLY (J.N.D.) **Golden mouth. The story of John Chrysostom - ascetic, preacher, bishop.** London: Duckworth, 1995. Pp. x + 310. £35. 0715626434.

KENNEDY (G.A.) **A new history of classical rhetoric.** Princeton UP, 1994. Pp. xii + 301. £45 (£14.95, paper). 0691034435 (hb), 069100059X (pb).

KENNELL (N.M.) **The gymnasium of virtue. Education and culture in ancient Sparta.** Chapel Hill/London: U North Carolina P, 1995. Pp. xi + 241. $43.95. 0807822191.

KHAN (H.A.) *Ed.* **The birth of the European identity. The Europe-Asia contrast in Greek thought, 490-322 B.C.** (Nottingham Classical Literature Studies 2.) U Nottingham, 1994. Pp. vii + 161. 0904857077.

KILIAN-DIRLMEIER (I.) **Die Schwerter in Griechenland (ausserhalb der Peloponnes), Bulgarien und Albanien.** (Prähistorische Bronzefunde Abt. IV Bd. 12.) Stuttgart: Steiner, 1993. Pp. viii + 197. DM 166. 3515060200.

KINGSLEY (P.) **Ancient philosophy, mystery, and magic. Empedocles and Pythagorean tradition.** Oxford UP, 1995. Pp. ix + 422. £40. 0198149883.

KINZL (K.H.) *Ed.* **Demokratia. Der Weg zur Demokratie bei den Griechen.** (Wege der Forschung 657). Darmstadt: Wissenschaftliche Buchgesellschaft, 1995. Pp. vii + 452. DM 128. 3534092163.

KITROMILIDES (P.M.) and EVRIVIADES (M.L.) *Ed.* **Cyprus.** (World bibliographical series 28.) Rev. ed. Oxford: Clio Press, 1995. Pp. 264.

KLOSS (G.) **Untersuchungen zum Wortfeld "verlangen/begehren" im frühgriechischen Epos.** (Hypomnemata 105.) Göttingen: Vandenhoeck & Ruprecht, 1994. Pp. 204. DM 58. 3525252056.

KNELL (H.) **Die Nike von Samothrake. Typus, Form, Bedeutung und Wirkungsgeschichte eines rhodischen Sieges-Anathems im Kabirenheiligtum von Samothrake.** Darmstadt: Wissenschaftliche Buchgesellschaft, 1995. Pp. viii + 130, ill. DM 49.80. 3534125479.

KOLB (F.) *Ed.* **Lykische Studien. 1. Die Siedlungskammer von Kyaneai.** (Asia Minor Studien 9.) Bonn: Habelt, 1993. Pp. vii + 174. DM 79. 37749-25585.

KOLB (F.) *Ed.* **Lykische Studien. 2. Forschungen auf dem Gebiet der Polis Kyaneai in Zentrallykien. Bericht über die Kampagne 1991.** (Asia Minor Studien 18.) Bonn: Habelt, 1995. Pp. x + 244, ill. DM 145. 3774926409.

KONDIS (B.) and MANDA (E.) *Ed.* **The Greek minority in Albania. A documentary record (1921-1993).** Thessaloniki: Institute for Balkan Studies, 1994. Pp. 130. 9607387023.

KONSTAN (D.) **Greek comedy and ideology.** New York: Oxford UP, 1995. Pp. xi + 244. £35. 01950-92945.

KRISELEIT (I.) and ZIMMER (G.) *Ed.* **Burgerwelte hellenistischen Tonfiguren und Nachschöpfungen im 19. Jh.** Berlin: Staatliche Museen zu Berlin, Preussischer Kulturbesitz Antikensammlung/Mainz am Rhein: von Zabern, 1994. Pp. 167, ill. DM 58. 3805316275 (Museum edition), 3805316399 (von Zabern).

KUNZE (M.) and others **Bericht über die Ausgrabungen in Olympia, 9. Herbst 1962 bis Frühjahr 1966.** Berlin/New York: de Gruyter, 1994. Pp. vii + 229, ill. DM 230. 3110142430.

KYRIAKOU (P.) **Homeric** *hapax legomena* **in the** *Argonautica* **of Apollonius Rhodius. A literary study.** (Palingenesia 54.) Stuttgart: Steiner, 1995. Pp. x + 276. DM 124. 3515065962 m.

LAFFINEUR (R.) and NIEMEIER (W.-D.) *Ed.* **Politeia. Society and state in the Aegean Bronze Age. Proceedings of the 5th International Aegean Conference.** (Aegaeum: Annales d'Archéologie Égéenne de l'Université de Liège et UT-PASP 12.) Liège: Université de Liège, Histoire de l'Art et Archéologie de la Grèce Antique/Austin: University of Texas at Austin, Program in Aegean Scripts and Prehistory, 1995. Pp. 674 in 2 vols, ill.

LAKMANN (M.-L.) **Der Platoniker Tauros in der Darstellung Aulus Gellius.** (Philosophia antiqua 63.) Leiden: Brill, 1995. Pp. xi +294. Fl. 140, $80. 9004100962.

LA MATINA (M.) **Il testo antico. Per una semiotica come filologia integrata.** (Working papers Circolo Semiologico Siciliano 1.) Palermo: L'Epos, 1994. Pp. 181. L 24,000. 181 p. 2 cm.

LANZA (L.) **Ritorno ad Omero. Con due appendici sulla poesia africana.** Venezia: Supernova, 1994. Pp. 129. L 20, 000.

LARSON (J.J.L.) **Greek heroine cults.** Madison, Wis.: U Wisconsin P, 1995. Pp. xv + 236, ill. £33.50 (£16, paper). 0299143708 (hb), 0299143740 (pb).

LATEINER (D.) **Sardonic smile. Nonverbal behavior in Homeric epic.** Ann Arbor: U Michigan P, 1995. Pp. xxi + 340. $47.50. 0472105981.

LAW (V.) and SLUITER (I.) *Ed.* **Dionysius Thrax and the *techne grammatike*.** (The Henry Sweet Society Studies in the History of Linguistics 1.) Münster: Nodus Publikationen, 1995. Pp. 160. DM 42. 3893234519.

LAWTON (C.L.) **Attic document reliefs. Art and politics in ancient Athens.** Oxford UP, 1995. Pp. xxi + 167, ill. £65. 0198149557.

LEIWO (M.) **Neapolitana. A study of population and language in Graeco-roman Naples.** (Commentationes humanarum litterarum 102.) Helsinki: Societas Scientiarum Fennica 1995. Pp. 236. 9516532721.

LENDLE (O.) **Kommentar zu Xenophons Anabasis (Bücher 1-7).** Darmstadt: Wissenschaftliche Buchgesellschaft, 1995. Pp. xxx + 523, ill. DM 78. 3534128133.

LEONTIS (A.) **Topographies of Hellenism. Mapping the homeland.** Ithaca/London: Cornell UP, 1995. Pp. xi + 257. £23.50. 0801430577.

LETOUBLON (F.) **La Ruche grecque et l'empire de Rome.** Grenoble: Ellug, 1995. Pp. 368. Fr. 165. 2902709757.

LICHTENTHAELER (C.) **Neuer Kommentar zu den ersten zwölf Krankengeschichten im III. Epidemienbuch des Hippokrates.** (Hippokratische Studien 15. Hermes Einzelschriften 65.) Stuttgart: Steiner, 1994. Pp. 188. DM 76. 3515063617.

LIM (R.) **Public disputation, power, and social order in late antiquity.** (The transformation of the classical heritage 23.) Berkeley: U California P, 1995. Pp. xvii + 278. £40. 0520085779.

LINK (S.) **Das griechische Kreta. Untersuchungen zu seiner staatlichen und gesellschaftlichen Entwicklung vom 6. bis zum 4. Jahrhundert v. Chr.** Stuttgart: Steiner, 1994. Pp. 149. DM 46. 3515065547.

LOCK (P.) **The Franks in the Aegean, 1204-1500.** London/New York: Longman, 1995. Pp. xiii + 400. £45 (£18.99, paper). 0582051401 (hb), 0582051398 (pb).

LORAUX (N.) **The experiences of Tiresias. The feminine and the Greek man.** Tr. P. Wissing. Princeton UP, 1995. Pp. viii + 348.. £24.95. 0691029857.

LORD (A.B.) **The singer resumes the tale.** Ed. M.L. Lord. Ithaca, N.Y/London: Cornell UP, 1995. Pp. xiii + 258. £31.50. 0801431034.

LOTZE (D.) **Griechische Geschichte von den Anfangen bis zum Hellenismus.** Munich: Beck, 1995. Pp. 113, ill. DM 14.80. 3406395007.

LURAGHI (N.) **Tirannidi arcaiche in Sicilia e Magna Grecia da Panezio di Leontini alla caduta dei Dinomenidi.** (Studi e testi della Fondazione Luigi Firpo, Centro di studi sul pensiero politico 3.) Florence: Olschki, 1994. Pp. 430. L 84,000. 8822242386.

LYNE (R.O.A.M.) **Horace. Behind the public poetry.** New Haven, Conn./London: Yale UP, 1995. Pp. viii + 230. £19.95. 0300063229.

MACDOWELL (D.M.) **Aristophanes and Athens. An introduction to the plays.** Oxford UP, 1995. Pp. xiii + 362. £40 (£12.99, paper). 0198721587 (hb), 019872-1595 (pb).

MCNEAL (R.A.) *Ed.* **Nicholas Biddle in Greece. The journals and letters of 1806.** University Park, Pa.: Pennsylvania State UP, 1993. Pp. x + 243, ill. $35. 0271009144.

MCQUEEN (E.I.) **Diodorus Siculus. The reign of Philip II. The Greek and Macedonian narrative from Book xvi: a companion.** London: Bristol Classical P, 1995. Pp. vi + 202. £9.95. 1853993859.

MACTOUX (M.-M.) and GENY (E.) *Ed.* **Mélanges Pierre Levèque. 8. Religion, anthropologie et société.** Paris: Les Belles Lettres, 1994. Pp. xxix + 408. 2251604995.

MADDOLI (G.) *Ed.* **L'*Athenaion politeia* di Aristotele, 1891-1991. Per un bilancio di cento anni di studi.** (Incontri Perugini di Storia della Storiografia Antica e sul Mondo Antico 6.) Naples: Edizioni Scientifiche Italiane, 1994. Pp. 311. L 40,000. 8871049136.

MAGUIRE (H.) *Ed.* **Byzantine magic.** Washington, D.C.: Dumbarton Oaks Research Library and Collection (distr. Harvard UP), 1995. Pp. vii + 187, ill. $30. 0884022307. US 30.00.

MANGAS (J.) and ALVAR (J.) *Ed.* **Homenaje a Jose Ma. Blazquez. Vol. 2.** Madrid: Ediciones Clasicas, 1994. Pp. xi + 519. 8478821201.

MANNING (S.W.) **The absolute chronology of the Aegean early Bronze Age. Archaeology, radiocarbon and history.** (Monographs in Mediterranean archaeology 1.) Sheffield Academic P, 1995. Pp. 370, ill. £40. 1850753369. 40.00/US 70.00.

MANSFELD (J.) **Prolegomena. Questions to be settled before the study of an author, or a text.** (Philosophia antiqua 61). Leiden: Brill, 1994. Pp. vii + 246. Fl. 100, $57.25. 9004100849.

MARCELLINUS: **The *Chronicle*.** Tr. and comm. B. Croke. (Byzantina Australiensia 7.) Sydney: Australian Association for Byzantine Studies, 1995. Pp. xxvii + 152. 326. 0959362665.

MARCONI (C.) **Selinunte. Le metope dell'Heraion.** Modena: Franco Cosimo Panini, 1994. Pp. 355. L 140,000. 8876864547.

MARTINEZ MANZANO (T.) **Konstantinos Laskaris. Humanist, Philologe, Lehrer, Kopist.** (Meletemata 4.) U Hamburg, Institut für Griechische und Lateinische Philologie, 1994. Pp. xvi + 382, ill. 3925793049.

MANGO (C.) and DAGRON (G.) *Ed.* **Constantinople and its hinterland. Papers from the twenty-seventh Spring Symposium of Byzantine Studies, Oxford, April 1993.** (Society for the Promotion of Byzantine Studies Publications 3.) Aldershot: Variorum, 1995. Pp. xi + 426, ill. £39.50. 0860784878.

MAURER (K.) **Interpolation in Thucydides.** (Mnemosyne Supplement 150.) Leiden/New York: E.J. Brill, 1995. Pp. xxiv + 242. Fl. 130, $74.50. 9004103007.

MEIKLE (S.) **Aristotle's economic thought.** Oxford UP, 1995. Pp. viii + 216. £25. 0198150024 m.

MENANDER: *The Bad-Tempered Man (Dyskolos)*. Ed., tr. and comm. S. Ireland. Warminster: Aris & Phillips, 1995. Pp. iv + 185. £35 (£11.95, paper). 0856686107 (hb), 085668225X (pb).

MESCH (W.) **Ontologie und Dialektik bei Aristoteles.** (Neue Studien zur Philosophie 7.) Göttingen: Vandenhoeck & Ruprecht, 1994. Pp. vii + 203. DM 60. 3525305079.

MICOZZI (M.) "White-on-red." Una produzione vascolare dell'orientalizzante etrusco. (Terra Italia 2.) Rome: Gruppo Editoriale Internazionale, 1994. Pp. 327, ill. L 160,000 (L 120,000, paper). 8880110-11X.

MILLER (F.D.) Nature, justice, and rights in Aristotle's *Politics*. Oxford UP, 1995. Pp. xvii + 424. £40. 0198240619.

MOELLENDORFF (P. von) Grundlagen einer Ästhetik der alten Komödie. Untersuchungen zu Aristophanes und Michail Bachtin. (Classica Monacensia 9.) Tübingen: Narr, 1995. Pp. 297. DM 58. 382334868X.

MOON (W.G.) *Ed.* Polykleitos, the Doryphoros and tradition. Madison, Wis.: U Wisconsin P, 1995. Pp. xii + 363, ill. £44.95. 0299143104.

MONLOUP (T.) Salamine de Chypre. 14. Les Terres cuites classiques. Un sanctuaire de la grande déesse. Paris: de Boccard, 1994. Pp. 215, ill. Fr. 350. 2903264929.

MORA (F.) Il pensiero storico-religioso antico. Autori greci e roma. 1. Dionigi d'Alicarnasso. (Storia delle religioni 12.) Rome: "L'Erma" di Bretschneider, 1995. Pp. xviii + 464. L 4000,000. 8870628876.

MORAITOU (D.) Die Äusserungen des Aristoteles über Dichter und Dichtung ausserhalb der Poetik. (Beiträge zur Altertumskunde 49.) Stuttgart/Leipzig: Teubner, 1994. Pp. 163. DM 58. 3519074982.

MORAVCSIK (J.M.E.) Plato and Platonism. Plato's conception of appearance and reality in ontology, epistemology, and ethics, and its modern echoes. (Issues in ancient philosophy 1.) Oxford: Blackwell, 1992. Pp. xrup + 342. £45. 1557862028.

MORRIS (C.) *Ed.* Klados. Essays in honour of J.N. Coldstream. (Bulletin of the Institute of Classical Studies Supplement 63.) London: Institute of Classical Studies, 1995. Pp. xiii + 310, ill. £40. 0900587-660.

MORRIS (R.) Monks and Laymen in Byzantium, 843-1118. Cambridge UP, 1995. Pp. xxii + 330. £40. 0521265584 m.

MORWOOD (J.) *Ed.* The Oxford Latin mini-dictionary. Oxford UP, 1995. Pp. xi + 693. £3.99. 01986-42253.

MOSER (P.K.) and VANDER NAT (A.) Human knowledge. Classical and contemporary approaches. Ed. 2. New York: Oxford UP, 1995. Pp. xi + 463. £35 (£17.99, paper). 0195086260 (hb), 0195086252 (pb).

MOSSMAN (J.) Wild justice. A study of Euripides' *Hecuba*. Oxford UP, 1995. Pp. xiii + 283. £35. 0198147899.

MUELLER-GOLDINGEN (C.) Untersuchungen zu Xenophons Kyrupädie. (Beiträge zur Altertumskunde 42.) Stuttgart/Leipzig: Teubner, 1995. Pp. xvi + 308. DM 136. 3519074915.

MURRAY (O.) and TECUSAN (M.) *Ed.* In vino veritas. London: British School at Rome, 1995. Pp. xviii + 317. £39.99. 0904152278.

MUSS (U.) Die Bauplastik des archaischen Artemisions von Ephesos. (Sonderschriften des Österreichisches Archäologisches Instituts in Wien 25.) Vienna: Österreichisches Archäologisches Institut, 1994. Pp. 128, ill. 3900305161.

NESBITT (J.) and OIKONOMIDES (N.) *Ed.* Catalogue of Byzantine seals at Dumbarton Oaks and in the Fogg Museum of Art. Vol. 2. South of the Balkans, the Islands, south of Asia Minor. Washington, D.C.: Dumbarton Oaks Research Library and Collection, 1994. Pp. xiii + 233, ill. $35. 0884022269.

NEUMANN (U.) Gegenwart und mythische Vergangenheit bei Euripides. (Hermes Einzelschriften 69.) Stuttgart: Steiner, 1995. Pp. 191. DM 74. 3515066012.

NICHOLSON MUSEUM. Classical art in the Nicholson Museum, Sydney. A. Campitoglou and E.G.D. Robinson. Mainz: von Zabern, 1995. Pp. vii + 273, ill. DM 238. 3805314906.

NIGHTINGALE (A.W.) Genres in dialogue. Plato and the construct of philosophy. Cambridge UP, 1995. Pp. xiv + 222. £32.50. 052148264.

NONNUS: *Les Dionysiaques*. 5. Chants XI-XIII. Ed. and tr. F. Vian. Paris: Les Belles Lettres (Budé), 1995. Pp. xiv + 280. Fr. 360. 2251004475.

NOTH (A.) and CONRAD (L.) The early Arabic historical tradition. A source-critical study. Tr. M. Bonner. Ed. 2. (Studies in late antiquity and early Islam 3.) Princeton, N.J.: Darwin Press, 1994. Pp. xi + 248. £18. 0878500820.

OBBINK (D.) Philodemus and poetry . Poetic theory and practice in Lucretius, Philodemus, and Horace. New York: Oxford UP, 1995. Pp. xiv + 316. £35. 0195088158.

OBERLEITNER (W.) Das Heroon von Trysa. Ein lykisches Furstengrab des 4. Jahrhunderts v. Chr. (Zaberns Bildbände zur Archaologie 18.) Mainz am Rhein: von Zabern, 1994. Pp. iv + 68, ill. DM 39.80. 3805316402.

OIKONOMIDES (N.) *Ed.* Studies in Byzantine sigillography. 4. Washington, D.C.: Dumbarton Oaks Research Library and Collection, 1995. Pp. xi + 216, ill. $24. 0884022293.

OLSON (D.S.) Blood and iron. Stories and storytelling in Homer's *Odyssey*. (Mnemosyne Supplement 148.) Leiden/New York: Brill, 1995. Pp. x + 260. Fl. 125, $71.50. 9004102515 m.

O'NEIL (J.L.) The origins and development of ancient Greek democracy. Lanham, Md.: Rowman & Littlefield, 1995. Pp. ix + 189. $54.50 ($22.95, paper). 084767956X (hb), 0847679578 (pb).

O'SULLIVAN (J.N.) Xenophon of Ephesus. His compositional technique and the birth of the novel. (Untersuchungen zur antiken Literatur und Geschichte 44.) Berlin/New York: de Gruyter, 1995. Pp. x + 215. DM 140. 3110143100.

The Oxyrhynchus papyri. Vol. 61. Ed. T. Gagos and others. London: Egypt Exploration Society (for the British Academy), 1995. Pp. xii + 163, ill. 08569-81265.

PADEL (R.) Whom gods destroy. Elements of Greek and tragic madness. Princeton UP, 1995. Pp. xviii + 276. £19.95. 0691033609.

PADUANO (G.) and others Aurelio Peretti, maestro di letteratura greca nell'Ateneo pisano (1901-1994). Pisa: Giardini, 1994. Pp. 28.

PAPANASTASSIOU (G.C.) Compléments au dictionnaire étymologique du grec ancien de Pierre Chantraine (L-O). Thessaloniki: Magia, 1994. Pp. 149. £30. 9607244095.

PAPPAS (N.) **Plato and the** *Republic.* London/New York: Routledge, 1995. Pp. xiv + 230, ill. £25 (£6.99, paper). 041509531X (hb), 0415095328 (pb).

PAQUET (L.) and LAFRANCE (Y.) **Les Présocratiques. Bibliographie analytique (1450-1879). 3e Supplément.** Montreal: Bellarmin, 1995. Pp. 429. 2890078043.

PARKINSON (R.) and QUIRKE (S.) **Papyrus.** London: British Museum P, 1995. Pp. 96, ill. £9.99. 07141-09797.

PATOURA (S.) **Oi aichmalotoi os paragontes epikoinonias kai plerophoreses (4os-10os ai.).** Athens: Ethniko Idryma Erevnon, Kentro Vyzantinon Erevnon, 1994. Pp. 174. 9607094425.

PATRICH (J.) **Sabas, leader of Palestinian monasticism. A comparative study in eastern monasticism, fourth to seventh centuries.** (Dumbarton Oaks Studies 32.) Washington, D.C.: Dumbarton Oaks Research Library and Collection, 1995. Pp. xv + 420, ill. $50. 0884022218.

PATTERSON (R.) **Aristotle's modal logic. Essence and entailment in the Organon.** Cambridge UP, 1995. Pp. ix + 291. £35. 052145168.

PATZER (H.) **Sprache und Dichtung im homerischen Epos.** (Sitzungsberichte der Wissenschaftlichen Gesellschaft an der Johann Wolfgang Goethe-Universität, Frankfurt am Main 31. 4.) Stuttgart: Steiner, 1994. Pp. 23. DM 24. 3515065113.

PELLICCIA (H.) **Mind, body, and speech in Homer and Pindar.** (Hypomnemata 107.) Göttingen: Vandenhoeck & Ruprecht, 1995. Pp. 389. DM 98. 3525252072.

PERBELLINI (G.M.) **The fortress of Nicosia, prototype of European renaissance military architecture.** Nicosia: Anastasios G. Leventis Foundation, 1994. Pp. 29, ill. 996356013X.

PERKINS (J.) **The suffering self. Pain and narrative representation in the early Christian era.** London/New York: Routledge, 1995. Pp. ix + 254. £40 (£12.99, paper). 0415113636 (hb), 0415127068 (pb).

PHEGOS. **Timetikos tomos gia ton kathegete Sotere Dakare.** Ioannina: Panepistemio Ioanninon, 1994. Pp. 588, ill.

PIGEAUD (J.) **L'Art et le vivant.** Paris: Gallimard, 1995. Pp. 463, ill. Fr. 170. 2070731359.

PINDAR: **Le Pitiche.** Ed. and tr. B. Gentili; comm. P.A. Bernardini and others. Milan: Mondadori/Fondazione Lorenzo Valla, 1995. Pp. cxx + 712. L 48,000. 88043-9143X.

PINDAR: **Victory odes.** *Olympians* **2, 7, 11;** *Nemean* **4;** *Isthmians* **3, 4, 7.** Ed. and comm. M.M. Willcock. Cambridge UP, 1995. Pp. viii + 181. £37.50 (£13.95, paper). 0521430550 (hb), 0521436362 (pb).

PIZZOCARO (M.) **Il triangolo amoroso. La nozione di "gelosia" nella cultura e nella lingua greca arcaica.** (Le Rane Studi 13.) Bari: Levante Editori, 1994. Pp. 192. L 28,000. 887949077X.

PLANA MALLART (R.) **La Chora d'Emporion. Paysage et structures agraires dans le nord-est catalan à la période pré-romaine.** (Centre de Recherches d'Histoire Ancienne 137. Espaces et Paysages 2.) Paris: Les Belles Lettres, 1994. Pp. 228, ill. 2251605444.

PLATO: *Phaedrus.* Tr. and comm. A. Nehamas and P. Woodruff. Indianapolis: Hackett, 1995. Pp. xlvii + 94. £19.95 (£4.95, paper). 0872202216 (hb), 087220-2208 (pb).

PLATO: *Parmenide.* Tr. and comm. L. Brisson. Paris: Flammarion, 1994. Pp. 333. 2080706888.

PLATO: *Politicus.* Tr. R. Waterfield; comm. J. Annas and R. Waterfield. Cambridge UP, 1995. Pp. xxix + 89. £27.95 (£9.95). 0521442621 (hb), 052144778X (pb).

PLATO: *Politicus.* Ed., tr. and comm. C.J. Rowe. Warminster: Aris & Phillips, 1995. Pp. vi + 245. £35 (£14.95, paper). 0856686123 (hb), 0856686131 (pb).

PLATO: *Opera.* **Vol. I.** Ed. E.A. Duke and others. Oxford UP (OCT), 1995. Pp. xxxi + 572. £17.50. 0198145691.

PLATO: *The Works.* **Vol. I.** Tr. T. Taylor and F. Sydenham. (The Thomas Taylor series 9.) Frome: Prometheus Trust, 1995. Pp. xv + . 1898910081.

PLOTINUS: *Collected writings.* Tr. T. Taylor. (The Thomas Taylor Series 3.) Frome: Prometheus Trust, 1994. pp. ix + 484. 1898910022.

PLOTINUS: **Les Deux Matières (Ennéade II, 4 [12]).** Ed., tr. and comm. J.-M. Narbonne. (Histoire des Doctrines de l'Antiquité Classique 17.) Paris: J. Vrin, 1993. Pp. 378. Fr. 235. 2711611574.

PLOTINUS: *Ennead* **III. 6 on the impassivity of the bodiless.** Tr. and comm. B. Fleet. Oxford UP, 1995. Pp. xxiv + 314. £40. 0198149654.

POLIGNAC (F. de) **Cults, territory, and the origins of the Greek city-state.** Tr. J. Lloyd. U Chicago P, 1995. pp. xvi + 187. £31.95 (£11.95, paper). 022667-3332 (hb), 0226673340 (pb).

POLYBIUS: *Histoires.* **Vol. 10. Livres XIII-XVI.** Ed. E. Foulon, tr. R. Weil. Paris: Les Belles lettres (Budé), 1995. Pp. 141. Fr. 270. 2251004432.

POOLE (A.) and MAULE (J.) *Ed.* **The Oxford book of classical verse in translation.** Oxford UP, 1995. Pp. xlix + 606. £19.99. 0192142097 m.

PORPHYRY: *De l'abstinence.* Ed., tr. and com. M. Patillon and A.P. Segonds. Paris: Les Belles Lettres (Budé), 1995. Pp. lxiv + 177. Fr. 285. 2251004440.

PORPHYRY: *The Homeric questions.* Tr. R. Schlunk. (Lang Classical Studies 2.) New York: Lang, 1993. Pp. xi + 99. £24. 0820416061.

PORRO (A.) **Vetera alcaica. L'esegesi di Alceo dagli alessandrini all'età imperiale.** (Biblioteca di Aevum Antiquum 6.) Milan: Vita e Pensiero, 1994. Pp. viii + 283. L 32,000. 8834317378.

PORTER (S.E.) **Idioms of the Greek New Testament.** (Biblical Languages Greek Series 2.) Sheffield: JSOT Press, 1992. Pp. 339. £27.50 (£14.95, paper). 18507-53571 (hb), 1850753792 (pb).

POWELL (A.) *Ed.* **The Greek world.** London/New York: Routledge, 1995. Pp. xiv, + 622, ill. £100. 0415060311.

PRICE (A.W.) **Mental conflict.** London/New York: Routledge, 1995. Pp. xiv + 218. £35 (£12.99, paper). 0415041511 (hb), 0415115574 (pb).

PRITCHARD (P.) **Plato's philosophy of mathematics.** (International Plato Studies 5.) Sankt Augustin: Academia Verlag, 1995. Pp. vii + 191. DM 58. 3883456373.

PRITCHETT (W.K.) **Essays in Greek history.** Amsterdam: Gieben, 1994. Pp. ix + 293, ill. Fl. 110. 905063316Ϊ.

PROCLUS: *Elements of theology.* Tr. T. Taylor. (The Thomas Taylor Series 1.) Frome: Prometheus Trust, 1994. Pp. viii + 133. 1898910006.

PROCLUS: *The theology of Plato.* Tr. T. Taylor. (The Thomas Taylor Series 8.) Frome: Prometheus Trust, 1995. Pp. xxxiv + 695. 1898910073.

PSEUDO-ALEXANDER OF APHRODISIAS: *Trattato sulla febbre.* Ed., tr. and comm. P. Tassinari. (Culture antiche. Studi e testi 8.) Alessandria: Edizioni dell' Orso, 1994. Pp. x + 141. L 25,000. 8876941673.

PSEUDO-JUSTIN. **Ps.-Justin (Markell von Ankyra?):** *Ad Graecos de vera religione* (bisher *"Cohortatio ad Graecos"*) Ed. C. Riedweg. (Schweizerische Beiträge zur Altertumswissenschaft, Heft 25.1-2). Basel: Reinhardt, 1994. Pp. x + 711 in 2 vols. SFr. 128. 372450859X

PUELMA (M.) **Labor et lima. Kleine Schriften und Nachträge.** Ed. I. Fasel. Basel: Schwabe & Co, 1995. Pp. 589. SwFr. 96, DM 115. 3796509762.

PUPPA (P.) **Le coppe megaresi in Italia.** (Studia archaeologica 78.) Rome: "L'Erma" di Bretschneider, 1995. Pp. 189, ill. L 270,000. 8870629074.

RADICKE (J.) **Die Rede des Demosthenes für die Freiheit der Rhodier (Or. 15).** (Beiträge zur Altertumskunde 65.) Stuttgart: Teubner, 1995. Pp. 214. DM 72. 3519076144.

RAUTH (T.) **Erotesis - apokrisis. Grammatikregeln in Frage und Antwort.** Bochum: Universitätsverlag Dr. N. Brockmeyer, 1995. Pp. viii + 291. DM 24.80. 3819603301.

REDEN (S. von) **Exchange in ancient Greece.** London: Duckworth, 1995. Pp. x + 244, ill. £35. 0715626000.

REDHEAD (B.) *Ed.* **Plato to Nato. Studies in political thought.** Ed. 2. London: Penguin Books/BBC Books, 1995. Pp. 222, ill. £6.99. 0140246770.

REHAK (P.) *Ed.* **The role of the ruler in the prehistoric Aegean. Proceedings of a panel discussion presented at the annual meeting of the Archaeological Institute of America, New Orleans, Louisiana, 28 December 1992.** (Aegaeum. Annales d'Archéologie Égéenne de l'Université de Liège et UT-PASP 11.) Liège: Université de Liège, Histoire de l'Art et Archéologie de la Grèce Antique/Austin: University of Texas at Austin, Program in Aegean Scripts and Prehistory, 1995. Pp. 211, ill.

RENGAKOS (A.) **Apollonios Rhodios und die antike Homererklärung.** (Zetemata 92.) Munich: Beck, 1994. Pp. 205. DM 88. 3406377181.

RHODES (R.F.) **Architecture and meaning on the Athenian Acropolis.** Cambridge UP, 1995. Pp. xvi + 218, ill. £40 (£13.95, paper). 0521470242 (hb), 0521469813 (pb).

RILEY-SMITH (J.) *Ed.* **The Oxford illustrated history of the Crusades.** Oxford UP, 1995. Pp. xi + 436, ill. £25. 0198204353 m.

RIZZO (F.P.) **I "formulari di Mosè" in un documento acrense. Paure e speranze dell'uomo tardo-antico.** Università degli Studi di Palermo, 1995. Pp. 63.

ROBB (K.) **Literacy and paideia in ancient Greece.** New York: Oxford UP, 1994. Pp. x + 310. £35. 0195059050.

ROBERTS (J.T.) **Athens on trial. The antidemocratic tradition in Western thought.** Princeton UP, 1994. Pp. xix + 405. $39.50. 0691056978.

ROBINSON (T.A.) **Aristotle in outline.** Indianapolis: Hackett, 1995. Pp. 125. £19.95 (£4.45, paper). 0872203158 (hb), 087220314X (pb).

ROBINSON (T.M.) **Plato's psychology.** Ed. 2. (Phoenix Supplement 8.) U Toronto P, 1995. Pp. xxxii + 202. £39 (£22.95, paper). 0802006353 (hb), 0802075908 (pb).

RODNEY S. YOUNG GALLERY. **The ancient Greek world. The Rodney S. Young Gallery.** Philadelphia: University of Pennsylvania Museum of Archaeology and Anthropology, 1995. Pp. 40, ill. $8.95. 0924171375.

ROLLEY (C.) **La Sculpture grecque. 1. Des origines au milieu du Ve siècle.** Paris: Picard, 1994. Pp. 438, ill. Fr. 580. 2708404482.

ROMILLY (J. de) **Alcibiade ou les dangers de l'ambition.** Paris: Editions de Fallois, 1995. Pp. 286. Fr. 125. 2877062465.

ROMILLY (J. de) **Rencontres avec la Grèce antique. 15 études et conferences.** Paris: Editions de Fallois, 1995. Pp. 298. Fr. 125. 2877062368.

ROMILLY (J. de) **Tragédies grecques au fil des ans.** Paris: Les Belles Lettres, 1995. Pp. 233. Fr. 125.

ROSSETTI (L.) *Ed.* **Understanding the *Phaedrus*. Proceedings of the II Symposium Platonicum.** (International Plato Studies 1.) Sankt Augustin: Academia Verlag, 1992. Pp. 328. DM 98. 3883456306.

ROSSETTO (P.C.) and SARTORIO (G.P.) *Ed.* **Teatri greci e romani alle origini del linguaggio rappresentato.** Censimento analitico. Rome/Turin: SEAT - Divisione STET, 1994. 3 vols, ill. L 230.000 (set).

ROSTOVTZEFF (M.I.) **Scripta varia. Ellenismo e impero romano.** Ed. A. Marcone. (Munera 3.) Bari: Edipuglia, 1995. Pp. xxxiii + 490. L 130,000. 88722-81431.

RUPKE (J.) **Kalender und Öffentlichkeit. Die Geschichte der Repräsentation und religiosen Qualifikation von Zeit in Rom.** (Religionsgeschichtliche Versuche und Vorarbeiten 40.) Berlin/New York: de Gruyter, 1995. Pp. 740, ill. DM 338. 3110145146.

RUTHERFORD (R.B.) **The art of Plato. Ten essays in Platonic interpretation.** London: Duckworth, 1995. Pp. xv + 335. £40. 0715626418.

SACKS (D.) **Encyclopedia of the ancient Greek world.** New York: Facts on File, 1995. Pp. xiii + 306, ill. $40. 0816023239.

SANCHEZ DE LA TORRE (A.) **La tirania en la grecia antigua.** Madrid: Real Academia de Jurisprudencia y Legislacion, 1994. Pp. 201. 8460518183.

SANCISI-WEERDENBURG (H.), KUHRT (A.) and ROOT (M.C.) *Ed.* **Continuity and change. Proceedings of the last Achaemenid history workshop, April 6-8, 1990 - Ann Arbor, Michigan.** (Achaemenid history 8.) Leiden: Nederlands Instituut voor het Nabije Oosten, 1994. Pp. xv + 442, ill. Fl. 216 (Fl. 195 subscribers). 906258408X.

SAPOUNA-SAKELLARAKIS (E.) **Die bronzenen Menschenfiguren auf Kreta und in der Ägäis.** (Prähistorische Bronzefunde I. 5.) Stuttgart; Steiner, 1995. Pp. xi + 178, ill. DM 196. 3515061533.

SAPRYKIN (S.I.) **Ancient farms and land-plots on the khora of Khersonesos Taurike (Research in the**

Herakleian Peninsula - 1974-1990). (McGill University Monographs in Classical Archaeology and History 16. Antiquitates Proponticae, Circumponticae et Caucausicae 1.) Amsterdam: Gieben, 1994. Pp. xi + 153, ill. Fl. 125. 9050633269.

SARISCHOULI (P.) **Berliner griechische Papyri. Christliche literarische Texte und Urkunden aus dem 3. bis 8. Jh. n. Chr.** (Serta Graeca 3.) Wiesbaden: Ludwig Reichert, 1995. Pp. x + 217, ill. DM 98. 3882268247.

SCARDIGLI (B.) *Ed.* **Essays on Plutarch's** *Lives.* Oxford UP, 1995. Pp. v + 403. £45. 0198140762.

SCARRE (C.) **The Penguin Historical Atlas of Ancient Rome.** London: Penguin Books, 1995. Pp. 144. £13. 0140513299.

SCHACHTER (A.) **Cults of Boiotia. 3. Potnia to Zeus. Cults of deities unspecified by name.** (Bulletin of the Institute of Classical Studies, Supplement 38.3). London: Institute of Classical Studies, 1994. Pp. 194. £30. 0900587415.

SCHARTAU (B.) **Codices graeci haunienses. Ein deskriptiver Katalog des griechischen Handschriftenbestandes der königlichen Bibliothek Kopenhagen.** (Danish Humanist Texts and Studies 9.) Copenhagen: Museum Tusculanum Press/The Royal Library, 1994. Pp. 614, ill. DKr. 500, $83. 8772892668.

SCHEIBLER (I.) **Griechische Topferkunst. Herstellung, Handel und Gebrauch der antiken Tongefässe.** Ed. 2. Munich: Beck, 1995. Pp. 224, ill. DM 44. 3406393063.

SCHILBACH (J.) **Elische Keramik des 5. und 4. Jahrhunderts.** (Olympische Forschungen 23.) Berlin/New York: de Gruyter, 1995. Pp. xii + 143, ill. DM 190. 3110141019.

SCHMIDT-COLINET (A.) *Ed.* **Palmyra. Kulturbegegnung im Grenzbereich.** (Zaberns Bildbände zur Archaologie 27.) Mainz am Rhein: von Zabern, 1995. Pp. iv + 82, ill. 3805317794.

SCHNEIDER BERRENBERG (R.) **Hand und Fuss. Anmerkungen zu den Massen des metrologischen Reliefs aus Salamis.** Bonn: Die Berrenberg Presse, 1995. Pp. 30, ill.

SCHOCH (M.) **Die minoische Chronologie. Möglichkeiten und Grenzen konventioneller und naturwissenschaftlicher Methoden.** (Documenta Naturae 94.) Munich: Documenta Naturae, 1995. Pp. vi + 256. DM 66.

SCHOTTROFF (L.) **Lydia's impatient sisters. A feminist social history of early Christianity.** Tr. B. and M. Rumscheidt. London: SCM Press, 1995. Pp. xvi + 298. £19.95. 066422072x.

SCHUBERT (C.) and BRODERSEN (K.) *Ed.* **Rom und der griechische Osten. Festschrift für Hatto H. Schmitt zum 65. Geburtstag dargebracht.** Stuttgart: Steiner, 1995. Pp. xii + 375, ill. DM 148. 3515066632.

SCOTT (D.) **Recollection and experience. Plato's theory of learning and its successors.** Cambridge UP, 1995. Pp. x + 289. £35. 0521474558.

SCULLION (S.) **Three studies in Athenian dramaturgy.** (Beiträge zur Altertumskunde 25.) Stuttgart/Leipzig: Teubner, 1994. Pp. ix + 147. DM 58. 3519074745.

SEGAL (C.) **Singers, heroes, and gods in the** *Odyssey.* Ithaca/London: Cornell UP, 1994. Pp. xiii + 244. £28.50. 0801430410.

SEGAL (C.) **Sophocles' tragic world. Divinity, nature, society.** Cambridge, Mass./London: Harvard UP, 1995. Pp. xii + 276. £25.50. 0674821009.

SENECA. **Seneca. Moral and Political Writings.** Ed. and tr. J.M. Cooper and J.F. Procopé. Cambridge UP, 1995. Pp. xl + 324. £40 (£14.95, paper). 0521342910 (hb), 0521348188 (pb).

SEXTUS EMPIRICUS: *Contro gli etici.* Ed, tr. and comm. E. Spinelli. (Elenchos 24.) Naples: Bibliopolis, 1995. Pp. 450. L 60,000. 8870883507.

SHANKS (M.) **Classical archaeology of Greece. Experiences of the discipline.** London/New York: Routledge, 1996. Pp. xiii + 199, ill. £35. 0415085217.

SHARPLES (R.W.) *Ed.* **Theophrastus of Eresus. Sources for his life, writings, thought and influence.** Commentary, Volume 5. Sources on biology (human physiology, living creatures, botany): texts 328-435. (Philosophia antiqua 64.) Leiden: Brill, 1995. Pp. xvi + 273. Fl. 135, $77.25. 9004101748.

SHAW (J.W) and SHAW (M.C) *Ed.* **Kommos. An excavation on the south coast of Crete, Vol. 1: The Kommos region and houses of the Minoan town. Part I: The Kommos region, ecology and Minoan industries.** Princeton UP, 1995. Pp. xxxvii + 809, ill. £120. 069103334X.

SHEEDY (K.A.) *Ed.* **Archaeology in the Peloponnese. New excavations and research.** (Oxbow monographs 48.) Oxford: Oxbow Books, 1994. Pp. viii + 117, ill. £12.95. 0946897778.

SHEPHERD (R.) **Ancient mining.** London/New York: Elsevier Applied Science (for the Institution of Mining and Metallurgy), 1993. Pp. xv + 494, ill. £69. 1858610117.

SIEBER (M.) **Troia. Geschichte, Grabungen, Kontroversen.** (Zaberns Bildbände zur Archäologie 17.) Mainz am Rhein: von Zabern, 1994. Pp. iv + 120, ill. DM 49.80. 3805316267.

SIHLER (A.L.) **New comparative grammar of Greek and Latin.** New York: Oxford UP, 1995. Pp. xxii + 686. £37.50. 0195083458.

SMITH (R.B.E.) **Julian's gods. Religion and philosophy in the thought and action of Julian the Apostate.** London/New York: Routledge, 1995. Pp. xvii + 300. £40. 0415034876.

SOUBIRAN (J.) **Prosodie et metrique du Miles Gloriosus de Plaute. Introduction et commentaire.** (Bibliotheque d'Études Classiques 2.) Louvain/Paris: Peeters, 1995. Pp. xi + 311. Fr.b. 1,400. 2877231933, 9068316974.

SOURVINOU-INWOOD (C.) **"Reading" Greek death to the end of the Classical period.** Oxford UP, 1995. Pp. xiii + 489. £50. 019814976X.

SOWERBY (R.) **The Greeks. An introduction to their culture.** London/New York: Routledge, 1995. Pp. x + 216. £35 (£9.99, paper). 0415120411 (hb), 041512-042X (pb).

SPELLMAN (L.) **Substance and separation in Aristotle.** Cambridge UP, 1995. Pp. ix + 131. £30. 0521471478.

SPENCER (N.) *Ed.* **Time, tradition, and society in Greek archaeology. Bridging the 'great divide.'** London/New York: Routledge, 1995. Pp. xx + 179. £35. 0415114128.

SPHETAS (S.) and KENTROTES (K.) **Skopia se anazetese. Tavtotetas kai diethnous anagnorises.** Thessaloniki: Institute for Balkan Studies, 1994. Pp. 67. 9607387015.

SPYRIDONIDOU-SKARSOULI (M.) *Ed. and comm.* **Der erste Teil der fünften Athos-Sammlung griechischer Sprichworter.** (Texte und Kommentare 18.) Berlin/New York: de Gruyter, 1995. Pp. xliv + 487. DM 298. 3110144565.

STEPHENS (S.A.) and WINKLER (J.J.) *Ed.* **Ancient Greek novels. The fragments.** Princeton UP, 1995. Pp. xvi + 541. £39.50. 0691069417.

STERN (E.M.) and SCHLICK-NOLTE (B.) **Early glass of the ancient world, 1600 B.C.-A.D. 50.** Ernesto Wolf Collection. Ostfildern: Verlag Gerd Hatje, 1994. Pp. 430, ill. 3775705031 (English edn.), 3775705023 (German edn.).

STERN-GILLET (S.) **Aristotle's philosophy of friendship.** Albany: SUNY P, 1995. Pp. vii + 233. $16.95. 0791423417 (hb), 0791423425 (pb).

STIBBE (C.M.) **Laconian drinking vessels and other open shapes. Laconian black-glazed pottery, part 2.** (Allard Pierson Series, Scripta Minora 4.) Amsterdam: Allard Pierson Museum, 1994. Pp. 288, ill. Fl. 249. 9071211223.

STRONK (J.P.) **The Ten Thousand in Thrace. An archaeological and historical commentary on Xenophon's** *Anabasis***, Books VI.iii-vi - VII.** (Amsterdam Classical Monographs 2.) Amsterdam: Gieben, 1995. Pp. xiv + 356. Fr. 150. 905063396X.

STUPPERICH (R.) *Ed.* **Lebendige Antike. Rezeptionen der Antike in Politik, Kunst und Wissenschaft der Neuzeit. Kolloquium für Wolfgang Schiering.** (Mannheimer historische Forschungen 6.) Mannheim: Palatium Verlag im J & J Verlag, 1995. Pp. 223. 3920671155.

SYLLOGE NUMMORUM GRAECORUM: **Staatliche Munzsammlung München. Heft 20. Ionien. 1. Nr. 1-882.** Ed. D.O.A. Klose. Munich: Hirmer, 1995. Pp. iv + 29, ill. DM 132.

SYRIOPOULOS (K.T.) **Apo ton Omeron eos ton Erodoton. From Homer to Herodotus.** Athens [Author], 1995. Pp. 182, ill.

SYRIOPOULOS (K.T.) **He proistorike katoikesis tes Hellados kai he genesis tou hellenikou ethnous.** (Bibliotheke tes en Athenais Archaiologikes Hetaireias 139.) Athens: Athens Archaeological Society, 1994-95. Pp. cxxiii + 1717 in 2 vols. 9607036425.

TATAKI (A.B.) **Macedonian Edessa. Prosopography and Onomasticon.** (Meletemata 18.) Athens: Research Centre for Greek and Roman Antiquity, National Hellenic Research Foundation/Paris: de Boccard, 1994. Pp. 128, ill. Fr. 190. 9607094832.

TEMKIN (O.) **The falling sickness. A history of epilepsy from the Greeks to the beginnings of modern neurology.** Ed. 2. Baltimore/London: Johns Hopkins UP, 1971 (repr. 1994). Pp. xvii + 467. £20.50. 0801848490.

THOM (J.C.) *Ed., tr. and comm.* **The Pythagorean** *Golden Verses.* (Religions in the Graeco-Roman world 123.) Leiden/New York: E.J. Brill, 1995. Pp. xv + 277. Fl. 125, $71.50. 9004101055.

THOME (J.) **Psychotherapeutische Aspekte in der Philosophie Platons.** (Altertumswissenschaftliche Texte und Studien 29.) Hildesheim/New York: Olms-Weidmann, 1995. Pp. xii + 287. DM 58. 3487099888.

THUNGEN (S.F. von) **Die frei stehende griechische Exedra.** Mainz: von Zabern, 1994. Pp. ix + 183, ill. DM 275. 380531471X.

THUR (G.) and TAEUBER (H.) **Prozessrechtliche Inschriften der griechischen Poleis Arkadien (IPARK).** Vienna: Verlag der Österreichischen Akademie der Wissenschaften, 1994. Pp. xxiv + 362, ill. öS 880, DM 135. 3700121415.

TOLLE-KASTENBEIN (R.) **Das archaische Wasserleitungsnetz für Athen und seine späteren Bauphasen.** (Zaberns Bildbände zur Archäologie 19.) Mainz am Rhein: von Zabern, 1994. Pp. iv + 120, ill. DM 39.80. 3805316194.

TOLLE-KASTENBEIN (R.) **Das Olympieion in Athen.** Cologne: Bohlau, 1994. Pp. 238, ill. DM 178. 34120-27944.

TOMLINSON (R.A.) **Greek and Roman architecture.** London: British Museum P, 1995. Pp. 128, ill. £9.99. 0714122041.

TONER (J.P.) **Leisure and ancient Rome.** Oxford: Polity Press, 1995. Pp. x + 198, ill. £39.50. 0745614329.

TOO (Y.L.) **The rhetoric of identity in Isocrates. Text, power, pedagogy.** Cambridge UP, 1995. Pp. xiii + 274. £35. 052147406X.

TORRES-GUERRA (J.B.) **La** *Tebaida* **homerica como fuente de** *Iliada* **y** *Odisea.* Madrid: Fundacion Pastor de Estudos Clasicos, 1995. Pp. 91. 8492046503.

TOUCHETTE (L.-A.) The **dancing maenad reliefs. Continuity and change in Roman copies.** (Bulletin of the Institute of Classical Studies Supplement 62.) London: Institute of Classical Studies, 1995. Pp. x + 119, ill. £35. 0900587652.

TOURNAVITOU (I.) **The "ivory houses" at Mycenae.** (British School at Athens, Supplementary Volume 24.) London: The British School at Athens, 1995. Pp. xx + 341. £65 (£60, BSA members). 090488712X.

TOWNSEND (R.F.) **The Athenian Agora, vol. 27. The east side of the Agora. The remains beneath the stoa of Attalos.** Princeton, N.J.: American School of Classical Studies at Athens, 1995. Pp. xxi + 248, ill. $120. 0876612273.

TRACY (S.V.) **Athenian democracy in transition. Attic letter-cutters of 340 to 290 B.C.** (Hellenistic culture and society 20.) Berkeley/London U California P, 1995. Pp. xiv + 206. £40. 0520200187.

TSETSKHLADZE (G.R.) *Ed.* **Greek and Roman settlements on the Black Sea coast. A workshop held at the 95th annual meeting of the Archaeological Institute of America, Washington DC, USA, December 1993.** (Colloquenda Pontica 1.) Bradford: Loid Publishing, 1994. Pp. 71, ill. £7.50 (£6, paper).

TSOURKA-PAPASTATHI (D.-I.) **E ellenike emporike kompania tou Sibiou Transylvanias 1636-1848. Organose kai dikaio.** Thessaloniki: Institute for Balkan Studies, 1994. Pp. 446. 960738704X.

TSUJI (S.) *Ed.* **The survey of early Byzantine sites in Oludeniz area (Lycia, Turkey). The first preliminary report.** (Memoirs of the Faculty of Letters, Osaka University 35.) Osaka University, 1995. Pp. v + 167, ill.

TUANA (N.) *Ed.* **Feminist interpretations of Plato.** University Park, Pa.: Pennsylvania State University

Press, 1994. Pp. xiv + 286. £31.50 (£12.95, paper). 0271010436 (hb), 0271010444 (pb).

TUNA-NORLING (Y.) **Die attisch-schwarzfigurige Keramik und der attische Keramikexport nach Kleinasien. Die Ausgrabungen von alt-Smyrna und Pitane.** (Istanbuler Forschungen 41.) Tübingen: Wasmuth, 1995. Pp. ix + 180. 3803017629.

TUSA (V.) **I sarcofagi romani in Sicilia.** Ed. 2. (Bibliotheca Archaeologica 14.) Rome: "L'Erma" di Bretschneider, 1995. Pp. xvi + 119, ill. L 250,000. 8870628957.

TYLDESLEY (J.) **Daughters of Isis. Women of ancient Egypt.** London: Penguin Books, 1994. Pp. xvii + 318. £7.99. 0140175962.

TZIATZI-PAPAGIANNI (M.) *Ed. and comm.* **Die Sprüche der sieben Weisen. Zwei byzantinische Sammlungen.** (Beiträge zur Altertumskunde 51.) Stuttgart/Leipzig: Teubner, 1994. Pp. xxv + 497. DM 154. 3519076004.

ULF (C.) *Ed.* **Griechische antike und deutsche Geschichtswissenschaft in biographischen und bibliographischen Daten von der französischen Revolution 1789 bis zum 2. deutschen Kaiserreich 1871.** Berlin: Akademie Verlag, 1995. Pp. 115. DM 58. 3050025409.

VANDENABEELE (F.) and LAFFINEUR (R.) **Cypriote stone sculpture. Proceedings of the Second International Conference of Cypriote studies, Brussels-Liège, 17-19 May, 1993.** Brussels-Liège: A.G. Leventis Foundation, Vrije Universiteit Brussel - Université de Liège 1994. Pp. 178, ill. Fr. b. 2200. 9963560202.

VAN DER EIJK (P.J.), HORSTMANSHOFF (H.F.J.) and SCHRIJVERS (P.H.) *Ed.* **Ancient medicine in its socio-cultural context. Papers read at the Congress held at Leiden University, 13-15 April 1992.** (Clio medica 27-28.) Amsterdam/Atlanta, Ga.: Rodopi, 1995. Pp. xxiii + 637 in 2 vols, ill. Fl. 55, $34 (v.1); Fl. 50, $31 (v.2). 9051835256 (v.1: hb), 9051835353 (v.2: hb), 9051835728 (v.1: pb), 9051-835825 (v.2: pb).

VAN DER TOORN (D.), BECKING (B.) and VAN DER HORST (P.) *Ed.* **Dictionary of deities and demons in the Bible.** Leiden: Brill, 1995. Pp. xxxvi + coll. 1774. Fl. 225, $128.75. 9004103139.

VAN STRATEN (F.T.) **Hiera kala. Images of animal sacrifice in archaic and classical Greece.** (Religions in the Graeco-Roman world 127.) Leiden: Brill, 1995. Pp. ix + 374, ill. Fl. 215, $123. 9004102922.

VANOTTI (G.) **L'altro Enea. La testimonianza di Dionigi di Alicarnasso.** (Problemi e Ricerche di Storia Antica 17.) Rome: "L'Erma" di Bretschneider, 1995. Pp. 343. L 220,000. 8870629082.

VEREMIS (T.M.) and DRAGOUMIS (M.) **Historical dictionary of Greece.** (European historical dictionaries 5.) Metuchen, N.J./London: Scarecrow Press, 1995. Pp. xvii + 258. £29.95. 081082888X.

VERMES (G.) **The Dead Sea scrolls in English.** Ed. 4. London: Penguin, 1995. Pp. lvii + 391. £8.99. 01402-37305.

VERNANT (J.-P.) *Ed.* **The Greeks.** Tr. C. Lambert and T.L. Fagan. U Chicago P, 1995. Pp. vii + 318. £33.95 (£12.75, paper). 0226853829 (hb), 022685-3837 (pb).

VIACAVA (A.) **L'atleta di Fano.** (Studia archaeologica 74.) Rome: "L'Erma" di Bretschneider, 1994. Pp. 154, ill. 887062868X.

VIAL (C.) **Les Grecs de la paix d'Apamée à la bataille d'Actium, 188-31.** Paris: Ed. du Seuil, 1995. Pp. 292, ill. 2020131315.

VIDAL-NAQUET (P.) **Politics ancient and modern.** Tr. J. Lloyd. Oxford: Polity Press, 1995. pp. vi + 209. £39.50. 0745610803.

VIKAN (G.) **Catalogue of the sculpture in the Dumbarton Oaks collection from the Ptolemaic period to the Renaissance.** Washington, D.C.: Dumbarton Oaks Research Library and Collection, 1995. Pp. xxxii + 149, ill. $80.

VILLALBA I VARNEDA (P.) **Olimpia. Origens dels jocs olimpics.** (Ciencia i Tecnica 2.) Bellaterra: Universitat Autonoma de Barcelona, Servei de Publicacions, 1994. Pp. 663. Pt. 6500, $66. 8449000874.

VINOGRADOV (IU. G.) and KRYZICKIJ (S.) **Olbia. Eine altgriechische Stadt im nordwestlichen Schwarzmeerraum.** (Mnemosyne Supplement 149.) Leiden/New York: Brill, 1995. Pp. x + 168, ill. Fl. 135, $77.25. 9004096779 m.

VLASTOS (G.) **Studies in Greek philosophy. 1. The Presocratics.** Ed. D.W. Graham. Princeton UP, 1995. Pp. xxxiv + 389. £40. 0691033102 (hb), 0691019371 (pb).

VLASTOS (G.) **Studies in Greek philosophy. 2. Socrates, Plato and their tradition.** Ed. D.W. Graham. Princeton UP, 1995. Pp. xxiv + 349. £40. 0691033110 (hb), 069101938X (pb).

VLEEMING (S.P.) **Ostraka varia. Tax receipts and legal documents on demotic, Greek, and Greek-demotic ostraka, chiefly of the early Ptolemaic period, from various collections (P. L. Bat. 26).** (Papyrologica Lugduno-Batava 26.) Leiden: Brill, 1994. Pp. xiii + 172, ill. Fl. 185, $105.75. 9004101322.

WALKER (H.J.) **Theseus and Athens.** New York: Oxford UP, 1995. Pp. x + 224. 0195089081.

WANNAGAT (D.) **Saule und Kontext. Piedestale und Teilkannelierung in der griechischen Architektur.** Munich: Biering & Brinkmann, 1995. Pp. 154, ill. 393060907X.

WARTENBERG (U.) **After Marathon. War, society and money in fifth-century Greece.** London: British Museum P, 1995. Pp. 64, ill. £8.99. 0714108820.

WEBSTER (T.B.L) **Monuments illustrating New Comedy.** Ed. 3, rev. J.R. Green and A. Seeberg. (Bulletin of the Institute of Classical Studies Supplement 50.) London: Institute of Classical Studies, 1995. 2 vols: pp. xvi + 264; viii + 515, ill. £90. 0900587768; 0900587733 (v.1), 0900587741 (v.2).

WHITBREAD (I.K.) **Greek transport amphorae. A petrological and archaeological study.** (Fitch Laboratory occasional paper/British School at Athens 4.) London: British School at Athens (distr. Oxbow Books, Oxford), 1995. Pp. xxiv + 453, ill. £40. 0904887138.

WIEMER (H.-U.) **Libanios und Julian. Studien zum Verhältnis von Rhetorik und Politik im vierten Jahrhundert n. Chr.** (Vestigia 46.) Munich: Beck, 1995. Pp. xii + 408. DM 168. 3406393357.

WILKINS (J.), HARVEY (D.) and DOBSON (M.) *Ed.* **Food in antiquity.** U Exeter P, 1995. Pp. xiii + 459. £35. 0859894185.

WILL (E.) **De l'Euphrate au Rhin. Apects de l'hellén-
isation et de la romanisation du Proche-Orient.**
Beirut: Institut Français d'Archéologie du Proche-
Orient, 1995. Pp. viii + 975, ill. Fr. 500. 270536722.

WINCKELMANN (J.J.) **"...die Augen ein wenig zu
öffnen." Eine Anthologie mit Bildern aus Johann
Joachim Winckelmanns Geschichte der Kunst des
Altertums.** Ed. and comm. M. Kunze and M.R.
Hofter. Mainz am Rhein: von Zabern, 1993. Pp. xii
+ 120, ill. DM 39.80. 3805315244.

WINNIFRITH (T.) **Shattered eagles, Balkan fragments.** London: Duckworth, 1995. Pp. 171. 07156-
26353.

WINTER (N.A.) Ed. **Proceedings of the international
conference on Greek architectural terracottas of
the Classical and Hellenistic periods, December
12-15, 1991.** (Hesperia Supplement 27.) Princeton,
N.J.: American School of Classical Studies at Athens,
1994. Pp. xiv + 340, ill. $120. 0876615272.

WOHLERS-SCHARF (T.) **Die Forschungsgeschichte
von Ephesos. Entdeckungen, Grabungen und
Persönlichkeiten.** (Europäische Hochschulschriften
Reihe XXXVIII, Archäologie 54.) Frankfurt am
Main: P. Lang, 1995. Pp. x + 337, ill. £31. 36314-
79646.

WOHRLE (G.) **Hypnos, der Allbezwinger. Eine
Studie zum literarischen Bild des Schlafes in der
griechischen Antike.** (Palingenesia 53.) Stuttgart:
Steiner, 1995. Pp. 123, ill. DM 64. 3515067388.

WORRLE (M.) and ZANKER (P.) **Stadtbild und
Bürgerbild in Hellenismus. Kolloquium, Munchen,
24. bis 26. juni 1993.** (Vestigia 47.) Munich: Beck.
1995. Pp. vii + 273, ill. DM 198. 3406390366.

WRIGHT (M.R.) **Cosmology in antiquity.** London/New
York: Routledge, 1995. Pp. x + 201, ill. £40 (£12.99,
paper). 0415083729 (hb), 0415121833 (pb).

XENOPHON: **Hellenika II.3.11-IV.2.8.** Ed., tr. and
comm. P. Krentz. Warminster: Aris & Phillips, 1995.
Pp. iv + 220. £35 (£14.95, paper). 0856686417 (hb),
0856686425 (pb).

ZAGAGI (N.) **The comedy of Menander. Convention,
variation and originality.** London: Duckworth, 1994.
Pp. 210. £35. 0715626221.

ZANKER (P.) **Die Maske des Sokrates. Das Bild des
Intellektuellen in der antiken Kunst.** Munich: Beck,
1995. Pp. 383, ill. DM 78. 3406390803.

ZIERL (A.) **Affekte in der Tragödie. Orestie, Oidipus
Tyrannos und die Poetik des Aristoteles.** Berlin:
Akademie Verlag, 1994. Pp. 288. DM 98. 305002-
6413.

ZIMMERMANN (B.) **Griechisch-römische Komodie
und Tragödie.** (Drama. Beiträge zum antiken Drama
und seiner Rezeption 3.) Stuttgart: M & P Verlag für
Wissenschaft und Forschung, 1995. Pp. 191. DM
29.80. 3476450597.

ZOJA (L.) **Growth and guilt. Psychology and the
limits of development.** Tr. H. Martin. London/New
York: Routledge, 1995. Pp. viii + 235. £37.50
(£13.99, paper). 0415116600 (hb), 0415116619 (pb).

ZUNTZ (G.) **Greek. A course in classical and post-
classical Greek grammar from original texts.** Ed.
S.E. Porter. (Biblical Languages, Greek Series 4.)
Sheffield Academic P, 1994. 2 vols: pp. 704, 433.
£55 (£25, paper). 1850753415 (hb), 1850757208 (pb).

ZUSANEK (H.) **Rhodos und Helios. Mythos, Topos
und Kultentwicklung.** Ed. S. Hoffmann. Frankfurt
am Main: P. Lang, 1994. Pp. 561. £48.

ZWIERLEIN-DIEHL (E.) **Magische Amulette und
andere Gemmen des Instituts für Altertumskunde
der Universität zu Köln.** (Papyrologica Coloniensia
20.) Opladen: Westdeutscher Verlag, 1992. Pp. 140,
ill. DM 98. 3531099345

INDEX OF BOOKS REVIEWED

Note: various titles are cited here in abbreviated form

MUSEUM SUPPLEMENT

(PLATES II-IV)

Classical Antiquities in Swansea

There are two main holdings of classical antiquities in Swansea. The first, and oldest, is at the Swansea Museum, formerly owned by the Royal Institution of South Wales and now owned by the City and County of Swansea Museums Service. The second, officially opened in June 1976, is the Wellcome Museum, which forms part of the Department of Classics and Ancient History at the University of Wales Swansea. It was established following the transfer in 1971 of some 2,000 objects, mostly Egyptian, but with a little classical, from the former collection of Sir Henry Wellcome who died in 1936. For the formation of the collection see R. Janssen, *The First Hundred Years: Egyptology at University College, London 1892-1992* (London 1992) 83; see also R.M. de Peyer and A.W. Johnston, 'Greek antiquities from the Wellcome Collection: a distribution list', *JHS* cvi (1986) 286-94 (although Swansea had been allocated its material prior to this dispersion and therefore does not feature). Many pieces from the Royal Institution of South Wales are now on loan to the Wellcome Museum.

Classical collections in Swansea date from at least the nineteenth century. Several items were acquired by the Royal Institution of South Wales. For example, a series of objects collected on Cyprus by Lt.-Col. W. Ll. Morgan, Royal Engineers, FSA, principally from tombs around Nicosia and Kyrenia, was acquired in 1878. One of the main private collections, which also went to the RISW and consisted of a number of Greek and Roman pots as well as 'Tanagra' terracottas, was collected in Italy by John Henry Vivian (1785-1855) whose family lived in Singleton Abbey (and which was later to become part of the University of Wales Swansea). The objects were apparently on display at Singleton until 1919. Vivian himself toured Europe during the 1820s and 1830s and it is likely that the objects were acquired at that time (see R.A. Griffiths, *Singleton Abbey and the Vivians of Swansea* (Llandysul 1988) 32-39). Some material was added by his son R. Glynn Vivian who seems to have acquired material in the 1890s and the early twentieth century (R. Ling, 'A note on five inscriptions in Swansea', *PBSR* xxxix [1971] 49).

Some classical antiquities had been acquired by the Department of Classics and Ancient History to form a teaching collection. After the formation of the Wellcome Museum, a number of the classical objects were given on loan by the Swansea Museum. It does however retain a number of objects, many linked to local archaeology. The Swansea Museum also holds a number of Egyptian items, notably the Ptolemaic coffin and mummy of Hor. At the time of writing it has not always been possible to ascertain the origins of all the antiquities held by the Wellcome Museum.

The Wellcome and Swansea Museums are now Registered Museums with the Museums and Galleries Commission. It thus seems unlikely that any major classical acquisitions will be made due to the recognition that the archaeological record is being damaged to supply antiquities for the market. This report is intended to provide a cross-section of the Greek, Cypriot and Etruscan collections, though not every piece has received a mention. There are also a number of Roman antiquities including inscriptions, pottery, lamps and coins. At the time of writing the possibility of creating a new display area with the help of the European Regional Development Fund is being actively pursued.

The Wellcome Museum has its own set of publications, *Pictures from the Wellcome Museum.* Further information about find-spots and the museum are published on the World Wide Web: http://www.swan.ac .uk/classics/mushp.htm; *cf.* D.W.J. Gill, 'Archaeology on the World Wide Web', *Antiquity* lxix (1995) 626-30. Relevant parts of the computer catalogue, prepared using MODES, will be published in this format.

We would like to acknowledge the work of Dr Kate Bosse-Griffiths, not only the previous Honorary Curator of the Wellcome Collection, but also Egyptological adviser to the Swansea Museum, without whose endeavours there might not be such varied collections of antiquities in the city. Jennifer Sabine has also commented on an earlier draft.

The following abbreviations have been used: RISW = Royal Institute of South Wales; SM = Swansea Museum; WM = Wellcome Museum.

Sculpture

1. WM GR-. Marble head. Bearded figure, perhaps of god. Band in hair. H. 0.30. (PLATE II *a*).

Pottery

Mycenaean

2. WM GR-23. Stirrup jar. Brown paint. H. 0.098, D. 0.097. Wellcome Collection.

3. WM GR-24. Krater. Orange-red decoration. Cross hatching on shoulder. Three looped handles on shoulder. LH III. H. 0.116, D. 0.135. Perhaps from Rhodes.

Cypriot

4. WM GR-34. Stringhole flask. Flat, lentoid shaped body. String-hole projections at bottom of neck. Four-holed projection lower on body. In slight relief, encircling lines and triple wavy line. Middle Cypriot. H. 0.178. Found on Cyprus; gift of Col. W. Ll. Morgan (SM 1878.18.27); loan to WM.

5. WM GR-12. Jug, with vertical looped handle. Painted red and white patterns. White Painted Ware. Middle Cypriot. H. 0.115, D. 0.110. Found on Cyprus; gift of Col. W. Ll. Morgan (SM 1878.68.24); loan to WM.

6. WM GR-10. Bowl, with horizontal wishbone handle. Brown decoration. Late Cypriot I. H. 0.082, D. 0.195, W. 0.257. Found on Cyprus; gift of Col. W. Ll. Morgan; loan to WM.

7. WM GR-11. Ladle-cup, with vertical handle; bird on top. Chequered pattern on body. Cross on flat base. Brown lines. H. 0.058, (with handle) 0.13, D. 0.08. Found on Cyprus; gift of Col.W. Ll. Morgan; loan to WM.

8. WM GR-45. Barrel-jug. H. 0.100.SM AX 100; loan to WM.

9. WM GR-41. Krater. Piriform, with three small vertical handles. Hache pattern on shoulder. Red paint. c. 1350 BC H. 0.110, D. (rim) 0.058, (base) 0.035. Found on Cyprus; gift of Col. Morgan (SM A 78.12); loan to WM.

10. WM W2061. Flask, with vertical handle. Base ring ware. H. 0.135, W. 0.08. Probably Wellcome Collection.

Corinthian
11. WM GR-25. Aryballos. Siren and swan (under handle). H. 0.097, D. 0.090. Purchased for the Department of Classics and Ancient History.

East Greek
12. WM GR-5. Pomegranate perfumed-oil container. Black and red paint. Incised pattern. Fifth century BC. H. 0.065, D. 0.050. From Siana (K40), Rhodes; purchased at auction, lot 68/3 'a Balsamarium in the form of a poppy-head, from Rhodes (rare)'; Wellcome Collection.

Attic
13. WM GR-. Alabastron. Black-glazed. Banded, in three zones, with added red and white lines. Sixth century BC. L. 0.236. Marked, no. 132.

14. WM GR-29. Black-figured lekythos. Maenad flanked by two satyrs moving right, but looking left, single maenad moving left. Grazing deer and lion, in silhouette, on shoulder. 500 BC. H. 0.147. Purchased for the Department of Classics and Ancient History. (PLATE II *b*).

15. WM GR-31. Red-figured cup (Type B). In tondo, seated satyr, facing right, with drinking horn-in his right hand, and wine-skin over his left shoulder. Misfired on outside. Restored from sherds; some repainting over fill. Early fifth century BC. H. 0.067, D. 0.177, W. 0.235. Purchased for the Department of Classics and Ancient History. (PLATE II *c*).

16. WM GR-15. Red-figured squat lekythos. Draped woman looking right, on base line. Handle missing. c. 400 BC. H. 0.106. SM AX 90; loan to WM. Marked, '6/-'. (PLATE III *a*).

17. WM GR-44. Lebes. Two vertical handles. Banded. Fifth century BC. H. 0.080, D. (Neck) 0.043, (foot) 0.035. Said to be from Athens.

18. WM GR-36. Skyphos (Type A). Reserved underside with circle and dot. Fifth century BC. H. 0.084, W. 0.175. Probably purchased in Italy c. 1825; John Henry Vivian collection; RISW (SM AX 88); loan to WM. See B.A. Sparkes and L. Talcott, *Black and plain pottery of the 6th, 5th and 4th centuries BC* (Athenian Agora xii, 1970) 84-85.

19. WM GR-46. Bolsal. Four linked palmettes inside. Black-glazed, but misfired to red on parts of outside. Reserved underside with band and circle. One handle missing. c. 410-400 BC. H. 0.065, D. 0.123.

20. WM GR-35. Feeder. Black-glazed. Fifth century BC. H. 0.060, D. 0.052. Found on Cyprus; gift of Col. W. Ll. Morgan (SM 1878.18.37); loan to WM. Other feeders from Cyprus include one from Kition (*Kition* iv, 96 no. 119) and another from Marion (tomb K47: Cambridge, Fitzwilliam Museum GR.161.1890: D.W.J. Gill, *Attic black-glazed pottery in the fifth century BC.: workshops and export*, D.Phil. Diss. 1986, 458, pl. 125, no. V60).

21. WM GR-. Small bowl, later and light. Black-glazed. H. 0.024, D. 0.77. Purchased at auction, lot 67/8; Wellcome Collection. See Sparkes and Talcott, *Black and plain pottery*, 134; Gill, *Attic black-glazed pottery*, 152. This was a particularly popular shape.

22. WM GR-. Small bowl, later and light. Black-glazed. H. 0.022, D. 0.077. Apparently from Egypt ('86' in white); Wellcome Collection. There are numerous examples from Cyrenaica and Cyprus although there are no previsouly recorded examples from Egypt (Gill, *Attic black-glazed pottery*, 417-20).

23. WM GR-. Saltcellar. Black-glazed. Flat base. Fifth century BC. H. 0.022, D. 0.055. See Sparkes and Talcott, *Black and plain pottery*, 136, fig. 9, esp. No. 913; Gill, *Attic black-glazed pottery*, 152-3, pl. 103 (with examples from Rhodes).

Etruscan
24. WM GR-. Olla. Body divided into four main zones by horizontal lines; these are decorated with triangular patterns, squares and wavy lines. Red paint. c. 750-690 BC. H. 0.379, W. 0.33. Wellcome Collection (52727/21345). For a similar example, but with simple figured scenes, see the example from Bisenzio, necropolis of Olmo Bello (t. 24): M. Cristofani, *Civiltà degli etruschi* (Milan 1985) 63, 78, no. 2.10.5. (PLATE III *b*).

25. WM GR-37. Kantharos, with high handles. Bucchero. Sixth century BC. H. 0.072, H. (With handles) 0.11, D. (rim) 0.122. Acquired in Italy c. 1825; John Henry Vivian collection; SM AX 88; loan to WM. (PLATE IV *a*).

South Italian
26. WM GR-6. Chous. Satyr, facing left, seated on rocks. He is holding a tray on his right hand, and grasps a thyrsos in his left. Wave pattern below scene; ovules above. Apulian. Fourth century BC. H. 0.244. Purchased for the Department of Classics and Ancient History. (PLATE IV *b*).

27. WM GR-30. Sessile kantharos. Laurel wreath in white. Orange lines below rim and on lower body. Gnathian ware. Third century BC. H. 0.086, W. 0.118. Probably acquired in Italy c. 1825; John Henry Vivian collection; SM AX 91; loan to WM.

28. WM GR-38. Stemless cup. Four stamped and linked palmettes inside. Black-glazed. One handle missing. Third century BC. H. 0.054, D. (rim) 0.159, (base) 0.065. Purchased in Italy c. 1825; John Henry Vivian collection; SM AX 35; loan to WM.

29. WM GR-43. Skyphos. Black-glazed. Two near vertical handles. H. 0.095, D. (rim) 0.081, (foot) 0.031. SM AX 93; loan to WM.

30. WM GR-39. Bowl. Black-glazed. Stamped decoration inside which includes a bearded face at centre (silen?), surrounded by a circle of maeander stamps, six palmettes linked by two rows of dots; five bands of rouletting. Plain rim. Light brown fabric. Third century BC. H. 0.065, D. (rim) 0.182. Purchased in Italy *c.* 1825; John Henry Vivian collection; SM AX 98; loan to WM.

31. WM GR-27. Lekanis (lid missing). Loop handles. Vertical white lines below rim. Added red on stem. Fourth century BC. H. 0.062, D. 0.181. Purchased at auction, lot 69/11 (with Etruscan objects); Wellcome Collection.

32. WM GR-28. Basket-shaped vessel. Thick white slip. H. 0.055, D. 0.074. Purchased at auction, lot 67/8 ('a vase in form of a workman's basket'); Wellcome Collection.

Black-glazed and plain, various fabrics
33. WM GR-47. Sessile kantharos with two high handles. Possibly Boeotian. Mid fifth century BC. H. 0.073, (with handles) 0.113.

34. WM GR-40. Bowl. Ring-shaped foot. Black-glazed. Third century BC. H. 0.035, D. (Rim) 0.080, (foot) 0.030. SM AX 97; loan to WM.

35. WM GR-42. Jar with two vertical handles. Inicised ivy pattern on shoulder. Buff terracotta. H. 0.100, D. (mouth) 0.089. SM AX 101; loan to WM.

36. WM GR-. Votive oinochoe. Black-glazed on top of spout. H. 0.025. Purchased at auction, lot 69/11; Wellcome Collection.

Lamps

In addition to these Greek lamps, there are a number of Roman relief lamps in the collection.

37. WM GR-14. Lamp. Black-glazed. Third century BC. H. 0.055, D. 0.035. Found on Cyprus; gift of Col. W. Ll. Morgan (SM 878.36); loan to WM.

38. WM GR-16. Lamp, with relief. Second-third century AD. D. 0.075. Found on Cyprus; gift of Col. W. Ll. Morgan (SM 878.35); loan to WM.

Terracottas
Cyprus
39. WM GR-1. Man carrying object. Flaring base. Hollow inside. Two holes on lower part of body above base. Detail of face (eyes, eyebrows, beard) and hands in thin glaze; horizontal lines decorate the lower body. H. 0.166, D. 0.084. Purchased at auction, lot 95/5; Wellcome Collection.

40. WM GR-7. Goat. Green paint. H. 0.096, L. 0.120. Found on Cyprus; gift of Col. W. Ll. Morgan (SM 878.29 = AX 103); loan to WM.

41. WM GR-4. Animal with handle. Buff coloured clay. H. 0.081, L. 0.136. Sold at Sotheby's 18 July 1919, lot 33; Wellcome Collection.

Boeotia
42. WM GR-9. Standing female figure. Flat body. *Polos* on head. Curl over forehead. Pomegranate amulet around neck. Detail in matt black paint. Vertical lines above hem of dress. Mid sixth century BC. H. 0.125. Wellcome Collection. See R.A. Higgins, *Greek Terracottas* (London 1967) pl. 18, c (British Museum, from Tanagra).

43. WM GR-2. Horse and rider. The horse and rider are decorated with a series of brown glazed lines. 550 BC. H. 0.084, L. 0.095. Wellcome Collection. Compare Higgins, *Greek Terracottas*, pl. 19, e (British Museum, from Tanagra).

44. WM GR-8. Standing female figure. Flat body. Chequer pattern of red and white squares, yellow and white triangles on dress. Late sixth century BC. H. 0.230. Wellcome Collection.

45. WM GR-105. Goat. White slip. Sixth century BC. L. 0.084. 'From Thebes' (perhaps in 1885); purchased at auction, lot 98/10; Wellcome Collection.

46. WM GR-26. Draped female figure. Fourth century BC. H. 0.198. Probably acquired in Italy by John Henry Vivian who acquired 'some Tanagra figurines' around 1825 (A. Stewart, *Family Tapestry* [1961], 127); loan to WM.

Attica
47. WM GR-101. Enthroned female figure. Only upper body and top of throne preserved. *c.* 400 BC. H. (present) 0.073, W. 0.070. Found in the Piraeus; sold at Sotheby's 22/23 May 1885, lot 108; Wellcome Collection. Compare Higgins, *Greek terracottas*, pl. 31, e (Louvre); R.V. Nicholls, 'Two groups of archaic Attic terracottas', in D.C. Kurtz and B.A. Sparkes (ed.), *The eye of Greece. Studies in the art of Athens* (Cambridge 1982) 114 K2; D.W.J. Gill, 'Recent acquisitions by the Fitzwilliam Museum, Cambridge, 1971-1989', *JHS* cx (1990) 293 no. 29.

Cyrenaica
The terracottas and related ceramic votives from Cyrene were part of a votive deposit excavated on the slope of the acropolis of Cyrene in 1910-11: see R. Norton and C. Densmore Curtis, 'The excavations at Cyrene: first campaign, 1910-1911', *BullArchInstAmer* ii (1911) 155-57. They were acquired by Dr A.F.S. Sladden, medical officer to the expedition (and later a pathologist in Swansea), who presented them to the RISW in 1962; then on loan to WM. The American expedition concentrated on the acropolis where, on the northwest slope, were found thousands of terracotta figurines. The excavators reported that 'early in November [1910] an Arab brought-to camp a basketful of interesting archaic terracotta figurines. He had dug them up in his garden, the westernmost of the cultivated patches which girdle the hill at the level of the fountain. The place is a flat strip below a ledge of rock'. They will feature in a

monograph on terracottas from Cyrene, *Il santuario delle ninfe*, with contributions by L. Bacchielli, J. Uhlenbrock, D.W.J. Gill and others. For the present time see L. Bacchielli, 'Un santuario di Frontiera, fra *Polis e Chora*', *Libyan Studies* xxv (1994) 45-59 (= J. Reynolds, ed., *Cyrenaican Archaeology: an International Colloquium*).

48. WM GR-48. Naked youth with chlamys over shoulder. H. 0.158. From Cyrene; loan to WM. (PLATE IV *c*).

49. WM GR-50. Standing youth. H. 0.157. From Cyrene; SM 962.2.6; loan to WM.

50. WM GR-53. Standing youth. Head and lower legs missing. H. 0.080. From Cyrene; SM 962.2.11; loan to WM.

51. WM GR-57. Standing youth. Head and feet missing. H. 0.087. From Cyrene; SM 962.2.12; loan to WM.

52. WM GR-58. Standing youth. Head and lower legs missing. H. 0.083. From Cyrene; SM 962.2.13; loan to WM.

53. WM GR-59. Standing youth. Head and lower legs missing. H. 0.087. From Cyrene; SM 962.2.15; loan to WM.

54. WM GR-. Standing male figure. Head missing. H. 0.080. From Cyrene; SM 962.2.21; loan to WM.

55. WM GR-49. Female figure holding silphium and animal. H. 0.138. From Cyrene; SM; loan to WM.

56. WM GR-51. Standing female figure. H. 0.155. From Cyrene; SM 962.2.5; loan to WM.

57. WM GR-52. Standing female figure. H. 0.118, W. (base) 0.032. From Cyrene; SM 962.2.7; loan to WM.

58. WM GR-54. Standing female figure. Head missing. H. 0.083. From Cyrene; SM 962.2.16; loan to WM.

59. WM GR-55. Standing female figure. Lower body missing. H. 0.121. From Cyrene; SM 962.2.15; loan to WM.

60. WM GR-56. Standing female figure with silphium plant. Head missing. H. 0.122, W. (plinth) 0.053. From Cyrene; SM 962.2.10; loan to WM.

61. WM GR-60. Standing female figure with fawn (?) by legs. Upper part of body missing. Stands on plinth. H. 0.126, W. (plinth) 0.077. From Cyrene; SM 962.2.4; loan to WM.

62. WM GR-61. Standing youth. Head and feet missing. H. 0.079. From Cyrene; SM 962.2.14; loan to WM.

63. WM GR-62. Head of female figure wearing *polos*. H. 0.043. From Cyrene; SM 962.2.20; loan to WM.

64. WM GR-63. Head of female figure wearing *polos*. H. 0.033. From Cyrene; SM 962.2.22; loan to WM.

65. WM GR-66. Seated female figure. Upper body missing. H. 0.069. From Cyrene; SM 962.2.17; loan to WM.

66. WM GR-67. Standing female figure holding offerings. Head and lower body missing. H. 0.061. From Cyrene; SM 962.2.18; loan to WM.

67. WM GR-68. Hand of goddess holding silphium plant. From Cyrene; SM 962.2; now missing. Publ. *Evening Post* 11 July 1962.

68. WM GR-64. Cylindrical loomweight. H. 0.053. From Cyrene; SM 962.2.31; loan to WM.

69. WM GR-69. Offering plate. From Cyrene; SM 962.2.29A; loan to WM.

70. WM GR-70. Offering plate. H. 0.008, L. 0.075. From Cyrene; SM 962.2.28B; loan to WM.

71. WM GR-71. Offering plate. From Cyrene; SM 962.2.29C; loan to WM.

72. WM GR-72. Offering tray. H. 0.007, L. 0.089, W. 0.023. From Cyrene; SM 962.2.28D; loan to WM.

Tarentum
73. WM GR-102. Priapos. Purchased at auction, lot 108/11; Wellcome Collection.

74. WM GR-104. Head of black, probably from a flask. Reddish clay. Possibly made at Tarentum. *c.* 350-325 BC. H. 0.05. Compare the example of a black boy asleep next to an amphora in Oxford: C.E. Vafopoulou-Richardson, *Greek terracottas* (Oxford 1981) 28-29, no. 27.

Other
75. WM GR-106. Female head. H. 0.135. Wellcome Collection.

76. WM GR-103. Small figure reclining on back of sow. Rectangular plinth. Possibly East Greek.

77. WM GR-3. Horse. Decorated with red and black stripes. Possibly Cypriot. Sixth century BC. H. 0.113. Sold at Sotheby's 18 July 1919, lot. 33/8; Wellcome Collection (HMM 26374).

Reliefs
78. WM GR-20. Architectural relief with bearded male head in relief, facing left. Perhaps second century AD. H. 0.130, L. 0.250. Discovered at Ephesus on Easter Day 1890 in the presence of Revd E.W. Boley; SM; loan to WM.

Glass

79. WM GR-32. Unguentarium. Second century AD. H. 0.165. Found on Cyprus; gift of Col. W. Ll. Morgan (SM A 878.33 = AX 119); loan to WM.

Inscriptions

There is a general book on inscribed material in the Wellcome Museum: Kate Bosse-Griffiths, *Five ways of writing between 2000 BC and AD 200*, Pictures from the Swansea Wellcome Museum 3 (Swansea 1994). See also R. Ling, 'A note on five inscriptions in Swansea', *PBSR* xxxix (1971) 47-51.

80. WM GR-. White marble plaque. Gift of R. Glynn Vivian, 1904; SM; loan to WM. Published: Ling, 'Five inscriptions in Swansea', 48-49 no. 5, pl. xi, c. Possibly a forgery.

81. WM GR-90. Funerary stela of Arisa daughter of Aristomenes. 7 lines of text. Ptolemaic. H. 0.27, W. 0.19. From Egypt; Mr D.L. Gibbs; gift to WM. Publ. Bosse-Griffiths, *Writing*, 20-21, Greek Writing: 2.

Mummy labels
There are three mummy labels with Greek inscriptions in the collection: D. Mueller, 'Three mummy labels in the Swansea Wellcome Collection', *JEA* lix (1973) 175-80.

82. WM W549. Mummy label. Seven lines of text which can be translated: 'Hermiysis, (son) of Kollouthos, farewell! Kollouthos to Kallistos: when the mummy of my child reaches you, keep guard until I arrive'. Four holes. L. 0.108, W. 0.085. Wellcome Collection.

83. WM W540. Mummy label of Ammonarion, died aged 25 years. Two lines of text. Two holes. L. 0.075, W. 0.042. Wellcome Collection.

84. WM W550. Mummy label of Senpeteminis, (daughter) of Petetriphis. Three lines of text. One hole. L. 0.112, W. 0.042. Possibly from Akhmin. Wellcome Collection.

Jewellery

85. WM GR-. Bronze finger ring. Intaglio design of human figure. On each side a crescent and star, and on the other a star. Rectangular bezel. Part of loop missing. Purchased in London; gift of Prof. G.M. Petersen; WM. For the crescent and moon on gems: M. Henig, *Classical gems ...in the Fitzwilliam Museum* (Cambridge 1994) 272 no. 582.

Coins

WM has a good collection of Parthian coins as well as a small number of Hellenistic and Roman ones.

86. WM GR-. Coin of Elis. Mid fourth century BC. Obverse: head of Zeus with laurel wreath. Gift of Dr C.A. Stray.

DAVID W.J. GILL
The Wellcome Museum
University of Wales Swansea

ROSALYN GEE
Swansea Museum

Postscript
After this Museum Supplement had gone to press additional funding was secured to build a new Egypt Centre. This new building, which will house the Egyptian and Classical collections, will adjoin the Taliesin Arts Centre at the University of Wales Swansea.

NEW AND FORTHCOMING PUBLICATIONS FROM THE INSTITUTE OF CLASSICAL STUDIES

Andokides and the Herms:
A study of crisis in fifth-century Athenian religion

William D Furley   BICS Supplement 65   ISBN 0 900587 72 5
October 1996: viii + 162pp; 175mm × 245mm; paperback; £25

Bulletin of the Institute of Classical Studies 41 1996

includes articles in memory of Dale Trendall
by Dyfri Williams, David Ridgway, and J. R. Green,
and contributions from John Crook, Robin Lane Fox, Luca Giuliani,
Freya Martin, Susanna Morton Braund, and Dimitris Plantzos.
November 1996: ISSN 0076-0730; £28

Aristotle and after

Edited by Richard Sorabji:
includes contributions by Susanne Bobzien, Travis Butler, Andrea Falcon,
Michael Frede, Richard Gaskin, Hans Gottschalk, Brad Inwood,
A. A. Long, Dirk Obbink, Marwan Rashed, Heinrich von Staden, M. B. Trapp.
December 1996:   BICS Supplement 68   ISBN 0 900587 79 2;   approx. £35

All Institute publications may be ordered from the Publications Office, Institute of Classical Studies, 31-34 Gordon Square, London WC1H 0PY: FAX 0171 383 4807. A catalogue of books in print is also available, free of charge, from the Institute.

Attic red-figure amphora by Phintias: (a) Apollo, Tityos, Leto, Artemis; (b) athletes and companions (Louvre G42; photograph by M. Chuzeville, reproduced by kind permission of the Louvre Museum)

(a) Marble head of god (1)

(b) Attic black-figured lekythos (14)

(c) Attic red-figured cup (15)

(a) Attic red-figured squat lekythos (16)

(b) Etruscan *olla* (24)

PLATE IV   MUSEUM SUPPLEMENT   *JHS* cxvi (1996)

(a) Etruscan bucchero kantharos (25)

(c) Terracotta youth from a votive
    deposit at Cyrene (48)

(b) Apulian chous (26)